N. Billings

McDougal, Littell
English

To the Student,

When was the last time you had a textbook that you felt was written just for you, with your interests and experiences in mind? When was the last time you felt challenged to stretch your own talents, solve difficult problems, or seek out new ideas?

McDougal, Littell English encourages you to do all of these things and more. Even while teaching you the skills necessary for effective thinking, writing, and speaking, the book takes learning one step further. It invites you to explore the world around you as well as the potential of your own mind.

Briefly skim through the book. Images dealing with our history, our culture, and even our sense of humor appear throughout each lesson. Each one is designed to intrigue, challenge, or amuse you, to broaden your range of experiences and provide you with starting points for writing and discussion.

We hope you will enjoy exploring the images and ideas in this book. We also hope you will enjoy a similar sense of discovery as you develop your own unique talents and abilities.

The Editors

"*We have tomorrow*
Bright before us
Like a flame."

Langston Hughes

McDougal, Littell
English

Blue Level

ℳℒ

McDougal, Littell & Company

Evanston, Illinois
New York   Dallas   Sacramento   Raleigh

Senior Consultants

Linda Flower, Professor of Rhetoric at Carnegie-Mellon University and Co-director, Center for the Study of Writing, the University of California at Berkeley and Carnegie-Mellon University

Barbara Sitko, Researcher, Center for the Study of Writing, the University of California at Berkeley and Carnegie-Mellon University

Consultants

Dr. Patricia A. Aubin, Director of English/Language Arts, Watertown Public Schools, Watertown, Massachusetts

John Barrett, Language Arts Coordinator, Farmington Public Schools, Farmington, Michigan

Shelley T. Bernstein, Subject Area Coordinator, Mater Dei High School, New Monmouth, New Jersey

John J. Elias, English Supervisor, Wilkes-Barre Area School District, Wilkes-Barre, Pennsylvania

Kay Lunsford, English Teacher and Department Chairman, North Kansas City High School, North Kansas City, Missouri

Jack Pelletier, Chair, English Department, Mira Loma High School, Sacramento, California

William J. Peppiatt, District Director of English and Language Arts, Suffern High School, Suffern, New York

Robert W. Salchert, Language Arts Coordinator, Valley High School, Las Vegas, Nevada

Dr. Jane S. Shoaf, C.E. Jordan High School, Durham, North Carolina

Acknowledgments: Sources of Quoted Materials   **53:** Simon & Schuster, Inc.: For an entry from *Webster's New World Dictionary, Student Edition,* copyright © 1976, 1981 Simon & Schuster, Inc. **56:** Random House, Inc.: For an entry from *The Random House Thesaurus,* copyright © 1984 Random House. **158:** The University of New Mexico Press: For excerpts from *The Way to Rainy Mountain* by N. Scott Momaday, © 1969 The University of New Mexico Press. **176:** May Swenson: For "A Navajo Blanket" by May Swenson, copyright © 1977 May Swenson, used by permission of the author. **210:** Little, Brown and Company in association with the Atlantic Monthly Press: For excerpts adapted from Chapter 11 in *Never Cry Wolf* by Farley Mowat, copyright © 1963 Farley Mowat, Limited. **234:** Houghton Mifflin Company: For excerpts from "Death of An Island," from *The Water Is Wide* by Pat Conroy, copyright © 1972 Pat Conroy. **268:** Scott Meredith Literary Agency, Inc.: For excerpts from "We'll Never Conquer Space" by Arthur C. Clarke, reprinted by permission of the author and the author's agents, Scott Meredith Literary Agency, Inc., 845 Third Avenue, New York, New York 10022. **290:** Marian Reiner: For "How to Eat (continued on page 869)

ISBN: 0-8123-5175-4

Composition

Developing Writing Skills

For a list of literature selections and special features, see the last section of this table of contents

Writing for Different Purposes

Resources and Skills

Grammar, Usage, and Mechanics

Special Features

Other Featured Writers

Woody Allen

Dave Barry

Doris Betts

Alan S. Blinder

Hal Borland

James Boswell

Stephen P. Breslow

Montgomery Brower

Pearl S. Buck

James Burke

Edgar Rice Burroughs

Lewis Carroll

Willa Cather

Bruce Catton

John Cheever

Anton Chekhov

Bruce Chatwin

John Henrik Clarke

Doug Cornell

Constance Crawford

e.e. cummings

Will Cuppy

Barbara Cushman

Albert A. Dekin, Jr.

Emily Dickinson

Annie Dillard

Bob Dotson

Gerald Durrell

Roger Ebert

Willard Espy

Martha Fay

Joshua Fischman

F. Scott Fitzgerald

Myron Flindt

Robert Francis

Nicholas Gage

Boyd Gibbons

Stephen Jay Gould

Sanche De Gramont

Sydney J. Harris

Moss Hart

William Least Heat Moon

Sue Hubbell

Mickey Kaus

Ken Kesey

Rudyard Kipling

Charles Kuralt

Anne LaBastille

Frederick Laing

Jerome Lamb

Ring Lardner

Jack London

Malcolm Lowry

Richard B. Manchester

Jan Mason

Helen Hynson Merrick

Sy Montgomery

H. H. Munro

Bob Mytkowicz

Kimon Nicolaides

S. A. Nigosian

Joyce Carol Oates

Iris Noble

Flannery O'Connor

John Poppy

Katherine Anne Porter

Ezra Pound

Jim Robbins

Edward Arlington Robinson

Andrew A. Rooney

Galen Rowell

Mari Susette Sandoz

Wilbur Schramm

Bernard Shanks

Julian Simon

Jack Smith

Mordecai Spektor

Bruce Springsteen

John Steinbeck

May Swenson

Lewis Thomas

Frank Trippett

Philip Trupp

Edith Wharton

Thomas Wolfe

Tom Wolfe

Jade Snow Wong

L a n g u a g e   F e a t u r e s

Writing Inside Out

Language Lore

On the Lightside

Composition

1

Responding to Your World

*C*ompare the image above with the one on the facing page. Each represents someone's perception of a relay race.

You are not a camera, objectively recording your world. Rather, you respond to and interact with it, experiencing it in a way that is uniquely your own. One way to share your world with others and to enter their worlds is through an expressive medium such as painting, music, writing, or even photography.

In this chapter you will take the first steps toward more effective communication. You will learn to use all your senses to become an astute observer of the world. You will also learn techniques to help you think about and organize your observations and record them clearly and creatively.

Munich Olympic Games, Jacob Lawrence, 1971.

5

Observing and Reflecting

Did you ever read a book or a story and wonder how the writer came up with such an original idea? Did you ever listen to the lyrics of a song and think, "That's *exactly* how I feel!" Ideas for stories and song lyrics—in fact, all writing ideas—depend, to some extent, on observing and reflecting. **Observing** is paying close attention to your environment and using your senses to gather information about it. **Reflecting** is using your reasoning skills, experience, and imagination to react to what you have observed. When you reflect, you make connections between things or ideas. Good writing communicates both what you have observed and how you interpret it.

Using Your Senses

Your five senses are always picking up information about the world that surrounds you. Good writers constantly try to sharpen their senses to heighten their awareness of how a thing looks, sounds, feels, tastes, and smells.

Sight Much of what we learn about the world comes to us through our vision. Although we often form impressions of what things *look* like, we seldom observe things carefully enough to *see* them in detail. To really see an object is to note every aspect of its appearance, its position relative to its surroundings, and whether it is in motion or at rest. Writers use special "sight words" to communicate detailed observations like these. In the following description of the Australian outback after a storm, notice how sight words convey details about color, appearance, and movement.

Literary Model

A pair of rainbows hung across the valley between the two mountains. The cliffs of the escarpment, which had been a dry red, were now purplish-black and striped, like a zebra, with vertical chutes of white water. The cloud seemed even denser than the earth, and, beneath its lower rim, the last of the sun broke through, flooding the spinifex [a type of Australian grass] with shafts of pale green light.

From *The Songlines* by Bruce Chatwin

Hearing It is easy to be aware of loud noises, but we often miss the softer, nearly inaudible sounds that comprise the rhythm of everyday life. To sharpen your sense of hearing, try closing your eyes and concentrating on sounds. "Hearing words," such as those in the following paragraph, give immediacy and impact to descriptions.

Literary Model

In the living room the mail slot clicked open and envelopes clattered down. In the back room, where our maid, Margaret Butler, was ironing, the steam iron thumped the muffled ironing board and hissed. The walls squeaked, the pipes knocked, the screen door trembled, the furnace banged, and the radiators clanged. This was the fall the loud trucks went by.

From *An American Childhood* by Annie Dillard

Touch, Taste, and Smell Words that communicate whether something is slippery or gritty, spicy or sweet, or fragrant or rancid help your reader share vicariously in what you are describing. Notice the words that evoke textures, tastes, and smells in the following paragraph about an ice-cream parlor.

Student Model

I slid onto a slick oilcloth seat. The shiny spigots gleamed and were reflected in the polished mirror facing me. The air was heavy with ripening bananas, hot fudge, and malted

7

milk. I drummed my fingertips impatiently on the cool marble countertop. With a jerk of a handle, the counter boy whooshed carbonated water into a tall glass and set it down in front of me. I picked up a straw and peeled back the paper wrapper. I raised the glass. The bubbles tickled the inside of my nose.

Reacting

Have you ever heard the question, "If a tree falls in a forest and no one hears it, does it make a sound?" The question suggests that an event takes on meaning only when someone reacts to it. Similarly, you must react to what you experience before it becomes meaningful for you. How you react is determined by who you are and what you already know or have experienced. For example, imagine that a fire truck—sirens blaring—has just raced down a residential street. Here's how several observers might react.

Observer	Reaction
baby in stroller	starts to cry
newspaper reporter	runs to the telephone
house painter on a ladder	pays little attention
group of children	chases after the fire truck

Point of View We can see that one event—a fire truck answering a call—elicited four different reactions, each representing a different

How birds see the world.

point of view. The baby, for example, became frightened by the loud sirens. The reporter sensed a story in the making and ran to phone in the tip to the newsroom. How someone reacts depends entirely on that individual's experience and frame of reference, as in the bird's-eye view of the world on page 8. What is important is that you become aware of your own reactions and the meaning of an event to you.

Objective and Subjective Another factor that affects reactions is your level of objectivity. When you react objectively to something, you observe it as it is, without "seasoning" it with your own experience, attitudes, or opinions. Good journalists are trained to report the news objectively. The following news report is an example of objective writing.

▬ Professional Model ▬▬▬▬▬▬▬▬▬▬▬
There were 640 reported incidents of bikes colliding with pedestrians in New York City last year, up from 339 in 1981. Three New York City pedestrians were killed by cyclists in 1986, while nine bikers were killed by motorists.

From "Scaring the Public to Death" by Frank Trippett

A subjective reaction, on the other hand, is colored by the observer's experience, frame of reference, and opinions and attitudes. When you write subjectively, you inject personal feelings into your work. While a piece of subjective writing may or may not cite facts or statistics, it always includes opinions and attitudes. The following letter to the editor is an example of subjective writing.

A recent story in *Time* said that nine bicyclists were killed by motorists in New York City in 1986. I'm just surprised that the number wasn't higher. Bike riders are careless commuters; they don't follow the rules of the road and I wish my community would ban them altogether.

Kelly Janowicz, Oak Grove, Illinois

Your reactions—objective or subjective—can affect your writing. They can also create an impact in the person who reads your writing. You will learn more about the uses of objective and subjective writing in Chapter 7.

Writing Activities *Observing and Reflecting*

A Think of a familiar place that you cannot see at this moment, such as a fast-food restaurant, your favorite spot at home, the lobby of a movie theater, or the inside of a garage. From memory, write a brief paragraph that describes this place. Next, spend some time observing the place. As you observe, list words or phrases that appeal to all five senses. Using your list, write a second description. Compare the two paragraphs. How are they alike? How are they different?

B Think of something that can be considered from several different points of view—for example, a touchdown pass in a football game as viewed by the quarterback, by a sports reporter, by the fans on the home team or the visiting team, or by the football itself. Describe your scenario in a paragraph, using the point of view of your choice.

C Look around you. As objectively as possible, describe what you see: a desk, a bulletin board. Then, take a second look at the same surroundings. This time, observe your surroundings subjectively. Do you see an old desk, its surface scarred with carved initials? a bulletin board vacant except for a few tattered scraps of paper? What feelings do you have in this setting? Try to inject those feelings into a second list. Compare the two lists. Using the best details on both lists, write a paragraph describing your surroundings.

Part 2
Thinking

Observing and reacting are just the beginning steps in making sense of the world. Thoughtful observers go beyond what they see and how they feel about it to create and explore new ideas. This process leads to the creation of a painting, a drawing, a story, an invention, or a piece of music.

Processing Ideas

The "raw data" supplied by your senses during observation can be processed to yield ideas for writing. When you see or read something interesting, ask yourself a number of questions about it. Here are a few suggestions:

What does this mean?
What can I learn from this?
How does this relate to other things I know?
How can I use this idea?

Let's consider an example. Suppose that you are looking for writing ideas for articles for your school magazine. You see a TV report about an American rock star's successful tour of the Soviet Union. To process what you've observed, you might ask yourself the following questions:

Why was this tour so successful?
Do Soviet teen-agers like rock music as much as American teens do?
Do they have rock bands in the Soviet Union?
Could I write an article about rock music in the Soviet Union?

Asking questions about what you observe paves the way for gleaning. *Gleaning* is the gathering of bits and pieces of information for the purpose of formulating writing ideas. You will learn more about gleaning—and other useful information-gathering techniques—in Chapter 2.

Exploring Ideas

The ideas that you first gather by observing and then process by questioning can in turn be used to explore and create new ideas. You can use several thinking techniques to build on what you have observed or to gain a better understanding of the information you've gathered. These techniques include freewriting, clustering, analyzing, inquiring, and imaging.

Freewriting The technique of **freewriting** uses continuous writing to generate new ideas. To use freewriting, follow these steps:

1. Choose a focus or starting point.
2. Write whatever comes to mind as you think about your focus. Continue writing without stopping for ten minutes. If you get stuck, keep your pen or pencil moving by drawing loops or doodles on your paper until you get another idea.
3. Don't worry about using complete sentences or proper spelling and punctuation.

Here is some freewriting Chris did to generate ideas for a report about American architecture.

American architecture . . . houses . . . office buildings . . . my favorites are skyscrapers—buildings that scrape the sky. Who thought of that name? The Empire State Building, the Sears Tower, the pyramid building in San Francisco—what's it called? All those windows, all that glass—some almost seem made of glass. What holds them up, anyway? I could ask Jan's mother—she works for the company that's building that new office tower downtown.

Clustering Another technique for generating ideas is **clustering.** When you use this technique, you make a visual map of your thoughts. To use clustering, follow these steps:

1. Write your focus in the center of your paper, and circle it.
2. Think about your focus, and jot down related ideas. Circle them. Connect these ideas by lines to the focus idea.
3. Write down and circle other ideas that occur to you. Connect these to ideas already on your chart.

Jolene was planning a report about the Olympics. To generate ideas for the report, she created this cluster diagram.

Analyzing The technique of **analyzing** involves dividing an idea into parts and examining each part. You might think of this technique as dissecting an idea, as you would dissect a frog in biology lab. Dissecting, or analyzing, helps you discover what parts make up the whole and how the parts are connected to each other. Separating the parts allows you to study each one in more detail.

Analyzing is a useful technique for organizing information as you prepare a report or presentation. Suppose you are planning a presentation about choosing a career. You've chosen journalism as your subject. To begin your analysis, divide your subject into several parts and then categorize relevant information.

> *Places to work:* newspapers, radio or TV stations, magazines, company publicity departments, wire news services
>
> *Types of jobs:* reporter, foreign correspondent, copy editor or proofreader, photographer, layout and design artist, on-air newscaster
>
> *Skills needed:* writing or design talent, interest in current events, ability to meet deadlines, self-confidence
>
> *Preparing for a journalism career:* work on high-school newspaper or yearbook, write for community newspaper, submit articles to magazines, study journalism in college

Inquiring The technique of **inquiring** involves gathering information through systematic questioning. As you think about your idea, list as many questions as you can, beginning with the words *who, what, where, when, why,* and *how.* These questions help you to assess what you already know about a topic and what you still need to find out.

Jason listed the following questions about the *Titanic* to develop ideas for a report:

> Who was aboard when the ship sank?
> What happened on the night of the sinking?
> Where was the *Titanic* when it sank?
> When did the sinking occur?
> Why did so many people die?
> How did the survivors escape?

Imaging Much of what you know is stored in your mind as whole pictures, or images. In **imaging,** you "call up" these pictures to gather ideas from them. To practice imaging, follow these steps:

1. Clear your mind and focus on your subject.
2. Try to picture in your mind the image you want to recall. Imagine approaching the image from a distance, gradually moving closer.
3. Jot down details as you remember them. Ask yourself questions about the image to recall more details.

Beth used imaging to gather details for a story. She focused on a time when she and her brother were cutting firewood and listed the following details:

June sun high in the sky
jeans and shirt soaked with sweat
wedge-shaped notch in white oak tree
high-pitched whine of chain saw
smell of leaf mold and gasoline

Writing Activities Exploring Ideas

A Choose a writing topic from the following list. Develop a clustering diagram (as shown on page 12) to generate ideas about the topic.

1. television detectives
2. Benjamin Franklin
3. Australia
4. *The Wizard of Oz*
5. rodeos
6. percussion instruments

B Choose another topic from the list above. Using the technique of inquiring (as described on page 13), list questions that you would ask an authority on the subject, in order to gather ideas about it.

C Think of a momentous day in your life, such as your first day of high school or a memorable birthday. Use the technique of imaging to list details about that day.

D Study the illustration on this page. Using this image, do ten minutes of freewriting.

Part 3
Personal Writing

Careful thought and observation can lead to exciting ideas, but these ideas can disappear in a week, a day, even an hour, unless they are recorded somehow. You can gather ideas in many ways, but one of the best and most personal ways is writing. Your writing need not be shared with others; instead, it can be **personal writing**—writing meant only for you. Personal writing is a way of savoring and exploring your ideas and feelings, to free up your writing skills and become comfortable with a pen or pencil in your hand.

Keeping a Journal

Some of your best writing can be done in a **journal,** a notebook in which you write regularly. Your journal can fulfill a variety of needs. It can be a diary—a narrative account of your life for a period of time. It can also be a sourcebook of writing ideas—your impressions, observations, reactions, and feelings. Use your journal to practice writing skills. If you keep your journal faithfully, it can be a "growth chart" of your progress—as a writer and a person.

Some writers set aside a particular time each day for journal writing. Others carry their journal with them and write whenever inspiration strikes. Most writers find it helpful to date their journal entries for future reference.

Writers have always kept journals. For example, James Boswell, the biographer of English author Samuel Johnson, kept a journal of his life in London in 1762 and 1763. Hidden for years, the journal was first published in 1950. Here is one of the entries.

▬ *Literary Model* ▬

Saturday 30 July [1763]. Mr. Johnson and I took a boat and sailed down the silver Thames . . . We landed at the Old Swan and walked to Billingsgate, where we took oars and moved smoothly along the river. We were entertained with the immense number and variety of ships that were lying at anchor. It was a pleasant day, and when we got clear out into the country, we were charmed with the beautiful fields on each side of the river.

From *Boswell's London Journal 1762–1763*

Here is a journal entry written by a high-school student.

Today when I was doing my laps, I felt like a swimming machine. My arms were pistons, rising and falling in rhythm. I ripped through the water, hardly aware of who I was. It was just me and the blue water and the empty sky. Afterwards, I clung to the cold tile of the pool edge, breathing hard. It was like waking up from a dream.

Your journal can take any form you want—a composition book, a loose leaf notebook, even an artbook. Set aside some time each day to write in your journal.

Other Types of Personal Writing

Journal writing is not the only way to release your thoughts and feelings onto paper. Your personal writing can take the form of a **memoir,** a **mood essay,** a **personal viewpoint,** or a **poem** or **song lyric.** In these kinds of writing as well, you write to please only yourself.

Memoirs When you want to capture a moment or an event in your life, you might try writing a **memoir.** An autobiography, a more comprehensive piece of writing, often spans a writer's lifetime.

Literary Model

I was bitten by a brown recluse spider a couple of weeks ago and lived to tell about it, so I shall. . . . [It] was hiding between the folds of a towel that I picked up and flung over my shoulder as I got ready to go for a swim with a friend. We were walking along the pathway down to the river when I felt a sharp, burning bite on my upper arm. I dropped the towel and saw a brown recluse scurry away. . . . My friend was horrified when I told him it was a brown recluse that had bitten me. He asked if I wanted to go back to the cabin. "Why?" I said. "If I'm going to die, I might better die down at the river than back in the cabin." So we continued on our way and spent the afternoon swimming and lying on a gravel bank.

From *A Country Year* by Sue Hubbell

Mood Essay Try writing a **mood essay** when you experience deep or unsettling feelings or a powerful event. Like descriptive writing, mood essays are rich in sensory details and impressions. Choose details to fit the particular mood you are trying to create.

After Ted saw his uncle's name on the Vietnam Veterans Memorial in Washington, D.C., he wrote a mood essay to express his feelings. Here is part of his essay.

Student Model

> I ran my finger across his name, very slowly. It was like reading Braille—each letter traveled like an electric current from my fingertip to my brain. At that moment, I knew my uncle for the first time.

Personal Viewpoint You probably hold opinions about a number of different issues. You can write a **personal viewpoint** about an issue or event that is important to you in a letter to the editor.

> Pit-bull terriers should be outlawed as pets. My eight-year-old daughter was bitten by one when she tried to give it a hug. She required plastic surgery on her face and will always have physical—and emotional—scars. Regardless of how lovingly these animals are raised, pit bulls revert to their vicious nature when threatened, even by the innocent play of a child.
>
> Anne Newberg, Rochester, Michigan

Poems or Song Lyrics Poetry can be a very special way to express your personal feelings. Sometimes your poetry is intended for musical accompaniment, as is the following song lyric.

━━ *Literary Model* ━━━━━━━━━━━━━━━━━━━━

Message keeps getting clearer
Radio's on and I'm moving 'round the place
I check my look in the mirror
I wanna change my clothes, my hair, my face
Man, I ain't getting nowhere just living in a dump like this
There's something happening somewhere
Baby I just know there is . . .

From "Dancing in the Dark" by Bruce Springsteen

Writing Activities Personal Writing

A Choose one of the following sentence beginnings. Use it to start a journal entry. You should write for ten minutes.

1. When I am a senior in high school . . .
2. When I was a child, I loved to . . .
3. Right now what is important to me is . . .
4. If I could change one thing about myself, I would . . .

B Write in your journal for ten minutes on the topic "something that I learned today." Do this on five consecutive days.

C Choose a picture that has special meaning for you, such as a photo of a relative or of a place you visited or a reproduction of a work of art that evokes strong feelings. Write a mood essay, poem, or song lyric that expresses your feelings about it.

D Do a piece of personal viewpoint writing, such as a letter to the editor, expressing your opinion about one of the following topics:

1. a newspaper or magazine article you did/didn't like
2. a political candidate you do/do not support
3. a movie or television program you liked/disliked

E Choose a moment in your life. It need not be something others would find exciting or memorable. Use imaging to recall details about the event. Then spend fifteen minutes writing a memoir in your journal.

Sailing Expressions

Centuries ago, when the phrase "let the cat out of the bag" was first used, it had nothing to do with felines. Likewise, "mind your *p*'s and *q*'s" had nothing to do with the alphabet. And "the devil to pay" had nothing to do with Satan. These are just a few of the expressions that can be traced to life on early sailing ships.

"Letting the cat out of the bag" may seem like a harmless way to refer to giving away a secret, but its origin was far more ominous. On early sailing vessels, the "cat" in question was the cat-o'-nine-tails, and when the ship's bosun let it out of the bag, it meant some sailor was in for a flogging.

"Minding one's *p*'s and *q*'s" was not part of a spelling lesson, either. When sailors went ashore, they were likely to congregate in the waterfront bars, where bartenders would tally the number of pints (*p*'s) and quarts (*q*'s) each man drank. The ship's quartermaster would warn the men before they left the ship about their *p*'s and *q*'s, hoping they would return to the ship somewhat sober.

The devil in "devil to pay" referred to a long seam running from stem to stern below the ship's main deck. "Paying" the devil was the term for the arduous task of caulking the seam and covering it with pitch.

Many other expressions, such as "first shot out of the locker," "son of a gun," and "pipe down," also sailed the high seas before finding a home on dry land.

Chapter 1
Application and Review

Use the techniques you have learned in this chapter to complete the following writing activities.

A Imaging What kind of day is it? Think of a particular kind of weather that you especially like—or dislike. For example, you might choose the first snowfall of winter, a steamy summer night, an afternoon thunderstorm, or a crisp day in autumn.

Use the technique of imaging (as explained on page 13) to recall a specific time in your life when you experienced this kind of weather. Concentrate on remembering the sensory details that accompanied this kind of weather: how it looked, how it sounded, even how it smelled and felt.

Jot down your observations and reactions as you recall the scene. Use your notes to write a mood essay that expresses your feelings about this kind of weather.

B Personal Viewpoint Choose an issue or a question that is important to you, or a cause that you feel strongly about. For example, you might have strong opinions about the lyrics of popular music, the existence of life on other planets, the protection of endangered species, the use of capital punishment, or the passage of gun-control legislation. Use this issue as a topic for personal viewpoint writing.

Use the techniques of analyzing or inquiring (as described on pages 12 and 13) to explore your opinion. Create a clustering diagram (as described on page 12) to develop related ideas. Use these notes to write a personal viewpoint that expresses how you feel about the issue you have chosen.

When you have finished writing your viewpoint, think of a person you know who disagrees with you. If you cannot think of someone, imagine a person who would hold a different point of view. Posing as that person, write a letter to yourself, expressing the opposing view. For example, if you have written your personal viewpoint in favor of gun-control laws, you might write a letter of rebuttal as an avid hunter who disagrees with such legislation.

Be sure to explore the opposing viewpoint carefully and thoroughly, using the techniques you learned in this chapter, before writing your rebuttal letter.

C *Starting Points for Writing* People, places, things, and experiences are constantly causing people to remember other people, places, things, and experiences. Any one of these memories is a good starting point for writing. What memories do you associate with the subjects, settings, and experiences suggested by the images and quotes below? Make a list of these memories.

"She always had her nose in the steam from a soup pot, she always thought their cat smelled bad, . . . she always wore heavy perfume."

Ann Beattie

I was really frozen. My ears were hurting and I could hardly move my fingers at all.

J. D. Salinger

2
Clear Thinking and Writing

*Y*ou don't have to be an astronaut or scientist to make fascinating discoveries. All you need to know is how to think. Questions, like space probes, can yield fantastic results.

For example, brainstorm to develop a list of questions triggered by looking at the picture of Saturn's rings on the opposite page. Then write freely to explore possible and even impossible and absurd answers to these questions.

Good writing begins with clear thinking. In this chapter you will learn thinking techniques that will help you generate and explore ideas. You will also begin to discover how to translate your ideas into writing.

Thinking About Thinking

As you experience the world, you are constantly thinking. An internal "camera" clicks away, recording everything around you and developing images in the form of thoughts. Much of your thinking occurs automatically. However, just as a photographer first learns about the process of photography in order to master its techniques, you must learn about the process of thinking. The mastery of thinking techniques will help you in all aspects of life, from taking a test to problem solving. In particular, thinking techniques can help you to assemble and write your thoughts.

Your writing actually begins in your mind. The "writing" portion is a translation of your thoughts onto paper. The clearer your thinking, the clearer the writing that you produce.

Types of Thinking

Your world is full of possibilities. Like a photographer, you can manipulate the countless images it presents to you. You can choose to focus on specific areas, to view things from near or far, even to mix images. In other words, you can guide the course of your own thoughts.

By opening your mind to different kinds of thinking, you can guide your ideas in interesting, innovative directions. This chapter will discuss creative thinking and critical thinking.

Creative Thinking Creative thinking is the process of creating new ideas from old ideas or from the circumstances and events around you. For example, composers initially wrote only light, delicate music for the piano. Then in the 1800's German composer Ludwig van Beethoven broke with tradition and composed piano concertos full of passionate, thunderous chords. In 1891, a Massachusetts teacher hung a peach basket at either end of a gymnasium to challenge his restless students—and invented the game of basketball.

Creative thinking can produce new art, new inventions, new discoveries—ideas that change the world. But creative thinking can also produce a fund-raising strategy for your club, a new way to comb your hair, or a topic for a composition. Many of the situations you encounter daily demand creative thinking. To meet that demand, you need not wait for inspiration to strike; you need only observe things with fresh eyes and concentrate on your thoughts.

Here's how some Nevada residents used creative thinking.

Highway 50 covers 287 long, empty miles in the state of Nevada—a stretch so barren that a national magazine dubbed it "the loneliest road in America." At first, residents of the sparse communities along the highway reacted to the description with fury. After a little time and a lot of creative thinking, however, they turned the bleak description to their advantage. They persuaded the state to officially designate Highway 50 "the loneliest road in America" and erected road signs bearing the slogan. To travelers along the route, they distributed Highway 50 Survival Kits, containing first-aid supplies and maps, and certificates from the governor testifying to the travelers' frontier spirit. As a result, tourism along the road rose 40 percent in just one year. Now local citizens are concerned that the highway may become too crowded to retain its designation!

Critical Thinking New ideas are exciting, but they are not always workable. Critical thinking must go hand in hand with creative thinking: you think of an idea, evaluate it, adjust it, evaluate it again, and continue to adjust and evaluate as long as necessary.

Critical thinking is a part of everyday life. You engage in some form of critical thinking when you review a TV program, vote in a school election, seek someone's advice, or even select a shampoo. The most difficult ideas to judge, however, are those you think of yourself. Few ideas, even brilliant ones, emerge perfectly formed. Practice in judging the ideas of others will help you develop the confidence and skill to judge—and adjust—your own ideas.

Leon, a high-school student, was writing to Ms. Ryan, the principal of his elementary school, about the National Youth Fitness Test. After meeting students from elementary and middle schools that had participated in the test, Leon was impressed. He wanted to tell Ms. Ryan about the testing program in the hope that she would encourage her school to join. Here are his thoughts on his first draft. Note how Leon uses critical thinking to evaluate and adjust his ideas.

Let's see. Should I explain why I think the test is so good? I could explain how the kids at my high school who are in the best physical shape were in fitness testing programs in grade school. Then I could tell about how they say that the test gave them a reason to get into shape. That's clear, and specific too. I wonder, though. Does Ms. Ryan know exactly what the test is? Maybe I should describe it. That would help my argument, too, by showing how interesting it is and how students get all involved in charting their progress. Okay, I'll add details about the test. Now, what about my language? It should be pretty formal. I'd better change *terrific* to *excellent*. . . .

Writing Activities Thinking About Thinking

A These questions and the questions on page 826 in the Writer's Handbook can help you think creatively and critically about any work of art. Use them to write your thoughts about the art on this page.

1. How does the scene affect you? Why?
2. How would changing the subjects, colors, or shapes change how you feel about this scene?
3. In what other ways could an artist depict such a scene?

B In your journal list some good ideas you have had in the past few weeks and how you arrived at them. (The following questions will help jog your memory.) Evaluate your ideas. What made them work? Could they have been improved?

1. Have you solved any problems lately—yours or someone else's?
2. Have you created a song, painting, or other work of art?
3. Did you find a new use for an old item?
4. Did you have an original idea for a story or other composition?

Bovine Park, Roy De Forest, 1977.

Part 2

Finding Ideas

The types of thinking you have just considered, creative thinking and critical thinking, can be used together to produce ideas. In fact, you can view thinking as a kind of manufacturing process, with ideas as the product. Like many products, ideas are constructed out of both raw materials and processed parts. The raw materials are the sensations and situations around you. The processed parts are the experiences, information, and thoughts inside you. Unlike a factory assembly line, however, your thinking is designed to produce products that are unique. Each time you view or experience something new, you increase your ability to create new and different ideas.

To generate these ideas—to retrieve and assemble information from inside you and around you—you may only need to focus your attention. Concentrating on something, even something familiar, can bring forth a huge array of ideas. Choose any object and focus on it—your pencil, for instance. What thoughts might come to mind?

> This pencil has a blunt point and tooth marks.
> What if a pencil could write its own stories?
> I wonder why most pencils are painted yellow? How are they made?
> Graphite wears down quickly. Could some stronger material be found?
> Pencils are so convenient. What was it like to use a quill pen?
> What was it like to live at the time of quill pens?
> Now writing with pencils is being replaced by word processors. How else is technology changing simple tasks?
> I remember a colored-pencil set I had when I was little. I drew. . .

To help you tap the worlds inside you and around you for ideas, you can use the skills of recalling and observing.

Recalling

"Memory is the mother of all wisdom," wrote the ancient playwright Aeschylus. All your life you have been storing thoughts, sensations, experiences, and facts. Calling upon those memories provides you with the raw material for new thoughts. A new connection, a new experience, a new application can transform a memory into an idea. Recalling your childhood toys, for example, might give you an idea for a new toy or a safe-toy campaign or a greeting card or a lyric or a story character.

From Chapter 1 you are already familiar with freewriting, an effective strategy for retrieving your own thoughts. In freewriting you start with an idea and write nonstop, letting your thoughts lead you.

In this chapter, you will learn about several more thinking techniques. You may use these techniques—and the ones discussed in Chapter 1—in a variety of combinations and for many purposes besides the ones described here.

Observing

While recalling helps you find ideas inside yourself, observing helps you discover ideas in the world around you. Observing means more than merely looking; it means becoming aware of the features that distinguish one person, place, thing, or situation from another.

For example, after getting off a bus, you probably cannot describe the other passengers. If you were a novelist seeking descriptive details, however, you might take more careful note. You might focus on one passenger or a few, zeroing in on features that characterize their clothing, physical appearance, and mannerisms. That is observing.

As you observe, general features like these will help you focus.

Sight	size	shape	color	weight
	age	number	height	depth
Other Senses	sound	feel	smell	taste
Other Features	duration	function	condition	value

Listing Listing enables you to observe more effectively by helping you select and characterize the most important features. Here is part of Leeann's list for a description of an elderly man she saw on a bus. Note how she focuses on some features, becoming increasingly specific. Notice also how this person's appearance suggests a story to her.

over 6 feet tall	peacock blue shirt
husky	booming voice
broad chest	loud laugh
jacket buttons straining	high-pitched
thick hands	sitting on rear of bus
blue-veined	hale and hearty
roughened by work?	talkative
white hair	not prosperous-looking
ruddy face	worn-out clothes
bright green pants	hole in shoe
pink and green plaid jacket	button missing from jacket

Leeann asked herself the following questions as she observed the man: *Wonder who this guy is, what he does? Does he realize how bizarre his clothes look? He doesn't look as if he has money, but he seems happy. Or maybe he's one of those eccentrics—lots of money hidden under a mattress somewhere. What would happen if that kind of guy suddenly lost his money? How would he act then?* By asking herself these questions, Leeann hit upon a writing idea.

Gleaning/Conducting Research During every waking moment —and also some sleeping moments—you are bombarded with possible ideas. Learn to "glean," or gather, those that might prove valuable. Become a collector of interesting sights, sensations, words, and thoughts. Like a collector, savor and examine the items in your collection. Ask yourself which are worth exploring.

When you encounter an idea that has potential, keep it in mind as you observe the world. Be on the lookout for related ideas. Conduct research. Prepare questions and answer them by reading, interviewing, and experimenting. Some exciting new ideas will inevitably result—not only writing ideas but other ideas as well. Here is an example.

> As a cereal company executive, Steve was always on the lookout for new ideas. One morning as he ate breakfast with friends, he watched them mix fruit into their oatmeal. Noting how appetizing the cereal looked, Steve had an idea. Suppose the fruit came with the oatmeal! He took the idea to his company. Could it be done? Yes, dried fruit could be added, which would soften in the cooked cereal. Did people want it? Interviews revealed that people preferred fresh fruit but did not mind dried fruit, and people in a hurry were willing to sacrifice freshness for convenience. Other suggestions were made, such as adding flavorings. A year after Steve's breakfast, the company introduced its new breakfast product.

Knowledge Inventory Observation is a give-and-take process, for you bring to it the wealth of knowledge you have accumulated. Something Steve knew, for example, was that a fruit-and-cereal combination is nutritious. This fact added to the merit of his idea.

When you observe something that might be of interest, ask yourself, "What do I know about this?" Make a list and see how it affects your observations—and the ideas that grow out of them. For example, when you observe an ocean beach in search of writing ideas, what knowledge do you bring to the scene? You might mention tides, salty water, pollution problems, and seasons.

By reminding yourself of what you already know, you become more sensitive to the details of the scene. How, for instance, does the change of seasons affect a beach? Is the tide high or low? What tells you this? Is there evidence of pollution?

Studying the things around you can activate your knowledge; that knowledge, in turn, can help you use your observations to create and refine your ideas.

Associating

You can "find" ideas by remembering them or by observing them. You can also generate ideas by associating them—that is, by re-combining what you know in new and different ways.

Associating is like the process of rearranging furniture. When you associate, you attempt to create a new idea by rearranging what you already know. Similarly, when you rearrange furniture, you try differ-ent groupings of chairs, tables, and lamps to achieve a new "look." Some combinations seem promising; others don't work at all. You might even experiment with bringing in posters or a bowl of flowers from another room. You use the trial-and-error method, combined with what you already know about the room, to produce the best result.

You learned one associating technique—clustering—in Chapter 1. Two others are creative questioning and brainstorming.

Creative Questioning The technique of creative questioning helps you to look at things—and ideas—differently. For example, suppose you were examining a common, everyday item like a paper cup. Using creative questioning, you might ask yourself "What if this were made of another material?" or "What if I changed the shape of this item?" or even "With what other item could I combine this in order to create something new and different?" Creative questions are limited only by your imagination.

Brainstorming The technique of brainstorming is similar to clus-tering in that you let your thoughts run free. In clustering, however, you use a diagram to connect your thoughts on a subject; in brainstorming, you write down every idea that occurs to you, whether related or not. In fact, one of the rules in brainstorming is that every idea—no matter how unrelated it seems—is valid and acceptable.

You can use the techniques of creative questioning and clustering on your own. You can also brainstorm alone, but it is far more pro-ductive when done in a group.

Bus Riders,
George Segal,
1964.

Writing Activities *Finding Ideas*

A Study the piece of art on this page. Use the skills of recalling and observing to help you extract new ideas from it. In your journal write answers to the following questions, challenging yourself to find something new.

1. Of what personal experience does this scene remind you?
2. Does it bring to mind certain people in your life?
3. What places or things does it bring to mind?
4. What do you know about it?
5. What would you like to know about it?
6. What could you do to get more information about the picture?
7. What are the main features? Make a list.
8. Choose one part. What are its features? Choose two other parts. What are their features? Zero in closely on one feature.
9. What do you like about it? What do you dislike about it?
10. How would you change it if you could?

B Choose one of the following subjects or a "trigger word" from the list on page 826 of the Writer's Handbook. Using it as a starting point, freewrite for ten minutes in your journal.

1. competition
2. sports fans
3. affection
4. cartoons
5. sunshine
6. envy

C Form a small group with some classmates who chose the same freewriting subject as you did in Activity B. As a group, brainstorm additional ideas on that subject. Afterward, compare the results of your freewriting and brainstorming in terms of the number and types of ideas generated.

Part 3
Developing Ideas

You have just examined ways in which you can generate ideas. Unfortunately, though, your ideas do not spring to mind fully formed and ready to go. You need to explore them, to take them beyond the obvious to discover what they are made of and where they might lead. Here's how two artists explored and developed an idea that resulted in an important art form.

In the early 1900's, painters Georges Braque and Pablo Picasso conceived of a new way to represent things: to present different views of a subject simultaneously on one canvas. Exploring this idea, they visually broke their subjects into parts and portrayed these parts from varying perspectives—from above, from the side, from inside out. From these attempts the painting style called *cubism* developed.

The artists found, however, that most viewers could no longer recognize the subjects of the paintings. To maintain a link between their subject and the viewer, they added a recognizable object, letter, or word to the painting. Braque and Picasso then carried this idea further by pasting real objects onto the canvas, and the collage was born—a new art form in which real materials and objects are pasted onto a painted or unpainted surface.

Artists may use their eyes, imagination, and skill to peer into an idea, and they may use new forms and materials to expand it. Scientists make use of microscopes, computers, and controlled experiments. The tools available to you for developing your ideas include describing, analyzing, and questioning.

Describing

Describing means breaking something down into the crucial details that allow you to re-create it for someone else, almost like taking a model airplane apart and reconstructing it piece by piece. Scrutinizing a

subject—taking it apart—can help you not only generate ideas but also describe them. Charting can help you to accomplish this task.

Charting In Part 2, you learned about listing, a technique that can help you describe. When you use listing, you simply write down all that you observe. In charting, however, you arrange the features and other observations in a certain order.

To construct a chart, select the most important features, make them column heads, and fill in the details. Arranging details in the form of a chart forces you to focus on them in an orderly way.

Emily was writing a short story set in a restaurant. Here is part of the chart she put together to help her visualize the scene.

Time and Place	Characters	Major Props
summer night	teen-age	wooden picnic
1970's	customers:	tables and
a southern city	five girls	benches
pizza	three boys	smell of garlic
restaurant	two female	and oregano
	cooks	plastic
	one waiter/	grapevines and
	owner	tiny colored
		lights
		rock music
		blaring from
		jukebox

Analyzing

Analyzing, an extremely important thinking skill, involves dividing an idea into its main parts and then examining each part. Mastering the techniques of analysis will allow you to explore any reasonable idea, no matter how complicated it seems.

For example, imagine that you live in a large housing complex. Although there are many community concerns, no vehicle exists for expressing them. You are interested in exploring the idea of publishing a community newspaper. Where do you start? You start by breaking the idea down into its main parts.

To begin, you might ask yourself, "What do I need in order to publish a newspaper?" You need (1) money, (2) a printing method, (3) a distribution system, (4) contents, and (5) staff. Now you are ready to consider each part in detail. Your idea is beginning to take shape.

You can use several techniques for analyzing. The first, charting, was discussed in the last section. Another technique, questioning, will be discussed in a section of its own. A third technique is the idea tree.

Idea Trees   Similar to the technique of charting, an idea tree serves as a visual way to analyze an idea. Like a blueprint of a house, an idea tree graphically displays the parts and how they fit together.

Here's how you would use an idea tree to analyze the newspaper idea. The subject appears at the base of the tree, which then branches into five main parts, each of which can branch into details, which in turn can branch. Only part of the tree is shown here.

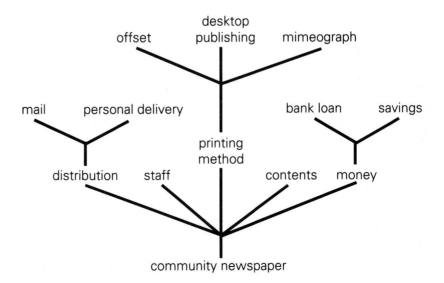

Questioning

When you want to know about something, you ask questions. Analyzing an idea is essentially a matter of asking the right questions. In fact, just forming the questions increases your understanding of the idea, for it forces you to consider exactly what it is important to know about a particular topic.

Here are some questions you might ask to begin your analysis of an idea that interests you.

1. What do I already know about this idea?
2. What must I find out about it?
3. What are the major parts?
4. What details are involved in each part?
5. How could I expand the idea? How could I narrow it?
6. How would I explain the idea to someone else?

These are general analysis questions. Other kinds of questions can be grouped into **action questions** and **category questions.**

Action Questions The basic information questions, as all journalism students learn, begin with the five *W*'s—*who, what, where, when,* and *why*—and the word *how.* If you are planning a newspaper article, a story plot, an election campaign, a TV ad, or anything that revolves around an action of any sort, these are the most direct questions to ask. Out of these basic questions, you can create others that allow you to investigate an idea in greater depth. Here are some examples.

1. *What?* What happened? What is it? What does it mean?
2. *Who?* Who is responsible? Who else is involved?
3. *Where?* Where does it happen? What is the place like?
4. *When?* When does it happen? What else is going on?
5. *Why?* Why does it happen? What causes it? What is its purpose?
6. *How?* How does it come about? How does it work?

In preparing a story for his high-school newspaper, Matt asked himself—and others—the following questions.

1. *What?* a collection of hazardous waste items from households: paint, paint thinner, pesticides, used motor oil, batteries, and so forth; first such collection planned here; has been held in neighboring towns
2. *Who?* sponsors: town and League of Women Voters; for residents only
3. *Where?* Center Street, Department of Public Works parking lot

4. *When?* Saturday, October 27, 9 A.M. to 3:30 P.M.; no other
   townwide activities planned that day
5. *Why?* increased use of hazardous household chemicals; need to
   provide for their safe disposal
6. *How?* residents drop off items at collection point; Carter Solvents
   Services picks them up for disposal; announcement in town paper
   and mailed to all residences, posters throughout town

Category Questions Other kinds of questions can also prove useful for investigating an idea in detail. Like action questions, category
questions help you divide a subject into its relevant parts. The parts in
this case have to do with categories, that is, with the different ways in
which you can view things.

To begin with, you might base your questions on how you categorize the subject itself. Is it a physical object? Is it an event? Is it a place?
Is it an opinion? Your questions will vary accordingly.

Suppose you have a brilliant idea for something the world has long
needed—a bicycle seat that will remain both soft and sturdy in use. To
develop your idea, what questions should you ask yourself? Here are
some examples.

1. What are its physical features—its shape, length, material, . . . ?
2. How is it put together? How is it made?
3. Who will use it and for what?
4. How does it differ from others of its kind?

Suppose you had to analyze a painting for an art-appreciation class.
Asking—and answering—the following questions would provide you
with a better understanding of the work.

1. What shapes are used? How are they arranged?
2. What colors are used? Where?
3. What is the scene, impression, mood, or tone?
4. How do the shapes and colors affect the mood?
5. What attracts my attention?
6. How does the work affect me?
7. What does the work depict or express?
8. How does this depiction relate to the real scene?
9. How would changing the shapes, colors, or subjects change the
   mood or meaning?

Other questions focus on the various aspects of an idea—how it
relates to other things, where it comes from, what it brings to mind, and
so on. Some of them appear in the chart on page 37.

Category Questions

Definition
1. How does the dictionary define it?
2. How would I define it?
3. To what group does it seem to belong?
4. How does it differ from others in that group?
5. What are some specific examples of it?
6. What are its parts? How might they be divided?

Comparison
1. What is it similar to? in what ways?
2. What is it different from? in what ways?
3. What is it better than? in what ways?
4. What is it worse than? in what ways?

Cause and Effect
1. What causes it?
2. What effects does it have?
3. What is its purpose?
4. Why does or did it happen?

Conditions and Events
1. Is it possible or impossible? Why?
2. Is it practical? Why or why not?
3. Has it happened before? When? How?
4. Who has done or experienced it?

Documentation
1. What facts or statistics do I know about it?
2. What laws are there about it?
3. What have I heard or read about it?
4. What have I heard people say about it?
5. What saying, proverb, song, or poem do I know about it?
6. How would I find out more about it?

Here's how an advertising copywriter used category questions to help her develop a campaign.

Lin was assigned to the Smoothee pots account—a new line of cookware that claimed to be spatterproof. Her first task was to come up with a concept. To do this, Lin took out her trusty list of questions and, with Smoothee pots in mind, answered each question briefly. Next, she went over her answers, marking the ones that showed the most promise in terms of campaign ideas. Then she returned to those answers, following up on the lines of thought they suggested.

Normally, Lin spent a great deal of time on this stage, working through the answers in great depth and detail and perhaps even re-asking certain questions to look for a different answer. This time, though, almost as soon as she had jotted down an answer to the question about famous sayings, a campaign theme came to her: "Out of the frying pan into the fire? Not with a Smoothee pan!"

Writing Activities *Developing Ideas*

A Choose one of the following subjects. Make a chart to describe its features.

1. the opening scene of a movie about a storm
2. a real automobile or other vehicle
3. an imaginary automobile or other vehicle
4. a busy street in your community
5. a table set for a child's birthday party
6. a baseball team's dugout during a playoff game

B Choose one of the following subjects. Analyze it by constructing an idea tree.

1. your dream career
2. a shopping mall
3. your favorite kind of music
4. types of movies
5. advertising for part-time work that you can do—babysitting, lawn mowing, typing term papers, and so on
6. your favorite novel

C Choose one of the following subjects. Develop the idea by using the questioning techniques described in this chapter. Write your questions and answers.

1. an ad campaign for a car
2. a plan for a party
3. a plan for a new TV game show
4. a photograph, drawing, or statue
5. a new solution to an old problem
6. a better mousetrap

Part 4

Organizing Ideas

Now that you have learned how to develop ideas, you must learn to organize them. Without effective organization, good ideas can founder and die.

For example, consider the library, where literally millions of facts are stored and made accessible to people. If the library were not organized—if its contents were not arranged so that people could find them—it would not be nearly as useful a resource. The same holds true for most good ideas, from telephone directories to chemical elements to story plots. Organization is needed to make them work.

Organizing means arranging and structuring ideas so that they can be used and understood. There are basically two ways to accomplish this—ordering and classifying. Ordering involves arranging things in a sequence. Classifying involves arranging things according to their similarities and differences.

Ordering

When you order things, you arrange them in a sequence based on some principle, such as time or importance. The sequence provides a logical organization that helps to make the idea comprehensible.

Can you make sense of these notes taken at the scene of an accident?

pedestrian stepped out of way
pedestrian's vision blocked
part of street blocked off
cat suddenly ran out
traffic light was changing
car turned corner quickly
suffered sprained ankle
carrying two bags of groceries
groceries all over street
pedestrian slipped on icy street

Did the blockade, cat, groceries, ice, or car cause the accident? If the events had been arranged in a logical sequence, the sequence itself would tell you "this happened next" or "this caused that." Three of the most useful arrangements are **chronological order, causal order,** and **cumulative order.**

Chronological Order To order things chronologically, arrange them in the sequence in which they occur. Actions, processes, and events lend themselves to a chronological arrangement.

Wes had been interested in deep-sea diving for a long time, so when he had to write a report, he decided to use it as his topic. From his notes, he constructed the following time line to help him trace the development of deep-sea diving as a sport.

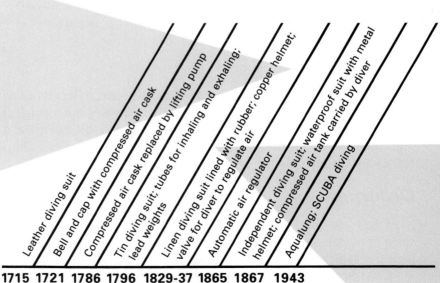

Leather diving suit
Bell and cap with compressed air cask
Compressed air cask replaced by lifting pump
Tin diving suit; tubes for inhaling and exhaling; lead weights
Linen diving suit lined with rubber; copper helmet; valve for diver to regulate air
Automatic air regulator
Independent diving suit; waterproof suit with metal helmet; compressed air tank carried by diver
Aqualung; SCUBA diving

1715 1721 1786 1796 1829-37 1865 1867 1943

Causal Order When the temperature falls below freezing, water turns to ice. When a baby becomes hungry, it cries. The first event (the cause) brings about the second event (the effect). An event like an election victory can have multiple causes and multiple effects. Some events create a chain of causes and effects. By ordering appropriate ideas as a chain, you can demonstrate clearly how they are connected, as in the events outlined below.

1. Every spring, heavy rains fell near the source of the Nile River.
2. This caused the river to swell and flood in Egypt each summer.
3. This flooding created a fertile strip of land in the desert.
4. As a result, Egyptian farmers could plant one crop every fall—but only one.
5. This limitation led to the building of the giant Aswan Dam.
6. The dam provided a year-round water supply and put an end to the flooding.
7. The absence of flooding caused the flow of tiny plants to the sea to stop.
8. With no tiny plants, the sardines lost their food supply.
9. This led to the collapse of Egypt's large sardine fishing industry.

Cumulative Order Ideas can be ordered so that they build up, or accumulate. For example, they can be arranged by degree of familiarity or importance—from most to least or from least to most.

Suppose you were writing a report on cures for the common cold. You might start by discussing familiar measures, such as resting and drinking plenty of liquids. Then you might discuss popular over-the-counter medications like aspirin, and physicians' varying opinions on their usefulness. Finally, you might mention recent research findings.

Classifying

Classifying means grouping things into categories on the basis of what they have in common. A system of classification can make things easier to understand and use. For example, stores classify the products they sell so customers can quickly locate the items they want to purchase. To make your writing clearer, look for relevant and logical ways to classify your ideas—into problem and solution, similarities and differences, and so on.

Here is how Irina used classifying techniques to plan a brochure.

Irina's publishing service had volunteered to develop an informational brochure for the tenth anniversary of Sadie's Place, a shelter for homeless families. A meeting was held at the shelter to discuss the brochure. At the meeting, residents and staff members enthusiastically contributed their ideas—stories of struggles, friendships, and plans. To impose some order, Irina proposed that they divide the brochure into three sections: the history of the shelter, personal stories, and plans for the future. Her idea was unanimously accepted.

Main Idea and Supporting Details Probably the most important way to organize your writing ideas is to classify them into main ideas and supporting details. Your main idea will be the principal message you want to get across. Your details will be the ideas, examples, or facts that help to explain, describe, or support the main idea. The more clearly you make this classsification, the clearer your writing is likely to be.

Here are some of Eric's notes for a report on the history of radio in the United States.

> 1925–1950: radio a major source of entertainment
> many comedians and reporters became famous on radio
> today, four times more radio stations than newspapers
> more national radio networks than TV networks
> increasing portability of radios
> TV more prominent but radio audience still growing
> about nine times more radio stations than TV stations
> specialized—news, classical music, ethnic . . .
> up-to-the-minute reports—traffic, weather . . .
> families buying multiple TV's now too

Eric realized that many of his notes had to do with the continued popularity of radio today despite the prominence of TV. He decided to make that idea the main idea of his report. Then he selected the details that would support the main idea.

Similarities and Differences When you make comparisons between two or more things, you are concerned with their similarities and differences. What are the reasons for choosing one political candidate over another, or one job offer over another? How do two computer programs compare? What do all of William Shakespeare's plays have in common? Which compact disc player produces the best sound for the lowest price?

The most effective way to deal with questions like these is to list the relevant features of the things being compared and then divide the features into those that are shared and those that are not.

Lena was writing a press release about Dr. Paul Ekman's research on smiles. To summarize his findings about genuine smiles and those that actually mask unpleasant feelings, Lena prepared the following three lists.

Both	True Smiles	False Smiles
designed to show pleasure	cheeks move up	furrow between eyebrows
corners of mouth curve up	crow's feet form around mouth	no crow's feet
	skin around eyebrows droops	no drooping skin around eyebrows

In the press release, Lena stated that the subtle but detectable differences can be useful in understanding social situations and in cases where physicians or therapists are looking for clues to a patient's real feelings.

Writing Activities *Organizing Ideas*

A Establish two methods of classifying the following sports.

football	diving	field hockey
volleyball	water skiing	figure skating
soccer	ice hockey	slalom skiing
swimming	baseball	water polo
tennis	badminton	basketball

B Arrange these facts about the history of New Zealand in chronological order.

as an independent nation, fought in both World War I and World War II on the side of the Allies

Maoris prevented the landing of a Dutch navigator, first European to sight New Zealand

Niue, 400 miles west, became self-governing in 1974

Britain declared New Zealand a colony and began organized settlement

British Captain James Cook explored coasts of New Zealand during the eighteenth century

in 1965 Cook Islands became self-governing

colony finally became a dominion—independent member of the British Commonwealth

Maoris, Polynesians from the eastern Pacific, were the first inhabitants of New Zealand

C Look at the picture on this page. Try to imagine what has just happened. Write about it in your journal, using the ordering method of your choice.

Part 5

Making Inferences and Drawing Conclusions

You want to be more than a storage place for someone else's ideas. You want to go beyond them to ideas and creations that are uniquely yours, to ask "What does this mean?" or "Where does this lead?" Then *you* can become the research scientist with the new discovery or the moviemaker with the startling vision.

Sir Isaac Newton could not actually see the force of gravity; he inferred it from observations about how objects fall and planets move. When Dr. Edward Jenner noticed that people who had had cowpox did not contract the deadly smallpox, he concluded that a cowpox vaccine would protect against the more serious disease. Like Newton and Jenner, you make inferences and draw conclusions constantly.

Going Beyond the Facts

Gathering experience, observations, and facts is a basic part of education and life, but it is not enough. You need to go beyond the facts—to see new connections and meanings—in order to learn, grow, and discover. Scientists realize this; they are always searching for new insights, always asking, "What might this mean?"

Here's how one American scientist went beyond the facts and made an important discovery.

> One day, research scientist Michael Zasloff was idly watching one of his laboratory frogs swimming in an aquarium full of brown, murky water. Because Dr. Zasloff had made a surgical incision on the frog's abdomen only a few days before, he expected to find the cut inflamed and infected from exposure to the bacteria-laden water. Yet, to his surprise, the frog's incision was healing nicely and showed no sign of infection.
>
> Suddenly Dr. Zasloff realized that something about the frog's body had protected it from almost certain infection. After five months of testing and analyzing, he was able to present his discovery: two antibiotics that occur naturally in a frog's skin. Called *magainins* (the Hebrew word for "shield"), the antibiotics kill a wide range of bacteria, fungi, and parasites, and may also prove effective in treating some cancers and viruses.

Dr. Zasloff's experience was similar to those of Newton, Jenner, and countless others who not only knew to go beyond the facts but also knew what to do when they got there. Like them, Dr. Zasloff used his knowledge to draw a conclusion from an observation. That is, he made an inference.

1. Observation: frog's incision is healing despite bacteria in water
2. Conclusion: something in the frog is protecting it from bacteria

As both a practicing physician and a scientist, Dr. Zasloff was able to bring exactly the right experience to his observation and make an inference that he knew to be significant. He had to demonstrate this significance, however. An inference, even a sound one, is not a fact; it must be tested. Dr. Zasloff spent months extracting chemicals from the frog's skin and testing them on different bacteria before he located the antibiotics. Tests on humans still lie ahead.

Here's how another person used her experience to make inferences and draw a conclusion.

> The eastern city in which Dina lived seemed to be turning into one massive construction site. While she missed some of the familiar old houses, Dina found herself constantly fascinated by the sight of a tall building rising piece by piece out of a hole in the ground. Each day after school, she made a detour to watch the latest building go up.

One day, watching the earth-moving equipment, she noticed what appeared to be broken pieces of pottery in the earth. She idly wondered why as she turned to head home. Then she caught sight of some other fragments at the edge of the site, and she picked one up. It resembled an old piece of pottery she had once broken. Curious, she examined some of the other fragments. One seemed to be the handle of a cup. Then an idea struck her. Hers was an old city, dating back to the time of colonial America. Could a colonial house have stood here? Were these dishes once used by a colonial family?

The next day, at the suggestion of her parents, Dina called the mayor's office and learned that a law protected building sites having possible historic value. The fragments did prove to be old, and construction was halted as archaeologists investigated further.

How did Dina go beyond the facts to make her discovery? Here are the steps she followed.

1. **She made an observation.** She noticed some unusual pottery fragments.
2. **She speculated about the meaning of the observation.** Rather than ignore it, she actively addressed her thoughts to it.
3. **She combined what she'd observed with other facts.** From her visits to other construction sites, Dina knew that these fragments were unusual. From a familiarity with her city's history, she knew that they might date back to colonial times.

At this point, Dina made an educated guess. While her discovery was dramatic, the process that led to it was not. It involved the same steps that you or anyone takes to make an inference. The first and third steps, in fact, are taken fairly automatically. It is step two—going beyond the facts—that provides the key to special discoveries. Train yourself to look at facts and ask "What does that mean?" for this is the question that can open doors.

Follow these guidelines to draw conclusions from your observations and experience.

Guidelines for Drawing Conclusions

1. Study your observation and the facts surrounding it.
2. Compare the information with what you already know and have previously observed.
3. Think about how all the differences of information might fit together. Look for similarities and inconsistencies.
4. Draw your conclusion.

Writing Activities Making Inferences

A Read each of the following statements. Then write two inferences that you can make from each one.

1. Grover Cleveland was the twenty-second and twenty-fourth President of the United States.
2. French is the official language of Gabon, a country located in central Africa.
3. In Canada, Thanksgiving is celebrated each year on the second Monday in October.
4. Gabriel Fahrenheit was an eighteenth-century physicist.
5. Karen Cahill just got her driver's license.
6. Pedro García speaks English as a native language and knows no Spanish.

B Read the following groups of facts and observations. Then, for each group, write a conclusion.

1. Your next-door neighbor Mr. Panetta tells you that he is planning to visit Italy. You know that Mr. Panetta's father, who lives in Naples, is recovering from surgery.

2. You notice several low-calorie frozen dinners in the freezer at your aunt's house. Your aunt tells you that she is five pounds overweight.
3. On your way home through the park yesterday evening, you noticed five or six people stretched out asleep on park benches. In the newspaper you read that twelve hundred people applied for ten apartments that had become available in public housing.
4. You occasionally hear meowing in the apartment next door. You have never seen a cat go in or come out.
5. You begin sneezing, coughing, and running a temperature. You remember that your little sister had the flu a week before.

C Read the following information. Do you draw the same conclusion as Lupe, the "detective"?

When Lupe arrived at her friend Ronald's house to work on homework, she discovered an unexpected scene. Gathered were Ronald, his father, a police officer, and Ronald's neighbor, Mr. Olsen, who was wearing a large bandage on his nose.

"This is an outrage!" sputtered Mr. Olsen. "Twenty minutes ago I was hammering a nail into the wall, getting ready to hang a mirror. Suddenly a ball came sailing through my open window and hit me on the nose. Then, it landed on the mirror beside me and shattered it. By the time I got to the window, I saw a kid with a red jacket running into this house. I yelled at him, but he didn't stop."

Mr. Olsen turned to the police officer. "I want these people to pay for my mirror—and my broken nose!"

"I admit that I have a red jacket and that I got home twenty minutes ago," said Ronald, "but I wasn't playing ball. In fact, nobody was playing ball!"

The three adults conferred while Lupe tried to comfort her miserable friend. She felt certain that Ronald was innocent; he didn't even like baseball! Lupe thought hard about what Mr. Olsen had said, trying to visualize the scene. If only she could find something. . . and suddenly it occurred to her.

"Excuse me a minute, Mr. Olsen," Lupe interrupted the adults, "but if you were hammering a nail into the wall, your back was to the window. How could the ball have hit you on the nose?"

It was the police officer's turn to play detective. "I'd like you to remove that bandage, sir," he told the neighbor. Sheepishly, Mr. Olsen removed the bandage, revealing a perfectly healthy nose. He left quietly, knowing that he would have to replace the mirror that he himself had dropped.

LANGUAGE LORE
Palindromes

L anguage buffs have devoted uncounted hours to inventing new *palindromes*—words or phrases that are identical whether read left-to-right or right-to-left.

Because they were reputedly invented by Sotades, a Greek poet of the third century B.C., palindromes are sometimes called *sotadics*. Short ones are easy to find: "deed," "eye," "kayak," "level," and "noon." The longest such word in English, "redivider," falls short of the longest known palindromic word, *saippuakauppias*, a 15-letter Finnish word meaning "soap seller."

The challenge of finding palindromic words pales before the complexity of creating palindromic sentences or stories. Humorists have even described the first conversation as an exchange of palindromes:

He: "Madam, I'm Adam."

She: "Eve."

Once they grow longer than about fifty letters, palindromes usually make little sense, although Penelope Gilliatt used fifty-one to say: "Doc, note I dissent. A fast never prevents a fatness. I diet on cod." A less ambitious writer mused, "Was it a car or a cat I saw?"

John Taylor probably created the first English palindromic sentence in the seventeenth century: "Lewd did I live & evil I did dwel." Napoleon Bonaparte is associated with one of the most famous: "Able was I ere I saw Elba," while history also comes alive in a palindrome attributed to Leigh Mercer: "A man, a plan, a canal—Panama."

Chapter 2
Application and Review

Use the thinking techniques that you have learned in this chapter to complete the following activities.

A Types of Thinking What good ideas have you heard or read about lately? Make a list, using the phrases below to help jog your memory. Then, choose one of the ideas and imagine that you are the person who thought of it. Describe the process by which the idea might have occurred to you.

an invention	a joke
a design or style	a book
a combination of colors	a movie
a solution to a problem	a TV program
a drawing or painting	a sculpture
a piece of advice	a piece of music

B Analyzing Think about a time in your life when you really worked hard at a task or some other effort and accomplished more than you thought was possible. Use analyzing techniques to recreate the incident for another person.

C Ordering Using causal ordering, write the major steps in the creation or development of one of the following.

1. a natural phenomenon, such as an earthquake, volcanic eruption, or thunderstorm
2. a historical event, such as the signing of a treaty, a revolution, or a cultural movement
3. a personal event, such as an achievement, a setback, or a relationship

D Classifying Choose one of the pairs listed below. Compare the two items by classifying their relevant features into similarities and differences.

1. Greece and Great Britain
2. alligators and crocodiles
3. cassette players and tape recorders
4. friends and pets

E *Starting Points for Writing* Writers unearth their freshest, most exciting ideas when they explore and expand upon unlikely, unbelievable, absurd thoughts and possibilities. Brainstorm about the images, headlines, and quote below to generate a list of questions that begin with "What if," trying not to limit your questions to the believable and possible. The list you produce should contain some unusual thoughts and possibilities that you can use as starting points for writing.

In certain rooms, bats congregate by the thousands, and they hang there in one vast, furry, silver-gray colony.

Tim Cahill

Town OKs Animal Rule

The Asheville Citizen 3/2/77

Shut-ins Can Grow Indoors With Lights

The *Miami Herald* 7/21/78

Focus On
THE DICTIONARY

A word isn't really your own until you can pronounce it and use it correctly. Your appreciation of it is not complete without an understanding of its history.

A Bestseller

Every year, two and a half million dictionaries are sold in the United States. What accounts for this popularity? Is it the spine-tingling plot, the lively characters, the full-page illustrations? No, it's the book's usefulness. Think of how often you go to the dictionary to "look it up." You may have noticed, though, that the dictionaries you've been using in school have grown increasingly complete and even more complex to match your expanding language and reference needs. As familiar as you may be with the dictionary, do you know about all its features?

Compact, Midsize, or Deluxe: Which Model Do I Need?

Dictionaries, like cars and many other products, come in a variety of sizes, and each size has certain unique features. The following sections describe several kinds of dictionaries.

Abridged Dictionaries The workhorse of dictionaries, the one you have probably used most often in school, is the abridged dictionary. A sample entry from an abridged dictionary is shown on page 53.

Available in various editions, such as student, college, and pocket editions, abridged dictionaries contain entries for all the words you are likely to need in everyday use. However, the amount of information given under each entry may vary among editions. Choose the kind of dictionary that will be most helpful to you. Also be alert to certain other features that may make one dictionary the best choice for a specific task. For example, notice how well your dictionary is keeping up with the times. Older editions may not contain such con-

temporary words as *microchip, ultralight, camcorder,* and *pixel.*

Would illustrations be helpful? If you are looking for the meaning of *minaret,* it might be useful to see a picture too.

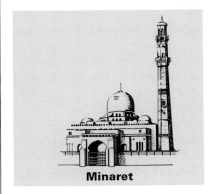

Minaret

Unabridged Dictionaries These are the largest and most complete dictionaries. These uncut versions can tell you more about a word than you ever wanted to know. They contain more entries of all kinds, and the entries include more information than do those in abridged editions. You might need to use an unabridged dictionary, for example, to find the meaning of the phrase *"lost his bark"* in a Shakespearean play. You would find that one meaning of the term *bark* is "boat." An unabridged dictionary includes words and phrases that are no longer in common use but that may be found in older literature.

Specialized Dictionaries To research a report or to pursue a hobby, you might use one of the 250 specialized dictionaries that concentrate on a particular aspect of the language or on a particular field of knowledge. For example, a report on ancient Greece might take you to the *Dictionary of Classical Mythology.* Likewise, an interest in word games might draw you to the *Dictionary of Difficult Words,* or one in ornithology might lead you to the classic *Dictionary of Birds.*

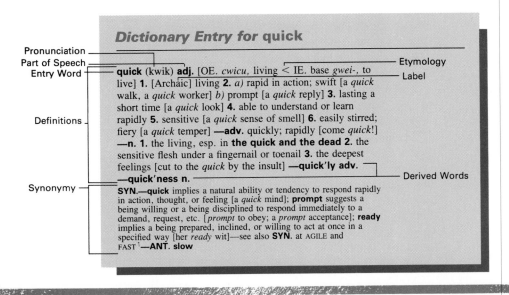

Dictionary Entry for **quick**

Pronunciation
Part of Speech
Entry Word
Etymology
Label

quick (kwik) **adj.** [OE. *cwicu,* living < IE. base *gwei-,* to live] **1.** [Archaic] living **2.** *a)* rapid in action; swift [a *quick* walk, a *quick* worker] *b)* prompt [a *quick* reply] **3.** lasting a short time [a *quick* look] **4.** able to understand or learn rapidly **5.** sensitive [a *quick* sense of smell] **6.** easily stirred; fiery [a *quick* temper] **—adv.** quickly; rapidly [come *quick*!] **—n. 1.** the living, esp. in **the quick and the dead 2.** the sensitive flesh under a fingernail or toenail **3.** the deepest feelings [cut to the *quick* by the insult] **—quick'ly adv.** **—quick'ness n.**

Definitions

Derived Words

Synonymy

SYN.—quick implies a natural ability or tendency to respond rapidly in action, thought, or feeling [a *quick* mind]; **prompt** suggests a being willing or a being disciplined to respond immediately to a demand, request, etc. [*prompt* to obey; a *prompt* acceptance]; **ready** implies a being prepared, inclined, or willing to act at once in a specified way [her *ready* wit]—see also **SYN.** at AGILE and FAST [1]**—ANT. slow**

What's the Good Word? The Parts of an Entry

Even though you may be an experienced dictionary user, a brief review of basic dictionary organization will be helpful, especially before you go on to explore the dictionary's rich resources.

To locate the page of the entry you need, look at the guide words at the top of each page. Next, scan the boldfaced main entries, or entry words, until you find the one that you want. Then take a fresh look at each part of the entry. You may discover new ways to use the information you find. Refer to the sample entry for *quick* on page 53 as you review each of the items in a dictionary entry.

How do you say gnu*? A word isn't really your own until you can pronounce it and use it correctly.*

Pronunciation How do you learn how to pronounce a word you have never seen before? How do you say *gnu,* for example? After each entry word, its pronunciation is shown in parentheses. A word isn't your own until you can both pronounce it and use it correctly.

Familiarize yourself with the dictionary symbols used to indicate pronunciation. In many dictionaries, explanations of the symbols are given in a key at the bottom of the right-hand pages.

Parts of Speech Many English words may be used as more than one part of speech, and the definition will vary accordingly. Are you reading the definition you really need?

Plural Forms How do you spell the plural of *octopus*? Is it *octopuses* or *octopi*? Irregular plurals can be bothersome. In this case, the dictionary shows *-puses, -pi,* which indicates that both spellings are correct and that the first form is preferred. If no plural is shown, add an *-s* to the singular form.

Etymology If etymologies, or word histories, seem to be all Greek to you, it is because many are. For example, *okto,* the root of *octopus,* comes from the Greek word meaning "eight." This knowledge can help you unlock the meanings of other words with the same root.

The etymology of an entry word is shown in brackets following the part of speech. The symbols and

"Fellow octopi, or octopuses ... octopi? ... Dang, it's hard to start a speech with this crowd."

abbreviations used in etymologies are explained in a key found in the front or the back of the dictionary. Study the etymology in the entry for *quick*.

Definition At last! The meat-and-potatoes part of the entry. Choose a dictionary with definitions that you can understand. A definition will include all the meanings of a word. Usually, the most common meanings are listed first. It is wise to read all the meanings for a word to find the one that best matches the word in its particular context.

Homographs Send in the clones. Sometimes you may see what appears to be two entries for the same word. Such entries are known as homographs—words that are spelled alike but have different meanings. The entries are distinguished by small raised numbers. For example, *story*[1] may be defined as "tale or narrative"; *story*[2], as "floor of a building."

Synonymies A rose is a rose is a rose. Sometimes you need a different word! A synonymy, marked by the abbreviation *SYN.*, appears after some entries. A synonymy consists of a list of synonyms, with explanations of the differences in their meanings. The abbreviation *ANT.*, found at the end of some synonymies, introduces antonyms. Examine the synonymy in the sample entry for *quick*.

Lagniappe—A Little Something Extra In some parts of the South, a *lagniappe,* or small gift, is pre-sented by a store owner to a customer with his or her purchase. When you use a dictionary, you often get something extra, too: useful information that goes beyond the definition of a word.

When you use a dictionary, you often get something extra: useful information that goes beyond the definition of a word.

Labels A label on a pair of jeans sends out a message about status and class. Words, too, have labels, identifying the status of their usage. The terms *obsolete* or *archaic,* for example, describe seldom-used words; the terms *colloquial* or *slang* describe words not accepted in formal English. Special symbols are used as labels. The symbol ‡ may be used to mark foreign words and phrases; the symbol ☆ often indicates a word or phrase that has originated in the United States.

Derived Words Many words belong to word families. Word families are a group of words that share a common root. A derived word is one in which a suffix is added to the root word. Derived words generally appear in boldface at the end of an entry. For example, the entry for *quick* includes *quickly* and *quickness*.

Cross-References Always read the fine print, or in this case, the small capital letters. Sometimes a notation directs you to another entry for more information. For example, at the end of the synonymy for the entry word *quick,* you will see the cross-references AGILE and FAST. These words direct you to two entries where you will find additional synonyms for *quick.*

Front and Back Matter From the front of the dictionary to the very last page, you can find useful information. The front matter includes the table of contents, special direc-

---

Thesaurus Entry for *equivalent*

equivalent *adj.* **1** *A dime is equivalent to ten pennies:* equal, the same as, comparable, commensurate with, tantamount, corresponding, correspondent, correlative; even, one and the same, of a piece. **—n. 2** *That dress cost the equivalent of a week's salary:* equal amount, comparable sum; correspondent, peer, counterpart, parallel, match.
Ant. 1 unequal, dissimilar, incomparable, incommensurate, different.

---

tions for using the dictionary, and explanations of the symbols and abbreviations used. The front matter may also include historical and usage information.

The back matter may include a list of foreign words and phrases; convenient tables, such as metric conversion tables; a list of universities and colleges; and biographical and geographical information.

Finding a Treasure: The Thesaurus

People who use language well search for the best word to convey a particular meaning. This is where a second "wordbook" can help you. The thesaurus (Greek for "treasure") is a special dictionary of synonyms and antonyms. In it you will be able to find related and contrasting words to use as replacements when you don't want to sound repetitious or when the word you're using doesn't convey the right shade of meaning.

Drawing by M. Stevens; © 1985 The New Yorker Magazine, Inc.

A Treasure Map: Finding Your Way

To use some thesauruses, you must first locate a word in the index and note the number that is printed beside the word. Then you must look under that number in the text to find the synonyms for the word. Other thesauruses, like dictionaries, are arranged in alphabetical order.

When Only the Best Will Do

Remember that the synonyms of a word cannot always be used interchangeably. Sometimes one synonym is more specific than the others, or one synonym has a different shade of meaning from the others. In some thesauruses, the word is used in a sentence, as in the entry for *equivalent*, shown on the facing page. Check the meanings of any unfamiliar synonyms in the dictionary.

At the end of an entry, antonyms are listed under the abbreviation *ANT*. Study these features in the entry for *equivalent*.

Are You Word Wise?

Refer to the sample entries and to your own dictionary and thesaurus to answer the following questions.

1. In which sense is the adjective *quick* no longer used very often?

2. Which definition of *quick* relates to anatomy?

3. Choose a synonym for *quick* that denotes "being prepared." Use it in a sentence.

4. Write a sentence using a noun synonym for *equivalent*.

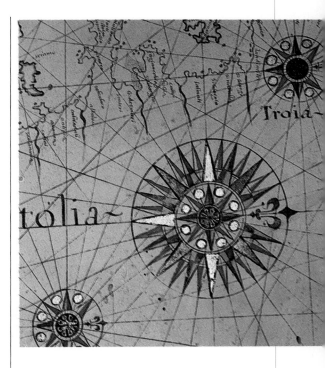

A thesaurus is a modern treasure map.

5. Using a thesaurus, find a word to replace each italicized word in the following passage. Check a dictionary to make certain that the replacement fits the context in the passage.

Early explorers were often at the mercy of unpredictable winds. Ferdinand Magellan and Juan Sebastián del Cano benefited from the gentle *winds* of the South Pacific. Leif Erickson and the Vikings weren't so fortunate. Frequently, they had to contend with *winds* of forty to fifty miles an hour. Such winds from the cold North made sailing extremely unpleasant. Unexpected *strong winds* were the dread of any explorer. Sailors much preferred the gentle and predictable western *winds*.

3

The Writing Process: Prewriting and Drafting

W hat do the researchers above and the diver on the opposite page have in common with you as a writer? The researchers and the diver follow certain steps—planning, exploring, gathering and organizing information—as they pursue their archaeological studies. These steps mirror those you follow during the prewriting and drafting stages of the writing process.

The prewriting and drafting techniques you learn in this chapter will help you explore possibilities for writing topics, gather information, organize it, and then use it to create the first draft of a composition.

What Is the Writing Process?

Perhaps you wonder about the title of this lesson. After all, you've been writing for years; and whenever you write, you no doubt follow steps that resemble the writing process. However, it may be helpful now to analyze exactly what you do when you write. In that way you will gain greater control over the process, and you will be able to adapt it to your own personal style and needs. Basically, the **writing process** involves three things.

1. A series of stages
2. A type of problem solving
3. A process of clear thinking

A Series of Stages

Individual writers adapt the writing process to suit their own unique style and to tackle different writing tasks. However, most writers complete four basic stages, called *prewriting, drafting, revising or editing,* and *publishing and presenting*.

Prewriting During prewriting the focus is on planning. The writer explores possibilities for topics and then begins gathering and organizing details to develop the main idea.

Drafting The goal of drafting is to set ideas down on paper, without much concern about errors in grammar, usage, and mechanics. The drafting stage often overlaps with other stages. For example, many writers do some revising while they draft. Many return to the prewriting stage to find additional information on their topic or to reorganize the presentation.

Revising or Editing During revising, or editing, a writer attempts to make sure that ideas are stated clearly and organized logically. Revising also involves proofreading to find and correct errors in grammar, usage, and mechanics.

Publishing and Presenting Although some writing is private, most writing is a way to communicate ideas to others. For example, you might read your essay aloud to your history class or submit your short story to the school newspaper for possible publication.

A Type of Problem Solving

The problem-solving method presented below can be applied to writing projects. As you will see, problem solving takes place in stages. The following chart shows how these stages correspond to the overlapping stages of the writing process.

Stages of Problem Solving and Writing

Problem Solving	Writing Process
Identify the task or problem	Confirm assignment or task
Analyze the task and examine alternatives	Prewriting
Choose one approach	
Try out or test approach	Drafting/Revising
Evaluate results	Revising/Presenting

One student used the problem-solving method to complete a writing project. His **task or problem** was an assignment given by his science teacher: to write a report about the space program. During prewriting, he analyzed the task by thinking about some decisions he had to make.

Next, he **examined possible alternatives.** He listed several possible topics, such as communications satellites, exploring Mars, space stations, and U.S. vs. Soviet space programs. He thought about possible audiences and purposes for his report. He considered various forms, methods of finding ideas, and ways of organizing and developing information. After this analysis, he **chose an approach**: to compare the U.S. and Soviet space programs.

In the drafting stage, the student **tried out the approach** by experimenting with several different ways of organizing and expressing his ideas. He created a time line on which he placed the key events in the U.S. and Soviet space programs, and he referred to his time line in his report.

Next, he **tested his approach** by asking a classmate to comment on his unfinished draft. During the revising stage, he **evaluated** his report. He sought input from classmates and friends and made the needed changes. At any time during the process, the student could have circled back to the prewriting stage to rethink his topic and begin anew. Finally, he prepared a final copy and **presented** it to his teacher and classmates to read.

A Process of Clear Thinking

Since writing is thinking, it follows that to write well, you must think clearly. The thinking techniques you learned in Chapter 2 can help you develop and organize ideas for writing. Skills such as **listing, inquiring, analyzing,** and **charting** can help you answer such questions as: What is my purpose in this piece of writing? How can I best communicate my ideas? What connections do I see between my ideas?

You apply these thinking skills during the overlapping stages of the writing process. As the following chart shows, the boundaries between stages may overlap. You adapt the process and use various thinking skills according to your individual style and purpose.

The Writing Process

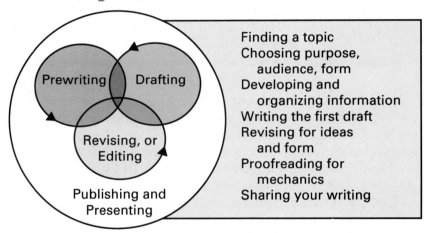

Finding a topic
Choosing purpose, audience, form
Developing and organizing information
Writing the first draft
Revising for ideas and form
Proofreading for mechanics
Sharing your writing

Writing Activity Thinking and Writing

Answer the following questions to help you understand how you use thinking skills while writing.

1. How do you usually get ideas for writing? Have you ever used free-writing or brainstorming?
2. What kind of planning or prewriting do you generally do? Do you use thinking skills such as analyzing or inquiring?
3. How do you usually develop ideas about a topic?
4. Do you usually organize ideas before writing? How?
5. Do you generally revise as you draft? Have you ever asked a reader to comment on a draft? What revising techniques have you used?
6. Have you ever started over on a writing project? Why?
7. Who have been your audiences?

Part 2
Prewriting: Focusing

Focusing is thinking clearly about a writing project before you start writing. As you focus, answer the following questions to determine your topic, purpose, audience, and form: What will I write about? Why am I writing about this topic? For whom am I writing? How can I present my ideas most effectively?

Finding a Topic

Sometimes your choice of writing topics is unlimited, but at other times topics are suggested by an assignment. For instance, the editor of your school newspaper may ask you to write an article about an exchange student from Japan who is visiting your school. Within the limits set by the assignment, a number of topics are possible. For example, you could focus on the differences between high schools in Japan and in the U.S. Or you might find an interesting subject in the background or experiences of the exchange student.

Whether or not the topic is assigned, the thinking skills you learned in Chapter 2 can help you think of a number of topic choices. Brainstorming alone, with a partner, or in a group can often turn up new angles on assigned topics. Interviews and other research can help you explore topic possibilities. Reflecting and freewriting can help you find and explore topics for free-choice writing.

Photographer Margaret Bourk-White chose to focus on one detail of the Chrysler Building in New York City, a gargoyle outside her studio on the sixty-first floor.

No two writers use the writing process in exactly the same way. One class read and discussed an account of Sir Edmund Hillary's 1953 conquest of Mt. Everest. Afterwards, their teacher asked them to write papers using mountains as a general theme. The rest of this chapter will follow two students, Kate and Jon, as they prepare their papers. You will discover how they use the writing process in two entirely different ways.

Kate got an idea while reading the Sunday paper. She noticed an article about the 1987 Snowbird Expedition, in which a group of Americans, led by women climbers, set out to climb Mt. Everest. The story made Kate wonder whether other women had made the climb successfully. She decided to do some research about women climbers to look for a topic. Research is most fruitful when you decide in advance what kind of information you are seeking. Inquiring—listing questions about a subject—is a good way to direct research. Here is Kate's list.

Kate   What women climbers have attempted Mt. Everest?
What happened on their expeditions?
When did the first woman reach the summit?
Why are more women climbing mountains today?
How do women climbers differ from men climbers?

Writing **Inside Out**
Christina Adachi, Radio/TV Journalist

When Christina January Adachi visits a restaurant, goes to a movie, a play, or even a dance club, she reports her experiences on Chicago's WLS radio and in a column she writes for a local newspaper. Known as the "Woman About Town," she also specializes in interviewing well-known women and has hosted local television talk shows.

"I think of myself as a radio and TV personality first, and a writer second," says Ms. Adachi. "I'm very good at getting people to talk about themselves; writing is difficult for me. But whatever I say on the air, I write myself." Explains Ms. Adachi, "You're a much more effective broadcast journalist when you speak your own words. Writing ability is important."

Through her research, Kate found that several women had climbed Mt. Everest since 1975. However, her reading revealed that no American woman had actually reached the top. Kate then decided to focus on successful and unsuccessful women's expeditions to Mt. Everest.

Jon used a different approach to selecting and narrowing his topic. While looking at an album of photographs he had taken on a camping trip to Wyoming, he remembered how impressed he had been by Devil's Tower, an unusual rock formation in northeastern Wyoming. He recalled that this mountain had been the landing site of the alien spacecraft in the movie *Close Encounters of the Third Kind*. This gave Jon the idea of writing a story with Devil's Tower as the setting.

Next Jon did some freewriting to narrow his topic further. Here is what he wrote.

Jon   Devil's Tower—long, vertical stripes, as if a huge cat had sharpened its claws on it. No, not a cat—it was a bear! The ranger told us that story at the campfire program. Stone spirits raised the Tower to save Sioux girls from an attacking bear. I could use that legend as the basis for my story.

Ms. Adachi relies on prewriting techniques in order to write well. When she attends an event or visits a restaurant, she takes careful notes and asks a lot of questions. She has even learned to write in the dark so that she can take notes at movies. She also spends a lot of time getting information over the telephone.

Before doing an interview, she reads as much as she can about her subject. Then she comes up with forty questions. She may not use them all, but she'd rather have too many questions than not enough. "You never know which question is going to lead to the most exciting information."

She saves the hardest questions until the interview is well under way. "First you have to build a foundation," she says.

Ms. Adachi says she has an inquisitive nature that makes her particularly good at her work. "I've always asked a lot of questions," she says. She laughs about the time she met a man who didn't know about her job. "After a few minutes of conversation, the man confided 'I feel like I'm on a radio talk show.'"

Though writing is not an easy task for her, Ms. Adachi emphasizes that she gets "great satisfaction" out of having written something she knows is good.

Establishing a Purpose

There are four main purposes for writing: **to express yourself, to entertain, to inform,** and **to persuade.** Sometimes a piece of writing has just one main purpose. For example, the purpose of an article explaining how weather affects climbers would be to inform. However, some pieces of writing have more than one purpose. For example, a personal narrative by an adventurer who has spent several months in the mountains of Alaska might have several purposes. The first purpose might be to express the writer's feelings about the experience. The second might be to persuade readers to support efforts to preserve the Alaskan wilderness.

As part of your prewriting planning, you should determine the purpose of your writing. You can do this by asking yourself questions such as the following:

1. What do I want to accomplish in this piece of writing?
2. What effect do I want my writing to have on my audience?
3. How can I best accomplish this?

Let's see how Kate and Jon determined the purposes of their papers. Here is how Kate answered the questions above.

Kate   Women have been allowed to join expeditions to the highest peaks only in the last fifteen years. I want to inform people about this change and to explain why women are now <u>leading</u> expeditions, such as Snowbird. Because I want my readers to appreciate what women climbers are accomplishing, I should explain the problems they face.

Jon's answers to the same questions are given below. Notice how his answers led him to a different set of purposes.

Jon   Devil's Tower was an eerie and impressive place. I remember thinking that something remarkable could happen there at any moment. Since I want to convey that atmosphere to my readers, my story should be more than just an entertaining adventure. The events should be magical, like the Sioux legend. Maybe some campers could hear about the legend and then have a similar experience happen to them.

Know Your Audience

Another part of prewriting is identifying your audience. You want to know as much about your readers as possible before you begin to write. Decisions about what details to include and which ones to develop fully will be based on what you think your readers will need.

For instance, for readers of *Climbing* magazine, you would not need to define specialized terms like *belay* (to secure a hold for a rope) and *rappel* (to descend a steep cliff using a rope). On the other hand, suppose you are a reporter for your school newspaper, and you are writing up an interview with a student who spent two weeks at climbing school. You would have to explain such terms in detail.

To know your audience, ask yourself questions such as these:

1. Who is my audience?
2. What do I know about this audience?
3. How much does the audience already know about the subject?
4. What part of the subject will they be interested in? Why?
5. What level of language would be most appropriate?

Here is how Kate answered these questions.

Kate   The next issue of the school magazine will be on the theme of "adventure." My paper would fit in perfectly. Since the readers of the magazine may also have seen the article about the Snowbird Expedition in the newspaper, I should be careful that I don't just repeat the information that was there. Instead, I will research other expeditions and compare them to Snowbird.

Here is how Jon analyzed his audience.

Jon   Our public library sponsors an annual creative writing contest, and this year's entries are due in just three weeks. The library accepts any kind of imaginative writing—poems, realistic stories, fables, fantasies. I know from reading last year's winners that the judges like suspense, vivid detail, and dramatic dialogue. I've chosen an exciting topic. I want to write my story in such a way that it will have some of the magic and excitement of the original Sioux legend.

Choosing a Form

Some common forms for writing are stories, plays, poems, journal accounts, articles, essays, letters, and school reports. To choose a form, think about what you want to accomplish. For example, if your purpose is to explain how to make or do something, you will probably write an article or report. If your purpose is to relate an event, you will probably write a letter, a story, or a journal account.

Kate's purpose was to inform her readers about women climbers and to compare recent expeditions to Mt. Everest, so she decided to write an article. Jon's purpose was to tell an eerie and exciting tale based on a Sioux legend. He chose to write a suspense story.

Writing Activities Focusing

A Read the list of general subjects below. Alone or with a partner, use brainstorming to list several limited topics related to each one.

1. living in families
2. careers
3. hobbies
4. the great outdoors
5. imaginary worlds
6. animals

B *Writing in Process* Choose a topic that you listed for Activity A. If you prefer, use a topic suggested by the picture below, by your journal, or by a thinking technique such as observing or freewriting. Be sure to limit your topic so that it is narrow enough to be covered thoroughly in a short paper. Establish your purpose, identify and analyze your audience, and choose a form. Make a special writing folder and save your prewriting notes in it.

Part 3
Prewriting: Developing and Organizing Information

The next step in prewriting is to gather information and organize it so that the relationship between ideas is clear.

Gathering and Developing Information

Depending on your topic, you might use one or a combination of methods to gather and develop information.

Analyzing and Inquiring Kate **analyzed** her topic, dividing it into parts. This technique helped her decide which ideas to develop and what information she would need.

> **Kate** Topic: Women Climbers and Mt. Everest
>
> Parts: 1. problems facing women climbers
> 2. women's expeditions that succeeded
> 3. women's expeditions that failed
> 4. the 1987 Snowbird Expedition

Jon developed his story by **inquiring,** asking questions about the topic. He answered his own questions by **inventing,** that is, by freeing his imagination to come up with creative ideas.

> **Jon** Who are the characters? Stan, 18, and his brother Mike, 15.
>
> Where does the story take place? On a backpacking trip near Devil's Tower, Wyoming.
>
> What happens in the story? The boys meet an old man on the trail. He tells them the Sioux legend of the Great Bear, whose claws made the ridges in the Tower. The boys stalk the bear. The bear stalks them. Stan and Mike hurriedly climb the Tower to escape.
>
> How does it end? Stan falls. Mike climbs to the top and finds him. Stan can't explain his magical rescue.

Gleaning Probably the most useful technique for developing information for an article or report is **gleaning.** You can also use gleaning to generate ideas for a narrative.

Kate started gleaning information about her topic when she read the article about the Snowbird Expedition in the newspaper. Next, she read parts of several books from the school library about expeditions to Mt. Everest. She looked for information about women's expeditions that succeeded and women's expeditions that failed. She took brief notes when she found relevant information.

Kate also read an article in *National Geographic* magazine by the American woman who was the leader of the 1978 American Women's Himalayan Expedition. From this source, she gathered details about problems facing women climbers. Gleaning information from written materials helped Kate understand her subject.

Another way to glean information is to **interview** someone who knows about your topic. Kate arranged to talk to a member of the Summit Club, a group of local climbing enthusiasts. Following are Kate's questions and the notes she took during the interview.

> *Kate* Question: What does it take to be a good climber?
>
> Answer: A good mountaineer has strength, endurance, technical skill, and the ability to handle high altitudes.
>
> Question: How do women climbers differ from men climbers?
>
> Answer: The success of several women's expeditions has shown that women can climb as well as men. Today both men and women have equal opportunities to attempt the highest peaks.

You can also glean information from **photographs, filmstrips, records,** and **videocassettes.** Jon used several of these sources. He studied photographs of Devil's Tower and made notes of descriptive details. Then he watched a filmstrip from the library about free rock climbing—climbing without technical aids—so that he could describe his characters' climb realistically. Finally, he listened to a record of a Native American storyteller retelling ancient legends. From this, Jon gathered ideas about how the old man in his story might tell Stan and Mike the legend of the Tower.

Organizing Information

To organize information for writing, use the thinking skills **ordering** and **classifying.** Examine the ideas you have gathered to determine how they are related. Ideas may be related by position, time, or degree of importance or familiarity. They may also be related by similarities, differences, or some other means. Sometimes the details you have gathered will not fit neatly into any standard order. If this is the case, you will need to devise an arrangement that makes sense to you and that helps you communicate your ideas clearly.

Ideas Related by Position If your ideas are related by position, you can arrange them in **spatial order**. For example, Kate gathered the following descriptive details about landmarks on the Snowbird climb of Mt. Everest. The numbers next to the ideas show how she arranged them in spatial order.

Kate

(2) The Khumbu Icefall, a jagged glacier with deep crevasses, between Base Camp and the supply depot at 19,300 feet.

(5) Final encampment at 26,000 feet on the South Col (a gap between peaks, used as a pass). Teams will attempt to reach the summit from here.

(3) A high altitude base at 21,500 feet, with living quarters, a mess tent, and a full-time cook.

(1) Base Camp at 18,000 feet, a sprawling, rocky tent city shared with climbing teams from France and Austria.

(4) A camp at 23,500 feet on the face of Lhotse, a peak near Everest, from which climbers can reach the South Col.

Ideas Related by Time If your ideas are related by time—for example, steps in a process or events in a narrative—you will usually want to arrange them in **chronological order.** A useful technique for organizing ideas chronologically is to place them in sequence on a **time line,** beginning with the earliest idea or event and ending with the latest. For example, the time line Jon made to organize the events for one part of his story is shown on the following page.

Jon Climbing Devil's Tower

8 P.M.	8:45	9:15	9:45
scramble over rocks at foot of cliff	climb to crack in leaning column	ascend crack by jamming toes into crannies	Mike reaches ledge; Stan disappears

Ideas Related by Degree If one idea you have gathered is more important or more familiar than another, you can arrange your details in **order of importance** or **order of familiarity.** For example, Kate might write a paragraph about the qualities of a good mountaineer—strength, endurance, technical skill, and the ability to handle high altitudes. She could arrange the details in order of importance, ending with endurance, which she considered to be the most important quality.

Later in her article, Kate might arrange the details in a paragraph about the problems facing women climbers in order of familiarity. She could start with the least familiar problem—women climber's limited high-altitude experience—and end with the most familiar problem—the heavy loads women climbers must carry.

Ideas Related by Similarities or Differences Sometimes ideas you have gathered are related because they are similar to or different from each other. If so, you can organize the ideas by **comparison and contrast.** For example, Jon wanted the events of his story to be similar to the events of the Sioux legend he had heard. To organize the details, he created the chart on the following page.

Jon

Comparing Events	
Sioux Legend	My Story
Sioux girls playing by a stream are attacked by a bear	Stan and Mike are fishing; bear they stalked chases them
They flee to top of small rock	They scramble over rocks at foot of Tower
Stone spirits cause rock to rise into air; becomes Devil's Tower	As they climb, Stan falls; magically, he wakes up at top of Tower
Angry bear claws tower in frustration, making vertical cracks	They imagine they hear bear clawing Tower

Combining Methods of Organization Some types of details are better suited to one method of organization than to another. For this reason, you might use different methods to arrange details of different types within a piece of writing. For example, Kate arranged the landmarks on the Snowbird climb of Mt. Everest in spatial order. She organized the problems facing women climbers in order of familiarity.

Jon also used more than one method of organization. Since Jon was writing a story, he knew that his basic method would be chronological order. However, his story included a paragraph describing Devil's Tower. There he arranged the details in spatial order, from the bottom of the tower to the top. In general, you should choose the method of organization that is appropriate for the details in a particular paragraph or section of your writing.

Writing Activity Organizing Information

Writing in Process Take out the notes you wrote for Activity B on page 68. Gather details about your topic by using one or a combination of the following methods: analyzing and inquiring, inventing, gleaning from books or non-print sources, and interviewing. Think about the various methods of organization, and decide which is best suited to each part of your writing. Create visual aids to help organize your details. Keep all of the notes in your writing folder.

Part 4
Drafting

Drafting is writing down your ideas in sentences and paragraphs. It is an experimental stage of the writing process, in which you try different methods of expressing your thoughts. Many writers revise as they draft by crossing out ideas, adding details, and reorganizing information. You do not need to worry about correcting errors in grammar, usage, and mechanics at this point, unless you want to. If you get stalled, you can always go back to prewriting to rethink your topic or to gather new ideas.

As you prepare to draft, review the planning notes you took during the prewriting stage. Ask yourself whether you are satisfied with decisions you made about your topic, purpose, audience, and form. Check to see whether your notes contain enough information to fulfill your purpose. Make sure that you have organized your information, and that your plan of organization is logical.

Next, choose a method of drafting. Several drafting methods are described in this section. Experiment with these methods to find the one that is best suited to your style of writing and to the goals of your writing project.

Loosely Structured Draft When you write a loosely structured draft, you work from rough prewriting notes. You experiment with ideas and organization as you work. This method works well when you are not quite sure what you want to say or how you want to say it.

One type of loosely structured draft is called **bridge building.** You begin with three or four main ideas. As you draft, you build "bridges" or logical connections between them. You ask yourself questions like, "What details will get me from idea A to idea B? How can I shape the writing so that I will be able to make a logical connection between the two?" This method is useful for writing in which research is not important and you discover what you want to say as you go along. Some writers begin drafting their short stories or personal narratives as a loosely structured draft.

Jon used the loosely structured method for drafting his story. He used the time line and comparison chart he had created to guide him. As he drafted, he tried to give each of his characters an individual personality. He also tried to make his story exciting by adding dialogue and by including vivid description.

Whether you use a highly structured draft or a loosely structured draft depends on you.

Highly Structured Draft In a highly structured draft, you work from very complete prewriting notes and follow your writing plan carefully. This writing method works well when you want to include a large amount of detailed information.

Kate chose the highly structured drafting method. This method was best because she had planned her article carefully during prewriting and because she had many details to include.

Quick Draft or Slow Draft In general, you can use whichever drafting method you choose by writing either a quick draft or a slow draft. In a **quick draft,** you can use your prewriting notes if you wish. However, your goal is to get your ideas down on paper quickly. This method works well for writers who find that frequent stops make them lose track of the flow of ideas. In a **slow draft,** you write one sentence or paragraph at a time, revising as you go along. This method works well for writers who are uncomfortable about leaving an idea unfinished or for projects that require information from many sources.

Writing Activity Drafting

Writing in Process Take out your writing folder from Activity B on page 68. Review your prewriting planning. Decide whether your writing style and topic are better suited to a quick draft or a slow draft. Write a first draft, using either the loosely structured or the highly structured method. Keep the draft in your folder.

Chapter 3

Application and Review

Use what you have learned about prewriting and drafting to complete one or more of the following activities. Activity A leads you step by step, Activity B leaves more choices to you, and Activity C provides starting points only. Save your drafts for the editing activities at the end of Chapter 4.

A Writing a Composition Is there intelligent life on other planets? Does life elsewhere conform to our ideas about extraterrestrials? What methods are being used to determine whether there is life in outer space? Have extraterrestrials ever visited our planet? Plan and write a composition that expresses your views about some aspect of the subject of extraterrestrial life. Your audience is an official from NASA who will respond to student essays on this subject during an assembly at your school.

Prewriting With a partner, brainstorm to create a list of possible topics, such as aliens in the movies or on television, searching for life with radio telescopes, or UFO's. Choose one topic and narrow it so that you can cover it in a short paper. Freewrite about your topic for five minutes. Use inquiring to make a list of questions about your topic. If necessary do a little research to answer questions you have listed. Organize your notes logically.

Drafting Choose a drafting method. Using your notes, write a first draft of your composition.

B Writing a Narrative Use the following guidelines to write a narrative explaining how some place or some thing came to be what it is today.

Prewriting Brainstorm alone or with other students to list things that had interesting beginnings. You might list historical subjects, such as how the Pyramids were built; scientific subjects, such as how the Grand Canyon was formed; or legendary subjects, such as how the leopard got its spots. Choose a topic and use a thinking technique, such as gleaning or inventing to develop ideas.

Drafting Decide on a method of drafting. Using your notes, write a first draft of your narrative.

C *Starting Points for Writing* Anything you feel strongly about—even things you fear, worry about, or get embarrassed by—can make an interesting writing topic. Based on the images below, brainstorm to create a list of things that might concern you. Add to this list any fears, worries, or embarrassments you are reminded of by the quote. The items on your list that you would be willing to reveal to others are excellent starting points for writing.

. . . one of the earliest problems is the inability of some . . . to say, "I love you." . . . Why should they once again lay their whole lives out on the line just so they can run the risk of hearing the person in question come back with "You do?" or "Don't be ridiculous" or "I've got a train to catch"?

Charles A. Monagan

4

The Writing Process: Revising and Presenting

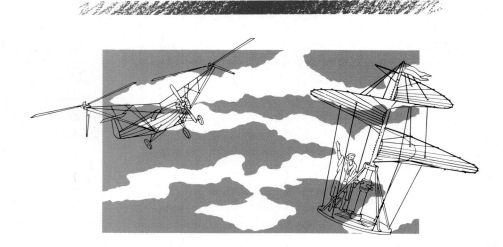

L eonardo da Vinci, the Italian artist and inventor, made these sketches of rotor-powered flying machines in 1483. However, before his invention could get off the drawing board and into the air, its design had to be tested and refined many times.

Writing is also a process of reworking and refining. Writers are constantly revising their work so that it will be more forceful, clear, vivid, and concise.

In this chapter you will learn techniques for revising your writing to improve its effectiveness. You will also learn how to present your revised writing to others.

Revising or Editing

Revising, or **editing,** is the evaluation stage of the writing process. During this stage, you evaluate what you have written and rework your draft to solve problems in three areas: ideas, form, and mechanics. To aid you in this process, you often ask someone else to read and comment on your draft.

It is a good idea to put your draft aside for a day or two before you start to revise it. This period of **reflecting** can help you gain distance and objectivity. As you reflect, ask yourself whether you are satisfied with the decisions you made during prewriting. Rather than trying to solve specific problems, think about the paper as a whole to identify its strengths and weaknesses.

Revising for Ideas

Revising for ideas is a writer's most important task. If the ideas are not well thought out or clearly expressed, your draft may need major changes. You may even need to rethink your topic or start over.

To revise for ideas, you must decide whether your focus is clear. You will waste time reorganizing an article that lacks a clear main idea or adding details to a story that doesn't go anywhere. Next, read your draft with your purpose in mind. If you decide that you have not accomplished what you set out to do, think about whether you need to develop ideas more fully or add new ideas.

Finally, ask yourself whether you have kept your audience in mind. Check to see if you have included all the information your audience needs. Make sure your details are appropriate for your audience.

When you revise your composition for ideas, think about the following questions.

Revising for Ideas Checklist

1. Does my draft have a clear focus or main idea?
2. Do I need to develop my ideas more fully?
3. Do I need to add ideas to accomplish my purpose?
4. Have I included all the information my audience needs?
5. Are my examples and details appropriate for my audience?
6. Have I expressed my ideas clearly and accurately?

Revising for Form

When you revise for form, you make sure your draft is unified, well-organized, and coherent. In a **unified** draft, all ideas and details relate directly to the main idea or focus. You should eliminate irrelevant ideas that may confuse your reader. You should also make sure that your examples, comparisons, and illustrations are clearly connected to the points you are making.

A draft that is **well-organized** is easy to read and understand. Ask yourself whether you have organized your material in the best and most logical manner. If necessary, move sentences or paragraphs around to improve the organization.

In a **coherent** draft, all ideas are smoothly and clearly connected. Read your draft aloud and listen to the flow of sentences and paragraphs. You can often improve the coherence of your composition by adding transition words and phrases to make the relationship between ideas clear.

When you revise your draft for form, you should think about the following questions.

Revising for Form Checklist

1. Do my details relate directly to my focus or main idea?
2. Have I explained clearly how examples and illustrations are connected?
3. Have I organized my ideas in the best and most logical manner?
4. Are my ideas smoothly and clearly connected?
5. Have I used transition words and phrases to make the relationship between my ideas clear?

Proofreading

Proofreading is the last step in the revising process. During this stage, you read your draft closely to find and correct any errors you might have made in punctuation, capitalization, spelling, grammar, and usage. Your aim is to create a final draft that is ready to present to an audience.

When you proofread, think about the questions in the checklist on the following page. (Additional information on these concepts can be found on the pages indicated in the checklist and in the Writer's Handbook, which begins on page 823.)

1. Does each sentence end with the proper punctuation mark? (See pages 733-734.)
2. Are commas, semicolons, colons, apostrophes, hyphens, dashes, and quotation marks used correctly? (See pages 736-749, 757-767, 775-784.)
3. Is the first word in each sentence capitalized? Are proper nouns and proper adjectives capitalized? Are all other rules of capitalization followed? (See pages 711-725.)
4. Are all words spelled correctly? Have I checked unfamiliar words in a dictionary? (See pages 792-804.)
5. Are all possessive and plural forms spelled correctly? (See pages 775-777, 802-804.)
6. Are there any run-on sentences or sentence fragments? (See pages 577-586.)
7. Do all verbs agree with their subjects? (See pages 635-651.)
8. Are all pronouns used in the correct form? (See pages 661-665.)
9. Are all adjectives and adverbs used correctly? (See pages 687-689, 692-701.)

Using Proofreading Marks

When you mark corrections on your draft, you use a set of standard symbols to indicate changes you want to make. These symbols, called **proofreading marks,** make it easy for you and anyone who reads your draft to understand exactly how you want your draft corrected. Study the proofreading marks on the following chart.

Proofreading Marks

∧ Add a letter or word.	◯ Close up.
⊙ Add a period.	¶ Begin a new paragraph.
≡ Capitalize a letter.	⋏ Add a comma.
/ Make a capital letter. lowercase.	∩∪ Trade the position of letters or words.
——— or ✗ Take out letters or words.	

Improving Spelling and Vocabulary

Revision provides many opportunities to sharpen your vocabulary and spelling skills. It is a good idea to set aside a section of your journal for a Personal Vocabulary List. In researching and writing your paper, you will come across new words and definitions. Record these in your list. Then set aside another section of your journal for a Personal Spelling List. Include both new words and the common but often-misspelled words called "spelling demons."

Writing Activities Revising

A Rewrite the following paragraph, using the Revising for Form Checklist on page 81. Remove irrelevant details. Rearrange sentences to improve organization. Add transitions for smoothness and clarity.

> Skiing was a way of getting from place to place in cold countries. Millions of people ski for fun. In 950 A.D., King Haakon the Good of Norway sent tax collectors on skis to far-off parts of his kingdom. In 1855, "Snowshoe" Thompson skied across the mountains south of Lake Tahoe to deliver mail. From the fifteenth to the seventeenth centuries, ski troops were part of the Scandinavian armies. Skiing is a sport, but it was a necessity.

B Study the proofreading marks in a paragraph from a science report. Refer to the chart on page 82. Then rewrite the corrected paragraph.

> The brain has fascinated people for centuries. scientists have only recently begun to discover how it works. Physically, the brain is just three and a half pounds of pinkish-gray tissue, but it controls who we are and how we perceive our world. The brain may contain as many nerve cells, called neurons, as there are stars in the milky way galaxy. Scientists are using their brains to understand how the brain works.

Part 2
Self-Editing

Self-editing is the process of taking a fresh look at your writing to evaluate how well you have fulfilled your goals and to correct any problems. You might wish to self-edit your draft in a series of readings. First, use the Revising for Ideas Checklist on page 80 to see whether your focus and its development meet the needs of your audience. Next, use the Revising for Form Checklist on page 81 to make sure your draft is unified, well-organized, and coherent. Finally, use the Proofreading Checklist on page 82 to find and correct mechanical errors.

Let's see how Kate used self-editing to revise the paragraph below for ideas and form. Kate's thoughts are shown in the margin.

Kate

Several woman have reached the top of

> State the main idea.

the world. On May 16, 1975, a Japanese

climber, Junko Tabei, stood atop Mt.

> Explain more clearly how he helped.

Everest. Her Sherpa guide ~~helped her to~~ *reached the top first. Then he pulled her up.* ~~complete the climb.~~ A Tibetan named

Phanthog reported that the women in her

expedition climbed as ~~well~~ *quickly* as the men. ~~Each~~

> This is irrelevant.

~~climber carried 35 pounds of equipment~~. She

attributed the success of the expedition to

> I should add transitions.

men and women working together. *Since 1975,* Five

women--from China, Poland, West Germany,

India, and Canada--have *also* made the climb.

> This idea is out of place.

However, ~~Phanthog was~~ the second woman to reach the

top in 1975.

After Kate revised her article for ideas and form, she used the Proofreading Checklist on page 82 to find and correct mechanical errors in her draft. Below is a paragraph from Kate's article.

Kate   Mt. Everest has been deadly for ~~several~~ other women climbers. Two women at least have died on the ~~M~~ountain. A ~~g~~erman climber, Hannelore Schmatz, was the fo~~u~~rth woman to reach the summit, in 1979. However, she and her male climbing partner died on ~~there~~ _their_ descent when they were forced to stop for the night at 28,000 feet with out tents or ox~~y~~gen. In 1982, American climber Marty Hoey died when she fell from a rope, her companions were certain that she had fallen down the entire face of the mountain.

85

Writing Activities Revising

A The paragraph below was revised for ideas and form. Decide why each revision was made, and write the reasons on your paper. Rewrite the paragraph to include the revisions, creating a clean final draft.

The Rosetta stone~~was~~ uncovered in 1799. Carved

in the stone is the same message in

hieroglyphics, Demotic, and ancient Greek.

~~Scholars~~ compar~~ed~~ *By* *ing* the Greek text to the

scholars figured out the meaning of the symbols.

hieroglyphics. ~~The stone~~ is the key to reading

Egyptian hieroglyphics.

B Using the appropriate checklists, revise the paragraph below for ideas and form. Rewrite the paragraph, showing your changes.

An asteroid is a rock tumbling in space. Between the orbits of Mars and Jupiter is an asteroid belt. Asteroids may be the shattered remains of a planet that exploded. Many craters, such as those on the moon, are caused by meteorites. The asteroid belt may be where a planet was prevented from forming by the gravity of Jupiter.

C Study the proofreading marks in the following paragraph, referring to the chart on page 82. Then rewrite the paragraph as a final draft.

America's newest national park is Great basin.

the park contains many kind of terrain, such as

dessert, alpine tundra, a stand of 3000 year old

bristlecone pines, glacial lakes, and a

permanent ice field. It's highest point is a

beautiful snowcaped mountain, Wheeler peak, that

rises abruptly from the nevada dessert.

Part 3
Peer Editing

Peer editing is a revision technique in which you ask a classmate to read and comment on a draft you have written. Because a peer editor is often a member of your potential audience, your peer editor's questions can help you judge in advance how well you have met your readers' needs. A peer editor can tell you whether your main idea or focus is coming across, what parts of your draft need more development, whether your organization is clear, and whether your details are well suited to your purpose and audience. A peer editor can also tell you what parts of your draft are successful. Both positive and negative feedback are valuable as you revise your draft.

Peer editing is most useful when you are revising a draft for ideas and for form. You will want your peer editor to concentrate on your ideas and how you present them, not simply to point out mechanical errors you have made.

Methods of Peer Editing

There are two basic methods of peer editing. In the **individual method,** you exchange drafts with a partner. Your partner reads your draft and comments or asks questions about any of the issues on the Revising for Ideas and Revising for Form Checklists. Both partners benefit. As a reader, you help another writer, and at the same time you sharpen your own evaluation skills.

In the **group method** of peer editing, a small group of students works together. Each group member concentrates on a different aspect of a draft under consideration. For instance, one student might consider the development of ideas. This reader would think about such questions as these: *What parts of this draft need more development? What kinds of information should the writer add?* Another reader might examine the organization, using such questions as these: *How is this draft organized? Does this method of organization help me follow the writer's ideas?*

Jon used the group method to gather input about his story. The reader who was concerned with development commented that Jon should add more details about Stan and Mike's feelings. The reader who examined the organization suggested that Jon might use flashbacks during Stan and Mike's climb to show the old man telling the Sioux Indian legend.

Peer Editing Responses

A peer editor can respond to a draft in several different ways. In an **oral response,** a peer editor asks the writer questions about a draft and talks with the writer about its strengths and weaknesses. For instance, Jon's peer editor might ask, "Is a *monolith* the same thing as a *tower*?" or say, "I liked the fact that Stan and Mike never see the bear. This really appealed to my imagination." Another type of response is **notes and queries** written in the margin of the draft. For example, Jon's peer editor could write, "You should explain why Stan and Mike decide to stalk the bear."

In a **written response,** a peer editor writes answers to questions posed by the writer. For example, Jon might ask a peer editor to answer the question, "What feeling or mood does my story convey?" A peer editor can also respond to a draft by filling out an **evaluation form.** A sample evaluation form for Jon's story appears on page 90.

Devil's Tower, Wyoming.

Qualities of a Good Evaluator

Keep the following points in mind when you act as a peer editor.

- A good evaluator is courteous, sensitive to the writer's feelings.
- A good evaluator points out strengths as well as weaknesses.
- A good evaluator supplies constructive criticism and offers suggestions for improvement.
- A good evaluator does not simply proofread but instead focuses on ideas and form.

Peer Editor Questions

To be an effective evaluator, you should come to a piece of writing with specific questions in mind. The questions on the following checklist can be applied to any kind of writing.

Checklist of Peer Editor Questions

1. What is the focus or main idea of the draft?
2. Are the supporting details related directly to this focus?
3. What additional details should the writer add?
4. Does the draft have a clear plan of organization?
5. Is there anything I find confusing?
6. Are there any awkward or unclear sentences or paragraphs?
7. What do I think or feel after reading the draft? Are these the effects that the writer intended?
8. What do I like best about the draft?

Following is part of Jon's draft. The comments his peer editor made, using the checklist above, appear in the margin.

Jon

You should describe his voice and appearance.

The old man drew the blanket around his shoulders and began to speak. The firelight illuminated his face with an unearthly glow. "Once, long, long ago," he said, "when the Sioux lived and hunted on these plains, two young girls were playing beside a stream. A great bear fishing in the stream was startled by their splashing. Without warning, the bear attacked them.

"The girls fled to the top of a small rock. They begged the stone spirits to save them. Suddenly, the rock began to grow. Taller and taller the rock grew, bearing the girls into the air.

Tell how Stan and Mike react to the story.

"As the rock grew, the bear became a giant as well. It clawed the tower in its rage, tearing the furrows that you can see today.

What are furrows?

"From that day the tower has been known to the Sioux as the Mateo Tepee, the Lodge of the Bear. Some say you can still hear the growling of the great bear on the night winds."

A good touch.

Using an Evaluation Form

A peer editor can also fill out an **evaluation form.** Here is an evaluation form that a classmate filled out about Jon's story.

Evaluation Form	
Questions About Ideas	**Comments**
Is there a clear focus or main idea?	*The focus is a legend about Devil's Tower that comes true.*
Does the content suit the audience and purpose?	*The content is appropriate for a suspenseful adventure story.*
What information should the writer add?	*He should add dialogue to show what Stan and Mike are thinking.*
Questions About Form	
Is the information arranged clearly and logically?	*The chronological organization of the events is clear.*
Are the details relevant to the focus or main idea?	*The part about stalking the bear isn't needed. The bear could just attack.*
What parts are unclear or confusing?	*I still don't understand how Stan got to the top of the rock.*

Evaluating a Reader's Comments

A peer editor's comments are valuable because they show how others react to your writing. However, before using the comments to revise your draft, you should evaluate each suggestion, asking yourself questions such as: Would this change help me fulfill my purpose? Would these details make my paper better or just longer? Act only on the suggestions that seem valuable.

Writing Activity Revising

Writing in Process Gather comments about the draft you wrote for the activity on page 75. Begin with peer editing. Work with a partner or an editing group, using the checklist on page 89. Then self-edit your draft, using the checklists on pages 80 and 81. Study the comments you have gathered and use them in revising your draft. As a final step, proofread, using the checklist on page 82.

Part 4
Publishing and Presenting

The final stage of the writing process is sharing your writing with others. Like Kate and Jon, you will want to find ways of presenting your work that go beyond your English classroom.

You could submit a poem or a short story to your school magazine. Your class could publish its own magazine or booklet. You could submit an article on your hobby or sport to a specialized magazine. You could write a letter to the editor of your local or school newspaper. You could present your work orally—in skits, in short plays, in oral readings. The photo above suggests a way of presenting that you may not have thought of—mock (or real) radio and TV broadcasts. Remember, most oral presentations begin with a writer using the writing process.

Kate submitted her article on women's expeditions to Mt. Everest to her school magazine. She also gave an oral presentation about the Snowbird Expedition at a meeting of the Summit Club in her town. Jon submitted his story about Devil's Tower to the library for its annual creative writing contest. The judges liked the way Jon used the old Sioux legend as the basis for a contemporary short story.

Writing Activity Publishing and Presenting

Writing in Process Brainstorm alone or with your classmates about ways of presenting your paper, both orally and in writing. Then choose the best option for sharing your work with an audience.

Chapter 4
Application and Review

A Revising a Composition   Act as a peer editor and review the following composition for ideas and form, using the checklists on pages 80 and 81. Make notes on your paper about changes you think the writer could make to improve the composition.

One of the most common, most useful, and least expensive tools you use is the pencil. But pencils did not always exist. In fact, they are only a little over four hundred years old.

Pens go back thousands of years, although the first ones were not much like yours. Early pens were sharpened reeds, or pieces of ivory or bone. Quill pens, or sharpened bird feathers, were the most common writing tools for hundreds of years.

The newest kind of pen has a soft point. It is the felt-tipped pen, and it comes in many colors.

In 1850 children were still carrying penknives to school to sharpen their quill pens. In 1884 a usable fountain pen was invented. In 1945 a ball point pen was marketed. It cost $12.50, it leaked, and it didn't write well.

Unlike the pen, the pencil is a fairly new invention. Its origin can be traced to England in 1564. A huge tree was uprooted by a storm, and a deposit of graphite was found in the cavity underneath. In 1565 Konrad von Gesner put graphite into a wooden holder and used it for sketching and note-taking. Gesner's invention may have been the world's first pencil.

The ball point pen has been greatly improved. For a few cents, you can buy one that works well.

After the invention of the typewriter, some people predicted that pencils would disappear. The typewriter did not replace the pencil. Neither did the word processor. The pencil will probably survive the invention of any writing tool of the future.

B Rewriting a Paragraph The following paragraph has been revised for ideas and form. Rewrite it, responding to the comments in the margin. Then prepare a final draft, using the Proofreading Checklist on page 82 to identify any mechanical errors.

> **Wrong focus. Add "as soldiers" to sentence 1.**
>
> **Idea is irrelevant.**
>
> **Idea is out of order.**

Throughout history dogs have served humans. They were used against enemy foot soldiers as early as 700 B.C. The ancient Gauls used dogs as soldiers, and they even made armor for them. In World War II, dogs belonged to the K–9 Corps and were used as messengers, sentries, and pack animals. It has been estimated that Americans feed their dogs five billion pounds of dog food annually. Dogs were also used as soldiers in Korea and later in Vietnam. In the fifth century A.D., Attila the Hun used dogs to guard his camps.

C Proofreading a Paragraph Use the chart on page 82 to identify the errors in the paragraph below. Then rewrite the paragraph correctly.

There is an ancient chinese legend that explains

the origin of tea. It was the year 2737 B.C. and

Shen Nung was the emperor. Some one was boiling

drinking water for him over an open fire leaves

from the burning branches fell into the pot of

boiling water. Shen Nung liked the fragrance and

took a drink of the World's first tea.

D Preparing Your Final Draft Take out the draft or drafts that you wrote for the Application and Review activities on pages 76 and 77. Revise and proofread one or more of your drafts. First, work with an editing partner or an editing group, and peer edit each other's draft, using the checklist on page 89. Then self-edit your own draft, using the checklists on pages 80 and 81. As a final step, proofread your draft, using the checklist on page 82.

5

From Paragraphs to Compositions

A stereo system, a marching band, a written composition—what do they have in common? Each is only as strong as its component parts. In the case of a composition, those components are paragraphs. Each paragraph, like each musician in a band, must perform well on its own before it becomes a valuable part of the whole.

In this chapter you will learn to improve the performance of individual paragraphs. Then you will discover how to integrate these paragraphs to create strong compositions.

Part 1
Understanding the Paragraph

A **paragraph** is a group of related sentences that explain or describe a single idea. Read the following paragraph and notice how the sentences fit together.

▬ *Literary Model* ▬

> Of all boxers it seems to have been Rocky Marciano (still our only undefeated heavyweight champion) who trained with the most monastic devotion; his training methods have become legendary. . . . Marciano was willing to seclude himself from the world, including his wife and family, for as long as three months before a fight. . . . Every minute of his life was defined in terms of the opening second of the fight. . . . In the final month Marciano would not write a letter, since a letter related to the outside world. During the last ten days before a fight he would see no mail, take no telephone calls, meet no new acquaintances. During the week before the fight he would not shake hands. Or go for a ride in a car, however brief. No new foods! . . . For all that was not *the fight* had to be excluded from consciousness. . . .

From *On Boxing* by Joyce Carol Oates

Paragraphs rarely exist in isolation, except in essay tests or similar situations. Although you will be writing single paragraphs during this chapter, remember that most paragraphs are part of a larger work.

The Structure of Paragraphs

A key word in the definition of a paragraph is the word *related*—all of the sentences in a paragraph must be related. To ensure this relatedness, good writers usually use one of three paragraph structures.

Paragraphs with a Topic Sentence In the model paragraph above, one sentence states the main idea, that Rocky Marciano's training methods became legendary. This is the **topic sentence**. In general, the other sentences in a paragraph contribute to the topic sentence, either by introducing it or by providing supporting details.

Paragraphs Without a Topic Sentence Not all paragraphs need a topic sentence. In some paragraphs, the topic sentence is *implied*. You know the main idea, but it is not stated explicitly. For example, the following paragraph compares the songs of four species of birds, but it does not state this in a topic sentence.

▬ *Professional Model*

The robin sings flexible songs, containing a variety of motifs that he rearranges to his liking; the notes in each motif constitute the syntax, and the possibilities for variation produce a considerable repertoire. The meadow lark . . . arranges these in phrases of three to six notes and elaborates fifty types of song. The nightingale has twenty-four basic songs, but gains wild variety by varying the internal arrangement of phrases and the length of pauses. The chaffinch listens to other chaffinches, and incorporates into his memory snatches of their songs.

From *The Lives of a Cell* by Lewis Thomas

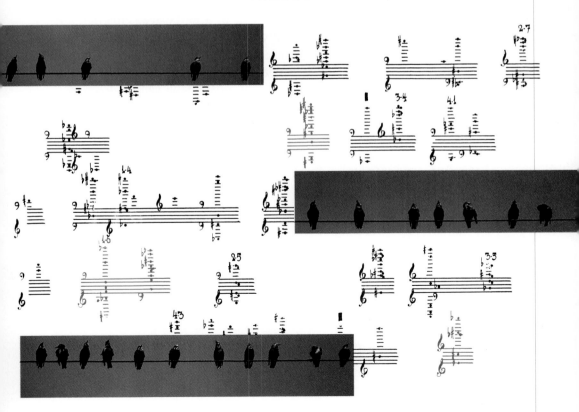

Paragraphs with Logical Progression Some paragraphs have no single main idea. In such paragraphs, each sentence builds logically on what came before and leads the reader to the next idea. Such paragraphs are typically used in narrative writing.

Student Model

Luis and I approached the dilapidated house warily. A hand-lettered sign on the door read, "Doorbell out of order. Please knock." I tapped lightly, hoping that no one would answer. Luis frowned and said, "What are you—chicken?" Making a fist, he knocked three times, rattling the door in its weatherbeaten frame. Still nothing. "That's good enough for me!" I shouted, poking the extinct doorbell once to empha-size my point. "Let's go." Then, from behind the door some-one growled, "Cancha read? Da bell's busted!"

Types of Paragraphs

Think of the many types of materials you read and the types of paragraphs they contain. A paragraph in a newspaper editorial, for example, is quite different from one in a motorcycle repair manual. How do we classify paragraphs?

One convenient way is according to **purpose.** At some time or other, you have probably learned that a paragraph can be *descriptive* (describing something), *narrative* (telling a story), *expository* (ex-plaining something), or *persuasive* (changing the reader's mind). Yet, there are really more than just four purposes for paragraphs. There are, in fact, almost as many purposes as there are subjects and reasons for writing. Consider the types of paragraphs you might write based on the following purposes.

To Narrate A narrative paragraph tells part of a story by presenting a series of events in chronological order. A good writer will use vivid description while laying out these events. The Student Model on this page is an example of a narrative paragraph.

Most narrative paragraphs have no topic sentence. Instead, the first sentence introduces a series of events. Succeeding sentences add to the action, piece by piece.

To Describe In a descriptive paragraph, you tell the reader what you have observed with your five senses. Note, for example, how the following paragraph tells what certain objects look like and how they are arranged in space.

▬ *Literary Model* ▬

The first snowfall came early in December. I remember how the world looked from our sitting-room window as I dressed behind the stove that morning: the low sky was like a sheet of metal; the blond cornfields had faded out into ghostliness at last; the little pond was frozen under its stiff willow bushes. Big white flakes were whirling over everything and disappearing in the red grass.

From *My Ántonia* by Willa Cather

To Define and/or Classify A definition paragraph tells what something is. It may also explain words or phrases that are crucial to the reader's understanding of the rest of the work. A classification paragraph explains the categories into which a defined item can be placed. You can begin either kind of paragraph with a general definition and then expand upon it.

▬ *Professional Model* ▬

When I say "ecologist," I have in mind those who are interested in (and usually also concerned about) the overall order of living things and their relationship to the environment. Persons interested in conserving or preserving some particular aspect of our environment, . . . are a very different type of person. . . .

From "Now (I Think) I Understand the Ecologists Better" by Julian L. Simon

To Explain a Process This type of paragraph uses chronological order to explain the steps involved in a process.

▬ *Professional Model* ▬

Sit close to the model or object which you intend to draw and lean forward in your chair. Focus your eyes on some point—any point will do—along the contour of the model. . . . Place the point of your pencil on the paper.

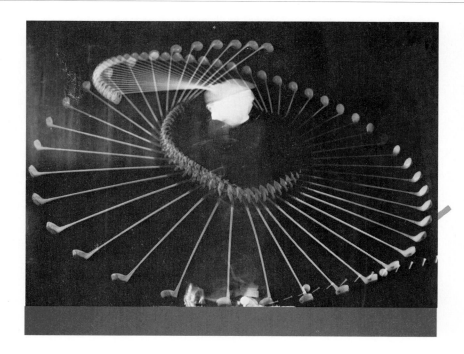

Imagine that your pencil point is touching the model instead of the paper. Without taking your eyes off the model, *wait* until you are *convinced* that the pencil is touching that point on the model upon which your eyes are fastened.

From *The Natural Way to Draw* by Kimon Nikolaïdes

To Analyze To write about complex subjects, writers often use analysis paragraphs, in which they break the subject into smaller parts and examine each part. The explanation should clarify the relationship between these parts.

A well-known writer once noticed that his sons, when watching a football game, always rooted for one of the teams—even if neither team was a local one. This paragraph represents part of his analysis of the phenomenon.

Literary Model

This [idea of partisanship] is a harmless attitude in sporting contests, but I think it represents a widespread human tendency that gets us into trouble more often than not. There is no psychological challenge or excitement in remaining neutral; lack of partisanship is boring compared to the fervor of

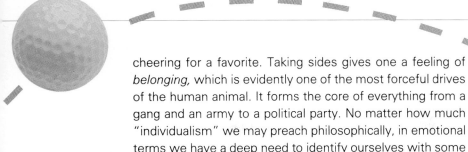

cheering for a favorite. Taking sides gives one a feeling of *belonging,* which is evidently one of the most forceful drives of the human animal. It forms the core of everything from a gang and an army to a political party. No matter how much "individualism" we may preach philosophically, in emotional terms we have a deep need to identify ourselves with some specific goal.

From *Clearing the Ground* by Sydney J. Harris

To Compare or Contrast A comparison paragraph discusses the similarities between two or more related items; a contrast paragraph discusses differences.

Professional Model

Yet on the whole, taking it by and large, and allowing for individual exceptions, you are smarter than the Fly. You know more than he does about more things. Above all, you possess the power of abstract reasoning, a faculty which distinguishes mankind from the merely brute creation, such as Flies. You can listen to the radio, look at television, and go to the movies. You can read mystery stories and try to guess who done it. Keep your chin up and always remember that if you are not the Fly's superior in every single respect one might mention, you are at least his equal, mentally. . . . The key is his imperfect memory. You can remember as far back as yesterday. The Fly cannot. He forgets. The particular Fly of whom we were speaking will be out of his dark corner in a few brief moments. . . .

From *How to Attract the Wombat* by Will Cuppy

To Persuade The persuasive paragraph attempts to change the reader's opinion about something. In a persuasive paragraph, the writer takes a stand on some issue and then presents reasons to support his or her thinking.

Student Model

The teen-age curfew in this community should be changed from 10:30 P.M. to midnight on weekdays. There are plenty of reasons to support this change. Many high-school students hold evening jobs and may work until 11 P.M. or later. Some community activities, such as attending a play, would keep students out late. Some students must work in groups on special projects for classes. Working as a group usually requires that the teen-agers meet at some central location. As a result, they may not be able to get home by 10:30 P.M.

Writing Activity *Analyzing Paragraphs*

Read the following paragraphs. Is the topic sentence implied or stated? Identify the purpose of each paragraph.

1. Back east they name towns Willow Springs and Elmhurst and Appleville. Out here, where willows, elms, and apples will not grow, there's a town named Greasewood and another named Cuckelbur, and another named Hackberry. That's the honest truth, you see. Yucca, Arizona. It doesn't sound as pretty as Willow Springs, but it's the truth: no willows, lots of yucca. Charles Kuralt

2. The late moon arose before the first rooster crowed. Kino opened his eyes in the darkness, for he sensed movement near him. . . . in the pale light of the moon that crept through the holes in the brush house Kino saw Juana arise silently from beside him. He saw her move toward the fireplace . . . and then she was gone. John Steinbeck

3. The old man wore the simplest cottons, faded from long use and countless washings. His skin was as parched and brown as the slopes above his high pasture in Baltistan's Karakoram Range. Only the old man's eyes, twinkling like diamonds behind thick glasses, hinted that this was no ordinary farmer.

    Galen Rowell and Barbara Cushman Rowell

4. Cross-country skiing is an economical sport that is easy to learn. Most people can pick up cross-country skills after only one lesson. You don't need special skiwear for cross-country skiing; a medium-weight parka and snow pants will do. You also don't need to buy costly lift tickets or travel to an expensive ski area. Cross-country skiing can be enjoyed in a forest preserve, along a road, in a city park—almost anywhere that you find snow.

5. No one could escape from the city. The mainland was two miles away, across an expanse of wild water that no boat could survive. All four bridges were down. Men, women, and children crouched in their houses, staying close to the walls because that was the safest place if the roof came down. Houses were collapsing; people were dying. No one knew how many; no one knew when his or her turn would come. The wind blew on—and on—and on.

Part 2

Developing and Organizing Paragraphs

After the general structure and purpose of the paragraph are established, the writer must determine the type of information to present and the best way to present it.

Developing Your Paragraph

You develop your paragraph by writing sentences that support your main idea. Depending on the purpose of the paragraph, the supporting details may take the form of anecdotes, examples, facts, statistics, sensory details, or narrative details.

Anecdotes An anecdote—a brief but interesting narrative—can support the main idea of a paragraph.

Professional Model

There is a story. . . that Charlie Chaplin once entered a "Charlie Chaplin look-alike" contest—and came in third. . . . If the judges had known it was Chaplin, he would have won the contest. . . . It is the reputation that is rewarded, more than the exhibition of talent. The name makes the game, in the eyes (and ears) of the public.

From *Clearing the Ground* by Sydney J. Harris

Examples Notice how the examples in the following paragraph provide concrete instances that support the main idea.

▬ *Professional Model* ▬▬▬▬▬▬▬▬▬▬▬▬

We learn fastest when we get responses, and in some situations it is possible to get feedback from inanimate objects. Bicycles, airplanes, and cars, for example, can let you know quickly when you do something right or wrong. The human body is a superb feedback mechanism, too, and such a subtle one that any athlete can profit immensely from a good instructor's help. . . .

From "The Keys to Mastery" by John Poppy

Facts and Statistics A fact is a statement that can be proved either by the use of reference materials or by firsthand observation. Statistics are quantifiable facts—that is, they are facts that are expressed in numbers.

▬ *Professional Model* ▬▬▬▬▬▬▬▬▬▬▬▬

That mass whale strandings are such a recurrent behavior—at Cape Cod alone, there have been seven in the past five years—seems to endow these strange events with a mysterious sense of ritual. Since 1913, when the British Museum first established stranding records, more than 10,000 porpoises, whales, and dolphins are known to have come ashore worldwide. Scientists estimate that the actual number of strandings may be 10 to 20 times that high, taking into account those that go unreported.

From "Beached! The Saga of Stranded Whales"
by Sy Montgomery

Sensory Details Often you can develop a paragraph by including relevant details that appeal to your reader's senses—sight, smell, taste, touch, and hearing.

▬ *Professional Model* ▬▬▬▬▬▬▬▬▬▬▬▬

It was dawn on the third day of our voyage. I pushed hard against the cabin door and thrust myself out on deck where a blast of warm wet air nearly blew me off my feet. I felt as if I were in a wind tunnel. Rubbing my sleepless eyes, I focused on the mainsail: It had ripped away from its rope-edged foot, and was flapping wildly in the wind-driven rain.

From "Plying the Java Sea" by Stephen P. Breslow

Narrative Details A paragraph that tells a story requires narrative details. Each narrative detail relates another incident in the story.

Literary Model

. . . The airplane from Minneapolis in which Francis Weed was traveling East ran into heavy weather. The sky had been a hazy blue. . . . Then mist began to form outside the windows, and they flew into a white cloud [that] reflected the exhaust fires. The color of the cloud darkened to gray, and the plane began to rock. . . . [Then] the plane began to drop and flounder wildly. A child was crying. . . . The exhaust fires blazed and shed sparks in the dark. . . . Then the lights flickered and went out.

From "The Country Husband" by John Cheever

Organizing Your Paragraph

After choosing the supporting details, decide how you will organize them. In most cases, the method you use will be related to the purpose of your writing. There are several ways to organize a paragraph, as described below.

Chronological Order This method presents a series of events in the order in which they occurred. Chronological order is most appropriate for a narrative paragraph or for one that develops its ideas with an incident or anecdote. The paragraph on this page about the turbulent plane ride is written in chronological order.

Spatial Order Sometimes, the details of a paragraph are presented in spatial order—that is, the order in which they are arranged in space. Spatial order can be accomplished in many ways—describing something from left to right, from top to bottom, from the inside out, and so forth. The paragraph from *My Ántonia* that appears on page 99 uses spatial order. In it, author Willa Cather describes a wintry scene from top to bottom.

Comparison or Contrast Comparison points out the similarities between two or more items; contrast focuses on the differences. This method of organization can be used with almost any kind of paragraph development. In the paragraph on page 97, the writer compares the songs of four species of birds.

Cause and Effect Often in expository writing, paragraphs are organized to demonstrate cause and effect—that is, because of event *A*, event *B* happened. In the following model, the writer reflects on why his high-school basketball team lost so many games.

━━ *Professional Model* ━━━━━━━━━━━━━━━

    Like all teams that lose, we were accomplished excuse-makers. For one thing, [our school] had no gym; we had to borrow gyms from other schools. . . . Also, we had no bus, so cars had to be commandeered for out-of-town games, and given our record, we did not attract the better class of automobile. What we got were mostly prewar models with leaky doors and inoperative heaters; our caravan crept over icy roads, past snow-filled fields, the team members and coach huddled inside with earflaps down and collars high. Sometimes the game was well into the second quarter before our feet thawed out into something resembling the standard five-toe model with moving parts.

From "Nostalgia" by Jerome D. Lamb

Order of Familiarity Under this method of organization, a paragraph begins with the most familiar facts and then moves to less familiar ones.

━━ *Student Model* ━━━━━━━━━━━━━━━

    As you think about the last movie you saw, you probably recall a series of images, much like the images you see in real life. But what you really saw was a series of photographs in rapid succession. What fools you is a characteristic of your eye called *persistence of vision.* Any image you see stays in your mind—and in your eye—for a tiny fraction of a second. Because of this delay in the human mind and eye, movies can create the illusion of continuing motion, a phenomenon known as the the *cinematic effect.*

Other Logical Orders These five organizational methods aren't the only ones you can use, however. Any format that will make sense to your reader is usable. When your purpose is to make a specific point, for example, you might use **order of importance.** Under this format, you begin with the least important idea and end with your strongest idea, bringing your argument to a climax and emphasizing your point. Another logical method of organization is **general to specific,** in which you begin with a general statement and support it with specific details.

Writing Activities *Developing a Paragraph*

A Choose a topic from the list below and identify the method of organization you would use to develop a paragraph on that topic. What kinds of information would you need to develop the paragraph?

1. irritating TV commercials
2. the sky before a storm
3. the results of jealousy
4. old music versus new
5. what it's like outside the school building at 7:00 A.M.
6. computers of the 1950's
7. a fashionable outfit
8. how I overcame my fear of _____
9. how a VCR works
10. a ride in a hot-air balloon

B *Writing in Process* Write a paragraph, using either the topic you chose in Activity A above or another topic. Remember to complete the stages of the process of writing (page 62).

Part 3
What Is a Composition?

Only rarely will you have to write just one isolated paragraph. More often, you will need to put together a group of closely related paragraphs to develop a single idea. In doing this, you are writing a **composition.**

The paragraphs that make up your composition will be one of three specialized types. Most compositions begin with an **introduction,** one or more paragraphs that state the main idea and tell the reader what the composition will be about. In a sense, the introduction performs the same function that a topic sentence does for a paragraph. The **body paragraphs** of a composition develop the idea presented in the introduction. The final paragraph, or **conclusion,** lets the reader know that the composition is coming to an end. The writer may use the conclusion to restate the main idea, to summarize the supporting information, or to provide a general comment. In addition to fulfilling one of these three functions, each paragraph in a composition has its own purpose.

Read the following composition, noting how it is organized with an introduction, a body, and a conclusion.

Student Model

Introduction

If you've ridden in elevators dozens of times without giving it another moment's thought, you might be interested to know that the elevator isn't just another "modern convenience." It has been with us, in one form or another, for centuries.

Body

In actuality, the first elevators were nothing more than a crude rope-and-pulley machine in the days of ancient Rome. Vitruvius, an architect and engineer, wrote about platforms powered by animals, humans, or water.

Descriptive paragraph

That design was gradually refined to a basket-and-rope idea rigged up on the outside of a building, a device often seen at monasteries and other remote places. Basket riders had to leap from their perch to the windowsill of their choice—and hope for the best.

Explanatory paragraph

In France during the the seventeenth century, the "flying chair" evolved. This early form of the elevator was really another pulley operation. It consisted of a rope wrapped around a wheel at the top of a building. On one end of the rope was a chair and on the other end, a weight. To make it work, the rider would sit in the chair and throw out a sandbag. This would cause the weight on the other end of the rope to fall. The speed of the ride depended on the weight of the rider, and a lighter person would very nearly fly! Unfortunately, however, no one had yet come up with a cure for motion sickness.

Use of cause and effect

Descriptive paragraph

Use of an example

As time passed, elevators eventually "came inside" and more sophisticated equipment evolved. In the mid-1800's, for example, an American named Elisha Graves Otis developed an important safety device for the elevator. This device, for which Otis became known as the "Father of the Elevator," consisted of two hooks and a spring attached to the cable at the base of the platform. In the event that the cable tension changes, the hooks catch and hold the platform,

Use of an
anecdote

preventing it from dropping. Otis presented his device at the 1854 Crystal Palace Exposition in London. He was so confident of the elevator's reliability that he would stand on the platform and personally cut the cables, allowing the hooks to save him from a fall.

Use of facts
and statistics

According to reports from the elevator industry, elevators are nearly 100 percent safe—five times safer than stairways. Although Otis's 1850's safety device may appear rather simple by space-age standards, the basic design is still used today. To safeguard against cable failure, elevators have eight woven steel cables that can support a load eight times greater than the car's capacity.

Conclusion

But perhaps you yearn for the "good old days" when people rode in baskets? If so, you might enjoy riding in a glass-walled elevator located on the outside of a building. These "stairways to the stars" are featured in many structures built since the 1970's, most notably in luxury hotels in larger U.S. cities. The glass elevators have at least one important difference from the basket, however: they open into the building. No leaping required!

Types of Compositions

Like paragraphs, compositions can be classified into types according to their purpose. Moreover, as with paragraphs, there are probably as many purposes for compositions as there are writers and reasons for writing. Generally, however, compositions fall into four broad categories based on the following purposes:

1. A **descriptive composition** relates an image, communicates a mood, or describes the impact of a subject on the writer. For instance, you might describe a beautiful old mansion on Rhode Island's shore.
2. A **narrative composition** tells a story. For example, you might relate how your school's hockey team won the state championship.
3. An **expository composition** informs or explains. For example, you might tell how sleet is formed, explain how to operate a minicomputer, or outline the similarities and differences between two diseases.
4. A **persuasive composition** attempts to influence the reader's opinion. For instance, you might write a composition supporting an "underdog" candidate for president of your class.

Stating the Thesis

After you determine the overall purpose of your composition, clarify your topic even further with a thesis. Your **thesis** is a concise statement of the controlling purpose or central idea of the composition. A thesis can also express your attitude, as in this example:

> Without immediate attention, acid rain could quickly become Planet Earth's environmental version of the "Black Death."

Developing a thesis helps you organize your composition. It forces you to focus your thinking and may point you to the best method of development for the composition. It may even suggest some of the main divisions for your outline.

In developing or evaluating a thesis statement, ask yourself the following questions: Does the thesis focus on one specific point? Does it give the main idea of the composition? Will readers find this statement interesting?

In the drafting stage, you might find it helpful to use what is called a *working thesis*—that is, a flexible statement of purpose. Once you have completed the first draft, you might revise the working thesis to fit more closely with what you've written. Often, writers work the thesis statement into the composition itself.

Writing Activities *What Is a Composition?*

A Evaluate the following pairs of statements. In each pair, one statement would make a good thesis for a composition and the other would not. Identify the better thesis statement in each pair and explain why you chose it.

1. I liked visiting the Grand Canyon.
   A backpacking trip to the Grand Canyon with my dad has fostered a new and special relationship between us.
2. Comic books are an interesting form of communication.
   Under the right circumstances, reading comic books can be an educational experience.
3. Some public buildings are not accessible to people in wheelchairs.
   With some minimal architectural changes, our community library could be made accessible to people in wheelchairs.

B *Writing in Process* Use the picture on this page to help you think of a topic for a short composition. Then, develop a working thesis that expresses your central point and suggests an organizational form. Start to gather ideas and organize details according to whether they would fit best within the introduction, the body, or the conclusion of your composition.

Part 4

Paragraphs to Compositions

You have learned that paragraphs perform different specialized functions within a composition. Some introduce ideas; others develop them; still others provide concluding statements. The most effective way to write your composition is to consider, in turn, each of these specialized functions.

Writing the Introduction

The introduction, as you have learned, must clearly state the main idea of the composition. However, the introduction has another equally important purpose: it must catch the reader's attention. It must be interesting enough to make the reader want to continue reading.

There are a number of strategies you can use in writing your introduction. The subject and purpose of your composition will help you determine the most effective one.

Address the Reader Directly In this strategy, you "speak" directly to the reader as you introduce your topic.

> Have you ever entered a store or restaurant and felt totally ignored? Have you ever stood at a checkout counter while the cashier talked on the phone with a friend instead of helping you?

Provide a Benefit An introduction can suggest that there are benefits to the reader's learning what you present. Such an introduction is appropriate in compositions that attempt to persuade the reader or that explain a process.

> If slow reading is your problem, you might be surprised to learn that you are not alone. Follow these simple guidelines and your reading speed will increase in just a few weeks.

Ask a Question Similarly, a thought-provoking question can draw the reader into your composition. Note the comical twist a famous humorist adds to this method.

> How many of you have ever wondered where certain slang expressions come from? Like "She's the cat's pajamas," or to "take it on the lam." Neither have I. Woody Allen

Repeat an Interesting Quotation An intriguing quote will often catch your reader's interest.

> Thomas Henry Huxley once defined science as "organized common sense." Stephen Jay Gould

State an Interesting Fact Another effective method is to teach the reader something new about your topic in the first few lines—something that leads into your central idea.

> Believe it or not, the Beatles created most of their extraordinary music on stock, off-the-shelf, production-model guitars.
>
> Bob Mytkowicz

Take a Stand Controversy can also work to attract the attention of your readers. If you begin your composition by taking a stand on a controversial issue, a reader may become interested because he or she strongly agrees or disagrees with your point of view.

> A number of probes and communications beams search endlessly for intelligent life beyond our own planet. They may just find what they are looking for—a lot sooner than most people expect.

Writing the Body

The body is the major part of the composition, where you develop and explain your main idea. Earlier in this chapter, you learned about the different purposes of paragraphs. Body paragraphs in a composition often have different purposes as well. Choose the types of body paragraphs that best suit your information, and be sure that they flow together logically.

Professional Model

Narrative Jack London captured the importance of a simple fire in his tale "To Build a Fire." Traveling during the bitter arctic winter, a man stops to build a fire. The terrible cold has numbed his brain as well as his hands. In desperation, he uses the entire supply of matches. As the fire builds and begins to warm and comfort him, snow cascades off the overhanging tree, burying the flames and the man's hope for survival.

Analysis A fire has many uses. As well as preventing death by hypothermia, it provides comfort and security. A fire soothes the body and returns the mind to rational and practical solutions for whatever problem has developed. Even if lost or panicked, the person who can build a fire will almost surely survive. . . .

Compare and contrast (persuasive)

The single most important survival tool, after a person's own intellect and knowledge, is the simple match. In a wilderness setting, matches should always be carried. A hunter can start a fire with his rifle and shells. A bird watcher can use binoculars to focus the sun's rays. A camper can use flashlight batteries or flint and steel. But the best, most dependable survival tool is a match. . . .

Anecdote (narrative)

Recently the evening news carried the story of two boys lost in the mountains above Salt Lake City. They were young, but they carried a few matches and a survival book. When evening came, snow began to fall, and the boys stopped to start a fire. They consulted their book and tried to find suitable fuel for the fire. Nothing seemed to work. Everything was wet and their matches were almost gone, and the night grew darker and colder. Then they made a wise choice. They tore up the survival book and used it for tinder. Soon they had a warm fire which also guided rescuers to them.

From *Wilderness Survival* by Bernard Shanks

Writing a Conclusion

The conclusion signals the end of your composition. It also ties your ideas and details together and presents a final statement for the reader to consider. There are a number of techniques you can use to conclude your composition.

Ask a Question Concluding with an interesting question is an effective way to keep the topic on your reader's mind and encourage the reader to think about what you have said.

> Can the Okefenokee survive? The sound of the swamp—the croaking and cawing of a huge discordant symphony—overwhelms a man's thoughts on that question. But it reminds us that in the end, nature does not play by man's rules.   Bob Dotson

Suggest a Solution A good way to conclude a composition that poses a problem is to suggest a solution.

> We *can* make our students better readers, but first, we need to change some habits. Good reading begins at home. Parents should set

an example by reading often. They must provide books for their children; the public library is a good place to start.

Summarize Important Points Sometimes the most effective conclusion is a summary of your information.

> Keeping a journal, then, can do a lot more than simply improve your writing. It can help you identify problems and see where you might be going wrong. It may even help you solve some dilemmas.

Restate the Central Idea Another way to conclude your composition is simply to restate the central idea.

> Feet have gotten a dirty deal over the years. We haven't paid half as much attention to them as we've paid to our hands. Feet are what Howard Cosell would call the unsung heroes of our bodies. We ought to give them a better break and the women walking to work in sneakers or running shoes are taking a big step in that direction. If I wore a hat, I'd take it off to them.   Andrew A. Rooney

Relate an Anecdote An interesting anecdote can also tie together the points you have made. The composition on pages 113–114 uses an anecdote as a conclusion.

Writing Activities Developing a Composition

A Read the following sentences. Sentences 1 through 5 come from composition introductions, and 6 through 10 are from conclusions. Identify the strategy that each sentence illustrates (for example, providing a benefit or restating the central idea).

1. You probably put away your bicycle when the weather gets cold, but a few tips on cold-weather bike gear can help you enjoy cycling in all types of weather.
2. The word *juke* in *jukebox* originally comes from a slang word that meant "wicked" or "disorderly."
3. The federal government must pass legislation to ban the sale of aerosol sprays immediately.
4. What kinds of new careers will be open to college graduates ten years from now?
5. Like most people, you probably have had the dream that you walk into class in the middle of an exam for which you are unprepared.
6. Most of the evidence, then, indicates that the typical high-school student in Japan leads a more sheltered life than an American student.

7. The power of political cartoons is far-reaching; they can affect public opinion and public policy.

8. Something must be done about the unsafe intersections around our school; additional crossing guards and new traffic lights would be a step in the right direction.

9. Isn't it worth the effort now to preserve one of the last remaining habitats of the mountain lion?

10. For many settlers in Australia's rugged outback, the weekly arrival of the "Tea and Sugar" train with its cargo of food and needed supplies is the only contact with the outside world.

B *Writing in Process* In Part 3 you wrote a thesis statement. Write a composition based upon that thesis statement (or another one). Make sure that your composition includes an introduction, a body, and a conclusion.

write a intro cartoon
b why disneys are the
movies best

Part 5

Unity and Coherence

Effective writing flows; it has a momentum of its own. To achieve a smooth flow, your own writing will need two essential qualities: unity and coherence.

Achieving Unity

In a composition with **unity,** each paragraph is related to the thesis statement or main idea presented in the introduction. Supporting details in each paragraph relate directly to that paragraph's topic sentence or main idea. To maintain unity as you write, check each paragraph's main idea against the introduction. Within each paragraph, check each sentence against the paragraph's main idea or topic sentence. Notice how the unrelated sentence destroys the unity in the following paragraph.

Spiders find a variety of uses for the silk they produce; two of the best uses are webs and draglines. Using its fingerlike spinnerets, the spider creates beaded strands of sticky silk. Woven into a web, these

Unrelated sentence   trap unsuspecting insects. Some spiders line their burrows with silk. The dragline, also crucial to the spider's survival, helps it move around. Using this long thin strand, the spider can hang in the air to avoid danger, swing to the ground to attack its prey, and find its way "home" on flat ground.

Achieving Coherence

A composition has **coherence** when the reader can follow the connections between paragraphs. Words and phrases called **transitional devices** provide such links between paragraphs. Transitional devices can show time or place (*always, before, above, around*), a relationship between ideas (*also, therefore*), or an opposite point of view (*but, on the other hand*).

Another transitional device is word repetition. You can create a transition by repeating a word used earlier. This device also has two variations. You can link paragraphs or ideas through the use of a synonym of a word used earlier. You can also create a transition by using a pronoun in place of a word used earlier. For example, suppose you are describing an *ocelot*—a jungle cat. You can begin your second paragraph by referring to the ocelot as "the sleek creature." Later you may simply refer to the ocelot by the pronoun *it*.

The Completed Composition

After you have checked for unity and coherence, read your composition as if you were not the writer. Does it make a point? Does it accomplish its goal? Is it interesting to read?

Writing Activities Unity and Coherence

A Rearrange the sentences in each group below to create a unified paragraph.

1. They are always encouraging you to do well. Parents, grandparents, aunts, and uncles all seem to pay more attention to you. There are many advantages to being a family's firstborn child. It's no wonder that more than half our presidents have been firstborns. This gives the firstborn child a lot of self-confidence and a belief that he or she will be taken seriously.

2. Dense forests covered most of its 11,000-foot splendor. Matching the whiteness of the peak was one isolated, billowy cloud that created a sharp contrast with the clear blue western-Canadian sky. Above the timberline was the snowy-white peak—the purest white I had ever seen. There stood the mountain, regally dwarfing all the others in the range.

B *Writing in Process* Review the composition you wrote in Part 4 of this chapter. Does each paragraph relate to the thesis statement or main idea? Have transition devices been used effectively to link paragraphs? Revise your composition as necessary.

Chapter 5
Application and Review

The following activities will give you practice writing compositions. Activity A leads you through the steps involved in writing a descriptive composition. Activities B and C offer you more choices for writing.

A Describing a Scene Use the following guidelines to plan and write a descriptive composition.

Prewriting With a small group of students, brainstorm to create a list of topics that describe a specific area at a particular time of day. Possible topics might include a busy newsstand at rush hour; the local post office/general store on a Saturday morning; or the school cafeteria at lunchtime. Choose one topic and observe the scene that you plan to describe. Take notes as you observe. Review your notes to find unifying themes. Determine what details should be presented and decide on the best form of organization for your composition. Write a thesis statement; then write an outline for your composition.

Drafting Use your outline to write a first draft. As you write, be sure your composition has an interesting introduction, body paragraphs that support your main idea, and an effective conclusion.

Revising As you revise, ask yourself these questions: Does my introduction state the main idea *and* catch the reader's attention? Do my body paragraphs develop and explain the main idea? Does my conclusion tie together all my information and present a strong final statement? Does my composition show unity and coherence?

B Writing an Expository Composition Use the following guidelines to write a composition that explains a process.

Prewriting Use freewriting (page 11) to think of a topic for an expository composition. Sample topics include how to read music, how to find an after-school job, why a certain animal has become extinct. Once you select a topic, use clustering (page 12) to decide on the details you will present. Think about your topic and then write an outline.

Drafting and Revising Write your first draft and read it to a group of students. Use the group's comments to guide your revision. Proofread your revised composition and make a clean final copy.

c *Starting Points for Writing* List anything you have tried to do—or are presently trying to do—but at which you haven't been successful. Free-associate with the images and quotes below to recall anything else that you worked very hard at but still failed to accomplish. Add these items to your list. The items on this list are good starting points for writing.

*I turned around, walked up the
path and grabbed for the cashews.*
Geneen Roth

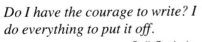

*One part of me was saying: Well,
if I have to do it, I have to do
it, and another was thinking:
What happens if they make a joke
of it—or ignore me?*
Sharon Wysocki

*Do I have the courage to write? I
do everything to put it off.*
Gail Godwin

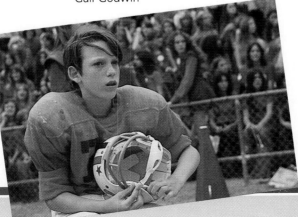

Focus On

SPEED WRITING

Speed writing—an informal system for writing faster—can be your secret code for taking better notes.

Drawing by Chas. Addams, © 1973, The New Yorker Magazine, Inc.

The famous archaeologist Nebraska Smith finds a message written on a cave wall. Agent 000 immediately transcribes the message into secret code to prevent discovery by enemy agents. This is the "stuff" of novels of intrigue. What has this to do with you? As you engage in the less dangerous tasks of listening to lectures and note taking, you too may have use for a special kind of secret code of your own.

Faster Than a Speeding Bullet: A Way to Get It All on Paper

Have you ever put your pen down in frustration from not being able to take notes fast enough? Certainly you have had writer's cramp. Speed writing can help you with your note-taking problems.

Speed Writing is an informal system for writing faster. It is not as structured as shorthand and does not depend on the special characters that shorthand uses. Instead, speed writing consists of a mixture of shortened words, symbols, abbreviations, and words written in their entirety. It offers a solution to your note-taking frustrations.

OK, What's the Catch? To be effective, speed writing must pass two tests. With some practice, you must be able to write faster using speed writing than you normally can, and you must be able to decipher what you've written. Otherwise, the rules for speed writing are wide open and you can do whatever works best for you.

There are some tried-and-true strategies for writing fast, accurate, readable notes. Begin by using some of what you already know.

Take a Cue from the Post Office: Abbreviate

All state names and some cities can be written in abbreviated form. For example, New York City, New York, may be written NYC, NY. Use such standard abbreviations whenever possible to speed up your writing.

Many fields of study, such as math and science, also have symbols and abbreviations that you can utilize in your method of speed writing. For example, try using the following symbols.

therefore   ∴
greater than   >
less than   <
plus or minus   +   −
reaction $r \times n$
change   △

Numbers offer another way of shortening what you write. The numeral *1* is easier to write than *one*. Also, use symbols, such as the following, that appear on the top row of keys on a typewriter.

number   #
at or about   @
percent   %
and   &

You should incorporate other commonly used symbols and abbreviations whenever possible: *ft.* for feet, *in.* for inches, *lb.* for pound, and A.M. for morning.

Some words lend themselves to shortening even without official abbreviations. Important can become *imp;* government, *gov;* manager, *mgr;* regarding, *re;* with, *w;* and without, *w/o.* Make use of these examples in your own speed-writing code, and be on the lookout for more that you can add to your list of abbreviated words.

Spell Creatively! Spell By Sound

Another speed-writing technique takes advantage of the connections between certain letters and sounds. "You" can become *u,* "through" can be *thru,* and "are" can become *r.*

In English, some sounds are made by more than one letter. To aid your speed writing, you can use a more uniform system that represents these sounds.

A System for Sounds

c   as in cat, cough
s   as in saw, cent
g   as in great
f   as in pheasant, farm
j   as in gentle, joy
q   as in quick, request

I Don't Want To Buy a Vowel

Consonants provide a framework for words. Speed writing takes advantage of the fact that vowels can be eliminated from most words without making those words unrecognizable. To prove this, the vowels have been omitted from the following familiar passage, and some symbols have been used. Translate the passage and you will see that it doesn't take long for your mind to replace the vowels.

4 scr & 7 yrs ag r 4fthrs brght 4th 2 ths cntnt a nw ntn.

Such deletions may leave some words represented by the same symbol. For example *ran, run, ruin,* and *rain* would all look like *rn.* Context plays an important role in these cases. Seldom would *rain* and *ruin* be used interchangeably. Consider "I *rn* to the beach." *Rain* and *ruin* are not reasonable choices. *Ran* and *run* are both possible. However, it is important in speed writing to remember that if deleting a vowel will cause confusion in translating what has been written, then the entire word should be used.

Ritual, Gwen Knight, 1987.

Alpha and Omega: Beginnings and Endings

Certain letters in English are often used together to form the beginnings and endings of words. As you devise your personal system of speed writing, develop an easy way to write often-used word beginnings and endings. For example, you could represent the prefix *-un* with the letter *u.* To write the often-used prefix *under-,* you might underscore the *u*. You could use the letter *n* to represent the prefix *non-.*

Word endings can also be represented by letters and symbols. Some systems of speed writing suggest using a dash to represent the ending *-ed* and a *-y* to stand for the endings *-ary* and *-ery.* Plurals can be shown in the usual way, by adding an *s.* You may also wish to use symbols for *-ment* and *-ing* and for other common endings.

Remember, you are devising your own system of writing shortcuts. Since you are the one who will use this system, find out what works best for you.

One Last Word of Advice

It's a good idea to review any notes in speed writing shortly after they are written to be sure you understand everything you wrote. Also, as you use speed writing, don't bother erasing a mistake. Simply draw a line through the mistake and write the correct word beside it. Since your code is only for you, neatness doesn't matter. You may never use speed writing to fool enemy agents, but you will find it to be a practical and

effective skill both in and out of school.

Using Your Code

A Practice using speed writing to write the following sentences and phrases.

1. The colonel wondered if there would be an attack.

2. Doublecheck on the chemical reaction in your experiment.

3. Thomas Willow is a vice-president of a large corporation.

4. Both angles must measure ninety degrees.

5. Why did the railroads change from steam to diesel?

6. The professor said you have two weeks to make up your work.

7. Therefore, $3.00 a pound is not an unfair price.

8. A meter is a little longer than a yard.

9. Roger and Terry do not have an equal voice in the matter.

10. We wired a number of messages to you.

11. Please estimate how long it will take to get to New York.

12. Four important dates are marked on the calendar.

B Try your hand at decoding a sample of speed writing. Transcribe the following passage from speed writing into customary text.

I d nt blv tht any f us wld xcj plses w ny othr pepl r jnrshn. t nrj, t fth, t dvsn wch w brng 2 ths ndvr wl lt r cntr & al wh srv it & t glw frm tht fr cn trl lt t wrld.

& so, m flw Amers—ask nt wht yr cntr cn d 4 u—ask wht u cn d 4 yr cntr.

C Practice speed writing as you take notes in your next class lecture. Review your notes soon afterward to make sure you understand the material.

6

Improving Sentence Style

What elements do you suppose the judges above consider as they evaluate a gymnast's performance? Would you have guessed technique and style?

Technique and style are as important to writers as they are to gymnasts. Writers who haven't mastered basic writing techniques tend to construct clumsy sentences that obscure their meaning. Furthermore, writers who do not make use of the elements of style cannot communicate their message as forcefully or elegantly as they otherwise might.

In this chapter you will master techniques for improving sentence style that will help you to convey what you mean, create specific moods, and add variety to your writing.

Combining Sentences and Sentence Parts

Too many short sentences can make your writing choppy, boring, and unclear. When you read over a first draft, watch for short sentences that express related ideas. As you revise, combine these short sentences to make your writing smoother, livelier, and clearer.

Combining Sentences

Two short sentences may express related ideas of equal importance. You can combine these sentences by using a comma and a conjunction. A **conjunction** is a word that connects words or groups of words.

If the ideas are similar, use a comma and the conjunction *and*.

> London is the capital of England.
> Madrid is the capital of Spain.
> London is the capital of England, **and** Madrid is the capital of Spain.

Similar ideas can also be joined by a *semicolon*.

> The doctor is in surgery.
> She cannot see any more patients today.
> The doctor is in surgery; she cannot see any more patients today.

If the ideas contrast, use a comma and the conjunction *but*.

> The emu is a bird.
> It does not have the capacity to fly.
> The emu is a bird, **but** it does not have the capacity to fly.

If there is a choice between two ideas, use a comma and the conjunction *or*.

> You can take the bus to the concert.
> We can walk to the concert together.
> You can take the bus to the concert, **or** we can walk to the concert together.

Grammar Note When sentences with ideas of equal importance are combined into a single statement, they form a **compound sentence**. For more information about compound sentences, see page 565.

By joining related ideas in a compound sentence, you can make your writing easier to understand. Sometimes through haste or carelessness, however, you may join unrelated ideas. The reader is then confused and has to stop and ask, "What is the connection between the two ideas?" You can eliminate this problem by expressing the omitted connecting thought. You may need to write two sentences in order to clarify your writing.

Confusing   The rain came down in torrents, and Mrs. Meyers had to entertain their dinner guests alone.

Improved   The rain came down in torrents. Because Mr. Meyers was helping victims in the flooded areas, Mrs. Meyers had to entertain their dinner guests alone.

Combining Sentence Parts

Sometimes the ideas expressed by two sentences are so closely related that some words in the first sentence are repeated, or are replaced by synonyms, in the second sentence. As you revise, you can combine sentences like these by eliminating the words that are repeated. You can then combine the remaining sentence parts with just a conjunction. No comma is needed.

For similar ideas, use *and*.

Ken put crisp lettuce in the salad. *He put* juicy tomatoes *in the salad.*
Ken put crisp lettuce **and** juicy tomatoes in the salad.

For contrasting ideas, use *but*.

The wild ponies of Chincoteague gallop fast. *They* tire fairly quickly.
The wild ponies of Chincoteague gallop fast **but** tire fairly quickly.

For a choice between ideas, use *or*.

Customers can climb the stairs near the rear of the store. *They can* use the escalator.
Customers can climb the stairs near the rear of the store **or** use the escalator.

Compare the following sentences. Notice how combining sentences differs from combining sentence parts.

Combining Sentences   Dolphins travel in family groups, and they communicate with clicks and whistles.

Combining Sentence Parts   Dolphins travel in family groups and communicate with clicks and whistles.

Writing Activities *Combining Ideas*

A Combine each pair of sentences. Follow the directions in parentheses and eliminate any italicized words.

1. Death Valley in California is a desert. Many plants and animals thrive there. (Use *but*.)
2. The dinosaurs disappeared about 65 million years ago. Scientists cannot explain why. (Use a semicolon.)
3. The jet streaked down the runway. *The jet* rose gracefully into the air. (Use *and*.)
4. A few spiders are poisonous. Most *spiders* are harmless. (Use *but*.)
5. Visitors to China can walk along the top of the Great Wall. *Tourists can also* explore the Forbidden City. (Use *or*.)

B Rewrite the following passage by combining the sentences enclosed in parentheses. Eliminate the words in italics and use the combining techniques you learned in Part 1.

(Crossword puzzles are brain teasers. *Crossword puzzles are also* entertainment for millions of people.) (Crossword puzzles are included in newspapers all over the world. They were not always a part of the newspaper.) (In 1913, the editor of the New York World was looking for an idea to spice up his newspaper. *He* came up with a puzzle called the "wordcross.") (Puzzle fever grew, and railroad companies put dictionaries on their trains. Railroads also *put* puzzles on their dining car menus.)

Part 2
Adding Words to Sentences

When you read a first draft, you may find that two sentences contain related ideas that are not equally important. As you revise, you may be able to incorporate a key word from one sentence into the other. The resulting single sentence may express your thoughts more effectively.

Inserting Words Without Changes

Often, you can add the key word in one sentence to another sentence without changing the form of the word. However, you must place the word near the person, thing, or action the word describes.

The meteor was brilliant. The meteor raced across the dark, eastern sky.
The **brilliant** meteor raced across the dark, eastern sky.

The scientist worked with the dangerous explosives. *She worked* carefully.
The scientist worked **carefully** with the explosives.

You can combine more than two sentences if one of the sentences states a main idea and each of the others adds just one important detail. When you add more than one word to a sentence, you may have to use a comma or the conjunction *and*.

Anteaters have tongues. *They are* long. *They are* sticky.
Anteaters have **long, sticky** tongues.

The windsurfers glided on the lake. *They glided* smoothly. *They glided* gracefully.
The windsurfers glided **smoothly and gracefully** on the lake.

The earthquake created a tidal wave. *The quake was* violent. *The wave was* huge.
The **violent** earthquake created a **huge** tidal wave.

Inserting Words with Changes

Sometimes you must change the form of a word before you can add it to another sentence. The most common changes involve adding endings such as *-y*, *-ed*, *-ing*, or *-ly*.

She walked slowly along the path. *It had many* rocks.
She walked slowly along the **rocky** path.

They spotted the lion near the wildebeest herd. *The lion* slept.
They spotted the **sleeping** lion near the wildebeest herd.

I found a trunk in the attic. *It was covered with* dust.
I found a **dusty** trunk in the attic.

The mayor greeted the visitors. *She was* pleasant.
The mayor greeted the visitors **pleasantly**.

Writing Activities Adding Words

A Combine each group of sentences. In sentences 1–5, eliminate the words in italics and follow the directions in parentheses. In sentences 6–10, you should decide which combining techniques to use.

1. A snake slithered under the door. *The snake was* long. *It was* speckled. (Use a comma.)
2. The soup was full of vegetables. Steam *rose from the soup*. (Use -y.)
3. She showed us her gold medal. *She was* proud. (Use -ly.)
4. The fans leaped to their feet. *The fans* cheered. (Use -ing.)
5. The vase is very valuable. *It has a* crack. (Use -ed.)
6. The poodle next door sleeps on pillows. The pillows are silk. That poodle is pampered.
7. The employee stood at the door of the office. He seemed hesitant.
8. An army of ants moved silently through the jungle. It moved steadily.
9. The deer ran from the hunter. The deer had a wound.
10. The raccoons come to our back door. They are hungry. They come daily.

B Rewrite the following passage. Combine the sentences in parentheses, eliminating the words in italics. Use conjunctions and change the forms of words wherever necessary.

(The Navajo are Native Americans. *They are also* United States citizens.) (Their reservation covers areas of the states of Arizona, New Mexico, and Utah. *The reservation is* enormous.) (Today, some Navajo farm or herd sheep on their reservation. Many *Navajo* have jobs in cities.)

(Navajo craft workers display their work to visitors. *They are* proud *of their work*. *The work is* artistic.) (The visitors watch the fingers of the workers who weave wool blankets. *The workers' fingers* fly. *The workers* fascinate *the visitors*.) (Visitors buy the jewelry made by other craft workers. *They are* eager *to buy the jewelry*. *It is* silver and turquoise.)

Part 3
Inserting Word Groups

When you are reading over a first draft, you may find that a group of words from one sentence can be used in another sentence. As you revise, you can combine the sentences in several ways.

Inserting Word Groups Without Changes

You can sometimes insert a group of words into another sentence without changing their form. When you revise, place the words close to the person, thing, or action they describe.

> NASA is creating a space station. *The station is* for lunar research.
> NASA is creating a space station **for lunar research.**

> A family moved in next door. *They are* from Vietnam.
> A family **from Vietnam** moved in next door.

> The neighbors have a huge barbecue. *They have it* once a year.
> **Once a year,** the neighbors have a huge barbecue.

A group of words in one sentence may rename a noun in another sentence. A group of words that renames a noun is known as an **appositive phrase.** Notice the appositive phrases in these examples.

> The Grand Canyon measures about 215 miles long and up to 12 miles wide. *It is* the largest canyon on the earth.
> The Grand Canyon, **the largest canyon on the earth,** measures about 215 miles long and up to 12 miles wide.

> The country of Japan is really an archipelago. *An archipelago is* a large group of islands.
> The country of Japan is really an archipelago, **a large group of islands.**

> The saguaro can grow taller than a five-story building. *The saguaro is* a cactus that thrives in the American Southwest.
> The saguaro, **a cactus that thrives in the American Southwest,** can grow taller than a five-story building.

Punctuation Note Set off appositive phrases with a comma or a set of commas. For more information about appositives and how to punctuate them, see pages 537–538.

Inserting Word Groups with -ing or -ed

When you add a group of words to a sentence, you may have to change the form of one of the words by adding *-ing* or *-ed*. As the examples below show, more than one group of words may be added to a sentence in this way.

Look at Harvey. *He is* telling his corny jokes again.
Look at Harvey **telling** his corny jokes again.

Everyone on the boat got seasick. *The boat had* a round bottom.
Everyone on the **round-bottomed** boat got seasick.

At the gate stand two soldiers. *The soldiers* guard the castle.
At the gate stand two soldiers **guarding** the castle.

A man burst into the room. *The man* breathed hard. *He* shouted the news of the victory.
A man burst into the room, **breathing** hard and **shouting** the news of the victory.

Writing Activities Adding Word Groups

A Combine the following sentences. In sentences 1–5, eliminate the words in italics and follow any directions in parentheses. In sentences 6–10, you should decide how to combine the sentences.

1. The firefighter rushed into the burning house. *She* hesitated just a moment at the door. (Use *-ing* and a comma.)
2. Flight 933 is now expected to depart for Chicago. *It should depart* at approximately 9:45 P.M.
3. In 1565, people from Spain founded St. Augustine. *It was* the first permanent European settlement in America. (Use a comma.)
4. The mayor called an emergency meeting. *He had* concerns about the pollution of the harbor. (Use *-ed* and commas.)
5. The people of the town are watching the raging forest fire. *The fire* creeps slowly toward their homes. (Use *-ing*.)
6. A gym teacher invented basketball. His name was James Naismith.
7. Carla joined a skydiving club. Carla is my cousin.
8. If you want to taste something delicious, try a tangelo. This fruit is a cross between a grapefruit and a tangerine.
9. Joel visited the memorial to the Holocaust victims. It is in Israel. He visited it with his aunt and uncle.
10. We crossed over the deep canyon on a bridge the Indians built. The bridge swayed. The Indians had built it with thick vines.

B Rewrite the following passage by combining the sentences in parentheses and eliminating the words in italics. You may need to use commas to set off a group of words or change the form of a word by adding *-ing* or *-ed*.

(Some favorite American fruits are immigrants. *They came here* from various parts of the world.) (An early favorite was the apple. *This fruit* arrived in 1629. *It came* from England.)

(The apple was relished by people long before 1629. *It is* an ancient food.) (Scientists have found the remains of apples in Stone Age villages. *These scientists are* interested in prehistoric peoples.)

(The orange is an immigrant too. *The orange is* another American favorite.) (This fruit was first grown in China. *It was grown* before the year 2000 B.C.) (Muslims brought orange trees with them when they conquered Spain. *Muslims were* also called Moors.) (The Spanish settlers introduced the fruit to the Americas. *They were settlers* of Florida. *They came* in the 1500's.)

Part 4
Combining with Who, Which, *or* That

In Part 3, you learned that a group of words in one sentence often describes a person or thing in a related sentence. As you revise, you can eliminate repetition by using the introductory words *who, which,* or *that* to combine sentences.

Inserting Word Groups with Who

Use the word *who* to add related details about a person or group of persons in a sentence. In the first example below, the two sentences are combined into one sentence using *who*. Notice that the additional details tell what kind of supporters a candidate needs to be successful. Since these details are essential to the meaning of the sentence, no commas are necessary. The additional details in the second example are not essential to the meaning of the sentence, and are therefore set off with commas.

To be successful, a candidate needs supporters. The supporters must be willing to work long and hard for victory.

To be successful, a candidate needs supporters **who** are willing to work long and hard for victory.

William Golding was awarded the Nobel Prize for literature in 1983. He is best known for the novel *Lord of the Flies*.

William Golding, **who** is best known for the novel *Lord of the Flies*, was awarded the Nobel Prize for literature in 1983.

Inserting Word Groups with That or Which

You can use *that* or *which* to add related details to a sentence when those details refer to things.

I like any movie. *The movie must* make me laugh hard.
I like any movie **that makes me laugh hard.**

The Taj Mahal took twenty years to build. *It* is in India.
The Taj Mahal, **which is in India,** took twenty years to build.

In the first example, the added details are necessary to the meaning of the sentence, so *that* is used. The related details in the second example are not essential to the main idea of the sentence, so *which* is used, and the details are set off with commas.

Grammar Note When a subordinate clause acts as an adjective, it is called an **adjective clause.** For more information, see pages 554–556.

Adjective Clause   Willis dragged the box *that contained the gold.*

Writing Activities Combining Sentences

A Combine each pair of sentences. In sentences 1–5, eliminate the words in italics, and follow the directions in parentheses. In sentences 6–10, use *who, which,* or *that* and commas.

1. Here is the novel. Jim said we should read *it*. (Use *that*.)
2. Scotland Yard is a part of the London police force. *Scotland Yard* is not in Scotland. (Use *which* and commas.)
3. A dentist in Italy pulled over seventy thousand teeth in thirty-six years! *He* grew up with my father. (Use *who* and commas.)
4. The firefighter is courageous. *That firefighter* rescued two young children from a burning house. (Use *who*.)
5. The first movie theater was called a nickelodeon. *This theater* seated ninety-two people. (Use *which* and commas.)

6. Samuel Johnson wrote an entire dictionary by himself in only eight years. Johnson lived in England during the 1800's.
7. The diamond tiara is priceless. The queen wears it.
8. The players were the honored guests at a city-wide celebration. The players won the world championship.
9. A house in California has 2,000 doors, 10,000 windows, and stairways leading nowhere. It may be the weirdest building on earth.
10. The white roses were gorgeous. You sent them to me for graduation.

B Rewrite the following passage by combining the sentences in parentheses. Eliminate the words in italics and use *who, which,* or *that.* If necessary, insert commas.

(Many scientists focus their attention on the solar system. *These scientists* study the skies.) (They have discovered that the solar system contains objects of various types. *The solar system* occupies a small area at the edge of the Milky Way.)

(One medium-sized star is our sun. *This star* shines brilliantly at the center of the solar system.) (Several orbiting planets receive varying amounts of heat and light from the glowing sun. *The planets* are the second-largest objects in the solar system.) The light and heat make a great variety of life forms possible on Earth.

(Other objects take their places in the sun's family. *They* are not as large as the planets.) Satellites orbit Earth and other planets. (In addition, asteroids orbit the sun between the planets Mars and Jupiter. *Asteroids* are small, rocky bodies.)

Computer-generated image of a spiral galaxy.

Part 5
Combining with When, Because, *and* Although

In a first draft, you may find that two sentences contain related ideas, but that one idea is less important than the other. That is, the idea in one sentence is subordinate to the idea in the other. As you revise, you can combine the two sentences by using certain words to show the relationship between the two ideas.

Showing Relationships

When you combine two sentences, there are several words you can use to indicate the subordinate relationship of one idea to another. Use *when* to show time, *because* to explain why something happened, and *although* to show under what conditions something happened. In the examples, notice how the boldface word in the combined sentence helps clarify the relationship between the ideas in the original pair of sentences.

> The cabin attendants started serving dinner. The captain of the jet turned off the seat-belt sign.
> The cabin attendants started serving dinner **when** the captain of the jet turned off the seat-belt sign.

> All the lights in the city are out. Lightning struck the main power plant.
> All the lights in the city are out **because** lightning struck the main power plant.

> We had a great time in Hawaii. Rain fell every day.
> We had a great time in Hawaii **although** rain fell every day.

When you wish to emphasize a subordinate idea, you can place it at the beginning of the combined sentence. Use a comma to separate the subordinate idea from the rest of the sentence.

> Although rain fell every day, we had a great time in Hawaii.

Grammar Note A word group that contains a subject and a predicate and is subordinated to explain when, why, or under what conditions is called a **subordinate clause.** For more information about subordinate clauses, see pages 551–561.

The following words can also be used to introduce subordinate clauses that express relationships of time, cause, and condition.

Words to Introduce Subordinate Clauses		
Time	**Cause**	**Condition**
after	as	considering (that)
before	consequently	whether (or not)
until	for	however
while	since	unless
during	thus	yet

Faulty Coordination and Subordination

When joining ideas, you may coordinate and subordinate ideas inaccurately. **Faulty coordination** occurs when you incorrectly coordinate two ideas that are not of equal value and cannot be joined by *and*. To correct faulty coordination, you should change one of the clauses into a subordinate clause, a phrase, or an appositive.

Faulty   The windows were left open, and the carpeting got wet.
Revised   Because the windows were left open, the carpeting got wet.

Faulty subordination occurs when you state the main idea in the subordinate clause.

Faulty   Since the workout was too strenuous for me, the aerobics class was an hour and a half long.
Revised   Since the aerobics class was an hour and a half long, the workout was too strenuous for me.

Writing Activities *Subordinating Ideas*

A Combine or revise the following pairs of sentences. In sentences 1–5, follow the directions in parentheses. In sentences 6–10, you should decide whether to use a subordinate clause and, if needed, a comma or a semicolon.

1. We postponed the yard sale. It was raining. (Use *because*.)
2. The crowd on both sides of the street cheered loudly. The President's car rolled by. (Use *when*.)
3. The hikers kept going. They were very tired. (Use *although*.)

4. Al cancelled his date. He had the flu. (Use *because*.)
5. The ski lift was closed, and there was no snow. (Use *since*.)
6. Our dog always howls. The moon is full.
7. Pandas are highly valued. They are becoming rare.
8. Few people agreed with Galileo. He explained that Earth was not at the center of the universe.
9. Iguanas can outwit their enemies, and they blend in with their environment.
10. In Columbus's time, people used spices to preserve food. Refrigeration had not been invented yet.

B Revise the following passage. Use techniques that you learned in Parts 1 through 5 of this chapter.

Whitcomb Judson had a difficult time with his invention. He was the man who invented the zipper. His invention was remarkable. Gideon Sundback helped Judson with the zipper. Judson is remembered as the originator of this invention.

In 1891, Judson introduced the Clasp Locker. He introduced it with pride. It was his first zipper. Judson tried hard to sell the zipper. Few people were interested. The inventor went back to his workshop. He introduced the C-Curity zipper in 1905.

Sundback came along at this time. He was a young engineer. The two men worked on the C-Curity. They were determined. The work was tedious. They finally perfected a zipper with parts. The parts of the zipper interlocked. The parts did not stick or burst open. Judson and Sundback put the improved zippers on the market. They sold thousands of them.

Part 6
Avoiding Empty Sentences

Combining sentences is not the only way to add quality and variety to your writing. You can also eliminate any empty sentences you discover in your first draft. Some empty sentences repeat ideas you have already expressed. Others make statements that are not supported by facts, reasons, or examples.

Repeating an Idea

As you revise, you can avoid repetition by omitting words that express similar ideas or by combining groups of sentences if they contain related ideas.

Faulty   Sandy is a volunteer, and she gets no money for her work. (The words *volunteer* and *gets no money for her work* express similar ideas. Omit the second clause of the sentence.)

Revised   Sandy is a volunteer.

Faulty   My friends took a plane. They took the plane last year. The plane was going to Rome. It was hijacked. It was forced to land. It landed in an empty desert area. (Combine related ideas and sentences.)

Revised   Last year, the plane my friends took to Rome was hijacked and forced to land in an empty desert area.

Sometimes a writer may try to prove a statement simply by repeating it in other words. This is called *circular reasoning*. To avoid circular reasoning, make sure you provide support for any statements you make.

Faulty   The reason I like kayaking is because it is my favorite sport. (*I like kayaking* and *it is my favorite sport* mean roughly the same thing.)

Revised   Kayaking is my favorite sport because it challenges me to manipulate the rapids.

Making Unsupported Statements

As you are revising a first draft, you might find opinions that are not supported by facts, reasons, or examples. Your readers have a right to understand why you hold these opinions. In the following paragraph, find the sentence that states an unsupported opinion.

The exploration of space began only recently. Yet, piloted and unpiloted space vehicles have already investigated the moon as well as several of the planets. Some people think that this activity should stop. However, I believe it should continue.

The writer gives no clue as to why he or she believes space exploration should continue. To make the paragraph more persuasive, the writer needs to provide reasons that support the stated opinion. For example, the writer might add the following:

First, space exploration satisfies an old and natural human longing to investigate the unknown. Furthermore, space explorers might discover planets with supplies of resources that are growing scarce on Earth.

Writing Activities Revising Sentences

A Revise the following sentences. Omit repeated ideas, or combine sentences to avoid repetition.

1. Maria is a talented guitarist. She plays the guitar with an exceptional amount of skill.
2. Hawaii is an enjoyable vacation spot and it is my favorite place to visit.
3. Neither of the two police detectives could find anything to believe about the suspect's alibi. Both of the officers agreed that the alibi the suspect gave was unbelievable.
4. Passengers can travel from New York to London. They can travel on supersonic aircraft. The aircraft are swift but noisy. Passengers can make the trip from New York to London in only $3\frac{1}{2}$ hours.
5. It was early Tuesday morning. Rachel got a telephone call. The call was surprising. It came from a disc jockey named Boppo Lewis. He has a radio show in San Francisco.

B Revise the following statements by adding supporting reasons, facts, or examples. If necessary, use reference materials.

1. Some of Shakespeare's best plays were comedies.
2. As President of the United States, Abraham Lincoln faced many difficult problems.
3. Precipitation is moisture that falls on Earth. It takes different forms in different locations.
4. Earth has a natural satellite called the moon. However, Earth is not the only planet that is orbited by satellites.
5. Many nuclear power plants have been built to provide electricity for people's use. These plants are dangerous and should be closed.

6. Today, many young people have large amounts of free time. The government should build recreation centers for these young people.
7. The Great Depression began in 1929 and lasted until World War II. It was a difficult time.
8. A phobia is a long-term, unreasonable fear of something. Such fears can deeply affect people's lives.
9. Greece is one of the oldest nations in the world. I would like to visit this Mediterranean country.
10. Rock music is very popular these days. Some older people do not like it very much.

Part 7
Avoiding Overloaded Sentences

As you read a first draft, watch for overloaded sentences. An overloaded sentence expresses several main ideas loosely connected by the conjunction *and*. Readers may find it difficult to figure out how these ideas are related to one another. To revise the draft, begin by reorganizing your ideas. Then use transition words and other combining methods to reveal the relationships between ideas.

Overloaded	The cat sniffed the canned food, and she was fussy, and then she turned up her nose, and she walked away.
Revised	The fussy cat sniffed her canned food. Then she turned up her nose and walked away.
Overloaded	Roberto banged on the door, and he banged frantically, and no one answered.
Revised	Roberto banged frantically on the door. However, no one answered.
Overloaded	Wilma accepted the gold medal, and she had a sober look on her face, and then the band played the national anthem, and tears slid down her cheeks.
Revised	Wilma had a sober look on her face as she accepted the gold medal. When the band played the national anthem, tears slid down her cheeks.

Other types of overloaded sentences carry too many ideas, combining important ideas with unimportant ones. These ideas may be connected by a number of different conjunctions.

Faulty	I want to teach piano because I want to help people discover their talents as musicians, but it doesn't matter if they are good, although it makes teaching easier, as long as they enjoy playing.
Revised	I want to teach piano because I want to help people discover their talents as musicians. It doesn't matter if they are good, as long as they enjoy playing.

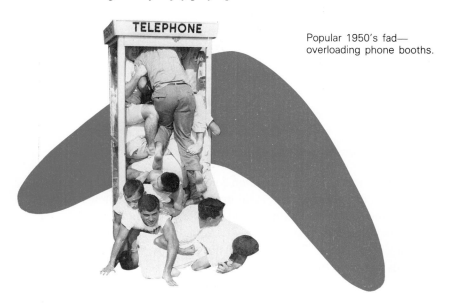

Popular 1950's fad—
overloading phone booths.

Writing Activities Overloaded Sentences

A Revise these overloaded sentences. Keep these techniques in mind:

- Divide each sentence into two or more phrases, clauses, or sentences, using sentence-combining techniques when possible.
- Reduce the number of *and*'s and other conjunctions.
- Show a logical connection between ideas. Use transition words such as *when, first, then, finally, however, as, but,* and *because.*

1. I was watching through the window, and the raccoon came into the yard, and it tipped over the trash barrel.
2. Every morning, he raised the shade in his bedroom, and he looked out the window, and he would fervently hope to see his lost dog playing in the yard.
3. We stopped at the music store, and then we picked up some nails at the hardware store, and then we had lunch.
4. We were waiting for an important call, and we were anxious, and then

the phone rang, and we all jumped.

5. Elena anchors a news program, but she has always wanted to write for a newspaper, although she has more experience in television news, and she has an interview with a local paper tomorrow.

6. The electricity went off, and we could not watch TV, and we spent an evening talking to each other, and the evening was enjoyable, and, afterwards, we decided to do this more often.

7. Ying-Ying is a panda and Pei-Pei is a panda, and the two pandas are in the Mexico City Zoo, and they were gifts from the people of China, and they became parents of twin cubs recently.

8. The capybara lives in the tropical regions of South America, and it is a large rodent, and it looks like a guinea pig.

9. That girl seems very rebellious, and she has purple streaks in her hair, but she is actually a kind person, and she is an outstanding student, and she gets excellent grades.

10. The door flew open, and in tore my dog, and he was yelping, and he was being pursued by the cat next door.

11. The horned toad is a desert animal, and it squirts blood from its eyes, and it does this when it is frightened or angry.

12. The mongoose attacked the deadly cobra, and it avoided the snake's fangs, and it lunged at its head, and the cobra was doomed.

13. The safety pin is a useful item, and it was patented by a man in New York, and he patented it in 1849, and his name was Walter Hunt.

14. Becky thought she wanted to be a nurse, and she thought this as a young girl, and she changed her mind in high school, and decided to become a doctor instead.

15. Andrea walked on the stage, and the scenery fell down at the same time, and the audience roared with laughter.

B Revise the following passage. Break up overloaded sentences. Use transition words and sentence-combining techniques to show connections between ideas.

Some people are extremely superstitious. My brother Al went for a job interview, and the interview was last Monday, and he took his rabbit's foot, and he thought of the rabbit's foot as a good-luck charm. He never lets a black cat cross his path, and he denies that he is a superstitious person, and he denies it firmly.

My friend Paula broke a mirror, and she did it accidentally, and the mirror was in her bathroom, and she worried all day, and she worried because she thought she would have seven years of bad luck. Whenever she spills some salt, and she throws some over her right shoulder, and she does it immediately.

Part 8

Avoiding Padded Sentences

A **padded sentence** contains unnecessary words and phrases. Because a padded sentence is unnecessarily wordy, the reader cannot easily understand its meaning. When you read a first draft, be on the lookout for padded sentences. As you revise, remove the padding and shorten wordy expressions.

Taking Out Extra Words

The following expressions are unnecessarily wordy. Next to each expression is a more direct way of communicating the same idea.

"Fact" Expressions	**Reduced**
because of the fact that	because, since
on account of the fact that	because, since
in spite of the fact that	although
the fact of the matter is	(Just say it!)

"What" Expressions	**Reduced**
what I want is	I want
what I mean is	(Just say it!)
what I want to say is	(Just say it!)
what I believe is	(Just say it!)

Other Expressions to Avoid

the point is	the thing is	it happens that
the reason is	being that	personally, I think

Your sentences will be much clearer and less wordy if you avoid the types of sentence padding shown in the following examples:

Padded   Don can't come to the phone *because of the fact that* he's in the shower.

Revised   Don can't come to the phone because he's in the shower.

Padded   *The thing is* Suzanne has decided to study acting instead of modeling.

Revised   Suzanne has decided to study acting instead of modeling.

Padded   *What I want to say is* we want to go to the National Football League playoffs.

Revised   We want to go to the National Football League playoffs.

Repetition of That

Often you may repeat the word *that* in a sentence, when it would have been sufficient and more effective to use it only once.

Lengthy   The varsity swim coach thought *that* if she held an extra practice meet *that* her students would be more prepared for the summer trials.

Revised   The varsity swim coach thought that if she held an extra practice meet, her students would be more prepared for the summer trials.

Lengthy   It is obvious *that* I did not have time to knit the sweater *that* I promised her.

Revised   It is obvious that I did not have the time to knit the sweater I promised her.

Reducing Clauses to Phrases

Very often clauses beginning with *who is, that is,* or *which is* can be simplified or reduced to phrases. Study the following examples.

Lengthy   Marilyn *who is the captain of the soccer team* scored seven goals in yesterday's game.

Revised   Marilyn, the captain of the soccer team, scored seven goals in yesterday's game.

Lengthy   The goose *that is in Barbara's yard* attacks all her visitors.
Revised   The goose in Barbara's yard attacks all her visitors.

Lengthy   The painting, *which is regarded as Monet's masterpiece,* disappeared from the museum.

Revised   The painting, regarded as Monet's masterpiece, disappeared from the museum.

Writing Activities Padded Sentences

A Revise each of the following sentences. Omit extra words that do not contribute to the meaning of the sentence. Remember that clauses beginning with *who, that,* and *which* can often be simplified.

1. What I mean is that Olga sprained her ankle and cannot dance.
2. The thing is that Bob can play the guitar and the drums, but he can't play the piano at all.
3. Wanda Loft, who is a member of the student council, volunteered to set up decorations for the dance.

4. Dana left work early on account of the fact that he lost one of his contact lenses.
5. Being that the play was scheduled to open in less than one hour, the cast was nervous.
6. It was obvious that he could not climb the rope that hung down the mountainside.
7. The fountain that stands in the center of the pavilion is still not working very well.
8. What I think is that the jazz festival was crowded but the musicians were very entertaining.
9. Due to the fact that it was snowing heavily, we decided to postpone our card game.
10. Donna believed that she could finish the puzzle that she received for her birthday.

B Revise the following passage. Omit extra words that repeat ideas. Keep in mind that clauses beginning with *who, that,* or *which* can often be simplified.

My brother, who is an American history teacher, is very interested in quilts. The reason is that quilts played an important part in our country's history. It happens that Sarah Sedgwick Everett made the first quilt in 1704. Mount Vernon, which was the home of George and Martha Washington, had many fancy quilts. The quilt that is hanging on one of the walls of my brother's home was stitched during the Revolutionary War. On account of the fact that many old quilts are so beautiful and full of detail, visitors come from all over the world to see them displayed in American museums.

C Revise the following passage. Use the techniques you learned in Parts 1 through 8.

In spite of the fact that Benjamin Franklin helped to found the United States, he occupied his time with many other activities. This citizen of early America won fame. He was extraordinary. He won fame throughout the world.

Franklin ran a printing business, and he published a newspaper, and he started a fire department, and he founded the University of Pennsylvania. Yet, he managed to write *Poor Richard's Almanac*. He wrote it in his spare time. The almanac was a book of sayings. They were wise and praised virtues such as thrift and honesty. One of the sayings in the almanac was "Make hay while the sun shines." Franklin lived by this saying.

Part 9
Keeping Sentence Parts Together

When you read over your first draft, check to make sure that you have not separated sentence parts that belong together. Separating such parts may make the sentence choppy and difficult to understand. Notice the improvement in the examples below when related sentence parts are placed closer together.

Awkward	*Margo,* after calling the police department, *went* next door to the neighbor's house.
Better	After calling the police department, Margo went next door to the neighbor's house.
Awkward	*I will,* when I save enough money, *buy* an acoustic guitar with twelve strings.
Better	When I save enough money, I will buy an acoustic guitar with twelve strings.
Awkward	*José saw,* near the top of the canyon, *an eagle* soar through the trees.
Better	José saw an eagle soar through the trees near the top of the canyon.

Writing Activities *Keeping Parts Together*

A Use the following steps to revise each of the sentences below.

• Read the sentence carefully.
• Reread the sentence, bringing related sentence parts closer together.
• Write the revised sentence on your paper.

1. Darlene, no matter how hard we tried to convince her, would not change her mind about the date of the party.
2. I would like to go to the movies, if I have time, to see *Rebel Without a Cause*.
3. Patrick's brother, although he's in college, came to see Patrick play in the game against Central High.
4. News reporters, since they're assigned to cover a city for years on end, get to know their posts well.
5. Dina's parents volunteer, for the holiday season, their time at a shelter for the homeless.

6. I traveled, after I graduated from school, across the continental United States.
7. Stuart, since he got married Saturday, is a lot more relaxed.
8. Eric, although he is only in a training program, will one day become general manager of a large corporation.
9. Student chefs, traveling all over the world as apprentices, learn from some of the greatest gourmets.
10. I saw, near the subway station, one of my friends from high school.

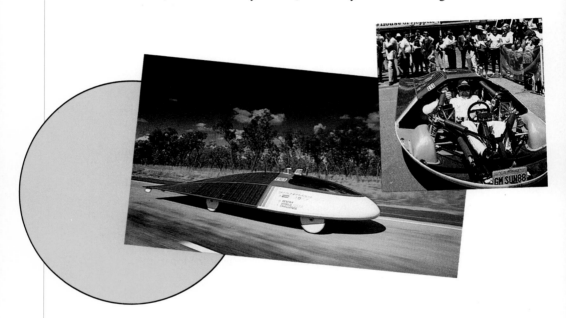

B Rewrite the following passage by moving the related sentence parts closer together.

A sun-powered passenger car, although it cost 8 million dollars to produce, can cross a continent almost as fast as a gasoline-powered automobile. The Sunraycer, named after its source of power, triumphed in the one-time event called the World Solar Challenge. The cockroach-shaped car, because of its aerodynamic shape, finished 600 miles ahead of its nearest competitors.

The race, across vast Australian highways, lasted five days. The car, slightly slower than gasoline-powered cars, averaged 43.5 miles per hour. Competitors from several countries, since this was an international event, were involved in the cross-country trek.

The Sunraycer, using photovoltaic cells that power satellites, triumphed over the competition. The other cars, because they relied on current technology, did not perform as well as the Sunraycer.

Making Sentence Parts Parallel

In Part 1 you learned how to use the conjunction *and* to combine sentences and improve your writing style. Keep in mind that the conjunction *and* should be used to join parallel sentence parts, that is, words or groups of words that are alike in structure and function. Note the ways in which the sentences below were revised to make the constructions parallel.

Faulty	Anita wanted a *sweater* for her birthday and *to travel* to her cousin Mark's house in southern California. (noun and infinitive)
Revised	Anita wanted to receive a sweater for her birthday and to travel to her cousin Mark's house in southern California. (infinitive and infinitive)
Faulty	Everyone needs a certain amount of *sympathy* and *to be noticed*. (noun and infinitive)
Revised	Everyone needs a certain amount of sympathy and attention. (noun and noun)
Faulty	My friend Yusi requested *assistance* with her social studies homework and *that I help her outline the objectives of the chapter*. (noun and clause)
Revised	My friend Yusi requested that I assist her with her social studies homework and that I help her outline the objectives of the chapter. (clause and clause)

Lack of parallelism often occurs when the pronouns *which* and *who* are used in a sentence. Try not to use *and who* or *and which* unless there is a preceding *who* or *which* to balance it.

Faulty	This is an award-winning *Broadway play* and *which you have to order tickets months in advance*. (noun and clause)
Revised	This is an award-winning Broadway play for which you have to order tickets months in advance.
Simpler	You have to order tickets months in advance for this award-winning Broadway play.
Faulty	Benjamin is a brilliant *engineer* and *who has an important job with the government*. (noun and clause)
Revised	Benjamin is a brilliant engineer who has an important job with the government.

Writing Activities *Achieving Parallelism*

A Revise the following sentences to make the constructions parallel.

1. Theresa had to choose between taking ballet lessons and to play on the softball team.
2. Our friends are the Blairs and who are going to Hawaii for their honeymoon.
3. My sister wanted to attend the University of Massachusetts and that she get into John Adams dormitory.
4. At Camp Edgewater you will learn surviving in the wilderness and to canoe down the Black River.
5. Everyone wants to enjoy the holidays and visit with friends they have not seen for a while.
6. The ambassador is a fine diplomat and who is knowledgeable about the country where she resides.
7. Miguel drove through the dense fog and which severely hampered the visibility.
8. When you get to know the store owner, you will consider him to be kind and that he is also helpful.
9. Television talk shows usually have fascinating guests and who have experiences to relate to the audience.
10. Many endangered animals are placed in animal reserves and which provide a fairly natural habitat for them.

B Revise the following passage. Study how the conjunction *and* is used incorrectly and then change the sentence construction to achieve parallelism.

Imagine going to school year-round and to be vacationing year-round as well. In order to ease classroom crowding and alleviate financial cutbacks, Los Angeles decided to operate classrooms year-round. This means students attend school on a rotating basis and that they have rotating vacations. Students attend school for three months and are vacationing or working for one month.

Plenty of parents and students are opposed to the idea and which is presently in use for only one percent of the student population. Many students have jobs during the summer and which they would lose if they could not commit a large amount of their time. Summer camps will also be hurt by the year-round schools and that they may have to close their doors permanently. Teachers are divided over the concept and who disagree over the impact year-round schools will have on the quality of education.

Sophomore

Classic "wise fools," the
Three Stooges.

Each school year, you take a step up the ladder, from freshman to sophomore, to junior, to senior. What is behind those names?

Some of the meanings are obvious. Seniors have reached the highest rung of the educational ladder, and juniors are a step below them. The *fresh* in freshmen shows they are new or inexperienced, so they are at the bottom of the ladder. But what about sophomores?

Sophomores have taken one step up the ladder, but juniors and seniors are quick to tell them they have a long way to go. According to one explanation of the word's origin, so does *sophomore*. Some language experts claim the name comes from the Greek words *sophos*, meaning "wise," and *moros*, meaning "foolish." The combination indicates that sophomores have gained some wisdom, but that they have much more to learn. Taken literally, it means sophomores are "wise fools." Other experts, however, claim the word comes from a form of the Greek word *sophism*, which means "to become wise." So a sophomore is someone who is learning. These experts say it has evolved through such forms as *sophy moors, sophumer,* and *soph mor* before taking on its present form.

Whatever the origin of the word, however, sophomores soon enough leave the controversy behind and move another step up the educational ladder.

Chapter 6
Application and Review

A Combining Sentences Combine the following sentences. Use the techniques you learned in Parts 1 through 5.

1. At 20°F, you would probably feel cold. You would be likely to feel warm at 20°C.
2. A laser beam can burn a hole through even a diamond easily. A laser beam is powerful. A diamond is tough.
3. The sound of the birds awakened Dan. The birds chirped. He awoke at 5:30 A.M. today.
4. George Simenon has sold more than 300 million of his books. He writes mostly crime stories.
5. The first drive-in movie theater was opened by Richard Hollingshead. It had room for only 400 cars. Hollingshead opened the theater in Camden, New Jersey.
6. This watch keeps good time. It has a musical alarm. Ed gave it to me for my birthday.
7. The crowd rushed into the theater. The doors opened at 7:30 P.M.
8. Tyler played a sonata at the recital. The sonata challenged him. His performance was perfect.
9. The koala looks like a teddy bear. It is one of the unusual mammals of Australia.
10. The pitcher continued with the game. She injured her leg in the fall.

B Improving Sentences Revise the following empty, over-loaded, and padded sentences.

1. I'm very sorry, but what I mean is you can't ride with us on account of the fact that the car is already full.
2. The cruise ship rocked and dipped violently in the stormy sea. In spite of the fact that the ship was tossed up and down and sideways, only a few passengers got seasick.
3. Paula was in the rain forest, and the forest was in the Amazon River Valley, and it was in June, and she was almost crushed to death by an anaconda, and the snake was unusually long.
4. Chris felt embarrassed and the reason was that he was wearing two different shoes on his feet.
5. The antique cars that are on display at the convention center are worth a great deal of money, and the cars are very old.

C Revise the following three passages. Use any of the techniques listed below.

- Combine sentences and parts of sentences.
- Add words and groups of words to sentences.
- Use *who, which,* and *that* to combine sentences.
- Combine or condense empty sentences.
- Separate overloaded sentences.
- Remove unnecessary words from padded sentences.
- Keep related sentence parts together.
- Make sure sentence constructions are parallel.

1. Lightning is a current, and the current is electrical. The current flashes in the sky. It flashes with a bright glow. A bolt of lightning can leap from one cloud, and it can go to another cloud. On the other hand, a lightning bolt can streak from the cloud to the ground. It reaches the ground, and it causes things to happen. It causes these things often. Some of these things are weird. One man tells a strange story. The man was bald. He was struck by lightning. The lightning did not hurt him. However, his hair started growing again. It started growing in a few weeks.

2. The *Clermont* was a steamboat built by Robert Fulton. Skeptical people jokingly called it "Fulton's Folly." Many predicted the failure of the *Clermont* and that Robert Fulton would go bankrupt. The steamboat successfully chugged up the Hudson River, and it went for 150 miles, and it made the trip on August 17, 1807. What's more, the boat moved at the speed of 5 miles per hour. The *Clermont* began its voyage in New York City. The voyage set a record. The *Clermont* arrived in Albany. Albany is the capital of the state of New York. The vessel arrived in Albany after 32 hours of struggle. It struggled against the strong current of the Hudson River.

3. Marrakech is the name of a city. It is an old and exotic city. Marrakech is in southern Morocco. The city, although it is modernized, is more of a marketplace than an urban area. Marrakech is called the "red city." The buildings and ramparts are made from beaten clay. The heart of Marrakech is called the Place Jema al Fna, and it is a colorful marketplace, and this place attracts people from morning until night. The marketplace is always teeming with activity and it is a bustling scene. Every day, you can see entertainers. They fascinate tourists with their legends. Water sellers who wear bright-colored clothes carry water in skin bags that they offer to people that are thirsty from the dusty air.

7
Writing Effective Description

*Genius . . . is the capacity to see ten things where the ordinary
[person] sees one. . . .*

Ezra Pound

What details might you mention in describing the photograph on the opposite page? Would you select the same features that the artist highlighted? What mood would your particular set of details evoke?

In this chapter you will learn to notice, select, and heighten significant sensory details as you describe people, places, and things. Improving your descriptive skills will enable you to convey whatever impression and mood you intend.

Part 1

Analyzing Description

There's an old saying that a picture is worth a thousand words. There might be some truth to the saying, if words described only what people see. Good descriptive writing, however, reveals not only appearance, but also the sounds, smells, tastes, and textures of things. More importantly, descriptive writing can get below the surface of things and tell us what people are thinking, what kind of mood a place creates, or how an object came into existence. Descriptions appear in almost every type of writing, from instruction manuals to poetry. Each description is shaped by the author's purpose.

The following models show two common uses for descriptive writing. One was written by a student for a geography paper, and the other was written by a professional writer. As you read each of the models, think about how the writer's purpose affects the description.

▬ *Student Model*

California's central valley is about 500 miles long. It lies between the moderately high Sierra Nevadas and the mountains that run along the coast from north to south. Much of the valley is level, and it is used as one of America's most fertile farming areas. California farmers grow more artichokes, tomatoes, and broccoli than farmers anywhere else in the United States.

The valley and the nearby foothills are dotted with occasional oak trees. The grass turns green in the wet winters and brown in the dry summers. The valley floor would also be brown in the summer, were it not for the two rivers that flow through the peaceful valley and irrigate it.

Discussing the Model Discuss the following questions with your classmates.

1. What senses does the student refer to in his description? How do those references contribute to the description?
2. Which features does he describe first? Which does he describe last? Why do you think he begins and ends with those features?
3. What details help you to view the report as a factual, objective description?

Recently . . . I took [my grandfather's] old deerskin hunting vest out of the closet and on an impulse pressed it to my face and sniffed. Abruptly there came over me a rush of emotion and memory as intimate as it was compelling. No longer was I an adult squinting across a chasm of years at dim events: Suddenly I was a boy again, and there in all but the flesh was my grandfather, methodically reloading his shotgun as the flushed quail sailed beyond the mesquite.

This was no hazy reverie. I could feel his whiskered cheek against mine and smell his peculiar fragrance of age, wool, dust, . . . the epoch slowly faded as I lay curled up in the backseat of my grandfather's Ford, returning from a long hunt in Mexico, half-listening to the men up front and Fred Allen on the radio, drifting into a sweet exhausted sleep.

From "The Intimate Sense of Smell" by Boyd Gibbons

Discussing the Model Use the following questions to focus your discussion.

1. How does the description above appeal to your senses? Which sense is most prominent in this passage?
2. What precise words does the writer use to describe how his grandfather smelled?
3. What sort of mood does the description create? How does it compare to the mood of the description in the student model?

Understanding Descriptive Writing

The authors of both of the descriptions you just read used precise details to appeal to the senses. Both writers established a mood at the beginning of the passage and included details and expressions to support the mood. Different uses of details helped the student to create a mood suitable for a report and helped the professional writer portray a nostalgic scene.

Description in Literature The following excerpt includes a number of effective descriptive passages designed to create a specific mood. As you read the selection, think about the way in which the description is organized and the mood it creates. Look for striking or memorable descriptions.

Description in Literature

from *The Way to Rainy Mountain*
N. Scott Momaday

In the following excerpt from The Way to Rainy Mountain, *N. Scott Momaday recalls his first visit back to the grave of his late grandmother and the home that she had lived in while she was alive. This account of Momaday's journey is a description of a man's memories, as well as a tribute to his heritage.*

Specific image

Figurative language

Precise details

A single knoll rises out of the plain in Oklahoma, north and west of the Wichita Range. For my people, the Kiowas, it is an old landmark, and they gave it the name Rainy Mountain. The hardest weather in the world is there. Winter brings blizzards, hot tornadic winds arise in the spring, and in summer the prairie is an anvil's edge. The grass turns brittle and brown, and it cracks beneath your feet. There are green belts along the rivers and creeks, linear groves of hickory and pecan, willow and witch hazel. At a distance in July or August the steaming foliage seems almost to writhe in fire. Great green and yellow grasshoppers are everywhere in the tall grass, popping up like corn to sting the flesh, and tortoises crawl about on the red earth, going nowhere in the plenty of time. Loneliness is an aspect of the land. . . .

I returned to Rainy Mountain [one day] in July. My grandmother had died in the spring, and I wanted to be at her grave. . . .

O nce there was a lot of sound in my grandmother's house, a lot of coming and going, feasting and talk. The summers there were full of excitement and reunion. The Kiowas are a summer people; they abide the cold and keep to themselves, but when the season turns and the land becomes warm and vital they cannot hold still; an old love of going

Evening Sing, Lee Tsatoke.

returns upon them. The aged visitors who came to my
grandmother's house when I was a child were made of lean
and leather, and they bore themselves upright. They wore
great black hats and bright ample shirts that shook in the
wind. They rubbed fat upon their hair and wound their
braids with strips of colored cloth. Some of them painted
their faces and carried the scars of old and cherished en-
mities. They were an old council of warlords, come to remind and be reminded of who they were. Their wives and
daughters served them well. The women might indulge
themselves; gossip was at once the mark and compensation
of their servitude. They made loud and elaborate talk among
themselves, full of jest and gesture, fright and false alarm.
They went abroad in fringed and flowered shawls, bright
beadwork and German silver. They were at home in the
kitchen, and they prepared meals that were banquets.

Sensory
details

*T*here were frequent prayer meetings, and great
nocturnal feasts. When I was a child I played with my
cousins outside, where the lamplight fell upon the ground
and the singing of the old people rose up around us and
carried away into the darkness. There were a lot of good

things to eat, a lot of laughter and surprise. And afterwards, when the quiet returned, I lay down with my grandmother and could hear the frogs away by the river and feel the motion of the air.

Now there is a funeral silence in the rooms, the endless wake of some final word. The walls have closed in upon my grandmother's house. When I returned to it in mourning, I saw for the first time in my life how small it was. It was late at night, and there was a white moon, nearly full. I sat for a long time on the stone steps by the kitchen door. From there I could see out across the land; I could see the long row of trees by the creek, the low light upon the rolling plains, and the stars of the Big Dipper. Once I looked at the moon and caught sight of a strange thing. A cricket had perched upon the handrail, only a few inches away from me. My line of vision was such that the creature filled the moon like a fossil. It had gone there, I thought, to live and die, for there, of all places, was its small definition made whole and eternal. A warm wind rose up and purled like the longing within me.

Figurative language

*T*he next morning I awoke at dawn and went out on the dirt road to Rainy Mountain. It was already hot, and the grasshoppers began to fill the air. Still, it was early in the morning, and the birds sang out of the shadows. The long yellow grass on the mountain shone in the bright light, and a scissortail hied above the land. There, where it ought to be, at the end of a long and legendary way, was my grandmother's grave. Here and there on the dark stones were ancestral names. Looking back once, I saw the mountain and came away.

Trying Out Descriptive Writing Now that you have read and discussed some examples of descriptive writing, try writing some descriptions of your own in your journal. Look at some of the things you use every day. How can you describe those things so that others can imagine them fully? What sense words can you use? What comparisons can you make?

After writing in your journal, decide which of your descriptions were most effective. What made them interesting and memorable? What elements do they have that you can use in other descriptions? The rest of the chapter will teach you more techniques for writing lively, effective description.

Part 2

Developing a Strong Description

A house is made up of thousands of parts—boards, nails, wires, pipes—organized in such a way that they create a single, unified structure. The details that make up a strong description should work together in the same way. A description may have just a few details, or it may have dozens, but the important thing is that they all work together to create a vivid image in the reader's mind.

Finding Details

Whenever you observe an object or a scene, you use some or all of your five senses—seeing, hearing, feeling, tasting, and smelling—to take in these details and find out what the object or scene is really like. When you write a description, you want your readers to perceive the things you are describing. To do that, you need to provide your readers with details to help them imagine these things. A description without details is like a frame without a picture: you can't expect your readers to see anything if you don't give them something to look at. You can find details through observation, research, memory, or through your own imagination. The method that you use depends on what you want to describe.

The Human Condition,
René Magritte, 1933.

Observation Use observation if you want to describe something that you can actually see, such as a construction site. Go to the site and observe it as closely as you can. What is your overall impression of the place? What colors predominate? What sounds do you hear? How does the upturned soil smell and feel? To what could you compare the machinery?

Research If you want to describe something you can't actually observe, such as a rare bird or a faraway place, research can help. Visit the library in your school or neighborhood. Encyclopedias and other reference sources contain detailed information about almost every conceivable subject. You can use the information in these sources to find the details you need.

Memory Use your memory if you want to describe something that you observed in the past, such as a horse show. In your mind, create an image of the show based on everything you remember. What did the arena look like? What sounds did you hear? How did it smell? What did the winning horse look like? When you have completed your mental picture, let your mind review it, noting details.

Imagination Finally, use your own imagination if you want to describe something that doesn't exist, such as a time/hyperspace travel machine. Once again, create an image of the thing in your mind and examine it closely. Because the image is imaginary, you can make up all the details you need.

Organizing a Description

Once you have collected details, you will need to put them in order. Begin by asking yourself the questions in the following guidelines. Your answers can help you define your purpose, and select and organize details to support it.

Guidelines for Selecting Details

1. What is the overall purpose of this paper?
2. What am I trying to accomplish in my descriptions?
3. What is the main impression I want to create?
4. What sensory details best bring my subject to life?
5. What details do I want to emphasize?

Spatial Order When you want to provide a simple, straightforward description of something, you will probably want to use a spatial order, which shows how the details are arranged in space. For example, you might arrange your description from top to bottom or from bottom to top. Other spatial orders include left-to-right, inside-to-outside, front-to-back, and near-to-far.

Order of Importance When you begin with details you feel are most important and end with the least important—or vice versa—you are organizing your description by order of importance. In this kind of description, your organization depends on your purpose.

Order of Impression In a poem or story, you would probably want to emphasize certain details. You might begin with the detail that first catches your eye and then move to the detail that next attracts your attention. Your description would reflect your changing impressions of your subject.

In the following description, notice how the writer uses order of impression to organize the details.

Literary Model

First impression

Supporting details

He's got on work-farm pants and shirt, sunned out till they're the color of watered milk. His face and neck and arms are the color of oxblood leather from working long in the fields. He's got a primer-black motorcycle cap stuck in his hair and a leather jacket over one arm, and he's got on boots gray and dusty and heavy enough to kick a man half in two.

From *One Flew Over the Cuckoo's Nest* by Ken Kesey

Writing Activities *Developing a Description*

A The details in the previous model were placed in a certain sequence in order to create a specific mood. Decide on a new mood for the paragraph and change the order of the details to establish that mood. You may add details from your imagination, if necessary.

B *Writing in Process* Pick an object you can observe closely and list at least twenty details. Then organize one group of details, using one of the orders you have learned—spatial order, order of importance, order of impression—to support a specific mood. Outline a description and then save your outline for a later activity.

Part 3

The Language of Description

You have learned that effective descriptions appeal to the senses and to the imagination. In this section you will learn how to use the language of description to enliven your writing. The language of description includes sensory images, specific words, and figurative language employed in fresh, even startling ways.

Sensory Images

You can create sensory images by using words or phrases that appeal to one or more of the reader's senses. The phrase "a bellowing flood," for example, appeals to the reader's sense of hearing. Notice how sensory images in the following paragraph from a fictional story help you to imagine the danger for three people journeying through the Yukon.

Literary Model

From every hill slope came the trickle of running water, the music of unseen fountains. All things were thawing, bending, snapping. The Yukon was straining to break loose from the ice that bound it down. It ate away from beneath; the sun ate from above. Air-holes formed, fissures sprang and spread apart, while thin sections of ice fell through bodily into the river. And amid all this bursting, rending, throbbing of awakening life, under the blazing sun and through the soft-sighing breezes, like wayfarers to death, staggered the two men, the woman, and the huskies.

From *The Call of the Wild* by Jack London

We not only see the ice-bound Yukon but also hear the sounds of water and life, and feel the sun and the breezes. Almost every word or phrase in the paragraph appeals to our senses in some way. For example, words such as *trickle, music,* and *snapping* appeal to our sense of hearing. *The blazing sun* and *soft-sighing breezes* appeal to our sense of touch. The effect is startling and powerful: like the three travelers, we become a part of the scene.

tied up ... lacks and still
navy blue ... but the grandm
n the brim ... h a bunch of
e print. He ... s with a sma
ith lace and ... were white
loth violets ... had pinnec
nyone seeing ... In case
... on the highway woul

Specific Words

Vivid descriptions depend on specific words. The more specific your words are, the stronger your image will be. "The room smelled," for example, doesn't tell what kind of room or exactly how it smelled. "The kitchen was drenched in the hearty smell of Dad's homemade chili," though, helps you imagine the scene. Take care to avoid simply tacking on modifiers, however. Adjectives and adverbs can help a scene come alive, but specific nouns and verbs are more powerful tools. In the following paragraph, notice how specific words contribute to our image of the grandmother.

■ *Literary Model*

The children's mother still had on slacks and still had her head tied up in a green kerchief, but the grandmother had on a navy blue straw sailor hat with a bunch of white violets on the brim and a navy blue dress with a small white dot in the print. Her collars and cuffs were white organdy trimmed with lace and at her neckline she had pinned a purple spray of cloth violets containing a sachet. In case of an accident, anyone seeing her dead on the highway would know at once that she was a lady.

From "A Good Man Is Hard to Find" by Flannery O'Connor

Figurative Language

Adjectives and adverbs are the heart of literal descriptions. Figurative language, however, emphasizes comparisons. Try to avoid stale, clichéd comparisons like "cold as ice" or "smooth as silk." Instead, look for fresh new comparisons, like those in the model below.

▬ Literary Model ▬

Comparison through use of similes

It was Bagheera the Black Panther, inky black all over, but with the panther markings showing up in certain lights like the pattern of watered silk . . . . he was as cunning as [the jackal], as bold as the wild buffalo, and as reckless as the wounded elephant . But he had a voice as soft as wild honey dripping from a tree, and a skin softer than down.

From *Jungle Book* by Rudyard Kipling

The box below shows some common types of figurative language, which are also called *figures of speech*.

Types of Figurative Language

Figure of Speech	Example
Simile	The grass felt like steel wool.
Metaphor	The grass was steel wool.
Personification	The sod hugged his feet as he walked.
Hyperbole	The turf was sharper than razors.

Writing Activities Descriptive Language

A Rewrite the following paragraph, replacing the clichés with fresh language.

Joe's face was as white as a sheet. The deafening roar in the hallway scared the daylights out of him. But he braced himself and lifted the chest, which weighed a ton. The dough inside was worth it.

B *Writing in Process* Using the outline from the writing activity on page 163, write a description that uses sensory images, specific words, and figurative language.

Part 4
Objective Description

Descriptions can be subjective or objective. Subjective descriptions create moods and express feelings; objective descriptions present facts in a clear and logical way. Objective descriptions are found in textbooks, reports, and other factual writing. They rely upon literal language. Notice how the writer of the model below organizes facts to create clear images of Central Africa.

Professional Model

Specific, literal
language

Villages in the inner delta are made of sun-baked brick, and every two or three years a new coating of clay is added. The mosques are made of the same material, built into conical towers. The wooden spikes on the outside walls, which seem to be a decorative element, are there so that workers can climb up the sides after each rainy season and apply a new layer of puddled clay. The towers of the most important mosques are topped with ostrich eggs.

From *The Strong Brown God* by Sanche De Gramont

Define Your Purpose

The first step in writing an objective description is to define your purpose. Ask yourself what you want your description to accomplish. Your answers will help you decide what details your readers will need to know. If you want to convey the glamor of flying, for example, you might want to describe the first-class cabin. If you want to describe the more mundane aspects of flying, you might focus on the baggage claim area. Because your purpose is different in each case, your focus is different, as well.

Observe and Gather Details

Once you have defined the purpose of your description, you can begin gathering details, as you learned to do in Part 2 of this chapter. For an objective description, which deals mostly with facts, you will want to use research and careful observation. Remember to select specific, detailed facts that are suited to your purpose. The following box suggests details to look for in describing people, places, or objects.

Details for Descriptive Writing	
People	height, weight, clothes, skin, hair, eyes, lips, facial expressions, scars, tone of voice, gestures, walk, smell, mannerisms
Places	location, weather, temperature, time of day, atmosphere, surrounding activities, vegetation, buildings, animals
Objects	color, shape, size, weight, texture, smell, taste, sound, location, quantity, unusual features

Writing Activities Objective Description

A Using the chart above as a guide, carefully observe a person, a place, and an object and gather a list of details to describe each one.

B *Writing in Process* Imagine that archaeologists found a prehistoric woman frozen in the tundra of Mongolia and were able to revive her. Of course she would not be familiar with the names of many contemporary objects, but she might be able to describe them. Imagine you are this prehistoric woman. Choose one of the scenes below and write an objective description of it.

Part 5

Subjective Description

Objective descriptions use facts or imaginary details to convey information. Subjective descriptions, on the other hand, use the same elements to express a mood or evoke one in the reader. Subjective descriptions are a major part of fiction and poetry, and they are also part of editorials, essays, and other forms of writing that express opinions or emotions. When you are writing a subjective description, it is extremely important to choose only those details that support the mood you want to create. The following description consists almost entirely of details that create a lonely mood.

Literary Model

Details to suggest lonely mood

About a mile farther, on a road I had never travelled, we came to an orchard of starved apple-trees writhing over a hillside among outcroppings of slate that nuzzled up through the snow like animals pushing out their noses to breathe. Beyond the orchard lay a field or two, their boundaries lost under drifts; and above the fields, huddled against the white immensities of land and sky, one of those lonely New England farm-houses that makes the landscape lonelier.

From *Ethan Frome* by Edith Wharton

Define Your Purpose and Mood

In all subjective descriptions, purpose and mood are closely related. In stories, for example, subjective descriptions create moods and characters. In persuasive essays, they strengthen the writer's arguments. Notice how the following two descriptions of people evoke two very different moods.

Student Model

Light, cheerful mood

My lively old aunt hurried toward me, gasping and panting and smiling all at the same time. She looked very glad to see me. She shoved a mangled bunch of sweet-smelling roses at me. They resembled the flowers on the wild print dress that was peeking out the bottom of her worn but cheerful yellow coat.

Haunting,
melancholy
mood

At the table a man unlike ordinary people was sitting mo-
tionless. He was a skeleton with skin drawn tight over his
bones, with long curls like a woman's and a shaggy beard.
His face was yellow with an earthy tint in it, his cheeks were
hollow. his back long and narrow, and the hand on which his
shaggy head was propped was so thin and delicate that it
was dreadful to look at it. His hair was already streaked with
silver, and seeing his emaciated, aged-looking face, no one
would have believed that he was only forty.

From "The Bet" by Anton Chekhov

Show Rather Than Tell

After you have defined your purpose and mood, you need to *show*
the mood through precise details, rather than just *tell* about the mood
with vague, abstract words. By using precise details, you let your
readers figure out for themselves what an object, person, or scene is
like. The following examples point out the differences between showing and telling.

Telling Riley's Place is a loud and busy restaurant during lunchtime.

Showing Waiters banged dishes onto bare metal tables; knives and forks
clattered together; customers shouted above the din. It was
lunchtime at Riley's Place, and there wasn't a seat in the
house.

Select Appropriate Details

As you learned in Part 2 of this chapter, you can use observation,
research, memory, or your own imagination to gather details for a
subjective description. In a subjective description, it is especially important to select only those details that are appropriate for your purpose
and mood. If you decide that a detail doesn't support the mood, eliminate it. If you end up with just a few details for your description, try to
gather more.

You may also choose to use any of several types of figurative
language such as simile, metaphor, or personification, depending upon
the purpose and mood of your description. Notice how the writer of the
following passage uses figurative language to describe an impressive
seaside estate.

Their house was even more elaborate than I expected, a cheerful red-and-white Georgian Colonial mansion, overlooking the bay. The lawn started at the beach and ran toward the front door for a quarter of a mile, jumping over sun-dials and brick walks and burning gardens—finally when it reached the house drifting up the side in bright vines as though from the momentum of its run.

From *The Great Gatsby* by F. Scott Fitzgerald

In the passage above, the author focuses the reader's attention on the immensity of the estate. He uses personification and concrete detail to show the lawn rather than just tell about it. The lawn runs, jumps, and finally, drifts up the side of the house.

Punctuation Note When a series of modifiers appears in a sentence, a comma is often inserted between each modifier in the series. See page 737 for information on how to determine when a comma is needed between modifiers.

The red, yellow, and violet print on the dress in the window screamed for attention.

Writing Activities *Subjective Description*

A The following sentences tell about something rather than show it. Make the sentences "show" by adding details, specific words, and figurative language.

1. The basketball game was very exciting.
2. My mother was angry with me.
3. We were pleasantly scared by the amusement park ride.
4. It's boring to sit in the doctor's waiting room.
5. The child in the photograph looked very poor.
6. It looked cold outside.
7. I could tell that Lena was as nervous as I was about the upcoming psychology test.
8. The curtain went up as the dancers appeared on stage.

B *Writing in Process* Look again at the photographs on page 168. Focus on the scene you described in Activity B on that page. Now write a subjective description of the same scene. Use specific details and figurative language to establish a definite mood in your description.

Part 6
Revising a Description

When you have completed the first draft of a description, you will want to revise it to make it as effective as possible. To revise, simply go over the steps that you used in writing the first draft of your description. Make sure your purpose is clear and well supported with details. Instead of padding your description with vague adjectives and adverbs, make sure you have used precise nouns, verbs, and modifiers. Try to find sensory words that state exactly what you mean. The checklist below shows some of the important questions to ask yourself as you revise.

Also consider using a peer evaluator, a fellow student, to get another opinion of your description. A peer evaluator can provide valuable insight into your descriptions, and may also suggest helpful changes. In addition, being someone else's peer evaluator allows you to develop your reading and revising skills, and thus can help you improve your own work.

Revision Checklist: Descriptive Writing

Purpose
1. Is the purpose of the description clear?
2. Is the description subjective or objective?
3. Is the mood clearly related to the purpose?
4. Does the language support the mood and purpose?

Organization
1. How is the description organized?
2. Is the organization logical and consistent?
3. Does your chosen method of organization match the purpose of the description?
4. Does it support the mood?

Language
1. Does the description create sensory images?
2. Have I chosen details to support the mood?
3. Are the words precise and specific?
4. Is the figurative language fresh and imaginative?
5. Does the description include lively nouns and verbs as well as modifiers?

Leslie revised the following description of an old globe with the help of a peer evaluator and the Revision Checklist. Notice her thoughts as she worked.

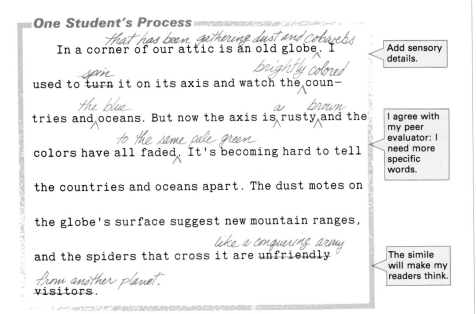

One Student's Process

that has been gathering dust and cobwebs
In a corner of our attic is an old globe. I

spin *brightly colored*
used to ~~turn~~ it on its axis and watch the coun—

the blue *a* *brown*
tries and oceans. But now the axis is rusty and the

to the same pale green
colors have all faded. It's becoming hard to tell

the countries and oceans apart. The dust motes on

the globe's surface suggest new mountain ranges,

like a conquering army
and the spiders that cross it are ~~unfriendly~~

from another planet.
~~visitors~~.

> Add sensory details.

> I agree with my peer evaluator: I need more specific words.

> The simile will make my readers think.

To complete the revision process, proofread your revised draft and check for any spelling or grammatical errors. Use the Proofreading Checklist in Chapter 4. Make a final copy of the revised and proofed draft. Your description is now ready for its final test: your readers.

Writing Activities *Revising a Description*

A Revise the following description by adding details, sensory images, precise nouns, verbs, and modifiers, and figurative language. Consult the Revision Checklist on page 172 for questions to ask yourself during the revision process.

> The house looked pretty bad from the outside. There was something wrong with the front door, and the bell didn't look too good either. The porch was in a shambles. Some of the steps were missing. The paint looked old, particularly near the ground. The roof had lots of holes, and the gutters did too. There was an old chimney, but it was crumbling. The yard was full of trash. Lots of the windows were broken. It didn't look to me like the kind of place anybody would ever want to live in.

B *Writing in Process* Revise the descriptions you wrote in Parts 4 and 5. If possible, find a peer evaluator to read the descriptions and help you with your revisions. Use the Revision Checklist and the Proofreading Checklist. Make final copies of your revised drafts on clean sheets of paper.

Writing **Inside Out**
Suzi Grad, Songwriter

Suzi Grad received her first guitar when she was eleven years old. Soon afterwards, she started writing songs. She would strum a few chords, wait for words to come into her head, and then try to sing them. As a young adult she began performing in local clubs and hotels. Recently she has moved into two new musical directions: she writes catchy jingles for radio commercials and, with her partner, she writes pop songs that they hope to sell to major record companies for stars like Madonna and Tina Turner to sing.

Each new project challenges her differently as a writer. For jingles she creates a tune, then takes the words the client gives her and makes them fit. Pop songs allow her more creativity. "Lyrics are very important in

Part 7

Uses of Descriptive Writing

You can use description to entertain, explain, convince, or portray. The chart below shows a few common uses of description.

Uses of Descriptive Writing

Type	Purpose	Example
Poem	To create a vivid scene	Poetic description of a city street
News story	To supply supporting details	Description of an escaped convict
Report	To present facts	Description of a chemical process
Editorial	To express opinion	Compelling description of a community problem

pop music," Suzi says. "I try to tell a story that makes the listener feel something. The story has to make sense, be something people can relate to; it can't be just a bunch of rhymes. It also has to be descriptive in setting, place, and time.

"People often ask me what comes first, the words or the music? There's no one way," she says. Usually Suzi gets an idea for a song, and that idea becomes the title. She keeps a file of titles and when she wants to write something, she picks a title and tries to build a catchy melody and chorus around it. "They call this catchy part of the song the *hook,*" she explains. "The hook is the part that people will remember."

"Sometimes I sit down at the synthesizer, play a couple of musical chords, and try to come up with a melody around the chords. I use a lot of filler words while writing the melody." Thus the melody can be written independently of the lyrics.

By the time she and her partner finish composing, the lyrics may change completely. "The words have to fit the music," she says. "We hardly ever write them alone. With our slow songs we use words that get emotions going; we really look into things. Our up-tempo songs are more hip, hoppy; they don't say as much. But with every lyric we find a real, universal feeling."

Notice how the following two models use descriptive language in very different ways. Read the models carefully and compare the purpose, language, and mood of the two pieces.

Literary Model

Eye-dazzlers the Indians weave. Three colors
are paths that pull you in, and pin you
to the maze.. Brightness makes your eyes jump,
surveying the geometric field. Alight, and enter
any of the gates—of Blue, of Red, of Black.
Be calmed and hooded, a hawk brought down,
glad to fasten to the forearm of a Chief.

You can sleep at the center,
attended by Sun that never fades, by Moon
that cools. Then, slipping free of zigzag and
hypnotic diamond, find your way out
by the spirit trail, a faint Green thread that
secretly crosses the border, where your mind
is rinsed and returned to you like a white cup.

"A Navajo Blanket" by May Swenson

Literary Model

The walls of the town, which is built on a hill, are high, the streets and lanes tortuous and broken, the roads winding. A fine American-style highway leads in from the north but is lost in its narrow streets and comes out a goat track.

From *Under the Volcano* by Malcolm Lowry

Writing Activities Uses of Description

A Look in books, magazines, or newspapers to find two contrasting descriptions. Write a few sentences in which you explain the use for each description.

B *Writing in Process* Pick a subject to describe. Then choose two forms of writing, such as a journal entry and a poem, in which to describe the subject. Use sensory images, specific words, and figurative language in your descriptions.

Guidelines: *Descriptive Writing*

Planning
- Define your purpose. Figure out what you want to describe and why. If you are writing a subjective description, determine the mood you want to create. *(See pages 161–163, 167.)*
- Gather details. Use observation, research, memory, or imagination to discover your subject's sensory details. Record the details on a list or a chart. *(See pages 161–162.)*
- Select appropriate details. Review the details you have gathered and select those that are appropriate to the purpose and mood of your description. If you do not have enough appropriate details, gather more. *(See pages 162–163, 170.)*
- Organize the description to reflect your purpose. Use spatial order, order of impression, or order of importance. *(See pages 162–163, 167.)*
- Arrange the details in an outline that you can follow as you complete the drafting stage. *(See pages 162–163, 167.)*

Drafting
- Show rather than tell. Use details to show what something actually looks like, rather than just telling about its appearance with abstract words. *(See pages 164–165, 170.)*
- Create sensory images. Use details to show how something looks, sounds, tastes, smells, or feels. *(See page 164.)*
- Use specific words. Find nouns, verbs, adjectives, and adverbs that describe your subject exactly. *(See page 165.)*
- Use figurative language such as similes, metaphors, personifications, or hyperboles to stimulate your reader's imagination. *(See page 166.)*

Revising
- Review each step in the planning and drafting stages and look for possible improvements.
- Use the Revision Checklist to evaluate the purpose, organization, and language of your description. *(See page 172.)*
- Use a peer evaluator to get a second opinion. *(See pages 172–173.)*
- Use the Proofreading Checklist to check your grammar and spelling. *(See page 82.)*
- Make a final copy of the description on a clean sheet of paper.

Chapter 7
Application and Review

Now you can use your knowledge about descriptive writing to enliven your own work. Read the instructions below and use your knowledge and imagination to write lively, vivid, thought-provoking descriptions.

A Describing a Familiar Place Write two subjective descriptions of a shopping mall or a shopping district in your community. For the first description, pretend you are a shopper who is buying items in a number of different stores. Choose a mood you would like to create and support it with facts and imaginary details. For the second description, pretend you are a salesperson in one of the stores. Decide upon another mood and express it by choosing different details. Your purpose for each description is to describe the mall or district as each person experiences it. Use the following guidelines.

Prewriting Visit a mall or shopping district and gather details through observation. For the first description, visit several stores and record the details that a shopper might be aware of. For the second description, spend a long time in a particular store and record the details that a saleperson might observe. Determine the mood that each description should create and choose the details that are appropriate for each mood. Then put all of your details in order and outline the description.

Drafting Use your outline to write a first draft of each description. Remember to show rather than tell. Try to create sensory images. Use specific words and figurative language.

Revising Use the Revision Checklist to evaluate your first drafts. Exchange your descriptions with a peer evaluator and consider his or her comments, too. Make your revisions and then proofread your revised drafts, using the Proofreading Checklist on page 82. Finally, make a clean copy of each description.

B Writing a Subjective Description Choose an object in a place you know well and observe it carefully. Note the object's sensory details and the mood you want to create. Then write a paragraph describing the object. Make sure you include the details that fit your opinion or feelings about the object and the place.

C *Starting Points for Writing* Strong images are good starting points for writing descriptions. You can find these images in literature or create them yourself. Generate some sensory images by asking yourself how you would describe a person, place, or thing shown below. What similes or metaphors might you use? What specific words? Use the Springboards to help you generate figurative language.

. . . he looked about as inconspicuous as a tarantula on a slice of angel food.
Raymond Chandler

Untitled, Tison Keel, 1986.

She walks in beauty, like the night . . .
George Gordon, Lord Byron

Springboards
- What does this remind me of?
- How would I describe this place?
- What does this person resemble?

8

Writing a Short Story

*W*hat do you think is going on in the scene pictured here? What do you think might happen next?

Stories are everywhere. However, you must decide which one to tell, what characters to include, and where the action takes place. You might choose to focus more on the setting, as in the photo on the opposite page, or on a character, as in the photo above.

In writing a short story you can invent characters, re-create people you've known, and control what happens to them. You can participate in the action as narrator or act as observer and reporter. Only you can tell your particular stories, and in this chapter you will learn the skills you need to make your fictional world real for your readers.

Part 1

Analyzing Narrative Writing

Writing that tells a story is called **narrative writing.** Narrative writing appears in many forms and is used for many different purposes. For example, a newspaper article about the views of a political candidate might include an anecdote, or brief story, about the candidate's life. A sports magazine story about a professional football player might use narrative to review some of the important moments in the player's career. But narrative writing doesn't have to deal only with things that have actually happened. It can also ride the rockets of imagination—for instance, a science fiction story might deal with time travel or an interplanetary war.

Here are two examples of narrative writing. The first is from a story written by a student named Rita. The second is from a magazine story about an unusual baseball star.

▬*Student Model*

The canoe trip did not go quite as planned. The first thing Janet did was climb into the canoe, and Nate got in behind her. No problem. Then suddenly the current started to turn them sideways. Nate stuck his paddle in to push the rear of the canoe to the left. At the same time, Janet grabbed an overhanging branch and tried to pull the front of the canoe to the left.

Fortunately, Phil and Linda were already on the river in the other canoe. They reached out and grabbed the empty canoe just before it disappeared into the white water. Meanwhile, Nate and Janet were bobbing along in their lifejackets, spitting out river water and blaming each other for the first of their eleven spills.

Discussing the Model Consider the following questions about the model. Then discuss the answers with your classmates.

1. Who are the characters in this narrative?
2. What situation are the characters involved in?
3. Is the narrator a character in the story?
4. Where does this narrative take place? What can you tell about when it takes place?

When we felt able, we hunted up the Brooklyn manager, who was a chunky, red-haired individual with a whisper like a foghorn. A foghorn with a Brooklyn accent. His name was Pop O'Donnell.

"I see that you've noticed," Pop boomed defensively.

"What do you mean," the Herald said severely, "by not notifying us you had a horse playing third base?"

"I didn't guess you'd believe it," Pop said.

Pop was still bewildered himself. He said the horse had wandered on the field that morning during practice. Someone tried to chase it off by hitting a baseball toward it. The horse calmly opened its mouth and caught the ball. Nothing could be neater.

From "My Kingdom for Jones" by Wilbur Schramm

Discussing the Model Read the following list of questions. Think about how you would answer them and then discuss your answers with your classmates.

1. What unusual situation is this story about?
2. Who are the characters?
3. Is the narrator a character in the story?
4. Where is much of this story likely to take place?

Understanding Narrative Writing

You have read and discussed examples of narrative from two short stories. In one example the narrator is outside the story; in the other example the narrator is one of the characters, a participant in the events. In both stories, however, you find the three elements common to all narratives—**plot,** the sequence of events; **characters,** the people involved in the story; and **setting,** the specific time and place of the story.

Narration in Literature A **short story** is almost all narrative. Read the short story on the following pages. After you have read it, you will learn how to plan and write a short story of your own. You will discover how you can use thinking skills to find a story idea based on a character, setting, or plot. Then you will learn how to develop these three elements to create an interesting short story that other people will want to read.

Narration in Literature

The Cub

Lois Dykeman Kleihauer

"No one in the world was as strong, or as wise, as his father." The small boy was certain of it. Did the young man really want to prove that he was now the stronger of the two?

Characters introduced

O ne of his first memories was of his father bending down from his great height to sweep him into the air. Up he went, gasping and laughing with delight. He could look down on his mother's upturned face as she watched, laughing with them, and at the thick shock of his father's brown hair and at his white teeth.

Then he would come down, shrieking happily, but he was never afraid, not with his father's hands holding him. No one in the world was as strong, or as wise, as his father.

Details developing characters

He remembered a time when his father moved the piano across the room for his mother. He watched while she guided it into its new position, and he saw the difference in their hands as they rested, side by side, upon the gleaming walnut. His mother's hands were white and slim and delicate, his father's large and square and strong.

Details of setting

As he grew, he learned to play bear. When it was time for his father to come home at night, he would lurk behind the kitchen door. When he heard the closing of the garage doors, he would hold his breath and squeeze himself into the crack behind the door. Then he would be quiet.

It was always the same. His father would open the door and stand there, the backs of his long legs beguilingly close. "Where's the boy?"

He would glance at the conspiratorial smile on his mother's face, and then he would leap and grab his father about the knees, and his father would look down and shout,

"Hey, what's this? A bear—a young cub!"

Then, no matter how tightly he tried to cling, he was lifted up and perched upon his father's shoulder, and they would march past his mother, and together they would duck their heads beneath the doors.

*A*nd then he went to school. And on the playground he learned how to wrestle and shout, how to hold back tears, how to get a half-nelson[1] on the boy who tried to take his football away from him. He came home at night and practiced his new wisdom on his father. Straining and puffing, he tried to pull his father off the lounge chair while his father kept on reading the paper, only glancing up now and then to ask in mild wonderment, "What are you trying to do, boy?"

He would stand and look at his father. "Gee whiz, Dad!" And then he would realize that his father was teasing him, and he would crawl up on his father's lap and pummel him in affectionate frustration.

And still he grew—taller, slimmer, stronger. He was like a young buck, with tiny new horns. He wanted to lock them with any other young buck's, to test them in combat. He measured his biceps with his mother's tape measure. Exultantly, he thrust his arm in front of his father. "Feel that! How's that for muscle?"

1. **half-nelson:** a wrestling hold

His father put his great thumb into the flexed muscle and pressed, and the boy pulled back, protesting, laughing. "Ouch!"

Sometimes they wrestled on the floor together, and his mother moved the chairs back. "Be careful, Charles—don't hurt him."

After a while his father would push him aside and sit in his chair, his long legs thrust out before him, and the boy would scramble to his feet, half resentful, half mirthful over the ease with which his father mastered him.

"Doggone it, Dad, someday—" he would say.

He went out for football and track in high school. He surprised even himself now, there was so much more of him. And he could look down on his mother. "Little one," he called her, or "Small fry."

Sometimes he took her wrists and backed her into a chair, while he laughed and she scolded. "I'll—I'll take you across my knee."

"Who will?" he demanded.

"Well—your father still can," she said.

His father—well, that was different.

*T*hey still wrestled occasionally, but it distressed his mother. She hovered about them, worrying, unable to comprehend the need for their struggling. It always ended the same way, with the boy upon his back, prostrate, and his father grinning down at him. "Give?"

"Give." And he got up, shaking his head.

Beginning of conflict

"I wish you wouldn't," his mother would say, fretting. "There's no point in it. You'll hurt yourselves; don't do it any more."

So for nearly a year they had not wrestled, but he thought about it one night at dinner. He looked at his father closely. It was queer, but his father didn't look nearly as tall or broad-shouldered as he used to. He could even look his father straight in the eyes.

"How much do you weigh, Dad?" he asked.

His father threw him a mild glance. "About the same; about a hundred and ninety. Why?"

The boy grinned. "Just wondering."

But after a while he went over to his father where he sat reading the paper and took it out of his hands. His father glanced up, his eyes at first questioning and then narrowing to meet the challenge in his son's. "So," he said softly.

"Come on, Dad."

His father took off his coat and began to unbutton his shirt. "You asked for it," he said.

His mother came in from the kitchen, alarmed. "Oh, Charles! Bill! Don't—you'll hurt yourselves!" But they paid no attention to her. They were standing now, their shirts off. They watched each other, intent and purposeful. The boy's teeth gleamed again. They circled for a moment, and then their hands closed upon each other's arms.

They strained against each other, and then the boy went down, taking his father with him. They moved and writhed and turned, in silence seeking an advantage, in silence pressing it to its conclusion. There was the sound of the thumps of their bodies upon the rug and of the quick, hard intake of breath. The boy showed his teeth occasionally in a grimace of pain. His mother stood at one side, both hands pressed against her ears. Occasionally her lips moved, but she did not make a sound.

After a while the boy pinned his father on his back. "Give!" he demanded.

His father said, "Heck no!" And with a great effort he pushed the boy off, and the struggle began again.

*B*ut at the end his father lay prostrate, and a look of bewilderment came into his eyes. He struggled desperately against his son's merciless, restraining hands. Finally he lay quiet, only his chest heaving, his breath coming loudly.

The boy said, "Give!"

The man frowned, shaking his head.

Still the boy knelt on him, pinning him down.

"Give!" he said, and tightened his grip. "Give!"

All at once his father began to laugh, silently, his shoulders shaking. The boy felt his mother's fingers tugging fiercely at his shoulder. "Let him up," she said. "Let him up!"

Climax of plot

The boy looked down at his father. "Give up?"

His father stopped laughing, but his eyes were still wet. "Okay," he said. "I give."

Male Head, Linda King, 1987.

The boy stood up and reached a hand to his father to help him up, but his mother was before him, putting an arm about his father's shoulders, helping him to rise. They stood together and looked at him, his father grinning gamely, his mother with baffled pain in her eyes.

The boy started to laugh. "I guess I—" He stopped. "Gosh, Dad, I didn't hurt you, did I?"

"Heck, no, I'm all right. Next time . . . ."

"Yeah, maybe next time . . . ."

*A*nd his mother did not contradict what they said, for she knew as well as they that there would never be a next time.

For a moment the three of them stood looking at one another, and then, suddenly, blindly, the boy turned. He ran through the door under which he had ducked so many times when he had ridden on his father's shoulders. He went out the kitchen door, behind which he had hidden, waiting to leap out and pounce upon his father's legs.

It was dark outside. He stood on the steps, feeling the air cool against his sweaty body. He stood with lifted head, looking at the stars, and then he could not see them because of the tears that burned his eyes and ran down his cheeks.

Trying Out Narrative Writing Use your journal to try out some narrative writing. Decide how you will proceed. Where will you get an idea? What details will you include? How will you organize your narrative? After drafting your story, think about what worked and what didn't work. In this chapter, you will learn to develop your skill at narrative writing.

Part 2
Understanding the Short Story

As you have learned, narratives can be written in many styles and for different reasons.

Short stories are narratives that are written to entertain, purely for the pleasure people find in telling and reading about "what happened." Stories can be realistic, centered around ordinary people and events—for example, "The Cub," which you read in Part 1. Other stories take place in an imaginary world. For example, in Ray Bradbury's story "All Summer in a Day," settlers on Venus are waiting to see the sun, which appears only once every seven years. The places and events in this story are out of the ordinary. Short stories usually begin with a minimum of background. The characters appear in a situation that involves some kind of problem or conflict that makes you want to find out what will happen next. Making readers curious and then satisfying their curiosity is what a short story is all about.

Characteristics of the Short Story

In Part 1 you examined three elements of narrative writing—characters, plot, and setting. In a short story, these elements can be used in various ways. Depending on the purpose of the narrative, writers may describe characters at length or hardly at all. Plots can be intricate or simple. A ghost story set in a dark old house may emphasize setting; a sports story may focus on plot or characters.

The development of characters, plot, and setting also depends on a fourth element—point of view. If the narrator—the voice telling the story—is an observer outside the events, the point of view is third-person. A third-person narrator can know everything—even the thoughts of the characters. The details of character, setting, and plot can therefore be developed in as much depth as the writer wishes.

■ *Literary Model* ■

Narrator's knowledge of Mildred's thoughts

George did not exactly snort but Mildred was sure if he had not been at a public telephone he would surely have snorted. He was an expert at this noise; it always sounded like a mule drinking, having suddenly got water up his nostrils. It was. . . an exceedingly irritating sound. . . .

From "The Proud and Virtuous" by Doris Betts

In a first-person narrative the narrator is one of the characters in the story. Therefore, the elements of the story must be developed so that they are consistent with what that narrator experiences.

■ *Literary Model* ━━━━━━━━━━━━━━

Setting
affected
by narrator's
feelings

I remember that to all of us the move to San Tomas was like the drawing of fresh breath. With relief, we turned our backs on the stony hills; . . . the house echoing with my parents' worry, the failure of my father's job. In San Tomas, where orange groves sprang from the desert and the California mountains towered blue, gold, gray above us, there was a new job. . . .

From "Victor" by Constance Crawford

Writing Activity The Short Story

Writing in Process In Part 3 you will start to write a short story. Begin collecting ideas for characters, plot, and setting. Glean ideas from people, places, newspapers, TV, your journal, and your imagination. There need not be any relationship among these elements. Later, you will have the opportunity to find a connection or create a new one where none exists.

Part 3
The Short Story: Prewriting and Drafting

How would you like to think of something no one ever thought of before? Here is your chance. When you write a story, you can imagine people and situations that never existed before. This lesson and the next one will lead you through the steps of writing a short story.

Finding a Story Idea

The first step in writing a short story is getting an idea. Since your story can be about almost anything, the array of choices may be bewildering. Your first problem is to find a focus, something to narrow the possibilities. You can use as your starting point one of the elements common to all narratives—characters, plot, or setting.

Ideas from Character A main character could provide a focus for your story. See what your journal contains about people. Make **lists** of individuals who have interested you or surprised you. Consider people you know, people in fiction, people in history, people in the news— even someone on the street whose face or gesture intrigued you. Use the thinking technique of **clustering** to gather details. Think of a name and write it in the center of a blank sheet of paper. Surround it with details about the person's appearance, personality, character traits, hobbies, jobs—anything that will bring the person to life. Some of the details about a character may suggest a story idea.

Ideas from Plot The plot of a story is made up of a series of events based on a conflict, or problem, and leading to a climax. You can start by **listing** problems or conflicts that are familiar to you and your friends—curfew, grades, relationships with family and friends, finding a job. You might use **gleaning,** looking through magazines and newspapers to find a story idea. You might ask yourself some **"what if" questions:** What if four friends were snowbound for a week in a small mountain cabin? What if hearing a song could transport you in time to the year when you first heard it? Such questions can suggest a focus for a short story.

Ideas from Setting A particular time or place can provide a focus for a story. The place can be one you know personally, one you have read about, one that is entirely imaginary, or one that combines the imaginary and the real. The time can be past, present, or future. Use clustering or draw a map to help you develop a clear mental picture of the setting. Then imagine a story that might take place there.

It may be helpful now to look at one particular writer's process. This writer, Kim, got her idea from setting, recalling a place she had enjoyed on her summer vacation. Here is some **freewriting** she did to develop her idea. Where can you see the germ of a story idea?

One Student's Process

Jane and I visited the Spectacular Spray Water Amusement Park one day last August. It's a great place to go on a hot summer day. The wave pool was fun, and the water slides were exciting. Some lucky kids even have jobs there as lifeguards. They must enjoy it up on those high towers. I guess most people would—unless they were afraid of heights.

Purpose and Audience

Once you have an idea, or focus, you can complete the plan for your story. Ask yourself what kind of story you're going to write. Will it be a funny story? a romantic story? a mysterious story? Who will be your readers, and how do you want them to react?

You don't have to answer these questions now, but thinking about them will help you shape your story. The answers will help you make decisions about characters, plot, and setting.

Planning the Story

You got your idea by using plot, character, or setting as a starting point. Now you should develop all three aspects of your story.

Developing Setting Kim got her idea from a setting, the water amusement park. Later, she made a list of sense impressions, such as *hot sun, cool water, misty spray, smells of chlorine and suntan lotion,* and *shrieking, laughing, screaming children.* As you think about your setting, consider the specific place, the time of day, the season, and the mood, such as somber or lively. Note any other details about the setting that will affect your characters and plot.

Writing Inside Out

Dr. David Houghton, Meteorologist

Most people just talk about the weather, but Dr. David Houghton does something about it. As a professor of meteorology at the University of Wisconsin in Madison, he is always involved in research projects that will help us better understand and forecast the weather. In order for other scientists to use his findings, he writes papers that are published in professional journals. It is very important that these papers be clearly written so that other scientists will want to read them.

Dr. Houghton has strong writing skills, but he does not find it easy to write. He likes to begin by choosing a title. For more complicated papers, he also makes an outline of everything he wants to cover. Then he follows his outline point

Developing Characters Kim needed a main character. She had seen lifeguards at the water amusement park, so she made up a lifeguard named Todd. She asked herself questions about Todd: How old is he? What does he look like? What makes him likable? What problems does he face? Questions like these can help you round out your characters.

Developing Plot A plot is what happens in a story. In most stories the plot is built around a conflict or problem that someone faces. The problem becomes increasingly serious, but it is solved at the end. Kim's description of her setting had suggested the following problem.

> **One Student's Process**
>
> Part of Todd's job as a lifeguard will be to watch out for people at the top of the water slide, but he is terrified of heights. How will he keep his job?

Creating a Chain of Events The problem your character faces gives you the beginning of your plot. The middle and the end come from thinking about possible solutions. Alone or with a friend, **brainstorm**

by point to develop a strong narrative.

Once the paper is finished, Dr. Houghton begins rewriting. "I like to do it all the way through once, then read through my paper, go back, and begin a revision process. There might be quite a few versions. . . before the final."

"All scientific papers have the same basic format," Dr. Houghton says. "First you introduce the subject and state the purpose of the paper or study. Then you go into what's been done before in this area. Next, you discuss your own procedures and the data you have found. Finally, you explain your conclusions."

Dr. Houghton, who often spends time helping his students write clearly, emphasizes "the basic business of the paragraph." "It's amazing how many people will write a paragraph that is not well-structured," he says. "A good topic sentence is the key."

Dr. Houghton's work has taken him to England, Russia, and China, and his studies have produced important information on such things as cloud structures and seasonal cycles. Besides papers, he writes reports, memos, summaries of meetings he attends, and "lots of letters." He also edited a book about jobs in meteorology. "There is no end to the importance of good English for a meteorologist," he says.

some possibilities. Ask these questions: What will my character do? What will happen next? Then work your way along, event by event, until your character's problem is solved. Write down your chain of events, and you will have the outline of your plot. What follows is the chain of events that Kim wrote.

One Student's Process

Chain of Events

1. Todd is hired to be a lifeguard at Spectacular Spray Water Amusement Park.
2. When he finds out that part of his job is to stand at the top of the water slide, he starts thinking of ways to get out of it, and arranges to work elsewhere in the park.
3. The manager finds out that Todd always works at the wave pool and tells him he has to guard the water slide the next day.
4. Todd considers quitting the job but decides not to.
5. He makes it to the top of the water slide, where he tries to do his job without looking down.
6. A little boy gets caught on the slide, and Todd has to decide whether to go down after him or get help.
7. Todd overcomes his fear and goes after the little boy.

From Prewriting to First Draft

You are ready to draft your story by expanding your chain of events. You may wonder how much you need to add. The answer is, enough to *show* what happens. Use sensory language, dialogue, and active verbs. Here are some other things that you should keep in mind as you write.

Keep a Consistent Point of View You need to decide on a point of view. Once you choose the point of view, you must remember to keep it consistent throughout the story. Kim didn't want to take Todd's fears too seriously, so she decided to use a third-person point of view. This point of view would allow the narrator to know Todd's thoughts and fears while remaining somewhat objective.

Use Chronological Order Most stories are told in chronological order, or the order in which events happened. It's possible, however, to start somewhere in the middle and use a **flashback** to tell what happened before. Kim could start her story with the manager telling Todd he has to work on the water slide. The earlier events would be told in a flashback. This plan would create suspense by letting readers in on Todd's problem.

Be Selective Be choosy about your details. Stick to the main story line, and select only details that support it. Kim decided to include details about Spectacular Spray park to help her readers picture the setting—the wave pool, the kiddy pool, and the three towering water slides. She did not include details about Todd's friends or other jobs he had held in the past.

Show, Don't Tell Develop characters through their actions and through dialogue, not just description. Instead of telling about a setting ("It was a hot day"), work in vivid details that show how the heat affected your characters: "Joe's shirt clung to him as beads of sweat trickled down his face." Give your readers action instead of summaries of events. This doesn't mean that you have to fill your story with car chases and exploding buildings. Just focus on the actions, gestures, and movements of characters. Notice how Kim introduced action in the following dialogue.

One Student's Process

Dialogue

"You wanted to see me, Ms. Argueta?" Todd said, a little anxiously.

"Yes," she said briskly. "I've been talking to some of the other lifeguards, and it seems that you haven't been doing your part."

Active verbs

Todd squirmed a little, and his wet swim trunks stuck to the lawn chair he was sitting in.

"I know," she continued, "that it's boring to stand up there on the water slides, but you have to take your turn with the others."

Todd felt a queasy sensation in his stomach.

Use of dialogue to advance plot

"First thing tomorrow," said Ms. Argueta, "I expect to see you on slide number 1. OK?"

Todd nodded weakly. "OK," he said in a voice that sounded to him like someone else's.

"Good. That's fair." Ms. Argueta took off her

sunglasses and seemed to Todd to be looking
closely at him. "There isn't anything else you
need to tell me about this business, is there?"

For a split second, Todd considered telling
her why the mention of the water slides made his
knees weak and his head spin. Then he thought
maybe he should quit on the spot. Finally, he
said, "No. Everything's fine." Except, he said
to himself, that first thing tomorrow I'm going
to die.

Grammar Note When you write a short story, you should use verb tenses consistently. Avoid tense changes such as this: After the game the autograph collector *was waiting* by the locker room. Suddenly he *sees* a player he *recognizes*.

Writing Activity Prewriting and Drafting

Writing in Process In the picture below is a character and a setting. You might even see a suggestion for a plot. Find a story idea in the picture, in another image in this book, in your collection of ideas from page 190, or on page 824 in the Writer's Handbook.

Next, decide what kind of story you want to write. Consider your purpose and audience. Use thinking skills to develop your setting, characters, and plot. Write your main character's problem in a sentence, and expand your idea into a chain of events. Write your first draft, using your chain of events as an outline. Save all your work.

Part 4

The Short Story: Revising and Proofreading

Once you have a first draft, you should try to look at your story from the point of view of your readers. This viewpoint will help you revise your draft.

First, you have to be sure that the events are clear and that they make sense. Readers won't enjoy your story if they don't know what's going on. Second, you want your story to be lively, so part of your revising process may involve adding dialogue and action. In this way, you can turn a drab sentence like "She was very angry about my letter" into something interesting: "'I'm not going to take it anymore!' she screamed, throwing the crumpled pages against the wall."

Find an editing partner to help you make your revisions. A reader who doesn't know the story as you do can tell you whether your story is clear and where you could add dialogue and action. Finally, you and your editing partner should consult the revision checklist below.

Revision Checklist: The Short Story

Purpose
1. Do you tell your story in a way that makes your purpose clear?
2. Do you keep your audience in mind as you write?

Organization
1. Do you start the story by getting directly into the events?
2. Do you follow chronological order?
3. If you use flashbacks, do you indicate the sequence clearly?

Development
1. Do you maintain a consistent point of view?
2. Do you choose details carefully, keeping to the story line?
3. Do you tell as much of the story as possible through action and dialogue? Do you show rather than tell?
4. Do your characters seem like real people?
5. Do you solve the main character's problem in an interesting and believable way?
6. Do you describe the setting clearly?

Here's how Kim, with the help of her editing partner, revised part of her first draft. The notes in the margin explain Kim's revisions.

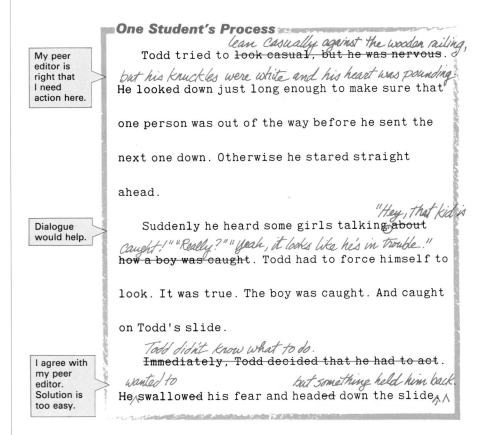

One Student's Process

My peer editor is right that I need action here.

Todd tried to ~~look casual, but he was nervous~~. *lean casually against the wooden railing,* *but his knuckles were white and his heart was pounding.* He looked down just long enough to make sure that one person was out of the way before he sent the next one down. Otherwise he stared straight ahead.

Dialogue would help.

Suddenly he heard some girls talking ~~about how a boy was caught~~. *"Hey, that kid is caught!" "Really?" "Yeah, it looks like he's in trouble."* Todd had to force himself to look. It was true. The boy was caught. And caught on Todd's slide.

I agree with my peer editor. Solution is too easy.

Todd didn't know what to do. ~~Immediately, Todd decided that he had to act.~~ He *wanted to* ~~swallowed~~ his fear and headed down the slide *but something held him back.*

Kim's first draft was easy to understand, and the sequence of events was clear. Her peer editor helped her to see, however, that her story needed more action and dialogue and that the solution to the problem came too soon and too easily. The revised version shows what Todd did instead of just telling how he felt. The revisions also let characters speak for themselves. These changes make the story livelier. Finally, holding off on Todd's decision keeps readers in suspense longer.

When you have finished revising your short story, proofread the revised draft. This is the final step of the revision process and an important one, since you want readers to pay attention to your story, not to your mistakes. Check your spelling, grammar, and punctuation. Refer to the Proofreading Checklist on page 82. Then make a clean copy you can share with your audience.

Writing Activities *Peer Evaluation*

A Select an editing partner, and evaluate each other's draft. Refer to the Revision Checklist on page 197 and the following guidelines to evaluate your partner's story.

1. Use the Revision Checklist to guide you in thinking about the short story in terms of its purpose, organization, and development. Write your reactions neatly in the margins of the paper.
2. In a sentence or two, write what you like best about the story.
3. Write one or two brief, general suggestions for how the writer might improve the story.

B *Writing in Process* Referring to the Revision Checklist and to your editing partner's comments, revise your first draft. Proofread, make a clean copy, and share the finished story with your classmates by reading it, by publishing it, or by putting it on tape.

Part 5
Uses of Narrative Writing

Narrative writing is used in many ways, often within other kinds of writing. The following chart lists some of these.

Uses of Narrative Writing

Type	Purpose	Example
History textbook	To bring history to life	Incident from Lewis and Clark expedition
Article in news magazine	To inform and persuade	Story about one girl in Special Olympics
Friendly letter	To communicate with a friend	Story of the writer's moving day
Sports section of newspaper	To inform and entertain	Description of highlights of Super Bowl game
Editorial in nature magazine	To inform and to win support	Story of efforts to save the panda
Article in family magazine	To inform and persuade	Story of child hurt by dangerous toy

The following narrative tells an imaginary story. It re-creates what might have happened to a group of Inupiat Eskimos whose remains were found in 1982, almost 500 years later, in Barrow, Alaska. What kind of book or article do you think this excerpt is from?

▬ *Professional Model* ▬

As night approached, the sea ice crashed against the shore, hurling occasional chunks high across the bluff toward the village. These tongues of rafted ice had thrust into the village in other storms, but they had only rarely caused significant damage.

In one small house close to the bluff edge two women— one in her 40's, the other in her 20's—slept fitfully near a teenage boy and two young girls. The five occupants of the house tossed and turned as the storm raged outside, seeking comfort in the knowledge that they were prepared as they had been taught to weather such storms. As long as the house was intact, they had nothing to fear.

Suddenly and without warning, a giant tongue of jumbled ice chunks, which had massed against the shore, burst free, carrying up and over the top of the bluff in a violent surge

known to the Inupiat as an *ivu*. Within seconds the surge sent tons of ice down on the tiny house near the edge.

Under this onslaught, the roof bent and then collapsed, hurling sod and roof timbers down into the house along with the ice. . . .

The ice advance stopped. Almost as soon as it had begun, it was over. Life and light were snuffed out beneath a pile of jumbled ice in the debris of a once safe and snug winter house. There was no sound or movement other than that of the still raging storm. By morning, the cold and lifeless house lay beneath a cap of ice congealed into a white shroud that covered all but the entrance tunnel and adjoining kitchen.

From "Sealed in Time" by Albert A. Dekin, Jr.

Dekin, an anthropologist, studied the buried remains of this group of Eskimos. The article tells what he saw and what he thought about it. By including a narrative, Dekin reminds his readers that those far-off events were real, and that they happened to real people.

The following narrative is the introduction to a magazine article about the fate of America's wild horses.

▀ *Professional Model* ▀

Our saddle horses gallop, snorting, down a dry wash below a ridge and out of sight of a herd of wild horses grazing quietly above us. The pounding hooves of our horses throw bits of red clay into the air as we ride through dense clumps of silver-green juniper and sagebrush. Ahead of us lie the flat, timbered peaks of Montana's Pryor Mountains, the sky above them a nickle-gray, pregnant with snow.

Lynne Taylor, a wild-horse specialist for the federal Bureau of Land Management [BLM] at the Pryor Mountain Wild Horse Refuge, reins his horse up and ties him to a small shrub. He motions us to do the same.

"Stay down," he says in a gravelly, trail-boss voice.

Taylor is the archetypal cowboy and at 51 may have spent more time in the saddle—either working or at rodeos—than out of it. A quiet man, he has been working with wild horses in the Pryors since 1971.

Stealthily we creep over a rust-colored ridge, then head up another. As we crest the second ridge, we can see the wild horses grazing, still unaware of us, a band of perhaps 13 led by a large black stallion. Then they see us and are spooked, their ears at attention, their nostrils flared. Wheeling back, their manes flowing and tails waving behind them in the wind, they gallop along the next ridge. After running for perhaps a quarter of a mile, they stop at a point where they can keep a wary eye on us.

From "On the Run" by Jim Robbins

To many readers, opposing views concerning the fate of America's wild horses might seem an uninteresting subject. But the narrative by Jim Robbins captures our attention and draws us into a discussion of the issues.

This narrative serves more than one purpose. It provides an interesting lead into the article, making readers want to read on. It also gives a splendid view of the objects of the controversy, the wild horses. The writer never takes sides, but the narrative encourages readers to feel concern about the fate of these horses, which are viewed by some as a "scourge" and by others as a "national treasure."

You can use narrative in other kinds of writing, as you have seen in these two excerpts. The occasional use of narrative will make your descriptions and your explanations livelier and more readable.

Writing Activities Using Narrative Writing

A Explain how a narrative might be used to enhance one of the following types of writing.

1. A report on hydroponic gardening
2. A persuasive article about street people
3. A news article on the aftermath of a flood
4. A historical piece about the Roaring 20's

B Look through some magazines and find one or two examples of narrative that is used in another kind of writing, such as those listed in the table on page 199. Bring your examples to class. Be prepared to explain how the author used the narrative—as an interest-catching introduction, as a way of bringing a character to life, to illustrate a persuasive argument, and so forth. Discuss the examples with your classmates. Then talk about how you might use narrative for similar purposes in papers you write for classes you are taking now, such as history, science, or computers.

Guidelines: Narrative Writing

Prewriting
- Use thinking skills such as freewriting to find a story idea based on character, plot, or setting. *(See pages 190 and 191.)*
- Decide what kind of story you will write, who your readers will be, and how you want your readers to react. *(See page 192.)*
- Use thinking skills to develop the plot, characters, and setting of your story. *(See pages 192 and 193.)*
- State in one sentence the problem your main character faces. *(See page 193.)*
- Using the problem as a starting point, create a chain of events that leads to a solution to the problem. *(See pages 193 and 194.)*

Drafting
- Choose a point of view for your story. *(See page 194.)*
- Begin by getting immediately into the action. *(See page 189.)*
- Provide enough information about the setting. *(See page 192.)*
- Use the chain of events to write a first draft. *(See pages 193 and 194.)*
- Use action and dialogue to bring your characters and events to life. *(See page 195.)*

Revising
- Do you give your readers enough information about the characters and setting? *(See page 197.)*
- Do you stick to the main story line, including only details that support it? *(See page 194.)*
- Do you show the characters in action rather than summarizing what they do? *(See page 195.)*
- Do you let the characters speak for themselves, using dialogue to bring them to life? *(See page 195.)*
- Do you maintain suspense by not giving away the end of the story too soon? *(See page 198.)*

Proofreading
- Do you maintain a consistent point of view? *(See page 194.)*
- Do you use verb tenses consistently? *(See page 196.)*
- Have you punctuated your dialogue correctly? *(See pages 780–782.)*
- Is your story free from errors in grammar, usage, capitalization, and spelling? *(See page 82.)*

Chapter 8
Application and Review

Use your narrative writing skills to complete one or more of the following activities. The instructions for Activity A lead you through the steps of the writing process. Activity B leaves more choices up to you, and Activity C provides several starting points.

A Writing a Story About a Hero You have read about heroes in literature—Ulysses, Beowulf, and King Arthur, for example. Heroes like these may have their origins in fact, but the stories about their exploits are probably mostly fictional. Create a hero of your own, perhaps a modern hero, and write a short story about one of his or her exploits.

Prewriting Begin by giving your hero a name, and use clustering to add details about the person's appearance, personality, and achievements. Or start with a situation, maybe even one you found in the daily paper, and freewrite about it to develop a plot idea. Or start with a setting. Think of one of the many places that could use heroic actions today, and invent a hero to fill the need.

Once you have an idea, flesh it out with details about plot, characters, and setting. Write a sentence stating the hero's problem. Then brainstorm alone or with a partner to create a chain of events.

Drafting Using your chain of events as an outline, draft your story. Bring the characters and events to life through action and dialogue.

Revising Be sure your story shows your character's heroism. Refer to the Revision Checklist on page 197 as you revise your first draft. Proofread your revised draft, using the checklist on page 82.

B Writing a Story About the Future Follow these steps to write a story about what life might be like in the future.

Prewriting Brainstorm a list of things that might be invented in the twenty-first century. Choose one invention. Working alone or with a partner, list some events that might occur because of it.

Drafting and Revising Tell your story as if the time is 100 years from now. Use your list of events to write a story that shows how the invention affects the lives of your characters. Revise your draft, using the Revision Checklist on page 197.

C *Starting Points for Writing* Brainstorm to generate a list of conflicts suggested by the images and quotes below. Add to this list any conflicts you can imagine occurring in the settings below. Include on your list everything that comes to mind, even those conflicts that might strike you as unlikely to occur between those characters or in that particular setting. Some of the items you list will be good starting points for writing short stories.

Needmore, Kentucky, . . . Population $6\frac{7}{8}$, and Harry had been among that wretched number since his parents took him out of the fifth grade . . . in Dayton, Ohio, and trundled him down to Needmore. . . .

Ed McClanahan

Liberation,
Ben Shahn, 1945.

The land seemed almost as dark as the water, for there was no moon. All that separated sea from shore was a long, straight stretch of beach—so white that it shone.

Peter Benchley

9

Exposition: Process and Definition

C an you describe the process by which this actor was transformed? If someone else can duplicate the process after listening to your description, you are a good communicator. For, when a person can explain a process clearly and precisely, fewer misunderstandings arise, and individuals are better able to quickly grasp what is being said.

The techniques of expository writing that you will learn in this chapter will help you to explain the steps in processes more effectively. They will also aid you in writing definitions.

Part 1

Analyzing Expository Writing

Writing that informs or explains is called **expository writing.** This is the type of writing that you most often use in school assignments. For example, a science teacher may ask you to write a lab report that explains the procedure and results of an experiment that you performed. You will also use expository writing outside school. Many jobs require such writing skills. As a bank employee, for example, you might need to write down the procedure used by security officers when they pick up the night deposit.

In expository writing, your purpose is always the same—to share knowledge. You can use the following techniques to present the information you wish to share.

Five Techniques Used in Expository Writing

1. Explaining a process—telling how something happens or how something is done, using step-by-step instructions.
2. Definition—explaining what something is by pointing out its qualities, characteristics, and uses.
3. Comparison and contrast—examining similarities and differences between things.
4. Cause and effect—showing how something came about or what the results were.
5. Problem and solution—examining aspects of a problem and finding possible solutions.

In the following model, notice the different types of expository techniques that a student named Luis uses in his explanation of subliminal communication.

Student Model

Since the 1950's, an unusual and controversial method has been used to send hidden messages. This method, called *subliminal communication,* sends messages that can be recorded by the human brain without the receiver being conscious of them.

Both the fascination with and the fear of subliminal communication come from the ways in which the messages are sent. A message can be an image "hidden" in a photograph, an inaudible message underneath the background music in stores and businesses, or a brief visual image between the frames of a movie or in a television show.

Those who support subliminal messages say that they are a harmless and efficient means of reaching goals. In one supermarket, for example, broadcasting the subliminal message Be Honest underneath the store's background music was said to have cut shoplifting by nearly 70 percent.

Critics argue that harmful or dangerous messages can be sent to the public without anyone being aware of them. In addition, critics charge that the messages can take away freedom of choice by planting a desire in a person's mind without his or her knowledge.

Discussing the Model After reading and answering the following questions about Luis's composition, discuss your answers with your classmates.

1. What is the purpose of Luis's composition?
2. What technique of explanation is used in the first paragraph? In the second?
3. What is the main idea of each paragraph? How would you describe the way this composition is organized?

Understanding Expository Writing

Most expository writing is a synthesis (combination) of various techniques of development. Although the purpose—to share knowledge—is always the same, you will frequently use more than one technique in an expository composition. Each subject is unique. It is up to you to decide what aspects of a subject you need to cover and what techniques you should use to present the information.

In this chapter and in Chapter 10, you will study five techniques used in expository writing. This chapter focuses on two of these techniques: explaining a process and developing a definition.

Exposition in Literature The following selection by Farley Mowat explains the process he went through in conducting an unusual scientific experiment.

Exposition in Literature

from *Never Cry Wolf*
by Farley Mowat

Isolated in the frigid Arctic, an inventive scientist studies the dietary habits of wolves and the nutritional value of mice, trying to prove that the wolves were not responsible for the decline in the local caribou population.

Introduction

*T*he realization that the wolves' summer diet consisted chiefly of mice did not conclude my work in the field of dietetics. I knew the mouse-wolf relationship was a revolutionary one to science and would be treated with suspicion, and possibly with ridicule, unless it could be so thoroughly substantiated that there would be no room to doubt its validity.

I had already established two major points:

1. That wolves caught and ate mice.
2. That the small rodents were sufficiently numerous to support the wolf population.

Purpose: to describe an experiment

There remained, however, a third point vital to the proof of my contention. This concerned the nutritional value of mice. It was imperative for me to prove that a diet of small rodents would suffice to maintain a large carnivore in good condition.

I recognized that this was not going to be an easy task. Only a controlled experiment would do, and since I could not exert the necessary control over the wolves, I was at a loss how to proceed.

For some days I pondered the problem, and then one morning, while I was preparing some lemmings and meadow mice as specimens, inspiration struck me. Despite the fact that man is not wholly carnivorous, I could see no valid reason why I should not use myself as a test subject. It was true that there was only one of me; but the difficulty this

Explanation of structure of experiment

posed could be met by setting up two timed intervals, during one of which I would confine myself to a mouse diet while during a second period of equal length I would eat canned meat and fresh fish. At the end of each period I would run a series of physiological tests upon myself and finally compare the two sets of results. While not absolutely conclusive as far as wolves were concerned, evidence that *my* metabolic functions remained unimpaired under a mouse regimen would strongly indicate that wolves, too, could survive and function normally on the same diet.

Beginning of procedure

There being no time like the present, I resolved to begin the experiment at once. Having cleaned the basinful of small corpses which remained from my morning session of mouse skinning, I placed them in a pot and hung it over my primus stove. The pot gave off a most delicate and delicious odor as the water boiled, and I was in excellent appetite by the time the stew was done.

*E*ating these small mammals presented something of a problem at first because of the numerous minute bones; however, I found that the bones could be chewed and swallowed without much difficulty. The taste of the mice—a purely subjective factor and not in the least relevant to the experiment—was pleasing, if rather bland. As the experiment progressed, this blandness led to a degree of boredom and a consequent loss of appetite and I was forced to seek variety in my methods of preparation.

Of the several recipes which I developed, the finest by far was Creamed Mouse . . .

Souris à la Crème

One dozen fat mice	Salt and pepper
One cup white flour	Cloves
One piece sowbelly	Ethyl alcohol

(I should perhaps note that sowbelly is normally only available in the Arctic, but ordinary salt pork can be substituted.) Skin and gut the mice, but do not remove the heads; wash, then place in a pot with enough alcohol to cover the carcasses. Allow to marinate for about two hours. Cut sowbelly into small cubes and fry slowly until most of the fat has been rendered. Now remove the carcasses from the alcohol and roll them in a mixture of salt, pepper, and flour; then place in frying pan and sauté for about five minutes (being careful not to allow the pan to get too hot, or the delicate meat will dry out and become tough and stringy). Now add a cup of alcohol and six or eight cloves. Cover the pan and allow to simmer slowly for fifteen minutes. The cream sauce can be made according to any standard recipe. When the sauce is ready, drench the carcasses with it, cover and allow to rest in a warm place for ten minutes before serving.

During the first week of the mouse diet I found my vigor remained unimpaired, and that I suffered no apparent ill effects. However, I did begin to develop a craving for fats. It was this which made me realize that my experiment, up to this point, had been rendered partly invalid by an oversight—and one, moreover, which did my scientific training no credit. The wolves, as I should have remembered, *ate the whole mouse;* and my dissections had shown that these small rodents stored most of their fat in the abdominal cavity, . . . It was an inexcusable error I had made, and I hastened to rectify it. From this time to the end of the experimental period I too ate the whole mouse, without the skin of course, and I found that my fat craving was considerably eased.

Trying Out Expository Writing Farley Mowat describes the process that he used to study the wolves' diet. Now think of a process that you know well. Write details in your journal, organize them, and then write a short composition in which you clearly explain the process.

Part 2

Explaining a Process

Writing that explains a process tells the reader how to do something or explains how something happens or works. For example, the explanations you have read in this book about the process of writing—prewriting, drafting, revising, and proofreading—are examples of process writing that teaches a skill. An explanation in a biology textbook of the process of photosynthesis is an example of process writing that shares knowledge.

In school, at work, and in everyday life you will find many opportunities to explain processes, either to teach others a skill you have developed or to share your knowledge about some subject. The following passage is part of a Georgia high-school student's published account of how an Appalachian craftsman named Garrett Arwood makes a fiddle.

Student Model

With all the pieces laid out, Garrett begins gluing the neck and back together, and then concentrates on attaching the dried sides. This must all be clamped and set to dry overnight. The lining strips and reinforcing blocks are added next, and everything is sanded to accommodate the top. When snugly fitted, the top is glued and clamped, as is the finger board. The setting of the sound post comes next and must be handled delicately. The bridge, tailpiece, and pegs are the only remaining items to be attached before the final step of either varnishing or staining. Garrett's fiddles have a tone and feeling all their own.

From *Foxfire 4* by Doug Cornell

Discussing the Model Think about the following questions, and discuss your answers in class.

1. How has Doug Cornell organized the steps in the process of making a fiddle?
2. What words or phrases does Doug Cornell use to link together the steps of the process that he describes? What purposes do these words serve?

The following article from the *Chicago Tribune* uses process writing to explain how frosted jeans are made by the H.D. Lee Company.

▬ *Professional Model* ▬▬▬▬▬▬▬▬▬▬▬▬▬▬

The process is more elaborate for "frosted" jeans—also called "iced" or "acid-washed" jeans.

Each five-gallon bucket of lava rocks is soaked for an hour with a beet-colored chemical mixture, the contents of which are a closely held company secret.

Then they're tumbled on a short dry cycle with the jeans in 125-pound washing machines to extract the excess moisture. Next, the rocks and jeans go through a full wash cycle with water and more chemicals, and then the jeans are taken out and dried.

After they're laundered, inspectors check for frays, tears and split seams.

The process—which pulls out the dye and starch that the fabric mills put in—gives a blotchy blue effect.

From the *Chicago Tribune,* December 1, 1987

Discussing the Model Read and discuss the following questions.

1. Is the writer's purpose to share knowledge or to teach a skill?
2. How has the writer enlivened the description of the steps?

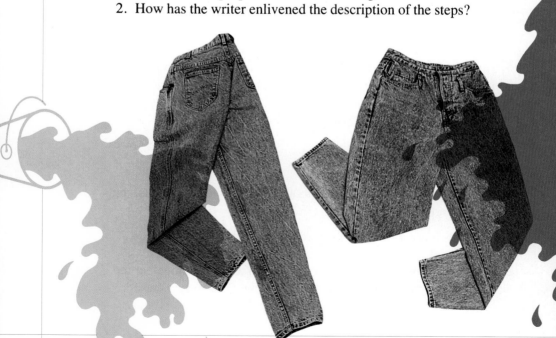

Prewriting: Explaining a Process

To explain a process successfully, your writing must be thorough and clear. Prewriting is crucial in expository writing since it is important to organize your ideas early in the writing process. Chapter 2, "Clear Thinking and Writing," and Chapter 3, "The Writing Process: Prewriting and Drafting," contain prewriting strategies to help you get started.

Choosing a Topic You can find topics in many areas of interest. For example, process explanations could be written describing how to make origami paper animals, how sneakers are made, and how a nuclear reaction occurs. As you choose your topic, consider the interests and needs of your audience.

Gathering and Organizing Information You can gather information through research, observation, experimentation, and interviews. Organize your information in chronological order following the steps in the process you are explaining.

Some processes require information in addition to the description of the process. For example, to explain a creative process such as how to make pen and ink drawings, you need to include information on the special materials used. When explaining natural or scientific processes, you should note the technical terms to be defined. Include all available facts and follow the list below.

Gathering and Organizing Information

1. List what you already know about the process.
2. Identify any missing steps or unclear information.
3. Gather missing information through reading and research.
4. Arrange the steps in chronological order.
5. Show your completed list to a classmate to check for missing steps or confusing information.

Analyzing Your Audience The information you provide and the way you present it will vary depending on your audience—their interest in the topic and how much they already know about it. For example, before you can prepare an explanation of a new computer program, you need to know how familiar your audience is with computers in general.

Drafting: Explaining a Process

Although a process explanation is fairly straightforward, your writing should not sound stiff and mechanical. Your explanation should be interesting and lively.

Writing an Introduction Your introduction should capture your readers' interest and let them know the purpose of your explanation. The following model from a high-school biology book gives an example of an introduction to the process of operating a microscope.

▬ *Professional Model*

> In this lab, you will learn how to use a compound light microscope to observe structures too small to see with the unaided eye. In future labs, you will use the techniques you learn in this lab to observe microscopic organisms.

Modern Biology Investigations

See Chapter 5, pages 112–113, for specific strategies for writing effective introductions.

Writing a Body Using your prewriting notes, explain your process step by step. Keep your audience in mind and think about ways to make your writing lively. Can you help the readers "see" the process through description? Might humor help to get your ideas across? As you write, check to see that your explanation is clear, logical, and thorough. Be sure to use clear transitions between the steps in the process to show the relationship and the time sequence between them.

Writing a Conclusion As you can see from the professional model below, the conclusion to a process explanation can be quite brief, as short as two or three sentences. Simply state the result of the process or explain the value of knowing the process.

▬ *Professional Model*

> In almost every type of biological research, the microscope plays a fundamental role. By allowing the exploration of a once-hidden world, the microscope has contributed immeasurably to our understanding of the earth's life forms.

Modern Biology Investigations

Revising: Explaining a Process

For strategies to help you revise, see Chapter 4, pages 80–81. Then, consider the following checklist.

Revision Checklist: Explaining a Process

Purpose
1. Have you clearly stated the purpose of your explanation?
2. Have you identified a specific audience and considered what information your audience needs to know?

Organization
1. Have you clearly explained each step in chronological order?
2. Have you used transitions to guide your readers?
3. Have you used details to explain the process?

Development
1. Have you made your writing lively and engrossing?
2. Have you included information on materials needed, and have you defined unfamiliar terms?
3. Have you included an introduction and conclusion?

Writing Activity Explaining a Process

Brainstorm to develop a list of topics, and then plan, write, and revise a composition that explains a process.

Prewriting and Drafting Determine your purpose and identify your audience. Then gather and organize your information.

Peer Evaluation and Revising Ask a peer editor to respond to your draft, using the following guidelines. Then revise your work, using the Revision Checklist and the comments of your peer editor.

Guidelines for Peer Editors

1. Using the Revision Checklist above, determine whether the writer has included all steps and explained each one clearly.
2. Identify what you thought was most effective about the draft.
3. Suggest one or two ways the writer could improve the draft.

Part 3
Writing a Definition

Another type of expository development is definition. A **definition** introduces readers to an unfamiliar term, object, or idea. Dictionary definitions are a simple example of this kind of writing. More detailed examples are commonly found in encyclopedias and reports. In compositions, definitions describe something by presenting details and distinguishing characteristics. A definition can be the subject of an entire composition, or it might be part of a larger explanation. A composition that defines something in a general way is usually organized in the following manner.

How to Structure a Definition

1. Put the subject in a larger class.
2. Identify the features that make it unique in its class.
3. Discuss the features or characteristics in detail.

Notice how a student follows the steps above to define *iceboats* in the following example.

Student Model

Iceboats are small, speedy boats resembling sailboats that are used for winter sports. An iceboat has a long body and is supported by three runners. One runner is attached to the body of the boat, and the other two are attached at the end of an *outrigger,* or crosspiece, that runs across the boat. The sail of an iceboat resembles that of a sailboat, and is fastened with steel wires to hollow masts and spars. Iceboats can be as short as ten feet, but most of them are somewhat longer.

Discussing the Model Discuss the following questions in class.

1. In what general class does the writer put iceboats?
2. What features make iceboats unique in their class?
3. What types of details does the writer use to describe iceboats?

Professional writers Martha Fay and Jan Mason use definition in a magazine article about the disorder called autism.

■ Professional Model ▬▬▬▬▬▬▬▬▬▬▬▬▬▬▬

Autism, which affects 15 of every 10,000 children in the U.S., is a disorder of extreme withdrawal. . . . Theories as to its cause range from an inheritable structural weakness in the X chromosomes to chemical imbalance. In clinical practice, however, . . . autism remains a maddening collection of symptoms: a refusal to make eye contact; absence of speech or a senseless parroting of the speech of others, called echolalia; apparent deafness or blindness; mental retardation; repetitive behavior that ranges from teeth-tapping to head-banging.

From "Child of Silence" by Martha Fay and Jan Mason

Discussing the Model Read and discuss the following questions.

1. In what general class do the authors put autism?
2. What characteristics do the writers identify to distinguish autism from other disorders of withdrawal?

Prewriting: Writing a Definition

Begin by writing a one-sentence definition that puts your subject in a class and then sets it apart from others in that class. Consider the following example:

A kangaroo is one kind of mammal that has a marsupium, or pouch.

The sentence puts the *kangaroo* in the class of *mammals,* and sets it apart from other mammals by noting that it has a marsupium.

Next, list distinguishing features of your subject. You might arrange them in the following format:

Subect: kangaroo
Class: marsupials
Distinguishing features: hops on hind legs; offspring complete
    development in mother's pouch

Finally, organize the details by placing them in categories. The chart on the next page shows how details about the kangaroo can be organized.

The details in your definition will usually progress from general to specific, but the features of your subject will influence the organization. For example, in the kangaroo composition, each group of details would be covered in a separate paragraph.

Drafting: Writing a Definition

Try to avoid a dry dictionary-like definition. As you write, use precise and vivid words, technical descriptions, humorous examples, or comparisons to enhance your explanation.

Writing an Introduction Your introduction should capture the attention of your readers. Following are three effective ways to begin:

- Start with a one-sentence definition.
- Start with a description.
- Start with an example.

The following example uses a familiar term in an unfamiliar way to capture the reader's attention.

> In Australia, hungry mobs hunt for food at night.

Writing a Body Use your prewriting chart to organize your paragraphs. Start with the most general categories and proceed to specific details. Use vivid descriptions, personal experiences, and colorful comparisons to make your definition come alive. If your definition includes abstract words or ideas, think of concrete examples to illustrate them.

Writing a Conclusion You might end your composition with a final illustration that adds perspective to your definition. Other possibilities are to end with a summary of the information or with a generalization about the important qualities of your subject.

Revising: Writing a Definition

After you have completed your composition, it is important to go back over what you have written and to make necessary revisions. Refer to the following checklist as you revise your work.

Revision Checklist: Writing a Definition

Purpose
1. Have you chosen a term, object, or definition that you are able to define?
2. Have you identified a specific audience and considered what information your audience needs to know?

Organization
1. Have you presented the features that make your subject unique within its class?
2. Have you organized the details and placed them in appropriate categories?

Development
1. Have you included a one-sentence definition of your subject that places it in a larger class?
2. Have you used descriptions, examples, and comparisons to hold the interest of your readers?

Writing Activity Writing a Definition

Brainstorm to develop a list of terms, objects, or ideas that could be defined in a composition. Choose one of them and develop a prewriting chart like the one on page 220. Then plan, write, and review a composition about your topic, keeping in mind your intended audience.

Prewriting and Drafting Write a definition that places your term in a larger class and also sets it apart from others in its class. Use general-to-specific organization of details, and include descriptions, examples, comparisons, or contrasts to interest your readers.

Peer Evaluation and Revising After you have carefully reread your draft, have a peer editor read and respond to it, using the guidelines on page 217. Use the responses of your peer editor and the Revision Checklist above as you revise.

Part 4

Synthesis: Combining Methods of Exposition

During any writing project, you must decide how to gather and organize your thoughts, write a first draft, and then revise it. One writer, Jean, chose to write about holography, combining process explanation and definition.

Prewriting: One Students's Process

Jean's first step was to develop a one-sentence definition for the topic of her composition.

```
                    , similar to photography,
Holography is the process by which a
                            ^

three-dimensional image is created.
```

> I need to place holography in a larger class.

Then she used the following format to identify her topic's distinguishing features.

```
Subject: holography
Class: photographic processes
Distinguishing features: creates
three-dimensional images
```

Finally, she created the chart on the following page to organize special details.

Types	How They are Formed	Uses

Types

transmission
reflection
integral

> I need to define these terms.

How They are Formed

1) image is recorded on a light-sensitive plate
2) plate is exposed to a laser beam
3) light patterns are picked up by viewer
4) viewer's eye "tricks" the brain into "seeing" the three-dimensional image

Uses

> I need to gather information about uses.

Drafting: One Student's Process

Jean began her introduction with an example of holography.

Imagine going to a movie where the characters

appear in three dimensions around you. This may

be possible in the near future because of an

, *a process similar to photography by which*

exciting technique called holography˄

a three-dimensional image is created.

Holography records on a light-sensitive plate or

that has the depth and appearance of a real object.

film an image˄

> I need to include my definition.

> This sentence makes the description clearer.

In the body of her composition, Jean related holography to a process readers would be familiar with—sight.

In order to understand how a hologram is created, it is helpful to understand how the human eye "sees" things. When you look at an object, your eye receives patterns of light reflected from the object's surface. Next, your eye sends these patterns to the brain. Finally the brain interprets them, creating an image of whatever you are looking at.

Revising: One Student's Process

As Jean revised her work, she made sure that she had presented all the information her audience needed, that her explanation was clear and complete, and that she had explained all unfamiliar terms. Here is how she revised two paragraphs.

> I need to define the terms better.

the simplest form of holograms,

To make a transmission hologram, a beam of

laser light is split into two parts. ~~The image~~

~~created is so lifelike that it appears to be a~~

~~real scene.~~ One part of the beam is used to

illuminate an object placed in its path. The

Then

> I need a transition here.

other part is sent on a separate path. The two

parts of the beam are brought together again,

creating an interference pattern. This pattern

is recorded on a special light-sensitive plate

and then developed like an ordinary photograph.

When a laser beam is passed through the

special plate, it reproduces the light patterns

recorded on it. These patterns appear to the

, which "tricks" the brain into seeing the object

viewer's eye as though actually present.

Writing Activity Synthesis

Think of a topic that combines aspects of definition and process explanation. For example, you might define a sport like jai alai and explain how it is played. Once you have chosen a topic, plan, write, and revise your composition using the steps described in this chapter.

Part 5

Uses of Process Explanations and Definitions

You will frequently encounter process explanations and definitions. The instructions that come with products, the definitions in encyclopedias and the directions in cookbooks are just a few examples. In addition, process explanations and definitions are included in many larger writing projects, from business reports to novels. The following chart lists some of the many ways they can be used.

Uses of Process Explanations and Definitions

Type	Purpose	Example
News media reports	To clarify an unknown term	Magazine article defining the Russian term *glasnost*
Information pamphlets	To teach a skill	Red Cross pamphlet explaining CPR
Instruction booklets	To give instructions for operation	Instruction guide explaining how to use a tape recorder
Reference books	To provide detailed information	Encyclopedia article explaining how hurricanes and tornadoes occur
Textbooks	To teach skills and share knowledge	Biology textbook explaining cell division
Stories	To entertain and share knowledge	Science fiction novel defining black holes

In his book on the U.S. space program, *The Right Stuff,* Tom Wolfe explains a complex concept—the unique qualities possessed by America's finest test pilots. Rather than using a formal process explanation, Wolfe uses a more informal technique involving comparison and description.

A young man might go into military flight training believing that he was entering some sort of technical school in which he was simply going to acquire a certain set of skills. Instead,

Comparison

he found himself all at once enclosed in a fraternity . . . the world was divided into those who had it and those who did not. This quality, this *it,* was never named . . . [The idea]

Description of process

seemed to be that a man should have the ability to go up in a hurtling piece of machinery and put his hide on the line and then have the moxie, the reflexes, the experience, the coolness, to pull it back in the last yawning moment—and then to go up again *the next day,* and the next day, and every next

Comparison

day, . . . A career of flying was like climbing one of those ancient Babylonian pyramids made up of a dizzy progression of steps and ledges . . . and the idea was to prove at every foot of the way up that pyramid that you were one of the elected and anointed ones who had *the right stuff* . . .

From *The Right Stuff* by Tom Wolfe

Writing Activity *Explanation and Definition*

Find examples of process explanations and definitions and analyze the organization of the selections. Evaluate their clarity and the techniques used to capture the reader's interest. Then rewrite one of the examples that you chose. Organize it in a different way, and interest your readers using a different technique.

Characters from the 1983 film
The Right Stuff.

Guidelines: *Expository Writing (1)*

Prewriting
- Decide your purpose—to share knowledge or teach a skill. *(See page 208.)*
- Address your writing to a specific audience, and consider the needs of your audience. *(See page 215.)*
- Develop prewriting notes that list the steps to be explained or the features of the item to be defined. *(See pages 215 and 219.)*
- Choose a logical pattern for organizing your information—usually chronological order for process explanations and general-to-specific order for definitions. *(See pages 215 and 220.)*

Drafting
- Write an introduction that captures the attention of your readers and either lets them know the purpose of your explanation or presents a definition of your subject. *(See pages 216 and 220.)*
- Explain unfamiliar terms, and include information on any special materials that may be needed. *(See page 215.)*
- Use precise and vivid words, descriptions, examples, and comparisons to enhance your explanation. *(See pages 216 and 220.)*
- Use transitions to show logical connections. *(See page 216.)*
- Write a conclusion that summarizes the information or illustrates its importance or usefulness. *(See pages 216 and 220.)*

Revising
- Ask a peer editor to review your draft. *(See pages 217 and 221.)*
- Refer to the appropriate Revision Checklist for the type of explanation you are writing. *(See pages 217 and 221.)*
- Keep your peer editor's comments in mind as you revise your work. *(See pages 217 and 221.)*

Proofreading
- Review your work for errors in grammar and usage.
- Review your work for errors in spelling and punctuation.

Presenting
- Prepare a final copy of your explanation.
- Share your work with your audience.

Chapter 9
Application and Review

The activities below let you practice what you have learned about writing. The first activity guides you through a process explanation. The second takes you through the process of writing a definition. The third gives you other starting points for expository writing.

A Explaining a Sport How would you explain a sport such as baseball to people who had never seen it before? Write an explanation of how to play one of the sports offered at your school. Your audience is a group of foreign-exchange students who are unfamiliar with American sports. Use the following guidelines as you write.

Prewriting Brainstorm to develop a list of sports. After choosing a topic, develop notes that list the steps in playing that sport. Also list the equipment needed and the terms you will need to explain.

Drafting Write a first draft, making sure that you present the steps in chronological order and use appropriate transitions to guide your readers. Also use examples, illustrations, and comparisons to make your writing entertaining as well as informative.

Revising Have a peer editor review your draft, using the Guidelines for Peer Editors on page 217. As you review your work, refer to the Revision Checklist on page 217, and keep in mind the comments of your peer editor. Proofread and prepare a final copy.

B Writing a Definition Plan, write, and review a composition that defines a term, object, or idea using the following guidelines.

Prewriting Brainstorm to think of topics that might make an interesting definition. For example, think about terms and ideas associated with recent scientific discoveries. Once you have chosen a topic, write a one-sentence definition that places it in a class and sets it apart from others in its class. Then prepare a prewriting chart to list its distinguishing features.

Drafting and Revising Use general-to-specific organization, and include examples, illustrations, or comparisons to make your writing vivid. Share your first draft with a peer editor, and refer to the Revision Checklist on page 221.

C *Starting Points for Writing* Brainstorm about the images below to generate a list of inventions that you use often but never think about, inventions that you wish you possessed, or inventions that you would like to create. Add to your list a few of the activities you might perform with the aid of these inventions. Then, when you want to use an item on your list as a starting point for writing exposition, freewrite answers to the questions given as Springboards below. You may need to do some research to answer the first of these questions.

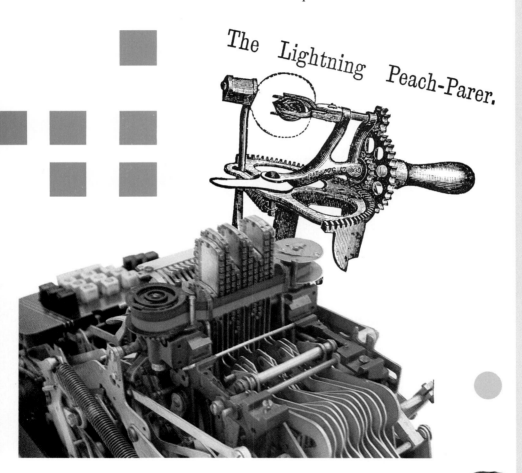

The Lightning Peach-Parer.

Springboards
- How does this item work?
- What steps do I follow when I perform this activity?
- Were I to try to explain what this item or activity is to someone unfamiliar with it, how would I define it?

10
Exposition: Exploring Relationships

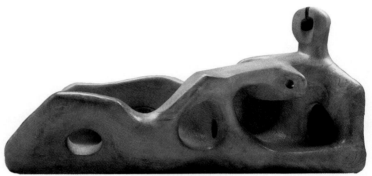

Reclining Figure, Henry Moore, 1939.

*C*ompare the sculpture by Henry Moore on this page with the paper cut by Henri Matisse on the opposite page. At first glance, the two works of art might not seem to have much in common. Yet here is how Matisse described the process he used in creating *Icarus*: "To cut to the quick in color reminds me of direct cutting in sculpture." With Matisse's words in mind, you might reexamine your comparison and discover other, more subtle relationships between the sculpture and the paper cut. Thus, the process of comparison and contrast can deepen your understanding of the two works of art.

Comparison and contrast is just one of the expository techniques you will explore in this chapter. In addition you will learn how to use cause-and-effect and problem-and-solution techniques to explore and present complex relationships.

Icarus, Henri Matisse, 1947.

Part 1
Analyzing Expository Writing

In Chapter 9, you studied two techniques used in expository writing: explaining a process and writing a definition. In this chapter you will explore three additional techniques: comparison and contrast, cause and effect, and problem and solution. As you develop a composition, you may find that one of these techniques is best suited to the topic you are exploring. For example, you might use comparison and contrast in a paper comparing the Civil War generals Ulysses S. Grant and Robert E. Lee. The cause-and-effect technique would be more appropriate in a composition explaining the relationship between cigarette smoking and lung cancer. The problem-and-solution analysis might be used in an essay presenting possible solutions to the problem of DDT contamination.

In many writing situations, you will not be using just one technique of exposition. Instead, you will use a combination of these and other techniques. Most expository writing is a synthesis, or combination, of techniques; each writer's purpose determines the methods he or she will use.

Notice the expository techniques a student named Ben uses in the following composition.

▬Student Model

Damaged trees in New England and lifeless lakes in Scandinavia are two examples of a serious international problem—acid rain.

Acid rain is a form of pollution that can have serious consequences. Unlike many other forms of pollution, it is difficult to trace. We can see pollutants rising from industrial smokestacks, and we can measure pollutants given off by automobiles. These sources of pollution can be easily identified, and steps can be taken to reduce pollution levels.

In contrast, acid rain comes from many sources in many locations. Its elements are carried hundreds or thousands of miles in the air. Therefore, tracking down the initial sources of acid rain is difficult. Finding solutions to the problem then becomes much more challenging.

Acid rain is formed when rain falls through polluted air and dissolves the pollutants in the air. Chemicals such as sulfur oxides, which are produced when fossil fuels are burned, and nitrogen oxides, which are produced when certain fertilizers are used, are released into the atmosphere and carried by the winds. As the dissolved chemicals fall to the ground, they can have harsh effects on the environment. Some plants and fish die when they absorb the chemicals. The metal and stone in buildings and bridges can start to crumble after years of exposure to acid rain. People who suffer from asthma, emphysema, and chronic bronchitis are also sensitive to acid rain.

What can be done? The key is to reduce the sulfur and nitrogen in the air. Steps can be taken to remove the chemicals from fuels before they are burned, or to remove them from smoke before the smoke is allowed to enter the air. In agricultural areas where fertilizers are needed, less polluting forms of fertilizers can be used.

The solutions to this problem are expensive and often difficult to carry out, but through international cooperation and local legislation we can begin to eliminate the destruction of acid rain.

Discussing the Model Think about the following questions concerning the student model above, then discuss your answers with your classmates.

1. How does Ben compare acid rain to other forms of pollution?
2. What causes of acid rain are discussed? What effects does Ben go on to discuss?
3. How does Ben examine the problem of acid rain? What solutions does he present?

Understanding Expository Writing

As you learned in Chapter 9, most expository writing is a synthesis of various techniques of development. You must decide which techniques to use in your composition. This chapter focuses on three of these techniques: comparison and contrast, cause and effect, and problem and solution.

Exposition in Literature The following selection explains the economic and social effects of an industrial factory on a small island and its people.

Exposition in Literature

from *Death of an Island*

by Pat Conroy

These paragraphs are from an autobiographical account of the author's year on a small island off the coast of South Carolina.

Effect

Cause

[Yamacraw] is not a large island, nor an important one, but it represents an era and a segment of history that is rapidly dying in America. The people of the island have changed very little since the Emancipation Proclamation. Indeed, many of them have never heard of this proclamation. They love their island with genuine affection but have watched the young people move to the city, to the lands far away and far removed from Yamacraw. The island is dying, and the people know it.

In the parable of Yamacraw there was a time when the black people supported themselves well, . . . Each morning the strong young men would take to their bateaux and

search the shores and inlets for the large clusters of oysters, which the women and old men in the factory shucked into large jars. Yamacraw oysters were world famous. . . . and the oyster factories operating on the island provided a substantial living for all the people. Everyone worked and everyone made money.

*T*hen a villain appeared. It was an industrial factory situated on a knoll above the Savannah River many miles away from Yamacraw. The villain spewed its excrement into the river, infected the creeks, and as silently as the pull of the tides, the filth crept to the shores of Yamacraw. As every good health inspector knows, the unfortunate consumer who lets an infected oyster slide down his throat is flirting with hepatitis. . . . Soon after this, little white signs were placed by the oyster banks forbidding anyone to gather the oysters. Ten thousand oysters were now as worthless as grains of sand. . . .

Since a factory is soulless and faceless, it could not be moved to understand the destruction its coming had wrought. When the oysters became contaminated, the island's only industry folded almost immediately. The great migration began. A steady flow of people faced with starvation moved toward the cities. They left in search of jobs. . . . Houses surrendered their tenants to the city and signs of sudden departure were rife in the interiors of deserted homes. Over 300 people left the island. They left reluctantly, but left permanently and returned only on sporadic visits to pay homage to the relatives too old or too stubborn to leave. As the oysters died, so did the people.

Trying Out Expository Writing Pat Conroy describes the destruction of an island and the causes of that destruction. Now try some of your own expository writing using the cause-and-effect technique. Choose a topic that you are interested in. For example, you could discuss the effects of the news media on presidential campaigns or the causes of high blood pressure. Write in your journal what you already know about the topic. Research any questions that you need answered. Organize your ideas and write a short composition describing the cause-and-effect relationship.

After you have finished, go back and reread your journal entries. Which parts were the most enjoyable to write? Which were difficult? Write your thoughts in your journal.

Part 2

Explaining Through Comparison and Contrast

When you examine the ways in which ideas are similar, you are **comparing** them. When you point out their differences, you are **contrasting** them. The comparison-and-contrast technique, however, can be used to go beyond showing similarities and differences. It can be used to draw conclusions about the relationships between ideas, introduce new concepts to the reader by comparing them to concepts with which the reader is already familiar, and refine the reader's understanding of similarities and differences. For example, two situations may seem similar at first, but after close examination they prove to be different, just as some situations that seem different may prove to be similar.

Now how Beth uses comparison and contrast in the following example.

Student Model

Mystery buffs fall into two categories—the fans of the English "whodunits" and the fans of American "hard-boiled detective" stories. The whodunit fans enjoy the works of Agatha Christie, while the hard-boiled fans read Raymond Chandler.

The fans of each type of mystery view society in different ways. In the whodunits, a crime temporarily disrupts a basically orderly society. In a hard-boiled detective story, on the other hand, the detective is continuously trying to "fix" a corrupt society.

Fans of both types, however, are generally not too interested in the crime itself. Instead they are fascinated by the twists and turns that lead to solving the mystery.

Discussing the Model Read the following questions and discuss them with your classmates.

1. What is compared in Beth's essay?
2. What features are examined in the comparison?
3. How are the features in the comparison arranged?

Now consider how movie critic Roger Ebert compares two ways of watching movies. Pay particular attention to the organization of the composition and to the way Ebert uses details and examples to support his ideas.

Professional Model

Like most other people whose tastes began to form before television became the dominant entertainment medium, I have a simple idea of what it means to go to the movies. You buy your ticket and take a seat in a large dark room with hundreds of strangers. You slide down in your seat and make yourself comfortable. On the screen in front of you, the movie image appears—enormous and overwhelming. If the movie is a good one, you allow yourself to be absorbed in its fantasy, and its dreams become part of your memories.

Television is not a substitute for that experience, and I have never had a TV-watching experience of emotional intensity comparable to my great movie-going experiences. Television is just not a first-class way to watch movies. The screen is too small. The image is technically inferior. The sound is disgracefully bad. As the viewer I can contain television—but the movies are so large they can contain me. I can't lose myself in a television image, and neither, I suspect, can most other people. That is why people are forever re-creating movie memories in great detail, but rarely bring the same passionate enthusiasm to made-for-TV films.

From *A Kiss Is Still a Kiss* by Roger Ebert

Discussing the Model Read and discuss the following questions with your classmates.

1. What is the main point of Roger Ebert's comparison?
2. Does Ebert concentrate on presenting similarities or differences between television and movies?
3. How does Ebert use details and examples to build the comparison between his subjects?
4. How does he arrange the features of the subjects that he is comparing and contrasting?
5. Compare the organization of Ebert's composition to that of Beth's composition.

Prewriting: Comparison and Contrast

Comparison and contrast can be used to analyze many topics, including literature, politics, sports, and science. It is also a useful technique for decision making. If, for example, you were planning to buy a VCR, you would want to compare and contrast the features of various VCRs before deciding which one to buy. As you plan a composition, you need to decide whether comparison and contrast will serve your purpose. For example, if you are trying to persuade someone, you might want to compare opinions on an issue. In discussing a problem, you could compare and contrast possible solutions to the problem.

Choosing a Topic When you are choosing composition topics to develop through comparison and contrast, make sure that the topics have enough characteristics in common to make the comparison worthwhile. For example, a comparison of rock music and chamber music might not be appropriate because the two types of music have little in common. Rock and blues music, however, have many common characteristics that could be compared and contrasted.

Left: The Beatles.
Right: Muddy Waters.

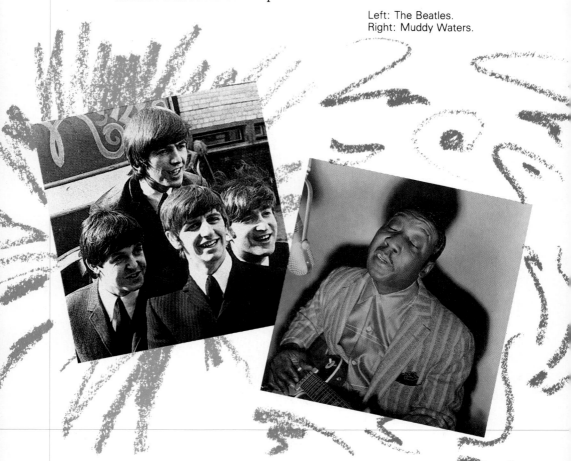

Writing a Clear Thesis Statement A well-crafted thesis statement can help you to narrow your topic and to decide what details to include in your comparison. The thesis statement should identify the subjects and the purpose of your comparison. To help you formulate your thesis statement, ask yourself the following questions: Do I want to show that the subjects are similar, or that they are different? Am I introducing a subject that may be unfamiliar to my readers, or am I attempting to refine my readers' understanding of the similarities and differences between two subjects?

Gathering and Organizing Information Using your thesis statement as a guide, identify the most important points of comparison—the **relevant features**. Develop a chart that lists the relevant features, and then compare each subject on each of those features. For example, in a comparison of rock music and blues music, relevant features might include rhythm, instrumentation, lyrics, audience, and performers.

There are two basic patterns for organizing a comparison. With subject-by-subject organization, you fully discuss one subject, and then the other. With the feature-by-feature pattern, you address each feature in turn and show how the subjects are similar or different. The chart below shows the two patterns of organization.

Subject-by-Subject	*Feature-by-Feature*
Introduction	Introduction
Subject 1	Feature 1
Feature 1	Subject 1
Feature 2, 3, etc.	Subject 2
Subject 2	Feature 2
Feature 1	Subject 1
Feature 2, 3, etc	Subject 2
Conclusion	Feature 3, etc.
	Conclusion

Drafting: Comparison and Contrast

As you write, keep your thesis statement in mind. Be sure to discuss each relevant feature you've identified. Choose one pattern of organization and follow it throughout your composition.

Writing an Introduction The introduction to your composition should present the subjects being compared and state the purpose of your comparison. To draw your readers into your composition, you might begin by showing a striking contrast or an often overlooked similarity between your subjects. You also might begin your composition with your thesis statement.

Using Transitions As you write the body, remember that transitions are effective signals to the reader to show whether you are discussing similarities or differences. Transitions that show similarities include *also, in the same manner, similarly, just as, likewise,* and *too.* Transitions that show differences include *although, but, in contrast, on the other hand, nevertheless, yet, despite,* and *however.*

Writing a Conclusion End your composition on a strong note. In addition to restating the main idea, draw a conclusion about the subjects you have compared.

Revising: Comparison and Contrast

Consider the questions presented in the following checklist as you revise your work.

Revision Checklist: Comparison and Contrast

Purpose
1. Have you chosen subjects for your composition that have enough features in common to make the comparison worthwhile?
2. Does your thesis statement clearly present the purpose of your comparison and narrow your topic?

Organization
1. Have you used appropriate transitions to show similarities and differences between the subjects of your comparison?
2. Have you used subject-by-subject or feature-by-feature organization?

Development
1. Have you identified the relevant features to be compared, analyzed them thoroughly, and used details clearly?
2. Have you drawn a specific conclusion and ended your composition on a strong note?

Writing Activities *Comparison and Contrast*

A Think of two actors or comedians you enjoy. How are they similar? How are they different? Develop a prewriting chart that could be used for an essay about the entertainers you have chosen. Start by making a list of relevant features or characteristics of each entertainer, then compare them.

B *Writing in Process* Refer to the prewriting chart you prepared in Exercise A or develop a new topic. Using the comparison-and-contrast technique, plan, write, and revise your composition.

Prewriting and Drafting Write a thesis statement that tells the purpose of your comparison and limits your topic. Then follow the steps presented in this section to gather and organize your information.

Peer Editing and Revising Ask a peer editor to review your draft and to answer the following questions: What was the most effective part of the comparison? What is one way in which the draft could be improved? (Make a specific suggestion.)

Now revise your work, using the Revision Checklist on page 240 and the comments of your peer editor as guides.

Part 3
Explaining Causes and Effects

When you explain what caused an action or event, or when you examine the effects of an action or event, you are using the **cause-and-effect** technique of exposition. Sometimes you may examine one cause that results in several effects, or one effect that stems from several causes. Other times you may examine a chain of causes and effects as shown below:

cause
↓
effect → cause
↓
effect → cause
↓
effect

Before you begin writing, however, you must make sure that your topic has a true cause-and-effect relationship—that one action actually *causes* another to happen. A composition that explains how the polio vaccine virtually eliminated the threat of polio is an example of cause-and-effect writing. A composition that explains how the polio vaccine was developed is merely a process explanation.

Consider the cause-and-effect relationship that Nora examined in the example below.

▬Student Model

When an earthquake strikes, its effects are immediately apparent on the earth's surface. Yet its causes are buried deep within the earth.

According to one theory, earthquakes can be traced to rigid plates below the earth's surface that slowly rub together. The motion squeezes the rocks at the edges of some plates, and if the force becomes too great, the rocks rupture and shift, causing a quake.

However, another theory contends that the movement of the plates is a secondary factor. According to this theory, steam and gases escape from the boiling mass deep in the earth, and force their way toward the surface, causing quakes.

Discussing the Model Read the following questions and discuss them with your classmates.

1. Does Nora's topic have a true cause-and-effect relationship? Why?
2. Does Nora concentrate on examining causes or effects?

In the following example, television commentator and author James Burke examines the effects of one modern invention.

▬Professional Model

The jet aircraft has probably done more than any other modern product of science and technology to bring change to the global community. . . .

It has undoubtedly changed the concept of distance. When the modern airline passenger takes off he leaves the reality of his surroundings, passes a period of time in a travelling capsule, and returns to reality at the other end of his flight: the reality of the terrain and the ocean that lies between his point of departure and destination is removed. With the advent of supersonic flight, the concept of time has

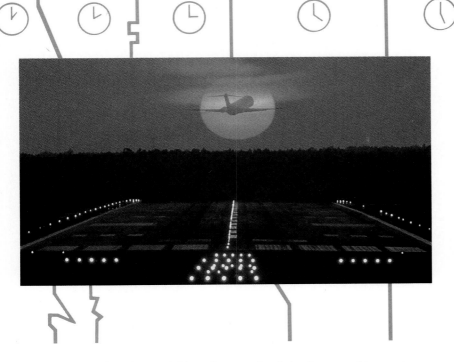

also changed. Now the traveller flying from east to west may arrive at his destination before he has left his point of departure, and in so doing experience the one bodily condition created by the development of the aircraft—jet lag.

From *Connections* by James Burke

Discussing the Model Consider the following questions.

1. What effects does Burke say air travel has brought about?
2. How does Burke use examples to explain his points?
3. How does the organization of Burke's essay differ from Nora's?

Prewriting: Causes and Effects

Cause-and-effect development is particularly effective in examining issues in the natural and social sciences.

Choosing a Topic When you choose a topic, consider the following questions to ensure that it has a true cause-and-effect relationship: (1) What caused _____ ? (2) What was the effect of _____ ? Remember that often you will not be choosing a topic but will be using the cause-and-effect technique to discuss subjects within your composition.

Writing a Clear Thesis Statement State the relationship you will explore and indicate whether you will focus on causes, effects, or both. Your thesis statement can help you set limits on the topic.

Gathering and Organizing Information The following steps will help you investigate your topic:

1. Write down what you already know about your topic, listing causes in one column and effects in another.
2. Research your topic to identify additional causes and effects.
3. Decide which points will help you to build the strongest relationship between causes and effects.

Cause-and-effect compositions generally follow one of two patterns of organization. In the **cause-to-effect pattern,** you state the cause first, and then proceed to the effect. In the **effect-to-cause pattern,** you begin with the effect and then examine what caused it.

Cause-to-Effect Patterns		*Effect-to-Cause Patterns*	
A	**B**	**A**	**B**
Introduction	Introduction	Introduction	Introduction
Cause	Cause 1	Effect	Effect 1
Effect 1	Cause 2	Cause 1	Effect 2
Effect 2	Cause 3, etc.	Cause 2	Effect 3, etc.
Effect 3, etc.	Effect	Cause 3, etc.	Cause
Conclusion	Conclusion	Conclusion	Conclusion

With either pattern, you can use **chronological order, order of importance,** or **familiar-to-unfamiliar order.**

Drafting: Causes and Effects

As you write, make sure that your composition shows a true cause-and-effect relationship, not merely a series of actions that occur in chronological order.

Writing an Introduction Present your topic and establish whether you will explain causes, effects, or both. You might begin by stating the relationship to be explored, providing background information, or asking a question.

Writing a Body Use specific examples and details to help your readers understand the cause-and-effect relationship. Use transitions, such as *therefore, due to,* and *consequently,* to show logical connections between causes and effects.

Writing a Conclusion You might end your composition by summarizing, drawing a conclusion, or making a prediction.

Punctuation Note Explaining causes and effects often involves using conjunctive adverbs such as *accordingly, hence, therefore, consequently,* and *thus* as transitional devices. When conjunctive adverbs are used to join two main clauses, they are preceded by a semicolon and followed by a comma. (See page 500.)

Revising: Causes and Effects

The following checklist can help you revise your work.

> ### Revision Checklist: Causes and Effects
>
> **Purpose**
> 1. Does your topic have a true cause-effect relationship?
> 2. Does your thesis statement set limits on the topic and indicate whether you will focus on causes, effects, or both?
>
> **Organization**
> 1. Which type of organization have you used, cause-to-effect or effect-to-cause?
> 2. Have you presented details in chronological order, order of importance, or familiar-to-unfamiliar order?
>
> **Development**
> 1. Do the introduction and conclusion create a strong impression?
> 2. Have you included specific examples and used transitions to show logical connections?

Writing Activities Causes and Effects

A Which statements indicate a true cause-and-effect relationship?

1. A car stalled on the freeway. Traffic is backed up.
2. I overslept this morning. I was late for my first class.
3. George lit the coals in the grill. He cooked dinner.

4. The rain began unexpectedly. We got soaked.
5. The pitcher warmed up. The pitcher entered the game.

B *Writing in Process* How has the weather affected your life? Think about an event, such as a major snowstorm or a heat wave, that had an impact on you. Then plan, write, and revise a composition using the cause-and-effect technique.

Prewriting and Drafting Make sure that your topic has a true cause-and-effect relationship, and then follow the steps presented in this section to gather and organize your information.

Peer Editing and Revising Ask a peer editor to answer these questions: What is the most interesting part? What could be changed to make the cause-and-effect relationship stronger?

Use your peer editor's comments and the checklist on page 245 to revise your work.

Part 4
Explaining Problems and Solutions

One of the most common experiences in life is facing problems and devising solutions. School assignments, news articles, political speeches, and many other forms of writing require the ability to explain problems and their solutions.

When using the problem-and-solution technique, you may emphasize the problem or the solution or fully develop both. Your topic and your purpose for writing will determine how you proceed. You can use this technique for an entire composition or for one or more sections within a composition.

Consider the problem that Anita examined in the following example.

▬Student Model

> Why is it so hard to find something worthwhile to watch on television? Isn't there something we can do to convince television stations to present better programs?
>
> I think there is. It is up to viewers to take a more active role. Viewers can call their local stations to complain about

offensive programs. We can send petitions to the networks to voice our displeasure.

If all else fails, there is one final step we can take to eliminate bad television. We can just turn off our sets.

Discussing the Model Read the following questions and discuss them with your classmates.

1. What is the problem that Anita is addressing?
2. Does she emphasize the problem, the solution, or both?

Read the following professional model. What problem does the writer address in this passage?

■ *Professional Model* ■

An economist rarely has the opportunity to recommend a policy that benefits 225 million people and saves the government money to boot. But I have such a suggestion: let's abolish the penny.

Problem

Yes, the old one-cent piece has outlived its usefulness and is now a public nuisance. . . . Pennies get in the way when we make change. They add unwanted weight to our pockets and purses. . . .

I used to dump my pennies into a shoe box. About two years ago. . . . I offered the box to my son William, then eight. I warned him that the bank would take the pennies only if he neatly wrapped them in rolls of 50. William, obviously a keen, intuitive economist, thought the matter over carefully for about two seconds before responding, "Thanks, Dad, but it's not worth it." If it's not worth the time of an eight-year-old to wrap pennies, why does the U.S. government keep producing the things?

Anecdote to illustrate author's point

. . . Only tradition explains our stubborn attachment to the penny. Sure, it has sentimental value. So, rather than call in all the pennies and melt them . . . . the government should simply announce that it is demonetizing the penny . . . . and let collectors take many of the pesky things out of circulation. After hobbyists and investors accumulated whatever stockpiles they desired, the rest could be redeemed by the government—wrapped neatly in rolls of 50, of course.

Solution

From "Cents Are Nonsense" by Alan S. Blinder

Discussing the Model Read and discuss the following questions with your classmates.

1. Does Blinder emphasize the problem, the solution, or both?
2. How does he use examples to develop his points?

Prewriting: Problems and Solutions

As you consider topics for a composition, be careful to avoid problems that are too large or too complex. A discussion of the world hunger problem, for example, would require a lengthy essay. A composition about what could be done to feed the hungry in your community, however, might be manageable. Also avoid topics that are obvious or clichéd, such as "littering is a big problem."

Often, the best topics are the ones with which you have first-hand experience. When you use your own expertise to examine problems and solutions, you can write with more authority.

Writing a Clear Thesis Statement Your thesis statement should identify the problem you are addressing and indicate whether you will focus on the problem, the solution, or both. An effective thesis statement can serve as a guide during the drafting stage.

Gathering and Organizing Information The following steps can help you investigate your topic.

Exploring the Problem
1. What is the problem?
2. Why should the reader care about the problem?
3. What is the extent of the problem?
4. What are the causes of the problem?
5. What are the effects of the problem?
6. Is the problem getting worse? How do you know?

Exploring the Solution (or Solutions)
1. Is there an ideal solution?
2. Is this solution feasible? Why?
3. What are other possible solutions?
4. What are the merits and drawbacks of these solutions?
5. Which solutions are significant enough to be included in your composition?

You should also gather as many facts, examples, and illustrations as possible to help your readers see the problem as you see it and understand your solution.

Drafting: Problems and Solutions

A problem-and-solution analysis is fairly simple to write—provided that you have chosen a topic with which you are familiar and you have fully researched it. Use the following steps as you draft your analysis:

1. Identify the problem.
2. Explain why the reader should care about the problem.
3. Give a full description of the problem, including as many examples as possible.
4. Give a full description of the solution (or solutions), including examples.
5. Tell what action is needed to implement a solution, or what the next step in finding a solution should be.

Writing an Introduction A strong introduction will make readers want to understand the problem. Starting your composition with an example or an anecdote is an effective way to personalize the problem and make it seem real to your readers.

Writing a Body Use the examples and illustrations you collected during prewriting to develop your composition. Keep the following guidelines in mind:

1. Use examples and illustrations to clarify general statements.
2. Use concrete words and images that help readers picture abstract ideas.
3. Choose examples and illustrations that mean something to your particular audience.
4. Choose examples and illustrations that appeal to your readers' senses and help them "see" your point.
5. Use at least one example or illustration for each general statement.

Writing a Conclusion An effective conclusion reinforces the significance of the problem and establishes the importance of the solution. You might make a prediction or call on your readers to take a specific action. You might end with your strongest illustration of the problem or a description of how things could be if the problem were solved.

Revising: Problems and Solutions

Refer to the following checklist as you revise your work.

Revision Checklist: Problems and Solutions

Purpose
1. Have you chosen a problem that is of a manageable size and that you are familiar with?
2. Does your thesis statement clearly identify the problem?
3. Does your thesis statement establish whether you are concentrating on the problem, the solution, or both?

Organization
1. Does your composition proceed logically from the problem to the solution?
2. Have you used examples and illustrations to clarify each general statement and help your readers "see" your point?

Development
1. Have you established reasons why the reader should care about the problem?
2. Have you fully described the problem and its solution or solutions?
3. Does your conclusion reinforce the significance of the problem and establish the importance of the solution?

Writing Activities Problems and Solutions

A What problems in your school or community need to be solved? What problems have already been solved? Use brainstorming to develop a list of topics for an essay you could write for your school newspaper. Try to generate ideas with which you have first-hand experience so that you will be able to write with authority.

B *Writing in Process* Select one of the essay topics you generated in Exercise A. Then plan, write, and revise a problem-and-solution essay for your school newspaper, using the strategies discussed in this section.

Prewriting and Drafting Write a thesis statement that identifies the problem and indicates whether you will emphasize the problem, the solution, or both. Next, explore the problem and solution, using the questions in the chart on page 249. Use the guidelines on page 249 to help you organize your draft. Include examples and illustrations to help your readers "see" the problem.

Peer Editing and Revising Ask a peer editor to review your draft and to answer the following questions: Was the problem understandable and the solution believable? What was the most effective part of the essay? How could the essay be improved? (Give two specific suggestions.)

Review the responses of your peer editor and refer to the Revision Checklist on page 250 as you revise your work.

Part 5
Synthesis: Combining Techniques of Exposition

Writing a composition generally involves a combination of the steps and techniques presented in this chapter and Chapter 9. It is up to you as a writer to decide which techniques to use in each part of your composition. In the following example, Rosa was asked to write an essay for her community newspaper about the problem of vandalism. Here are some of the decisions she made as she prepared her essay. Notice how Rosa used the cause-and-effect and definition techniques throughout her problem-and-solution composition.

Prewriting: One Student's Process

First Rosa developed a thesis statement that identified the problem she was addressing.

> Vandalism is costing the nation more than one billion dollars a year, but many communities are developing programs to reduce the problem.

Next, she answered these questions as she gathered information.

1. What is the problem? Vandalism costs the nation more than a billion dollars a year.
2. Why should the reader care about the problem? In addition to the financial burden, the senseless destruction defaces the community and shows a breakdown of community values.
3. What is the extent of the problem? FBI reports more than 224,000 incidents a year.
4. What are the causes?
5. Is the problem getting worse? How do you know? Government statistics show a threefold increase in arrests over the past two decades.

I need to gather information on causes.

Rosa also explored the solution and began to gather examples and illustrations.

Drafting: One Student's Process

For her introduction, Rosa chose to use an incident that would impress upon her readers the serious consequences of vandalism. Then she addressed the solutions.

Cause

Effect

Effect

Recently in New Jersey, several youths opened a valve in an aqueduct. But their prank had serious results. Before the valve was closed again, the city had lost 50 million gallons of water, and much of the city's water supply had been cut off. In addition, the city was forced to spend $2.5 million for repairs and for purchasing water.

Solution   Communities nationwide are developing
innovative programs to deal with problems. One
Definition   approach is to establish "youth juries" so that
offenders are tried and punished by their peers.
Solution   Another program has vandals assigned to
clean-up crews as a form of restitution. Another
plan involves strictly enforced probation
programs for offenders.

Revising: One Student's Process

Next Rosa examined the causes of vandalism. Note the revision she
made to clarify a point.

There is no single cause of vandalism;

instead, experts blame several factors. Some

cite a declining respect for authority and a lack

of discipline in schools. Others blame our

I need to
explain
this point.   mobile society. *When children don't get to know
their community, they care less about people
and property.*

Writing Activity *Synthesis*

Think of composition topics that you could develop using a combination of the exposition techniques you have studied in this chapter and in Chapter 9. For example, you might compare the process of cooking eggs in a microwave oven with the conventional cooking process, or you might define *rhinoviruses* and examine their effects on the respiratory system. Once you have chosen a topic, plan, write, and revise a composition using the steps you have studied.

Part 6
Uses of Expository Writing

As you have learned, many techniques can be used to develop expository writing. In your everyday reading, you are likely to encounter expository writing that combines the techniques presented in these chapters with other techniques. Expository writing often involves a synthesis of several techniques, and a writer's purpose will determine which techniques he or she uses. The following chart lists some of the many uses of exposition.

Uses of Expository Writing

Type	Purpose	Example
Editorials	To examine issues of public concern	Newspaper editorial that examines the problem of school crowding and proposes solutions
Public service announcements	To inform a general audience	Television announcement on the causes and effects of alcoholism
Political speeches	To inform and persuade voters	Campaign speech comparing the positions of two candidates on various issues
Nonfiction books	To share knowledge with a general audience	Book comparing the auto industries in the U.S. and Japan

Notice how different methods of exposition allowed one newspaper reporter to describe the emergence of a new software "virus," discovered at Hebrew University.

▬ *Professional Model* ▬

A newly diagnosed software "virus" that nearly killed valuable scientific files at Hebrew University here has alerted the computer world to the possibility of saboteurs wreaking chaos on personal computer systems everywhere. . . .

Definition

The invisible scourge, known as a virus in computer jargon, is a tiny self-propagating set of orders infiltrated into a computer system as part of the contents of a normal program. It is designed to wipe out the memory of a given computer's hard disc, and also to reproduce itself in all other computer programs within the system it attacks.

The consequent and inevitable damage it can do makes it an ideal device for criminals, spies and terrorists.

Process

Israel's strain of the virus was programmed to disrupt IBM-PC computers and cause periodic malfunctions that were timed by its unknown designer to take place every Friday and on the 13th day of each month. Ultimately, the

Cause/effect

program would erase the computer system's storage in toto the next time a Friday coincided with the 13th day of a month. This would designate May 13, 1988, as doomsday for 80 percent of the IBM-PC users in this country and for their colleagues abroad who interfaced with the contaminated program. . . .

Nothing is known about the person responsible for spreading the virus or the motive behind this effort. Ofer Ahituv, head of a leading computer software firm in Tel Aviv, suspects it may have originated with a programmer who thinks he has a score to settle with former employers. . . .

Other computer experts in Israel believe the emergence of this hazard may terminate the illegal copying of computer software that has become common throughout the world, especially among Israel's advanced computer users. . . .

Said Shai Bushinsky, a self-employed computer expert knowledgeable about the virus, "The current free flow of information will stop. Everyone will be very careful who they come into contact with and with whom they share their information." . . .

Cause/effect

A defect in the virus led to its discovery last week. Instead of infecting each program or data file once, the malignant orders copied themselves over and over, consuming increasing amounts of memory space. . . .

Process

[Hebrew University computer experts] succeeded in isolating the virus within a contaminated program by running it through a blank computer.

This enabled them to ascertain that the virus had copied itself into the computer's operating system. Their next step was to disassemble the core memory and expose the method by which the virus operates.

Once they had reached this stage, it was possible for them to develop an antidote program.

From "Virus Hits Computers" by Jay Bushinsky

Writing Activity Using Exposition

Find examples of comparison-and-contrast, cause-and-effect, and problem-and-solution writing in books, magazines, newspapers, and other sources. Bring an example of each type to class and exchange them. As a class, develop a list of the ways each technique is used.

Guidelines: *Expository Writing (2)*

Prewriting
- Decide which technique or techniques of exposition are appropriate for your composition: comparison and contrast, cause and effect, or problem and solution.
- Consider your audience and how to get your point across effectively and clearly.
- Develop a controlling purpose that determines the techniques you use and that directs your research.
- Choose a strategy for organizing that fits the technique of exposition that you have chosen.

Drafting
- Write an introduction that captures the attention of your readers and that clearly establishes the purpose of your composition. *(See pages 240, 244, and 249.)*
- Use transitions to show logical connections. *(See pages 240 and 245.)*
- Use specific, well-chosen examples and illustrations to help your readers "see" your points. *(See pages 245 and 249.)*
- Write a conclusion that ends your composition on a strong note, restates your main point, and summarizes your information or draws a conclusion. *(See pages 240, 245, and 250.)*

Revising
- Ask a peer editor to review your draft. *(See pages 241, 246, and 251.)*
- Refer to the appropriate Revision Checklist for the technique of exposition you have chosen. *(See pages 240, 245, and 250.)*
- Consider the comments of your peer editor as you revise your work. *(See pages 241, 245, and 250.)*

Proofreading
- Review your work for errors in grammar and usage.
- Review your work for errors in spelling and punctuation.

Presenting
- Prepare a final copy of your composition.
- Share your work with your readers.

Chapter 10
Application and Review

Use the expository techniques you learned in this chapter to complete the following activities.

A Writing a Review You have been chosen by the local newspaper to write a restaurant review comparing two of the restaurants that are favorites among high school students. Use the comparison-and-contrast technique to plan, write, and revise your review.

Prewriting As you choose restaurants, be sure they have enough in common to make the comparison worthwhile. Write a thesis statement that establishes the point of your comparison. Next, develop a chart of the relevant features and analyze each restaurant. Decide whether you will use subject-by-subject or feature-by-feature organization in your restaurant review.

Drafting Write an introduction that draws your readers into your review. Use your prewriting chart to make sure your comparison is complete on each relevant feature. Use transitions to signal comparisons and contrasts; include examples and illustrations. Write a conclusion that ends your review on a strong note.

Revising Ask a peer editor to review your draft, using the Revision Checklist on page 240. Consider your peer editor's comments and the Revision Checklist as you revise. Proofread and prepare a final copy of your composition.

B Techniques of Expository Writing Plan, write, and revise an essay using the cause-and-effect or problem-and-solution technique.

Prewriting Use brainstorming to develop a list of topics. You might write about the effects of different types of music on your mood, for example, or about the problem of balancing schoolwork and a job. Once you have chosen a topic, write a thesis statement, gather information, and decide on an appropriate method for organizing your draft.

Drafting and Revising As you write, be sure to include examples and illustrations to help your readers understand your points. Share your first draft with a peer editor, and refer to the appropriate Revision Checklist to guide your revision.

c *Starting Points for Writing* What cause-and-effect relationships come to mind when you think about the images and the quotes below? What subjects that you might compare and contrast occur to you? List these cause-and-effect relationships and the subjects you might compare and contrast to compile starting points for writing exposition.

In Bulgaria, a nod means no and a shake of the head means yes.
Do's and Taboos Around the World

Once I made my own clothes. What drove me to it, those seams endlessly sewn and ripped out and sewn again, the index finger needlepointed, thread all over the floor?
Margaret Atwood

Focus On

ESSAY TESTS

Mastering the essay test is just like running the perfect race. It takes previewing, pacing, and strategy.

When taking an essay test, have you ever felt that you were running a losing race against the clock? You can win this race, but to do so you need to be wise as well as swift. This mini-chapter will help you become "test wise."

Get a Jump on the Test—Five Steps for Success

1. Preview the test. Like a good runner, you need to know what lies ahead. Read the directions and look over the entire test. See how many questions need to be answered and how many points each one is worth. If some questions are optional, decide which ones you're going to answer.

2. Plan your time. To reach the finish line, you'll need to pace yourself. If you have forty minutes to answer two questions of equal worth, plan to spend twenty minutes on each, and stick to your plan! This way you can give each question equal attention.

3. Analyze the questions. Here is where you can make or break your race. Before you start to write an answer, determine exactly what the question is asking. Study the chart on the following page to see how key words can help you do this.

4. Make informal notes or an outline. Some students like to take notes in a modified outline form. Others find it helpful to quickly jot down words and phrases without worrying about logical order. Then they organize these notes by numbering them.

The following notes show how one student used the method of jotting down words to respond to the question "Discuss how transportation changed during the Industrial Revolution in Britain."

- railroads (the *Rocket*)   *3*
- new roads constructed   *1*
- canals built (3,000 miles)   *2*
- steamships

Continued on page 262.

Analyzing Essay Questions to Develop Writing Strategies

There are a number of different types of essay questions. Each type of question requires a different strategy. Note these different strategies as you read.

Question: *Analyze* the composition of the earth's atmosphere and the function of each element.
Strategy: When you analyze something, you break it down into its parts to explain how it works. To answer the question, you need to discuss the most important gases in the atmosphere one at a time, explaining how each is important to life on earth.

Question: *Compare and contrast* the goals of W.E.B. DuBois and Booker T. Washington.
Strategy: To compare and contrast you need to discuss both similarities and differences. Here, you could initially discuss what goals these two black leaders shared. Then you could discuss differences between their goals.

Question: *Discuss* how transportation changed during Great Britain's Industrial Revolution.
Strategy: When you are asked to discuss or describe, you need to make a general statement and support it with facts and details.

Question: *Explain* the origins of the Korean War.
Strategy: Most essay questions are asking you to explain something, even when *explain* isn't in the question. An explanation requires that you make a problem, relationship, process, or term clear and understandable. Use examples, facts, quotations, and reasons to help support your explanation. To review different methods for developing a clear explanation, see Chapter 9 and Chapter 10.

Question: *Identify and define* the various types of triangles.
Strategy: To identify or define, list the distinguishing characteristics of the subject. Here, your first sentence might define a triangle and tell how many types there are. The following sentences could define each type.

Question: *Interpret* the line "And miles to go before I sleep" in Robert Frost's poem, "Stopping by Woods on a Snowy Evening."
Strategy: To interpret something, you need to give your opinion of what it means and to support your opinion with reasons and details. Here, use specific details from the rest of the poem you are interpreting for support.

Question: *Summarize* the plot of the play *A Raisin in the Sun.*
Strategy: Summarizing requires that you present a condensed version of a story or process. Concentrate on the major events or main points of the topic, but be careful not to leave out too much. A summary must be complete. One part should lead to the next, so that your reader will be able to see how the story or process was presented.

Choose whatever organizing strategy works best for you. Your choice may vary depending on how much time you have or how well you know your subject. To review organizing strategies, see the discussion in the Writer's Handbook, pages 823–848.

5. Develop a thesis statement. A good thesis statement sets a goal and keeps you on track. A thesis is usually the opening sentence of an answer.

You can often restate the essay question to create a thesis statement. Here's a restatement of the question about the Industrial Revolution: "The Industrial Revolution changed transportation in Great Britain." That's not bad. But you can make it stronger by thinking about how transportation changed. The following thesis statement

gives the readers a better idea of what the essay will be about: "Great Britain's Industrial Revolution brought about improvements in nearly every area of transportation." Just from reading the thesis, the reader knows that the transportation improved and that the changes were wide-ranging.

Thesis statements can often help organize your answer. Study the following thesis statement: "Though W.E.B. DuBois and Booker T. Washington both wanted to improve the social and economic status of blacks, their goals were otherwise very different." Here, you might begin by briefly discussing the similarity between their goals. Then you could discuss the differences.

Use transitions between points to keep your reader on track.

Running the Good Race—Tips for the Writing Stage

1. Be guided by your thesis. All parts of your essay should be connected to your thesis. If you find your essay wandering from your thesis, go back to your outline.

2. Move smoothly from one idea to the next. Use transitions between points to keep your reader on track.

3. End with a strong conclusion. Don't just repeat your thesis. Study the last sentence of the sample student essay to see how you can restate without repeating.

Sample Student Essay

Study the following essay to see how it utilizes the notes, outline, and thesis statement described in this chapter.

Thesis   Great Britain's Industrial Revolution brought about improvements in nearly all areas of transportation.

First Main Point   In 1815, John McAdam devised a method of constructing smooth and durable roads. As a result, roads were constructed rapidly throughout Great Britain. Around this time,

Second Main Point   canal building became common, and by 1830 Great Britain had more than 3,000 miles of canals. The canals connected various water-ways and made it easier to ship materials and products by boat.

     In 1830, a locomotive called the Rocket pulled a string of rail cars from Liverpool to Manchester. Before long, railroads connected

Third Main Point   the nation. In the middle part of the century,

Fourth Main Point   steamships also became commonplace. They made it possible to transport all kinds of goods quickly and safely over great distances, across England and across the oceans of the world.

Conclusion   Improved roads, canals, steamships and railroads made it easier and faster to reach nearly all parts of Great Britain and many other parts of the world.

The Final Kick—Revising and Proofreading

As you revise your work, check your notes to make sure you've covered everything. Concentrate on content and organization first. Then tackle mechanics.

Try Your Skill

What follows is a poorly written answer to the question, "Describe the long-term effects of cigarette smoking." Using what you have learned, revise and finish the essay (you may need to do some research at the library). "Smoking is not good for you. Doctors say it is bad for your heart and lungs. Another bad thing about smoking is that it smells up clothes. And it's bad for people around you."

11
Writing Effective Persuasion

W hether we should always support our leaders' decisions and
actions without question or hold unswervingly to what
we believe is right and just is a topic of controversy.
What would you do? Would you follow a leader without question? Before responding, consider what might
happen if one of these climbers, attached to each other
by a length of rope, decided to head off in a direction
different from that of the leader.

In this chapter you will explore the many sides of
subjects such as this one as you gather information in
support of particular arguments. Then you will learn to
present your arguments persuasively.

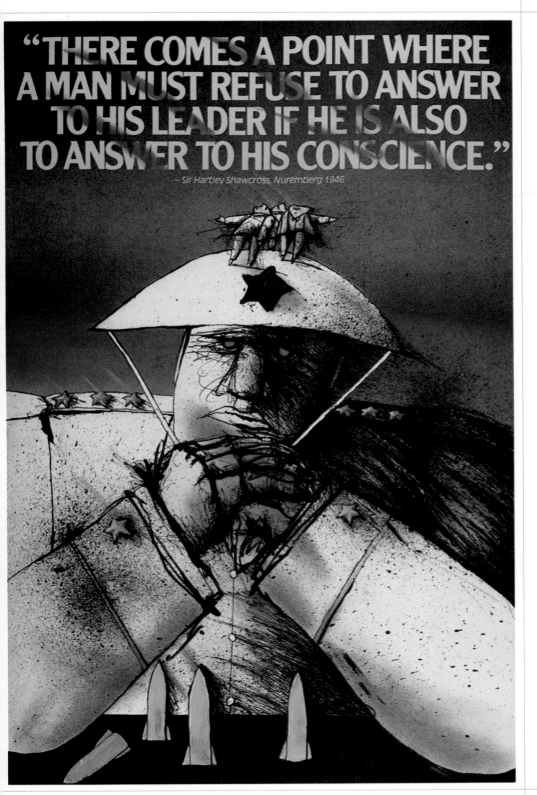

"THERE COMES A POINT WHERE A MAN MUST REFUSE TO ANSWER TO HIS LEADER IF HE IS ALSO TO ANSWER TO HIS CONSCIENCE."

— Sir Hartley Shawcross, Nuremberg 1946

Part 1

Analyzing Persuasive Writing

When you list reasons to be allowed to take a trip or you write a letter asking your friends to visit, you are attempting to persuade—to influence the opinions and behavior of others. Persuasive writing includes speeches, advertising copy, editorials, business proposals, and movie, book, or music reviews. The persuasive writer asks the audience to adopt a particular point of view and, often, to take a specific action. Effective persuasive writing supports a clearly stated position by presenting strong evidence and well-reasoned arguments.

The following models show two common uses of persuasive writing. One is a letter by a student. The other is by a professional writer. As you read, think about the techniques they use to persuade you.

Student Model

Dear Editors,

There has been a lot of talk about students not caring about the appearance of our school. You hear about trash in the hallways, about dirty walls covered with graffiti, about names carved on furniture. But if the school seemed more worth caring about, students would take better care of it. Most of the school building is very old. When was the last time it was painted? The hallways are dark because the walls are dingy and the lights don't work. If you drop something on the floor, it's lost. The newest part of our school is the gym. It is clean and bright, and for three years now students have kept it that way. New paint, lights, and furniture will make the difference. Let's try it.

Suzanna Montañez

Discussing the Model Answer the following questions.

1. What is Suzanna's position? How does she make it clear?
2. What arguments did Suzanna use to support her position? Which of the supporting arguments did you find most convincing?
3. Who is Suzanna's audience? How can you tell that she kept her audience in mind as she wrote?

Believe it or not, some runners feel the urge to hit the road the day after a marathon. But those who insist on running during the crucial postmarathon recovery period may be setting themselves up for injury or impaired performance. So say researchers at the Human Performance Lab in Muncie, Indiana, and the Work Physiology Lab at Ohio State University. . . .

Runners who rested completely (no running) recovered leg strength and work capacity more rapidly than those who jogged. . . .

To ensure your own speedy recovery, rest for at least a week after a marathon. . . . Light workouts, especially swimming, bicycling, and walking, are good substitutes. Such low-stress exercises loosen your muscles and may actually hasten your recovery.

From *Marathon: The Day After* edited by Kate Delhagen

Discussing the Model Discuss the following questions with your classmates.

1. How does this writer introduce her position?
2. What does she say in support of rest? Which argument did you find most effective? Why?
3. How do you know that this writer understands her audience?

Understanding Persuasive Writing

Effective persuasive writing always presents a clearly stated argument to a specific audience. Both of the models you just read were effective because the writers included a clearly stated position and supported it with appropriate, well-reasoned arguments. The student writer used her own observations, and the professional writer presented scientific evidence to support her view.

Persuasion in Literature A clear purpose, a sense of audience, and logical, well-organized arguments are features of all effective persuasive essays. As you read the following essay, notice how the writer presents his point of view. Watch for the kinds of supporting arguments he provides and the way in which he organizes those arguments. Finally, ask yourself who the writer is trying to reach.

Persuasion in Literature

from *We'll Never Conquer Space*
by Arthur C. Clarke

In the following excerpt, science-fiction writer Arthur C. Clarke uses logical arguments to suggest that the universe is not ours to conquer, as many people might like to think. The arguments he presents are based on facts. Clarke also presents images and creates unusual circumstances to catch the imagination of the reader. As you read this excerpt, ask yourself which arguments are most effective and why they are effective. Which images capture your imagination?

Thesis statement

*M*an will never conquer space. Such a statement may sound ludicrous, now that our rockets are already 100 million miles beyond the moon. . . . Yet it expresses a truth which our ancestors knew, one we have forgotten—and our descendants must learn again, in heartbreak and loneliness.

Our age is in many ways unique, full of events and phenomena which never occurred before and can never happen again. They distort our thinking, making us believe that what is true now will be true forever. . . . Because we have annihilated distance on this planet, we imagine that we can do it once again. The facts are far otherwise, and we will see them more clearly if we forget the present and turn our minds towards the past. . . .

First argument

The new stage that is opening up for the human drama will never shrink as the old one has done. We have abolished space here on the little earth; we can never abolish the space that yawns between the stars. Once again we are face to face with immensity and must accept its grandeur and terror, its inspiring possibilities and its dreadful restraints. From a world that has become too small, we are moving out into one that will be forever too large, whose frontiers will recede from us always more swiftly than we can reach out towards them. . . .

The marvelous telephone and television network that will soon enmesh the whole world, making all men neighbors, cannot be extended into space. It will never be possible to converse with anyone on another planet.

Do not misunderstand this statement. Even with today's radio equipment, the problem of sending speech to the other planets is almost trivial. But the messages will take minutes—sometimes hours—on their journey, because radio and light waves travel at the same limited speed of 186,000 miles a second.

*T*wenty years from now you will be able to listen to a friend on Mars, but the words you hear will have left his mouth at least three minutes earlier, and your reply will take a corresponding time to reach him. In such circumstances, an exchange of verbal messages is possible—but not a conversation.

Even in the case of the nearby moon, the $2\frac{1}{2}$-second time lag will be annoying. At distances of more than a million miles, it will be intolerable.

At this point, we will . . . deal with an obvious objection. Can we be sure that the velocity of light is indeed a limiting factor? So many "impassible" barriers have been shattered in the past; perhaps this one may go the way of all the others.

We will not argue the point, or give the reasons why scientists believe that light can never be outraced by any form of radiation or any material object. Instead, let us . . . take the most optimistic possible case and imagine that the speed of transporation may eventually become infinite.

P icture a time when, by the development of techniques as far beyond our present engineering as a transistor is beyond a stone axe, we can reach anywhere we please instantaneously, with no more effort than by dialing a number. This would indeed cut the universe down to size and reduce its physical immensity to nothingness. What would be left?

Everything that really matters. For the universe has two aspects—its scale, and its overwhelming, mind-numbing complexity. Having abolished the first, we are now face-to-face with the second.

What we must now try to visualize is not size, but quantity. Most people today are familiar with the simple notation which scientists use to describe large numbers; it consists merely of counting zeroes, so that a hundred becomes 10^2, a million, 10^6, a billion, 10^9 and so on. This useful trick enables us to work with quantities of any magnitude. . . .

Facts to weaken opposing argument

The number of other suns in our own galaxy (that is, the whirlpool of stars and cosmic dust of which our sun is an out-of-town member, lying in one of the remoter spiral arms) is estimated at about 10^{11}—or written in full, 100,000,000,000. Our present telescopes can observe something like 10 other galaxies, and they show no sign of thinning out even at the extreme limit of vision. . . .

Observation as evidence

Before such numbers, even spirits brave enough to face the challenge of the light-years must quail. The detailed examination of all the grains of sands on all the beaches of the world is a far smaller task than the exploration of the universe.

Thesis restated in conclusion

And so we return to our opening statement. Space can be mapped and crossed and occupied without definable limit; but it can never be conquered. When our race has reached its ultimate achievements, . . . even then we shall still be like ants crawling on the face of the earth.

Trying Out Persuasive Writing Now that you have read some examples of persuasive writing, think about some of the issues that interest you. For each issue, note your position and your reasoning. Organize your best reasons and write a persuasive composition of your own. After writing, decide which arguments were most convincing and why. The following pages will teach you more techniques for effective persuasive writing.

Part 2
Prewriting

You have learned that attempts to persuade others are a part of everyday experience. As such, they often occur casually in conversation, with little or no previous thought. Effective persuasion, however, requires careful thought and planning. It involves selecting a suitable topic, defining your position on a specific issue, understanding your audience, gathering and evaluating evidence to support your position, developing arguments, and organizing the composition.

Selecting a Persuasive Topic

The topic for a persuasive composition must contain an important and debatable issue—an issue about which people are likely to disagree. The first step in selecting a topic is to think of an issue you feel strongly about. When you have chosen a topic, check it against the following guidelines.

Guidelines for Choosing a Topic

1. Is the issue controversial? Is it arguable?
2. Is the topic broad enough to be interesting to my audience?
3. Is the issue narrow enough that I can find and use specific evidence?
4. Is the issue a matter of opinion, not personal preference?

You can find topics by noting your reaction to news items in the newspapers or on television. A topic might arise out of a situation at school, your workplace, or your community. You also might brainstorm topics with friends, or use clustering or other thinking strategies you learned in Chapter 2. Notice how Pat, a student writer, developed a topic from an issue that interested her.

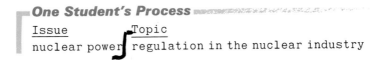

One Student's Process

```
Issue            Topic
nuclear power  regulation in the nuclear industry
```

Defining Your Position

Once you have chosen a suitable topic, define your position in a clear thesis statement that is interesting, debatable, and a matter of opinion. In a persuasive essay, the thesis statement is often a judgment or recommendation using the words *should, ought,* or *must.* A fact, such as "There are more than 300 nuclear plants in the world," is not a suitable thesis statement. Neither is a statement of personal preference, such as "I am horrified at the prospect of a nuclear plant meltdown." A debatable statement of opinion, such as Pat's, below, provides an effective thesis statement.

One Student's Process

Thesis Statement   Nuclear plants should be regulated by a committee of impartial scientists.

To test your thesis statement, try to write it in simple terms. If you cannot state it clearly, rethink your thesis or find a simpler issue. Then make sure the statement is debatable. If it is hard to think of counter-arguments, you probably have a poor issue and should search further. If the evidence you gather prompts you to modify your position, try it out. Your new position may be stronger than your original idea.

Determining Your Audience

To be effective, your persuasive strategy will depend on your understanding of your audience. If the topic you select is of little interest to the audience, your effort at persuasion will fail. Decide whether your audience is likely to agree or disagree with you. Perhaps it will be a mixed audience. In some cases it may be difficult or even impossible to anticipate an audience's reaction. But when clues are available, it is better to study them. The following guidelines will be useful in analyzing your audience.

Guidelines for Analyzing Your Audience

1. What are the interests and concerns of my audience?
2. What background does the audience have in regard to my topic?
3. Are there any sensitive topics that I should avoid?
4. Does my audience already agree with me, or do they disagree?

Gathering Evidence

Once you have chosen your topic and defined your position, you can begin gathering evidence. Most of your evidence will consist of facts, examples, anecdotes, observations, and authoritative opinions.

Facts Statements about things or circumstances that are known to be true or can be proven to be true are called **facts.** Statistics fall into this category. Facts are the most accepted forms of evidence.

Examples Statements about single instances that illustrate a general principle are known as **examples.**

Anecdotes Brief stories, usually illustrating a typical human situation, are called **anecdotes.** When anecdotes do not demonstrate a general truth, or when they illustrate a specific fact, they are thought to be weak evidence.

Observations Accounts of events that one has actually witnessed or reports of such accounts made by others are known as **observations.** First-hand observations can be very effective evidence.

Authoritative Opinions Points of view expressed by persons thought to have special knowledge of the topic at hand are called **authoritative opinions.**

Evaluating Evidence

Most evidence is presented in the form of factual statements. But facts can be twisted and evidence can be stacked to address only one point of view. To be sure that your evidence is valid, check for the following qualities.

Make sure your facts are **up-to-date.** Particularly in scientific areas or news-related fields, be certain that your facts are current. An encyclopedia published in 1965 may not be a good source.

Make sure that statements are **unbiased.** Take into account the possible motives or special interests of your sources. Airlines, for example, are likely to assert that air travel is extremely safe. They may be correct, but you will want to check their facts before relying on their claims.

Make sure your evidence is **consistent.** Consult more than one source for important pieces of evidence. When sources give contradictory evidence, check the reliability of each source.

Make sure the evidence is **complete.** No argument can be ultimately effective if it does not take objections into account.

Gather many kinds of evidence and evaluate them to determine the strength of your position. Pat filled out the following worksheet for her report. It lists the kinds of evidence she would need to support her argument that scientists should regulate the use of nuclear power.

One Student's Process

Persuasive Writing Worksheet

Kind of Evidence	Supporting Material
Fact	There are over 300 nuclear plants in the world.
Authoritative opinion	Einstein said the danger of nuclear power was almost more than its promise.
Observation	New discoveries are rarely kept secret.
Fact	Exposure to radiation can cause radiation sickness.
Example	The Chernobyl accident showed the potential for disaster.
Anecdote	Accidents at Chernobyl and Three Mile Island came from non-nuclear tasks.

Writing Activities Prewriting

A Imagine that you have chosen as a persuasive topic the dietary habits of teenagers. You have noticed concern about the soft drinks teenagers consume and have seen statements in the media and elsewhere promoting milk as a healthier beverage. You want to argue that milk is a beverage for infants, not adults. Write a paragraph analyzing the audience you will address.

B *Writing in Process* Use the prewriting skills you have learned to select a topic and choose an issue for a persuasive composition. Then gather evidence that supports your position, identify an audience, and draft a thesis statement with an audience in mind. Save your work for a later activity.

Part 3

Preparing Your Arguments

As you develop a thesis statement and gather supporting evidence, you are, in effect, preparing your case. Your readers will decide the merits of your position based on the quality of your evidence and the effectiveness of your arguments—that is, the language you use and the logic you apply. You have put together your evidence; now you can begin devising strategies for presenting it.

Precise Language

Effective persuasion involves saying exactly what you mean. Lack of precision can weaken your arguments and give the impression that you do not have facts to support your viewpoint. In fact, vague statements and undefined terms may signal that either your thoughts are unclear or your evidence is incomplete.

It also is a good idea to avoid using vague judgment words such as *good, bad, right,* and *wrong* unless you can defend your judgment with logical arguments. For example, imagine that you and a friend disagree on the usefulness of a new bowling alley. If you simply said your friend was wrong, your argument would not be very convincing. It would be more effective to discuss specifically which of your friend's facts were incorrect.

Precision in fiber-optics.

Denotation and Connotation One way to ensure precision in your writing is to choose words for both their *denotative* and *connotative* meanings. The denotative meaning of a word is generally limited to its dictionary definition. However, words often have connotative meanings that go beyond the dictionary definition. Consider the underlined words in the following sentences.

> Fleming *discovered* the miracle of penicillin.
> Fleming *stumbled on* the miracle of penicillin.

Both sentences tell you that Fleming found penicillin, but only one casts Fleming as an active participant in the process. The other implies that he was simply lucky. The **denotations** of the two words are similar, but their **connotations** are sharply different.

Loaded Language

Language that carries a heavy emotional charge is called *loaded language*. Such language usually contains words with strong positive or negative connotations. Read this paragraph twice, once using the first word in each pair, and again using the second word.

> You have asked for my views on the *(creature/man)* named Bumbling. He has been a *(clinging/faithful)* *(nuisance/aide)* here for *(ages/years)*. If you can find a *(crevice/position)* for him in the *(woodwork/structure)* of your *(sweatshop/company)*, I will be *(relieved/pleased)*.

The words in each pair have very strong—and very different— connotations. They are examples of loaded language. Which word you choose will determine the meaning of the sentence. Loaded language can be a useful tool in persuading your audience.

Take care, however, to back up emotional appeals in your composition with strong supporting evidence and arguments. Simply using loaded language is unfair. In addition, purely emotional appeals are almost always seen as substitutes for sound reasoning.

Logical Fallacies

No matter how many arguments you put forth or how precisely you word them, they will not withstand scrutiny unless they are based on sound reasoning. You have already learned that arguments can be built unfairly by stacking the evidence. Most other errors in reasoning are the result of logical fallacies. Avoid the following fallacies as you gather evidence and build arguments.

Circular Reasoning An attempt to support a statement by simply repeating the statement in different or stronger terms is known as circular reasoning. Read this statement: "Richardson is the most successful mayor the town has ever had, because he's the best mayor in our history." The second part of the sentence offers no evidence. It simply repeats the claim that was already presented. Don't think that using the word *because* in an argument automatically gives you a reason; make certain you provide real support for your statement.

Evading Issues If you are unwilling to confront issues closely related to the main topic of your persuasive composition, you may be evading issues. For example, you might want to argue that we should help third world nations develop nuclear technology. In order to argue convincingly, you would need to address the concern that nations could use the technology to create nuclear weapons. If you avoid that issue, you weaken your argument.

False Analogy Analogies are helpful when you want to explain something that is unfamiliar in familiar terms. Make sure the things you compare have essential features in common, however. It would be false, for example, to argue that, "Clogged arteries require surgery to clear them; our clogged highways require equally drastic measures." The image may be effective, but it does not take the place of sound facts or statistics.

Overgeneralization Generalizations are often useful in persuasion if there is evidence to support them. An example might be, "In times of crisis, the American people usually support the President." This statement is probably acceptable because it can be shown by public opinion polls to be true. Beware of generalizations that are too broad to be valid, however. The statement, "In times of crisis, every American supports the President," is an overgeneralization. Because every American cannot be contacted and surveyed, the statement cannot be proved.

Stereotyping The error of attributing to an individual, for purposes of argument, some characteristic that is said to be true of a group is stereotyping. Consider the following statement: "People who live in big cities are too busy making and spending money to care about each other." This statement is an example of stereotyping. Although it has dramatic appeal, proving that it is true with respect to any individual would be difficult. To claim that it is true of most or all individuals who live in cities is absurd.

Name-calling Making unsupported assumptions about people is name-calling, a fallacy similar to stereotyping. Name-calling directs attention to a person, rather than the person's ideas about an issue. Someone who claims that "Harry can't know anything about cooking because he's a truck driver" is committing the error of name-calling.

Bandwagon/Snob Appeal In old-time campaigns, politicians used to travel on bandwagons. They would urge citizens to "jump on the bandwagon"—or join the crowd—and vote for them. Advertisers who urge you to "Buy the brand that's number 1" are using bandwagon appeal. If they imply that the product is for a special few, they are using a form of bandwagon appeal called *snob appeal*.

Oversimplification It is always necessary to simplify issues and evidence to some extent as you build arguments in a persuasive essay. Yet, if you oversimplify, you destroy your credibility. Take care that when you simplify your arguments, you do not eliminate important steps in your reasoning. Oversimplification usually takes one of several different forms.

One kind of oversimplification is the **either/or fallacy.** This fallacy occurs when you assert that there are only two alternatives in a given situation. For example, the claim, "If banks didn't pay interest on savings, no one would save money" leaves out the possibility that people would save outside of the banks, or use banks simply because banks are insured.

The **cause-effect fallacy** is the result of assuming that when one event follows another, a cause-effect relationship exists between the two events. For example, if you found that two of your classmates had been sick shortly after science class, you might argue that science class was making students ill. Without investigating further, you might never find out that both students had been exposed to mumps.

False cause is a similar error in which a writer states reasons for an event or circumstance, even though the reasons given have no basis in fact. For instance, the statement, "Everyone forgets things, because there is only so much room for information in the brain" is an example of false cause.

Only reason is a form of oversimplification in which a writer states or implies that there was only one reason for an event, when there were probably many. An example might be, "The American Revolution was a revolt against the tax Great Britain put on imported tea."

Writing Activities *Identifying Fallacies*

A Examine each of the following statements. What kind of fallacy is illustrated in each statement? Which of the statements contain loaded words? Identify the fallacy in each statement and rewrite the argument so that it is logical.

1. Jack, don't take geometry; all artists hate subjects like math.
2. Please donate to the zoo's adopt-an-animal fund. Almost everyone in your class has contributed.
3. London has an unpleasant climate; it is always foggy there.
4. I really don't think we should plan to barbeque. As soon as we plan to cook out, it rains.
5. We have to see this movie because it's a movie we can't miss.
6. Please let me work on the school paper this year. If you don't, my career as a journalist will never get off the ground.
7. Don't let Sheri go to the amusement park; she's a coward.
8. My sister Maureen can't help you any more than a dog can teach a cat how to bark.

B Read the news section of your local paper or a major city's newspaper. Choose two news articles and two editorials about important issues to study in depth.

As you study the articles, find examples of loaded language and the fallacies you have studied in this chapter. Write several paragraphs discussing the fallacies you found and the ways in which they were employed.

Part 4
Drafting a Persuasive Composition

By the time you begin the first draft of your persuasive composition, much of the work is already behind you. Writing the first draft is largely a matter of assembling the prewriting materials into an effective form. Remember that the first draft is merely a rough draft. At this point, you are exploring ideas and methods. It is more important to get ideas onto paper than to write a perfect composition on the first try.

Organizing the Composition

The first step in drafting your persuasive composition is to organize your arguments for maximum impact on your audience. The order in which you present your arguments will depend partly on the strength of the arguments, and partly on your assessment of the audience. Does the audience already agree with you about the issue? Will they be skeptical? Pat decided that her audience would be reasonably open to her ideas, so she decided to begin with her weakest arguments and build to her strongest, most convincing points. The following chart shows five basic strategies for organizing a persuasive composition.

Methods of Organizing Arguments

Type of Audience	Method of Organization
Neutral	Weakest to strongest
Agreeable	Weakest to strongest
Opinion unknown	Strongest to weakest arguments, then restate strongest
Opinion well-known	Argument easiest to agree with, followed by difficult arguments
Hostile	Strongest arguments, then weaknesses of opposing views, then add remaining arguments, then restate strong arguments
	or
	Attack weaknesses of opposing views, then present weakest arguments, then stronger arguments

Presenting Your Arguments

Organizing your first draft will give you an overview of your composition. Your ideas may fit together nicely, or you may question the strength of your position and return to the prewriting stage.

Style You have already learned to avoid the use of loaded language. You also can make decisions about language style. Decide whether it would be more effective to reach your audience through a formal address or a more conversational style of language.

Introduction Your introduction will contain your thesis statement. Make sure that you state your thesis clearly and capture the attention of your readers. Your thesis should tell the audience what, if any, action you want them to take. You might want to create a sense of urgency about the issue as well as show a sharp contrast between your views and the views of others. Pat used these techniques to make her introduction captivating and to set the tone of her composition.

One Student's Process

Concrete image to capture attention

Clear thesis statement

> Nuclear power is like a gift given by a master practical joker. It is the source of tremendous potential. If we can find a way to use it safely, it can provide clean, inexpensive energy for centuries. Yet, it also contains more potential for disaster than any other current technology. For these reasons, we need to make sure that the use of nuclear power is supervised by knowledgeable, impartial, professionals. We should convene an international committee of scientists to regulate nuclear plants throughout the world.

Body The body of your composition should be a well-organized presentation of logical arguments supported by evidence. You have learned how to judge evidence and organize arguments. Also try to make the transitions between paragraphs smooth so that the audience can follow your reasoning.

Conclusion An effective conclusion summarizes your main arguments and restates your thesis. It may also repeat your request for action from the audience. Make sure that you do not add new information in your conclusion. It will muddy your point and distract the audience.

Writing Activities Drafting Your Composition

A Imagine that a local developer has just completed plans to build a concert stadium in an abandoned warehouse. She already has bought the property, which is zoned for industrial or commercial use. She did not reveal her plans for the property until recently, when blueprints were completed. Her plans have created controversy. Some people see them as early steps in the revitalization of a neighborhood. Others see it as a failure to support local industry and as a future source of traffic congestion. Choose your position on the issue and write a thesis statement. List the kinds of evidence you will need to support your position and then outline the order in which you would present your arguments.

B Look at the image at the bottom of this page. Discuss the image with your classmates, using the brainstorming techniques you learned in this chapter to help you think of a controversial issue. When you and your classmates have decided on an issue, write a clear, arguable thesis statement. Then discuss the evidence you would need in order to develop strong arguments. With your classmates, discuss ways to organize the composition.

C *Writing in Process* Develop logical arguments from the evidence you gathered in Part 2. Make sure your arguments support the thesis statement you wrote. Pay special attention to style and to the organization of your composition's introduction, body, and conclusion.

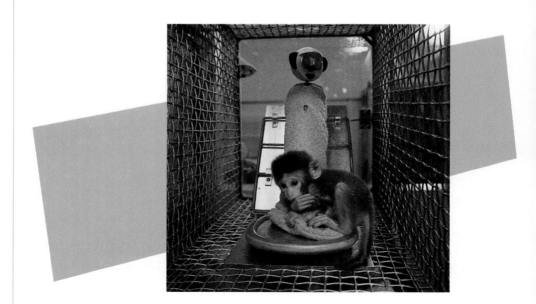

Part 5
Revising and Proofreading

No matter how much planning you did in the prewriting stage, your writing may take you in unexpected directions. You should probably put your first draft aside after you write it, so when you are ready for revision, you will have a clear perspective. Then read your first draft to yourself at least three times: once for logic, once for content and organization, and once for language and mechanics. Then get a new perspective by asking a classmate to act as a peer evaluator. Use your peer evaluator's comments to help you revise your draft.

The checklist below will help you focus on critical areas while you are revising.

Revision Checklist: Persuasive Writing

Purpose
1. What is your purpose in writing the composition? Does your composition accomplish its purpose?
2. Is your position arguable? Is it clearly defined in a supportable thesis statement?
3. Are your facts accurate and persuasive? Are your arguments logical?

Organization
1. Have you organized your arguments in a logical sequence?
2. Does the organization take into account your understanding of the audience?
3. Are your transitions clear?

Development
1. Have you stated your thesis in the introduction and restated it in the conclusion?
2. Have you consistently adopted an appropriate language style in your writing?
3. Have you presented enough solid evidence and logical arguments to persuade your audience?
4. Have you chosen strong, convincing language without using loaded language and logical fallacies?
5. Is your writing clear and grammatically correct?

Note how Pat used the comments of a peer evaluator, along with her own thoughts and comments, in revising a part of her first draft.

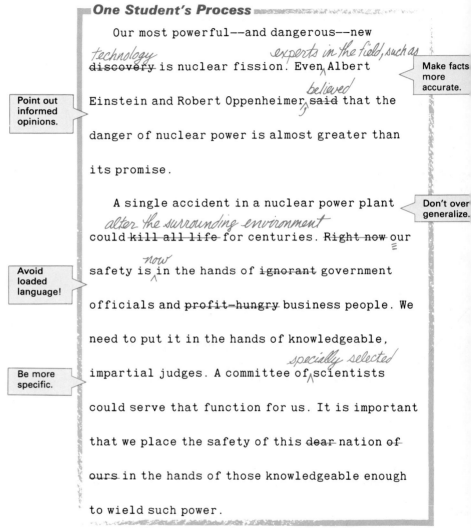

One Student's Process

Our most powerful--and dangerous--new

~~discovery~~ *technology* is nuclear fission. Even~~,~~ Albert *experts in the field, such as*

> Make facts more accurate.

Einstein and Robert Oppenheimer~~,~~ ~~said~~ *believed* that the

> Point out informed opinions.

danger of nuclear power is almost greater than

its promise.

A single accident in a nuclear power plant

> Don't over generalize.

could ~~kill all life~~ *alter the surrounding environment* for centuries. ~~Right now~~ our

safety is *now* in the hands of ~~ignorant~~ government

> Avoid loaded language!

officials and ~~profit-hungry~~ business people. We

need to put it in the hands of knowledgeable,

impartial judges. A committee of *specially selected* scientists

> Be more specific.

could serve that function for us. It is important

that we place the safety of this ~~dear~~ nation ~~of~~

~~ours~~ in the hands of those knowledgeable enough

to wield such power.

Writing Activities Revising

A Exchange persuasive compositions from Part 4 with a classmate. To comment on your classmate's composition, use the Revision Checklist on page 283. Next, describe what you like best about the ideas, organization, and language. Finally, suggest revisions.

B *Writing in Process* Revise your own first draft from Part 4, based on your peer evaluator's comments, the Revision Checklist, and the knowledge you gained in this part. Then proofread it.

Part 6

Uses of Persuasive Writing

You have seen that attempts to influence the opinions and behavior of others occur not only in conversation, but may appear in written forms of communication as well. In fact, whenever you write, you can use persuasive techniques to get your audience to see your subject from your perspective. The skills you have learned can be applied in many areas of your life, and eventually in your work. The following chart shows the ways persuasive writing can be used in everyday life.

Uses of Persuasive Writing

Type	Purpose	Example
Editorials	Express views of newspaper management	Article analyzing various pollution regulations
Advertisements	Persuade audience to buy product or service	Television commercial for breakfast food
Letters	Persuade the reader to act in your favor	Recommendation for an apprenticeship
Articles	Influence opinions and actions	Music review rating the top recordings of the year
Speeches	Influence political views or actions	Anti-pollution fund-raising speech

Two models of professional persuasive writing are given on the following page. The first is from an article about treasure hunters in the oceans. The second is part of an article about recycling trash. It includes solutions suggested by both interest groups and government institutions. Read both models and note the kinds of arguments and the organization each writer used. Think about the reasons why the authors of each piece chose to write in the style they did.

If an undisciplined treasure hunter were allowed to work a wreck like the *Fowey*, Fischer warns, it could only end in disaster. Huge holes would be blasted in the sand by large formidable-looking tubes called "mail-boxes." These devices direct the wash from a boat's propellers toward the bottom, and in 30 minutes can cut through about five feet of sand. The *Fowey*'s timbers would be scattered, artifacts would be collected without any particular relationship to each other or where they lay in the hull, so that the characteristics of the vessel would be jumbled and incomprehensible. The swords would be sold, the cannons left to rust in obscure marinas, and the non-negotiables swept aside in search of the mother lode. No marine archaeologist can endorse such methods.

From "Ancient Shipwrecks" by Philip Trupp

So what's to be done with the mountains of trash? Barry Commoner and others favor "a combination of several schemes," Bass explains in *Mother Jones*. "Composting food and yard waste; reusing construction waste as fill material, in roadbeds, for example . . . and expanding household recycling. . . ."

Such a solution is also endorsed by the Environmental Planning Lobby . . . "It takes far longer—and more money—to build an incinerator than it does to implement an integrated recycling and separation program."

From "Garbage Is a Burning Issue" by Mordecai Spektor

Writing Activities Using Persuasive Writing

A Review the categories and examples of persuasive writing listed in the chart on page 285. Think of additional categories of persuasive writing and find several examples of each category. Compare the examples you have thought of with those of your classmates and discuss them.

B Choose one of the categories from the chart on page 285. Brainstorm for a topic. Then develop a debatable thesis statement. After gathering and organizing your evidence, write, revise, and proofread your persuasive composition.

Guidelines: *Persuasive Writing*

Persuasive writing is writing that attempts to influence the opinions—and perhaps the actions—of others. Techniques for writing effective persuasive essays are summarized here.

Prewriting

- Develop a list of possible topics based on conversations, gleanings from television, newspapers, or other news sources, and your own thoughts concerning current events. *(See page 271.)*
- Choose an issue that interests you. Make sure it is an issue about which different people are likely to disagree. *(See page 271.)*
- Define your position on the issue in a logical, clearly worded thesis statement. *(See page 272.)*
- Evaluate your audience's interests and point of view. *(See page 272.)*
- Gather evidence to support your position. Evaluate each piece of evidence and label it as fact, example, anecdote, observation, or authoritative opinion. *(See pages 273–274.)*
- Develop your arguments on the basis of the evidence you have gathered, and check them for fallacies, excessive appeals to emotion, and loaded words. *(See pages 275–279.)*

Drafting

- Organize your arguments effectively. *(See pages 272, 280–281.)*
- Write a strong opening paragraph containing your thesis statement. Include a call to action, if you like. *(See pages 272, 281.)*
- Write the body of the composition, making sure that transitions are smooth and that your reasoning can easily be followed. *(See page 281.)*
- Write a concluding paragraph that summarizes your position and restates your thesis. Be sure to express clearly what action (if any) you would like the audience to take. *(See page 281.)*

Revising and Proofreading

- Give your composition three readings—once each for purpose, organization, and development. When possible, show your composition to a peer evaluator. *(See pages 283–284.)*
- Revise and proofread based on your own judgment and your evaluator's comments. *(See pages 283–284.)*

Chapter 11
Application and Review

You have learned to compose a debatable thesis statement and plan and write a variety of persuasive essays. Now use your skills to complete one or more of the following activities. Activity A is highly structured; Activities B and C offer you more choice.

A Writing a Proposal Imagine that you are part of a committee evaluating a proposal for a new program in which students would receive school credit for a half-day of community service each week. Some committee members want participation in the program to be voluntary. Other committee members want all students to be required to participate.

Prewriting Brainstorm about the issue described above. What kinds of experiences contribute to a well-rounded education? What would be the benefits of such a program for the individual? for the community? What are the drawbacks? Choose a position and develop arguments to support it. Then organize your arguments to appeal to those most likely to disagree with you.

Drafting Using your outline, write a first draft. Try to use strong arguments and specific examples. Take care to avoid using logical fallacies or loaded language.

Revising Use the Revision Checklist on page 283 to help you revise your first draft. Exchange your essay with a peer evaluator and consider his or her comments. After revising, proofread (using the Proofreading Checklist) and prepare a final copy to present to the committee.

B Writing a Review Use the guidelines below to plan and write a review of a popular magazine.

Prewriting Choose a magazine. Note in detail the things you like and dislike about the subject matter and style of the magazine, and why you think your readers should or should not subscribe. Organize your notes to help you appeal to a specific audience.

Drafting and Revising Use your notes to write a first draft. Try to tailor your arguments to your audience. Then revise your draft and share it with someone.

c *Starting Points for Writing*   What are you reactions to the images and the quotes below? List your strongest feelings and any beliefs or opinions you hold that the images and quotes bring to mind.

All you need is love.

John Lennon

Americans are all too soft. I am not soft. It is better to be hard, so that you can know what to do.

Pearl S. Buck

Anxiety is the dizziness of freedom.

Søren Kierkegaard

12

Writing About
Literature: Poetry

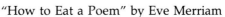

Don't be polite.
Bite in.
Pick it up with your fingers and lick the juice that
   may run down your chin.
It is ready and ripe now, whenever you are.

You do not need a knife or fork or spoon
or plate or napkin or tablecloth.

For there is no core
or stem
or rind
or pit
or seed
or skin
to throw away.

"How to Eat a Poem" by Eve Merriam

*C*an you taste the sweetness of these peaches, smell their ripeness, feel their texture as you take a bite?

That's what a poem gives you—a rich, multisensory experience to swallow whole. Everything counts in a poem—the sound, the meaning, the arrangement of the words. In this chapter you will learn to analyze and write about how these elements work together to make a poem come alive.

Part 1

The Process of Poetry Analysis

In this chapter, you will learn how to analyze a piece of literature. Although here you will focus on the analysis of poetry, the following procedure can be used with any form of literature:

1. Read the text closely.
2. Analyze the elements.
3. Organize and draft your thoughts and ideas.

Each form of literature—short story, novel, play, or poem—has certain elements that can be identified and studied. In the section that follows, you will examine the elements of poetry.

The Elements of Poetry

The basic elements of poetry include speaker, content, theme, shape and form, mood, figurative language, and sound effects. You may base your analysis upon one or more of these elements.

Speaker The poem's speaker is the person who is addressing the reader. Sometimes the speaker is the poet, who addresses the reader directly:

> My long two-pointed ladder's sticking through a tree
> Toward heaven still,
> And there's a barrel that I didn't fill.
>
> From "After Apple-Picking" by Robert Frost

The poet may also take on another personality or role, as in these lines:

> Yet when a Boy, and Barefoot—I more than once at Noon
> Have passed, I thought, a Whip lash
> Upbraiding in the Sun.
>
> From "A Narrow Fellow in the Grass" by Emily Dickinson

The poet reveals the identity of the speaker in various ways. Choice of words, focus of attention, and attitudes will indicate the age, perspective, and identity of the speaker. Once you have identified the speaker, try to understand the speaker's feelings regarding the poem's subject. This will give you a greater understanding of the poem's message.

Content To understand the content of the poem, first ask yourself "What happens in this poem?" The poem may be a narrative that tells a story as in "The Midnight Ride of Paul Revere," or the poem may express thoughts and feelings without telling a story, as in these lines:

> Three moves in six months and I remain
> the same
> Two homes made two friends
> The third leaves me with myself again.
> (We hardly speak.)
> Here I am with tame ducks
> and my neighbors' boats
> only this electric heat
> against the April damp
> I have a friend named Frank—
> The only one who ever dares to call
> and ask me, "How's your soul?"
>
> From "Three Moves" by John Logan

Theme The theme of a poem is the meaning of the poem—the main idea the poet is trying to communicate. The theme may be stated directly, or it may be implied. Learn how to identify an implied theme by paying attention to what is said and how it is expressed. The theme in the poem above by John Logan is that moving from place to place causes loneliness.

Shape and Form Because a poet has more freedom than a novelist, short-story teller, or dramatist, the actual shape and form of poems can vary dramatically from poem to poem.

Basically, you will encounter two forms: structured and free verse. Structured poetry has predictable patterns of rhyme, rhythm, line length, and stanza construction. Note the easy, regular, predictable rhythm of these four lines:

> I wish I could walk for a day and a night,
> And find me at dawn in a desolate place
> With never the rut of a road in sight,
> Nor the roof of a house, nor the eyes of a face.
>
> From "Departure" by Edna St. Vincent Millay

In free verse, the poet experiments with the form of the poem. The rhythm, number of syllables per line, and stanza construction do not follow a pattern. Punctuation, capitalization, and correct spelling may be abandoned. Even the arrangement of the words on the page may suggest the poem's theme or mood, as in the following lines:

> in Just-
> spring   when the world is mud-
> luscious the little
> lame balloonman
> whistles   far   and wee
> and eddieandbill come
> running from marbles and
> piracies and it's
> spring
> when the world is puddle-wonderful
>
> From "in Just-" by e.e. cummings

Mood The mood of a poem is the feeling that the poet creates and that the reader senses through the poet's choice of words, rhythm, rhyme, style, and structure. Poems may express many moods—humorous, sarcastic, joyous, angry, or solemn.

Figurative Language To create vivid images, a poet often uses figurative language. Such language presents literal facts in an unusual or distinctive way. A poet chooses words to create images the reader can visualize clearly. Notice the imagery in the following lines:

> It was beginning winter,
> The light moved slowly over the frozen field,
> Over the dry seed-crowns,
> The beautiful surviving bones
> Swinging in the wind.
>
> From "The Lost Son" by Theodore Roethke

Metaphor, simile, and personification are the most common examples of figurative language.

Metaphor A metaphor is an implied comparison of two things that are usually considered to be dissimilar. The comparison may provide deeper understanding by surprising the reader with similarities.

Hold fast to dreams
For if dreams die
Life is a broken-winged bird
That cannot fly.

From "Dreams" by Langston Hughes

Through the use of metaphor in the lines above, the poet suggests that life without dreams, like a broken-winged bird, is tragic.

Simile A simile is also a comparison of presumably unlike things, but it uses the words *like* or *as*. Notice how the poet uses simile to compare a mighty bird to the awesome power of nature in the following lines.

The wrinkled sea beneath him crawls;
He watches from his mountain walls,
And like a thunderbolt he falls.

From "The Eagle" by Alfred, Lord Tennyson

Often a simile can make a description more vivid. For example: "Like delicate ostrich feathers, frost covered the windowpane."

Personification Another figure of speech is personification, in which an animal, thing, or idea is given human characteristics. A cat, for example, may tell a lost little boy the way home. Personification may also be used in a short phrase such as "temperamental elevator."

What is the poet personifying in the following poem?

> I like to see it lap the Miles—
> And lick the Valleys up—
> And stop to feed itself at Tanks—
>
> From "I Like to See It Lap the Miles" by Emily Dickinson

If you guessed "a train," you guessed correctly.

Sound Effects A poet may also use sound effects to help convey the poem's message. The chart below explores various sound-effect devices used in Edgar Allan Poe's "The Bells."

Sound-Effect Devices

Device	Definition	Example
Repetition	Repeated words and phrases	From the bells, bells, bells, bells, Bells, bells, bells—
Rhyme	Repeated sounds, usually at the end of a line	How it swells! How it dwells On the Future!—how it tells Of the rapture that impels
Rhythm	Pattern of stressed and un-stressed syllables	While the stars that oversprinkle All the heavens, seem to twinkle With a crystalline delight; Keeping time, time, time, In a sort of Runic rhyme,
Onomato-poeia	Using a word or phrase to imitate a sound	From the jingling and the tinkling of the bells.
Alliteration	Repeating begin-ning consonant sounds	What a tale of terror, now, their turbulency tells!
Consonance	Repeating inter-nal consonant sounds	In a clamorous appealing to the mercy of the fire,
Assonance	Repeating vowel sounds	From the molten-golden notes,

Writing Activities Selecting Poems

A Get together with your classmates in small groups and gather several poems that are between ten and forty lines in length; everyone in your group should be familiar with each poem. Discuss the elements of poetry you have just studied as they relate to these poems and work together to identify speaker, content, theme, structure, mood, figurative language, and sound effects in each poem.

B *Writing in Process* Review the poems you discussed in Activity A. Select one or two poems from this activity or from another source to be the subject of an analysis. If you wish, you can choose two poems that focus on a similar topic, theme, or event.

Part 2
Analyzing Poetry

There are several ways to focus your analysis of a poem or poems. If you are studying a single poem, you can analyze one or more elements, such as the speaker, theme, structure, mood, figurative language, or sound effects. If you are studying two poems, you might compare these elements as they are used in the two poems.

The first step in any analysis is to read carefully and to think about what you are analyzing. You might use the following questions to help you focus your analysis: Who is speaking? Is anything happening in the poem or are personal feelings or emotions being revealed? What point is the poet trying to make? Are there predictable patterns of rhyme, rhythm, line length, and stanza construction? What is the mood of the poem? How does the poet use figurative language? Are sound effects an important element of the poem? If so, what devices does the poet use to create these sound effects?

After answering the questions above, you may find, for example, that the poem you have chosen lends itself to an analysis of figurative language. If you are studying two poems, you may find that answers to the above questions suggest a comparison of the use of rhyme and rhythm in the two poems.

On the following pages, you will find two poems: "Ex-Basketball Player" by John Updike and "To an Athlete Dying Young" by A. E. Housman. As you read each poem, try to answer the questions discussed above.

Ex-Basketball Player

Pearl Avenue runs past the high-school lot,
Bends with the trolley tracks, and stops, cut off
Before it has a chance to go two blocks,
At Colonel McComsky Plaza. Berth's Garage
Is on the corner facing west, and there,
Most days, you'll find Flick Webb, who helps Berth out.

Flick stands tall among the idiot pumps—
Five on a side, the old bubble-head style,
Their rubber elbows hanging loose and low.
One's nostrils are two S's, and his eyes
An E and O. And one is squat, without
A head at all—more of a football type.

Once Flick played for the high-school team, the Wizards.
He was good: in fact, the best. In '46
He bucketed three hundred ninety points,
A county record still. The ball loved Flick.
I saw him rack up thirty-eight or forty
In one home game. His hands were like wild birds.

He never learned a trade, he just sells gas,
Checks oil, and changes flats. Once in a while,
As a gag he dribbles an inner tube,
But most of us remember anyway.
His hands are fine and nervous on the lug wrench.
It makes no difference to the lug wrench, though.

Off work, he hangs around Mae's Luncheonette.
Grease-grey and kind of coiled, he plays pinball,
Sips lemon cokes, and smokes those thin cigars;
Flick seldom speaks to Mae, just sits and nods
Beyond her face towards bright applauding tiers
Of Necco Wafers, Nibs, and Juju Beads.

John Updike

To an Athlete Dying Young

The time you won your town the race
We chaired you through the market-place;
Man and boy stood cheering by,
And home we brought you shoulder-high.

Today, the road all runners come,
Shoulder-high we bring you home,
And set you at your threshold down,
Townsman of a stiller town.

Smart lad, to slip betimes away
From fields where glory does not stay
And early though the laurel grows
It withers quicker than the rose.

Eyes the shady night has shut
Cannot see the record cut,
And silence sounds no worse than cheers
After earth has stopped the ears:

Now you will not swell the rout
Of lads that wore their honors out,
Runners whom renown outran
And the name died before the man.

So set before its echoes fade,
The fleet foot on the sill of shade,
And hold to the low lintel up
The still-defended challenge cup.

And round that early-laureled head
Will flock to gaze the strengthless dead,
And find unwithered on its curls
The garland briefer than a girl's.

                              A. E. Housman

Prewriting

To organize your thinking in the preparation of a poetry analysis, it is helpful to break the process down into a series of logical steps. The first step is a close reading of the poem. Next, decide on a focus for your paper either by brainstorming with others or by asking yourself questions. Once you have identified a focus, you should formulate a thesis statement—the main point of your poetry analysis.

Close Reading Close reading is a technique or strategy that helps you begin your analysis of a poem and its elements. This analysis, ideally, will lead you to a thorough understanding of the poet's technique and the poem's meaning. Use the following guidelines in a close reading of a poem.

Guidelines for Close Reading

1. Read the poem once, slowly.
2. Read the poem again—more slowly than before!
3. Read the poem aloud carefully and listen to the sound of the words as you read.
4. Consult a reliable source such as a dictionary to help you understand the precise meaning of any unfamiliar words, phrases, or idiomatic expressions.
5. Pay attention to key words. Keep in mind that a very familiar word may be used in an unusual way. Be sure you understand both the denotation and the connotation of key words.
6. Figurative language may be difficult to interpret. Be sure you can translate each figurative expression into a meaningful idea.
7. Break the poem down into sections and try to create a summary statement for each section.
8. Notice which methods the poet uses in the poem. How do these methods appeal to your senses or heighten your understanding of the poem?
9. Decide if the structure and the form of the poem are important elements.
10. Notice how the rhyme scheme and the rhythm contribute to the impact of poem.
11. Try to formulate the main idea of the poem. Write it in one or two sentences.

Finding a Focus

In order to find a focus for your analysis of a poem, you have to explore the poem carefully and extensively. Make notes about the elements you discovered during the close reading process. Then think about the effect or meaning of each element as well as why the poet may have chosen it.

Brainstorming Group brainstorming is a helpful technique for uncovering the significance of various elements in a poem. Refer back to the thinking strategies that were introduced in Chapter 2. Graphic organizers can also be very useful in visualizing and exploring details of poetry.

Here you can examine how Jason used a cluster map to treat the similarities and differences in "Ex-Basketball Player" and "To an Athlete Dying Young."

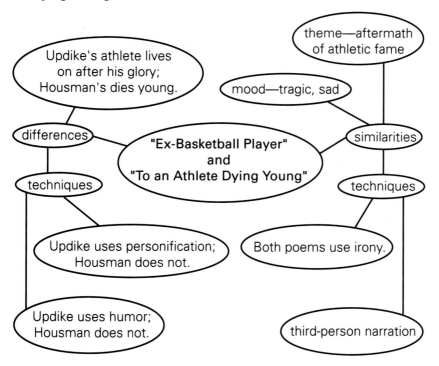

Asking Questions Another way to explore poetry is to develop and use a set of questions about the poetic elements. In the following chart Jason applies this technique to "Ex-Basketball Player" and "To an Athlete Dying Young." Notice how he answers each question as it relates to both poems.

One Student's Process

Question

Answer

1. Who is the subject of each poem?
In "Ex-Basketball Player," the subject
is a former basketball star, Flick
Webb, who now makes a living by
pumping gas at an Esso station.
In "To an Athlete Dying Young," the
subject is a former track star who
has died at a young age, while still a
champion basking in the glory of
athletic fame.

Question

Answer

2. Who is the speaker in each poem?
In "Ex-Basketball Player," the speaker
is a third-person narrator who
witnessed Flick's success in person
and who now sees the way Flick
occupies himself in the present. In
"To an Athlete Dying Young," the
third-person speaker addresses
himself to the deceased subject of
his poem. In addition, he witnessed
the athlete's glory days in person.

Question

Answer

3. What is the mood of the poem?
In "Ex-Basketball Player," the mood is
sad--Flick was a hero and now he's
reduced to a menial job and mediocre
existence. In "To an Athlete Dying
Young," the mood is also sad. A hero
has tragically died at a young age.

Question

Answer

4. What attitude does the poet take
toward his subject?
In "Ex-Basketball Player," Updike does
not make a direct statement, but by
contrasting Flick's former and
present lives he illustrates a
tragic loss of glory and fame. In "To
an Athlete Dying Young," Housman
tells the athlete that he is better
off having died before his fame had a
chance to fade--but it is a weak
consolation.

Question	5. How does the rhythm of the poem convey meaning?
Answer	In "Ex—Basketball Player," the rhythm is simple and regular——perhaps echoing Flick's present way of life. In "To an Athlete Dying Young," the rhythm is also regular——perhaps recalling the rhythm of a funeral procession.

Developing a Thesis Statement After you have examined the poem, the next step is to formulate a thesis statement, the main point of your analysis. To do this, you should identify the poetic element or elements that most interest you based on the questioning and brainstorming activities you have done. Your thesis statement should then be expressed in a clear sentence.

For example, a thesis statement like the following can be the focus for a comparison of "Ex-Basketball Player" and "To an Athlete Dying Young": *Updike and Housman express similar themes in their poems about yesterday's athletic heroes.*

Writing Activity Prewriting

Writing in Process Use the Guidelines for a Close Reading on page 300 for the poem or poems you selected in Part 1. Explore the poems by brainstorming or clustering. Also, examine the questions on pages 302 and 303 that were used to explore the poems by Updike and

Housman and answer them as they relate to your chosen poem or poems. You may also formulate and answer other questions relevant to your analysis. Finally, develop a single focus and use this focus to write a thesis statement.

Part 3
Organizing Your Analysis

Once you've decided on the main idea of your analysis, you should go back to your notes. Choose the main points you will use to support your thesis. Then list the supporting details from each poem under those main points. Organize the main points and details in a logical order. If you are discussing rhythm, you might choose to discuss the poem from the beginning to the end. If you are concerned with imagery, you may want to progress from the most vivid example to ones that have less impact. Also think about the similarities and differences you want to point out if you are comparing two poems.

Using a Chart

A visual device, such as a chart, may help you organize your ideas. Jason's chart below compares the subjects of each of the athlete poems:

One Student's Process

	Updike's Flick	Housman's Athlete
sport	basketball	track
example of success	300 points in 1946	won race for his town
current status	pumps gas; hangs out	dead at an early age

Creating an Informal Outline

An informal outline is another way to organize the material you have assembled. It may be used instead of, or in conjunction with, such visual devices as charts. Lay out your information logically and go back to the poems to acquire additional details as necessary. Here is Jason's informal outline for a comparative analysis of the two poems "Ex-Basketball Player" and "To an Athlete Dying Young."

Title: The Aftermath

I. Introduction
   A. Titles, authors—"Ex-Basketball Player" by John Updike and "To an Athlete Dying Young" by A. E. Housman
   B. Element to examine—theme
   C. Thesis statement—Updike and Housman express similar themes in their poems about yesterday's athletic heroes.

II. Body
   A. Updike's Flick has gone from fame to mediocrity.
      1. Flick was a basketball star who set a county record.
      2. Now Flick pumps gas and hangs out at Mae's Luncheonette.
   B. Only death has saved Housman's athlete from post-fame letdown.
      1. The young athlete won his town's race and the acclaim of many people.
      2. Because he has died young, he has not lived to see the glory slip away.
   C. Updike might think Flick better off dead, and Housman suggests that his young athlete would be unhappy if alive.
      1. Flick's hands are wasted pumping gas. He leads a meaningless life— empty compared to the glory days.
      2. Housman's athlete will not become a has-been who sees his name die before him.

III. Conclusion
   Restatement of thesis and closing remarks.

Writing Activity Organizing

Writing in Process Use a chart or an outline to organize the material you collected for your analysis of one poem or your comparative analysis of two poems.

Part 4
Drafting and Revising

Be sure that your poetry analysis accurately reflects the intent of the poem or poems you are examining. Do not shape facts to suit weak arguments. Use quotes from the poem or poems to support the points you want to make. Here are some other guidelines to keep in mind:

1. Verify that your thesis about the relationship is supportable.
2. Review the validity of your supporting details.
3. Check your organization and follow the device that is most helpful.
4. Tailor your presentation to suit your audience.

Here is Jason's comparative analysis of the poems by Updike and Housman based on his previously written thesis statement:

One Student's Process

Theme revealed by title

Titles, authors, and genre identified

Thesis statement

Examination of first poem

Use of quotation

Use of brackets

The Aftermath

"Ex–Basketball Player" by John Updike and "To an Athlete Dying Young" by A. E. Housman are two poems about athletes who have made their marks in a particular sport. The poems deal with what happens to each of them in the aftermath of their athletic fame. In fact, Updike and Housman express very similar themes in their poems about yesterday's heroes.

John Updike's Flick Webb has sadly gone from fame to mediocrity. As a high–school basketball player, Flick was quite a star. In 1946, we are told, "He bucketed three hundred ninety points, / A county record still." The speaker saw Flick score "thirty–eight or forty [points] / In one home game." The poet emphasizes Flick's ability by using personification and simile: "The ball loved Flick" and "His hands were like wild birds."

Now it is a different story. Flick pumps gas at Berth's garage. His hands are still "fine and nervous" as they work the lug wrench, though these qualities cannot be appreciated by this senseless tool. He "stands tall among the idiot pumps"––silent, dumb companions. At Mae's Luncheonette where Flick hangs out, his current audience can be found in the "applauding tiers / Of Necco Wafers, Nibs, and Juju Beads." A sad comedown from the fame of his school days.

Examination of second poem

A. E. Housman's athlete, however, has been saved from obscurity only by an early death. As a track star, he won a big race for his town. His fans carried him joyously through the crowded streets: "Man and boy stood cheering by, / And home we brought you shoulder–high."

Use of quotation

But the athlete has died young, and is now being carried in a funeral procession. The speaker finds consolation. The young man was wise to depart early "From field where glory does not stay." He will not see his record being broken or endure the silence that follows the cheers. Instead, the athlete will face "the strengthless dead," who will see upon his "early–laureled head" the victory garland.

Comparison of poems

Actually, Housman's words about the painful loss of athletic fame describe Flick Webb's current life:

Four-line quotation

> Now you will not swell the rout
> Of lads that wore their honors out,
> Runners whom renown outran
> And the name died before the man.

Use of Housman's lines to describe Updike's subject

Indeed, the young athlete is dead and shielded from losing his glory and fame. Flick is alive and aware of the fact that his name––once applauded by cheering crowds––is actually dead. Updike might agree with Housman that such an athlete may be better off dead; Flick leads an empty life compared to the days of his fame.

Conclusion

So in their treatment of the silence and emptiness that follows athletic acclaim, Housman and Updike address similar, sad themes in their poems. Both athletes have basked in the glory of success. One has died before his fame could fade. The other lives on to see his achievement buried in the mediocre life he lives.

Revising

Your next step is to revise what you have written. Though you may think you are thoroughly familiar with your work, be suspicious! Examine your analysis as if someone else had written it and be very critical. This will ensure that your final product will be well written.

Guidelines for Revising Poetry Analysis

1. Think about your purpose for writing. Verify that your thesis statement accurately and clearly reflects your main point.
2. Be sure you have written your analysis at the appropriate level for your audience.
3. Follow a logical plan of organization. If you chose a specific order, follow it throughout your analysis.
4. Make sure your tone is appropriate and consistent.
5. Check the validity of your arguments and conclusions. Your supporting details should be accurate and reinforce your thesis.
6. If you have paraphrased, make sure you have done so accurately.
7. Make sure your quotations are accurate. Insert slashes between quoted lines of poetry that are not set off in your text. If the quote runs longer than two written lines, do not use slashes. Set the poem off from the text and follow the poet's form line for line.
8. Be sure to follow these proofreading guidelines:
   • Capitalize the initial letter of every important word in the title of a poem.
   • Put the title of a poem within quotation marks.
   • Enclose direct quotes (two lines or less) from poems in quotation marks.
   • Set off, indent, and introduce longer quotations by colons.
   • Use an ellipsis to indicate missing words in a quotation.
   • Place words added to a quotation within brackets.

Writing Activity Writing and Revising

Writing in Process Write, revise, and proofread your analysis or comparative analysis. Collect and organize your material. Use quotes and examples to support your analysis. Write your paper, keeping your outline in mind. Finally, revise and proofread your analysis following the guidelines listed in the chart above.

Chapter 12
Application and Review

Analyzing Poems Compare and contrast the first stanza of Langston Hughes' poem "Dreams" on page 295 and these stanzas from Maya Angelou's poem "Caged Bird." Think of how both poets treat the same theme and how they use figurative language to convey this theme.

> The free bird thinks of another breeze
> and the trade winds soft through the sighing trees
> and the fat worms waiting on a dawn-bright lawn
> and he names the sky his own.
>
> But a caged bird stands on the grave of dreams
> his shadow shouts on a nightmare scream
> his wings are clipped and his feet are tied
> so he opens his throat to sing
>
> the caged bird sings
> with a fearful trill
> of things unknown
> but longed for still
> and his tune is heard
> on the distant hill
> for the caged bird
> sings of freedom.

From "Caged Bird" by Maya Angelou

Prewriting Brainstorm with other students or friends to discover connections between the two poems in relation to theme and figurative language. Ask questions to find similarities and differences and then create a chart on these points. Next, read these poems as many times as it takes to become thoroughly familiar with them. Form a thesis statement based on your impressions, prepare a list of supporting details from the poems, and devise an organization plan.

Drafting and Revising After deciding on a thesis statement and creating an outline for your paper, write a first draft. Then, read the draft critically. Has your main idea been clearly expressed and logically defended? Are your quotations accurate and appropriate? Finally, check for punctuation errors and revise your paper as necessary.

13
Writing a Report

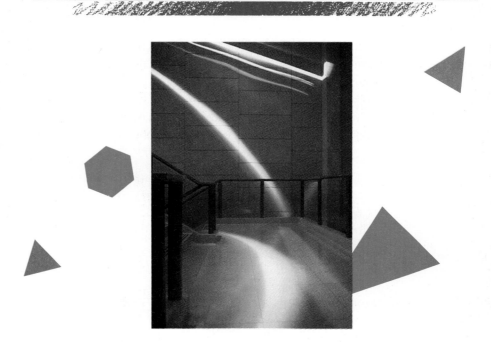

*H*ow, exactly, do the suspended prisms shown on the opposite page change sunlight into the rainbows swimming in the stairwell shown above? Why might Charles Ross, the artist who created this sculpture, have wanted to cast rainbows on walls? What do his other artworks look like? Such questions can be the stimulus for a challenging and interesting report.

In this chapter you will become familiar with the many kinds of resources from which you can obtain answers to questions like these. You will also learn to organize and present to others the information you obtain.

27 Prisms from the Origin of Color, Charles Ross, 1976.

Planning Your Report

Your science teacher assigns a paper on solar flares—explosions on the sun that have surprising effects on earth. Your English teacher asks you to report on slang terms used by teen-agers over the past twenty years. Your economics teacher assigns a paper on the advertising used for a particular product, and you choose designer jeans. What do these three assignments have in common?

In each assignment, you must write a **report,** a composition based on information from outside research. In writing a report, you gather materials from a variety of sources and then present your information clearly and accurately. As you prepare your report, you go through the usual stages of writing a composition—prewriting, drafting, and revising. These stages help you organize and present your facts clearly and logically.

A good report is more than just a recounting of facts and ideas, however. As you review the material you have gathered, think about it carefully. Consider which facts and ideas are most important. Decide how to organize your information. Look for new ideas, new insights, and fresh approaches to your subject.

As you plan your report, you begin to give it shape. You choose a subject, determine your purpose, limit your topic, prepare your research questions, and identify your audience.

Choosing Your Subject

Usually, your teacher will assign a report topic. Often, though, you will have some choice. In an American history lesson on early settlers, for example, you may choose to report on something that particularly interests you, such as the mysterious disappearance of the entire Roanoke Island settlement around 1590.

In order to **choose your subject,** first make a list of appropriate subjects. Be sure that these topics would interest both you and your readers. Remember that they should not involve you personally and that the subjects must require outside research. Examples of appropriate and interesting report topics would be "How Astronomers Measure the Moon," "Fashions of the 1950's," and "Origins of the English Language."

After you have listed about ten possible subjects, use these guidelines to choose one topic for your report.

Determining Your Purpose

As you think about your subject, you will notice that it probably can be approached in various ways. **Determining the purpose** of your report will help you decide how to approach your subject and will help focus your thinking and research.

The purpose of most reports is to inform. In writing such a report, you present facts and details to help the reader understand the subject. The following reports would be informative.

> How a Book Is Produced
> Saturn's Rings
> What Are Vitamins?

Comparing and Contrasting Some reports present information by comparing and contrasting two or more items. To do this, first read about the two items separately. Then think about their similarities and differences. (For more information on comparison and contrast, see Chapter 10, pages 236–240.) Here are some topics for compare and contrast reports.

> Popular Movies: Today and Thirty Years Ago
> Grant and Lee: Two Great Generals
> Records and Compact Discs

Explaining Causes and Effects Some reports explain cause-and-effect relationships—the connections between an event and its causes or effects. (For more information on cause and effect, see Chapter 10, pages 241–245.) The following reports would discuss cause-and-effect relationships.

> What Caused the Ice Age?
> How Does a Camera Produce a Picture?
> Computers in the Classroom: How Do They Affect Learning?

Analyzing Subjects When you write a report that analyzes, you break the topic into small parts and examine each of these parts. As you clarify the relationships between the different parts, your reader should be able to draw conclusions about the topic. The following reports analyze a topic.

> Poverty in the United States
> Do Competitive Sports Build Character?
> The Benefits of Year-Round Schooling

Limiting Your Topic

The chart on page 313 presents some guidelines for choosing a report subject. The third point on the chart explains that your subject must be narrow enough to be developed thoroughly. Often, you may find that a subject interests you but is really too broad for a short report. Therefore, an essential step in planning your report is **limiting your topic.** Which of the following subjects would make a good four-page report?

> The Aztecs
> The Architecture of Roman Houses
> Important Inventions
> Fashions of the United States

The second topic is the best choice because it concerns a limited subject, "The Architecture of Roman Houses," which can be discussed in a short report. The other subjects are too broad to be covered adequately and need to be narrowed. The following guidelines can help you in limiting topics.

Guidelines for Limiting a Report Topic

1. Consider how much information is available on the subject you have chosen.
2. Consider how long your report must be.
3. Do some preliminary reading to find out possible ways of limiting the topic.

How could you narrow some of the broad subjects listed above? To narrow the topic, "The Aztecs," for example, you might look in an encyclopedia for ideas. You might then choose a more focused topic like "The Spanish Conquest of the Aztecs," or "Aztec Influences on Modern Mexico." For "Fashions of the United States," you might write about the fashions of a certain period in history, compare the fashions of that time with contemporary fashions, or describe the fashions of different parts of the country.

In this chapter you will follow the processes through which Monica, a student writing a science report, approached her topic, did research, and then wrote her report. She originally planned to report on "The Uses of Lasers." After doing some reading, however, Monica realized that that topic was too broad for a short report. She found that there are important laser applications in manufacturing, communications, entertainment, medicine, and art. She decided that she wanted to learn more about how lasers are used in medicine.

Writing a Thesis Statement

After determining the purpose of your report, you can write a **thesis statement,** or statement of purpose. This statement helps you focus your thinking and research. You may even want to include the thesis statement in your introduction. As you plan and write your report, you can refer back to the thesis statement to be sure you are not straying from your purpose. Monica wrote the following thesis for her report on the uses of lasers in medicine:

One Student's Process

Among all the astounding applications of laser technology, perhaps the most important and most dramatic are in the field of medicine.

Preparing Your Research Questions

With your topic narrowed, you can clarify your thinking further by **preparing research questions** to answer in the report. Monica wrote the following research questions:

One Student's Process

1. What is a laser?
2. How was the laser developed?
3. How does it work?
4. What can lasers do?
5. What are some medical uses of lasers?
6. Are lasers a new "miracle cure"?

Determining Your Audience

Another important step in sharpening the focus of your report is **determining your audience.** Who will your readers be? How much will they already know about your topic? How much interest will they have in the topic?

Usually, you can assume that your audience knows very little about your topic and that you are the "expert." You will need to give your readers a clear overview and sufficient background on the topic, using language that is easily understood. Define any technical terms needed to discuss the topic.

You must also think about how interested your audience is in your topic. You may decide that it is up to you to make your readers interested in the topic you have chosen and that you must devise a strategy to catch their attention. For example, you can present the report in an unusual manner (such as following the format of a news report) or from an unusual viewpoint (perhaps that of an invisible bystander). Another strategy might be to draw a connection to another topic that you know already interests your audience.

Writing Activities Prewriting

A Read the following list of topics and decide which are too broad to cover in a short report. Narrow each broad topic so that it is suitable for a four-page report.

1. First Aid	6. Why the Town's Steel Mills Closed
2. Stars	7. Making a Hologram
3. Training for the Olympics	8. Ballet
4. Political Cartoons	9. Meteors
5. Choosing the Right College	10. The Rocky Mountains

B Choose five narrowed topics from Exercise A. Write an appropriate thesis statement and five research questions for each topic you chose.

C *Writing in Process* Select your own report topic. Begin with a general topic and limit it so that it is suitable for a four-page report. Explain the steps you went through in limiting your topic. Write a thesis statement for your report. Decide who your audience is and how much they know about the topic. Are they already interested in the subject, or is it an unfamiliar topic that will require you to capture your audience's attention? Next, prepare a list of five to ten questions to guide your research in preparing your report.

Part 2
Researching Your Topic

Do you enjoy putting together jigsaw puzzles? As you read or watch a mystery, do you try to list all the clues and solve the crime? Such methodical activities can be quite challenging, stimulating, and enjoyable. The research you do for your report, if you approach it in a logical, step-by-step manner, can be just as satisfying. Also, like those other complex activities, the research process may begin to make sense only after you complete a number of the required steps.

You can begin your research after you have narrowed your topic and written your research questions. A trip to the library will provide you with most of the material you need to prepare your report. Interviewing people is also an excellent way to gather information.

Locating Your Materials

In order to **locate information** for your report, you need to understand how materials are organized in the library. Following is a brief explanation of how to find the books, reference materials, and

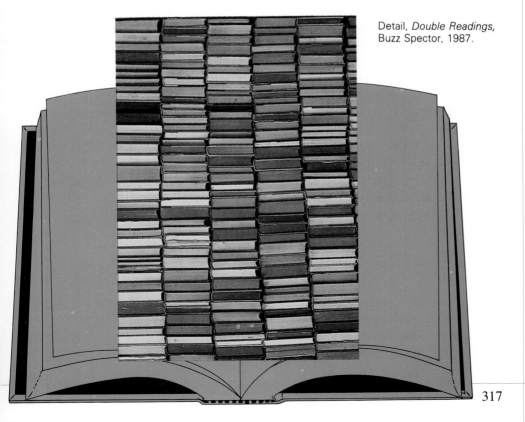

Detail, *Double Readings,* Buzz Spector, 1987.

periodicals (magazines, journals, and newspapers) you will need. See Chapter 16 for more extensive guidance in using the library.

Books In the library, books are arranged by subject. History books are shelved together, for example, as are books on music. Each subject is divided further into subsections. Under science, you will find subsections covering such fields as astronomy, biology, chemistry, earth science, and physics. Each book has a number or letter code, known as a call number, based on the book's subject. Call numbers, which you can find in the library's card catalog, can help you locate any book or subject area.

Reference Works For a good report, you will need to use reference works. Reference materials that must remain in the library building are shelved in a special section. The library's reference collection includes dictionaries, encyclopedias, almanacs and yearbooks, atlases, biographical dictionaries, and indexes of articles that have been published in magazines and other types of periodicals.

Periodicals In the *Readers' Guide to Periodical Literature,* you can find out about articles that have been written on your topic. The *Readers' Guide* directs you to specific articles in the library's collection of magazines, journals, and newspapers. These periodicals are often included in the general reference section.

When you go to the library to do research, decide what kind of source would most likely include information on your topic. If you are writing about the architecture of a Roman house, for example, you might find useful material in the encyclopedia entries for "Rome" and "Architecture." Look in the subject file of the card catalog for nonfiction books on Rome, house building, or architecture. Also check the periodical index for listings of articles on your topic that have been published in history journals or in art or architecture magazines. Remember that the librarian is one of the most valuable resources in the library and can also help you locate information.

Creating Your Working Bibliography

After you have gathered a number of possible source materials, skim each book or article to decide which ones will be helpful for your report. Then you can begin recording all the useful books, articles, and references on individual 3″ × 5″ index cards. This record is your **working bibliography.**

Study the following bibliography cards for Monica's report on laser medicine. The numbers in the upper right-hand corner will help the writer as she takes notes, documents her sources, and prepares a final bibliography. Notice that two of the cards are annotated with Monica's comments.

Bibliography Cards

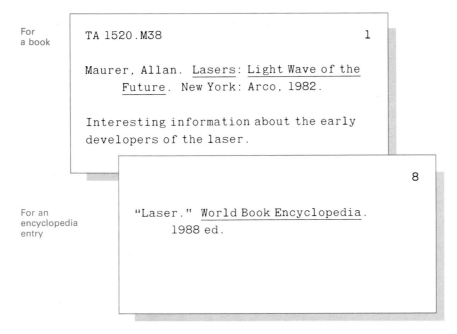

For
a book

TA 1520.M38   1

Maurer, Allan. <u>Lasers</u>: <u>Light Wave of the Future</u>. New York: Arco, 1982.

Interesting information about the early developers of the laser.

8

For an
encyclopedia
entry

"Laser." <u>World Book Encyclopedia</u>. 1988 ed.

19

Jacobs, Madeline. "The Light Fantastic:
    Lasers Brighten the Future."
    Futurist Dec. 1985: 36–39.

Gives an excellent description of how a
laser works.

Taking Notes

The next step in doing research is to read the sources listed in your working bibliography. Look for facts and ideas that are relevant to your report. On 3″ × 5″ index cards record the facts you plan to use. Write only one piece of information on each card. These **note cards** provide an efficient means of note taking. You can study each fact individually. As you consider various ways of organizing the information, you can change the order of the cards.

Look at the following note card that Monica wrote for her report. Notice that the card has a number and a letter in the upper right-hand corner. The number refers to the bibliography card. The letter *D* indicates that this is the fourth note from that source. Notice also that Monica has annotated the note card.

Note Card

1D

Laser diagnosis found an almost invisible
cancer in the lungs of a 70–year–old
Canadian farmer. Be sure to differentiate
between laser diagnosis and laser surgery.

Avoiding Plagiarism The facts that you write on note cards should be **paraphrased,** or written in your own words. If you take only the essential details and do not copy entire sentences or paragraphs, your report will be original. You will also avoid **plagiarism**—the uncredited use of another person's material. In published works, plagiarism is illegal; in school reports, it is often a cause for a failing grade. Notice how Monica paraphrased and summarized one fact about lasers.

Fact   Not only can [lasers] be very precisely directed, but a particular color can be chosen to destroy certain types of tissues while leaving others relatively intact. . . .

From Science 84 Nov. 1984: 153
by Charles H. Townes

Summary   A specific color of laser beam can be used to destroy certain tissues, bypassing other tissues.

Direct Quotes Sometimes you want to use the exact words of your source. **Direct quotes** strengthen your report as you support your own thesis with the ideas of others. When you find a useful quote, copy it accurately on a note card and put quotation marks around it.

Direct Quote

" . . . the applications of lasers seem limited only by the imagination of scientists and engineers."

From Futurist Dec. 1985: 39
by Madeline Jacobs

Writing Activities Researching Your Topic

A Read this quotation and paraphrase it for a note card.

As for the traits that characterize a "wilderness woman" . . . I'd say these are enthusiasm, youthfulness (regardless of age), idealism, a sense of commitment, a certain disregard for convention, capability, self-sufficiency, self-confidence, love of nature, and, in varying degrees, a sense of adventure. . . .

From *Women and Wilderness* by Anne LaBastille

B *Writing in Process* Research the report topic you began in Part 1 of this chapter. Use books, periodicals, and reference materials to create a working bibliography of at least seven sources. Next, read your sources and write note cards. Include at least two direct quotes in your note cards.

Part 3
Drafting Your Outline

Once you have researched your topic and compiled the information on note cards, you can begin to plan the organization of your report. Most of your notes can be categorized under certain key ideas. Identifying these key ideas is the first step in organizing your information.

Read the following facts from Monica's note cards on the uses of lasers in medicine and see how she put them in order.

One Student's Process

1. An atom or a molecule can be "excited" to a higher energy level by means of an external source of energy.
2. The laser is a "bloodless scalpel," cauterizing, or sealing, all blood vessels it touches that are less than 0.02 inches (0.5 mm) in diameter.
3. The work of physicist Charles H. Townes provided the basic idea for the laser.
4. With a laser scalpel, the surgeon is able safely to burn away surface tissues or to make deep incisions.
5. Unlike normal light, the light in a laser beam is coherent. All of the photons, or units of energy, move in the same direction and at the same wavelength. This explains the great intensity of laser light.
6. The future of lasers has its limitations—the expense of the equipment, for example.
7. Townes devised a practical way to obtain a very pure and extremely powerful form of energy from atoms of matter.

As Monica read through her notes, she saw that the information could be divided into four major topics: (I) origins, (II) definition and explanation, (III) uses in medicine, and (IV) future uses. She marked her notes with Roman numerals and organized them.

One Student's Process

    I. Origins and uses
   II. Definition and explanation
  III. Medical applications
   IV. The future of laser medicine

Logical Order Notice that Monica made sense of her facts by arranging them in a logical order. She saw that some notes gave information about what lasers are and how they work, whereas other notes focused on specific uses of lasers in medicine. She set up her outline to move from a discussion of the origin of lasers to an explanation of their uses in medicine now and in the future.

As you review your notes, you will see that you can use a number of different methods to organize the material you have gathered. You might put facts in order of importance, or you could order your facts according to how familiar the information is, moving from most familiar to least familiar.

Notes for a geography report on Easter Island, for example, could be organized according to spatial order, whereas chronological order might be most appropriate for a history report on the same topic. Generally, your material will not fit neatly into one of these orders. You may need to use a combination of methods.

Stone figures on Easter Island.

AD 1100

AD 1680

AD 1722

AD 380

Writing Your Outline

Any of the methods for writing outlines in the Writer's Handbook can help you organize your notes. In your outline, each of the key ideas that helped you organize your notes becomes the heading of a major division, which is labeled with a Roman numeral.

Subheadings, which summarize individual note cards for key ideas, are labeled with capital letters. There should be at least two subheadings of equal importance under each division. Under these are more specific subheadings, giving supporting details. These entries are labeled with numbers.

Study the outline that Monica prepared for her report on lasers in medicine.

One Student's Process

The Uses of Lasers in Medicine
I. Origins and uses
   A. Townes: ideas and plan
   B. Wide scope of uses today
II. What is a laser?
   A. Definition
   B. Basic principles
   C. How it works
III. Medical uses of lasers
   A. General advantages: the laser scalpel
   B. Eye surgery
      1. Selective beam
      2. Detached retina
   C. Dermatology
   D. Heart and circulatory treatments
   E. Internal bleeding
   F. Cancer
      1. Diagnosis
      2. Treatment
   G. Dentistry
   H. Acupuncture
IV. The future of lasers in medicine
   A. Not a miracle cure
   B. Promise for the future

After you finish your outline, you may decide that a section needs more facts. Return to the library and look for new sources.

Writing Activities Drafting Your Outline

A Read the following facts about King Tutankhamen. Group these facts and arrange them in a logical order. Then write an outline. Tell what form of logical organization you have used and explain why you chose that form.

1. King Tutankhamen's tomb contains four rooms.
2. King Tutankhamen's widow asked the Hittite king to help her retain the throne. The Hittite king accomplished this by sending one of his sons to marry the widow and thus unite the ruling families.
3. Tutankhamen was originally named Tutankhaton, which means "the life of Aton is pleasing."
4. "Tutankhamen was a boy of eight or nine when he became king."
5. The Hittite king sent his son, Prince Zannanza, to Tutankhamen's widow; the boy was attacked and slain by Egyptians.
6. The part of King Tutankhamen's tomb that contained his mummy was found to be undisturbed.
7. Tutankhaton changed his name to *Tutankhamen* because of pressure from the priests of Amon to do so.
8. There is a discrepancy among scholars over Tutankhamen's lineage.
9. King Tutankhamen's tomb was discovered in 1922 by Lord Carnarvon and Howard Carter after a five-year search.
10. "A new dynasty succeeded to the throne after Tutankhamen's death and the slaying of his potential successor, Prince Zannanza."
11. Tutankhamen may have been the son-in-law or brother of King Aton.
12. The greatest treasure was King Tutankhamen's burial mask of solid gold inlaid with stones.
13. Tutankhamen served as king of Egypt from about 1347 B.C. until his death in 1339 B.C.
14. Most of the items found in Tutankhamen's tomb are now displayed in the Egyptian Museum in Cairo.

B *Writing in Process* Group the note cards for the report you began in Part 1 of this chapter. Arrange your facts in a logical order. Tell what form of logical organization you have chosen and explain why. Then write an outline for your report. Be sure that each major heading is a key idea.

Part 4
Drafting Your Report

Once you have an outline and a complete set of note cards, you can begin drafting your report. To write your first draft, follow the organization of your outline and fill in the necessary details from your note cards. Each time you use a fact or idea from a note card, write the number of the card near the fact. These numbers will help you later on when you cite your sources.

Be sure that each section of your draft makes the point you want and that all of the sections fit together logically. Use transitional words and phrases to tie together your facts, paragraphs, and sections. These steps will help you achieve unity and coherence in your report and will help your readers understand the material you are presenting.

As you write your draft, remember that a report, like other compositions, has three main sections—the introduction, the body, and the conclusion.

The Introduction

You may introduce your report by presenting facts from the first part of your outline, or you may want to capture your audience's attention with a question, an interesting fact, or a quotation. (See Chapter 5, pages 112–113.) Whatever its form, your introduction has two basic functions: it should grab the reader's attention, and it should present the purpose of the report in a thesis statement. Look at this introduction that Monica wrote for her report on lasers in medicine.

One Student's Process

One morning in 1951, physicist Charles H. Townes sat on a park bench, gazing at his surroundings. Suddenly he had an idea—a practical way to obtain a very pure and powerful form of energy from molecules. This energy, Townes believed, would be useful in scientific research, allowing extremely accurate measurement and analysis. But Townes's discovery was much more earth shaking than he realized. It provided the basic idea for the laser, a device that today has an amazing variety of applications in such fields as manufacturing, communications, entertainment, and art. It is in the field of medicine, however, that lasers have had perhaps their most important and most dramatic effects.

In this paragraph, the writer introduces the topic and treats the factual material with a fresh approach. With her details about Townes's discovery and her thesis statement, Monica draws her readers's interest to the topic of laser medicine.

The Body

A good introduction makes the reader want to know more about the topic. The body of your report should provide this information. The body is made up of a series of paragraphs that follow the writing plan presented in your outline. Each main division of your outline becomes one or more paragraphs. Be sure that each paragraph has a topic sentence and supporting information.

In Monica's report on laser medicine, her introduction covers the first main division of her outline. The body of her report—contained in the following paragraphs—develops the next three major divisions:

II. Definition and explanation
III. Medical applications
IV. The future of lasers in medicine

Documentation

In the body of your report you will present, in your own words, facts and ideas from source materials. You must **document,** or cite the source of, each fact or idea that is not common knowledge.

Parenthetical Documentation One common method of citing sources is known as **parenthetical documentation.** You include the citation in your writing, inserting it in parentheses after the last sentence that presents the relevant information. Because your sources will be listed in a bibliography at the end of your report (see page 335), the author's last name and a page reference are usually sufficient documentation. The following example shows parenthetical documentation.

> **One Student's Process**
>
> The particular beam used is so precise that it can cut through the skin of a tomato without touching the meat (Maurer 4).

The parenthetical reference indicates that this information comes from page 4 of a book by Maurer.

To determine what information you need to document your sources, keep the following guidelines in mind.

Guidelines for Documentation

1. **Works with one author.** Give the author's last name in parentheses at the end of a sentence, followed by the page numbers (Jones 58).
2. **Works with more than one author.** List all the last names in parentheses, or give one last name followed by et al. (Smith, Jones, and Wilcox 87) or (Smith et al. 87).
3. **Works with no author listed.** When citing an article that does not identify the author, use the title of the work or a shortened version of it ("Robotics" 398).
4. **Two works by the same author.** If you use more than one work by the same author, give the title, or a shortened version, after the author's last name (Jones, Robots 398).
5. **Two works cited at the same place.** If you use more than one source to support a point, use a semicolon to separate the entries (Jones 398; Smith 87).

The body of Monica's documented report on laser medicine is the result of several drafts. Notice how Monica has blended different types of exposition with other writing forms.

Lasers and Medicine: A Bright Ray of Hope

Narrative style introduction

One morning in 1951, as physicist Charles H. Townes sat on a park bench, he had an idea—a practical way to obtain a very powerful form of energy from molecules. This energy, Townes believed, would be useful in scientific research, allowing extremely accurate measurement and analysis (Townes 153). Townes's discovery was more earthshaking than he realized. It provided the basic idea for the laser, a device that today has an amazing variety of applications in such fields as manufacturing, communications and en-

Thesis statement

tertainment. It is in the field of medicine, however, that lasers have had perhaps their most important and most dramatic effects.

Definition

A laser, most simply defined, is a device that produces an extremely intense beam of light. The beam is so strong that it can burn a hole in a diamond or travel as far as the moon ("Laser" 83).

Question as transition

How does the laser produce such a powerful beam? All substances are made up of atoms and molecules, which possess energy. The addition of

Process

more energy from an outside source "excites" or adds energy to atoms and molecules. When the energy source is removed, the substance's atoms and molecules become less "excited" and give off

Definition

their excess energy (Jacobs 37). This process is known as stimulated emission. Townes discovered how to use this stimulated emission to produce intense energy beams in the form of microwaves,

Parenthetical note

like those in a microwave oven (Hecht and Teresi 50-51). About six years later, Townes thought of producing light beams by stimulated emission. In 1960, physicist Theodore Maiman produced the first laser. Its name comes from the first letters of the words light amplification from stimulated emission of radiation (Townes 154).

Process

The laser works as follows. The atoms in a specially-prepared substance––it may be a solid, a liquid, or a gas––are excited by an outside energy source. As the atoms begin to lose energy, they emit photons, or units of light energy. The photon from one atom stimulates another atom to give off an identical photon. This process continues until a number of photons are proceeding

Definition of unfamiliar terms

coherently, in the same direction and at the same wavelength. This explains the great intensity of laser light, since ordinary light is incoherent; it goes off in a number of directions at many different wavelengths. The coherent laser light bounces between two mirrors in the laser, gaining tremendous power. The light released is thus a single intense beam ("Laser" 85; Jacobs 37).

Transition

This powerful beam, however, has proven a safe and delicate medical tool. Attached to a special arm, the laser can be a valuable surgeon's scalpel. The surgeon can burn away surface tissue at a less intense focus, or make

Writing Inside Out
Albert Smith, Consultant

The single most important ingredient necessary for good writing, according to Albert Smith, is information. Mr. Smith works in New York as a consultant, teaching business people how to improve their writing skills.

how smart you are or how much you know before you get an assignment. It depends primarily on your ability to gather all the information you can about a subject. Only when you have enough information can you draw a conclusion.

Q What is your theory about information?
A Writing has nothing to do with

Q How do you help people become better writers?
A I show them how to gather

deep incisions by focusing the beam to a fine
point. Surrounding tissues remain undamaged,
since human cells are poor conductors of heat.
The laser is also a "bloodless scalpel," sealing
all blood vessels that are smaller than 0.02
inches (0.5mm). The laser scalpel can be focused
finely enough to vaporize one single cell (Hecht
and Teresi 65). It is also fast and provides no
contact pressure. Thus, compared to a conventional scalpel, the laser reduces the trauma
that accompanies surgery (Maurer 7).

Transition

The laser scalpel has another important characteristic that makes it ideal for delicate eye
surgery. A specific color of laser beam can be
used to destroy certain tissues, bypassing other

Supporting
detail

tissues (Townes 155). One researcher demon-
strates this quite graphically as he shoots a
ruby-red beam at two balloons, a blue one inside
of a clear one. The beam passes through the clear
balloon and pops the blue one, which has absorbed
the red laser light (Maurer 1-2).

information and organize it in two
stages. In the first stage, they organize the information so that they
understand everything about the
subject. This is the you-to-you
stage, or first draft. It is important
the same way it is important for an
athlete to practice all week for one
game.

Next comes the you-to-reader
stage. Now they write a second
draft based on what they think
their audience needs to know. This
version is usually shorter than the
first. It still includes lots of information, examples, and ideas, but just
enough for the reader to use.
Thinking about another person using your information turns the writing process into a joy.

Q Why do you suppose that
many businesspeople need help
with their writing?
A I work with junior and senior
executives who are talented in
their fields, but who never learned
to write well in school. When they
have to make a presentation, they
crumble. I help them build their
confidence.

Q What is your background?
What made you decide to go into
the consulting field?
A For many years I taught ancient
Greek in colleges. Now I like helping people outside the classroom.
I like seeing how my clients make
immediate use of information I
give them.

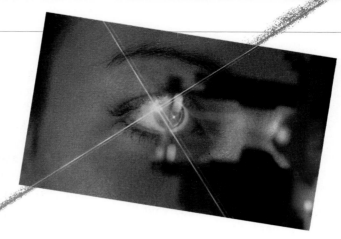

Transition

The first medical applications of a laser took advantage of this unusual property. In 1963, two doctors sent a laser beam through the transparent cornea of a patient's eye to repair a detached retina. The beam welded the retina to the back of the eyeball. The operation was a suc-

Parenthetical note

cess and the patient felt no pain (Maurer 1-2).

Also among the first to use lasers were dermatologists, or skin doctors. With lasers, these doctors can close the blood vessels that have caused deep-red birthmarks and break down the dye in unwanted tatoos. More recently, dermatologists have used lasers to speed up the healing of wounds (Hecht and Teresi 73-75).

Order of increasing importance

The major value of laser surgery, however, lies in its ability to perform delicate operations within the body in sensitive areas that are rich in blood vessels. For this reason, the laser has been a valuable tool in the treatment of heart and circulatory problems, internal bleeding, and some forms of cancer.

Definition

One common heart and circulatory problem is plaque, hardened materials and fat that clog arteries and restrict blood flow. A buildup of plaque can cause a stroke or heart attack. Laser surgeons are working on a process in which they thread a tube into the clogged blood vessel and vaporize the plaque with a laser. The doctor who thought of this technique insists that he got the idea while watching the laser-sword battle in the movie Star Wars (Zarley 268, 271).

In a similar manner, doctors can stop internal bleeding. The patient swallows a tube known as an endoscope, which contains optical fibers. These fibers allow the surgeon to see along the length of the tube. Next, the surgeon seals the bleeding vessels with a laser beam. The beam used is so precise that it can cut through the skin of a tomato without touching the meat (Maurer 3–6; Hecht and Teresi 71–72).

Lasers have also been used to cure and diagnose some forms of cancer. A dye or medicine taken by the patient is absorbed by the cancer cells. If the affected area is in the lungs, for example, the patient then swallows a bronchoscope, a fiber–optic tube that reveals the cancer. A laser beam is then directed at the cancer cells to vaporize them (Maurer 13).

Dentists are also beginning to benefit from laser technology. Dental surgeons are using lasers to vaporize damaged tooth material with amazing accuracy (Burroughs 41). Orthodontists are using holography——three–dimensional photographs made by laser light——to measure the ef-

fects of braces. They make holograms of the patient's mouth without braces and then a month after the braces are put in. Then they print both 3–D images on one photographic plate. Orthodontists are thus able to measure changes that other methods could miss (Hecht and Teresi 78–79).

Even some acupuncturists, practitioners who stimulate pressure points on the body with needles, have begun using low–power lasers in place of needles. Acupuncturists, who believe they can cure illnesses by stimulating these points, are finding lasers faster, cleaner, and more painless than needles. Acupuncturists in China report that laser treatment has relieved asthma symptoms in 72 percent of the patients treated (Hecht and Teresi 75–76).

Does the body of this report follow the outline? Remember that you may add, delete, or reorganize information to improve your report.

The Conclusion

As you read the introduction and body paragraphs about laser medicine, you probably noticed that something was missing. The last body paragraph does not provide an adequate ending for the report. It leaves you hanging, waiting for more.

An effective report needs an interesting conclusion, one that will stay in the reader's mind. The conclusion ties the report together and gives it a definite ending. In a conclusion the writer may summarize the report's main points or may evaluate the topic and its effects. Sometimes the conclusion will provide a general statement that points to possibilities of further examination of the subject.

Study the conclusion of Monica's report.

One Student's Process

    Lasers, it seems, have miraculous capabili-
ties in the field of medicine. Perhaps for that
very reason, many doctors and writers try to keep
this relatively new development in perspective.
Admitting only that it is "a new hope" with "bright
promise," many insist that it is not the "cure-all"
it may seem to be (Hecht and Teresi 62, 79). Nevertheless, even Charles H. Townes remains amazed
at the medical applications resulting from his
idea in the park in 1951 (Townes 155). The future
looks bright, according to one writer. "The applications of lasers seem limited only by the
imagination of scientists and engineers"
(Jacobs 38).

Notice that in the first line of her conclusion, Monica signals an end to the report and provides a general summary of the main point. Next, she evaluates the topic and looks to the future.

Writing Activity Drafting Your Report

Writing in Process Using the outline you prepared in Part 3 of this chapter, draft the report you began in Part 1. In your introduction, use a question, an interesting fact, anecdote, or quote to catch the reader's interest. Use transitional devices to link your paragraphs. Cite your sources with parenthetical documentation. In your conclusion, use a quote that will keep the topic in your reader's mind.

Part 5
Revising and Proofreading Your Report

Reread the draft of your report. Use the guidelines on page 337 to help you revise your writing. Also, note that there is one additional guideline that applies in particular to reports: *Check your facts to be sure they are correct.* You may even want to check each of your most important facts in a second source.

You must also be sure that you have cited all your sources in your documentation and in a bibliography at the end of your report. When compiling your bibliography, list only the sources you actually have used in your report. Study Monica's bibliography for her report on laser medicine. Notice that she has listed her sources in alphabetical order according to the author's last name (or the name of the article, when no author is given).

One Student's Process

Bibliography

Burroughs, Williams. Understanding Science:
    Lasers. New York: Warwick, 1984.
Hecht, Jeff, and Dick Teresi. Lasers:
    Supertool of the 1980s. New Haven:
    Ticknor, 1982.
Jacobs, Madeline. "The Light Fantastic:
    Lasers Brighten the Future." Futurist
    Dec. 1985: 36–39.
"Laser." World Book Encyclopedia. 1988 ed.
Maurer, Allan. Lasers: Light Wave of the
    Future. New York: Arco, 1982.
Townes, Charles H. "Harnessing Light."
    Science 84 Nov. 1984: 153–55.
Zarley, Craig. "Lasers Join the Medical
    Force." Esquire Sept. 1983: 268–71.

When you have finished revising your report and writing your bibliography, make a clean final copy. Then use the Proofreading Checklist on page 82 for proofreading your report. Check your grammar, capitalization, punctuation, and spelling.

Esperanto

O ne hundred years ago a young Polish man dedicated his life to using language to bring the people of the world together. Ludwig Zamenhof grew up in Bialystock, Poland, a city made up of people from diverse racial and cultural backgrounds who spoke many different languages. Zamenhof believed that many of the disagreements among people could be eliminated if everyone spoke a common language. So he invented one.

Zamenhof devised a new language made up of root words from many European languages. To promote his invention, he wrote about it extensively under the pen name Doktoro Esperanto, which means "Dr. Hopeful" in the new language. Soon, the language became known as Esperanto. It uses a twenty-eight letter alphabet, and each letter has only one sound (unlike English, in which vowels and some consonants can have several different sounds). It has only sixteen rules of grammar to remember and, unlike English, there are no exceptions to the rules. See if you can translate the following Esperanto sentence:

> La inteligenta persono lernas la interlingvon Esperanto rapide kaj facile.

Zamenhof's followers continue to promote Esperanto as an aid to international understanding. In addition, as the sentence above explains, "the intelligent person learns the international language Esperanto quickly and easily."

EL POPOLA
CINIO
7 1987

Esperanto speakers often wear lapel pins shaped like green stars. Right: Cover of an Esperanto magazine published in China.

Guidelines: Writing a Report

Planning Your Report
- Make a list of interesting and appropriate topics and select a subject from this list. *(See page 312.)*
- Determine your purpose by choosing an approach such as informing your audience, comparing and contrasting items, discussing cause and effect, or analyzing your topic. *(See pages 313–314.)*
- Limit and narrow your topic for a short report. *(See pages 314–315.)*
- Prepare your research questions. *(See page 315.)*
- Determine your audience so you know the amount of background information you will have to include. *(See page 316.)*

Researching Your Topic
- Locate your reference works in the library. *(See pages 317–318.)*
- Use reference works to gather information. *(See pages 317–318.)*
- Create a working bibliography for all your sources. *(See pages 318–319.)*
- Take notes from your sources, making sure to paraphrase the information or directly quote the material. *(See pages 320–321.)*

Drafting Your Outline
- Sort your facts into groups so you can arrange them in a logical order and then pick a type of organization. *(See page 323.)*
- Write an outline showing how your facts are arranged. *(See page 324.)*

Drafting Your Report
- Write an introduction, using the first part of your outline or using a question, fact, anecdote, or quotation. *(See pages 326–327.)*
- Write the body of your report, following the organization you chose for your outline. *(See page 327.)*
- Use parenthetical footnotes to document facts. *(See page 328.)*
- Write a conclusion that ties your report together. *(See page 334.)*

Revising and Proofreading Your Report
- Check that your facts are accurate and documented. *(See page 335.)*
- Create a bibliography, alphabetically listing only the sources from which you have taken information. *(See page 335.)*
- Proofread your final copy. *(See page 335.)*

Chapter 13
Application and Review

Use what you have learned about writing reports in completing the following activities.

A Limiting Your Topic The topic "The Use of Lasers" is too broad for a short report. There are many areas in which lasers are being used today—art, manufacturing, entertainment, and communications, as well as medicine. Plan and write your own report by first limiting this topic to an application other than medicine. Holography and tele-communications are two possibilities. Then write your report, using the following guidelines as you write.

Prewriting Read an encyclopedia article about lasers. Make a list of all the uses of lasers discussed in the article and choose an application that you find interesting. Be sure that your topic is suitable for a four- or five-page report. Focus your research by developing questions you want to answer. Then research the topic in the library, completing bibliography and note cards. Next, organize your note cards and write an outline for your report.

Drafting Use your outline to write a first draft. Be sure to use vivid language and to link your ideas with transitional devices. (See Chapter 5, page 117.) Use parenthetical documentation to cite your sources.

Revising Use the checklists on pages 80–81 to help you revise your first draft. Then prepare your final bibliography and proofread your report, using the guidelines on page 82.

B Writing a History Report Use the following guidelines to plan, research, and write a four- to five-page history report.

Prewriting Study the table of contents of a history textbook and choose a period of time that interests you. Skim the relevant chapters in the book and make a list of possible topics. When you have chosen and narrowed your topic, research the topic and write an outline.

Drafting and Revising Write a first draft from your outline. Ask another student to edit your work and use the student's comments to guide your revisions. Then write your final bibliography. Use the guidelines on page 82 to help you proofread your report.

C *Starting Points for Writing* To develop a list of interesting writing topics, brainstorm or freewrite about the images and the quote below, using the questions given as Springboards to aid you.

What do we know about the African warrior queens of Dahomey . . . who led their armies against colonial invaders? Or the market women of modern West Africa who run the daily businesses of their countries?

Gloria Steinem

Springboards
- What trade secrets are you curious to learn about?
- What careers might you like to investigate?
- Who else might you want to discover more about?

Resources and Skil

14
Strengthening Your Vocabulary

Two boys uncoached are tossing a poem together,
Overhand, underhand, backhand, sleight of hand, every hand,
Teasing with attitudes, latitudes, interludes, altitudes,
High, make him fly off the ground for it, low, make him stoop,
Make him scoop it up, make him as-almost-as-possible miss it. . .

From "Catch" by Robert Francis

Warm up, stretch your language ligaments. Words are made up of parts that can be tossed around and recombined, as Robert Francis has done in his poem, for the sheer fun of playing with sound and sense.

Learning how words are put together can also help you discover the meanings of unfamiliar words. In this chapter you will learn how understanding context clues and analyzing word parts can help you develop a winning vocabulary.

Inferring Word Meanings from Context

You are reading a passage and you encounter an unfamiliar word. What do you do? Race by it? Your understanding of the passage may suffer. Reach for a dictionary? What if you don't have one handy? You do have another option.

Often you can find clues to the meaning of a word by thinking about its **context,** the sentence or group of sentences in which the word appears. In some cases you may have to reflect on the entire passage and **infer,** or draw a conclusion about, the meaning.

Several types of context clues may help you determine the meaning of an unfamiliar word. These types of clues include definition and restatement, example, comparison, contrast, and cause and effect. Learning to recognize these clues can help improve your reading comprehension.

Definition and Restatement

The easiest context clues to detect are **definition** and **restatement** clues. Sometimes a writer will directly define a word, especially if the word is a technical term that may be unfamiliar to readers. Consider the following example:

> Metal can be made more flexible by *annealing,* which is a process of heating followed by slow cooling.

In the example above, the definition of *annealing* is given directly following the words *which is.* Annealing is a "process of heating followed by slow cooling."

More often, a writer will restate the meaning of a word in a less precise form than a dictionary definition.

> Throughout the trial the jury was *sequestered*—they were not allowed to contact anyone outside the courtroom.

Even if you do not know the word *sequestered,* the context of the passage suggests the definition, "not allowed to contact anyone." Indeed the dictionary definition of the verb *sequester* is "to keep away from others."

Definition and restatement are often signaled by certain key words and phrases such as those listed on the next page.

Definition and restatement clues can also be signaled by punctuation. An **appositive,** a noun or pronoun that follows another word and identifies or explains it, is set off by commas. Notice that the definition of appositive in the previous sentence is itself an appositive. The phrase "a noun or pronoun that follows another word and identifies or explains it" indicates what an appositive is.

Example

Less direct than definition or restatement are context clues in which the writer follows an unfamiliar word with an illustration or **example** of it. By examining these examples, you can often get a good idea of the word's meaning.

> The university had several excellent *entomologists* on its staff. These included Dr. Tower, a specialist on flying insects, and Dr. Mistri, an expert on ants.

Although the word *entomologist* is not directly defined, the two examples suggest that an entomologist is a person who studies insects.

Sometimes the example itself is the unfamiliar word. To find a context clue, you must look carefully at the words that introduce the example.

> Various forms of abstract painting, such as *cubism* and *expressionism,* developed in the early twentieth century.

Even if you do not know exactly what *cubism* and *expressionism* are, you do know that they are forms of abstract painting since they are introduced as examples.

The words listed below often signal examples.

Dream Lab,
André Heller,
1987 U.S. tour

Comparison

A writer may provide clues to the meaning of an unfamiliar word by drawing a **comparison** using other, more familiar terms. By noting the similarities between the things described, you can form a good idea of the meaning of the unfamiliar word.

> The *dirigible,* like a huge balloon, floated above the stadium with an advertising banner streaming out behind it.

Although the context does not fully reveal what a *dirigible* is, the comparison allows you to visualize what it might look like and leads you to conclude that a *dirigible* is a balloon-like aircraft.

Comparisons are often signaled by certain key words.

Key Words for Comparison				
like	in the same way	resembling	similarly	identical
as	similar to	likewise	also	related

Contrast

You may also find a clue to the meaning of an unfamiliar word when that word is discussed in **contrast** to something familiar. By knowing what the unfamiliar word *does not* mean, you can get some idea of what it *does* mean.

> Zinc is a naturally occurring element. *Einsteinium,* however, is not.

From the contrast developed in these two sentences you know that unlike zinc, *einsteinium* does not occur naturally. You can infer then that *einsteinium* is an artificially produced element. Notice that the word *however* helps to signal the contrast.

The following key words and phrases signal contrasts.

Key Words for Contrast

but	on the other hand	dissimilar
although	unlike	different
on the contrary	in contrast to	however

Cause and Effect

Another category of context clue is **cause and effect.** An action's cause may be stated in unfamiliar terms. The action's effect, stated in familiar terms, can help you understand the unfamiliar terms. Consider the following example:

> When the lake began to *encroach* on the shoreline, the townspeople met to discuss how to save the beaches.

The townspeople's reaction leads you to infer that the lake must be rising beyond its usual limits, which is one meaning of *encroach*.

Certain key words and phrases, such as the following, may signal cause and effect.

Key Words for Cause and Effect

because	consequently	when
since	therefore	as a result

Exercises

A Using the context clues that you have studied, determine the meaning of the italicized word in each passage. Write your own definition for each word. Then look in a dictionary to check your definition.

1. Gold is a *ductile* metal. It can be bent or hammered without breaking.
2. Julie was extremely *loquacious,* but her friend rarely said a word.

3. The president and the prime minister expressed *consonant* ideas; that is, they were in agreement on most issues.
4. Like a *catalyst* in a chemical reaction, Ralph's timely arrival and excellent advice helped speed up our meeting.
5. For years toxic waste had been dumped into the river, and now a thick, odorless *miasma* spread throughout the surrounding area.

B Write a passage using at least five of the following words. Suggest the meaning of each word by providing the type of context clue indicated in parentheses. Use the lists of key words provided in this chapter. Also use the picture on this page to start you thinking.

1. *sentinel:* a person set to guard a group (restatement)
2. *deciduous:* pertaining to a tree that sheds its leaves every year (example)
3. *pithy:* brief and full of substance and meaning (contrast)
4. *volatile:* explosive, unstable (cause and effect)
5. *balalaika:* an instrument with a triangular body and three strings (comparison)
6. *spectral:* ghostly (definition)
7. *predator:* an animal that hunts other animals (example)
8. *steppe:* a large area of flat land in which there are few trees (contrast)

Part 2

Drawing Inferences from General Context

Often you will have to infer the meaning of a word from the main idea or supporting details of an entire paragraph.

Inference from Supporting Details In the paragraph that follows, notice how the details help you infer the meaning of *eclectic*.

> You have only to turn on your radio to see how *eclectic* America's musical tastes are. At any time of the day you are sure to find jazz, show tunes, country-and-western songs, and several varieties of rock-and-roll. A twist of the dial may bring you "easy listening" music or a string quartet.

Since the idea is supported by details showing a wide variety of music, *eclectic* must have a meaning that is close to "widely varied."

Inference Based on Contrast The following paragraph develops a series of contrasts that help you to infer the meaning of the word *dour*.

> Throughout the first hour that I spent on the dock, the silent man fishing beside me wore a *dour* expression. The only sounds from him were long sighs. Suddenly he caught a flounder. At once he began to smile. He introduced himself and for the next hour kept up a constant stream of anecdotes and jokes.

Noting the contrast in the man's behavior, you can assume that earlier the man was not smiling or joking. Thus, you can conclude that a *dour* person is someone who is rather gloomy.

Exercise

Read each of the following passages carefully and infer the meaning of the italicized word. Write your own definition of the word. Then check the definition in a dictionary.

1. As a young man, Dennis decided that he was going to get ahead at all costs. He never did anyone a favor unless he felt certain that it would be returned twofold. He remembered a person's name only if the person could be useful to him. Largely because of his *calculating* attitude, Dennis had few friends.

2. I sat staring out the window at the willow trees. It was a warm, lazy day, and my thoughts drifted back to other such peaceful days in Louisville years before. I was suddenly shocked out of this *reverie* by the insistent ringing of the doorbell.

3. Sometimes the loss of one sense leads to *augmentation* of the others. People who lose their sight, for example, often have an increased ability to hear, smell, taste, and touch.

4. The defendant took the stand. He was neatly dressed in a gray suit, with a white shirt and a dark blue tie. He walked with a sure stride and took the oath in a calm and steady voice. When he turned his eyes to me, I saw that they had an open, honest look. I was surprised. He certainly did not appear to be the *malefactor* that I had imagined.

5. Roman *hegemony* reached its height under the Emperor Augustus. All Europe, with the exception of Germany, was under Roman rule. To the north, Roman power extended to nearly all of Great Britain. North Africa, Turkey, and much of the Middle East were also under the control of Rome.

6. My friend spends much of her time now reading and knitting. She rarely leaves her apartment these days. When she does make one of her infrequent visits, it is not without hours of planning and worrying beforehand. How unlike the free spirit she once was. She seems to have lost all of her old zest and *spontaneity*.

Part 3
Determining Word Meanings from Prefixes and Suffixes

Another way to determine the meaning of an unfamiliar word is to analyze the parts of the word. All English words are made up of one or more of the parts listed below:

Prefix	a word part that is added to the beginning of another word or word part
Suffix	a word part that is added to the end of another word or word part
Base Word	a complete word to which a prefix and/or a suffix may be added
Root	a word part to which a prefix and/or a suffix must be added to make a word

Consider the word *unquestionable*. It is made up of the prefix *-un,* the base word *question,* and the suffix *-able. Incredible* is made up of the prefix *in-,* the root *cred,* and the suffix *-ible.*

Recognizing Prefixes

Recognizing prefixes gives you a big advantage when you encounter unfamiliar words. Consider the word *intrastate.* If you know the meaning of the prefix *intra,* "within", then you can easily determine the meaning of the whole word, "within a state's boundaries."

The following chart lists prefixes that are helpful to know. These prefixes have only one meaning.

Prefixes That Have a Single Meaning

Prefix	Meaning	Example
bene-	good	benefit
circum-	around	circumvent
col-, com-	with, together	collapse
con-, cor-		compile
		construct
		correspond
contra-	opposed	contradict
equi-	equal	equidistant
extra-	outside	extralegal
hemi-	half	hemisphere
hyper-	over, above	hypercritical
inter-	between, among	international
intra-	within	intracellular
intro-	into	introvert
mal-	bad	maltreat
mid-	halfway	midday
mis-	wrong	misspell
non-	not	nonworking
pre-	before	predawn
retro-	backward, behind	retroactive
sub-	under, below	subzero

Many prefixes, however, have more than one meaning. Study the common prefixes with multiple meanings that are listed in the chart on the next page.

Prefixes That Have More Than One Meaning

Prefix	Meaning	Example
ab-, a-	not	abnormal
	away	absent
	up, out	arise
ad-	motion toward	adopt
	nearness to	adrenal
ante-	before, prior to	antecedent
	in front of	anteroom
anti-	against	anticensorship
	prevents, cures	antidote
	opposite, reverse	antimatter
de-	away from, off	derail
	down	decline
	reverse action of	defrost
dis-	lack of	distrust
	not	dishonest
	away	dispatch
em-, en-	to get into, on	embark
	to make, cause	enfeeble
	in, into	enclose
il-, im-, in-, ir-	not	immature
	in, into	investigate
pro-	in favor of	prolabor
	forward, ahead	propel
re-	again	replant
	back	repay
semi-	half	semicircle
	twice in a period	semiannual
	partly	semiconscious
super-	over and above	superhuman
	very large	supertanker
trans-	across	transatlantic
	beyond	transcend

"Actually I'm not even a real Modo, I'm only a Quasimodo."

Exercises

A Replace each italicized phrase with a single word. Each word should contain one of the prefixes you have learned. You may want to check the spelling in a dictionary.

1. Stealing is *not legal*. Stealing is _____ .
2. I will *not associate* with that group in the future. I will _____ myself from that group.
3. She was asked to *submit* her application *again*. She was asked to _____ her application.
4. The rolling hills *make a circle* around the valley. The rolling hills _____ the valley.
5. That ship *sails across the Pacific*. It is a _____ ship.
6. The check was *dated beforehand*. The check was _____ .
7. Jesse James was a *very famous* outlaw. James was _____ .
8. The factory had forty positions available for *partly skilled* workers. The factory was hiring _____ workers.
9. To reduce the speed of its descent, the space capsule had *rockets* that fired *backwards*, opposite to the direction of flight. The space capsule fired its _____ .
10. The rooms were first filled with water to *reverse* the *contamination* of the nuclear facility. The nuclear facility began the _____ of the rooms.
11. Looking over the sentence, the writer decided to *add* some modifiers to the *verb*. The writer will put some _____ in the sentence.
12. He had always been *overly sensitive* about his weight. He was _____ .

13. The playful cat became so *tangled in* the ball of yarn that she could not move. The cat was completely ⎯⎯⎯⎯⎯ in the yarn.
14. "That point is not relevant to the argument," the debate coach said. "The point is ⎯⎯⎯⎯⎯ ."

B For each of the following words, draw lines to separate the word into two parts—prefix and base. Determine the meaning of the prefix. Then add the meaning of the prefix to the base word and write the meaning of each complete word. Compare the meaning with the meaning given in a dictionary. Then use each word correctly in a sentence.

1. misjudge	6. confederation	11. malfunction
2. apolitical	7. equilateral	12. hyperventilation
3. extraordinary	8. circumnavigate	13. adjoin
4. intramolecular	9. antibacterial	14. deplane
5. nonpoisonous	10. subconscious	15. antebellum

Recognizing Suffixes

Another way to determine word meaning is to look for suffixes. Like prefixes, suffixes have their own meanings. Once you know the suffixes and their meanings, you can attach them to base words or roots to form new words. For example, the suffix *-ance* can be added to the base word *appear* to create the word *appearance*. Likewise, the suffix *-ist* can be added to the base word *zoology* to create the word *zoologist*.

Notice that the spelling of a base word may change when a suffix is added. In the example above, the *y* was dropped from *zoology* when *-ist* was added. For information about spelling rules for adding suffixes, see Chapter 33.

Noun Suffixes Noun suffixes are added to a base word or root to form nouns. Become familiar with the following common noun suffixes.

Noun Suffixes That Mean "One Who Does Something"

Suffix	Examples
-ant	commandant, occupant
-eer, -ier	auctioneer, cavalier
-er, -or	manager, counselor
-ist	geologist, somnambulist
-ician	beautician, statistician

Noun Suffixes That Form Abstract Words

Suffix	Examples
-ance, -ence	vigilance, independence
-ation, -ition	imagination, condition
-dom	freedom, kingdom
-hood	womanhood, brotherhood
-ice	cowardice, prejudice
-ism	realism, federalism
-ment	encouragement, commitment
-ness	kindness, fondness
-ship	ownership, worship
-tude	gratitude, solitude
-ty, -ity	frailty, sincerity

Adjective Suffixes Adjective suffixes are added to a base word or root to form adjectives—words that are used to modify nouns and pronouns. Various meanings are attached to these suffixes, as indicated in the chart that follows.

Adjective Suffixes

Suffix	Meaning	Example
-ous	full of	furious
-acious	full of	vivacious
-ful	full of	harmful
-al	relating to	musical
-ant	relating to	triumphant
-ic	pertaining to or like	heroic
-ical	pertaining to	economical
-ish	pertaining to or like	waspish
-ive	pertaining to	descriptive
-ly	like	scholarly
-ular	pertaining to	cellular
-able	able to	readable
-ible	able to	convertible
-less	without	senseless
-like	like	lifelike
-most	at the extreme	topmost

Verb Suffixes Verb suffixes change base words to verbs. The following chart lists four common verb suffixes.

Verb Suffixes

Suffix	Meaning	Example
-ate	to make	activate
-en	to become	lengthen
-fy	to make	simplify
-ize	to become	crystallize

Adverb Suffixes Adverb suffixes change base words to adverbs—words that modify verbs, adjectives, and other adverbs. The following chart lists the most common adverb suffixes.

Adverb Suffixes

Suffix	Meaning	Example
-ly, -ily	manner	quickly
-ward	towards	skyward
-wise	like	clockwise

Exercises

A From each of the words listed below, form another word by adding a suffix. Use a dictionary to check your words.

1. wise	5. home	9. profit	13. electric
2. equal	6. ideal	10. judge	14. liquid
3. correspond	7. grand	11. resign	15. report
4. exult	8. laugh	12. character	16. victory

B In each of the following sentences, there is a blank followed by a base word in parentheses. Add a suffix to the base word to form the correct part of speech to fit the sentences.

1. Elena's strongest asset was her _____ (thorough).
2. The embezzler returned at night to _____ (false) the bank records.
3. "Take back that _____ (slander) remark!" snarled Helen.

4. After five days of _____ (exhaust) looking, the search team finally found the missing spelunker.

5. The most spectacular view in North America was the _____ (culminate) and the reward of their three-day climb to the top of Mt. McKinley.

6. Dr. Benson is one of the _____ (fore) authorities in the field of microbiology.

7. Captain Ahab in Herman Melville's novel *Moby Dick* is one of the most fascinating _____ (fiction) characters.

8. Kenneth wore a coat and tie to the party although there was no need for such _____ (formal).

9. The Lincoln assassination remains one of the most _____ (enigma) historical episodes in American history.

10. *Disintegration of the Persistence of Memory* is a work by Salvador Dali, perhaps the best-known _____ (surreal) painter.

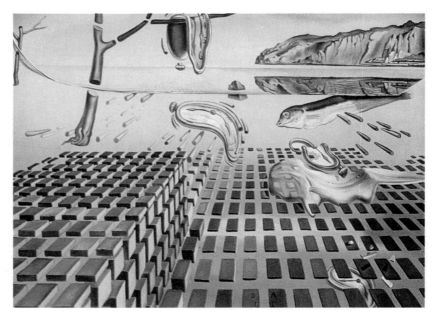

Disintegration of the Persistence of Memory, Salvador Dali, 1952–1954.

C Study the words in the following list. Determine their meanings from what you have learned about prefixes and suffixes. Then use each word in a sentence that shows your understanding of its meaning. Use a dictionary to check the meanings.

1. inexactitude
2. prematurely
3. nonconformist
4. immobility
5. misinformation
6. disillusionment

Part 4
Roots and Word Families

Another way to develop your vocabulary is to become familiar with **roots.** A root is the part of a word that contains its basic meaning. A root cannot stand alone. Many roots, such as those listed in the following two charts, originally came from Greek or Latin.

Useful Greek Roots

Root	Meaning	Example
anthrop	human	anthropology
aster, astr	star	asterisk
auto	self, alone	automobile
bibl	book	bibliography
bi, bio	life	biology
chron	time	chronology
crac, crat	govern	democracy
dem	people	epidemic
gen	birth, race	generation
geo	earth	geoscience
graph	write	paragraph
gram	write	grammar
hydr	water	hydrogen
log	word, reason	dialogue
logy	study of	geology
metr, meter	measure	barometer
neo	new	neophyte
nom, nym	name, word, law	economic
ortho	straight, correct	orthodontist
pan	all, entire	panorama
phil	love	philosopher
phobia	fear	claustrophobia
phon	sound	phonograph
psych	mind, soul	psychology
scope	see	telescope
soph	wise, wisdom	sophisticated
tele	far, distant	television
therm	heat	thermometer

Useful Latin Roots

Root	Meaning	Examples
capt	take, hold, seize	capture, captivate
cede, ceed, cess	go, yield, give away	recession, proceed
cred	believe	credit, creed
dic, dict	speak, say, tell	dictate, dictionary
duc, duct	lead	induce, conductor
fac, fec	do, make	factory, defect
ject	throw, hurl	eject, inject
junct	join	junction, conjunction
mit, miss	send	admit, dismiss
pon, pos, posit	place, put	component, deposit
port	carry	porter, portable
puls	throb, urge	pulsate, compulsory
scrib, script	write	description, scripture
spec	look, see	spectacle, spectator
stat	stand, put in a place	statue, stature
ten	stretch, hold	tendon, tenant
tract	pull, move	tractor, retract
vers, vert	turn	versatile, invert
vid, vis	see	video, vista
voc, vok	call	vocation, invoke
vol	wish	volunteer, malevolent
volv	roll	revolve, involve

These roots generate whole families of English words. A **word family** is a group of words with a common root. For example, all of the words in the following word family are derived from the Latin root *pas,* or *pat,* which means "feeling."

apathy	passion
compassion	impassive
compatible	patient
sympathy	pathos
dispassionate	empathetic
antipathy	pathology
passive	pathetic

By knowing word families, you can recognize roots in many related words and develop your vocabulary.

Exercises

A Each of the following words contains two or more Greek roots. Give the meanings of these roots. Then, define the word based on the meanings of its parts. Check the definition in a dictionary.

1. bibliophile
2. demography
3. autobiography
4. astrology
5. astronomy
6. philosophy
7. metronome
8. geothermal
9. autocratic
10. bibliophobia
11. technocrat
12. telephotography
13. chronometer
14. hydrology
15. orthography

B On your paper, complete the following sentences with definitions. Use the information given in the Greek roots chart on page 357 and in the first sentence of each item. Then check the answers in a dictionary.

1. The Greek word *adelphos* means "brother." Therefore, the name *Philadelphia* means _____ .
2. The Greek word *morph* means "shape" or "form." Therefore, the word *anthropomorphic* means _____ .
3. The Greek word *pseudes* means "false." Therefore, the word *pseudonym* means _____ .
4. The Greek word *psyche* means "mind" or "soul." Therefore, the word *psychology* means _____ .
5. The Greek word *acea* means "cure." Therefore the word *panacea* means _____ .
6. The Greek prefix *ana-* means, among other things, "backward." Therefore, the word *anagram* means _____ .
7. The Greek word *nautes* means "sailor." Therefore, the word *astronaut* means _____ .
8. The Greek word *kryptos* means "hidden." Therefore, the word *cryptogram* means _____ .
9. The Greek prefix *eu* means "good" or "well." Therefore, the word *euphony* means _____ .
10. The Greek prefix *syn-, sym-* means "together." Therefore, the word *synchronize* means _____ .

C Each of the following words contains one Latin root plus a prefix, a suffix, or both. Tell what each word part means. Write a definition for each word. Check the definition in a dictionary.

1. captive
2. export
3. incredulous
4. transpose
5. transmit
6. subversion
7. revoke
8. visible
9. convert
10. inspector
11. static
12. traction

In the Chinese game of mah-jongg, players try to form winning combinations of tiles engraved with drawings and symbols.

D Using your knowledge of Latin roots, choose words from the following list to complete the sentences below.

benediction	envision	receded
benevolent	evoked	remit
captivated	imports	reverted
conductor	intractable	stationary
credible	mission	vocation

1. The performer *took hold* of the audience. The performer _____ the audience.
2. Please *send back* your payment. Please _____ your payment.
3. The _____ *lead* the orchestra in a spirited rendition of Beethoven's *Ninth Symphony*.
4. She told a very *believable* story. Her story was _____ .
5. At low tide, the level of the ocean water *went back down*. The water _____ .
6. We were *sent* to find water. Finding water was our _____ .
7. A person who *wishes good* for others is _____ .
8. Teaching is my *calling* in life. Teaching is my _____ .
9. Dr. Jekyll *turned back* into Mr. Hyde. He _____ to his other personality.
10. Coffee is *carried into* our country from Brazil. Our country _____ coffee from Brazil.
11. The quarterback *stood in one place*. He remained _____ .
12. I can *see* many changes coming in the next few years. I _____ many changes over the next few years.

13. Alex has made his decision and *cannot be moved*. He is _____ .
14. The song *called forth* memories of her past. The song _____ memories of her past.
15. The chaplain *uttered a blessing*. The troops listened to this _____ .

E Listed below are several different word families. For each word family, identify the Latin root. Then add at least two other words to each family.

1. credence
   creditor
2. procession
   secede
3. specimen
   introspection
4. remit
   commit
5. diction
   predict
6. repose
   position
7. export
   portable
8. conduct
   reduce
9. vision
   visual
10. reject
    dejected
11. evolve
    revolving
12. tension
    tenet

Part 5
Activating Your Skills

You have now learned several helpful methods for determining the meanings of words. The following exercises feature words that may be unfamiliar to you. These are also the kinds of words that appear on standardized tests. The exercises will offer you another opportunity to activate the vocabulary skills that you have learned.

Section 1: Inferring Word Meanings from Context Use context clues to select the best definition for the italicized word in each passage. Write the letter of the best definition.

1. Leroy loved the *lugubrious* melodies of funeral marches.
   a. low
   b. frightening
   c. ancient
   d. mournful
2. After several crushing defeats, Wally started to lose his *zeal* for the basketball season.
   a. curiosity
   b. patience
   c. funds
   d. enthusiasm
3. Benjamin Franklin is noted for his *aphorisms,* short statements expressing wise observations.
   a. criticisms
   b. jokes
   c. sayings
   d. amendments

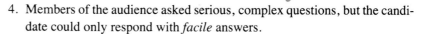

4. Members of the audience asked serious, complex questions, but the candidate could only respond with *facile* answers.
   a. honest
   c. superficial
   b. difficult
   d. misleading

5. Amid the remaining *flotsam* from the wrecked ship, rescue workers found only some timber and a single sailor's cap.
   a. floating debris
   c. nets
   b. water
   d. sailors

6. After the last meeting, Agent 008 had been followed and almost caught; therefore, she arranged for the next meeting to occur in a more *clandestine* place.
   a. expensive
   c. democratic
   b. hidden
   d. neutral

7. According to ancient legend, the Sirens' song was so *mesmerizing* that sailors hearing it would forget all about their duties.
   a. hypnotizing
   c. painful
   b. shocking
   d. revealing

8. Though Dr. Grumwald had great faith in the *salubrious* effects of the new medicine, his patient continued to get worse.
   a. dangerous
   c. long-lasting
   b. harmful
   d. healthful

9. Though the shopkeeper claimed the portrait of Washington was *bona fide*, there was something about it that seemed inauthentic.
   a. fake
   c. modern
   b. exotic
   d. genuine

10. The Bill of Rights is the *bulwark* of our civil liberties. It is our principal defense of our basic freedoms.
    a. test
    b. protection
    c. policy
    d. weakness

11. Ms. Bell prefers to spend her vacation in a *bucolic* place—a farm or a cabin in the woods.
    a. carefree
    b. friendly
    c. rural
    d. faraway

12. She did have one *idiosyncrasy,* an odd habit of winking.
    a. foolish act
    b. peculiar behavior
    c. hobby
    d. strange acquaintance

13. Marietta likes the quiet of the library, as opposed to the *cacophony* of the cafeteria.
    a. noise
    b. clutter
    c. crowd
    d. food

14. The whale came into existence fairly recently; but the shark, a truly *primordial* beast, has been around for millions of years.
    a. ancient
    b. frightening
    c. wild
    d. unknown

15. The minister's living quarters, or *manse,* was on the same street as the church.
    a. pulpit
    b. church
    c. home
    d. congregation

16. The speaker tried to *repress,* or hold back, her anger at the heckler's remarks.
    a. excuse
    b. control
    c. explain
    d. ignore

17. The local college is offering several classes in *horticulture,* including one on perennials and one on vegetable gardens.
    a. home improvement
    b. interior decorating
    c. growing plants
    d. outdoor recreation

18. *Terrestrial* animals, unlike their counterparts in the water, have to support their own weight.
    a. large
    b. land
    c. heavy
    d. warm-blooded

19. Because the school's halls were so *labyrinthine,* Mr. Bolenger drew up a detailed map to help the new students find their way.
    a. long
    b. like a maze
    c. narrow
    d. brightly decorated

20. The *euphoria* she felt was like a hot bath after two weeks of camping.
    a. anxiety
    b. impatience
    c. well-being
    d. unity

Section 2: Inferring Meaning from General Context Read each passage, noting the main idea and supporting details. Then write the letter that represents the best definition of the word in italics.

1. Rock music is *ubiquitous* nowadays. Not only do we hear it on television and radio, but also in cars, elevators, and stores.
   a. soothing
   b. everywhere
   c. modern
   d. loud

2. Many creatures undergo a complete *metamorphosis*. The butterfly, for example, begins life as a caterpillar and then changes into its adult form. The frog begins life as a tadpole and only later develops the shape and habits of the adult.
   a. awakening
   b. examination
   c. life
   d. transformation

3. Ancient Sumeria was a *hagiocracy*. All important decisions were made by priests. They passed laws, settled disputes, and collected taxes.
   a. country ruled by force
   b. country ruled by religious leaders
   c. city
   d. nation

4. *Arachnids* are sometimes good to have around. They help farmers by eating insects, and their webs can be beautiful.
   a. insects
   b. gardens
   c. spiders
   d. flowering plants

5. The use of *metonymy* is especially prevalent in political discussions. We frequently hear terms such as "the press" for "journalists" and "the White House" for the "President."
   a. an unoriginal expression
   b. substituting one word for a closely related word
   c. old-fashioned terms
   d. hard to understand jargon

6. Black lung disease is *endemic* among coal miners in the Welsh mountains. The disease is also prevalent among coal miners in the Appalachian Mountains.
   a. growing
   b. native to a region
   c. preventable
   d. originating in a rural area

7. Many people of the time considered Bach's music *ephemeral*. However, people still listen to his music today, over two hundred years later.
   a. beautiful
   b. complicated
   c. short-lived
   d. long-lived

8. Hyenas are cautious, cowardly creatures. Jackals, on the other hand, are known for their *temerity*.
   a. recklessness
   b. cowardliness
   c. friendliness
   d. behavior

9. The sloth may be the most *dilatory* animal in existence. Scientists have to combat boredom when studying these creatures because it takes them so long to do anything.
   a. slow-moving
   b. little-known
   c. gentle
   d. interesting
10. Carlotta and I both read the passage several times very carefully, examining each word. Nonetheless, her *exegesis* differed from mine largely because the author did not clarify what he meant by "courage."
    a. book
    b. interpretation
    c. author
    d. assignment

Section 3: Analyzing Word Parts Use your knowledge of prefixes, suffixes, base words, and roots to determine the meaning of each italicized word. Write the letter that represents the best definition.

1. *disclaim*
   a. deny any claim
   b. treat well
   c. be under obligation
   d. repeat a claim
2. *extragalactic*
   a. located within the galaxy
   b. deprived of a galaxy
   c. located outside the galaxy
   d. equal to the galaxy in size

3. *superstructure*
    a. a structure built below something else
    b. outside the structure
    c. a structure built on top of some other structure or on top of a foundation
    d. inside the structure
4. *presuppose*
    a. falsely believe
    b. support beforehand
    c. assume beforehand
    d. apply pressure to
5. *equipotential*
    a. having no potential
    b. having equal potential
    c. having great potential
    d. having potential for math
6. *atypical*
    a. like everyone else
    b. normal
    c. not like everyone else
    d. a kind or type
7. *intersperse*
    a. to scatter among things
    b. between a sphere
    c. to enter into
    d. a wide assortment
8. *concordance*
    a. like a concord
    b. a type of dance
    c. agreement, harmony
    d. a special meeting
9. *discourteous*
    a. with courtesy
    b. not courteous
    c. uncourtly
    d. a type of discourse
10. *neoclassic*
    a. a revival of classic style
    b. opposed to the classics
    c. the idea, or philosophy, that fine art should be appreciated for its own sake
    d. a new idea

11. *submerge*
    a. emerge
    b. above the head
    c. to place under water
    d. under someone's supervision
12. *manipulation*
    a. capable of handling
    b. skillful handling
    c. poor handling or operation
    d. opposed to an operation
13. *noncommittal*
    a. to pledge oneself to
    b. like a commitment
    c. not committing oneself to any course of action, not admitting knowledge or involvement
    d. an overwhelming sense of duty
14. *demotic*
    a. of the people, popular
    b. like a democracy
    c. against the people
    d. the philosophy of those people who belong to the Democratic political party
15. *juncture*
    a. a meeting house
    b. a joining
    c. a fork in the road
    d. against joining
16. *malocclusion*
    a. healthy teeth
    b. dental chart
    c. a poor meeting of the teeth
    d. relating to the jaw
17. *immeasurable*
    a. a unit of measure
    b. capable of measuring
    c. held in high esteem
    d. too much to be measured
18. *monochromatic*
    a. very colorful
    b. made up of a variety of colors
    c. having one color
    d. a type of shiny chrome

Shorn Words

Many new words are created by the addition of prefixes and suffixes to existing words, but one group of words is created through subtraction. Although the television was invented in the 1920's, it wasn't until the 1950's that the verb *televise* came into the language. Editors made changes in manuscripts long before *edit* existed as a word. These new words are examples of **back-formations.**

Back-formations occur when letters are trimmed from existing words. Often, they are words created by mistake. In the seventeenth century, for example, the word *pease* was mistaken for a plural word because of the "s" sound at the end. The word *pea* came into being as the singular version, even though *pease* was actually singular. (By the same logic, a new word *chee* might be invented as a singular form of *cheese*.) In other cases, such as the creation of *beg* from *beggar* and *scavenge* from *scavenger*, the letters deleted were mistaken for suffixes, although they really are not.

Mistaken or not, many back-formations have become accepted parts of English. *Revolt* came from *revolution, donate* came from *donation, baby-sit* came from *baby-sitter, diagnose* came from *diagnosis,* and *exclaim* came from *exclamation.*

In fact, it often seems more logical to assume that the back-formation came first, not the other way around.

Chapter 14
Application and Review

A Inferring Word Meanings from Context Read the following passage carefully, noting the italicized words. Based on your understanding of the passage, infer and write the meaning of each italicized word. Then, check the definition in a dictionary.

> August, 1931—The port town of Veracruz is a little purgatory between land and sea for the traveler, but the people who live there are very fond of themselves and the town they have helped to make. . . . They carry on their lives of alternate violence and *lethargy* with a pleasurable *contempt* for outside opinion, founded on the charmed notion that their ways and feelings are above and beyond criticism.
>
> When they entertain themselves at their numerous private and public feasts, the newspapers publish lyric *prose* saying . . . what lavish and *aristocratic*—the terms are *synonymous*, they believe—taste the decorations and refreshments [show]; and they cannot praise too much the skill with which the members of good society maintain in their *deportment*, the delicate balance between high courtesy and easy *merriment*. . . . "We are generous, warmhearted, *hospitable*, sensitive," they go on, and they mean it to be read not only by themselves but by the polyglot barbarians of the upper plateau who *obstinately* go on regarding Veracruz as merely a *pestilential* jumping-off place into the sea.
>
> From *Ship of Fools*, by Katherine Anne Porter

B Analyzing Word Parts Study the words in the following list. Determine their meanings from what you have learned about prefixes, suffixes, roots, and base words. Check the meaning of each word in a dictionary. Then use each word in a sentence.

1. absolve
2. predominant
3. subsequent
4. irrevocable
5. circumspect
6. chronometry
7. anomalous
8. teletypewriter
9. neologism
10. incapacious

15

Using Language Precisely

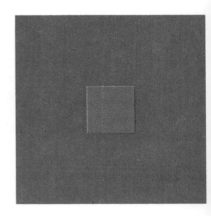

L ook carefully at the images above. Which inner square is the lighter shade of gray? Although they look different, both inner squares are exactly the same color.

Just as the color of the background against which the square is seen influences the way you perceive it, so does the context in which a word is used determine its shades of meaning. Ordinary words take on unique meanings when used by computer scientists, sportscasters, or musicians. People from different parts of the country have characteristic vocabularies and ways of speaking. A particular individual even uses language differently in different situations.

In this chapter you will learn about the many meanings of words and levels of language and how to use them to communicate clearly and effectively.

Part 1
Levels of Language

Diversity can make language more interesting and communication more effective. However, at times, differences in spoken or written English can be a barrier to understanding. In order to choose an appropriate form of English for an occasion, you must first identify both the situation and the audience. You can then suit your language to your purpose. The types of language that are used for different situations are called **levels of usage.** The terms *standard* and *nonstandard* are used to describe these levels.

Standard English

The language that follows the rules and guidelines accepted by English speakers everywhere is **standard English.** Standard English may be further divided into two accepted levels of usage: formal and informal.

Formal English is the language appropriate to circumstances that are serious, dignified, or ceremonial. You sometimes hear formal English in sermons and public speeches. However, formal English is used more often in writing than in speaking. You will find it in scholarly journals, legal papers, business reports, and many textbooks. The following passage from a textbook is an example of formal English:

> One of the oldest surviving religions in the world, with an unbroken succession of seers and teachers, is practiced by millions of people living in the vast subcontinent of India; it is known as Hinduism. Modern Hindus use this Western term [Hinduism] simply as a convenience when speaking or writing English. Among themselves they prefer to call their religion *sanatana dharma* ("eternal religion"), since it was not founded by any historical person but is based upon eternal principles that were "heard" by the *rishis* (sages or seers) who lived during a very remote period in history.
>
> From *World Religions* by S. A. Nigosian

Informal English is the comfortable, correct language commonly used in everyday situations. Also known as **colloquial English,** it is the language of conversation and informal talks as well as the written language of most newspapers and magazine articles. Consider the following example of informal English:

> The citizens of Farmington, Utah, will never forget the sound. "The trees were popping and the boulders rolling," recalls Steve Moon of the fire department. "Anybody who wouldn't be nervous listening to *that* coming down the hill would have to have something wrong with him." What came down that hill was mud: tons of soggy, slippery, onrushing mud. The same thing was happening in the neighboring town of Bountiful, where 1,000 people had to be evacuated. Mud slides and floods all last week caused millions of dollars of damage and the loss of 16 homes in Utah and in western Nevada, where a mucky avalanche descended from aptly named *Slide Mountain*.
>
> From *Time*

Think of formality and informality as opposite ends of the same scale. Most writing, even of a very serious nature, is somewhat mobile, sliding back and forth along a short range of the scale. However, just as combining very formal with very informal clothing would seem odd, jumping abruptly from very formal to very informal language would be confusing or disruptive.

The chart that follows lists the characteristics of formal and informal English. As you read it, remember that there are similarities as well as differences between formal and informal English. Both levels use correct grammar, spelling, and punctuation.

Characteristics of Formal and Informal English

	Formal	Informal
Tone	Serious, reserved, academic, ceremonial	Personal, friendly, casual
Vocabulary and Mechanics	Sometimes uses longer or more complicated words Avoids contractions, clipped words, and slang Uses correct grammar, spelling, and punctuation	Uses simpler words Often uses contractions and clipped words Avoids slang Uses correct grammar, spelling, and punctuation
Organization	Longer, carefully constructed sentences	Sentences of a great variety of lengths Similar to conversational English
Appropriate Uses	Reports or serious essays Business letters Legal, academic, religious, or other professional documents Formal presentations, speeches, debates, or interviews	Writing intended for a general audience Friendly letters Conversations, informal talks
Audience	Readers of scholarly material Readers of professional documents Persons in positions of authority	Friends, co-workers Most general audiences

Slang consists of new words or expressions as well as established words and phrases that have taken on new meanings. Slang is at the most informal end of the scale of language levels and is never found in formal English. In fact, slang is seldom part of informal writing except when it is used in dialogue and in writing meant to appeal to a specific group of people who are familiar with the specific vocabulary of a shared interest area.

Slang often seems colorful and interesting when it is first used, and sometimes it even becomes accepted in general use. For example, the words *carpetbagger, hobo,* and *killjoy* began as slang. However, most slang terms fade away quickly. It is best to avoid using slang in most situations.

Nonstandard English

Language that does not conform to the accepted standards of grammar, usage, and mechanics is called **nonstandard English.** It is chiefly a form of spoken English. If nonstandard English appears in print, it is usually in the dialogue of a character in a story or play. For example, in the following passage the author deliberately uses nonstandard English. Can you identify the examples of nonstandard English in this portion of a letter from a rookie baseball player?

> Next morning half the bunch mostly vetrans went to the ball park which isn't no better than the one we got at home. Most of them was vetrans as I say but I was in the bunch. That makes things look pretty good for me don't it Al? We tossed the ball round and hit fungos and run round and then Callahan asks Scott and Russell and I to warm up easy and pitch a few to the batters. It was warm and I felt pretty good so I warmed up pretty good . . . . So I went in and after I lobbed a few I cut loose my fast one. Lord was to bat and he ducked out of the way and then throwed his bat to the bench. Callahan says What's the matter Harry? Lord says I forgot to pay up my life insurance. He says I ain't ready for Walter Johnson's July stuff.
>
> From *You Know Me Al* by Ring Lardner

The misspelling of *veteran,* the incorrect verb forms *don't it,* and *ain't,* the double negative *isn't no better,* and the errors in subject-verb agreement and punctuation are typical of nonstandard English.

Exercise

The following passage contains several different levels of language. First, rewrite the passage in formal English as if it were part of a science report. Then rewrite the passage as though you were going to include it in a letter to a friend who shares your interest in telescopes and stargazing.

> By shining the light of distant stars through a spectrograph, astronomers can produce rainbowlike spectra for objects that are way, way out there in space somewhere. After studying these spectra, scientists can figure out lots of interesting things, like what stuff stars are made out of and how far away the stars are and how fast those stars are traveling through space. Given the value of such scientific information, one can conclude that sometimes things that look really great are also extremely useful.

Part 2
Using Words Precisely

Using levels of language correctly is one way of improving your communication skills. Using words precisely is another.

The rich vocabulary of English has evolved over the centuries. Existing English words have been altered, new words have been invented, and useful words have been absorbed from other languages. As a result, many English words have taken on more than one meaning, making it possible to use the same word in several ways. English also has many words that mean essentially the same thing—called synonyms—that allow you to select the precise word that best fits the specific context.

Multiple Meanings of Words

You probably feel that you are familiar with the word *front*. Would you be surprised to learn that *Webster's New World Dictionary* gives twenty-four definitions of this simple word?

Becoming familiar with the various meanings of a word is one way to increase your vocabulary. Learning to use these various meanings correctly can increase the precision of your language. The following sentences illustrate a few of the meanings of *front*. Notice how the meaning of the word changes as the part of speech changes. Consult your dictionary to discover other meanings of *front*.

Inwardly trembling, Martina put on a brave *front*. (noun)
Slowly, we worked through to the *front* row. (adjective)
The French windows *fronted* on a formal garden. (verb)

Synonyms

Think for a moment of the color blue. Perhaps you see royal blue, sapphire, aquamarine, sky blue, and navy blue. Each hue has its own distinct look and effect on you.

Just as there are various shades of the color blue, there are various shades of meaning for any group of synonyms. Knowing how to use synonyms effectively contributes to a writer's ability to express ideas precisely.

The shades of meaning of the synonyms in the following sentences differ. Notice how greater precision is achieved through word choice.

The aged monk *walked* through the abbey halls.
The aged monk *shambled* through the abbey halls.
The doctor emerged from the patient's room with a *serious* look on his face.
The doctor emerged from the patient's room with a *somber* look on his face.

A thesaurus or a dictionary synonymy can help you find synonyms for a word. You may wish to refer to the mini-chapter on pages 52–57 to review the use of these reference works.

Drawing by H. Martin; © 1986 The New Yorker Magazine, Inc.

"*Care to go for a short trudge?*"

Denotation and Connotation As you choose which is the best of several synonyms to use, consider the emotional impact each word will have on your listener or reader. Precise and effective usage is often dependent upon recognizing the denotations and connotations of words with similar meanings.

The denotation of a word is its dictionary definition. For instance, *chow, lunch,* and *repast* all have the same general denotation, "meal." But a word may also have a **connotation,** or meaning related to the feelings a word creates. For example, *chow* is slang and implies that the meal is very informal. *Lunch* implies a light meal, while *repast* is used to describe a more formal feast.

A writer or speaker can shape the attitude of an audience through the choice of a word or words with certain connotations. See how the connotations of the following synonyms help to shape the tone in each of these sentences:

Admiring	I was *loyal* and never left the family home.
Positive	You were *attached* and never left the family home.
Negative	He was *dependent* and never left the family home.

Exercises

A Consult a dictionary to find the many definitions for the word *slip.* Write ten sentences that use the word *slip* in ten different ways.

B Determine the meaning of each italicized word in the following sentences. Consult a dictionary if necessary.

1. The men *scoured* the countryside for the lost boy.
2. An American *school* of painting began with Benjamin West.
3. I could not find the book I wanted in the *stacks*.
4. He converted his assets to *liquid* form.
5. Because of the dangerous *list,* the captain called all *hands.*
6. The writer realized that he needed to *ply* his trade in order to improve.

C Using the model on this page, create groupings of three sentences for each of the words listed. The connotation must proceed from *I* to *you* to *he* or *she* and should become increasingly negative. Do not change the basic meaning of the first word. Look at this example:

> *Example*   I am *traditional.* You are *old-fashioned.* He is *reactionary.*

1. precise   2. dreamer   3. slender   4. cautious

Part 3
Writing and Speaking Clearly

The purpose of language is to communicate. The use of precise, easily understood words and the appropriate level of language help to achieve effective communication. Other types of language can detract from the clarity and directness of your message.

Jargon

Every technical or professional field creates its own specialized vocabulary. By using this vocabulary, or **jargon,** people in the same field can communicate efficiently with one another. To outsiders, however, jargon may seem unfamiliar and confusing. When deciding whether or not jargon is appropriate, a speaker or writer must consider how knowledgeable an audience is about a topic.

There is a second reason for learning how to handle jargon. In today's complex society, jargon finds its way into newspaper and magazine articles and eventually into everyday speech. Familiarity with these specialized vocabularies will enable you to comprehend more of what you read or hear and will help you to communicate more knowledgeably. Study the following specialized terms:

Specialized Terms

Vocabulary of Sports

bullpen	line drive	rebound	blitz	face-off
safety	gridiron	down	puck	squeeze play

Vocabulary of the Arts

harmony	soft shoe	abstract	ballad	melodrama
timbre	choreography	hue	epic	cast

Vocabulary of Science

black hole	nova	enzyme	molecule	anxiety
fission	holography	biosphere	quasar	quantum

Vocabulary of Business

capital	commodities	prime rate	recession	assets
debit	monopoly	wholesale	overhead	merger

Exercises

A Read the following paragraph. Identify each legal term, and, if you are unsure of its meaning, use a dictionary to find a definition. Rewrite the paragraph in language that can be understood by a group of students who are unfamiliar with technical legal terms. Be sure to use correct grammar, spelling, and punctuation.

> The framers [of the Constitution] allowed federal courts to hear suits between citizens of different states. They feared local judges and juries wouldn't do justice to outsiders. But do we really need to make a federal case out of a car crash between an Iowan and a Kansan? "Diversity" suits are 25 percent of the federal caseload. They encourage legal gamesmanship. While federal judges in diversity cases apply their own "procedural" laws, they must apply the state's (which state's?) "substantive" laws, guessing how state courts would decide issues they haven't decided yet.

From *Newsweek*

B Members of different professions and people involved in different activities may use the same terms but attach different meanings to them. Use a dictionary to find the meaning for each of the terms listed below as it is used in both of the fields given. Then use the term in a sentence as it would be used in each of the specialized areas listed.

1. season (sports, cooking)
2. issue (art, law)
3. charging (sports, finance)
4. flat (music, real estate)
5. ears (agriculture, journalism)
6. pack (travel, medicine)
7. cast (fishing, theater)
8. baste (cooking, sewing)
9. stock (merchandising, ranching)
10. slice (food service, sports)
11. root (mathematics, sports)
12. mace (cooking, weaponry)
13. justify (publishing, law)
14. yarn (literature, sewing)
15. temper (metallurgy, music)

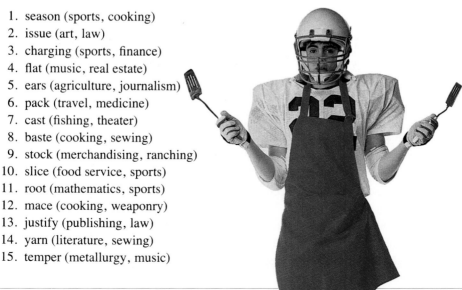

379

Gobbledygook

Sometimes in an effort to sound well-informed and impressive, people use long difficult words and complicated sentences. Such language is called **gobbledygook.** Gobbledygook frequently can be found in professional publications and public statements. Study the statement below from an insurance policy.

> This policy is issued in consideration of the application therefore, a copy of which application is attached hereto and made part hereof. Payment for said insurance is on file of the above-named issued.

This passage uses legal jargon and complicated sentence structure to "dress up" its simple meaning: Here is your insurance policy. Our records show that you have paid for this policy.

Avoid using jargon that is unfamiliar to your audience. Also, avoid padding your sentences or using big words when small ones will do. The use of gobbledygook prevents clear, direct communication of your message.

Cliché

Another type of ineffective language is the **cliché.** A cliché is an expression that was once fresh and powerful but through overuse has lost its impact and exactness of meaning. Read the following list of clichés. What original, more direct expression can you suggest to replace each cliché?

after all is said and done	busy as a bee
at a loss for words	deep, dark secret
easier said than done	as cold as ice
familiar landmark	needless to say
bored to death	crack of dawn
time is money	on the ball

Euphemisms

Euphemisms are expressions that are prettier or less harsh than the words they stand for. For example, the term *senior citizens* is less abrasive than the phrase *old people*. Writers and speakers should be sensitive to the effective use of euphemisms. Euphemisms are properly used when courtesy and tact are called for. If, however, the euphemism is misleading or being used to cover up the truth, it is better to use the more precise original term. Review the following list of euphemisms that may be used to replace unpleasant terms.

Common Euphemisms

Unpleasant Term	Euphemism
false teeth	dentures
to arrest	to detain
to spy	to do intelligence work
propaganda	information
retreat	strategic withdrawal
garbage collector	sanitation engineer

Exercises

A Match each passage of gobbledygook on the left with the corresponding famous quotation on the right.

1. Humankind, taken *in toto,* is such that the individuals comprising this group are coequal in their inceptive or primal state.

    a. "I know why the caged bird sings." Paul Laurence Dunbar

2. Past experience seems to indicate that the events concomitant to love are unlikely to proceed in an orderly or expected manner.

    b. "To err is human, to forgive divine." Alexander Pope

3. Indulgence in censurable behavior is an attendant human frailty in sharp contrast to the exoneration of others who indulge in censurable behavior, a quality associated with deity.

    c. "All men are created equal." Thomas Jefferson

4. The causal or determining factors that underlie the euphonious vocalizations of immured avifauna lie within the scope of my personal reasoning.

    d. "The course of true love never did run smooth."
        William Shakespeare

B These gobbledygook sentences are weighed down with excess baggage—unnecessarily ponderous words. Translate them into understandable English. Your dictionary will help you with unfamiliar words.

1. He gave up his employment because he came to the conclusion that the remuneration involved was not commensurate with his performance load.
2. Demand for parking does not appear to exceed significantly the supply of available parking spaces within our building's designated parking lots even during peak demand periods.
3. Before performance can be initiated on stage, all illumination in contingent areas must be lessened to the maximum extent.
4. Objects that scintillate are not necessarily auric in nature.
5. Extra supplies may be requisitioned by obtaining and completing an appropriate form.

C Identify the clichés or euphemisms in the following sentences. Translate the sentences into more direct, precise, or original language. Be prepared to discuss which version is preferable.

1. Like many young actors in New York, Edgar was between jobs .
2. This year's new football coach really has a lot on the ball .
3. Providing enough refuse containers helps to prevent litter.
4. Firefighters arrived just in the nick of time .
5. Portly gentlemen often have difficulty finding attractive suits.

Chapter 15
Application and Review

A Understanding Levels of Language The following passage contains mixed levels of language, slang, gobbledygook, and clichés. First rewrite the passage in the form appropriate for a newsletter to the Filmgoers Club. Then rewrite the passage as it would appear as part of a report on Western films.

> Let me tell you, in the last scene of the movie, everything goes wacko. The star foregoes his prior Western equestrian pursuits and accedes to the ingenue's matrimonial ambitions. It's hard to imagine that in this day and age folks will shell out a big wad of cash to see such mediocre performances and such a mundane plot. Take my word for it; you can miss this bomb.

B Understanding Jargon Read the following newspaper article. Identify and define any terms that could be considered jargon. Using a dictionary or another reference source, rewrite the article so it can be understood by people unfamiliar with the stock market and its specialized vocabulary.

Stocks were mixed throughout the day Thursday as the market modestly extended its slight advance in the previous session.

Steel, oil-service, and forest products issues rose, but several defense, mining, oil, and drug stocks fell back.

Gainers held a 9-7 edge over losers on the New York Stock Exchange, but the NYSE's composite index was up .04 to 95.93.

Big Board volume totaled 83.74 million shares, against 80.38 million on Wednesday.

C Using Synonyms Study the differences in meaning for the following groups of words. Use each word in a sentence that correctly reflects its connotations.

1. obese, plump, fat
2. renown, fame, notoriety
3. home, residence, pad
4. outdo, surpass, excel
5. economical, thrifty, stingy
6. oppose, resist, combat

Focus On

ADVERTISING

It is estimated that you encounter 1,500 ads every day. How well are you doing under this assault?

Let the Buyer Beware

The cartoon above, although a humorous exaggeration, suggests the lengths advertisers will go to to get your attention—and your money. To make sense of the information you're bombarded with and to become a smart consumer, you must learn how to question, analyze, and judge advertising.

Just the Facts, Ma'am

Advertising is tremendously useful, both to the advertiser and to the consumer. The seller has a way to make the product known, the buyer a way to learn about the product. There are two basic types of advertising: *informative* and *persuasive.*

Informative advertising is the kind you normally see in a merchandise catalog. Specific information is given about a product, including what it will do and how much it costs. Even though the

intent is to persuade you to buy, the information is presented without emotional appeals. You must judge the value of the product by studying the facts about it.

Study the ad describing a bicycle helmet. Most cyclists look for safety and comfort in a helmet. Which words indicate the helmet's safety features? What backs up the ad's claim about the "excellent ventilation system"?

Study the facts about a product before you judge its value.

The Price Is Right?

With certain advertising, especially informational ads, the product's price is highlighted. The price often sounds like a bargain, but consider carefully the wording used.

"List price . . ." This is the price suggested by the manufacturer. Sometimes a product is advertised as "selling at list price." However, many products sell for less than the list price and indeed are never intended to sell at what the manufacturer suggests.

"Originally . . ." When a price is quoted as "originally $24.99, now only $21.99," it means that at one time (perhaps as much as five years ago), the product sold at $24.99. The product may have been overpriced to begin with, however, or it may have been replaced by a better model.

"Below manufacturer's cost . . ." It may seem like a bargain, but find out *why* the manufacturer is willing to take a loss. The product may be poorly designed or a poor seller that desperately needs a sales boost. It may not have a guarantee, and spare parts may be virtually impossible to obtain. Ask yourself, "Why haven't others bought this product?"

When the Difference Is Only Skin Deep

Many products are very similar, both in price and quality. For example, laboratory tests show that all gasoline brands with the same octane rating perform equally well in car engines. Many brands of blue jeans are indistinguishable without their designer labels. Generic food products often differ from their name-brand counterparts only in their packaging and in their price.

To make their products seem different and more appealing than others, advertisers do more than just point out the facts about their product. They create persuasive ads which usually are more manipulative than informative. The advertisers employ careful wording to make their products seem better than others.

Persuasive advertisements also rely on various kinds of emotional appeals to sway your thinking. The advertisement shown on page 387 is a persuasive ad. Refer to it as you read about the following advertising techniques.

Watchwords

Weasel Words Qualifiers such as *almost, nearly,* and *close to* give the advertiser a convenient "out."

SUPRA
CYCLING HELMET

$56.95

Our popular Supra cycling helmet is made of a tough outer surface and a state-of-the-art inner liner, which make the Supra highly shock absorbent. The excellent ventilation system has six front vents and six rear vents to help circulate air within the helmet. Our new "gull's wing" design enhances the Supra's aerodynamics.

Color: **White.** Sizes: **S, M, L, XL.** Weight: **450g**

For example, a shampoo that leaves your hair "feeling like never before" could actually make your hair feel worse than ever without making the ad incorrect.

Purr and Snarl Words Ad writers consciously use words with strong positive or negative connotations to sway your feelings. Purr words have positive connotations. Words such as *golden, mother, home,* and *success* trigger pleasant thoughts and help create a favorable impression of a product or service.

Snarl words, which carry negative connotations, are also used in some advertising. In the phrase "prevents ugly blemishes," the word *ugly* helps trigger a negative reaction, not to the product itself, but to the situation that the product claims to remedy.

> *When you read an advertisement, look for the words and phrases that carry strong positive or negative connotations.*

Comparatives/Superlatives

Words such as *better, best, more,* and *most* are used liberally in persuasive ads, and you should be aware of what they really mean. According to accepted advertising standards, many similar products can say they are "the best," but what is usually meant is "among the best." With comparatives and superlatives be aware of the rele-

Su*purr*latives like *super mom* can be powerful persuaders.

vant questions that the wording often dodges: What facts are given to substantiate the claim? What is the product being compared with? Who made the comparison?

Unidentified Terms "The sportswear with polypropylene!" The fabric sounds wonderful—but what exactly *is* polypropylene? Ad writers realize that "scientific" terms and "special" numbers impress people. An ad may tell you that the special ingredient *YK7* is what makes brand *Z* better than Brand *X*. Before you buy, find out what that special ingredient is. If you aren't told, then you shouldn't let the term influence you.

Nothing But the (Half) Truth

Unfinished Claims These are statements such as "50 percent more pain reliever" and "nine out of ten doctors recommend." These claims are "unfinished" because not all of the context of the statistic is given. In the first case, you are not told whether the product has 50 percent more pain reliever than it used to have or 50 percent more than competing brands. In the second case, you might wonder how many doctors were sampled.

Implied Ideas In a television commercial for a popular breakfast cereal, you are told that the cereal is "part of a complete, balanced breakfast." The announcer intentionally places the emphasis on "complete, balanced breakfast" and de-emphasizes "part of." As a result, the commercial implies that the cereal is all the breakfast you need. As a hedge against this falsehood, the orange juice, milk, and toast are pictured, hiding behind the cereal.

Why Not Be Beautiful?

Advertisers use a variety of appeals to persuade you to spend your money on their products. Following are some of the most commonly used advertising appeals.

Emotional Appeals These appeals take advantage of the fact that people have certain nearly universal needs and desires. Some of these needs and desires include keeping ourselves and our families safe and happy, making ourselves more physically attractive, having friends and being popular, and attaining higher social status. Advertising slogans such as "Is your family as safe as you think?" and "Why not be your most beautiful?" appeal to the viewers' basic desires.

Appeal to Authority People tend to trust the word of an authority. A testimonial from an expert, such as an auto mechanic endorsing a motor oil, may suggest that the

Experts Agree

Bugs just can't resist

Fatal Attraction

Irresistible XTP Powder attracts bugs, then deals them a deadly blow.

Kills all household pests in just 10 days or your money back

product is effective. But frequently, this kind of ad oversimplifies or distorts the opinions of experts. The ads don't tell you that experts often disagree. In some cases, the "expert" may be only an actor or actress hired to play the part.

Appeal to Reason Some ads present facts about the product and urge you, as a reasonable consumer, to make the smart choice. Be careful to note what information has been provided. Is it relevant? Is it documented? Have any details been omitted? Are the claims different from those anyone else could make?

Also, watch for ads with circular reasoning. These simply repeat a claim in different words. "People like Cloud Nine ice cream because they really enjoy it" is circular reasoning.

Appeal by Association This appeal comes in four varieties. Bandwagon ads encourge you to be part of the crowd and to be like everyone else. "Everyone loves Can-Do Computers!" is a statement that appeals to the common desire to be like other people.

Be careful to note what information an advertisement provides.

Ads based on snob appeal use the opposite strategy: rather than be like everyone else, you sometimes want to be distinctive. You would rather be a member of a select group. "For those who dare to be different: the Skywalker Skateboard!" Ads such as these suggest that if you buy the item, you can be one of a chosen few.

Another kind of appeal by association is the false testimonial. Many companies hire celebrities to endorse their products. These companies hope that people will buy products because they identify with the star doing the testimonial. Of course, a celebrity doing a testimonial often works in a field completely unrelated to the product. You may wish you could be an Olympic gymnast, but don't get that desire confused with buying flashlight batteries promoted by an athlete!

A fourth ad strategy is called transfer. Picture the following soft drink ad: A group of happy people are enjoying a day at the beach— some of them are tossing a beach ball, others are splashing in the water, and some are listening to the radio and having a soft drink.

Advertisers hope that consumers will associate the coolness of water and the vitality and happiness of a group with the soft drink. With this ad technique, the very positive feelings evoked by certain images—happy groups, home, parties, America—are transferred to the product.

Try Your Skill

A Identify the advertising technique used in each of the following slogans.

1. Now that you've reached the top, you deserve a Wexter.

2. Put Z4000 in your tank. The gas with gusto.

3. Six out of seven professional mechanics use Black Gold on their own cars.

4. *Everyone* loves Claude's stone-washed jeans.

5. When Joe Wyoming isn't wearing a football uniform, he wears Saddle cologne.

6. Now you can earn up to $100.00 in one day!

B Write two advertisements for your favorite album, tape, or compact disk. Make one an informative ad, and the other a persuasive ad, using at least one of the appeals presented in this chapter.

C Even responsible advertisers use the techniques described in this chapter. Study the ad on this page. Find at least three examples of the advertising language you have been learning about. Write a paragraph, explaining each of the examples you've chosen.

16

The Library and Reference Works

*A*lmost anything you want to know can be found in a library. Sometimes, though, it's hard to know just where to begin looking.

Fortunately, libraries arrange their books more systematically than the haphazard array shown in the photograph. In this chapter you will learn how libraries are organized and how to use the card and computerized catalogs to find the information you are looking for. You will also learn about the library's many reference sources, such as atlases, encyclopedias, and various audiovisual materials, and how to use them most effectively.

Part 1
Organization of Libraries

Libraries follow a universal plan for organizing materials. Familiarity with this arrangement provides library users with easy access to the resources that they require. Perhaps the most important resource at the library is the librarian. To make the best use of your library, ask for the librarian's assistance.

Sections of the Library

All libraries organize their book collections into the same standard sections as described below.

Catalog Section Each item in the library is listed in the **card catalog** or in a **computer catalog.** All listings are arranged alphabetically by author, title, and subject. Computer catalogs can often provide a printed list of books available on a given subject.

Stacks The large bookcases where the fiction and nonfiction books available for checkout are shelved are called the **stacks.** Reference materials and items from special sections are not considered part of the stacks.

Periodical Section This section consists of current issues of magazines and newspapers and the indexes to them, such as the *Readers' Guide to Periodical Literature*. Check with the librarian to learn how older magazines are stored. The periodical section may be a part of the reference section or it may be found in a separate area.

Reference Section Dictionaries, encyclopedias, almanacs, yearbooks, and atlases are usually shelved in a separate room or area of the library. Most of these materials must remain in the library.

Special Sections Many libraries have special sections, such as a children's room or a section devoted to the local history of the area. Often, libraries also have special sections for nonprint materials such as record collections, art reproduction prints, videocassettes, and filmstrips. Many libraries provide audiovisual equipment and special areas for listening to or for viewing nonprint materials. Computers and typewriters may also be available for public use.

Exercise

Draw a map of the floor plan of your school library and one of your local library. Label the sections mentioned in this lesson. How are the libraries similar? How do they differ? What special sections does your local library contain?

Part 2
Classification and Arrangement of Books

Understanding the classification and arrangement of books in a library will enable you to find the resource you need quickly and efficiently.

Fiction

Novels and short-story collections are arranged alphabetically by the author's last name in a section of the stacks labeled *Fiction*. Multiple works by the same author are arranged alphabetically by title. Fiction may be further grouped into a classification such as mystery or science fiction.

Nonfiction

Works of nonfiction are classified in various ways.

Dewey Decimal System The **Dewey Decimal System,** which is named for its originator, Melvil Dewey, classifies all books by number in ten major categories. These categories and examples of the topics they include are listed below.

000–099	General Works (encyclopedias, bibliographies)
100–199	Philosophy (conduct, psychology)
200–299	Religion (the Bible, mythology, theology)
300–399	Social Science (law, education, economics)
400–499	Language (grammars, dictionaries, foreign languages)
500–599	Science (mathematics, biology, chemistry)
600–699	Technology (medicine, inventions, cooking)
700–799	The Arts (painting, music, theater, sports)
800–899	Literature (poetry, plays, essays)
900–999	History (biography, geography, travel)

Detail, *Numbers in Color*, Jasper Johns, 1959.

Each major subject area is divided into subcategories. For example, a book on circuses is categorized broadly under *the arts (700–799)* and specifically under *public performances (791)*.

Library shelves are prominently marked with the Dewey Decimal numbers. Within each section, books are arranged alphabetically by the author's last name. Biography may be shelved in the 920's or in a special section, in which case a *B* appears on the spine of the book and on the catalog card. Reference books are marked with an *R* on the catalog card and are shelved separately.

Library of Congress Classification Another method of classifying books, the **Library of Congress Classification,** or **LC,** is used primarily by large libraries. Books are classified by letter into twenty-one broad categories. These categories are listed below.

A	General Works	**M**	Music
B	Philosophy, Psychology, Religion	**N**	Fine Arts
		P	Language and Literature
C–F	History	**Q**	Science
E–F	American History	**R**	Medicine
G	Geography, Anthropology, Recreation	**S**	Agriculture
		T	Technology
H	Social Sciences	**U**	Military Science
J	Political Science	**V**	Naval Science
K	Law	**Z**	Bibliography and Library Science
L	Education		

Subdivisions within a category are indicated by adding a second letter. For example, science is labeled *Q* and botany, *QK.*

Exercise

Write the Dewey Decimal category in which books about each of the following would be found.

1. Development of the jet engine
2. Cost of a college education
3. Rules for soccer
4. Plays with only two characters
5. African art
6. Norse mythology
7. Algebra
8. Cajun cooking

Part 3
Understanding Library Catalogs

Every library follows a system for cataloging all available books and non-print sources. To determine whether the library has a particular book and where to find it, use the computer or the card catalog.

The Card Catalog

The **card catalog** is a cabinet of long, narrow drawers or file trays containing alphabetically arranged cards. There are usually three cards for each book in the card catalog: the author card, the title card, and the subject card. Each card carries a classification number, or **call number,** in the upper left-hand corner. Call numbers give the Dewey Decimal number or the Library of Congress letter code for a book. On some cards an additional letter code indicates that a book is kept in one of the special sections of the library. Such codes include REF, reference; J or JUV, juvenile; SC, short-story collection; and SF, science fiction. Call numbers help you locate where a book is shelved.

Author, Title, and Subject Cards Each of these three types of cards contains essentially the same information, although the arrangement of the information varies according to the type of card.

On an **author card** the author's name, last name first, appears as a heading on the card. A **title card** lists the book title as a heading with the author's name directly under the title. A subject heading appears at the top of a **subject card.**

The book's title and the author's name appear below this heading. Author, title, and subject cards for nonfiction books carry a call number in the upper left-hand corner of the card. These different cards allow you to look up a book no matter what specific information you begin with.

Cross-Reference Cards that read "See" and "See also" are cross-reference cards. "See" cards refer you to other subject headings in the catalog. For example, a subject card on movies may read "See *Moving pictures.*" This means that the library lists books on movies under the heading *moving pictures.*

"See also" cards refer you to other closely related subjects. For example, a subject card on moving pictures may read "See also *Comedy films.*"

Other Information About Catalogs

Here are some additional facts about catalogs that might be useful.

The Computerized Catalog Many libraries offer a computerized catalog system, which allows you to use a computer terminal to search for a book by the author, title, or subject. For example, if you were searching for books on windsurfing, you might type in the heading *water sports* on a terminal like the one shown below. A librarian will help if you require assistance using the computer.

Additional Catalog Information Both card catalog cards and computerized programs provide additional useful information about each book. Both catalog systems usually list the number of pages a book contains as well as a notation telling whether the book has illustrations, maps, tables, or other similar features. In addition, some catalogs provide a brief description of the plot or nature of the book. Often, the catalog card will also include a listing of other catalog cards for the book. When you have several sources from which to choose, such information can help you to select the book that is best suited to your needs.

Alternate Headings If you have difficulty finding information on a topic, or if you exhaust all the sources readily available, think about other ways information on the topic might be listed. For example, information for a report on off-shore drilling might also be found in articles or books about petroleum sources or energy sources. You would then look up subject cards under the headings *petroleum* and *energy*. Since off-shore drilling affects the surrounding environment, materials on ecology might also provide information. Always try to think of alternate headings and explore them when you have exhausted the available sources.

Exercises

A Find a title, author, call number, and publication date for a book in each of the categories described below. Use the catalog system that is available in your library.

1. A collection of American poetry
2. A history of education in the United States
3. A book on World War I
4. A collection of fine art reproductions
5. A book by Lewis Carroll

B Consider all possible headings and decide what subject cards might provide information on the following topics. Be prepared to discuss your answers.

1. Bali dances
2. The powers of the president
3. Jewelry designs
4. Automobile insurance
5. Writing a research paper
6. Physical fitness
7. Salem witchcraft trials
8. Civil War ballads
9. Life on Mars
10. Atomic submarines

Part 4
Using Reference Works

Reference works may be the most useful resources the library has to offer. Whether you are asked to write a brief biographical sketch of the American writer Carl Sandburg or to do a short report explaining black holes in space, you will find reference works helpful. Knowing the various types of reference works and where they are kept in the library can save you valuable time.

Reference Books

Using resources effectively means knowing which kind of reference work best suits a research task. You are already familiar with one kind of reference work, the dictionary, discussed on pages 52–57. Other reference works include encyclopedias, almanacs and yearbooks, biographical references, books about authors, literary reference books, pamphlets, handbooks, catalogs, atlases, and periodicals.

With so many resources available, you may find that after you have selected the type of reference work you need, you still need to make a choice from several sources of the same kind. To make the best choice from those available, first examine the publication date to locate the most recently published source. Skim the preface to learn what the book covers, how information is arranged, and to become familiar with any special symbols or abbreviations used.

Study the descriptions of the resources that follow to learn what kind of information each contains.

Encyclopedias These are collections of articles, arranged alphabetically by subject. Encyclopedia articles offer quick reference and a general overview of a topic. For in-depth research, you might begin with an encyclopedia, but you will also want to tap the storehouse of other sources on your subject available in the reference section. For up-to-date information on a topic, check the yearbook that many encyclopedias issue. Following is a list of some reliable general encyclopedias that are frequently used:

> *Encyclopaedia Britannica* (30 volumes; very complete but somewhat technical and difficult to read)
> *Encyclopedia Americana* (30 volumes)
> *World Book Encyclopedia* (22 volumes)

Special-purpose encyclopedias are encyclopedias that are devoted entirely to one subject. Check the reference section of your library for specialized encyclopedias such as the following:

> *Encyclopedia of World History*
> *LaRousse Encyclopedia of Mythology*
> *The Mammals of America*
> *The Baseball Encyclopedia*

Almanacs and Yearbooks When your research involves facts and statistics on current events, almanacs or yearbooks are useful sources of information. Published annually, these resources also provide current information on matters of historical record in government, economics, population, sports, and other fields. The following are widely used books in this category:

> *Guinness Book of World Records*
> *Statistical Abstract of the United States*
> *World Almanac and Book of Facts*

Biographical References Brief biographical notations may be found in dictionaries, and longer biographical articles may be found in encyclopedias. Often, however, the best source for information about a person is a specialized reference work that focuses only on biographies. Check the preface of the particular work to determine if the nature of the listings included is appropriate for your research. Some examples of biographical references follow:

> *Webster's Biographical Dictionary*
> *Current Biography*
> *Who's Who in America*
> *The International Who's Who*

Books About Authors Some biographical references contain information that is limited to authors. Some sources contain very brief entries, while others have more complete listings, including works published, awards won, and critical evaluations. Select a source according to the amount of detail that you are seeking. Following are some examples of these references:

> *Contemporary Authors*
> *Twentieth-Century Authors*
> *European Authors: 1000–1900*
> *American Authors: 1600–1900*

Literary Reference Books Certain reference books are especially helpful for doing research in literature. They provide information such as famous quotations by authors; sources for identifying and locating poems by their titles, first lines, authors, or subjects; and information about characters from literature. These are a few commonly used literary reference books:

> *Bartlett's Familiar Quotations*
> *Granger's Index to Poetry*
> *Cyclopedia of Literary Characters*
> *The Oxford Companion to American Literature*
> *The Oxford Companion to English Literature*
> *The Oxford Companion to the Theatre*

Atlases An atlas is often thought of mainly as a book of maps. However, atlases also contain interesting data on a number of subjects. The *National Geographic Atlas of the World,* for example, includes "Great Moments in Geography" and sections on population, temperatures, oceans, and place names. In addition, historical atlases often give an interesting view of how the maps of countries or sections of the world would have looked centuries ago. The following are some widely used atlases:

> *Atlas of World History*
> *The International Atlas from Rand McNally*
> *The Britannica Atlas*

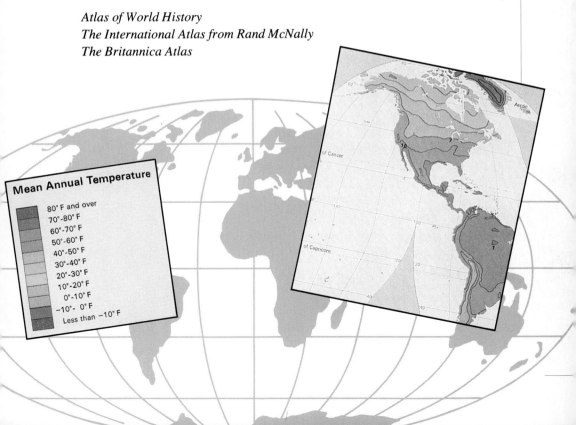

Mean Annual Temperature

- 80° F and over
- 70°-80° F
- 60°-70° F
- 50°-60° F
- 40°-50° F
- 30°-40° F
- 20°-30° F
- 10°-20° F
- 0°-10° F
- −10°- 0° F
- Less than −10° F

The Vertical File Many libraries offer current pamphlets, booklets, and clippings on a variety of subjects. These materials are often housed in file cabinets known as the **vertical file.**

Periodicals For information on current topics, magazines are an important resource. The *Readers' Guide to Periodical Literature* is a special index for magazine articles. This guide lists the titles of articles published in more than one hundred magazines. Articles are listed alphabetically under subject and author (and titles when necessary).

Excerpt from the *Readers' Guide*

	Cable television
Title of Article	Opportunities abound on PBS and cable [miniseries and movies based on novels] L. See. *Publ Wkly* 231:30 Ap 3 '87
	Comedy programs
Name of Magazine	Ranting, raving, doing the dishes. R. Zoglin. il *Time* 129:88–9 Ap 27 '87
	Shopping services
	See Electronic shopping
	Cactus
	Theft
Author of Article	Cactus rustlers. L. Frazer. il *Sierra* 72:15–16 Mr/Ap '87
	Cactus rustlers *See* Cactus—Theft
Author Entry	**Cahn, Robert**
Volume Number	Takeover at the Park Service. *Natl Parks* 61:53 Mr/Ap '87
	Cairo (Egypt)
	History
Date of Magazine	Cairo recalled [1940s] E. W. Said. il por *House Gard* 159:20+ Ap '87
	Cajun cooking *See* Cooking, Cajun
Subject Entry	**Cake**
Illustrated Article	We've got to come up with a better name than bird seed cake. il. *Sunset* 178:158 Mr '87
	Calcium blocking agents
"See also" Cross-reference	*See also*
	Verapamil
	Calcium in the body
	Teenagers and the calcium crisis. P. Mann. il *Saturday Evening Post* 259:68–71 Ap '87
"See" Cross-reference	**Calculi, Biliary** *See* Gallstones
	Caldwell, Erskine, 1903–1987
	about
	Obituary
	Natl Rev 39:21 My 8 '87

Nonprint Materials Libraries have many resources available in nonprint form for research. For example, the *CD-ROM* (Compact Disc-Read Only Memory) provides a computerized method of researching magazines. This disc contains a multiple-year index of approximately four hundred magazines as well as *The New York Times*. The user can search the computer alphabetically for the author, title, or subject of an article and then receive a display or printout of the required information.

Additionally, you may use microforms when doing research. **Microforms** are very small photographs of printed pages stored on either filmstrips called **microfilm,** or film cards called **microfiche.** These microforms save space in the library and can be viewed on a special machine that the librarian will demonstrate.

Finally, many libraries also have a variety of filmstrips, tape recordings, videocassettes, records, and art items that are available for library use and for circulation. Check with your librarian about the circulation policies for these materials.

Exercises

A Write which type of reference book would be the best source for finding the following information.

1. Who was awarded the Nobel Prize for physics last year?
2. How do bees make honey?
3. Are any cities located along the Apalachicola River?
4. At what age did Katherine Anne Porter publish her first work?
5. Who said, "Words are the only things that last forever?"
6. What is the tuition at the largest university in your state?
7. Who is Dame Ninette de Valois and for what is she known?
8. Who is the archenemy of Sherlock Holmes?
9. What are the populations of the three largest cities in your state?
10. What is the name of the poet who wrote "The Highwayman"?

B Use the *Readers' Guide to Periodical Literature* to find the following information.

1. Use the "Key to Abbreviations" to find the meaning of the following symbols:

   Ap   il   supp   jt auth   por

2. Using the list of "Abbreviations of Periodicals Indexed," give the complete titles of the following magazines:

   Mot Trend   Sci Am   Int Wildl   Sch Update   Wash Mon

What's Cooking?

C ookbooks are more than mere collections of recipes and household hints. They help shape the way we talk about food, and they have added the names of common dishes and cooking terms to the language.

The first American cookbook, published in 1796, was written by Amelia Simmons, and it was a standard part of American kitchens for the following thirty years. It was the first book to include recipes for such American dishes as cranberry sauce and pumpkin pie, and the first to use American terms such as *molasses* instead of the British *treacle, biscuits* instead of *scones,* and *cookies* instead of *biscuits.* During the 1820's and 1830's, many new cooking terms and names for American dishes, such as *chowder, succotash,* and *buckwheat cakes,* were added to the language.

Perhaps the most influential cookbook writer was Fannie Farmer. The cookbook she wrote in 1896 is still in use. In addition, she revolutionized kitchen terminology, replacing vague terms, such as *pinch* or *dash,* with her system of level measurement. Terms such as *level teaspoon, measuring cup,* and *oven thermometer* were brought into the language through Fannie Farmer's cookbook.

Chapter 16
Application and Review

A Using Reference Works Using the encyclopedias, almanacs, atlases, yearbooks, and the biographical and literary reference works noted in this chapter, find answers to the following questions. Write the name of the reference work you used after each answer.

1. In what literary work does the character Mercutio appear?
2. What was Thomas Jefferson's role in the American Revolution?
3. What is the title of the poem that begins, "Some say the world will end in fire"? Who wrote the poem?
4. Who were the parents of the Roman god Neptune?
5. What event took place in the United States on January 25, 1915?
6. How did the expression "the real McCoy" originate?
7. Does India use nuclear reactors to produce electricity?
8. What is the "Theater of the Absurd"?
9. In what country is the Great Sandy Desert located?
10. Who are the transitional poets of English literature?

B Using Biographical References Choose one of the following well-known figures. List the titles of at least four sources in your library that give biographical information about the person. Use no more than one encyclopedia. Write two or three paragraphs about the life of this person.

Simón Bolívar   Joan Benoit Samuelson
Robert Jarvick   Mary Wollstonecraft Shelley

C Using the *Readers' Guide* Follow the directions below.

1. Use the excerpt from the *Readers' Guide* on page 400 to answer the following questions:
    a. Under what heading is information on Cajun cooking found?
    b. What is the title of the article from the *Saturday Evening Post?*
    c. Give the author of "Teenagers and the Calcium Crisis."
    d. On what page or pages is the article "Cairo Recalled"?
    e. In what magazine does Erskine Caldwell's obituary appear?
2. Use the *Readers' Guide* to find three articles on a subject of interest to you. Give the title, author, magazine name, volume number, date, and page numbers for each article.

17

Establishing Study Skills

"*B* asketball practice, a science project, math homework, a band concert, an English theme . . . how am I ever going to find the time?"

Keeping up with your many responsibilities at school is a real challenge, and you may have often wished that you could squeeze a few more hours out of the day. You can't hold back the clock, but you can learn techniques to help you manage your time more efficiently.

In this chapter you will discover how to sharpen your reading, notetaking, and outlining skills. You will also see how knowing your individual learning style can help you choose the best way to study a particular topic.

Part 1
Managing Your Time

The first step in taking control of your learning is to become a better manager of your time. You are probably finding that, just when your school performance matters more than ever before, you seem to have less time for your studies. Imagine that your time is a bank account. Regularly ask yourself: "Is this worth spending my money (time) on?"

You can learn to manage your time more effectively by following these guidelines.

1. **Evaluate your present use of time.** For three days, keep a record of how you spend your time. Write down your activities each hour of each day. Then study the results, noting the time-wasters and the areas that deserve more time.

2. **Have a realistic study schedule.** As you consider your assignments, construct a schedule to guide you. On your schedule, note the due date for each assignment. Divide the assignments into smaller stages, making sure to allot enough time for each stage.

   The time allotment will vary depending on the task; for example, consider these two assignments:

Study Schedule

Assignment	Due in	Prewriting	Drafting	Revising
Composition A	4 days	2 days	1 day	1 day
Report B	3 weeks	13 days	3 days	5 days

   Remember to start assignments early—they often take longer than anticipated. Your schedule should be flexible so that you can adjust to unexpected demands. Also, be sure to allow yourself a healthy balance of work and play.

3. **Understand the directions before beginning an assignment.** Don't waste time doing a project incorrectly. If the instructions are written, read them carefully and completely before starting your assignment. If the directions are oral, take good notes. For each step in an assignment, find a key word describing what you must do. Key words include *answer, explain, research, memorize, write, read, draw, solve,* and *review*.

4. **Ensure productive study sessions.** Tackle the harder assignments first, while your mind is fresh. If one form of study gets monotonous, switch to another form—for example, switch from writing to reading. Give yourself regular study breaks.

Exercise

On a sheet of paper, design a study plan for the week. For this exercise you may use your own current assignments, or imagine that you have the following upcoming assignments:

1. Biology—read Chapters 8–10 by Wednesday.
2. English—read two short stories by Edgar Allan Poe and write a composition comparing them. Due Friday.
3. French—find a recipe for a French dessert and prepare the dish to share in class on Wednesday.
4. Math—study for a geometry test on Friday.
5. Social studies—work on research paper about emerging African nations. Due in two weeks.
6. Band—practice trumpet for concert on Saturday.

Allow time for daily assignments in each of these subjects as well.

Part 2
Improving Your Reading Skills

Managing your time is just one aspect of efficient study. Improving your reading skills is another. As you get older, you will encounter more and more printed materials, both in and out of school. Improving your reading skills enables you to keep up with and understand all the things you must read.

Varying Your Reading Rate

"Some books are to be tasted, others to be swallowed, and some few to be chewed and digested." This statement was made by Francis Bacon, a seventeenth-century English philosopher. His humorous comparison of food and books still makes sense today.

Different study purposes and reading materials require different kinds of reading. You do not read a newspaper, for example, the same way that you read a physics textbook. Your reading rate must be varied to suit your purpose and subject matter.

Three Ways to Vary Your Reading Rate

1. **Skimming** involves moving your eyes quickly over a page or selection, noting titles, topic sentences, and highlighted words or phrases, to get a general idea of the content of a selection. Skimming is helpful when you must look over a great deal of information quickly, as when you are doing research. This is the fastest type of reading.
2. **Scanning** involves moving your eyes quickly across a line or down a page to locate particular information, such as when looking up a fact in an encyclopedia. When scanning, look for key words and phrases that indicate that you are close to the information that you need. Then, stop scanning and read slowly.
3. **In-depth reading** means reading slowly and carefully. Much of your reading entails understanding new material and remembering details. Therefore a slower, more careful rate is necessary. As you read, search for main ideas expressed in headings and topic sentences. Then find supporting information, such as examples and statistics.

Think carefully about when to use these three reading rates. For example, your biology teacher may assign a chapter for you to read at home, with questions to answer at the end of the chapter. You might skim the chapter first, noting the subheadings and getting a general idea about the chapter's contents and organization. Then you could read the chapter carefully, noting the definitions of terms and the examples given. Finally, when answering the questions, you would scan parts of the chapter looking for the particular term, phrase, or idea you need.

If, on the other hand, your English teacher assigned a short story to be read and analyzed, you might use the reading rates differently. You might begin with in-depth reading, then scan the story to find specific elements of setting, character, and plot.

Finding the Main Idea

The most important point in a piece of writing is called the **main idea.** No matter which reading rate you use, you must be able to recognize main ideas to understand what you are studying. Sometimes the main idea in a paragraph is stated outright; other times the main idea is implied.

When the main idea is **stated,** often it will be contained in the first or last sentence of the paragraph. Sometimes, however, the main idea may appear in boldface or italicized type, or in a chapter heading or subheading. In the following paragraph about the Civil War, the main idea is clearly stated.

> In the Civil War, the common soldiers of both sides were the same sort of people: untrained and untaught young men, mostly from the country. There weren't many cities then, and they weren't very large, so the average soldier generally came from either a farm or from some very small town or rural area. He had never been anywhere; he was completely unsophisticated. He joined up because he wanted to, because his patriotism had been aroused. The bands were playing, the recruiting officers were making speeches, so he got stirred up and enlisted. Sometimes, he was not altogether dry behind the ears.
>
> From *Reflections on the Civil War* by Bruce Catton

The first sentence states the main idea, that most Civil War soldiers were young men from the country. The rest of the paragraph reinforces this idea by describing such soldiers in greater detail.

Civil War soldiers outside a training camp.

Sometimes the main idea is **implied,** or suggested. You must read the entire paragraph, noting the details, and infer the main idea. The following paragraph contains an implied main idea.

> Many scientists think dinosaurs were slow-moving, cold-blooded animals called ectotherms—animals whose body heat is controlled by the outside temperature. Other scientists now dispute this. They say some dinosaurs may have been speedy, warm-blooded creatures called endotherms—animals that generate their own body heat.
>
> From *What's Your Dino Score?* by Myron Flindt

After noting the contrasting statements in the paragraph above, you can readily infer its main idea: Scientists disagree about what dinosaurs were like.

Finding Information in Books

Knowing how to locate information in a book is another valuable study skill. When you are familiar with the parts of a book, you can find needed facts quickly. When you do research, this will help you to determine whether the book will be a useful source.

The Parts of a Book

The **title page** gives the complete title of the book, the names of authors or editors, and the name and location of the publisher.

The **copyright page** gives the copyright dates, the names of the copyright holders, and the dates of editions or printings.

The **foreword, preface,** or **introduction** is a written commentary that supplies background information.

The **table of contents** is a summary or outline of the contents of the book, arranged in order of appearance.

The **text** is the body of the book. It may be divided into chapters.

The **appendices** contain additional information such as maps, charts, tables, illustrations, or graphs.

The **bibliography** is a list of additional readings on the subject.

The **index** is an alphabetical list of subjects covered in the book. Each entry is followed by page numbers.

Exercise

Below is an excerpt about Viking ships. Follow the directions, one at a time.

1. Skim the article below. What is the most important clue about the general topic?
2. Scan the article. How many oarsmen sailed on Viking ships? Would this article be a good source for a report on modern shipbuilding techniques? Why or why not?
3. Now read the article carefully. What is the main idea in the first paragraph? Is this idea stated or implied? What is the main idea in the second paragraph? Is it stated or implied? What is the main idea in the third paragraph? Is it stated or implied?

Vikings: Sea Rovers and Their Ships

Viking ships were by far the best of the period, made to handle easily and to cleave the water swiftly. The men who sailed in them were both fearless and physically tough.

Without the help of even a crude drawing, depending on skilled hand and eye alone, the shipbuilder fashioned the shell and then fitted ribs to the planking. Low in the middle, and sweeping up at either end, the craft was propelled by a single, square sail and, as a rule, from twenty-eight to forty oarsmen.

The beautiful dragon ships were intricately carved, with a dragon rearing up from the stempost. The longships, however, were the most powerful war vessels. Rows of shields hung over the gunwales, handy in case of attack. Longships rarely had decks, but if a storm arose, tents might be set up at the stern. Merchant vessels were similar to the longships except that they were rather drab and carried no shields.

From *Sweden* by Helen Hynson Merrick

Part 3
Writing as an Aid to Study

Like reading, writing can be a powerful tool for learning. The act of writing things down can help you remember specific pieces of information and make sense of what you have learned. Two forms of writing in particular will help you clarify your thoughts and organize your studies: taking notes and keeping a learning log. Both of these forms are discussed on the following pages.

Taking Notes

Whether you are reading or listening, be alert for signals that indicate important points. *Most, important, first,* and *to review* are such signals. Speakers also make vocal signals, such as pausing for emphasis or repeating. Do not try to write every word that you hear or read.

There are various ways of organizing notes on your paper. One useful method is the modified outline. (For information about the formal outline, see The Writer's Handbook, pages 827–829.)

Here is a sample modified outline showing notes from a biology lesson.

Parts of a Cell

Cell wall & cell membrane
 — cellulose
 — diffusion / active transport
Nucleus
  — DNA molecules / chromosomes
  — Nucleolus / RNA
Endoplasmic reticulum
  — network of tubes found in cytoplasm
Golgi bodies
Mitochondria
  — powerhouses of cell / ATP
Chloroplasts
 — found in plant cells
 — contain chlorophyll
Vacuoles

Notice that you place the main ideas on the left and the supporting details beneath them. Write your notes in phrases, not complete sentences. You must be able to record the information quickly. Use abbreviations and symbols to help you save time. (For information regarding speed writing, see pages 120–123.)

Keeping a Learning Log

In a **learning log** you write about what you are studying, exploring questions such as, What did I learn? What questions do I still have? This writing helps you clarify concepts that are confusing or complex and increases your involvement in your learning.

You can put learning log entries in the notebooks you keep for your classes or in a special section of a writing journal. The following excerpt is from a student's learning log.

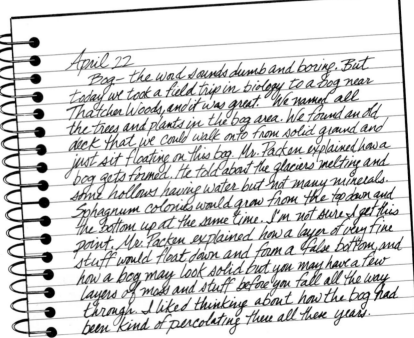

April 22

Bog – the word sounds dumb and boring. But today we took a field trip in biology to a bog near Thatcher Woods, and it was great. We named all the trees and plants in the bog area. We found an old deck that we could walk onto from solid ground and just sit floating on this bog. Mr. Packen explained how a bog gets formed. He told about the glaciers melting and some hollows having water but not many minerals. Sphagnum colonies would grow from the top down and the bottom up at the same time. I'm not sure I get this point. Mr. Packen explained how a layer of very fine stuff would float down and form a false bottom, and how a bog may look solid but you may have a few layers of moss and stuff before you fall all the way through. I liked thinking about how the bog had been kind of percolating there all these years.

Using the above learning log entry to reflect on a field trip, the student records some of the happenings, paraphrases the teacher's comments, and makes note of one point that is still unclear.

As you write about what you are learning, remember that you can **attack** a lesson from various angles. On the next page is a list of questions to consider.

Exercise

The following topics are writing ideas for a learning log. Write the entries in your journal or in your class notebooks.

1. Think of an interesting or curious thing that you learned in one of your classes, explain what it was, and explain your feelings about what you learned.
2. Write a how-to entry about an activity you did in a science class, such as growing a culture in a petri dish. Write the step-by-step instructions, but imagine your audience is a fifth-grade class.

Part 4
Styles of Learning

Think about your style of dress. Do you wear certain clothes often because they are comfortable and you feel good in them? Now think about how you learn things. Here too, you have a style. You prefer certain ways of learning because they feel right, and you know they work for you. It is important to take into account your learning style. By knowing your best learning styles, you will be able to study more efficiently and effectively.

How do you know what your best style of learning is? On the next page, five students are described. Consider which of these students sounds most like you.

Student A: Enjoys reading. Remembers things best after seeing them in print. Finds graphic devices and other visual aids helpful.
Student B: Likes to write. Remembers things best by writing them down. Keeps a journal. Enjoys sharing ideas by writing.
Student C: Likes class discussions. Learns best by going over the material orally with a friend. Enjoys tutoring other students.
Student D: Prefers to listen and watch. Can listen to people and easily follow and remember the points they make. Learns best from lectures and audiovisual materials.
Student E: Prefers to do "hands-on" projects. Is adept manually and physically. Likes to build, fix, draw, or sculpt.

Typically, you learn in all of these ways—through reading, writing, speaking, listening, and handling. The point is, when you can choose the way to study a topic, there are two important factors to take into account. First, consider using your strongest style so that you can capitalize on your strengths. For example, if you learn best by listening, and you are studying a novel, you would be smart to listen to a tape of the novel in addition to reading it. Second, consider how the task itself can best be learned. For example, learning historical dates is a task that lends itself to reading and writing, whereas learning about word processing is best accomplished by physical practice.

Exercise

Imagine that you have an extra credit project to do on the play *King Lear*. Your project can take the form of reading, writing, speaking, listening, or making something. Consider your best learning style and describe specifically the type of project you would do and why.

Production of Shakespeare's play *King Lear.*

Chapter 17
Application and Review

A Reading Skills Follow the directions below, one at a time.

1. Skim the article.
2. Next scan the article to answer this question: How large are the herds of Asiatic elephants?
3. Now read the article in depth. Write down the main idea of each paragraph and tell whether it is stated or implied.

The Life of an Elephant

Most elephants live in herds. The size of an elephant herd probably depends mainly on the amount of food and water available. A herd of African elephants may have up to 1,000 members, but Asiatic elephants live in groups of only 5 to 60 animals. A herd of elephants consists of a number of families, each of which is made up of several adults and their young. Most herds of elephants are led by an old cow called a *matriarch* . . . .

Elephants have no permanent homes. They roam wherever they can find enough food and water. A herd may wander over an area of about 390 square miles (1,000 square kilometers). Elephants in Kenya roam areas as large as 1,900 square miles (5,000 square kilometers). . . .

Wild elephants usually eat for about 16 hours every day. They bathe in lakes and rivers and like to roll in muddy water. After a mud bath, an elephant may cover itself with dirt. The dirt coating helps protect the animal's skin from the sun and insects. Elephants often play by tussling among themselves with their tusks and trunks.

Elephants communicate with one another in various ways. For example, they touch with their trunks as a greeting. A mother elephant calls to her young by slapping her ears against her head. Elephants also communicate by means of rumbling, grunting, and squealing noises.

The World Book Encyclopedia

B Writing Log In a textbook for one of your classes, find a paragraph that explains a concept. Choose a paragraph that you found difficult to understand the first time you read it.

Rewrite this paragraph in your own words to explain the difficult concept. You may find it helpful to review what you have written as you study this topic before a test.

18
Test-Taking Strategies

Nearly Hit,
Paul Klee,
1928.

A geometry test? Tomorrow? The announcement of an upcoming test may cause you some anxiety, but you don't have to lose your head.

Some nervousness before tests is natural because tests are important measures of your mastery of specific course material and of your overall academic growth. However, you can develop strategies that will enable you to approach any test confidently. In this chapter you will learn about various types of classroom and standardized tests and how to prepare for each type.

Classroom Tests

Because classroom tests cover a limited amount of specific information, you can usually anticipate the kind of preparation you will need to do. Effective review for classroom tests consists of several steps.

How to Study for a Classroom Test

1. **Write down all the information your teacher gives about the test.** Be sure you know what kind of test will be given, when it will be given, and exactly what it will cover. Then you will know what material to study, and how much time you have to study it.

2. **Study from the various sources of information that you have.** Your textbook, notes, assignments, and quizzes all contain information you may need to review. Skim the material, highlighting important information. You may find it useful to write down the key information. This will force you to concentrate on the content and organize it into categories that will help you retain the material.

3. **Devise study questions on the material to be covered on the test.** If questions are not provided, make them up yourself. Questions can include key terms; important names, dates, and events; relevant formulas; theories; and concepts.

4. **Test yourself by using the study questions from step 3.** Locate and review answers to any questions you could not answer on your self-test.

5. **Allow yourself plenty of time to study.** Last-minute cramming for a test is not helpful.

Types of Classroom Test Questions

There are several different types of classroom test questions. Each type of test question has its own special characteristics. Therefore, you should use a different strategy for answering each type of question.

The chart on the following page contains some helpful tips and strategies on how to answer the types of questions you regularly encounter on classroom tests.

Strategies for Answering Common Types of Test Questions

Multiple Choice

1. Read all the choices before deciding on your answer.
2. Eliminate incorrect answers.
3. Choose the most complete and accurate answer.
4. Look for words like *always*, *never*, and *only*. These words often indicate incorrect answers.
5. Consider carefully such choices as *none* or *all of the above*.

True/False

1. The whole statement is false if any part of it is false.
2. Absolute words (*all, never, only*) often make a statement false.
3. Qualifying words (*probably, usually, sometimes*) often make a statement true.

Matching

1. Note whether the number of items in each column is equal and how many times each item can or must be used.
2. Read all the items in both columns before pairing any of them.
3. Match easy items first, crossing them out as they are used (unless items are to be used more than once).
4. Keep in mind that if you change one answer, you may have to change several others in related questions.

Completion (Fill-in-the-Blank)

1. Use specific, not general, information.
2. Be sure your wording answers the question fully.
3. Be sure your answer fits grammatically in the sentence.
4. Write legibly. Check for and correct mechanical errors.

Short Answer

1. Answer in complete sentences.
2. Answer all parts of the question. Be specific.
3. Check grammar, spelling, punctuation, and capitalization.

Essay*

1. Be sure you understand what each question asks you to do.
2. Make a modified outline of the major points and the supporting details that you want to cover. Write your essay.
3. Carefully proofread your essay and make corrections.

*Essay tests are discussed in detail on pages 260–263.

Exercises

A Match the following items.

1. Outline the answer first.　　　　　　　a. multiple choice
2. Read all the choices first.　　　　　　b. completion
3. Match easy items first.　　　　　　　 c. essay
4. Make the answer grammatically correct.　d. matching

B Write a one-paragraph essay telling how to avoid test anxiety.

Part 2
Standardized Tests

A standardized test measures your performance against that of many other people who take the same test under similar conditions. Standardized tests do not cover specific course work. Instead, they assess academic abilities you have gained throughout your life.

The Scholastic Aptitude Test (SAT) and the American College Testing examination (ACT) are two tests designed to evaluate how well prepared you are to do college-level work. Both tests offer a preliminary version that may be taken for practice, the PSAT and the P-ACT Plus.

You can prepare for these tests by studying the types of questions they contain and by developing the skills that they measure: vocabulary, reading, computation, critical thinking, and English usage. The following pages give examples of the types of questions in these tests.

Antonym Questions

Antonym questions ask you to choose a word that is most nearly *opposite* in meaning to the given word.

Eulogize:
- a. praise
- b. usurp
- c. support
- d. malign
- e. undermine

To answer an antonym question, use the following strategies:

1. Remember to find a word that is *opposite* in meaning. Do not be thrown off by *synonyms*. In the sample above, choice *a* is a synonym.
2. Decide whether the given word is positive or negative, and then eliminate all the choices that are in the same category as the given word. *Eulogize* has a positive connotation. Therefore choices *a* and *c* can be eliminated. The correct answer is *d*.
3. Many words have more than one meaning. If no word fits your understanding of the opposite meaning, think of other meanings for the given word.
4. If you don't know a word's meaning, try to analyze its parts. See Chapter 14 for more information on word parts.

Analogy Questions

Analogy questions give you two words that are *related* in some way. You need to determine this relationship and find another pair of words that are related in the same way.

Stanza : Poem
- a. movie : script
- b. story : writer
- c. act : play
- d. novel : chapter
- e. song : melody

Follow these strategies in answering analogy questions:

1. Establish the relationship of the given pair of words by creating a sentence that contains the words and shows their relationship:

   A *stanza* is a section of a *poem*.

2. Find the pair of words among the answer choices that could logically replace the given pair in your sentence:

   An *act* is a section of a *play*.

3. Recognize the types of relationships that can be expressed in analogies. Several are listed on the next page.

Types of Analogies

Type	Example
cause to effect	virus : cold
part to whole	finger : hand
object to purpose	car : transportation
action to object	dribble : basketball
item to category	salamander : amphibian
type to characteristic	owl : nocturnal
word to synonym	antipathy : aversion
word to antonym	antipathy : attraction
object to its material	shoe : leather
worker to product	composer : symphony
worker to tool	carpenter : hammer
time sequence	sunrise : sunset

Sentence Completion Questions

A sentence completion question is a sentence with words missing. Your job is to select the word or words that best complete the sentence.

> Age did not _____ but actually _____ this artist's output.
> a. renew . . . furthered   d. slow . . . slacked
> b. decrease . . . increased   e. lengthen . . . narrowed
> c. publicize . . . secluded

To answer sentence completion questions, use these strategies:

1. Read the sentence carefully, noting key words or phrases. Words that signal contrast (*but, however*), similarity (*and, another*), or cause and effect (*because, as a result*) give clues to the relationships expressed in the sentence. For example, the word *but* in the question above is a clue that the answer will contain words with opposite meanings. Thus, the correct answer is *b*: *decrease . . . increased*.

2. Try each of the choices in the sentence. Eliminate choices that make no sense, are grammatically incorrect, or contradict some part of the sentence. In an item with two blanks, make sure the answer you choose correctly fills *both* blanks.

3. Look for grammatical clues in the sentence. Does the space call for a verb, an adjective, a noun? Should the word be plural? If it is a verb, what tense is required?

Reading-Comprehension Questions

Reading-comprehension questions assess your ability to interpret written material. You may be asked to do one of the following tasks:

1. Pick out the central idea.
2. Recall a specific detail.
3. Draw a conclusion from the information given.
4. Determine the meaning of a word.
5. Identify the mood of the passage.
6. Determine specific techniques that the writer has used.

To answer reading-comprehension questions, use the following strategies:

1. Before you read the passage, read the questions that follow it. Then you will have an idea of what information to look for as you read the material.
2. Read all the choices before you select an answer.
3. Choose the *best* answer based on the material in the passage, not based on your opinion.
4. Notice the reasoning the author uses and the facts and ideas that are presented. Also be aware of the author's tone and style.

Apply the above strategies to the following passage and questions.

Today, all bats fly at night, and it is likely that this was always the case, since the birds had already laid claim to the day. To do so,

however, the bats had to develop an efficient navigational system. It is based on ultrasounds like those made by shrews and other primitive insectivores. The bats use the ultrasounds for sonar, an extremely sophisticated method of echolocation. This is similar in principle to radar; but radar employs radio waves, whereas sonar uses sound waves. A bat flying by sonar emits sound waves of between 50,000 and 200,000 vibrations per second. It sends out these sounds in short bursts, like clicks, twenty or thirty times every second. On the basis of the echo each sound makes, the bat is able to judge the position of obstacles as well as of moving prey.

1. The best title for this passage would be
   a. Creatures of the Night
   b. Sonar Location Systems
   c. The Bat's Navigational System
   d. Hearing of the Bat
2. According to the passage, the major difference between sonar and radar is
   a. the fact that radar is used for radios
   b. the type of wave that each uses
   c. the number of vibrations per second
   d. the use of sonar for navigation
3. The passage mentions all of the following facts about bats *except* that they
   a. fly at night
   b. locate and capture food while flying
   c. have extremely acute hearing
   d. are the only mammals that truly fly

Standard English Usage Questions

Standard English usage questions require you to identify errors, such as incorrect verb tenses, improper agreement between pronouns and antecedents, lack of parallel structure, incorrect use of idioms, and improper word choice. In each sentence, four words or phrases are underlined and lettered. Choose the one underlined part that needs to be corrected. If the sentence contains no error, choose answer *e*, labeled "No error."

Her remarks <u>were</u> startling; <u>their</u> <u>affect</u> on the audience <u>was</u>
          a   b   c   d
immediately apparent. <u>No error.</u>
                       e

Use the following strategies to answer usage questions:

1. Read the entire sentence through completely.
2. Check to see that its parts are in agreement: Does the subject agree with its verb? Do pronouns agree with their antecedents? Are all the verbs in the correct tense?
3. Check the grammatical construction of the sentence. In particular, look for improper parallelism (see Chapter 6).
4. Look for misuse of modifiers and other words. Note any improper word choice. In the sample question, for example, *affect* has been used incorrectly; the proper word is *effect*.
5. Remember, the error occurs in an *underlined* part of the sentence.

Sentence Correction Questions

These items test your ability to *correct,* rather than just recognize, an error in a sentence. In a sentence correction question, the underlined portion of the sentence contains an element that is wordy, unclear, awkwardly phrased, ambiguous, or illogical. Below the sentence are five versions of the underlined part. You evaluate the sentence and its underlined part and then choose the best version. If you think the sentence is correct as written, choose answer *a*, which repeats the original underlined part without change.

More efficient, cost-effective solar power would be a great boon, since its source is readily available and the sun is a virtually inexhaustible supply.

a. and the sun is a virtually inexhaustible supply
b. and its supply is virtually inexhaustible
c. and the sun being a virtually inexhaustible supply
d. because of its inexhaustible supply
e. and since it is an inexhaustible supply

To answer sentence correction questions, use these strategies:

1. As you read the item, keep in mind that only the underlined portion of the sentence can change. Identify the error in the underlined portion first before you look at the choices.
2. Pay careful attention to grammar, punctuation, and word choice. In the example above, the underlined clause is not parallel to the clause that comes before it. "Its source is readily available" should be followed by a clause worded in a similar manner. Choice *b*, "and its supply is virtually inexhaustible," has a parallel structure and is, therefore, the correct answer.

Exercises

A Antonyms For each of the following antonym questions, write the letter of the word that is most nearly opposite in meaning to the given word.

1. Decry:
   a. condemn
   b. criticize
   c. change
   d. depend
   e. praise

2. Abhor:
   a. challenge
   b. admire
   c. settle
   d. encourage
   e. chide

3. Tolerate:
   a. uphold
   b. maintain
   c. forbid
   d. accept
   e. utilize

4. Belligerent:
   a. animated
   b. fervent
   c. bland
   d. peaceable
   e. jovial

5. Ambiguity:
   a. clarity
   b. extravagance
   c. luxuriousness
   d. distress
   e. injustice

6. Noxious:
   a. diffuse
   b. latent
   c. unique
   d. static
   e. beneficial

B Analogies For each of the following analogy questions, select the lettered pair that *best* expresses a relationship similar to the one expressed in the original pair.

1. Hurricane : Damage
   a. contamination : sickness
   b. memory : forgetfulness
   c. ocean : current
   d. wind : storm
   e. campfire : kindling

2. Teacher : School
   a. nurse : hospital
   b. traveler : journey
   c. lawyer : library
   d. artist : painting
   e. soldier : uniform

3. Trivial : Insignificant
   a. malicious : random
   b. invigorating : exhilarating
   c. irritable : agreeable
   d. site : design
   e. irrational : reasonable

4. Breakfast : Supper
   a. banquet : meal
   b. fruit : cheese
   c. preparation : completion
   d. appetizer : dessert
   e. lunch : sandwich

5. Elbow : Joint
   a. knee : foot
   b. eye : head
   c. stomach : eat
   d. skeleton : bone
   e. biceps : muscle

C Sentence Completion Choose the *best* word or words for each sentence.

1. Although she had never taken a single _____ lesson, Dionne could sing a song _____ at first sight.
   a. piano . . . shakily
   b. solo . . . alone
   c. music . . . adequately
   d. skiing . . . confidently
   e. voice . . . beautifully

2. Elizabeth was _____ ; she absolutely refused to speak against her friend.
   a. hesitant
   b. disloyal
   c. easygoing
   d. adamant
   e. uncaring

3. We are not told the nature of the illness, but we _____ from the patient's pallor and the large number of medicines on the nightstand that the illness has been lengthy and serious.
   a. infer
   b. decide
   c. elucidate
   d. deliberate
   e. imply

4. The novel is written in a _____ style that is _____ to read; however, the story that unfolds is so exciting that the reader willingly struggles with the elaborate sentences and formal diction.
   a. humorous . . . stilted
   b. lofty . . . difficult
   c. complex . . . easy
   d. profound . . . inspiring
   e. terse . . . impossible

D Reading Comprehension Read the following passage. Then choose the best answer to each of the questions.

> After his seventh birthday the Sioux boy never addressed his blood mother or sister directly again, speaking to them only through a third person. When he showed signs of coming manhood, he was prepared for his pubertal fasting by men close to the family, including some wise and holy ones. . . . When he was ready, the boy was escorted to some far, barren hill and left there in breechclout and moccasins against the sun of day, the cold of night, without food or water. The ordeal was to strip away every superficiality, all the things of the flesh, to prepare for a dreaming, a vision from the Powers. Usually by the third or fourth day, the youth had dreamed and was brought down, gaunt and weak. He was given a few drops of water at a time and some food, but slowly, and after he was restored a little and bathed and feasted, his advisors and the holy man tried to interpret the vision that was to guide him in this manhood he was now entering.
>
> From *These Were the Sioux* by Mari Susette Sandoz

1. The author treats her subject with
    a. awed amazement
    b. amused detachment
    c. active dislike
    d. affectionate good humor
    e. factual objectivity
2. It can be inferred that during the preparation the boy was
    a. treated with dignity and respect by the men
    b. largely ignored by the tribe
    c. given a great deal of advice by his parents
    d. looked upon as a hero and given many gifts
    e. often reduced to tears and entreaty
3. The main topic of the passage is
    a. the exclusion of women in the Sioux rituals
    b. the cruelty of the Sioux toward their adolescents
    c. the Sioux's theory about dreaming
    d. the Sioux manhood ritual
    e. the customs of the Sioux

4. The author states that the youth's fasting ritual
   a. took place before his seventh birthday
   b. lasted no more than three days
   c. was intended to strip away superficial things of the flesh
   d. allowed the boy water but no food
   e. was initiated by holy men and women of the tribe

E English Usage Write the letter of the underlined part that must be changed to make each sentence correct. If there is no error, write *e*.

1. Eager <u>to express</u> <u>there</u> appreciation, the cast <u>presented the</u> <u>director with</u>
        a   b   c

   a bouquet of roses, <u>while</u> the audience applauded tumultuously.
                       d

   <u>No error</u>
     e

2. When you <u>drive on icy roads</u>, remember to drive <u>slowly, to</u> apply the
               a   b

   <u>brakes by using short</u> pumping motions, and <u>you turn</u> in the direction of
            c   d

   a skid. <u>No error</u>
           e

3. Although naturalists <u>have studied</u> migration for years, the inner
                  a

   <u>mechanism that</u> prompts the migratory bird and <u>holds it on course</u> for
       b   c

   thousands of miles <u>remains</u> a mystery. <u>No error</u>
              d   e

4. <u>Not only</u> had both <u>sides sustained</u> heavy casualties, <u>but</u> neither
      a   b   c

   <u>can claim</u> a clear-cut victory for itself. <u>No error</u>
     d   e

5. As the <u>plot unfolds</u>, the reader of this story <u>come to</u> fear the cruel
          a   b

   Madame Defarge <u>and, finally,</u> to pity <u>her</u>. <u>No error</u>
             c   d   e

F Sentence Correction Select the answer that, when used to replace the underlined words, produces the most effective sentence. Select *a* if the original sentence needs no revision.

1. A bad accident occurred at the busy intersection, injuring several <u>people, and a traffic light was put up</u>.
    a. people, and a traffic light was put up
    b. people. The result is that a traffic light was put up
    c. people. As a result, a traffic light was put up
    d. people, then a traffic light was put up
    e. people, a traffic light was put up
2. Beyond the dunes, angry <u>clouds that seethed</u> on the horizon, like smoke above the flames of waves.
    a. clouds that seethed
    b. clouds, which seethed
    c. clouds, seething
    d. clouds seethed
    e. clouds, which were seething
3. California was declared a territory of the United States <u>on August15, 1848, it was admitted to the Union</u> as a state in September 1850.
    a. on August 15, 1848, it was admitted to the Union
    b. on August 15, 1848; but it was admitted to the Union
    c. on August 15, 1848; nonetheless, it was admitted to the Union
    d. on August 15, 1848, then it was admitted to the Union
    e. on August 15, 1848. It was admitted to the Union
4. The fort, <u>built in the tenth century to protect the coast,</u> has become a tourist attraction for the city.
    a. built in the tenth century to protect the coast,
    b. it was built in the tenth century to protect the coast
    c. being built in the tenth century and protected the coast
    d. that was built in the tenth century will protect the coast
    e. built in the tenth century and protecting the coast
5. Far from ending space travel, the shuttle accident actually increased the determination of space engineers, mission control, specialists, and astronauts to face the dangers, <u>meet new challenges, and expanding the frontiers of exploration.</u>
    a. meet new challenges, and expanding the frontiers of exploration
    b. meet new challenges, expanding the frontiers of exploration
    c. meeting new challenges meanwhile expanding the frontiers of exploration
    d. meet new challenges, and expand the frontiers of exploration
    e. so that challenges are met and frontiers are expanding

Part 3
Taking Tests

While it is important to have strategies for answering various types of questions on tests, it is equally important to have an effective overall strategy for taking the tests. As you take a test, keep the following guidelines in mind:

Basic Strategies for Taking Standardized Tests

1. **Budget your time carefully.**
2. **Read the directions for each section carefully.** For each question, read all answer choices before making a choice.
3. **Answer the questions you know first.** Mark the difficult ones and return to them later. The more difficult questions are often at the end of each section.
4. **Make only "educated" guesses.** Random guessing is unlikely to improve your score. In fact, on some standardized tests, points are deducted for incorrect answers. However, if you can eliminate one or more of the choices, then your chances of guessing the correct answer are increased.
5. **Mark the answer sheet carefully and correctly.** Most standardized tests are graded by computer. You record your answers on a separate answer sheet by filling in circles corresponding to the correct answers in the test booklet.

   23. ⓐ ⓑ ⓒ ⓓ ⓔ

   Follow these guidelines when using answer sheets that will be graded by a computer:

   • Fill in the circle for the correct answer completely.
   • Check your numbering on the answer sheet periodically, particularly if you skip an item.
   • Do not make stray marks on the answer sheet. Stray marks are often misread as wrong answers by the scoring machine.
6. **Try to maintain a relaxed, positive attitude.** Get a good night's sleep and eat a good breakfast before taking the test. Physical and mental fitness will significantly increase your chances of success.

Chapter 18
Application and Review

A Matching Questions On a sheet of paper, match the following items.

1. Antonym	a. Choose the best version of the underlined portion of the sentence.
2. Sentence correction	b. Choose words that fit the grammar and sense of the sentence.
3. Sentence completion	c. Choose the underlined part that needs to be corrected.
4. English usage	d. Find another pair of words with the same type of relationship.
5. Analogy	e. Choose the word most nearly opposite in meaning.

B Standardized Test Questions On a sheet of paper, write the letter of the best answer.

1. Find the word most nearly opposite in meaning to the given word.
   Obstacle: a. commitment   d. advantage
                  b. spitefulness   e. ailment
                  c. obstruction

2. Select the lettered pair that best expresses a relationship similar to that of the original pair.
   Coach : Team   a. umpire : pitcher   d. teacher : principal
                b. officer : troops   e. director : play
                c. football : basketball

3. Select the pair of words that best fits the meaning of the following sentence: Ill-fed, ill-clad, and uneducated, the children of these _____ countries are both unhealthy and _____ .
   a. unimportant . . . diseased   d. backward . . . strong
   b. small . . . warlike   e. impoverished . . . illiterate
   c. tragic . . . criminal

4. If there is an error in an underlined sentence part, write the letter that corresponds to it. If there is no error, write *e*.

   One of the <u>most compelling</u> arguments <u>were made</u> by the chief of
                    a   b

   <u>police, who</u> described a <u>gory accident scene</u>. <u>No error</u>
       c   d   e

19

Business Letters and Job Applications

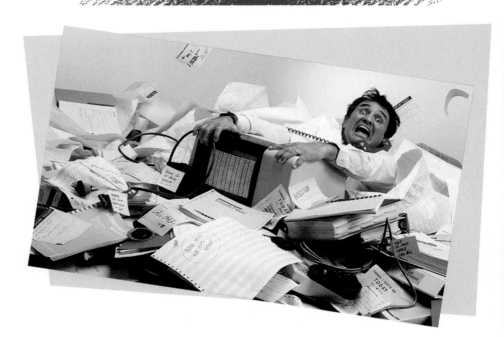

*B*usinesses may receive thousands of letters a day. Whether you are applying for a part-time job at a video store or ordering a paint-by-numbers kit for your little brother's birthday, you must make sure that your letter will not get lost in the shuffle.

In this chapter you will learn how to write a business letter so that it reaches the proper person and communicates your message clearly and concisely. You will also learn how to fill out employment forms and how to present yourself effectively in job interviews.

Forms of Business Letters

Most business letters are written for a very specific purpose, such as requesting information, ordering a product, or applying for a job. An effective letter is one that achieves its desired result. If you want your letter to get results, you should pay careful attention to its physical appearance and format. A neat, attractive letter will be easier to read. It will also create a favorable impression, and your reader will be more receptive to your message.

Use the following guidelines in writing business letters:

1. Use plain white paper, preferably $8\frac{1}{2}$ by 11 inches.
2. Type your letter and envelope, if possible. If you cannot type, write legibly in ink.
3. Frame your letter like a picture, allowing at least $1\frac{1}{4}$ inches on all sides for margins.
4. Be sure your letter is error-free and clean.
5. Make a photocopy of your letter for your records.

The Parts of a Letter

Every business letter has six basic parts. These parts are used to present information in an organized and predictable way.

The **heading** consists of three lines at the top of the page. The first line gives your street address (or your rural route or post-office box number) and apartment number. The second line lists your city, state, and ZIP code. The third line gives the date.

> 413 Acacia Avenue   P.O. Box 1792051
> Palo Alto, California 94306   St. Louis, Missouri 63141
> April 2, 19—   July 14, 19—

If you live in a small town that does not use street addresses for mailing purposes, the name of your town would be placed on the first line and your state and ZIP code on the second line.

The **inside address** follows the heading after a line of space. The name and title of the person to whom you are writing (or the name of the department, if you do not know the person's name) go on the first line; the name of the company or organization on the second line; the street address or post-office box number on the third line; and the city, state, and ZIP code on the fourth line.

Ms. Sara Lemoine, Director   Customer Service Department
Youth Employment Agency   SCM Office Supplies
816 W. Fluornoy Ave.   2409 W. Second St.
Oak Park, Illinois 60304   Marion, Indiana 46952

If possible, you should direct your letter to a specific person, using his or her full name and correct title.

The **salutation** is placed beneath the inside address with a line of space between them. It begins with *Dear*, is followed by the name of the person to whom you are writing, and ends with a colon. If you do not know the person's name, address the department or position within the company or organization. The following forms are acceptable:

Dear Mr. Randolph: Dear Mrs. Jackson: Dear Representative:
Dear Ms. Kreutzer: Dear Sir or Madam: Dear Editor:

The **body,** in which you convey your central message, begins beneath the salutation. Leave a line of space between them. Single space between the lines in each paragraph and double space between paragraphs. If your letter is very short, you may choose to double space the entire body.

The **closing** is placed two lines below the body. Only the first word is capitalized. The last word is followed by a comma.

Sincerely,   Very truly yours,   Respectfully yours,
Sincerely yours,   Yours truly,   Cordially,

The **signature** should be written in ink beneath the closing. If your letter is typed, type your name four spaces below your signature. Otherwise, print your name beneath the signature.

The **business envelope** is a standard $9\frac{1}{2}$ by 4 inches. The inside address should be placed near the center of the envelope front. The return address is positioned in the upper left-hand corner.

Full Block and Modified Block Forms

The two most frequently used forms of a business letter are full block and modified block. In **full block form,** all parts of the letter begin at the left margin. Paragraphs are not indented, but a line of space is left between them. In **modified block form,** paragraphs are indented with a line of space left between them. The heading, closing, and signature are aligned near the right margin. Pages 435 and 436 show an example of each form.

Full Block Form

Heading	413 Acacia Avenue Palo Alto, California 94306 April 2, 19—
Inside Address	Service Representative Leisure Time Publishing Company P.O. Box 87345 Walnut Creek, California 94597
Salutation	Dear Service Representative:
Body	I am writing to seek correction of a mistake that your company made. On September 15 I ordered the book <u>Great Moments in Rock and Roll</u> by Bill Fender from your company. I included a money order for $21.95. However, I have neither heard from your company nor received the book. Please either send me the book or refund my money as soon as possible. I have enclosed a copy of my money order and a copy of my original order letter.
Closing	Yours truly,
Signature	*Rosa M. Ortega* Rosa M. Ortega

Modified Block Form

Heading

Inside Address

Salutation

Body

Closing

Signature

718 Heffron Drive
Winona, Minnesota 55987
March 29, 19—

Order Department
Music Alive!
P.O. Box 216735
Minneapolis, Minnesota 55428

Dear Order Department:

I am interested in becoming a member of your

Compact Disc Discount Club. Please send me an

application form and a copy of your catalog.

Sincerely,

Robert Costello

Robert Costello

Exercise

Write a letter and envelope for two of the three free government publications listed below. For one letter, follow the modified block form. For the other, follow the full block form.

1. *One Step at a Time—An Introduction to Running.* Write to the President's Council on Physical Fitness and Sports, Department of Health and Human Services, Suite 7103, 450 5th St. NW, Washington, DC 20001.
2. *International Youth Exchange: Advisory List of International Educational Travel and Exchange Programs.* Write to Consumer Information Center-D, Department 41D, Pueblo, CO 81009.
3. *Student Guide—Five Federal Financial Aid Programs.* Write to Consumer Information Center-D, Department 41D, Pueblo, CO 81009.

Part 2
Writing Effective Business Letters

Business letters are written for many reasons. Whatever the purpose of your letter, the following guidelines apply:

1. Always be courteous and treat the reader with respect.
2. State your purpose directly.
3. Include only necessary details.
4. Use formal language, but keep it simple, clear, and sincere. Avoid informal language and slang.

Letters Requesting Information or Ordering Products

When you request information, your letter should specify what you need as well as when and why you need it. Make it as easy as possible for the reader to reply.

If you wish to order a product through the mail and no order form is available, you can write an order letter. Clearly describe the merchandise: include the exact name, size, color, model number, quantity, unit price, and total price. Tell how you are paying for the product and include sales tax or other fees that apply.

Letters of Complaint or Appreciation

If you are not satisfied with a product or service, you should write a letter of complaint. Begin by stating your purpose. Describe the service or product ordered, including the date ordered and the amount paid. Then identify the problem such as a wrong model, damaged or incomplete goods, late delivery, or poor service. Finally, explain what you would like the company to do to resolve your complaint. Include photocopies of all relevant documents, such as receipts and money orders, with your letter.

Study the letter of complaint on page 435. Note how the letter states essential information without using angry or sarcastic language.

Companies or organizations also like to know when their products or services are appreciated. If you are especially pleased with something, you can write a letter of appreciation.

Exercise

Think of a time when you were dissatisfied with a product or service. Write a letter to the appropriate person or company. Use an acceptable format and follow the guidelines on page 437.

Part 3
Finding Part-Time Jobs

If you decide to seek part-time employment, a business letter can help you establish initial contact. The following section will help you strengthen the language skills needed for writing letters of application, completing employment forms, and interviewing.

Letters of Application

A letter of application is written to request a job application and interview. It should be addressed to the personnel manager or department and should follow the guidelines listed below:

1. State the job for which you are applying and how you learned of it.
2. List your relevant experience and skills. State your age or grade in school and the date and times you can work.
3. List the names, positions, and phone numbers of adults who can attest to your character and ability. Be sure to obtain their permission first.
4. Ask for an application and interview, and give your phone number.
5. Thank the prospective employer for his or her time.

Letter of Application

555 Dover Street
Albuquerque, New Mexico 87101
April 23, 19—

Dr. Carla Manos
333 First Street
Albuquerque, New Mexico 87101

Dear Dr. Manos:

I would like to apply for a job as an assistant at your veterinary clinic. Ms. Siebers, my guidance counselor at Albuquerque High, told me that you may have an opening.

I am very interested in veterinary medicine and would welcome this opportunity to learn more about the field. At school, I have maintained a B average, worked as the treasurer of my sophomore class, and helped organize the school science fair. Both Ms. Siebers and Mr. Walters, our principal, have offered to act as references for me. They can be contacted at 555-1232.

I am available for work each day at 3:15. Also, I will be willing to work full time this summer.

I would appreciate your sending me an application form. I would also like to arrange an interview. I can be reached at home at 555-4321.

Thank you for considering me for the position.

Sincerely,

Alex Conner

Alex Conner

Completing Employment Forms

When you apply for a job, you will probably have to fill out an employment or application form that asks for essential information about you. Fill the form out completely and neatly, following the guidelines listed below:

1. Read all directions carefully. Then gather information such as your social security number; parents' birth dates; and names, addresses, and phone numbers of responsible adults or former employers who have agreed to serve as personal references.
2. Reread the directions and fill out the form line by line. You may wish to practice on a separate sheet of paper first.
3. Do not leave blank spaces. If the question does not apply to you, write *N.A.*, which means "not applicable."
4. List any special skills you have, such as typing, knowledge of computers, or data processing. Also list school achievements, volunteer activities, and awards, if appropriate.
5. Check the completed form for accuracy and thoroughness and return it to the designated person.

Interviewing

The interview is often the last step in a job hunt. It is your chance to sell yourself, to present your personality and skills as positively as possible.

Appearance is a key to a successful interview. Good grooming and neatness demonstrate attention to detail, a valuable asset for all good workers.

Promptness, another strong asset, can be demonstrated by arriving on time or a bit early.

Courtesy is a must during the interview. A polite, friendly introduction and handshake are appreciated by the interviewer. When the interview is over, thank the interviewer for his or her time.

Communication skills involve speaking, listening, and body language. Speak clearly, using correct grammar. Listen carefully and maintain eye contact with the interviewer. Sit up straight and avoid nervous hand gestures.

The following questions are similar to those often asked during interviews. How would you answer each one? Remember to answer all questions honestly and confidently.

Questions Frequently Asked by Interviewers

1. Why are you interested in this job?
2. Why do you feel you could handle the job? What experience do you have?
3. Tell me a little about yourself—your hobbies and interests, for example.
4. What do you like most about yourself? What do you like least?
5. Why would you be the best person for the job?

After an interview, it is appropriate to extend your thanks with a phone call or letter. This will show that you are considerate and interested in the job.

Exercises

A Using your own paper, write down the information required in the sample application form on page 442.

B Decide what type of job you might be interested in. Then, assume you are being interviewed for that position and write out the answers to the five questions listed in the chart above. Use your answers to write a letter of application to a prospective employer following the format shown on page 439.

APPLICATION FOR PART-TIME EMPLOYMENT

PLEASE PRINT

LAST

NAME

FIRST   MIDDLE

ADDRESS

STREET   CITY   STATE   ZIP

SOCIAL SECURITY NO.

LOCAL PHONE (   )

BIRTHDATE   MO   DAY   YR

Are you a U.S. veteran? YES_____ NO_____

Dates served_____

Military occupation _____

If hired, can you provide proof of citizenship?

YES_____ NO_____

If you are not a U.S. citizen, do you have the legal right to remain permanently and work in the U.S.?

YES_____ NO_____

Have you ever been convicted of a felony?

YES_____ NO_____

If yes, explain _____

SCHOOL	NO. OF YEARS ATTENDED	NAME OF SCHOOL	CITY	COURSE OF STUDY	DATE OF GRADUATION
GRAMMAR					
HIGH					
COLLEGE					
OTHER					

NAME AND ADDRESS OF EMPLOYER	DATES	JOB DUTIES	SALARY	REASON FOR LEAVING

LIST ANY SPECIAL SKILLS, ACHIEVEMENTS, OR VOLUNTEER ACTIVITIES THAT APPLY

LIST TWO REFERENCES WHO ARE NOT RELATIVES OR EMPLOYERS

PLEASE READ BEFORE SIGNING:
I certify that the information contained in this application is accurate. I know that giving false or incomplete information for employment is a serious matter and grounds for dismissal and forfeiture of benefits.

I authorize my former employers and other individuals to give information about me whether or not it is on their records, and I release them and their companies from any liabilities.

DATE_____   SIGNATURE_____

Chapter 19
Application and Review

A Rewrite the following business letter, correcting the errors in form and content. Make up any information that is necessary; delete any unnecessary information. Use polite, formal language. Then correctly address a mock envelope for the letter.

```
                              336 Monument Boulevard
                              Richmond Virginia 23226
                              May 2, 19—

Complaint Person
Leavit Jeans Co.
One Charles Center
Baltimore Maryland 21201

Dear sir,
Boy, did you mess up my order. I ordered two pairs of
jeans, but you sent me the wrong size. What a dumb thing
to do! My friends are making fun of my old jeans. They
call them dinosaurs because they're so old. Now I won't
have nothing new to wear on vacation.

I am returning both pairs of your stupid jeans. By
the way, I don't like your new commercials and neither
does my friend Nate.

                              Jerome Daley
```

B Choose one of the ads below and write a letter of application for that job. Give information needed such as your address and your qualifications. Make up the name and address of the employer.

Interviewers—Now hiring telephone interviewers for market research. Experience preferred, but will train. Evening and weekend hours.

Stock—Perm. part-time positions for packing and restocking school and art supplies.

Focus On

M E M O R Y

Researchers have learned that you can improve your memory using simple exercises and memory tricks.

Some people can read an article or book and later repeat what they read, word for word. Talent like that would certainly come in handy on tests, but unfortunately, such photographic memory feats are very rare.

Researchers say that the vast majority of us forget at least 25 percent of what we learn by the end of the day we learn it. But researchers have also discovered that much can be done to improve memory. This chapter focuses on several methods for helping you retain more of what you learn.

Rote Warriors

There are two ways you can go about remembering something— by a process called rote memorization or by one of the methods of association.

Rote memorization involves repeating information over and over again until it becomes solidly fixed in your mind.

Association entails making a connection between information you need to remember and something you already know. When you use association, you create pathways to information. Methods for using association will be presented in this chapter.

Most things you learn require both rote memorization and association, although some learning tasks emphasize only one method. Learning a character's lines in a play, for example, requires mostly rote memorization.

One important truth affects all memorization, and it is this: The greater your motivation for remembering something, the better your chance of remembering it. Before memorizing anything, therefore, spend a little time summoning your desire to learn it.

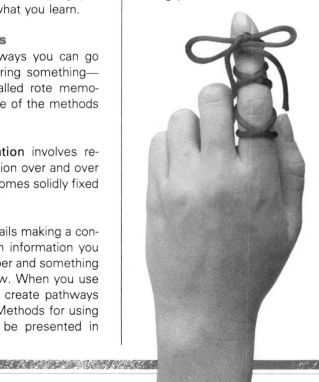

The Long and Short of It

You are equipped with both short-term and long-term memory. To remember what time to meet your friend tomorrow morning, you need to have that information in your short-term memory only. To remember twenty lines from *Julius Caesar* next week or next month or ten years from now, you must have the lines in your long-term memory.

Your brain forgets most things it feels it doesn't need anymore. Reviewing helps your long-term memory because, in effect, you tell your brain: "I'm not done with these facts yet." Current research indicates that the most effective strategy for long-term retention is to review material according to the following schedule:

- **right after learning**
- **later the same day**
- **one week later**
- **one month later**
- **just before the test**

There are several ways to make the most of your review sessions. First, keep your sessions short. Second, don't try to memorize too much at one time. Third, put sleep to work for you. Reviewing just before you go to sleep actually enhances your ability to remember because in sleep your brain tends to reinforce your most recent thoughts.

Flex Your Muscles

Memory research has indicated that the more ways you learn something, the better. Sticking only to reading and rereading breeds monotony rather than retention. Soon you find yourself just staring at the page, thinking about Saturday night.

The best cure for a wandering mind is to vary your approach to studying and learning. Here are a few strategies.

Repeat information out loud. Review with a friend and quiz each other on the material. Take notes on key pieces of information in your book and rewrite important material in your own words.

Other strategies include tape-recording the material you are learning and listening to the tape. You can also draw a diagram incorporating the information.

These additional activities will greatly reinforce your learning; they give the brain more chances to lock onto memories.

The more ways you learn, the more memory pathways you create in your brain.

Pathways to Memory

Some brain researchers claim that everything we experience is stored in the brain and that you need only to find a path to the memory among the ten billion neurons in the brain.

Mnemonics, or memory cues and associations, can create paths between the material you wish to remember and knowledge you already have. Following are some common associative devices.

The more outrageous the picture you create in your mind, the more memorable it will be.

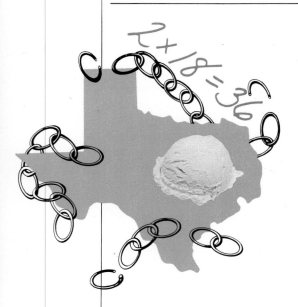

Use Your Imagination Memories stored as vivid scenes are often the most lasting. Create a mental image of the facts you want to remember. The picture above is an example of a mnemonic device. What historical fact does it show?

Suppose you need to remember that Napoleon was defeated by the Duke of Wellington at the Battle of Waterloo. You might imagine a tired, thirsty soldier (with *Napoleon* sewn on his coat) *dragging* himself up to a *well* only to find no *water*.

The picture above, by the way, shows that in 1836, Texas won independence from Mexico even after being defeated at the Alamo. (*a la mode!*)

Make a Connection Relate the memory to some other information that you know. One student remembered the year that the French Revolution began—1789—by thinking of the number on his football jersey (17) and the number of the street (89th) on which he lived.

Form Abbreviations Simple cues can help you remember key letters in a piece of information. In geometry, for example, remembering the letters *ASA* can help you recall **A**ngle, **S**ide, **A**ngle and the method for proving that two triangles are congruent.

To memorize a list, you can create words, phrases, or sentences using the first initials of the terms you need to remember. In biology, for example, if you compose a wacky sentence such as **K**ing **P**hilip **c**ame **o**ver **f**rom **G**ermany **s**lowly, you will have a device that will enable you to remember the scientific classifications of living things (**K**ingdom, **P**hylum, **C**lass, **O**rder, **F**amily, **G**enus, and **S**pecies).

Make a Rhyme Many television commercials are based on jingles or songs. Why? Because the rhymes in the songs or jingles stick in your mind and remind you of the product.

Rhymes are especially good for helping you to remember historical dates. With very little creativity you can make up rhymes for all kinds of facts. For example, consider the following: "1807 was steamboat heaven" and "In 1941 Pearl Harbor faced the gun."

Create Categories Information is easier to recall if it is divided into small chunks of similar information. If you have a list of items to remember, categorize the items according to their similarities. For example, to remember the names of World War II leaders, you could devise two categories:

Allied Leaders
Franklin D. Roosevelt
Winston Churchill
Joseph Stalin

Axis Leaders
Adolf Hitler
Benito Mussolini
Hideki Tojo

Count Items If you know that there are seven countries in Central America but you have thought of only six as you answer a test, you will remember at the very least that you need to search your mind to remember one final piece of information.

The memory strategies you choose should suit your learning style.

Experiment with Strategies Of course, there is no single right way to remember something. The memory strategy you choose should depend upon the type of material to be learned and your individual learning style. Experiment to find which strategies work best for you. Generally, the wisest strategy is to use more than one memory technique.

Lest You Forget
Employ the techniques you have learned in the following exercises.

1. Create a sentence or phrase to help you memorize the seven groups in the animal kingdom in the following order: sponges, coelenterates, worms, mollusks, echinoderms, arthropods, and chordates.

2. Use your imagination to create an image to help you remember the following fact: When Walter Payton retired in 1988, the Chicago Bears retired uniform number 34 as well.

3. Decide upon one or more memory techniques, other than diagrams, that you would use to learn the terms on the picture below. Write a short paragraph to explain the memory technique(s) you chose.

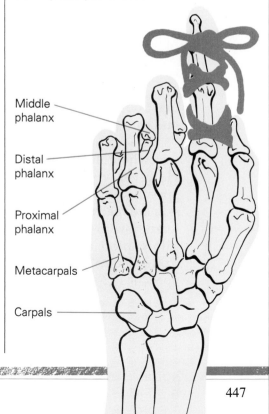

Middle phalanx

Distal phalanx

Proximal phalanx

Metacarpals

Carpals

20
Formal Speaking

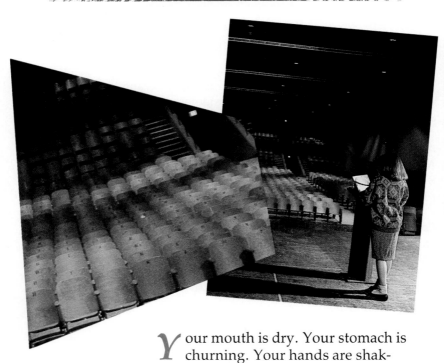

*Y*our mouth is dry. Your stomach is churning. Your hands are shaking. Soon all those empty seats will be filled and all eyes and ears will be turned expectantly toward you.

The fear of speaking formally before a group can be overwhelming for even the most experienced orator. However, you can develop the ability to present a speech knowledgeably and confidently, assured that you are reaching your audience. In this chapter you will learn how to select a topic, organize the appropriate information, and deliver your speech most effectively. You will also learn how to listen to and evaluate speeches given by others.

Part 1
Preparing a Formal Speech

You don't have to be the President of the United States addressing the nation, an athlete accepting a place in a hall of fame, or a lawyer presenting your closing remarks to a jury to need to know how to speak formally in front of a group. As a student, you may find yourself giving a formal talk or report in biology class, presenting a project to a committee, or making a speech at an assembly.

A formal speech is one delivered on a specific topic to a specific audience for a specific purpose. It is usually fairly long and generally requires a great deal of thought, time, and preparation. The process of preparing a speech is very similar to the prewriting stage of preparing a composition. However, the written form your speech takes will vary depending on the type of delivery you choose to give. You will learn more about types of delivery and methods of preparation later in this chapter.

Selecting and Narrowing a Topic

No one likes to listen to a dull speech. However, there is almost no such thing as a dull subject. Any topic can be appealing to an audience if the speaker is truly interested in the subject and can convey that interest to the audience. Choose a subject that interests you, and your interest will be contagious. You might find an interesting topic arising from a situation or assignment.

Keep the following guidelines in mind:

1. **Unusual subjects appeal to everyone.** People always like to hear about something "odd, but true."
2. **The familiar topic has value, but be sure to provide a fresh angle or new point of view.** Otherwise your speech will be dull. For example, if you were asked to welcome a group of incoming freshmen, you could enliven the topic of "school life" by focusing on "the hectic life of a freshman."

Narrowing a topic adequately is especially important for a formal talk. Since most formal talks have a time limit, you should strike a balance in your coverage of the topic you've chosen. In other words, the scope should be narrow enough to adequately discuss the topic within the time limit and detailed enough so that you keep your audience interested and do not run out of material too soon.

Defining Your Purpose

Almost any speech that you will be asked to give will serve one of the following purposes: to **inform** your listeners, to **persuade** your listeners, or to **entertain** your listeners. Decide which of these is the purpose of your speech. The information below will help you learn to identify your purpose.

The **informative speech** is the type you are most often asked to give. Most class reports, for example, are informative. In this kind of speech, you simply want your audience to understand or to appreciate what you are telling them. Speeches that inform might describe a tropical rain forest, explain the brake system of a car, or report on a recently published book.

The **persuasive speech** attempts to lead to some change in the listener's point of view, attitude, or course of action. Speeches that appeal for the election of a candidate, encourage support for a school or charitable activity, or argue against what the speaker considers an unwise course of action are all examples of persuasive speech.

In giving an **entertaining speech** you want your audience to enjoy what you say. A speech meant to entertain might be an after-dinner speech or a between-the-acts speech by a master of ceremonies.

Of course, any one of these types of speeches does not exclude aspects of the others. An informative speech, for example, should also be interesting and should persuade the audience that your information is worth listening to. A persuasive speech should contain information to support its points. And every speech must be entertaining enough to keep the audience awake.

Identifying Your Audience

Understanding your audience can influence the way you develop your material. Ask yourself the following questions as you prepare.

1. **How much does the audience already know about the material you will be presenting?** Determine the amount of background information you will have to supply and the terms you will need to define. Always try to include some new information. Audiences do not want to hear only what they already know.
2. **How does the audience feel about your topic?** The attitude of your audience toward the subject may influence the way you introduce your topic, the tone you use, and the kinds of details and reasons you choose to present. Adapting your material in this way may cause the audience to listen more favorably to a new idea.

Determining Your Main Idea

Begin the actual preparation of a speech by developing a statement of the main idea, or **thesis.** This thesis can usually be stated in one sentence. (See Chapter 5 for a discussion of the thesis.) As you can see in the following examples, the thesis may express an opinion or a general fact about your topic.

Unless we act now, the giant panda may soon perish.
Anorexia nervosa is a growing health problem among teen-age girls.
Good luck charms take on many unusual forms in different cultures.

The statement of your main idea is the key to your entire speech. The thesis must clearly communicate the point of your speech to your audience. Identifying this thesis helps you keep ideas unified during research and topic development.

Researching Your Topic

Many of the research and notetaking techniques you have used to write reports and other types of exposition can be used to prepare a speech. For more information on these techniques, see Chapters 13 and 17.

As you gather information, remember not to overlook yourself as an important reference source. Firsthand knowledge can add a great deal of interest to a speech. Someone who has actually been on a survival trip can enliven researched details about survival techniques with fascinating personal experiences.

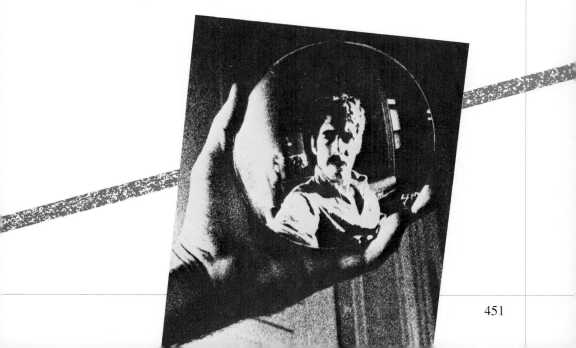

Organizing Your Speech

Before writing your speech or notes you must organize your material. Follow these guidelines as you organize:

Organizing Your Research Notes

1. Scan the subject headings of the note cards you took during research.
2. Based upon these subject headings, make a separate list of main ideas.
3. Divide your note cards into separate groups, one group for each main idea.
4. Confirm that you have several notes providing supporting details for each main idea. If you do not, you may have to eliminate some of your main idea groups, combine some groups, or do further research.

Now, make a modified outline of your speech. This outline will include the following components in shortened form: the **introduction,** the **body,** and the **conclusion.** You may wish to refer to the Writer's Handbook, pages 827–829, for information on making an outline.

Exercise

Choose one of the following topics or a subject of your own.

Magic tricks that everyone can do
A campaign speech for a classmate running for student office
How to register to vote
Robotics
Life in a space capsule
What to do before the paramedics arrive

Narrow the topic to fit a speech with a time limit of ten to fifteen minutes. Identify your purpose and audience. Then state your main idea. Gather material through reflection on your personal experience or through research.

Follow the guidelines above to organize the note cards that you prepared during research. Then make a list of main ideas, using the subject headings of your note cards. Based upon this list of main ideas, make a modified outline.

Part 2
Choosing a Method of Delivery

At this stage in the preparation of your speech, you should begin to think about the method of delivery you will use: extemporaneous, manuscript, or memorized. In what situations would each of these methods be appropriate? Weigh the benefits and drawbacks of each method of delivery, and choose one that matches the situation in which you are speaking.

Extemporaneous The extemporaneous speech is carefully prepared, but not memorized. The extemporaneous speaker has organized or outlined the information and has all key ideas firmly in mind. The speaker may use notes in order to recall details that support each major idea. Although the material has been planned and rehearsed, the specific words of delivery are spontaneous and may vary from those used during practice.

Extemporaneous Delivery

Benefits
1. Speaker has time to select, organize, and practice material.
2. Speaker has control over the material.
3. Speaker's delivery is fresh and natural.
4. Speaker can react to audience and adapt material on the spot.
5. Extemporaneous delivery can be successfully used by both professional and nonprofessional speakers.

Drawbacks
1. Speaker has notes but not the whole speech text. The speaker must depend on memory to supply some material.
2. Speaker must gauge delivery to fit the time span.

Manuscript A manuscript speech is written out in its entirety and read to the audience. Manuscript delivery is well suited to very formal occasions, such as a presidential speech. It is also useful when a great number of facts, statistics, or details must be covered, such as in a research report. Radio and television news broadcasters also use this method of delivery.

President John F. Kennedy addresses a joint session of Congress.

Manuscript Delivery

Benefits
1. No vital point or idea is omitted.
2. Carefully phrased wording is not garbled.
3. Speech can be tailored to fit time allotment exactly.
4. Delivery is the same every time the speech is given.

Drawbacks
1. It is difficult to sound natural while reading.
2. It is difficult to maintain eye contact with audience.
3. There is no possibility for change in response to audience reaction.

Memorized   A memorized speech is simply a manuscript speech that is delivered word for word from memory. This method is chosen when a speaker does not want notes to be visible. For example, the valedictorian of a graduating class will often present an address from memory. Memorized delivery is also used by people who introduce speakers. Occasionally, however, a speaker may choose to keep the manuscript of a speech available for reference while delivering it from memory.

Memorized Delivery

Benefits

1. This delivery ensures that the speaker knows exactly what to say and the order in which to say it.
2. Delivery can be tailored to match time restrictions perfectly.

Drawbacks

1. This method is suitable only for speakers with excellent memory skills.
2. It is very difficult for inexperienced speakers to appear and sound natural.
3. Memorized delivery leaves no room for change or addition in response to audience reaction.
4. Speech length may be limited by speaker's memorization ability. One lapse in memory may put the speaker in a loop repeating material already covered.

Exercise

Study the situations listed below, and indicate which method of delivery would be best suited to each situation. Be prepared to discuss your choices.

1. A scientist has developed a new drug for the treatment of high blood pressure, and will address several groups of doctors in various cities to explain the properties and uses of this drug.
2. Eun Lee is one of three candidates running for student body president of Gordon High School. He will speak at a pre-election assembly and plans to interrupt the text of the speech periodically to invite questions and audience response.
3. The mayor is giving a short speech dedicating a newly constructed library. The dedication will take place outdoors with no lectern or podium available. The library is being named in honor of a former prominent citizen.
4. A lawyer is making closing comments to a jury before it makes a decision on the case.
5. Juanita Soliz has been chosen to represent the local youth organization in their attempt to gain regular Friday night use of the Greater Pilsen Community Hall. Juanita will present the organization's request to the city council.

Part 3
Shaping Your Speech

The type of delivery you choose will determine whether you prepare prompt cards or write out your speech. Manuscript and memorized deliveries are given from written speeches. The extemporaneous speaker uses notes or prompt cards.

Drafting Your Speech

Drafting a written version of your speech aids all three methods of delivery. First, you can see whether you have thoroughly covered all your material and supported any broad statements with specific details. You can visually check for unity and clarity. You can also use the written speech to prepare prompt cards for an extemporaneous delivery.

Follow the steps in the process of writing to prepare your speech. A written speech, however, differs somewhat from a composition. Keep the following points in mind as you draft.

Guidelines for Drafting a Speech

1. Strive for a lighter, more conversational tone than you would use in a composition. For example, consider inserting humor into your introduction. Also, use contractions where natural.
2. Use short sentences, similar to those in conversation.
3. Keep statistics as simple as possible. Remember that your audience is listening not reading. For example, say "nearly ten thousand" instead of "nine thousand nine hundred and fifty."

Preparing Prompt Cards for Delivery

To prepare prompt cards you can utilize the informal outline you made earlier for your written draft.

On each note card write a phrase or sentence that states one of the main ideas of your speech. Along with this main idea, jot down some key words or phrases that bring details about that idea to mind. These key words will help you to recall all the points you want to include and, at the same time, will allow you to speak naturally, rather than reading from a prepared page.

The following excerpt from a student's written draft is the basis for a note card she will use for her speech. The phrases on her note card will remind her of details. With a key point firmly in mind, she will be able to speak confidently.

Student Model

Band membership leads to yet another benefit: the opportunity to travel. State competitions held each year provide an opportunity for the group to travel and play before parades, both in-state and out-of-state. Such trips offer the challenge and enjoyment of taking part in the event, as well as the pleasure of traveling to new places. Also, the sharing of meals, rooms, and laughs with fellow band members creates friendships that can last a lifetime and good memories that you will cherish for years.

Note Card

```
Benefits:

    opportunity to travel
    play for parades
    challenge and enjoyment
    sharing experiences: meals, rooms, laughs
    creates friendships and memories
```

Exercise

Use your informal outline or written draft as a guide. Prepare note cards that you can use as prompts for delivering the speech.

Part 4

Practicing and Delivering a Speech

Most performers experience some stage fright when they appear before an audience. Such feelings of uneasiness can occur whenever you care about doing something well. As a speaker, it is possible to take certain actions that will allow you to appear relaxed and will help you to create an effective impression.

Rehearsing Your Speech

Try to see and hear yourself as others will. If possible, videotape your speech as you practice. If something doesn't look or sound right, try it again with emphasis on a different word or phrase. If videotaping is not possible, practice in front of a mirror to evaluate your appearance and gestures. Use a tape recorder to listen to your delivery.

Rehearse your speech aloud many times. Practice before a sympathetic audience (friend, family member) to gain confidence. Ask for suggestions about how to improve your delivery and make adjustments as you rehearse.

Creating an Effective Impression

Whenever you talk to other people, you communicate your message through both what you say and how you look. The following chart provides helpful guidelines for creating an effective impression.

Guidelines for Creating an Effective Impression

1. **Dress appropriately.** Dress and groom yourself in a way that does not draw attention away from your speech. Your clothing should be appropriate to the audience and the occasion.

2. **Maintain direct eye contact.** Really look at people in all parts of the audience. Direct eye contact lets them know you want to communicate.

3. **Stand naturally.** Try to appear relaxed, but do not slouch or lean on the lectern. Putting one foot in front of another will help you maintain your balance.

4. **Keep gestures and facial expressions natural.** Your facial expressions and body movements should develop naturally from your feelings about your subject. Natural expressions and movements help emphasize meaning and can ease tension. A look of concern, for example, can communicate the seriousness of an idea.

5. **Use your voice to enhance your message.** Vary the volume, pace, and tone or pitch of your voice to suit the content of various parts of your speech. Be careful to speak loudly enough so that your audience will be able to hear you without difficulty.

6. **Strive for careful articulation, a comfortable pace, and effective pauses.** Speak more precisely than you do in ordinary conversation. Pronounce each syllable clearly and distinctly. Be careful to pronounce final consonants. Do not clip vowel sounds or hold *s* sounds. Also, speak more slowly than you would in ordinary conversation. For dramatic effect, try to pause before or after an important point in order to draw the listeners' attention to that point.

7. **Let your nervousness work for you.** Channel your apprehension into enthusiasm for your presentation. A little stage fright is helpful!

Exercise

Following your teacher's directions, choose a method of delivery and then practice and present the speech that you have prepared. You may want to rehearse with a classmate. Remember to use the Guidelines for Creating an Effective Impression.

Part 5
Listening to and Evaluating Speeches

There will be many occasions when it will be important to listen to speeches by others. Some will be informal, such as instructions from a coach or employer. Some may be formal, such as addresses in assemblies. Whatever the occasion, here are a few guidelines to help you be a good listener:

1. Do not speak when someone else is speaking.
2. Direct your attention to the speaker.
3. Give the speaker positive feedback by using appropriate facial expressions and maintaining eye contact.
4. Listen to the introduction and identify the main idea.
5. Listen for words and phrases like the following that signal major ideas: *first, next, another, similarly, in addition,* and *most importantly.*
6. If appropriate, take notes to help you remember main points.
7. Evaluate ideas and evidence. Draw your own conclusions about the material: Is the speaker's supporting evidence strong enough to make you accept the main idea of the speech?

Listening to Evaluate

In some classes you may be asked to evaluate another student's speech. Use a checklist similar to the following to help you pick out the strong and weak points.

Checklist for Evaluating Speeches

Content

Introduction
- Does it get the audience's attention?
- Is it brief and to the point?
- Is it appropriate to the topic?

Body
- Does it support the main idea?
- Does it contain only relevant material?
- Does it state supporting ideas clearly?
- Does it develop supporting ideas completely?

Conclusion
- Is it brief?
- Does it provide a summary of major points or draw attention back to main idea?

Presentation

Nonverbal
- Does the speaker have good posture?
- Is the speaker relaxed and confident?
- Does the speaker have good eye contact?
- Are gestures and facial expressions natural and appropriate?
- Is the speaker neither too quiet nor too loud?
- Is the speaker's articulation clear?

Verbal
- Is the speaker's pace neither too slow nor too rapid?
- Is the speaker's pitch neither too high nor too low?
- Does the speaker vary volume, pace, and pitch?
- Does the speaker use pauses effectively?

You may wish to add a section to your evaluation checklist entitled "Other Comments." It is always helpful to include specific constructive suggestions for improvement.

Exercise

Use the checklist above to critique a round of speeches in your class. Be sure your comments are specific and constructive.

Gullah

A bout 250,000 people living on the islands off the southeastern coast of the United States awake to "dayclean," not dawn. There, "tek e foot enn 'e han" means "to hurry away." "Onrabel e mout," which literally means "unravel his mouth," is the way to describe someone who talks a lot. The people on these islands speak Gullah, an English dialect that blends English vocabulary with West African grammar and intonations.

Gullah is an example of the type of language that develops when people from different cultures struggle to communicate. Its roots go back to the sixteenth century, when Africans who spoke hundreds of different local languages were captured by the slave traders. Since the Africans and the traders did not speak a common language, they developed a "pidgin" that combined aspects of their various languages. Pidgin English became the language of the slave ships. It continued to evolve on the plantations of the South and began to disappear when slavery ended. However, Gullah has survived, primarily because it is spoken on island communities that have remained relatively isolated for much of the past century.

West African ceremonial masks.

Chapter 20
Application and Review

A Adjusting Material to Your Audience Choose a controversial topic that can be argued from more than one side, such as nuclear energy or pass-fail grading systems. Write two speech introductions, one for a supportive audience and one for an audience opposed to your point of view.

B Supporting Your Ideas Write a statement that reflects both viewpoints of the topic you chose in Exercise A. Find supporting materials, such as examples or statistics, that support each way of viewing the topic. Be prepared to discuss which supporting materials are most effective.

C Improving Articulation and Pronunciation Practice articulation by pronouncing the following sentences. Articulate every syllable and pronounce final consonant sounds.

1. In the fiercest frosts we went in winter weather.
2. Which width, thick or thin, best suits the situation?
3. Naturally, I couldn't, wouldn't, and didn't do it.
4. Earl heard his bird's nervous words.
5. Manny insisted Otto utter many mutters and murmurs.
6. The six ships slunk into the slips.

D Analyzing Speeches In the library, listen to a recording or read a copy of a speech by a famous person, such as Winston Churchill or Ralph Nader. Make a modified outline that shows how ideas are introduced and developed in this speech. Are both an introduction and a conclusion used? In a few paragraphs, discuss what kinds of supporting evidence the speaker gives. Is this evidence effective in supporting the speaker's case?

E Preparing Speeches Prepare a ten-minute speech that you could present to your science or social studies class on a topic that interests you. Choose and limit your topic, keeping your time limit and audience in mind. Gather information and organize the information into a modified outline. Write out your speech or prepare prompt cards directly from your outline. Practice your speech and, as your teacher directs, present it to the class.

Grammar, Usage, and Mechanics

Grammar and Writing

When you opened your first language arts textbook in elementary school, you began a study of English grammar, usage, and mechanics that has continued throughout your school career. From time to time, though, you may have wondered, "Why am I studying this? What good does it do me?"

Teachers and students ask themselves these questions every year. *McDougal, Littell English* was written to help you find answers to these questions. In the chapters that follow, you will see that the study of language involves more than just rules and exercises. The study of language encompasses writing, thinking, speaking, understanding literature—even humor.

Grammar Does Help

The study of grammar, usage, and mechanics can have many benefits, depending on how you approach it.

Improved Skills in Usage The way you use language can affect many things, from a grade on a paper to the result of a job interview. The details of language—subject-verb agreement, pronoun usage, verb tense—directly affect the clarity of what you say or write. The rules of language, therefore, can make a tremendous difference in the impression you make on others through your school work, in any written correspondence, in interviews, and eventually in your career.

Improved Thinking Skills The study of grammar involves a number of thinking skills, especially the skills of analysis, classification, and application. As you dissect a sentence, classify a word, or apply a concept to a piece of writing, you are stretching your ability to think clearly and effectively.

A Vocabulary for Writing It would be difficult to learn to drive a car if you had to talk about "the round thing in front of the dashboard" instead of a *steering wheel*. Similarly, it would be difficult to discuss ways to improve your writing without the proper vocabulary. For example, you can add variety and interest to your writing through the appropriate use of participial phrases. Conjunctions and clauses can help you combine short, choppy sentences into longer, more graceful ones. Yet without these terms, a teacher or peer editor would have a hard time communicating suggestions to you, and you would have an even harder time trying to implement those suggestions.

More Effective Writing The artist Picasso understood the rules of color, shape, and perspective. Yet, when it suited his purpose, he bent those rules to create a certain effect or make a unique statement. Professional writers do the same thing. How often have you pointed out to a teacher that an author has used sentence fragments in dialogue or unusual capitalization and punctuation in poetry? These writers, however, bend the rules only after understanding how language works. The resulting sentences are still clear and effective. The more you understand the rules, the better you too will be able to use language as a powerful means of expressing ideas.

Appreciation of Literature A sport like football is much more enjoyable if you know something about the strategies that are used to play the game. Similarly, you can appreciate a work of literature much more if you are sensitive to the techniques and strategies that the author is using. For example, you might notice how a writer uses certain modifiers and verbal phrases to create an atmosphere of suspense. In another piece of writing, you might recognize how a writer uses punctuation to introduce rhythm and movement. Through an awareness of language, you can better enjoy and understand each story or poem you read.

Applications in This Book

In *McDougal, Littell English,* you will find lessons and activities designed to help you achieve all the benefits of language study.

Meaningful Explanations When you learn about a concept, you will be shown how it can affect your writing. You will also be told when everyday language departs from the rules.

Writing Opportunities Throughout the chapters, you will be given opportunities to apply what you have learned in creative writing activities that will stretch your imagination.

Literature-Based Activities Some exercises will give you the opportunity to work with the writing of famous authors, to see how they use the rules—and sometimes why they break them.

On the Lightside Language can be fun. The light essays included in these chapters will show you that words can have a sense of humor, too.

21

The Parts of Speech

P ig. Kingdom: Animalia; phylum: Chordata; class: Mammalia; order: Artiodactyla. In order to organize their study of living things, biologists classify animals with similar physical characteristics into groups such as these.

Words, too, are classified into groups called the *parts of speech.* However, unlike biologists, linguists classify each word according to its function in a sentence, which may vary every time the word appears.

In this chapter you will study the parts of speech. Once you become familiar with them, you will have a vocabulary with which to discuss your writing. You will also be able to recognize and correct errors in sentence construction.

Part 1
Nouns

Certain words in English are used as labels to name persons, places, things, and ideas.

A noun is a word that names a person, place, thing, or idea.

Persons   Edith Hamilton, author, friend, Caesar
Places   Athens, city, mall, Shea Stadium
Things   book, cassette, soccer, announcement
Ideas   happiness, democracy, sympathy, success

Concrete and Abstract Nouns

A **concrete noun** names something that can be seen, heard, smelled, touched, or tasted: *book, thunder, perfume, soup*.

An **abstract noun** names something that cannot be perceived through the five senses: *belief, joy, strictness, efficiency*.

Concrete Nouns	Abstract Nouns
Golden Gate Bridge	talent
fireworks	bravery
silk	friendship
smoke	peace
sofa	comfort

Common and Proper Nouns

A **common noun** is a general name for a person, place, thing, or idea. It is a name that is common to an entire group: *teacher, city, song*.

A **proper noun** is the name of a particular person, place, thing, or idea: *Ms. Sullivan, Detroit, "This Land Is Your Land."*

As you can see in the following examples, a proper noun always begins with a capital letter and may consist of more than one word.

Common Nouns	Proper Nouns
country	Costa Rica
valley	Star Valley
state	Wyoming
union	United Mine Workers
actor	Emilio Estevez
building	Lincoln Center

Compound Nouns

A **compound noun** contains two or more shorter words. Compound nouns may be written as one word, as separate words, or with hyphens.

One Word	Separate Words	With Hyphens
foodstuff	disc jockey	brother-in-law
grandmother	home run	rock-and-roll

Collective Nouns

A **collective noun** is a singular noun that refers to a group of people or things.

choir	team	family	herd	audience	council

Exercises

A Rewrite each sentence, substituting a proper noun for each italicized common noun and a common noun for each italicized proper noun. You may have to add or delete words.

1. The president of the *company* held a press conference.
2. The class read a passage from the *poem*.
3. Did you hear *Billy Joel* discuss creativity with the emcee?
4. The painting is one of *van Gogh's* most famous works.
5. I read a review of the movie in the *newspaper*.

B Application in Literature Write each italicized noun and identify it by type: *Concrete, Abstract, Compound, Collective*. Some nouns will fit more than one category.

(1) I was . . . disappointed to find the *shades* still drawn and the *family* fast asleep when I unlocked the door and stepped into the *apartment*. (2) I stood in the *doorway* of the kitchen . . . and gazed at the sleeping *figure* of my *brother* on the *daybed* in the *dining room*, and beyond it at the closed door of the one *bedroom* where my *parents* slept. (3) The frayed *carpet* on the floor was the carpet I had crawled over before I could walk. (4) Each *flower* in the badly faded and worn *design* was sharply etched in my *mind*. (5) Each *piece* of furniture in the cramped dim room seemed mildewed with

The Window, Henri Matisse, 1916.

a thousand double-edged *memories.* (6) The *ghosts* of a thousand leaden *meals* hovered over the dining-room table. (7) The dust of countless black-hearted days clung to every *crevice* of the squalid ugly furniture I had known since *childhood.* (8) To walk out of it forever . . . would give *meaning* to the *wonder* of what had happened to me, make *success* tangible, decisive.

From *Act One* by Moss Hart

Part 2
Pronouns

To avoid unnecessary repetition, pronouns are often used to replace nouns. Pronouns can be used in the same ways that nouns are used.

A pronoun is a word used in place of a noun or another pronoun.

The noun for which a pronoun stands and to which it refers is its **antecedent.**

Karen repaired *her* broken bicycle. (*Karen* is the antecedent of the pronoun *her.*)

Sometimes the antecedent appears in a preceding sentence.

Switzerland has many exports. *Its* cheeses and cuckoo clocks are popular around the world. (*Switzerland* is the antecedent of the pronoun *its.*)

There are seven kinds of pronouns: personal pronouns, reflexive pronouns, intensive pronouns, demonstrative pronouns, indefinite pronouns, interrogative pronouns, and relative pronouns. On the pages that follow, you will learn to identify these pronouns. (For problems in pronoun usage, see Chapter 27.)

Personal Pronouns

Personal pronouns are pronouns that change form to express person, number, and gender.

Person Pronouns that identify the person speaking are in the **first person.** Pronouns that identify the person being spoken to are in the **second person.** Pronouns that identify the person or thing being spoken about are in the **third person.**

Number Pronouns that refer to one person, place, thing, or idea are **singular** in number. Pronouns that refer to more than one are **plural** in number.

Singular	The *plant* has lost *its* leaves. (The singular pronoun *its* refers to the singular antecedent *plant.*)
Plural	The *plants* have lost *their* leaves. (The plural pronoun *their* refers to the plural antecedent *plants.*)

The following chart shows the person and number of the personal pronouns.

Personal Pronouns

	First Person	Second Person	Third Person
Singular	I, me	you	he, him (his)
	(my, mine)	(your, yours)	she, her (her, hers)
			it (its)
Plural	we, us	you	they, them
	(our, ours)	(your, yours)	(their, theirs)

Gender Pronouns that refer to males are in the **masculine gender.** Pronouns that refer to females are in the **feminine gender.** Pronouns that refer to things are in the **neuter gender.**

Although the neuter pronoun *it* refers to things, the female pronouns *she, her,* and *hers* are sometimes used to refer to countries, ships, and airplanes. Animals may be referred to by *it* and *its* or by *he, him, his, she, her,* and *hers.*

Possessive pronouns are special forms of personal pronouns that show ownership or belonging.

> That road map is *his*. (ownership)
> *Our* family likes to travel. (belonging)

In the chart on page 472, the possessive forms of the personal pronouns are in parentheses.

The possessive pronouns *mine, yours, his, hers, its, ours,* and *theirs* are used like other pronouns to replace nouns. The possessive pronouns *my, your, his, her, its, our,* and *their* are used as modifiers. Notice that *his* and *its* appear in both groups.

> This horse is *mine*. (used like other pronouns)
> This is *my* horse. (modifies the noun *horse*)

> The awards are *ours*. (used like other pronouns)
> We claimed *our* awards. (modifies the noun *awards*)

Exercise

On your paper, write the personal pronouns in the following sentences. After each pronoun write its antecedent.

1. Mary Cassatt was a well-known American painter who chose Paris as her permanent residence.
2. The speaker asked the delegates for their attention.
3. When Luis tried to move the trunk, he found it too heavy to lift.
4. Shirley Temple, the child actress, made a million dollars before she was ten years old.
5. Pygmy marmosets must be small indeed, for they can perch on a single blade of grass.
6. When Jim's power mower broke, the Dows let him use theirs.
7. Helen and Nita finished the math section first. They found it easier than the verbal section.
8. "I think these gloves are mine," said Allison.
9. The boys cooked their meals over an open fire.
10. The snake tests its surroundings with its tongue.

Reflexive and Intensive Pronouns

Reflexive and intensive pronouns are formed by adding *-self* or *-selves* to certain personal pronouns.

Singular   myself, yourself, himself, herself, itself
Plural   ourselves, yourselves, themselves

Grammar Note There are no other acceptable reflexive or intensive pronouns. *Hisself* and *theirselves* are never correct.

Reflexive pronouns reflect an action back upon the subject.

Mother treated *herself* to a microwave oven.

The guests helped *themselves* to the cold buffet.

Intensive pronouns add emphasis to a noun or a pronoun in the same sentence, but they are not essential to the meaning of the sentence. If they are removed, the meaning of the sentence does not change.

Have you written to the mayor *himself?*
We drew up the petition *ourselves.*

Usage Note Reflexive and intensive pronouns should never be used without antecedents.

Incorrect   Kip asked Sam and *myself* to go to the movies.
Correct   Kip asked Sam and *me* to go to the movies.

Exercise

Write an appropriate reflexive or intensive pronoun for each of the following sentences. After each pronoun write its antecedent and tell whether the pronoun is intensive or reflexive.

1. They certainly gave _____ the benefit of the doubt.
2. A lizard was sunning _____ on a flat rock.
3. The doctor _____ helped my grandmother into the car.
4. We bought _____ a new cabinet for the VCR.
5. Marianne Moore _____ said poetry should be pleasing to the mind.
6. The horses opened the gates by _____ and headed for the valley.
7. You will have to solve this problem _____ .
8. The President _____ answered our letter about the astronauts.
9. Our basketball players can certainly be proud of _____ .
10. I guess I'll have to finish staining the bookcase _____ .

Calvin & Hobbes. Reprinted with permission.
All rights reserved.

Demonstrative Pronouns

The **demonstrative pronouns** *this, that, these,* and *those* point out persons or things. *This* and *these* point out persons or things that are near in space or time. *That* and *those* point out persons or things that are farther away in space or time. Demonstrative pronouns may come before or after their antecedents.

Before   *These* are the *sneakers* I want.

After   Look at the *trophies. Those* were won by my father.

Indefinite Pronouns

Pronouns that do not refer to a definite person or thing are called **indefinite pronouns.** Indefinite pronouns often have no antecedents.

Someone returned my keys.
Several have applied, but *few* have been accepted.

The most common indefinite pronouns are listed below.

Indefinite Pronouns	
Singular	another, anybody, anyone, anything, each, everybody, everyone, everything, much, neither, nobody, no one, nothing, one, somebody, someone, something
Plural	both, few, many, several
Singular or Plural	all, any, more, most, none, some

Interrogative Pronouns

The **interrogative pronouns** *who, whom, whose, which,* and *what* are used to introduce questions.

Who is pitching today?   *What* is the schedule?

Relative Pronouns

A **relative pronoun** relates, or connects, a clause to the word or words it modifies. The noun or pronoun that the clause modifies is the antecedent of the relative pronoun. The relative pronouns are *who, whom, whose, which,* and *that*.

> Show me the *camera that* you bought. (The antecedent of the relative pronoun *that* is *camera*.)
> She is the *candidate whom* everyone prefers. (The antecedent of the relative pronoun *whom* is *candidate*.)

Grammar Note Certain pronouns can also function as adjectives.

Demonstrative Pronouns	*this* hat, *that* car, *these* suitcases, *those* curtains
Indefinite Pronouns	*many* awards, *few* supplies, *each* player
Interrogative Pronouns	*whose* jeans, *what* plans, *which* movie theater

Exercises

A On your paper, write the pronouns in the following sentences. Identify each pronoun according to its kind: *Personal, Reflexive, Intensive, Demonstrative, Indefinite, Interrogative,* or *Relative*.

1. We planned most of the rafting trip ourselves.
2. None of the shop's doors were locked, all of the windows were open, but no one was inside.
3. Is this the watch that you want for your birthday, or is it that one?
4. People hurt themselves when they do not face problems.
5. Did anyone besides you see the comet?
6. Those are handsome vases; they come from China.
7. Everyone who wants to can sign up for our class trip.
8. Whose are those?
9. Who played the part of Jean Valjean in *Les Misérables?*
10. Some of the members were angry, but everybody finally agreed to our plan.

B On your paper, write the pronouns in each of the following sentences. Identify each pronoun according to its kind.

(1) Who would have thought anyone could be fascinated by mushrooms? (2) I wouldn't have, at least not until a friend showed me an article in *Nature World*. (3) What exactly are mushrooms—plants or animals? (4) Technically, they are neither. (5) They are fungi. (6) I decided to find out for myself why people look for mushrooms. (7) I discovered four varieties in a nearby park, and one made a lasting impression. (8) That was the stinkhorn. (9) As I have told anyone who will listen to me, the stinkhorn is appropriately named. (10) Its odor left me breathless! (11) Many of the mushrooms I found were indeed beautiful. (12) Some resemble tiers of organ pipes. (13) Those belonging to the genus *Hercium* resemble icicles.

(14) Since certain mushrooms are poisonous, collecting them for eating is something one should leave to the experts. (15) I plan to admire mushrooms for their appearance only.

C *Write Now* Use the photos below as starting points for a paragraph or two about caves. First, decide on your purpose. Will you describe a cave you've visited, tell a story, or give factual information about caves? Will your tone be serious or humorous? As you write, see how many kinds of pronouns you can use.

Part 3
Verbs

A verb is a word that expresses an action, a condition, or a state of being.

There are two main categories of verbs: **action verbs** and **linking verbs**. Other verbs, called **auxiliary verbs**, are sometimes combined with action verbs and linking verbs.

Action Verbs

An **action verb** is a verb that tells what action someone or something is performing. The action may be physical or mental.

Physical Action   We *worked* hard on the fund drive.
Mental Action   Everyone *hoped* for success.

Linking Verbs

A **linking verb** does not express action. Instead, it links the subject of the sentence to a word in the predicate.

> Mr. Kachenko *is* our teacher. (The linking verb *is* links the subject *Mr. Kachenko* to the noun *teacher*.)
> That dog *looks* miserable. (The linking verb *looks* links the subject *dog* to the adjective *miserable*.)

Linking verbs may be divided into three groups.

Types of Linking Verbs

Forms of *To Be*
I *am* happy.
My sister *is* a pharmacist.
They *are* my cousins from Ireland.
Our shoes *were* wet.

Verbs That Express Condition
Everyone *looked* hot.
The tomatoes *grew* tall.
Our cat *seems* intelligent.

Sensory Verbs
The baby's skin *feels* smooth.
This yogurt *tastes* different.
The basement *smells* damp.
The music *sounds* loud.

The children *appeared* sleepy.
The audience *became* restless.
The salad *stayed* fresh.

Sometimes the same verb can be a linking verb or an action verb.

Linking Verb	Action Verb
The fish *tastes* delicious.	The cook *tastes* the fish.
Everyone *looked* hungry.	He *looked* for some herbs.

Note If you can substitute *is*, *are*, *was*, or *were* for a verb, you know it is a linking verb.

The fish *tastes* delicious.	The fish *is* delicious.
Everyone *looked* hungry.	Everyone *was* hungry.

Exercise

On your paper, write the verbs in the following sentences. Identify each verb according to its kind: *Action Verb* or *Linking Verb*.

1. The deadly funnel cloud appeared without warning.
2. The damage from the tornado appears serious.
3. Denise was the youngest competitor in the tournament.
4. The footprints under the window looked fresh.
5. The criminal investigators looked carefully at the footprints.
6. I am curious about your sudden resignation.
7. I just tasted my first papaya.
8. These apples taste unusually tart.
9. An echo sounded through the valley.
10. Your voice sounds hoarse today.

Auxiliary Verbs

An action verb or a linking verb sometimes has one or more **auxiliary verbs**, also called **helping verbs**. The verb that the auxiliary verb helps is the **main verb**. In the following examples, the auxiliary verbs are in italics. The main verbs are in boldface type.

The skies *should* **clear** by noon.
The wind *has been* **blowing** since midnight.

The most common auxiliary verbs are forms of *be*, *have*, and *do*.

Be	am, is, are, was, were, be, been, being	*Have*	have, has, had
		Do	do, does, did

Other common auxiliary verbs are listed below.

can	will	shall	may	must
could	would	should	might	

Together the main verb and one or more auxiliary verbs make up a **verb phrase**.

Auxiliary Verb(s)	+ Main Verb	= Verb Phrase
had	been	had been
have	had	have had
was	doing	was doing
could have	helped	could have helped
might have been	seen	might have been seen
is being	repaired	is being repaired

In the first three examples above, note that the auxiliary verbs *be*, *have*, and *do* may also be used as main verbs.

Often the auxiliary verb and the main verb are separated by one or more words that are not part of the verb phrase. In the examples that follow, note that the contraction *n't* is not part of the verb phrase.

> They certainly *were*n't *being* very helpful.
> We *had* just *left* for the airport.
> My parents *will* never *forget* your kindness.
> *Have* you really *been* to Saudi Arabia?
> *Could*n't rapid action *have helped* you avert this disaster?

Exercises

A On your paper, write the verb phrases in the following sentences. Underline the auxiliary verb once and the main verb twice.

> *Example*   I had never seen the ocean before. had seen

1. According to the forecast, the rain will soon stop .
2. Carmine must feel happy about the elections.
3. Have you ever been to Hawaii?
4. The tanker had apparently run aground in the fog.
5. The benches in the park have been freshly painted .
6. The oxygen supply in a submarine can last for several weeks.
7. No one has ever survived in that desert for more than three days.
8. The new zoning laws aren't being enforced properly.
9. The swimmers were obviously exhausted .
10. Do you have enough blankets for the camping trip?
11. The new gymnasium will surely be ready by September.
12. The driver must have been completely blinded by the rain.
13. The flaws can easily be seen with a magnifying glass.
14. The snow is slowly being cleared from the landing strip.
15. From the highway we could already smell the salty sea air.

B On your paper, write the verbs in the following paragraphs. Remember to include all the words that make up a verb phrase. Identify each verb as an *Action Verb* or a *Linking Verb*.

(1) In my mind's eye I can see the old stone house. (2) It stands about a hundred yards from the edge of the water. (3) The house has not been occupied for years. (4) Its walls are gray. (5) Wooden shutters are nailed over the windows. (6) A steady wind blows in from the sea. (7) Even in the summer the air feels cold. (8) The rains come down with great force; dark clouds bring an early twilight. (9) The house stands quietly amid the overgrown beach grass. (10) It appears indifferent to the forces of nature.

(11) I have never entered the house. (12) Perhaps I will gain admission one day. (13) Will I be frightened inside the gray and lonely house? (14) One can only imagine.

Transitive and Intransitive Verbs

Linking verbs are always intransitive. Action verbs are either transitive or intransitive. An action verb is **transitive** when the action is directed from the subject to the object of the verb. The object comes after the verb and tells *who* or *what* receives the action.

Subject	Transitive Verb	Object
Soula	painted	the fence.
My uncle	owns	a panel truck.
José	won	the trophy.

An action verb is **intransitive** when it does not have an object.

Subject	Intransitive Verb	
The tanker	exploded.	
Maria	sang	beautifully.
Ants	live	in colonies.

In the second example above, the action verb is followed by an adverb, not by an object. In the third example, the action verb is followed by a phrase, not by an object.

Some action verbs may be transitive in one sentence and intransitive in another. Remember that linking verbs are always intransitive.

Transitive Verb	Intransitive Verb
Everyone *applauded* the winner.	Everyone *applauded*.
Are you *selling* your home?	*Are* you *selling*?
Mr. Berra *called* the lawyer.	Mr. Berra *called* yesterday.

Verb or Noun?

Many words may be used either as nouns or as verbs. To distinguish between nouns and verbs, determine whether the word names a person, place, or thing, or expresses an action or state of being.

We chipped away at the ice with a *pick*. (noun)
Pick a melon that's not too ripe. (verb)

Our club is in good *shape* financially. (noun)
Everyone will *shape* up after spring training. (verb)

Exercises

A On your paper, write the verbs and verb phrases in the following sentences. Identify each verb as *Transitive* or *Intransitive*.

1. Deserts can become extremely cold at night.
2. We visited a replica of the *Mayflower*.
3. After seven weeks the sailors had finally sighted land.
4. All oceans contain salt water.
5. The murderer does not appear until the final scene.
6. Our team usually plays well during the first quarter.
7. Everyone seems confident about the outcome of the congressional investigation.
8. My sister Nita willingly accepts responsibility.
9. State troopers are now enforcing the speed laws.
10. The jet disappeared into the distant clouds.

B On your paper, write the verbs in the following sentences. Identify each verb as a *Transitive Verb* or an *Intransitive Verb*. Then write five new sentences using each transitive verb as an intransitive verb and each intransitive verb as a transitive verb.

> *Example*   Hugo played a beautiful melody on the
> French horn. played, Transitive
> Chris played on the tennis team.

1. The tall ships sailed into the harbor.
2. Will your work load lighten after this semester?
3. The Morrisons moved their furniture in a rented van.
4. Who kicked the winning field goal?
5. The explorers crossed the Andes by burro.

C *Write Now* Look at the dogsled driver in the picture below. Imagine that you have the training and endurance to participate in a rigorous activity like this. Who would you be? What would you do? Select an idea from the list below or invent your own. Tell about yourself and your abilities in one paragraph. In a second paragraph, describe one or two events that might occur during your day. Use verbs that will help your reader picture the action.

Olympic athlete	mountain climber
pro football star	white-water canoe guide
jungle explorer	race car driver
slalom ski racer	sunken treasure hunter

Checkpoint *Parts 1, 2, and 3*

A Write the italicized nouns in the following sentences. Identify each as *Concrete, Abstract, Common, Proper, Compound,* or *Collective.* Each noun will fit two or three categories.

> *Example*   My *sister-in-law* wrote a paper about *Babe Didrikson* and her *commitment* to sports.
>
> sister-in-law, Concrete, Common, Compound
>
> Babe Didrikson, Concrete, Proper
>
> commitment, Abstract, Common

1. Few mountains can compare in *splendor* with the *Grand Tetons.*
2. The *store* in the *shopping center* is like a huge *warehouse.*
3. The *pitcher* narrowed his eyes in intense *concentration.*
4. Most medical *breakthroughs* are the *result* of long *years* of blood, sweat, and tears.
5. The plot of that *soap opera* often involves *blackmail.*
6. *Andrew Wyeth* is known for his detailed paintings of rural *scenes.*
7. The *team* had its *picture* taken with the *mayor.*
8. The *screech* of skidding tires was followed by the sound of breaking *glass.*
9. A powerful *tribe* had settled in the *hills* that sloped up from the *riverbank.*
10. To triumph over a *challenge,* one has to overcome fear and *self-doubt.*

B On your paper, write the pronouns in the following sentences. Identify each pronoun according to its kind: *Personal, Reflexive, Intensive, Demonstrative, Indefinite, Interrogative,* or *Relative.*

1. This is the costume I am wearing to our Mardi Gras party.
2. Who is taller, your sister or my brother?
3. Even if Babe Ruth himself were on our team, we could not have beaten them.
4. We built the fire ourselves, so all could enjoy it.
5. We considered ourselves brave, but no one in the group would pet their tame tiger.
6. Is that the project you entered in the Science Fair?
7. She is a person whom one instinctively trusts.
8. Each of the plants is healthy, and several have new leaves.

9. Which of these is yours?
10. Nobody knows how they managed to pull themselves from the water onto the icy ledge.

C On your paper, write the verbs in the following sentences. If the verb is part of a verb phrase, underline the auxiliary verb once and the main verb twice. Identify each verb as an *Action Verb* or a *Linking Verb* and as a *Transitive Verb* or an *Intransitive Verb*.

1. Have you ever seen the classic movie *It's a Wonderful Life* starring James Stewart?
2. A journey in a space shuttle will soon seem as commonplace as a flight in an airplane.
3. By noon Kathy will have collected dozens of shells for her art project.
4. Ahmad's sister worked patiently without a break.
5. Alexander the Great had become a famous conqueror by the age of seventeen.
6. The elderly senator had often dreamed about the office of the Presidency.
7. What will you be doing in the year 2000?
8. Searchers had finally spotted the wreckage of the plane.
9. The exchange students sang a lively French song.
10. The mountains of the West must have seemed insurmountable to the original pioneers.

Part 4
Adjectives

Words that change or limit the meanings of other words are called **modifiers.** One kind of modifier is the **adjective.**

An adjective is a word that modifies a noun or a pronoun.

An adjective answers one of the following questions: *Which one? What kind? How many? How much?*

Which One	this, that, these, those
What Kind	huge, new, green, courageous
How Many	few, several, both, ten, most
How Much	more, less, sufficient, plentiful

Position of Adjectives

Adjectives usually appear before the nouns or pronouns that they modify.

Irate passengers have complained about the *dark* windows on the *new* buses.

Sometimes, for variety, a writer will put adjectives in other positions. Compare the following sentences.

The skier, *swift* and *powerful*, outdistanced his rivals.

Swift and *powerful*, the skier outdistanced his rivals.

Articles

The most common adjectives are the articles *a, an,* and *the.* The word *the* is called a **definite article** because it usually refers to a specific person, place, or thing. The words *a* and *an* are called **indefinite articles** because they refer to no particular person, place, or thing.

Use *a* before a word beginning with a consonant sound: *a check, a history paper.* Use *an* before a word beginning with a vowel sound: *an envelope, an hour.*

Proper Adjectives

A **proper adjective** is formed from a proper noun and is always capitalized.

Proper Noun	Proper Adjective
Spain	Spanish
Canada	Canadian
Shakespeare	Shakespearean
Jackson	Jacksonian

Predicate Adjectives

An adjective that follows a linking verb and modifies the subject of the sentence is called a **predicate adjective.** Unlike most adjectives, predicate adjectives are separated from the words they modify.

Some movies seem *endless.*

The pages of the diary were *yellowed* and *brittle.*

Other Parts of Speech as Adjectives

Nouns, pronouns, and certain verb forms sometimes function as adjectives. To understand the function of a word, decide how it is used in a sentence. If a word tells *what kind, which one, how much,* or *how many* about a noun or pronoun, it is functioning as an adjective. The nouns, pronouns, and verb forms below are functioning as adjectives.

Nouns	The Hawaiian dancers wore *grass* skirts.
	Dorothy walked down a yellow *brick* road.
Pronouns	*This* ticket will admit you to the football game.
	Marty played *her* new tape at least ten times.
Verb Forms	Ellie straightened up her *cluttered* room.
	Rod stirred the soup mix into some *boiling* water.

Exercises

A Write the adjectives in the following sentences. Do not include articles.

1. Honey has been a valuable substance since earliest times.
2. Most foods that early people ate were tough and bland; honey, in contrast, was smooth, sweet, thick, and delicious.
3. Early people began to gather raw honey when they discovered nests of wild bees.
4. The ancient lore about bees included many superstitions.
5. One myth was that loud noises attract bees, but actually bees have very poor hearing.
6. A Hittite law of about 300 B.C. established the value of honey.

7. A tub of honey was as valuable as a tub of butter or one sheep.
8. The ancient Chinese and the medieval Europeans were among those who used honey for medicinal purposes.
9. Honey has been eaten for quick energy since the days of the original Greek Olympic games.
10. There are still many people who eat honey for energy, including marathon runners and Arctic explorers.

B Application in Literature Find at least twenty adjectives in the following excerpt and write them on your paper. Do not include articles. The passage is from a letter written in 1520 by explorer Hernán Cortez to his king, Charles V of Spain. In it Cortez describes the Aztec capital Tenochtitlán (now Mexico City).

Detail, *The Great City of Tenochtitlán,* Diego Rivera, 1945.

(1) Most powerful Lord, an account to Your Royal Excellency of the magnificence, the strange and marvelous things of this great city . . . will, I well know, be so remarkable as not to be believed. (2) This great city is built on the salt lake. (3) There are four artificial causeways leading to it, and each is as wide as two cavalry lances. (4) The city itself is as big as Seville or Córdoba . . . . (5) This city has many squares where trading is done and markets are held continuously. (6) There is also one square . . . where more than 60,000 people come each day to buy and sell, and where every kind of merchandise produced in these lands is found.

c *Write Now* Test your ability to use adjectives effectively by writing a description of what you are wearing right now. Try to go beyond ordinary words such as *old, new, red,* or *blue*. Search for adjectives that can show why a pair of jeans or a sweater is unique. Are the jeans stiff, worn, faded, or patched? Is the sweater fuzzy, ragged, or stretched?

Part 5
Adverbs

Another kind of modifier is the **adverb**.

An adverb is a word that modifies a verb, an adjective, or another adverb.

Modifying a Verb	The ship sailed *slowly* out of the harbor.
Modifying an Adjective	We all had a *rather* hectic day of sightseeing in San Francisco.
Modifying an Adverb	The traffic moved *very* quickly.

Adverbs answer the questions *Where? When? How?* and *To what extent?*

Where	We moved the table *outside*.
When	The picnic begins *later*.
How	The storm came *unexpectedly*.
To What Extent	Everyone got *very* wet.

Grammar Note Adverbs that modify adjectives or other adverbs by adding emphasis are called **intensifiers**. These include *too, very, extremely, truly,* and *really*. Avoid overuse of intensifiers. Too many *very*'s and *really*'s can weaken your writing.

Forms of Adverbs

Many adverbs are formed by adding *-ly* to an adjective: *correct, correctly; prompt, promptly; easy, easily*. Some modifiers that end in *-ly*, however, are adjectives: *friendly* dog, *lonely* soldier, *ugly* bruise.

Some common adverbs do not end in *-ly*. These include the negatives *no, not,* and *never*, and time words such as *soon, later,* and *often*.

Position of Adverbs

An adverb usually follows the verb it modifies.

Their bus arrives *there tomorrow.*

Sometimes, however, an adverb comes before the verb.

Frequently, the bus leaves on time.

The bus *frequently* leaves on time.

Intensifiers or other adverbs that modify adjectives or other adverbs usually come right before the word they modify.

Ours is a *very* common name.

We worked *extremely* hard on his campaign.

Nouns as Adverbs

Several words that are generally thought of as nouns can also function as adverbs. These adverbs tell *where* and *when.* Look at the following examples.

Noun	Adverb
My *home* is in Tulsa.	She went *home* early. (where)
Tomorrow will be sunny.	I'll study *tomorrow.* (when)

Adjective or Adverb?

Words like *fast* and *early* have the same form when used as adjectives or as adverbs. To tell whether a word is an adjective or an adverb, determine which word it modifies. If the word modifies a noun or a pronoun, it is an adjective. If it modifies a verb, an adjective, or another adverb, it is an adverb.

Adjective   My grandmother has always been an *early* riser. (The adjective *early* modifies the noun *riser* and tells *what kind.*)

Adverb   My grandmother rises *early.* (The adverb *early* modifies the verb *rises* and tells *when.*)

Grammar Note Many adverbs are combined with verbs to make idioms. An **idiom** is a group of words whose meaning is different from the literal meanings of the individual words. Some idiomatic verb phrases are *break down, bottle up, check out, fill in, grow up, set up,* and *strike out.*

Exercises

A Each sentence below contains an adverb in italics. Write the word or words each adverb modifies. Tell which question the adverb answers: *Where? How? When? To what extent?*

1. Kelly tied the square knot *skillfully*.
2. It began to rain, and we all ran *indoors*.
3. Last summer was *extremely* hot.
4. The President will address the nation *tonight*.
5. After the long cold winter, the settlers' food supply was *completely* exhausted.

B Application in Literature Find at least fifteen adverbs in the following passage and write them on your paper. As you read the passage, notice how the adverbs add specific details that make the writing more vivid.

(1) "Nicholas, Nicholas!" she screamed, "you are to come out of this at once. (2) It's no use trying to hide there; I can see you all the time."

(3) Presently the angry repetitions of Nicholas's name gave way to a shriek, and a cry for somebody to come quickly. (4) Nicholas shut the book, restored it carefully to its place in a corner, and shook some dust from a neighboring pile of newspapers over it. (5) Then he crept from the room, locked the door, and replaced the key exactly where he had found it. (6) His aunt was still calling his name when he sauntered into the front garden.

(7) "Who's calling?" he asked.

(8) "Me," came the answer from the other side of the wall. (9) "Didn't you hear me? (10) I've been looking for you in the gooseberry garden, and I've slipped into the rain-water tank. (11) Luckily there's no water in it, but the sides are slippery and I can't get out. (12) Fetch the little ladder from under the cherry tree--"

(13) "I was told I wasn't to go into the gooseberry garden," said Nicholas promptly.

(14) "I told you not to, and now I tell you that you may," came the voice from the rain-water tank rather impatiently.

(15) "Your voice doesn't sound like aunt's," objected Nicholas. (16) "You may be the Evil One tempting me to be

disobedient. (17) Aunt often tells me that the Evil One tempts me and that I always yield. (18) This time I'm not going to yield."

From *The Lumber Room* by H. H. Munro (Saki)

c *Write Now* Visualize yourself traveling down the road pictured in the photo above. Write a description of your journey. Tell where you have been and where you are going. Use at least five of the words below in your writing. When you are done, underline these words and tell whether you have used them as adverbs or adjectives.

low	slow	right	late	straight
high	fast	north	early	far

Checkpoint Parts 4 and 5

A Write the modifiers in the following sentences and identify each as an adjective or adverb. Then write the word each adjective or adverb modifies. Do not include articles.

1. We were tense as our plane approached the thunderclouds.
2. Which of the runners had the fastest time?
3. A large calico cat crept silently across my yard.

4. A tiny tugboat slowly towed the enormous oil tanker out of the narrow harbor.
5. The game lasted much longer than most because of an extremely long half-time program.
6. Some rock stars are incredibly wealthy.
7. The audience laughed loudest at the antics of the sad clown with the baggy pants.
8. Yesterday we discovered a dinosaur fossil near the base of the mountain trail.
9. France is smaller than Texas.
10. The fishermen hauled the empty nets onto the deck of the boat and headed for home.
11. The trunk in the attic appeared rather old.
12. A very unpleasant odor gradually filled the chemistry lab and the hallway.
13. After the sudden storm, the crickets remained unusually quiet for several hours.
14. Maria operates the finest art gallery in town.
15. Usually, elephants move rather slowly.

B Application in Literature Find at least five adverbs and ten adjectives in the following paragraphs and write them on your paper. Identify each modifier as an adverb or adjective and tell what word each modifies. Notice how a careful choice of modifiers can create a strong, clear description. Remember that many words can function as more than one part of speech.

(1) In many ways he looked like something that was awkwardly put together. (2) Both his nose and his lips seemed a trifle too large for his face. (3) To say he was ugly would be unjust and to say he was handsome would be gross exaggeration. (4) Truthfully, I could never make up my mind about him. (5) Sometimes he looked like something out of a book of ancient history . . . looked as if he was left over from that magnificent era before the machine age came and marred the earth's natural beauty.

(6) His great variety of talent often startled the teachers. (7) This caused his classmates to look upon him with a mixed feeling of awe and envy.

From "The Boy Who Painted Christ Black" by John Henrik Clarke

What Is and Ain't Grammatical

In the excerpt below, humorist Dave Barry reflects upon the importance of English grammar and speculates about its "origins."

I cannot overemphasize the importance of good grammar.

Actually, I could easily overemphasize the importance of good grammar. For example, I could say: "Bad grammar is the leading cause of a slow, painful death in North America," or "Without good grammar, the United States would have lost World War II."

The truth is that grammar is not the most important thing in the world. The Super Bowl is the most important thing in the world. But grammar is still important. For example, suppose you are being interviewed for a job as an airplane pilot, and your prospective employer asks you if you have any experience, and you answer: "Well, I ain't never actually flied no actual airplanes or nothing, but I got several pilot-style hats and several friends who I like to talk about airplanes with."

If you answer this way, the prospective employer will immediately realize that you have ended your sentence with a preposition. (What you should have said, of course, is "several friends with who I like to talk about airplanes.") So you will not get the job, because airline pilots have to use good grammar when they get on the intercom and explain to the passengers that, because of high winds, the plane is going to take off several hours late and land in Pierre, South Dakota, instead of Los Angeles.

We did not always have grammar. In medieval England, people said whatever they wanted, without regard to rules, and as a result they sounded like morons. Take the poet Geoffrey Chaucer, who couldn't even spell his first name right. He wrote a large poem called *Canterbury Tales,* in which people from various professions—knight, monk, miller, reever, riveter, eeler, diver, stevedore, spinnaker, etc.—drone on and on like this:

> *In a somer sesun whon softe*
> *was the sunne*
> *I kylled a younge birde ande*
> *I ate it on a bunne.*

When Chaucer's poem was published, everybody read it and said: "Good grief, we need some grammar around here." So they formed a Grammar Commission, which developed the parts of speech, the main ones being nouns, verbs, predicants, conjectures, particles, proverbs, adjoiners, coordinates, and rebuttals. Then the commission made up hundreds and hundreds of grammar rules, all of which were strictly enforced. ***Dave Barry***

Part 6
Prepositions

A preposition is a word used to show the relationship between a noun or a pronoun and another word in the sentence.

> Several *of* America's best poets have come *from* New England. (The preposition *of* relates the pronoun *Several* to the noun *poets;* the preposition *from* relates the verb *have come* to the noun *New England.*)

Prepositions often express relationships of location (*by, near*), direction (*to, down*), and association (*of, with*). Look for prepositions like these as you study the following list.

Commonly Used Prepositions

about	before	down	of	throughout
above	behind	during	off	to
across	below	except	on	toward
after	beneath	for	onto	under
against	beside	from	out	underneath
along	between	in	outside	until
among	beyond	inside	over	up
around	but	into	past	upon
as	by	like	since	with
at	despite	near	through	within

Usage Note The words *but* and *as* are usually conjunctions. However, *but* is used as a preposition when it means "except." *As* functions as a preposition when it means "in the capacity of."

A **compound preposition** is formed by combining words.

Commonly Used Compound Prepositions

according to	by means of	in place of	on account of
aside from	in addition to	in spite of	out of
because of	in front of	instead of	prior to

Objects of Prepositions

A preposition never appears alone. It is followed by a word or a group of words called the **object of the preposition.**

> The box fell behind the *refrigerator*. (The word *refrigerator* is the object of the preposition *behind*.)
>
> Before *baking a cake,* you should read the recipe. (The group of words *baking a cake* is the object of the preposition *before*.)

A preposition and its object, plus any modifiers, form a **prepositional phrase.**

into the house	because of the icy roads
among her papers	on the northeast corner
near the train tracks	to the moon

In most prepositional phrases, the object follows the preposition. Occasionally, however, the object comes first. This usually occurs in sentences that have interrogative or relative pronouns.

> *Whom* did you write the letter *to?* (The interrogative pronoun *whom* is the object of the preposition *to*.)
>
> Is this the town *that* you came *from?* (The relative pronoun *that* is the object of the preposition *from*.)

Adverb or Preposition?

A number of words may be used either as prepositions or as adverbs. One simple test may help you to tell the difference. A preposition is never used alone. It is always followed by a noun or a pronoun as part of a phrase. If the word is in a phrase, it is probably a preposition. If the word has no object, it is probably an adverb.

> Sue put on her coat and went *out*. (*Out* is an adverb. It has no object.)
> Sue put on her coat and went *out* the door. (*Out* is a preposition. It has an object, *door*.)

> The sundial had been knocked *down*. (adverb)
> The cart rolled *down* the hill. (preposition)

> Will you all please stand *up?* (adverb)
> The mountaineers struggled *up* Pike's Peak. (preposition)

For more information on prepositional phrases, see Chapter 23, page 533.

Exercises

A On your paper, write the prepositions in the following sentences. After each preposition, write its object.

1. During the intermission, the crowd rushed toward the snack bar.
2. A man jumped onto the train and shouted at the passengers.
3. Everyone but me saw the car crash into the fence.
4. We all felt better after our talk with the coach.
5. Aside from the cost, we have no objection to your proposal.
6. Whom did you address the package to?
7. Is there a law against fireworks outside the city?
8. Because of the storm, most schools were closed on Friday.
9. Every night the dog sniffs around the kitchen for its dinner.
10. To the east sharp peaks rose above the floor of the valley.

B Write the prepositions. After each preposition, write its object.

1. Prior to 1689 Russia was an agricultural society controlled by nobles and farmed by peasants.
2. There was little contact with Western Europe.
3. A major problem was the lack of seaports.
4. During this time, Sweden blocked passage to the Atlantic Ocean in the west, while the Ottoman Empire (Turkey) controlled the waterways in the south.
5. When Peter the Great came to power in 1689, he immediately began plans for the introduction of Western culture throughout Russia, the capture of neighboring ports, and the creation of a navy.
6. Peter made extensive trips to Europe, where he observed, studied, and even worked as a carpenter for a shipbuilder.

Left: Peter the Great.
Right: Petrodvorets, the Grand Cascade, Leningrad, Russia (formerly St. Petersburg).

497

7. When he returned to Russia, he brought a number of European scientists and craftsmen with him. He also brought European ideas of dress, politics, education, and military training, which he forced upon his subjects.
8. Many of Peter's Western ideas were not popular among the nobility, but this did not stop him.
9. In 1721, four years before his death, Peter captured some Baltic seaports from Sweden and established the Russian navy.
10. Peter also built a new capital called St. Petersburg near the Baltic. He called the town his "window to the world."

Part 7
Conjunctions

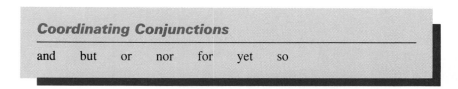

Prepositions show relationships between words. Conjunctions connect words or groups of words.

A conjunction is a word that connects words or groups of words.

There are three kinds of conjunctions: coordinating conjunctions, correlative conjunctions, and subordinating conjunctions.

Coordinating Conjunctions

A **coordinating conjunction** is used to connect words or groups of words that have the same function in a sentence.

Coordinating Conjunctions						
and	but	or	nor	for	yet	so

Coordinating conjunctions can connect the following:

Nouns	**Rain** *and* **fog** made travel impossible.
Pronouns	This package is for **you** *and* **me**.
Verbs	We **bathed** *and* **groomed** the dog.
Adjectives	Our principal is **strict** *yet* **fair**.
Adverbs	They worked **slowly** *but* **efficiently**.
Prepositions	Are you **with** *or* **against** us?

A coordinating conjunction can also connect phrases or independent clauses. Clauses are groups of words containing both a subject and a verb. For a discussion of clauses, see Chapter 23.

Phrases   The fog crept <u>over the water</u> *and* <u>toward the city</u>.
Clauses   <u>They acted human</u>, *yet* <u>their feet were definitely webbed</u>.

The conjunctions *for* and *so* always connect clauses.

<u>We know spring is coming</u>, *for* <u>the river is beginning to thaw</u>.
<u>We needed extra chairs</u>, *so* <u>we borrowed some from our neighbor</u>.

Nor is used as a coordinating conjunction only when it is preceded by such negative words as *no, not,* or *neither*.

The team has *no* coach, *nor* does it have a catcher.

Correlative Conjunctions

Correlative conjunctions are similar to coordinating conjunctions. However, correlative conjunctions are always used in pairs.

Correlative Conjunctions		
both . . . and	neither . . . nor	whether . . . or
either . . . or	not only . . . but (also)	

Both my grandfather *and* my aunt are physicians.
The peaches are *neither* in the refrigerator *nor* on the table.
Either that cat is grinning at us, *or* I am imagining things.
The lettuce is *not only* wilted *but also* moldy.
I wondered *whether* you would come by train *or* by bus.

Subordinating Conjunctions

A **subordinating conjunction** introduces certain subordinate clauses—clauses that cannot stand by themselves as complete sentences. A subordinating conjunction joins a subordinate clause to an independent clause—a clause that can stand by itself as a complete sentence.

┌independent ┐┌─────── subordinate ───────┐
A crowd gathers *whenever* there is an accident. (The subordinating conjunction *whenever* connects the subordinate clause to the independent clause.)

Subordinating conjunctions show various kinds of relationships including those of time, manner, place, reason, comparison, condition, or purpose.

Subordinating Conjunctions

Time	after, as, as long as, as soon as, before, since, until, when, whenever, while
Manner	as, as if
Place	where, wherever
Cause or Reason	because, since
Comparison	as, as much as, than
Condition	although, as long as, even if, even though, if, provided that, though, unless, while
Purpose	in order that, so that, that

Conjunctive Adverbs

A **conjunctive adverb** is an adverb that is used to connect clauses that can stand by themselves as sentences.

> We were not certain that this was the correct address; *nevertheless,* we rang the doorbell.
>
> Michelangelo is best known for his painting in the Sistine Chapel; *however,* he thought of himself primarily as a sculptor.

The words most often used as conjunctive adverbs are listed in the chart below.

Conjunctive Adverbs

accordingly	furthermore	nevertheless
also	hence	otherwise
besides	however	still
consequently	indeed	then
finally	moreover	therefore

Punctuation Note A conjunctive adverb is preceded by a semicolon and followed by a comma.

Exercises

A On your paper, write the conjunctions in the following sentences. Identify each conjunction according to its kind: *Coordinating Conjunction, Correlative Conjunction, Subordinating Conjunction,* or *Conjunctive Adverb.*

1. The search party worked quickly and carefully.
2. We must either sell more subscriptions or give up the early morning paper route.
3. Is Juan or Kate responsible for buying the tickets?
4. We were not at home when the mail carrier knocked; nevertheless, the package arrived safely.
5. The car stalled, so we hiked to the nearest service station.
6. She seemed confident before she gave her speech.
7. Neither the awards nor the speeches were very surprising.
8. The dictionary is a valuable tool; however, not all dictionaries agree on spelling and pronunciation.
9. We'll bicycle through the park Saturday unless it rains.
10. Because the sub was lying silently three hundred feet down, the planes could not detect it.
11. Although the army was starving, Washington led them forward.
12. The eggs were overcooked; otherwise, the breakfast was good.
13. The Japanese and the Italian delegates opposed the plan.
14. The traffic moves slowly whenever it rains.
15. The ride on the *Metroliner* was fast and comfortable.

B Write each pair of sentences as one sentence by joining the italicized words with the kind of conjunction indicated in parentheses. Delete words as necessary.

1. The rocket shot *off the pad.* It shot *into the air.* (coordinating)
2. *Mother sprained her ankle. She is not going to work tomorrow.* (conjunctive adverb)
3. Germanium is a *rare metal.* It is *useful.* (coordinating)
4. You may take *biology.* You may take *earth science.* (correlative)
5. The test was *fair.* The test was *difficult.* (coordinating)
6. *The museum was closed. We went to the zoo.* (subordinating)
7. *Dad tossed the salad. He made the dressing.* (correlative)
8. *I enjoyed the book. I wanted to see the movie.* (conjunctive adverb)
9. A stray dog crept *through the broken front gate.* It crept *into the yard.* (coordinating)
10. *Everyone rose. The judge entered.* (subordinating)

Part 8

Interjections

An interjection is a word or a group of words that expresses feeling or emotion.

An interjection may precede a sentence or appear within a sentence.

> *Good grief!* Are those your new sneakers?
> His new sneakers, *alas,* were ruined.
> *Well,* what are we going to do now?

Punctuation Note An interjection that precedes a sentence is followed by an exclamation point or a comma. An interjection within a sentence is set off by commas or a comma.

Exercise

On your paper, write the following sentences, replacing each blank with an appropriate interjection. Do not use an interjection more than once. Remember to use the correct punctuation and capitalization.

1. _____ it can't be six o'clock already.
2. _____ You just won first prize.
3. _____ Everyone is taking a nap.
4. _____ That skunk really smells.
5. _____ it's time to go.

Checkpoint *Parts 1–8*

A On your paper, write the adverbs and prepositions in the following sentences. After each adverb, write the word it modifies. After each preposition, write its object.

1. The lights of the distant airplanes were almost invisible among the stars.
2. In the Gettysburg Address, Lincoln firmly stated that ours was a government of the people, by the people, and for the people.
3. Jacques Cousteau "eavesdrops" on marine life by means of extremely sensitive sonar equipment.
4. Diane awoke early in the morning and went down to the beach looking for seashells.
5. The first kindergarten in the United States was begun by Margaretha M. Schurz in 1856.
6. The Yukon River flows down through Alaska and empties into the Bering Sea.
7. Many children in Zaire must row back and forth to school across dangerous swamps.
8. Tiles from Spain have been carefully installed on the ceiling of the Holland Tunnel in place of the original tiles.
9. The blue whale was nearly hunted to extinction in the late 1800's for its oil and meat.
10. Muscles will eventually become covered with fat if they are not exercised.

B On your paper, write the conjunctions in the following sentences. Identify each conjunction according to its kind: *Coordinating Conjunction, Correlative Conjunction, Subordinating Conjunction,* or *Conjunctive Adverb.*

1. Shakespeare did not attend college, but he did master several languages and both ancient and modern history.
2. A chemical waste dump was found near the reservoir; consequently, the water supply was shut off.
3. Elise told the guidance counselor that she wants to be either a concert violinist or a composer.
4. Firecrackers and similar explosives are illegal in this state; however, they are not illegal in the adjoining one.
5. Zeus was the foremost Greek god, yet even he was subject to fate.

6. Let's plan to spend a weekend camping in Wisconsin when the weather is warmer.
7. A cut usually requires stitches if the edges are jagged and uneven.
8. The motion of the boat made me seasick; nevertheless , I would not have missed the tour of the Gulf.
9. Neither rain nor sleet nor snow keeps my little sister from her daily newspaper route.
10. It was once believed that not only water but also canals existed on the surface of Mars.

C Identify the part of speech of each italicized word in the sentences below. Then, write a new sentence using the word as indicated in parentheses.

1. The gravitational *pull* of the sun and moon on the earth creates tides. (verb)
2. Of all the things we've discussed, *which* is the problem that bothers you the most? (adjective)
3. The wind blew *hard* all night long and by morning the lawn was littered with debris. (adjective)
4. At the North Pole, the sea is very *deep*. (adverb)
5. The crowds were so enormous that our tour guide was left *behind*. (preposition)
6. There will be no *afternoon* games next year unless the school board reconsiders its decision. (noun)
7. His last movie did not *further* his career. (adverb)
8. My grandparents have a very *fast* boat but they rarely use it anymore. (adverb)
9. By early afternoon, the yellow 1955 Chevrolet had taken the *lead* in the race. (verb)
10. A great crowd gathered *around* the movie star and began to ask for autographs. (adverb)
11. Do you know at *what* time the shuttle liftoff will occur this morning? (pronoun)
12. Because poor quality mortar had been used, the *brick* wall was already crumbling. (noun)
13. There's a part that's perfect for you, so *promise* me that you will come to auditions. (noun)
14. When we were in Africa last year, we visited a wildlife preserve *in* Kenya. (adverb)
15. A local ice-cream manufacturer is planning to *branch* out into other parts of the country. (noun)

Linking
Grammar & Writing

Think of a time when you were very frightened. Perhaps you were home alone in a storm or walking through a forest on a moonless night. Write a paragraph that describes your experience.

Prewriting and Drafting Try to remember the time and place of your experience along with as many sights, sounds, and other sensations as possible. To brainstorm for descriptive language, make columns for *Nouns, Adjectives, Verbs,* and *Adverbs.* Begin by listing a noun, and then list related words as shown below.

Nouns	Adjectives	Verbs	Adverbs
branches	shadowy	threatened	menacingly
wind	gusting	blew	eerily

Revising and Proofreading When revising, consider the following questions:

1. Have you used vivid, dramatic details?
2. Have you shown your reader *why* you were afraid?
3. Is the organization of your description easy to follow?

Additional Writing Topic Pretend that you are witnessing the final moments of an important sporting event such as the one in the picture below. Write two paragraphs. In the first, describe the crowd, the setting, and the general atmosphere. In the second, describe the action during the last moments of the event.

Chapter 21
Application and Review

A Understanding How Words Are Used Determine how the italicized words are used in each sentence. Tell whether each is a *Noun, Pronoun, Verb, Adjective, Adverb, Preposition, Conjunction,* or *Interjection.*

1. *Several* of the people *on* the beach played volleyball.
2. The campers *soon* learned that the *plant* with *three* leaves was poison ivy.
3. Although she *seemed* calm, Char was *nervous and* tense about appearing in the play.
4. *Wow! That* really sailed out of the stadium.
5. The lighthouse *keeper sounded* the foghorn.
6. Scientists *are finding* many *uses* for the *laser* beam.
7. Belinda *guided* the chestnut-brown horse *along* a wooded trail.
8. Carlos celebrated his *birthday* by going *to* the carnival.
9. For supper we *ate some* of the vegetables that grew in our garden.
10. *Who* actually discovered *America?*
11. *Ashley* used both *palms* and ferns *in* her terrarium.
12. The cafeteria serves hamburgers *or* hot dogs *nearly* every day.
13. *Frequently,* Lisa *uses* a jump rope to exercise.
14. The game stopped while Derek hunted *for* his contact *lens.*
15. *Aha!* You're the *one* making that noise!

B Recognizing Parts of Speech Determine the part of speech of each italicized word in the following paragraph.

(1) A *monsoon* is a seasonal wind often accompanied *by heavy* rainfall. (2) In Japan, monsoons are extremely important because they bring the moisture *that* nourishes *the* country's rice fields. (3) *Since* the Japanese depend *heavily* on this crop for food—the word "gohan" is used in Japan for both "food" and "rice"—failure of the monsoon to appear has *often* resulted in famine. (4) In other words, the monsoon is both a giver *and* taker of life. (5) In early fall, *it* often brings *typhoons,* Pacific Ocean counterparts to Atlantic hurricanes. (6) These roaring winds *sometimes* churn up *monstrous* tidal waves that wreak havoc *along* the shorelines of the *island* kingdom. (7) Monsoons also bring tremendous amounts of rain *to* the lands that *they* move across. (8) In fact, one *Asian* city receives an average of 240 inches of rain *annually.*

C Using Words as Different Parts of Speech Identify the part of speech of the italicized word in each of the following sentences. Then, write a new sentence using the same word as the part of speech indicated in parentheses.

1. "*Tomorrow* is the day we've all been waiting for," said Heather excitedly. (adverb)
2. The operator of the Ferris wheel assured me that no one had ever fallen *out*. (preposition)
3. Not only was *that* western novel a best seller, but it also won a Pulitzer Prize several years ago. (pronoun)
4. "*Wonderful!*" he said. "I thought you would win first place at the science fair." (adjective)
5. *Help* arrived in the form of a country doctor driving a battered 1963 Chevy. (verb)
6. When the tomato was first introduced to Europe, many people thought that the *plant* was poisonous. (verb)
7. When you're driving to work, *what* radio station do you listen to most often? (pronoun)
8. The pitch was *high* and outside, but the umpire called it a strike anyway. (adverb)
9. The swallows would *dart* back and forth between the feeder and the birdbath. (noun)
10. Spider monkeys *hold* onto tree branches with their tails to keep from falling. (noun)

D Identifying Parts of Speech Identify the part of speech of each of the italicized words in the following sentence pairs.

1. a. The home team's quarterback almost fumbled the ball but made a *fast* recovery.
   b. The line for tickets to the new movie was long, but it moved *fast* once it got started.
2. a. Will someone *time* Maria's speech for her?
   b. What *time* does the debate begin?
3. a. I always bring my bicycle *inside* when the weather forecaster predicts rain.
   b. The mailboxes are *inside* the lobby.
4. a. Have you already mailed *those* letters?
   b. *Those* are the letters she wrote.
5. a. Weighing up to 1,800 pounds, the North American moose is the largest member of the *deer* family.
   b. The smallest *deer* is the Chilean pudu.

22

The Sentence
and Its Parts

*T*ake the mainspring out of a
watch, and the rest of the clock-
works ceases to work. Take the verb out of a sentence,
and the remaining group of words no longer functions
as a sentence. Neither sentence nor watch is complete
without these essential parts. Furthermore, for the
watch to tell time accurately and the sentence to clearly
convey the message its author intended, these parts
must be arranged in proper working order.

In this chapter you will learn how the parts of speech
work together so that you can arrange them to express
your thoughts clearly.

Part 1
The Sentence

Sentences make statements, ask questions, give commands, and show feelings. Each sentence expresses a complete idea. As you learn more about sentences, you will expand on the following definition.

A sentence is a group of words that expresses a complete thought.

When part of an idea is missing from a sentence, the group of words is a **sentence fragment.**

Sentence Fragment	The owner of the car. (What about the owner?)
Sentence	The owner of the car filed an accident report.
Sentence Fragment	Seemed dull. (Who or what seemed dull?)
Sentence	The movie seemed dull.

You will work more with sentence fragments in Chapter 24.

Exercises

A On your paper, write *S* for each group of words below that is a sentence. Write *F* for each group of words that is a fragment.

1. A bearded man with a Seeing Eye dog.
2. The registered letter has already come.
3. Washed in on the tide.
4. Several highlights of his illustrious career.
5. Waited impatiently for the announcement.
6. Shelters for the disadvantaged and homeless.
7. Fortunately nobody in the life raft panicked.
8. An entirely new approach.
9. Will be constructed on the same spot.
10. A water main has broken.

B Some of the following groups of words are sentence fragments. Rewrite the fragments so that they are complete sentences.

1. Actually, were not at all surprised.
2. No clear-cut plan for creating school spirit.
3. Never spoke to us or even noticed us, though we were standing right next to him.

4. They scraped and painted the walls.
5. Disappearing in the fog and howling mournfully.
6. Always asking questions, but never getting a valid response.
7. Still trying to discourage the plan of the Indian Council.
8. Was too much emphasis placed on winning?
9. The change in demographics throughout the country.
10. Coming to a screeching stop in the middle of the intersection.

Part 2
Kinds of Sentences

A sentence may be classified according to the purpose it serves. Four principal purposes are listed below.

A **declarative sentence** expresses a statement of fact, wish, intent, or feeling. It ends with a period.

> Hulda Crooks climbed Mt. Fuji at the age of 91.
> Everyone wished the balloonist a successful flight.

An **interrogative sentence** asks a question. It always ends with a question mark.

> Why do some people wear sunglasses indoors?
> Will the Olympic pool be finished on time?

An **imperative sentence** gives a command, request, or direction. It usually ends with a period. If the command or request is strong, an imperative sentence may end with an exclamation point.

> You return that book as soon as possible.
> Follow that car.   *or*   Follow that car!

An **exclamatory sentence** expresses strong feeling. It always ends with an exclamation point.

> What a great time we had!
> I won first prize!

Punctuation Note When an exclamatory sentence is preceded by a separate exclamation, either a period or an exclamation mark can be used at the end of the sentence.

> Oh, no! I left the tickets at home! (*or*.)

Exercises

A Identify each sentence below according to its kind: *Declarative, Interrogative, Imperative,* or *Exclamatory.* Then indicate the end punctuation. Some sentences may be punctuated in more than one way.

1. Keep your seat belts securely fastened until the plane has come to a complete stop
2. Which design will be easiest to produce
3. Soprano Marjorie Lawrence sings from a wheelchair
4. What a wild landing that was
5. Don't wear those dirty sneakers and ragged jeans to school
6. My parents are taking a vacation from alarm clocks
7. B-r-r-r That lake water is like ice
8. A small creek wandered between tree-shaded banks near my friend's cottage
9. Who is our most reliable pitcher
10. Tyrone and I carefully maneuvered the canoe through the marshy channels

B Application in Literature The following passage contains all four kinds of sentences. The author uses them to vary the dialogue and help convey the feeling of the speaker. Note that the end marks for the sentences are missing. Number your paper from 1 to 15. Identify each sentence according to its kind. Then write the appropriate end mark for each sentence. Be sure to find at least one sentence that can end with an exclamation point.

(1) Cockerill ushered [Nellie] to the door (2) "You go home now and wait, Miss Bly (3) Leave your address at the desk downstairs as you go out"

(4) She turned to go (5) Again Joseph Pulitzer did an unprecedented thing (6) "Have you any money (7) Can you wait those few days or perhaps a week"

(8) "Oh . . . I forgot" (9) She told them the story of her lost purse (10) "I can't even pay my rent"

(11) Pulitzer fumbled in his pocket and . . . gave up (12) "Give her a voucher, John (13) Give her twenty-five dollars" (14) Then to Nellie: "This money, this is not a loan; it is an advance on your salary"

(15) She didn't walk downstairs; she floated

From *Nellie Bly: First Woman Reporter* by Iris Noble

c *Proofreading* On your paper, rewrite the following paragraph, correcting all errors in punctuation, capitalization, and spelling. Before you change any end punctuation, decide whether the sentence is declarative, interrogative, imperative, or exclamatory.

Have you seen this article. It tells about Rudyard Kipling, the English author who wrote novels, peoms, stories, and tails for children. Did you know that Kipling was borne in 1865 in india, the setting for much of his writeing! What an interesting life he must have lead. He traveled throughout the british Empire and spent several years in the United States. Read "Gunga Din" "The Rode to Mandalay," *The Jungle Book,* and *Just So Storys* to sample this Nobel prize winner's work?

Left: Rudyard Kipling's room in Allahabad, India, 1888–1889. Right: Rudyard Kipling.

Part 3
Complete Subjects and Predicates

A sentence has two parts: a complete subject and a complete predicate. The **complete subject** includes all the words that identify the person, place, thing, or idea that the sentence is about. The **complete predicate** includes all the words that tell what the subject did or what happened to the subject.

Complete Subject	Complete Predicate
Children	play.
The children on our block	always play in a nearby park.

Exercise

Write the following sentences on your paper. Underline the complete subject once and the complete predicate twice.

1. The trees along the nature trail are labeled.
2. A cocoon was attached to the underside of the leaf.
3. Our landlord has promised us a new refrigerator.
4. Several pages in this paperback are stuck together.
5. My parents became United States citizens recently.
6. Everything in the Edgar Allan Poe Cottage in the Bronx has been carefully restored by the County Historical Society.
7. Mt. McKinley attracts hundreds of climbers every summer.
8. The most popular sculpture in the museum is a forgery.
9. Most islands in the South Pacific are surrounded by coral.
10. The plants in an aquarium provide oxygen for the fish.

Checkpoint *Parts 1, 2, and 3*

A In all but two of the following groups of words, either the complete subject or the complete predicate is missing. Identify each sentence fragment and rewrite it as a complete sentence by providing the missing part. Then underline each complete subject once and each complete predicate twice. Write *Sentence* for those groups of words that are already complete sentences.

> *Example*   This year's country music special.
>
> This year's country music special was not as
> good as last year's.

1. Is working in the supermarket this summer.
2. The villain's face, partially hidden by a long, black moustache.
3. Parking spaces in our neighborhood are very scarce.
4. Gathered around the subway entrance.
5. Are making stuffed animals for all of the infants at Children's Memorial Hospital.
6. A bicycle with a quick-release front wheel.
7. The captain's desk was covered with charts and maps.
8. Usually directs traffic at that corner.
9. A thick Irish stew with lamb and potatoes.
10. Scrambled for a first down.

B On your paper, identify each of the following sentences according to its kind: *Declarative, Interrogative, Imperative,* or *Exclamatory.* Indicate the correct end punctuation by writing *Period, Question Mark,* or *Exclamation Point.* Then rewrite each sentence so that it is the kind indicated in parentheses. Use appropriate end punctuation.

> *Example*   Buy a ticket for the matinee. (Interrogative)
> Imperative, Period
> Did you buy a ticket for the matinee?

1. What a gorgeous day it is (Declarative)
2. It is illegal to hunt crocodiles in Florida (Interrogative)
3. Did Shakespeare write comedies and tragedies (Declarative)
4. You are lucky (Exclamatory)
5. Stop at the store on your way home (Declarative)
6. The gym is large enough for the flea market (Interrogative)
7. Does their school have a rugby team (Declarative)
8. He has written his grandparents a postcard (Interrogative)
9. Return your library books on time (Declarative)
10. Has that book become a best seller (Declarative)

Part 4
Simple Subjects and Predicates

The simple subject is the key word or words in the complete subject.

To find the subject, ask *who* or *what* before the verb.

> Holly called yesterday.   **Verb**   called
>   **Who called?**   Holly
>   **Subject**   Holly

The simple subject does not include modifiers. In the examples below, the simple subjects are in boldface type.

> Every **atom** in the universe has an effect on every other atom.
> The late **Roman Jakobson** could read in twenty-five languages.

Do not confuse the simple subject with other words that appear between the subject and the predicate. In the first example above, the subject is *atom*, not *universe*.

A simple subject made of two or more key words is a **compound subject.** The parts of a compound subject are joined by a conjunction such as *and* or *or*.

> The **Nile,** the **Amazon,** *and* the **Mississippi** are three of the world's longest rivers.

The simple predicate, also called the *verb,* is the key word or words in the complete predicate.

The verb may be a phrase consisting of more than one word: *had seen, should have seen, was singing, had been singing.* The words making up the verb phrase may be interrupted by a modifier. Such a modifier is not part of the verb. The verbs below are in boldface type.

> Hair **grows** more quickly in warm climates.
> Two bears **had ransacked** the garbage during the night.
> We **will** not **be going** to the lake this summer.

A **compound verb** is made up of two or more verbs or verb phrases joined by a conjunction.

> The park ranger **found** *and* **destroyed** the traps.
> The flowers **were swaying** *and* **dancing** in the breeze.

In this text, *subject* will be used to refer to the simple subject; *verb* will be used to refer to the simple predicate.

Sentence Diagraming For information on diagraming subjects, verbs, and their modifiers, see pages 812–822.

Exercises

A On your paper, write the subject and verb of each of the following sentences. Underline the subject once and the verb twice.

1. A flock of migrating ducks landed on the pond.
2. A long freight train was rumbling by.
3. The Secret Service protects the President of the United States.
4. The bear rose slowly, stretched, and shook itself.
5. Several of the club members are helping with the decorations.
6. Soup, whole-grain bread, and fruit make a nutritious lunch.
7. Several tenants cleaned the vacant lot and planted a garden.
8. Either the drummer or the violinist will perform a solo.
9. Most of Greenland is covered by a great icecap.
10. Aristotle was a tutor to young Alexander the Great.

B Application in Literature On your paper, write the subject and verb of each sentence in the following literature passage. Underline each subject once and each verb twice. Remember that sentence parts can be compound.

(1) Jade Snow's parents had conceded defeat. . . .
(2) [Now] Jade Snow came and went without any questions.
(3) In spite of her parents' dark predictions, her new freedom in the choice of companions did not result in a rush of undesirables. (4) As a matter of fact, the boys were more concerned with copying her lecture notes than with anything else.

(5) As for Joe, on the evening of Jade Snow's seventeenth birthday, he gave her as a remembrance a sparkling grown-up bracelet. (6) There under the stars he gently tilted her face and gave her her first kiss.

(7) Awkward in her full-skirted red cotton dress, Jade Snow was caught by surprise and without words. (8) She had been kissed at seventeen . . . a cause for rejoicing.

From *Fifth Chinese Daughter* by Jade Snow Wong

c *Write Now* Following are notes for a brief report about the life of Jade Snow Wong. As you can see, the notes are not written as complete sentences. Incorporate the notes into one or two paragraphs. Be sure to write complete sentences. Try to make some of the subjects and verbs compound.

born in 1922
parents from China
emigrated to San Francisco
only Chinese spoken in her home
worked in tailoring shop in San Francisco
unusual middle name
born during rare California snowfall
first college graduate in her family
chose chemistry as major

primarily interested in pottery and ceramics
autobiography, *Fifth Chinese Daughter*, published in 1950
admits her experiences may not be typical
wrote about struggle between Chinese ways and American customs
written in third person because of Chinese habit
second book, *No Chinese Stranger*, published in 1975

Part 5
Subjects in Unusual Positions

In most sentences the subject appears before the verb. In some types of sentences, however, this order is not followed.

Subjects in Inverted Sentences

Inverted sentences are those in which a verb or part of a verb phrase is positioned before the subject. Following are the three most common types of inverted sentences.

Questions In most questions, the subject appears between the words that make up the verb phrase. In the examples below, the subject is underlined once and the verb twice.

> Have you called yet?
> Are your neighbors moving to Detroit?
> Where should we put these boxes?

In most questions beginning with the interrogative words *where, when, why, how,* or *how much,* the subject falls between the parts of the verb. In questions beginning with an interrogative adjective or pronoun, the verb may follow the subject in normal order.

> Which picture fell off the wall?
> Who shouted?
> What happened?

Notice that *who* and *what* sometimes function as subjects.

Sentences Beginning with *There* and *Here* When a sentence begins with *there* or *here,* the subject usually follows the verb. Remember that *there* and *here* are never the subjects of a sentence.

> There are my red sneakers.
> Here is your passport.

In the examples above, *there* and *here* are adverbs. They modify the verb and tell *where*. To find the subject, reword the sentence.

> My red sneakers are there. (*Sneakers* is the subject.)
> Your passport is here. (*Passport* is the subject.)

Sometimes, however, *there* is used as an **expletive,** a word that merely helps to get a sentence started. If you can rearrange the sentence and drop the word *there,* you can assume it is an expletive.

> There is Ms. Dobkin's office.
> Ms. Dobkin's office is there. (*There* is an adverb.)

> There were several people in line.
> Several people were in line. (*There* is an expletive.)

Occasionally, a sentence beginning with the adverb *there* or *here* will follow regular subject-verb order.

> Here she comes.
> There he is.

Sentences Inverted for Emphasis For emphasis or variety a speaker or writer may intentionally place the verb before the subject. This technique focuses extra attention on the subject. When used sparingly, this type of sentence adds drama. When it is overused, the result can sound artificial.

Normal Order	A wall of flood water burst through the door.
Inverted Order	Through the door burst a wall of flood water.

Normal Order	An abandoned cottage was at the end of the path.
Inverted Order	At the end of the path was an abandoned cottage.

Finding Subjects in Inverted Sentences One way to find the subject in an inverted sentence is to find the verb first. Then ask *who* or *what* before the verb.

> From the distance came the howl of a timber wolf. (The verb is *came.* What came? Howl came. The subject is *howl.*)

Another way to find the subject is to reorder the sentence. Putting the words in a different order often makes the subject easier to identify.

After the rain <u>came</u> the <u>wind</u>.
The <u>wind</u> <u>came</u> after the rain.

Subjects in Imperative Sentences

The subject of an imperative sentence is always *you*. When the subject is not directly stated, as is usually the case, *you* is "understood" to be the subject.

<u>You</u> <u>look</u> at these pictures.
(<u>You</u>) <u>Speak</u> to the landlord tomorrow.

Sentence Diagraming For information on diagraming imperative sentences, see page 813.

Exercises

A On your paper, write the subject and verb of each of the following sentences. Underline the subject once and the verb twice. If the subject is understood, write *you* in parentheses and underline it.

> *Example*   Put this in your locker.
> (<u>You</u>) <u>put</u>

1. There in the mud lay my brand new scarf.
2. Don't forget to mow the lawn today, Mike.
3. How much money can we raise at the bake sale?
4. Could you see anything from the back row?
5. Ask Harrison for his five-alarm chili recipe.
6. Inside the elegant white florist's box was one perfect long-stemmed yellow rose.
7. There are very few pandas living in the wild.
8. The gentle call of the emperor's nightingale floated away on the evening breeze.
9. Should I have tried to see the doctor sooner?
10. Through the swirling mists appeared the outline of a long-deserted castle.
11. Please get me a ticket, too.
12. Here are the registration forms.
13. From the stands came a roar of approval.
14. How can I get from here to the auditorium?
15. There are six typing errors in your paper.

B On your paper, write the subject and verb of each of the sentences in the paragraph below. Underline the subject once and the verb twice.

(1) In the future, we will find robots as much a part of our daily lives as automobiles or television sets. (2) Where will robots be utilized? (3) You will find robots in homes, schools, and businesses. (4) What will these mechanical servants do for us? (5) They will perform many of our more tedious tasks. (6) Here are the only requirements for a basic robot. (7) It needs a computer, of course, and a mechanical arm with claws. (8) Along the arm run cables. (9) Instructions from the computer to the claws are transmitted through these cables. (10) Robots can only follow instructions programmed into their computer "brains." (11) Where can you learn more about robots? (12) Ask your librarian or science teacher.

C *Write Now* You are a musical composer in the 1800's working side by side with the great masters Beethoven and Brahms. Your first symphony, *Rock-and-Roll Rhythms in G Minor,* has just been performed, but it is not a success. The critics are outraged and the audience is confused. Write a brief essay that defends and explains your music. Make your writing as interesting as your music by including some inverted and imperative sentences.

Part 6

Complements

Some sentences, such as *Joan sings,* contain only a subject and a verb. Most sentences, however, require additional words placed after the verb to complete the meaning of the sentence. These additional words are called **complements.**

A complement is a word or a group of words that completes the meaning of the verb.

> Friction produces *heat*. (Produces what? Produces heat. *Heat* completes the meaning of *produces*.)
> The guide showed the *visitors* from Japan some unusual *minerals*. (Showed what to whom? Showed minerals to visitors. *Visitors* and *minerals* complete the meaning of *showed*.)
> Old Faithful is a well-known *geyser*. (Is what? Is geyser. *Geyser* completes the meaning of *is*.)
> Many volcanoes are *dormant*. (Are what? Are dormant. *Dormant* completes the meaning of *are*.)

Now you will study four kinds of complements: direct objects, indirect objects, objective complements, and subject complements.

Direct Objects

A **direct object** is a word or group of words that receives the action of an action verb. It answers the question *What?* or *Whom?* about the verb. Verbs that take direct objects are called **transitive verbs.** See page 481 for more information about transitive verbs.

> Everyone knows your *secret*. (Knows what?)
> The fans cheered *Paul Molitar*. (Cheered whom?)

Do not confuse a direct object with an adverb that follows an action verb. A direct object tells *what* or *whom*. An adverb tells *where, when, how,* or *to what extent.*

Direct Object   We followed the *trail*. (Followed what?)
Adverb   We followed *closely*. (Followed how?)

The direct object may be compound.

> I misplaced my *pad* and *pencil*. (Misplaced what?)
> The officer helped my *sister* and *me*. (Helped whom?)

Indirect Objects

An **indirect object** is a word or group of words that tells *to whom* or *for whom* the action of the verb is being performed. A verb has an indirect object only if it also has a direct object. The indirect object always comes before the direct object.

> The book club sent *us* a refund. (Sent a refund to whom?)
> My aunt made *Lisa* a sweater. (Made a sweater for whom?)

The indirect object may be compound.

> Our grandmother taught my *cousin* and *me* Greek.

The words *to* and *for* never appear before the indirect object. *To* and *for* are prepositions when they are followed by a noun or pronoun. The noun or pronoun is the object of the preposition.

Indirect Object	The team sent the *coach* a telegram.
Object of a Preposition	The team sent a telegram to the *coach*.

For more information on prepositions, see pages 495–497.

Exercises

A Make three columns labeled *Verb, Indirect Object,* and *Direct Object.* For each sentence, write the verb and the object or objects in the proper columns. If there is no indirect object, write *None.*

1. The reporter wrote the mayor a letter of apology.
2. Have you ever given an elephant a bath?
3. We found a magazine and several letters under the doormat.
4. The new vacuum has attachments that clean furniture and drapes.
5. We handed Rico and Paula the money for our tickets.
6. My aunt made Dad and me a huge pot of beef and barley soup.
7. Ernest lent Alice his trumpet for the band auditions.
8. Has the ticket agent guaranteed you good seats for the concert?
9. The rain brought little relief to the drought-stricken plains.
10. Those plants need fresh air and direct sunlight.

B Write the following sentences. Underline each subject once and each verb twice. Write *DO* over each direct object and *IO* over each indirect object.

1. One of the ushers found me a seat in the front row.
2. The judges awarded Melissa first prize in the piano competition.
3. The doctor has prescribed vitamins for the whole family.

4. Has Juan read you his letter to the editor?
5. My mother finally found my brother an affordable secondhand car in good condition.
6. The supervisor offered my cousin the job of assistant manager.
7. At the holidays we send our relatives a family photograph.
8. During the Soviet blockade, Western powers airlifted the people of West Berlin badly needed supplies.
9. The superintendent awarded five students scholarships.
10. A helicopter lowered a ladder to the survivors.

Objective Complements

An **objective complement** is a word or group of words that follows a direct object and renames or describes that object. Objective complements follow certain verbs and their synonyms: *appoint, call, choose, consider, elect, find, make, keep, name, think.*

An objective complement may be a noun or an adjective.

Noun	Tennis experts consider Steffi Graf a unique *player*. (*Player* renames or describes the object *Steffi Graf.*)
Adjective	Many even call her *unbeatable*. (*Unbeatable* describes the object *her*.)

Exercise

Identify each complement in the following sentences according to its kind: *Direct Object, Indirect Object,* or *Objective Complement.*

> *Example*   Our class elected Tricia Fox president.
> Tricia Fox, Direct Object
> president, Objective Complement

1. The new baseball coach considers Laura a reliable but mediocre pitcher.
2. Has the manufacturer sent Michael a new jacket?
3. We found the film long and dull, but my parents enjoyed it.
4. The superintendent handed Ursula the keys to the store room.
5. The senator appointed Dad her legal assistant.
6. Violence on television makes many people uncomfortable.
7. Chicago's voters elected him mayor for an unprecedented fourth consecutive term.
8. The jury must have thought the witness unreliable.
9. *Treasure Island* made Robert Louis Stevenson famous.
10. Automated assembly lines made Ford cars affordable.

Subject Complements

A **subject complement** is a complement that follows a linking verb and renames or describes the subject. Subject complements often come after a form of the verb *be*. For a discussion of linking verbs, see page 478. There are two kinds of subject complements: **predicate nominatives** and **predicate adjectives.**

Predicate Nominatives A **predicate nominative** is a word or a group of words that follows a linking verb and names or identifies the subject of the sentence. Predicate nominatives can be either **predicate nouns** or **predicate pronouns.**

Predicate Noun   My favorite sport is *football*.
Predicate Pronoun   The winner should have been *she*.

The predicate nominative may be compound.

Benjamin Franklin was a *statesman* and an *inventor*.

Predicate Adjectives A **predicate adjective** is an adjective that follows a linking verb and modifies the subject of the sentence.

Everyone on the team felt *confident* of victory.

The predicate adjective may be compound.

Medieval castles were usually *cold, damp,* and *gloomy*.

Sentence Diagraming For information on diagraming subject complements, see page 814.

Exercises

A Write each subject complement in the following sentences and identify it according to its kind: *Predicate Nominative* or *Predicate Adjective*. Remember that a subject complement may be compound.

1. "Does your chewing gum lose its flavor on the bedpost overnight?" was the first line of a song popular in the 1960's.
2. Gum-chewing has been popular in many cultures for over 2,000 years.
3. Spruce gums were the first ones available in the United States.
4. Some spruce gums used by early American settlers were waxy and tough.
5. The later chicle-based gums were sweeter and tastier.
6. Chicle is an ingredient in most modern gums.

7. Some people have become avid collectors of the baseball cards given away with certain gums.
8. Children have been fond of bubble gum since it was first put on the market in 1933.
9. Kurt Bevacqua was the winner of a 1975 bubble-blowing contest.
10. The size of his winning bubble was eighteen inches.

B Complete each group of words by adding a subject complement. Then tell whether the complement is a predicate nominative or a predicate adjective. Use at least three compound complements.

1. Two well-known singers are
2. Outer space is
3. The abandoned factory looked
4. Your excuse for missing class seems
5. The water in the pond appears
6. This salad tastes
7. My best friend is
8. A current fad is
9. The team remained
10. That tape sounds

Checkpoint Parts 4, 5, and 6

On your paper, write the following sentences. Underline each subject once and each verb twice. Identify each complement by writing *DO* (direct object), *IO* (indirect object), *OC* (objective complement), *PN* (predicate nominative), or *PA* (predicate adjective) over the appropriate word. Not every sentence has a complement.

1. The opening ceremony of the Olympics is usually very impressive.
2. Why do some people consider thirteen an unlucky number?

3. Along the shore the tourists found some unusual shells.
4. The coach appointed them co-captains of the B team.
5. Our neighbor gives his dogs and cats the run of the house.
6. The baseball manager considers the rookie outfielder a valuable addition to the team.
7. Dust and carbon monoxide can form a thick smog.
8. There are sandwiches and cold drinks in the refrigerator.
9. The first prize will be five hundred dollars and a trip to New York City.
10. Thunder crashed overhead and rattled the windowpanes.
11. The new owners of the cottage have planted geraniums and marigolds along the front walk.
12. They named their hamsters Napoleon and Josephine.
13. Vidkun Quisling was the Norwegian leader who betrayed his country to the Germans during World War II.
14. Did England award Florence Nightingale the Order of Merit?
15. Our new dog is both pugnacious and quarrelsome.

Part 7
The Sentence Redefined

Here and at the end of Chapter 23, you will add to the basic definition of the sentence given on page 509. You now know a sentence is a group of words that (1) expresses a complete thought, (2) contains at least one subject and verb, and (3) may contain a complement.

Exercise

Proofreading Combine the fragments in the following paragraph into complete sentences. Also correct any errors in punctuation, capitalization, or spelling.

Citadelle Henry is one of the largest forts. In the world. It sits atop a jungle peek. On the Caribbean island of haiti. The fort was begun in the early nineteenth Century. By Haitian liberator Jean-Jacques Dessalines. Under his leadership, the slaves of Haiti. Rebelled and defeated they're French masters. The next ruler, King henry Christophe, oversaw most of the Citadelles' construction. King Christophe hoped the forte would proteckt his subjects. From any future European invasions. He wiseley decided that fighting from the Hills. Was the best plan of defence for the island.

Linking
Grammar *&* Writing

Did you know that 92,000 Americans have reservations with Pan American Airlines for a trip to the moon? Imagine that you were on such a trip. What would the experience be like? Write one or more paragraphs in which you describe your voyage.

To make your description more interesting, use all four kinds of sentences (declarative, imperative, interrogative, and exclamatory).

Prewriting and Drafting Look at the photos below as you think about what you might see on your space voyage. Limit your description to the one part of the voyage that you think would be the most exciting—the take-off, the landing, or the flight itself. Imagine what you would see and hear and feel. Try freewriting or brainstorming to develop colorful details for your description.

Revising and Proofreading When revising your description, consider these questions:

1. Does your description include vivid, sensory details?
2. Does your description follow a logical order?
3. Have you used all four kinds of sentences?

Additional Writing Topic A local millionaire has decided to sponsor a writing contest at your school. He will award a prize of ten thousand dollars to the person who can write the most entertaining description of himself or herself. In one paragraph, describe who you are. Use several predicate nouns and predicate adjectives.

Chapter 22
Application and Review

A Writing Complete Sentences All but two of the following groups of words do not express complete thoughts. Identify these groups and change them into sentences. Write *Sentence* for those groups of words that are already complete sentences.

1. The scientist in the laboratory.
2. Swayed and trembled in the violent wind.
3. The girl with the short, curly hair.
4. Stopping abruptly, he turned and stalked away.
5. Offered Joyce one scoop of rocky road ice cream.
6. The scariest movie I have ever seen.
7. Rushed toward the goal post while the fans roared.
8. Is flying in tonight from Philadelphia on a DC-10.
9. Tried unsuccessfully to hold back his tears.
10. Working in the emergency ward is exhausting for the hospital staff.

B Finding Subjects and Verbs Find the verb and its simple subject in each of the following sentences.

1. There were thirty-two new players at the first football practice of the season.
2. Along the horizon twinkled the lights of the city.
3. Between the band and the next float rode sixteen clowns on multicolored motorbikes.
4. Rudolf Nureyev and Mikhail Baryshnikov were both born in Russia.
5. Maurice Sendak writes and illustrates many wonderful and popular children's books.
6. How are you getting to work during the bus strike?
7. Into the harbor sailed the double-masted schooner.
8. Here are the videotapes of the game.
9. From the cave entrance flew a cloud of bats.
10. On this island grow many carnivorous plants.
11. Are you in intermediate ballet or the advanced class?
12. St. Paul's Cathedral is located in London.
13. West Virginia became a state during the administration of President Abraham Lincoln.
14. Some lizards change color when frightened.
15. Who will wear the green jerseys?

C Identifying the Parts of a Sentence Label six columns *Subject, Verb, Direct Object, Indirect Object, Objective Complement,* and *Subject Complement*. Place those parts of the following sentences in the proper columns. Some of the sentence parts may be compound.

1. Our drama class wrote and produced a serious musical about substance abuse.
2. My aunt in Mexico sent me some hand-crafted silver jewelry.
3. A *B* on that paper would make me ecstatic!
4. During the trial, the defendant admitted her guilt.
5. I found your report confusing and misleading.
6. The magician showed Arleta several illusions.
7. The Latin class wore togas for their Roman banquet.
8. The baby sitter gave the children crackers and cheese.
9. My helicopter ride was rough and noisy.
10. Pigs and cattle were loaded onto railroad cars.
11. This cave looks treacherous.
12. A gust of wind scattered Jason's homework around the parking lot.
13. Three airplanes performed stunts for the crowd.
14. The gymnastics coach spotted Kendra during her back flip.
15. The politicians consider Ms. Weiss a prime candidate for nomination.
16. Billie Holiday was a famous blues singer.
17. Cindy asked the veterinarian questions about pet care.
18. Dad taught us a new dive.
19. Cassie seemed curious about the algebra assignment.
20. Whom did their class elect for president?

D Using Sentence Parts Complete the following sentences by adding the material indicated in parentheses.

1. The rescue volunteers distributed _____ to the flood victims. (compound direct object)
2. I made _____ peanut butter and banana sandwiches. (compound indirect object)
3. The President _____ at the photographers and the White House journalists. (compound verb)
4. Marnie _____ to make the decision on her own. (verb)
5. The game show contestants were _____ . (compound predicate adjective)
6. Christopher named his pet snakes _____ . (compound objective complement)
7. The nominees were _____ . (compound predicate nominative)
8. _____ are great qualities in a friend. (compound subject)

Cumulative Review

Chapters 21 and 22

A Identifying Parts of Speech Write the function of each italicized word, telling whether it is a *Noun*, *Pronoun*, *Verb*, *Adjective*, *Adverb*, *Preposition*, *Conjunction*, or *Interjection*.

1. It appeared that the battle was almost *certainly* lost.
2. *Whenever* she imagined the possibility of winning the scholarship, she worked even harder.
3. Only the crackling sound of footsteps on the snow interrupted the *still* beauty of the wintry night.
4. The final responsibility for all decisions belongs to *her*.
5. With each swish of the basket, the crowd's enthusiasm *mounted*.
6. If you only could have been *there,* you would have been amazed to see everyone working so hard.
7. *Which* of the desserts are you going to choose?
8. That woman's secretive manner and mysterious appearance remind me of a spy *that* I once read about.
9. Once you know him better, you will discover that *underneath* that tough, selfish exterior lies a tough, selfish interior.
10. After the storm, the captain went *below* to check the damage.
11. The Thomas Hardy poem "During Wind and Rain" repeats the phrase, "*Ah,* no; the years, the years" in each stanza.
12. Of all of those who had entered, only *fifteen* remained.
13. Either Sherry *or* Nathan will be able to tell you the answer to that question.
14. She seemed *confident* of her ability, though she had never played.
15. The human body can survive without food longer than it can survive *without* water.

B Recognizing Parts of a Sentence Study each italicized word or group of words in the sentences below. Write whether it is a *Subject*, *Verb*, *Direct Object*, *Indirect Object*, *Objective Complement*, *Subject Complement*, or *Object of a Preposition*.

1. Maria made herself a tostada with the fresh *tortilla*.
2. From the distance came the lively *sounds* of the street musicians.
3. Frederick Douglass *published* a famous abolitionist newspaper.
4. Many high-school students have read the *fiction* of John Steinbeck.

5. The French impressionists often painted outside in order to capture the immediacy of their *sensations*.
6. Augustus appointed himself first *emperor* of Rome.
7. Churchill's wartime speeches sounded *fearless* and *resolute* to the people of Great Britain.
8. While telling his imaginary story of a haunted house, he gave *himself* a good scare.
9. Margaret Atwood *wrote* a powerful poem about the accidental drowning of her young son.
10. Author Virginia Woolf and her friends once disguised *themselves,* impersonated foreign dignitaries, and fooled the British Navy.
11. Cable television reaches nearly 50 percent of the *households* in the United States.
12. The audience gave the long-winded *speaker* a lukewarm reception, even though they had paid an extravagant sum of money to see him.
13. The parents of the football player Jim Plunkett were both legally *blind*.
14. Who answered the front *door* when the mysterious, late-night visitors rang the bell?
15. She appeared *poised* and knowledgeable as she answered the questions from the senators.

C Using Parts of Speech and Parts of Sentences Complete the following sentences by adding the material indicated in parentheses.

1. After the party, the room looked _____ . (compound predicate adjective)
2. The war between Iran and Iraq had been intensifying; _____ athletes from the two countries competed in a volleyball match. (conjunctive adverb)
3. In his new role as team captain, he _____ dedicated and disciplined. (linking verb)
4. Her performanced showed _____ the astounding range of her voice. (indirect object)
5. The ruthless dictator named himself _____ . (objective complement)
6. _____ had already left the dance floor. (indefinite pronoun)
7. Her favorite spectator sports were _____ . (compound predicate nominative)
8. The father looked _____ at his playful child. (adverb)
9. Gandhi gave _____ to rich and poor alike. (direct object)
10. The old man saw in _____ a glimpse of his own past. (object of a preposition)

23

Using Phrases and Clauses

L ike kids hanging on a jungle gym, phrases and clauses can be attached anywhere in a sentence—at the beginning, at the end, or somewhere in between—to add information and interest to the basic message.

In this chapter you will learn to recognize the types of phrases and clauses and how they function in sentences. You will also discover how to use these flexible components to make your own writing and speaking come alive.

Part 1

Prepositional Phrases

A **phrase** is a group of related words that does not have a subject and a predicate and that functions in a sentence as a single part of speech. One kind of phrase is a **prepositional phrase**.

A prepositional phrase is a phrase that consists of a preposition, its object, and any modifiers of the object.

> The mockingbird imitates the calls *of other birds*. (*Birds* is the object of the preposition *of*.)

As you have learned, the object of a preposition is always a noun, pronoun, or a group of words used as a noun. A prepositional phrase may have two or more objects joined by a conjunction.

> Deliver the letter *to whoever answers the door*. (The group of words *whoever answers the door* is the object of the preposition *to*.)

> A majority of members *of both the House and the Senate* strongly supported the bill. (*House* and *Senate* are the compound objects of the preposition *of*.)

A prepositional phrase is a modifier and functions in a sentence as an adjective or an adverb.

Adjective Phrases

A prepositional phrase that modifies a noun or pronoun is called an **adjective phrase**. An adjective phrase can modify a subject, direct object, indirect object, or predicate nominative. The phrase usually tells *which one* or *what kind* about the word it modifies.

Modifying a Subject	The clock *in the church steeple* struck ten. (*Which* clock?)
Modifying a Direct Object	Kim repaired the shutter *on my camera*. (*Which* shutter?)
Modifying an Indirect Object	Mom gave the family *next door* a plum pudding. (*Which* family?)
Modifying a Predicate Nominative	A marmoset is a monkey *from South America*. (*What kind* of monkey?)

An adjective phrase sometimes modifies the object in another prepositional phrase.

Several scenes in the documentary *about grizzlies* were frightening. (*Which* documentary?)

Adverb Phrases

A prepositional phrase that functions as an adverb is called an **adverb phrase.** An adverb phrase modifies a verb, an adjective, or another adverb. Like an adverb, an adverb phrase tells *how, when, where,* or *to what extent* about the word it modifies.

Modifying a Verb	The milk spilled *on the floor.* (Spilled *where*?)
Modifying an Adjective	Charles Dickens was very skillful *at characterization.* (Skillful *how*?)
Modifying an Adverb	Autumn color begins soon *after the first frost.* (*How* soon?)

More than one adverb phrase may modify the same word.

Who knocked *on our door at dawn?* (Both phrases modify *knocked*. *On our door* tells where. *At dawn* tells when.)

Punctuation Note There are three times when a prepositional phrase at the beginning of a sentence is followed by a comma.

1. If the phrase is followed by a natural pause when read: According to the fire marshall, smoke detectors save lives.
2. After a series of prepositional phrases: After three weeks of heavy rain in April, the fields were wet and muddy.
3. To avoid confusion: Next to the school, houses were being built.

Placement of Prepositional Phrases

A prepositional phrase may come before or after the word it modifies. However, to avoid confusion, place a prepositional phrase close to the word it modifies.

Confusing	Edward explained how to raise earthworms in his report.
Clear	*In his report,* Edward explained how to raise earthworms.

Sentence Diagraming For information on diagraming prepositional phrases, see page 817.

A Cat in Underwear?

As anyone knows who has ever written so much as a letter home to mother, the English language is full of traps and pitfalls. It is harder to write a clear sentence than to keep a clear conscience.

Some time ago, while trying to explain why I thought my neighborhood had that exclusive quality known as ambience[1], I wrote this sentence. . . .

"A man chasing a cat with a broom in his underwear is ambience by any definition."

Oddly enough, several people evidently misunderstood that simple sentence. . . .

"It was with considerable interest," wrote Bob Byrne, "knowing that you also have long suffered with a back problem, that I read that you keep a broom in your underwear. Is this good?"

The problem seems to be that the reader's understanding is colored or distorted by his own experience. . . ."A gray tomcat with a broom in his underwear is ambience," wrote Mrs. Cecil T. Brown, "in anyone's language. Please call us collect the next time. We will take pictures."

"I do agree," wrote yet another, . . . "Mt. Washington must have ambience—a cat in underwear, indeed! And even more ambient—a cat with a *broom* in his underwear?"

"I have known cats for many years," wrote N. S. Elliott of Hollywood, "but have never seen one wearing underwear. Or outerwear, either, for that matter. Or was it you with the broom in your underwear? If so, why?"

What I would like to do now is to explain exactly what happened that night. . . .

We have a new tomcat in the neighborhood, and he had begun to exasperate me beyond the limits of my patience, if not my sanity. He would wait until I had gone to bed, or was about to, then skulk into our yard and crouch in the ivy under my windows to caterwaul his loathsome lovesong.

Among all my virtues, I like to think that tolerance for my fellow creatures is first. But the screech of a . . . tomcat strings me out. So that night, when he did it again, I snapped. I won't go into the ludicrous details.

But if you had been here, you would have seen a man chasing a cat with a broom in his underwear.

As you see, the difficulty of saying exactly what you mean, so that your reader can't fail to understand, is not a common skill, which is why most writing is not so much read as puzzled out.

Jack Smith

---

[1] **ambience:** a special atmosphere

Exercises

A On your paper, write the prepositional phrases in the following sentences. After each phrase write the word or words the phrase modifies and tell whether the phrase is used as an *Adjective* or *Adverb*. Each sentence has more than one prepositional phrase.

> *Example*   At the end of autumn, the lake is covered with ice.
> At the end, is covered, Adverb
> of autumn, end, Adjective
> with ice, is covered, Adverb

1. Lines of ginkgo trees have been planted along the parkway.
2. The birds of the evergreen forests have a varied diet of seeds, berries, and insects.
3. Georgia O'Keeffe is famous for her dramatic paintings of the American Southwest.
4. By the side of the road, a motorist was changing one of the tires of her car.
5. The identity of the man in the iron mask remained a mystery until the death of Louis XIV.
6. Before long, a spontaneous burst of applause rose from the bystanders.
7. For eight hours, the survivors clung to the small iron buoy.
8. A cloud of thick smoke appeared on the horizon.
9. An otter slithered down the riverbank into the water.
10. Before a holiday, a feeling of excitement pervades the school.

B Application in Literature List the prepositional phrases in the following passage. Tell whether the phrase is an adjective or adverb phrase. Notice how the writer uses prepositional phrases to add clarity and interest to the nouns and verbs in the passage.

> (1) The inhabitants of the wall were a mixed lot, and they were divided into day and night workers, the hunters and the hunted. (2) At night the hunters were the toads that lived among the brambles, and the geckos, pale, translucent, with bulging eyes, that lived in the cracks higher up the wall. (3) Their prey was the population of stupid, absent-minded crane-flies that zoomed and barged their way among the leaves; moths of all sizes and shapes . . . fluttered in soft clouds. . . .
>
> From "The World in a Wall" by Gerald Durrell

c *Write Now* Scientists believe that one answer to the world's hunger problems may lie in farming the sea. Imagine that you are a staff member of the first oceanic farm. Use a variety of prepositional phrases to write a paragraph describing your first harvest.

Part 2
Appositives and Appositive Phrases

An appositive is a noun or a pronoun that usually follows another noun or pronoun and identifies or explains it.

> The adventurous balloonist *Julian Nott* is planning an around-the-world flight. (The appositive *Julian Nott* identifies *balloonist*.)

An appositive phrase consists of an appositive and its modifiers.

> Nott's balloon, *a revolutionary new model with a pressurized gondola,* can ascend seven miles into the jet stream. (The appositive *model* explains the subject *balloon*. The adjectives *revolutionary* and *new* and the adjective phrase *with a pressurized gondola* modify the appositive *model*.)

© 1984 Universal Press Syndicate

"Dang it, Monica! I can't live this charade any longer! I'm not a telephone repairman who stumbled into your life— I'm a Komodo dragon, largest member of the lizard family and a filthy liar."

Sometimes the appositive phrase comes before the word it identifies or explains.

> *A noted pilot of her era,* Anne Morrow Lindbergh was also a writer of exceptional ability. (The appositive *pilot* explains the subject *Anne Morrow Lindbergh.*)

An appositive may be compound.

> Antoine de Saint-Exupéry, a *writer* and an *artist,* began his career in aviation as a mail pilot.

An appositive may be essential or nonessential. An **essential appositive** is one that is needed to make the intended meaning of a sentence complete.

> The aviator *Beryl Markam* wrote about her historic flight across the Atlantic. (Without the appositive, the intended meaning would not be complete.)

A **nonessential appositive** is one that adds extra meaning to a sentence in which the meaning is already clear and complete.

> Nevil Norway, *a British pilot,* wrote novels under the name of Nevil Shute.

Sometimes special circumstances affect whether an appositive is essential or nonessential. Consider the example below.

> My nephew Alex just graduated from college.

If the writer has several nephews, and only Alex graduated, then the appositive is essential. Usually, however, an appositive such as the one above would be considered nonessential.

Punctuation Note As shown above, nonessential appositives are set off with commas. Commas are not used with essential appositives.

Sentence Diagraming For information on diagraming appositives and appositive phrases, see page 819.

Exercises

A Write the appositive or the appositive phrase in each of the following sentences. A sentence may have more than one appositive.

1. Kim can do her math problems faster with an abacus, an ancient form of calculator, than I can with a modern calculator.

2. Robinson Crusoe and Friday are the principal characters in Defoe's classic novel *Robinson Crusoe*.
3. The metal tungsten is added to steel to make it hard.
4. Captain Kidd, a well-known pirate, may have buried treasure in New York.
5. The unforgettable actor Lionel Barrymore was also an accomplished musician.
6. The songstress Jenny Lind toured the United States under the management of P. T. Barnum, the world-famous showman.
7. Does the name Johnny Appleseed mean anything to you?
8. Herbert Pocket was a friend of Pip, the hero of *Great Expectations*.
9. A delicate, lacy-winged insect, the mayfly lives only a few days.
10. Yellowstone, the world's first national park, was established in 1872.

B On your paper, combine the following pairs of sentences into a single sentence by using an appositive phrase. Eliminate words as needed and use appropriate punctuation.

> *Example*   They entered their dog in the dog show. Their dog's name is Pockets.
>
>   They entered their dog Pockets in the dog show.

1. The highlight of our vacation was the logrolling contest in Itasca. Itasca is the source of the Mississippi River.
2. The *Nightingale* is named for Florence Nightingale. It is a U.S. Air Force hospital plane with a red cross on its tail.
3. Attila overran a large part of Eurasia in the fifth century. Attila was king of the Huns.
4. The Iditarod covers 1,100 miles from Anchorage to Nome and lasts twelve days. It is the most grueling dogsled race in the world.
5. Red Grange was the first football player to have his jersey retired. He was known as the Galloping Ghost of the University of Illinois.
6. Beyond the tundra, ice and snow remain year round. The tundra is a region of land in the Arctic.
7. Why would you visit a chiropodist? A chiropodist is a doctor who treats ailments of the feet.
8. Prince Otto von Bismark created the nation of Germany. Prince Otto was the Iron Chancellor.
9. Uranium is a radioactive element. Radioactive elements give off alpha, beta, and gamma rays.
10. Chess gets its name from a Persian word meaning "king." The Persian word for "king" is *shah*.

Part 3
Verbals and Verbal Phrases

A **verbal** is a verb form that functions as a noun, an adjective, or an adverb. A **verbal phrase** consists of a verbal, its modifiers, and its complements. There are three kinds of verbals: **infinitives, participles,** and **gerunds.**

Infinitives and Infinitive Phrases

An infinitive is a verb form that usually begins with *to* and functions as a noun, an adjective, or an adverb.

Noun	*To leave* was a difficult decision. (subject)
	King Edward did not choose *to rule*. (direct object)
	His choice was *to abdicate*. (predicate nominative)
Adjective	That is the game *to see*. (modifies the noun *game*)
Adverb	Everyone stood *to stretch*. (modifies the verb *stood*)
	Kiwis are unable *to fly*. (modifies the adjective *unable*)

Grammar Note Do not confuse an infinitive (*to* plus a verb form) with a prepositional phrase (*to* plus a noun or pronoun).

An infinitive is often used with one or more auxiliary verbs.

Selma was proud *to have been elected*.

To, which is called "the sign of the infinitive," is sometimes left out of the sentence.

Someone will help you *pack*. (Someone will help you [*to*] *pack*.)

Infinitives used with the following verbs do not usually include *to: dare, help, make, see, hear, let, please, watch*.

An infinitive phrase consists of an infinitive, its modifiers, and its complements.

Infinitives may be modified by adverbs and by adverb phrases.

Firefighters have *to practice daily*. (*Daily* is an adverb modifying *to practice*.)

We packed sandwiches *to eat on the bus*. (*On the bus* is an adverb prepositional phrase modifying *to eat*.)

Since an infinitive is a verb form, it can have complements.

> Rita offered *to make everyone pizza*. (*Everyone* is the indirect object of the infinitive *to make; pizza* is the direct object.)

When the infinitive is formed from a linking verb, its complement is a predicate adjective or predicate nominative.

> We tried *to look serious*. (*Serious* is a predicate adjective after the infinitive *to look*.)

Like infinitives, infinitive phrases can function as nouns, adjectives, or adverbs.

Noun *To chase after the dog* would be futile. (subject)

Adjective Ms. Lawry is the candidate *to watch in this election.*

Adverb We meet every Friday night *to play Scrabble™ or Trivial Pursuit.*™

Usage Note Careful writers avoid placing a modifier between *to* and the rest of the infinitive. A modifier in that position is said to "split the infinitive." A split infinitive usually sounds awkward and should be reworded.

Awkward The principal hopes to substantially increase our reading scores.

Improved The principal hopes to increase our reading scores substantially.

Exercises

A Write the infinitives and infinitive phrases in the following sentences. Do not confuse infinitives with prepositional phrases.

1. Some poetry is difficult to interpret.
2. Our neighbors helped us carry the tree stump to the dumpster.
3. The President seems to recognize the problem.
4. To get the frightened cat down from the tree, the firefighter used an extension ladder.
5. Vi watched the weaver bird skillfully construct the nest.
6. To escape the heavy rain, the cyclists rode into a deserted barn.
7. The proposal to table the motion failed.
8. The people downstairs want to sublet their apartment to us.
9. Most elected officials like to hear from their constituents.
10. Many actors also want to write and direct.

B On your paper, write the infinitives and infinitive phrases in the following sentences. Then tell how each infinitive or infinitive phrase is used in the sentence: as a *Noun,* an *Adjective,* or an *Adverb.*

1. In the eighteenth century, an Arab worker helped discover one of the most famous stones in history, the Rosetta Stone.
2. Thinking the oddly shaped black basalt stone was magical, the worker's first impulse was to destroy it.
3. Fortunately, the engineer in charge of the crew became interested in the stone and decided to clean it.
4. On its polished surface were three broad bands of etched writing that proved very difficult to read.
5. To decipher the writing on its surface, scholars examined it carefully.
6. Once they realized that the three messages were the same and that one was written in Greek, scholars were able to read the hieroglyphics.
7. However, it took more than twenty years to unlock the entire Egyptian script.
8. In time, the Rosetta Stone was so important it became booty, to be fought over by nations warring in Egypt.
9. Meanwhile, many people worked to piece together the puzzling facts and unlock the stone's message.
10. Finally, Jean François Champollion was to get credit for deciphering the hieroglyphics.

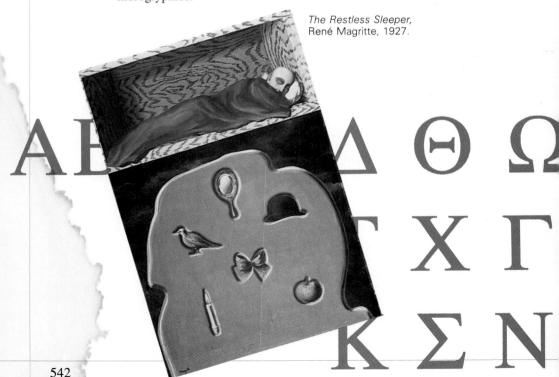

The Restless Sleeper,
René Magritte, 1927.

Participles and Participial Phrases

A participle is a verb form that functions as an adjective.

Like adjectives, participles modify nouns and pronouns.

Modifying a Noun   The *shaken* passengers talked about their escape. (*Shaken* modifies the noun *passengers*.)

Modifying a Pronoun   *Bored*, everyone soon became restless. (*Bored* modifies the pronoun *everyone*.)

There are two kinds of participles: **present participles** and **past participles.** For all verbs, the present participle ends in *-ing*. The past participle has several different forms but usually ends with *-d, -ed, -t,* or *-n*. See Chapter 25, pages 594–633, for lists of irregular verbs and their past participles.

When a present participle or past participle is used with an auxiliary verb to form a verb phrase, it functions as a verb. When it is used as an adjective, it is a verbal.

Verb Phrase   The child on the monkey bars *was laughing*.

Verbal   *Laughing*, the child swung from the monkey bars.

A participle used as an adjective is sometimes used with one or more auxiliary verbs.

Having finished, we turned in our test papers and left.

A participial phrase consists of a participle and its modifiers and complements. Participial phrases function as adjectives.

Participles may be modified by adverbs and by adverb phrases.

Already soaked by the rain, I struggled with my umbrella. (In the participial phrase, the participle *soaked* is modified by the adverb *already* and the adverb phrase *by the rain*.)

Since a participle is a verb form, it can have complements.

Handing the sailor the navigational charts, the captain went below. (*Sailor* is the indirect object of the participle *handing*; *charts* is the direct object.)

Punctuation Note Introductory participles and participial phrases are followed by a comma.

Participial phrases may be essential or nonessential. An **essential participial phrase** is one that is needed to make the meaning of a sentence complete. A **nonessential participial phrase** is one that adds extra meaning to the sentence.

Essential	The puppy *curled up in the corner* is ours. (The participial phrase points out a particular puppy.)
Nonessential	The puppy, *curled up in the corner,* slept through all the excitement. (The participial phrase adds to the description of the puppy.)

Punctuation Note Nonessential participial phrases within a sentence are set off by commas. Commas are not used to set off essential participial phrases.

Misplaced Participles A participle or participial phrase should be placed as close as possible to the word that it modifies. Otherwise, the meaning of the sentence may not be clear.

Confusing	Holsteins are the most popular cows among dairy farmers *producing the most milk.* (The participial phrase appears to modify *farmers.*)
Clear	*Producing the most milk,* Holsteins are the most popular cows among dairy farmers. (The participial phrase clearly modifies *Holsteins.*)

Dangling Participles A participle or a participial phrase that does not clearly modify anything in a sentence is called a **dangling participle.** A dangling participle causes confusion because it appears to modify a word that it cannot sensibly modify. Correct a dangling participle by providing a word for the participle to modify.

Confusing	*Peering through the microscope,* several amoebas wiggled across the slide. (Who is peering? The amoebas?)
Clear	Peering through the microscope, the biology student watched several amoebas wiggle across the slide.
Confusing	*Carefully calculating the danger,* the victims were rescued. (The participial phrase has no word to modify.)
Clear	Carefully calculating the danger, the paramedics rescued the victims.

Sentence Diagraming For information on diagraming participles and participial phrases, see page 818.

Exercises

A On your paper, write the participles and participial phrases in the following sentences. After each participle or participial phrase, write the word it modifies.

1. Can a broken promise ever be mended?
2. We visited a castle built in the twelfth century.
3. The witness carrying the umbrella will testify for the defense.
4. Best known for her novels, Willa Cather also wrote short stories.
5. The sunken treasure, encrusted with barnacles, certainly didn't look very valuable.
6. The school soccer team has a losing record.
7. Having heard the election results, Thomas Dewey retired for the night, thinking he was President.
8. Frothing beakers and smoking test tubes gave the laboratory an eerie atmosphere.
9. Walking in pairs, the elephants lumbered into the ring.
10. Movies intended for a general audience are rated *G*.
11. Wilting in the hot sun, both teams played listlessly.
12. The approaching band has won the state championship.
13. Crowded with colorful characters, *Shogun* depicts the life of samurai swordsmen.
14. Candidates running for public office must become experts at time management.
15. The cast appeared discouraged after the dress rehearsal.

B Each of the following sentences contains a misplaced participle or a dangling participle. On your paper, revise each sentence to make the meaning clear.

1. Walking across the front lawn, the geraniums and marigolds looked colorful.
2. Broken down and dented, Paul paid very little for the car.
3. The posters seemed beautiful to Laura hanging on the wall.
4. Pickled and chilled, the family enjoyed the kiwi fruit.
5. Swimming in the aquarium, the cat peered at the guppies.
6. Rowing steadily, the boat was maneuvered safely to shore.
7. The chimpanzees were observed by scientists swinging from the branches.
8. Having accidentally bumped the table, the lamp crashed to the floor.
9. Lying under the kitchen table, I found the note Dad had left.
10. Performing maneuvers in the air, we watched the Blue Angels.

c *Write Now* By using verbal phrases you can add energy and movement to your writing. For example, compare the following descriptions of an accident.

> The truck swerved wildly. It went around a corner. Then it jumped the curb and crashed through a storefront.
> Swerving wildly around a corner, the truck jumped the curb and crashed through a storefront.

Imagine that you are a reporter. You have just covered one of the following events (or one of your choice). Write a brief article that captures the action and contains at least four participial phrases.

> an earthquake in downtown Los Angeles
> a firefighter's rescue of a small girl
> a movie crew filming a chase scene through city streets
> a bear—having escaped from the zoo—rummages through the local produce market

Gerunds and Gerund Phrases

A gerund is a verb form that ends in *-ing* and functions as a noun.

A gerund can be used in a sentence in almost every way that a noun can be used.

Subject   *Jogging* is not recommended for everyone.
Direct Object Never cease *dreaming*.

Object of a Preposition	If you swim too soon after *eating*, you may get a muscle cramp.
Predicate Nominative	My favorite Olympic event is *kayaking*.
Appositive	Her hobby, *skydiving*, sounds risky.

A gerund phrase consists of a gerund and its modifiers and complements.

Like verbs, gerunds are modified by adverbs and adverb phrases.

> *Running away from a problem* won't solve it. (The adverb *away* and the adverb phrase *from a problem* modify the gerund *running*.)

Unlike a verb, however, a gerund may also be modified by an adjective.

> *Proper lighting on stage* is a necessity. (The adjective *proper* and the adverb phrase *on stage* modify *lighting*.)

Since it is a verb form, a gerund may have complements.

> *Telling me that story* has certainly changed my outlook. (*Me* is the indirect object of the gerund *telling*; *story* is the direct object.)
> *Being a dancer* requires great discipline. (*Dancer* is the predicate nominative after the gerund *being*.)

Like gerunds, gerund phrases function as nouns.

Subject	*Playing tennis on a tour* is not always fun.
Direct Object	The photographer tried *adjusting the shutter*.
Predicate Nominative	Their biggest mistake was *giving my brother a trombone*.
Object of a Preposition	Read everything carefully before *signing a contract*.
Appositive	On vacation we had one unforgettable experience, *fishing for tarpon*.

Sentence Diagraming For information on diagraming gerunds and gerund phrases, see pages 817–818.

Exercises

A Write the gerunds and gerund phrases in the sentences below.

1. We added to the resale value of the bike by painting it.

2. Counterfeiting is illegal.
3. For surfing, Hawaiian beaches are best.
4. Sleeping late in the morning is a great luxury.
5. Douse the fire thoroughly before leaving the campsite.
6. Watching the clock is a poor work habit.
7. Silas Marner was known for hoarding his money.
8. Concentration is important in playing chess.
9. Rattling the presents is half the fun of Christmas Eve.
10. At the dairy, some of us tried milking a cow by hand.
11. Our neighbor's hobby is raising tropical fish.
12. Her ambition, performing in a ballet, was never realized.
13. Glazing makes pottery waterproof.
14. Steel gets its strength from the process of tempering.
15. A method for turning metals into gold was sought by alchemists.

B Write the gerunds and gerund phrases in the following sentences. Tell whether each is a *Subject*, *Direct Object*, *Predicate Nominative*, *Object of a Preposition*, or *Appositive*. If there is no gerund or gerund phrase, write *None*.

(1) Batik, using wax to dye fabric in intricate patterns, is a process that originated in Java. (2) Planning the design is very important since some areas of the fabric will be colored, and some areas will remain plain. (3) Liquid wax, paraffin, or rice paste forms a coating that is painted onto the areas that are not to be dyed. (4) When the fabric is dipped into the dye, the covered areas resist the pigment. (5) After the

cloth is dry, the wax can be removed by boiling. (6) With no coating, the design stands out against the colored background.

(7) Two difficult tasks are achieving multiple shades of the same color and introducing a second color. (8) Two shades of one color can be made by protecting the parts that are not to be dyed darker. (9) The fabric is then dipped into the dye again. (10) Repeating the same process with a different dye, allows a new color to be added.

Checkpoint *Parts 1, 2, and 3*

A On your paper, write the phrases in the following sentences. Tell whether each phrase is a *Prepositional Phrase*, an *Appositive Phrase*, an *Infinitive Phrase*, a *Participial Phrase*, or a *Gerund Phrase*. Keep in mind that a prepositional phrase may be part of a verbal phrase.

1. Sitting on the roof, we watched the fireworks over Shea Stadium.
2. Crippled and already beaten, the Spanish Armada sailed north to its final battle.
3. The skillful gemcutter looked for a place to make the first cut in the diamond.
4. We hoped to see many of our former neighbors at the reunion.
5. Helen Hunt Jackson, a schoolmate and lifelong friend, was Emily Dickinson's literary champion.
6. Finding new sources of water is essential for our cities.
7. Marcia's hobby is carving chess pieces from blocks of wood.
8. To give their children a good education is the dream of parents around the world.
9. Some people enjoy going for a brisk hike before breakfast.
10. Sturdy and maneuverable vessels, Columbus's ships marked a major advance in the seafaring technology of the time.

B Write the verbals in the following sentences. Identify each as a *Gerund*, an *Infinitive*, or a *Participle*. Tell whether each gerund is acting as a *Subject*, *Direct Object*, or *Object of a Preposition*. Tell whether each infinitive is acting as a *Noun*, *Adjective*, or *Adverb*. Also tell which word each participle is modifying.

1. Cultivated for centuries, the aromatic vanilla plant has a long and fascinating history.
2. To the ancient Aztecs vanilla was a highly cherished gift from the gods.

3. Considered very precious, vanilla was once reserved for European royalty.
4. Classified as part of the orchid family, the vanilla plant must be pollinated by hand.
5. A plant needs four years to mature before producing beans.
6. Then the skilled workers pollinating the plants don't dare waste any time.
7. Having matured, the plants flower only one day a year.
8. Fertilizing the plants needs to occur between nine and ten in the morning when the blossoms are completely open; only then will the fertilized flower develop.
9. Treated like customers in an expensive spa, the beans then get a sunning treatment by day and a sweating session at night.
10. Once it undergoes the processes of drying and sorting, the valuable product goes to market branded with the owner's special mark to protect it from vanilla rustlers.
11. Buyers must also beware of counterfeiters who sprinkle white powder on inferior beans to make them resemble the frosted crystals on the outside of superior beans.
12. Could you dare call vanilla plain again?

C Application in Literature Write the phrases in the following passage. Tell if each phrase is *Prepositional*, *Participial*, *Gerund*, or *Infinitive*. Notice how the writer uses a variety of phrase constructions to create an interesting and vivid passage.

(1) Why he couldn't possibly recognize her. . . . (2) John would be looking for a young woman with a peaked Spanish comb in her hair and the painted fan. (3) Digging post holes changed a woman. (4) Riding country roads in the winter . . . was another thing: sitting up nights with sick horses and sick children . . . [but] it was time to go in and light the lamps. . . . (5) Lighting the lamps had been beautiful. (6) The children huddled up to her and breathed like little calves waiting at the bar in the twilight. (7) Their eyes followed the match and watched the flame rise and settle in a blue curve, then they moved away from her. (8) The lamp was lit. (9) They didn't have to be scared . . . any more. Never, never, never more.

From *The Jilting of Granny Weatherall*
by Katherine Anne Porter

Part 4
Clauses

A clause is a group of words that contains a subject and a verb.

There are two kinds of clauses: **independent** and **subordinate**.

Independent Clauses

A clause that can stand alone as a sentence is an independent, or main, clause.

The sentence below contains two independent clauses.

> <u>Beethoven</u> gradually <u>became</u> deaf; nevertheless, <u>he</u> <u>continued</u> to write great music.

In the example above, the subject of each independent clause has been underlined once, and the verb has been underlined twice. Each clause can stand alone as a sentence.

> Beethoven gradually became deaf. He continued to write great music.

Subordinate Clauses

A clause that cannot stand alone as a sentence is a subordinate, or dependent, clause.

Both of the clauses that are shown below have a subject and a verb. However, they are not sentences because they do not express complete thoughts.

> If <u>you</u> <u>like</u> houses with a history. (Then what happens?)
> Where <u>George</u> <u>Washington</u> <u>stayed</u> after the surrender at Yorktown. (What about where he stayed?)

To form a sentence, you must combine the subordinate clause with an independent clause.

> ┌─ subordinate clause ─┐   ┌──────────── independent
> If you like houses with a history, you will enjoy a trip through the
> clause ──┐
> Hudson Valley.

> ┌ independent clause ┐   ┌──────────────── subordinate
> We visited the house where George Washington stayed after the
> clause ──────┐.
> surrender at Yorktown.

Do not confuse a subordinate clause with a verbal phrase. A verbal phrase does not have a subject and a verb.

Subordinate Clause	Unknowingly, ancient Egyptians used treatments *that contained penicillin*. (The subject is *that* and the verb is *contained*.)
Verbal Phrases	Unknowingly, ancient Egyptians used treatments *containing penicillin*. (The participial phrase does not have a subject and a verb.)
	The treatments were used *to cure skin ailments*. (The infinitive phrase does not have a subject and a verb.)

The subject of a subordinate clause may be a relative pronoun such as *who, whom, whose, that,* or *which*. In the first example above, *that* is a relative pronoun.

Exercises

A On your paper, write the italicized group of words in each of the following sentences. Identify each group as a *Phrase* or a *Clause*. When you identify a clause, tell whether it is an *Independent Clause* or a *Subordinate Clause*.

1. Washoe, the ape, uses sign language *to ask for things*.
2. To photograph the ocean bottom, *the divers descended in a metal sphere*.

3. Scientists are now more hopeful of *finding a cure for muscular dystrophy*.
4. *When it clawed at the door*, the dog finally attracted its owner's attention.
5. *It is hard to believe* that they are moving to Alaska.
6. Tires must be inflated properly, or *they will not wear well*.
7. That player is a rookie *whose future looks very bright*.
8. The whale swam around the wrecked boat, *churning the water in its vengeful wake*.
9. Remember to turn off your stereo *before you fall asleep*.
10. Whenever there is a heavy snowfall in the city, *ground transportation comes to a halt*.
11. Set up the easel *wherever the light is best*.
12. Why is caviar, *which is just fish eggs*, so expensive?
13. *Found throughout Australia*, dingos are wild dogs.
14. *Interpret his comment* however you like.
15. Designed as a universal language, *Esperanto is spoken by few people*.

B Write the following sentences on your paper. Underline each independent clause once and each subordinate clause twice. Note that a sentence may contain two independent clauses or an independent clause and a subordinate clause.

1. Jane Addams was a social reformer who had led an aimless existence for several years.
2. Until she visited a settlement house in London, she did not find her vocation.
3. A settlement house is an institution that provides needed community services.
4. Miss Addams came to Chicago where she helped establish Hull House.
5. The story of Hull House, which is a long one, illustrates Ms. Addams's perseverance.
6. She was active in labor and social reform, but she remained the chief fund-raiser for Hull House.
7. Jane Addams soon became a public figure, and her early interest in woman's suffrage was revived.
8. When Theodore Roosevelt asked for help, she campaigned vigorously for the Progressive Party.
9. After Hull House moved its headquarters in 1963, most of the settlement buildings were demolished.
10. The house itself still stands, and it serves as a memorial to Jane Addams.

Part 5
Kinds of Subordinate Clauses

There are three kinds of subordinate clauses: **adjective clauses, adverb clauses,** and **noun clauses.**

Adjective Clauses

The single-word adjective, the adjective phrase, and the adjective clause are used in the same way. They modify a noun or a pronoun.

An adjective clause is a subordinate clause that is used as an adjective to modify a noun or a pronoun.

Like adjectives, adjective clauses tell *what kind* or *which one.* An adjective clause is usually placed immediately after the word the clause modifies.

The stamps *that commemorate American locomotives* feature four different models. (*what kind* of stamps?)

That is the wealthy collector *who bought the rare stamp.* (*which* collector?)

Words Used to Introduce Adjective Clauses Most adjective clauses begin with a relative pronoun: *who, whom, whose, that, which.* A **relative pronoun** relates the clause to the word it modifies. The modified word is the antecedent of the relative pronoun.

Isaac Newton, the English scientist, was born the same year *that Galileo, the famous Italian astronomer and physicist, died.* (*Year* is the antecedent of the relative pronoun *that* and is modified by the entire adjective clause.)

Sometimes the relative pronoun functions in the adjective clause as a subject, a direct object, an object of a preposition, or a modifier.

Subject	Westwater Canyon cuts through rock *that* is almost two billion years old. (The relative pronoun *that* is the subject of the verb *is* in the adjective clause.)
Direct Object	The artist *whom* I admire most is Mary Cassatt. (The relative pronoun *whom* is the direct object of the verb *admire* in the adjective clause.)

Object of *a Preposition*	The tourists to *whom* we spoke are from Germany. (The relative pronoun *whom* is the object of the preposition *to* in the adjective clause.)
Modifier	He is the friend *whose* father is an engineer. (The relative pronoun *whose* modifies *father*, the subject of the adjective clause.)

An adjective clause introduced by a relative pronoun is sometimes called a **relative clause.**

Usage Note As you use adjective clauses in description and other writing, be aware that the case of the pronoun, *who* or *whom*, is determined by the use of the pronoun in the adjective clause. *Who* can be used as a subject or predicate nominative within a clause. *Whom* can function as a direct object, indirect object, or object of a preposition.

The **relative adverbs** *after, before, since, when, where,* and *why* may also introduce adjective clauses. Like relative pronouns, relative adverbs relate the clause to the word it modifies. Unlike a relative pronoun, however, a relative adverb modifies the verb in the adjective clause.

> In Minnesota we visited a workshop *where birch bark canoes are made by hand.* (The adjective clause modifies the noun *workshop.* The relative adverb *where* modifies the verb *are made* in the adjective clause.)

Sometimes the introductory word in an adjective clause is omitted.

> The trail *the guide indicated* led to a mill. (The relative pronoun *that* is omitted: *that* the guide indicated.)

Essential and Nonessential Adjective Clauses An adjective clause may be essential or nonessential. An **essential adjective clause** is one that is needed to make the intended meaning of a sentence complete.

> We asked for a houseplant *that is not overly fond of direct sunlight.* (The clause is needed to complete the meaning of the sentence.)

A **nonessential adjective clause** is one that adds additional information to a sentence in which the meaning is already complete.

> The wax begonia, *which can be red, white, or pink,* blooms all year long. (The clause adds an idea to the sentence.)

That is always used to introduce essential clauses. In formal writing, *which* introduces nonessential clauses. *Who* may be used to introduce essential or nonessential clauses when the antecedent is a person. *Which* is never used to refer to people.

Punctuation Note As shown in the examples on the previous page, commas are used to set off a nonessential clause from the rest of the sentence. Commas are not used with essential clauses.

Sentence Diagraming For information about diagraming adjective clauses, see page 820.

Exercises

A On your paper, write the adjective clauses in the following sentences and the word each modifies. Then underline the relative pronoun or the relative adverb that introduces the clause. In two sentences the introductory word has been omitted.

1. The North and South poles belong to no time zone; therefore technically, there are places where time stands still.
2. Senator Bradley is the official to whom we wrote.
3. Early summer is the time of year when tornadoes most often strike.
4. The energy we are using came originally from the sun.
5. What is the most embarrassing thing that ever happened to you?
6. Easter Island, which is located off the coast of Chile, is noted for its colossal pre-Columbian statues.
7. Windsurfing requires participants who are agile.
8. Where are the peppers you sautéed for the pizza?
9. Julius Caesar was a Roman general whose success in the Gallic Wars earned him a loyal following.
10. The letter to which you refer must have been misfiled.

B Combine each of the following sentence pairs into a sentence with an adjective clause. Remember to punctuate the clauses correctly.

> *Example*   I read an article about Mount Olympus. Zeus was
> believed to have held court there.
> I read an article about Mount Olympus, where Zeus was
> believed to have held court.

1. The National Weather Service is part of the Department of Commerce. The service was established by Congress in 1871.
2. The representative was helpful. We spoke to her on the phone.

3. Elinor Wylie was known for the visual imagery of her poetry. Her published works include *Nets to Catch the Wind*.
4. Scientists have invented a light. It does not produce heat.
5. The man hosts a popular game show. We saw him in a restaurant.
6. Springs are fed by rain. The rain seeps through the soil.
7. E.H. Shepard is an artist. He did the illustrations for the Winnie the Pooh books.
8. I have seen the house. Betsy Ross lived in the house.
9. The mynah bird sings in two languages. My aunt bought the bird.
10. Verona is a town in northern Italy. It is the setting for Shakespeare's *Romeo and Juliet*.

c *Proofreading* Revise the following paragraph by using adjective clauses to combine some thoughts. Be alert for errors in existing adjective clauses as well as other errors in usage or mechanics.

The Incas were a South American indian people. These people ruled one of the largest and richest empires in the americas. Because the Incas did not develop a writing system before the Spanish conquest of thier civilization, archaeological remains provide the major source of information about them.

Historians know a number of interesting facts about the incas. The Incas had special officials to who was given the duty of record keeping. The officials used a *quipe*. The *quipe* was a cord. The cord was tyed with knotted strings of various lengths and colors. There were also surgeons. These surgeons performed an operation which involved cutting away part of the skull. They held the belief that this would relieve pressure on the brain and let out evil spirits.

Adverb Clauses

An adverb clause is a subordinate clause that is used as an adverb to modify a verb, an adjective, or an adverb.

Modifying a Verb	The sheriff posted the notice *where everyone could see it.*
Modifying an Adjective	In cooking class we learned that dough is proofed *when it has risen.*
Modifying an Adverb	The cave was darker *than you can imagine.*

Like adverbs, adverb clauses tell *where, when, why, how,* or *to what extent* about words they modify. Adverb clauses can also explain *under what circumstances* and *why.*

If demand exceeds supply, prices will go up. (Go up *under what circumstances?*)

He lost the debate *because he was not prepared.* (Lost *why?*)

Like verbs, verbals also may be modified by an adverb clause.

Modifying an Infinitive	Erin wants to visit Ireland *so that she can kiss the Blarney Stone.* (Why?)
Modifying a Participle	Waiting *until the nurse slept,* Juliet drank the potion. (Under what circumstances?)
Modifying a Gerund	Guessing *if you don't know the answer* may help. (Under what circumstances?)

Words Used to Introduce Adverb Clauses Most adverb clauses begin with subordinating conjunctions. A **subordinating conjunction** relates the clause to the word it modifies. Subordinating conjunctions can be used to show a variety of relationships between ideas.

Time	after, as, as soon as, before, since, until, when, whenever, while
Cause	because, since
Comparison	as, as much as, than
Condition	although, as long as, even though, provided that, unless
Purpose	in order that, so that
Manner	as, as if, as though
Place	where, wherever

Elliptical Clauses *Elliptical* comes from *ellipsis,* which means "omission of a word or words." An **elliptical clause** is an adverb clause from which a word or words have been omitted.

> *When applying for a job,* you should dress appropriately. (The words *you are* have been omitted: when *you are* applying.)
> You seem happier with the results *than I.* (The word *do* has been omitted: than I *do*.)

Punctuation Note An adverb clause at the beginning of a sentence is followed by a comma.

Sentence Diagraming For information on diagraming adverb clauses, see page 820.

Exercises

A On your paper, write the adverb clauses in the following sentences. Underline the subordinating conjunction. After each clause write the word or words that it modifies.

> *Example*   Whenever drought is a problem, people hope for rain.
>   <u>Whenever</u> drought is a problem, hope

1. Even though it seems difficult, if not impossible, humans have long tried to make rain.
2. When an ancient rainmaker cast a spell, people could not always count on rain.
3. More recent "pluviologists" have proved no better at the task than the ancient rainmakers were.
4. One rainmaker was almost lynched because he "caused" a twenty-inch rain and washed out a dam.
5. Until Vincent Schaefer had a happy accident, rainmaking remained a hoax.
6. Seeding clouds so that drops of water would form had been tried by many different scientists.
7. Would seeding work if the temperature of the clouds was below freezing?
8. After Schaefer tried out this idea in a series of almost comical experiments with his home freezer, he succeeded.
9. One day, as he was putting a block of dry ice into the freezer, Schaefer exhaled.
10. Soon his improvised laboratory looked as if a miniature snowstorm were in progress.

B Compose sentences that use the following adverb clauses. Underline the word or words each clause modifies.

1. Because nonpoisonous snakes destroy rodents
2. Because the judge entered the court
3. Until there was no sound or movement
4. When the Liberty Bell cracked
5. Since it is difficult to recognize harmful wild mushrooms
6. Provided that your registration fee is paid
7. If you have the sales receipt
8. Although the car needed repair
9. Unless more funds are raised
10. Where the soil is sandy
11. So that we can finish the experiment
12. While I am running errands

c *Write Now* Good horror films always seem to have dramatic special effects. For example, think of Dr. Frankenstein's lab. Whenever lightning strikes, electric arcs bounce around his mysterious machines. Describe a scene from one of your favorite horror films or devise a scene of your own. Use a variety of adverb clauses to add drama to your description.

Noun Clauses

A noun clause is a subordinate clause that is used in a sentence as a noun.

A noun clause may be used in any way that a noun is used. Consequently, noun clauses most frequently function as subjects, direct objects, indirect objects, predicate nominatives, objects of prepositions, and appositives.

Subject	*Where the hostages are* remains a mystery to the police.
Direct Object	Hoyle believed *that his theory would revolutionize the study of the universe.*
Indirect Object	Give *whoever comes in last* a consolation prize.
Predicate Nominative	My question is *how do I load this computer program.*
Object of a Preposition	We have to limit expenses to *whatever funds are available.*
Appositive	My parents vetoed the idea *that we buy a sports car instead of a wagon.*

A noun clause may function as the direct object of a verbal.

> Alice tried to decide *if she had been dreaming*. (The noun clause is
> the direct object of the infinitive *to decide*.)
> Henry VIII had no trouble deciding *whether he should remarry*.
> (The noun clause is the direct object of the gerund *deciding*.)

Words Used to Introduce Noun Clauses Noun clauses are
introduced by pronouns and by subordinating conjunctions.

Pronouns   who, whom, which, what, that, whoever, whomever,
               whatever

A pronoun that introduces a noun clause may also function as a subject
or an object within the clause.

> The American Red Cross provides shelter and emergency relief aid
> for *whoever needs it*. (*Whoever* is the subject of the verb *needs* in the
> noun clause.)

Subordinating Conjunctions   how, that, when, where, whether, why
                                       (For a complete list of subordinating
                                       conjunctions, see page 500.)

Notice that some of the same words that introduce noun clauses can
also introduce adjective and adverb clauses. To determine if a clause is
functioning as a noun, decide if the clause is doing the job of a noun in
the sentence. In the first example below, the clause is a noun clause
because it is functioning as a direct object. The clauses in the second
and third examples are modifying other words; therefore, they are not
functioning as noun clauses.

> The orchestra conductor announced *when the concert would begin*.
> (Announced *what*? The noun clause is the direct object of the verb
> *announced*.)
> This is the time of year *when the Canada geese fly over*. (*Which* time?
> The adjective clause modifies the noun *time*.)
> The engine knocks *when you use low octane gas*. (Knocks *when*? The
> adverb clause modifies the verb *knocks*.)

Sometimes the introductory word is omitted from a noun clause.

> The report said *unemployment was at an all-time low*. (The report
> said *that* unemployment was at an all-time low.)

Sentence Diagraming For information on diagraming noun
clauses, see pages 820–821.

Exercises

A Identify each noun clause. Tell whether it is used as a *Subject, Object of a Verb, Object of a Preposition, Predicate Nominative,* or *Appositive.*

1. The suspect would not tell us where she had been.
2. What the reporter really wanted remained a mystery to us.
3. Fred was apologetic about what he had said.
4. The doctor said that Marion could get up tomorrow.
5. Do you know who invented the microscope?
6. We had no idea of what might happen.
7. The police know who wrote the threatening letters.
8. Who will win the playoffs is anyone's guess.
9. Everyone wondered when the fog would lift.
10. The date of the surprise birthday party was what they did not write on the invitation.
11. What happened to the missing paintings was never discovered by the police or the FBI.
12. The neighborhood council will be grateful for whatever you do.
13. Who had the brilliant idea that we should clean out the attic during spring vacation?
14. We did not know Harold had such amazing powers of concentration.
15. Is your new job what you expected?

B On your paper, write the noun clauses in the following quotations. Tell how each clause functions in the sentence by writing *Subject, Object of a Verb, Object of a Preposition, Predicate Nominative,* or *Appositive.*

1. Genius does what it must, and talent does what it can. Owen Meredith
2. I regret that I have but one life to give for my country. Nathan Hale
3. Don't invent with your mouth what you don't see with a smile.
Mother Teresa
4. Whoever gossips to you will gossip about you. Spanish proverb
5. The best way to be thankful is to make use of what the gods have given you. Anthony Trollope
6. What is wanted is not more law, but a better public opinion.
James G. Blaine
7. A Bill of Rights is what the people are entitled to. Thomas Jefferson
8. Paradise is where I am. Voltaire
9. Remember that time is money. Benjamin Franklin
10. Whoever does not rise early will never do any good. Samuel Johnson

C Write sentences using the following noun clauses as indicated in parentheses.

1. what the excited witness was saying (direct object)
2. who the murderer was (subject)
3. when the treasure is buried (predicate noun)
4. whichever skater wins (object of preposition)
5. that all men are created equal (appositive)

D *Write Now* A good mystery or adventure novel can keep a reader intrigued for hours. Recount the plot of your favorite mystery or adventure story, using a variety of noun clauses.

Checkpoint *Parts 4 and 5*

A On your paper, write the italicized groups of words in the following sentences. Tell whether each group of words is a *Phrase* or a *Clause*. When you identify a clause, tell whether it is an *Independent Clause* or a *Subordinate Clause*.

1. *When I was last in New Orleans,* it was during Mardi Gras.
2. *After winning the Olympic gold medal,* the U.S. hockey team received congratulations from the President.
3. Poison ivy is a dangerous plant, but *it can be easily identified.*
4. *While Gina worked diligently on the crossword puzzle,* Renetta read the sports section.

5. *Charging out of the woods,* a six-pronged deer appeared on the path ahead of us.
6. Islam, *the official religion of many Arabic countries,* was founded in the seventh century A.D.
7. If the litmus paper turns blue, *the substance is basic.*
8. The professor, *who teaches at Rutgers University,* spoke to us about careers in the media.
9. *Caught in the monstrous traffic jam,* some drivers got out of their cars and began to chat.
10. Some caterpillars live in tentlike webs *that they spin among tree branches.*

B On your paper, write the subordinate clauses in the following sentences. Tell whether each is an *Adjective, Adverb,* or *Noun Clause.* For each adjective or adverb clause, tell the word it modifies. Tell whether each noun clause is used as a *Subject, Object of a Verb, Object of a Preposition, Predicate Nominative,* or *Appositive.*

1. Chief Inspector Holmes looked thoughtful as he inspected the contents of the safe.
2. Warm Springs, Georgia, is where President Franklin Roosevelt spent the last days of his life.
3. Many visitors go each year to Stratford, the town where William Shakespeare was born.
4. Paul Zindel's novel *Pigman* is as serious as it is funny.
5. Chaing did better on the history exam than she had expected.
6. Henry Ford, who was a pioneer in the automobile industry, called his first car the "quadricycle."
7. The stray cat that wandered into our yard has adopted us.
8. After *Brighton Beach Memoirs* became a hit on Broadway, it was made into a motion picture.
9. If the coach agrees, we will wear our jerseys for the homecoming game.
10. Queen Victoria ruled in an age when England was the head of a great colonial empire.
11. Although his native tongue was Polish, Joseph Conrad became a famous English novelist.
12. The shop teacher showed the class how an adz is used.
13. Most reputable scientists scorn the belief that earth has been visited by UFO's.
14. That Duke Ellington was a great musician is unquestionable.
15. Dr. Robert Goddard, whose inventions launched the Space Age, built the first liquid-fueled rocket in 1926.

Part 6
The Structure of the Sentence

You have learned that sentences may be classified according to their purpose: declarative, interrogative, imperative, and exclamatory. Sentences may also be classified according to their structure—the number and kinds of clauses they contain. The four kinds of structural classifications are (1) simple sentences, (2) compound sentences, (3) complex sentences, and (4) compound-complex sentences.

Simple Sentences

A simple sentence is a sentence that contains one independent clause and no subordinate clauses.

> The candidate is confident.

A simple sentence may have any number of phrases.

> The candidate, Mrs. Schulman from Queens, is confident about the outcome of the mayoral race.

The parts of a simple sentence may be compound.

Compound Subject	Both the *Montagues* and the *Capulets* contributed to the feud.
Compound Verb	Someone *had split* the logs and *stacked* the wood in the shed.
Compound Complement	Mark Twain was both a *writer* and an *inventor*.

More than one part of a simple sentence may be compound.

> The firefighters and several police officers rushed into the building and warned the tenants of the bomb threat. (simple sentence with a compound subject and a compound verb)

Compound Sentences

A compound sentence is a sentence that has two or more independent clauses that are joined together.

The clauses in a compound sentence may be joined with a comma and a coordinating conjunction: *and, but, nor, or, for, yet.*

> Everyone stopped work, **and** the factory became silent.

The independent clauses may be joined with a semicolon.

There is no joy in Mudville; Mighty Casey has struck out.

In some compound sentences the clauses may be joined by a semicolon and a conjunctive adverb. (For a list of conjunctive adverbs see page 500.)

Our library may be small; **however,** it has an extensive collection of reference books.

Punctuation Note As shown above, a conjunctive adverb is usually preceded by a semicolon and followed by a comma.

Sentence Diagraming For information on diagraming simple and compound sentences, see pages 812–821.

Exercises

A On your paper, write the following sentences. Underline the subject of each independent clause once and the verb twice. Label each sentence *Simple* or *Compound*. Keep in mind that a simple sentence may have one or more compound parts.

1. The governor will address the committee and endorse the bill.
2. The house itself is small, but the grounds are spacious.
3. In Norway, people drive or ski from one village to another.
4. Both strawberries and asparagus are in season.
5. The fans were ecstatic; their team had made it to the semifinals.
6. Hamilton and Washington wrote Washington's Farewell Address.
7. Plastics are nonconductors; therefore, they make ideal electrical parts.
8. The climbers reached the summit and spent the afternoon there.
9. Beavers help conserve soil; thus, they should be protected.
10. Gnats and mosquitoes are most numerous in early June and July.

B On your paper, rewrite the following sentences changing them to the structure indicated in parentheses.

Example Isaac Stern played at the benefit. Loretta Lynn played there too. (simple sentence with compound subject)
Isaac Stern and Loretta Lynn played at the benefit.

1. Two deer bolted across the road. They disappeared into a grove of birch trees. (simple sentence with compound predicate)

2. Birds are born blind. They can recognize their mothers by using their other senses. (compound sentence with conjunctive adverb)
3. For years the Great Lakes were very polluted. The situation is improving. (compound sentence with coordinating conjunction)
4. Da Vinci painted only a few pictures. They are all masterpieces. (compound sentence with coordinating conjunction)
5. The drought forced the price of citrus up. The early frost also forced the price of citrus up. (simple sentence with compound subject)

Complex Sentences

The complex sentence consists of one main clause and one or more subordinate clauses.

In a complex sentence, the subordinate clause is used as a noun or as a modifier. If it is used as a modifier, the subordinate clause usually modifies a word in the main clause.

> *When you leave,* shut the door. (Clause modifies *shut*.)
> *If he quits that job,* he will regret it later on. (Clause modifies *will regret*.)

In each preceding example, the main clause can stand as a sentence by itself: *Shut the door. He will regret it later on.*

The subordinate clauses, however, cannot stand alone because their meaning is incomplete.

> When you leave . . . (What then?)
> If he quits that job . . . (What will happen?)

The complex structure of the Georges Pompidou Center, Paris, France.

Complex sentences containing noun clauses are somewhat different from those with adjective or adverb clauses. The noun clause is used as a noun within the main clause. The noun clause, in other words, is part of the main clause.

> *What we saw* is impossible! (Noun clause is subject of *is*.)
> Kira is sorry about *what she said*. (Noun clause is object of preposition *about*.)

Usually, as in the examples above, neither the main clause nor the noun clause can stand by itself. Nonetheless, a sentence containing one main clause and noun clause is regarded as a complex sentence.

Sentence Diagraming For information on diagraming complex sentences, see page 821.

Exercises

A On your paper, write the following complex sentences. Underline each independent clause once and each subordinate clause twice.

1. Simmer the pudding until it thickens.
2. Is that the house Frank Lloyd Wright built for himself?
3. Our school, which has only 227 students, ordered more than 2,000 paperbacks last year.
4. Over two centuries have passed since the Constitution was signed.
5. In 1494 Spain and Portugal signed the Treaty of Tordesillas, which divided the New World between them.
6. Some scholars believe that writing began as a form of word magic.
7. If you finish your paper by Thursday, we can go to the movies.
8. I can't decide whether Charlie Chaplin or Groucho Marx is my favorite movie comedian.
9. What is science fiction today, may become real-life science tomorrow.
10. The city that had the first zoo in America was Philadelphia.

B On your paper, write the following sentences. Label each sentence *Simple, Compound,* or *Complex*. Underline the subordinate clauses in the complex sentences.

1. Anyone who has come under the spell of a great piece of music may have wondered what inspired the composer.
2. Many contemporary composers deny working from inspiration.
3. According to one, he composes because he can't help it!
4. As a rule, creative artists do not sit around waiting for inspiration.

5. They turn to their creative tasks, and they do their best.
6. Many composers, however, seem to write music as though they had the gift of automatic writing.
7. Mozart and Schubert, two of the most spontaneous composers, seemed to write music with little or no conscious effort.
8. Others started with an idea; they then labored long and carefully over their work.
9. Beethoven was busy with his *C Minor Symphony* for over five years, and it took Brahms over twenty-five years to write his great symphony.
10. It is a fact that each composer works in his or her own way.

Compound-Complex Sentences

A compound-complex sentence is a sentence that has two or more independent clauses and one or more subordinate clauses.

In the following examples, the independent clauses are underlined once, the subordinate clauses twice.

> The bicycle, which I repaired myself, had better work, for I certainly cannot afford a new one. (The subordinate clause interrupts the first independent clause.)
>
> When the ice melted, heavy rains began, and the streets flooded.

Sentence Diagraming For information on diagraming compound-complex sentences, see page 822.

Exercises

A Write the following compound-complex sentences. Underline each independent clause once and each subordinate clause twice.

1. Divers sometimes explore the sunken ships under Lake Superior, but they must be careful, because these wrecks can be dangerous.
2. The clown looked everywhere for his trumpet; since it was in his back pocket, he couldn't find it.
3. After the beaker was broken, spilled liquid extinguished the flame, and the Bunsen burner wouldn't work.
4. Richard Burbage, who was the son of an actor, played the first Hamlet; moreover, he was a shareholder in Shakespeare's theater.
5. While the captain and the first mate were below, a violent storm arose, and the whalespotter noticed a waterspout in the distance.
6. There are very few tickets left, but you can see the concert provided that you don't mind sitting in the second balcony.

7. Gauguin painted palm trees of orange and purple; nevertheless, many European critics agreed that his work showed genius.
8. We enjoyed the jousting at the Renaissance Fair; however, the madrigal singers, who were among the best we've ever seen, put on an even better show.
9. The White Rabbit, who wore a waistcoat and a pocket watch, scurried by, and Alice gasped in amazement.
10. It was a still night, and we heard a loon that nested by the lake.

B Application in Literature Make four columns with the headings *Simple*, *Compound*, *Complex*, and *Compound-Complex*. Read the passage. List the numbers of the sentences that fit under each heading.

(1) One day after school, twenty-five years ago, several of us were playing with a football in the yard at Randy Shepperton's. (2) Randy was calling signals and handling the ball. (3) Nebraska Crane was kicking it. (4) Augustus Potterham was too clumsy to run or kick or pass, [and] so we put him at center, where all he'd have to do would be to pass the ball back to Randy when he got the signal.

(5) It was late in October and there was a smell of smoke, of leaves, of burning in the air. (6) Nebraska had just kicked to us. (7) It was a good kick too—a high, soaring punt that spiraled out above my head, behind me. (8) I ran back and tried to get it, but it was far and away "over the goal line." (9) It hit the street and bounded back and forth with that peculiarly erratic bounce a football has.

From *The Child Tiger* by Thomas Wolfe

Checkpoint *Part 6*

A On your paper, write the following sentences. Underline each independent clause once and each subordinate clause twice. Then identify each sentence according to its kind: *Simple, Compound, Complex,* or *Compound-Complex.*

1. The ski resorts upstate will lose money unless it snows soon.
2. Cockroaches feed on plant and animal remains, but they also come indoors in search of food or even wood.
3. Since the monkey house opened, attendance at the zoo has increased, and peanut sales have skyrocketed.
4. The saraband, a slow, graceful dance, originated in Spain.
5. Before he reached the age of twenty-five, John Updike had published many articles; moreover, he had also written a novel.

B On your paper, write the following sentences. Underline each independent clause once and each subordinate clause twice. Then identify each sentence according to its kind: *Simple, Compound, Complex,* or *Compound-Complex.*

1. Aquaculture is the finny future of high-tech fish farming.
2. An Aquacell at the University of Arizona provides an ideal environment for raising fish and other aquatic animals.
3. The fish are raised both as a subject for study and as a food source that is high in yield.
4. Because conditions must be carefully controlled, a computer checks oxygen levels and food consumption, and computer readings are taken each morning.
5. Scientists know more about warm-water species than they do about cold-water fish.
6. Eels are included in the study, but not as a food source.
7. Eels have a terrible feed conversion ratio; eight pounds of food produces only one pound of eel.
8. Catfish, which outstrip their closest rivals, are the number-one fish in U.S. aquaculture, and their popularity is growing.
9. Paddlefish, which produce fine meat and are an excellent source of eggs for caviar, are also under study.
10. The world has many mouths to feed; perhaps aquaculture holds the answer to the food shortage.

Linking
Grammar *&* Writing

Think of an activity that you do well. It could be anything from bicycle repairing to studying for a test. Then think of a simple process that you go through as part of this activity. For example, you might use a warm-up and stretching routine to get ready for football or ballet. You might also follow a series of specific steps when you practice guitar or piano or when you prepare dinner. Write one or two paragraphs that explain this process. In your explanation, use adverb, adjective, and noun clauses.

Prewriting and Drafting First visualize the process that you have chosen to explain. List all the steps involved. If possible, read your list to someone who is familiar with the process and ask for suggestions. Add any steps you may have forgotten. Then write your draft using your list as an aid. Include transition words such as *first, next,* and *after* to connect the steps. Remember that your reader will know only what you tell him or her. Make your explanation so clear and easy to follow that the reader could repeat the process.

Revision and Proofreading As you revise, consider the following questions:

1. Does the explanation that you have written include all the steps that are part of the process?
2. Are the steps in your process arranged in the order in which they will be performed?
3. Do the transition words connect the steps in a logical way?
4. Is each step clear and easy to understand?
5. Did you use adverb, adjective, and noun clauses where appropriate? Did you use them correctly?

Additional Writing Topic You have just thought of an invention that the whole world is waiting for. You want to sell your marvelous idea to a respected manufacturer so that production can begin on a large scale. Write a few paragraphs to the president of the company explaining why he or she should buy your invention. First try to write an interesting and persuasive letter using only simple sentences. Then expand your letter using complex, compound, and compound-complex sentences. Notice how variation in sentence structure creates a more interesting letter.

Navaho

Though many Native American languages have been supplanted by English, the Navaho language continues to play an important role in the lives of the Navaho people. More than 100,000 people speak Navaho, principally on the sprawling Navaho Reservation covering fourteen million acres of Arizona, New Mexico, and Utah.

The Navaho language differs from English in many ways. It is a "tone" language, one in which the pitch used to pronounce a word helps determine its meaning. In addition, nouns are classified as either animate or inanimate, and words associated with active things have feminine gender while static things have masculine gender. Some verb forms change depending upon their direct object. For example, the verb form used to say *holding a ball* is different from the verb form used for *holding a stick*.

Instead of borrowing words from English, the Navaho adapt existing Navaho words and phrases to suit new needs. A car, for example, is a *chidi,* named after the noise a car makes when it starts. A car's headlights are "the eyes of the chidi," its wheels "the legs of the chidi," and its tires "the moccasins of the chidi."

Although many Native American languages are disappearing due to the dominance of English, the Navaho people are steadfastly holding on to their linguistic heritage.

Chapter 23

Application and Review

A Identifying Phrases On your paper, underline the phrases in the following sentences. Identify each phrase as *Prepositional, Participial, Gerund,* or *Infinitive.* Tell if each infinitive phrase is functioning as a *Noun, Adjective,* or *Adverb.* Tell if each prepositional phrase is functioning as an *Adjective* or *Adverb.*

1. *Moby Dick* is a book to be read slowly and carefully.
2. Mrs. Ling will be happy to show you her prize-winning orchids.
3. Ralph Waldo Emerson believed the only way to have a friend is to be one.
4. Hunted almost to extinction, the American buffalo is now protected in zoos and preserves.
5. Mr. Aldridge always wanted to see the spectacular geysers spouting in Yellowstone Park.
6. Climbing "El Capitán" will require training and perseverance.
7. Arachne was famous for weaving beautiful tapestries.
8. Hiking in the mountains helped William O. Douglas overcome a lung ailment.
9. Riding his bike, Alan can reach Jonesboro in two hours.
10. The ground, having become too dry, began to crack.
11. Finally the scuba diver emerged on the port side of the boat.
12. Having written several gothic novels, Mary Stewart is an author known to many.
13. Rosebushes of that kind need careful tending.
14. At the street fair, we enjoyed watching the mimes.
15. Shoppers laden with packages bustled here and there.

B Identifying Clauses Indicate whether each group of italicized words is an *Independent Clause* or a *Subordinate Clause.* For each subordinate clause, tell whether it is an *Adjective, Adverb,* or *Noun.*

1. *When you are shopping for winter clothes,* you should consider warmth as well as price and fit.
2. William Pitt was a statesman of great intellect, but *his physical health was poor.*
3. A history play on the career of Henry VIII was the last known work *that Shakespeare wrote.*
4. Our newspaper endorsed the candidate *who is the most qualified.*

5. *What career you pursue* will depend upon your interests.
6. *When the referee blows the whistle,* leap for the ball.
7. Although Francis Drake's treatment of Spanish ships sometimes amounted to piracy, *the Queen of England permitted and encouraged his activities.*
8. The family that you are born into and the people *that you meet* help shape your social behavior and attitudes.
9. Do you know *who wrote the biography of Carrie Chapman*?
10. While the band was playing, *several guards stood in front of the stage.*
11. Mark Twain said *that cauliflower is just a cabbage with a college education.*
12. A crampon is one of the tools *that a mountain climber uses.*
13. Ever since she read about Mark Twain's life, *she has wanted to ride on a riverboat.*
14. *Because some germs have become resistant to antibiotics,* it may be getting harder to fight disease.
15. *Can you tell* which mushroom is edible?

C Identifying Sentence Types Identify each sentence as *Simple, Compound, Complex,* or *Compound-Complex.* In addition, find each subordinate clause and tell what kind it is—*Adjective, Adverb,* or *Noun.*

1. Blane demonstrated how she weaves cloth on a loom.
2. The owl screeched as it captured its prey.
3. Black and white photographs can be very dramatic.
4. Did a court jester juggle, or did he just tell jokes?
5. A pilot must consider temperature, wind, and visibility.
6. Darryl dropped the bag that contained the two dozen eggs, and then he slipped and dropped the bottle of milk.
7. Since she was very young, Bernice has collected hats.
8. Some shoppers hurried through the aisles, but others browsed.
9. While the band members marched, they formed designs on the field.
10. Bert fed the horse oats, and then he placed a blanket on its back while Laura untangled the bridle.
11. The popular play *Cats* was based on a series of poems that T.S. Eliot wrote about cats.
12. What annoys Mr. Berman most is tardiness.
13. The Chicago Fire of 1871 destroyed much of the city.
14. If the ice caps melted, much of the earth would be flooded, and the temperature would change throughout the world.
15. Joshua wants to visit Russia, but he speaks only English.

24

Writing Complete Sentences

*T*ry to imagine what this picture would look like if it were complete. Could you have guessed that the girl in pink was actually holding a catcher's mitt? Could you have known that the boy in the red shirt had a hulahoop around his waist?

Whenever you have to guess at what is missing, you run the risk of guessing wrong. That is why writers try to express their ideas as completely as possible, rather than in fragments. One way they do this is by writing in complete sentences.

In this chapter you will learn to write in complete sentences as well as to recognize and revise sentence fragments and run-on sentences. This will lessen the possibility that your meaning will be mistaken.

Sentence Fragments

A sentence fragment is a group of words that is only part of a sentence.

As you learned in Chapters 22 and 23, a sentence must express a complete thought and must have at least one subject and one verb. Many sentence fragments lack either a subject or a verb.

Fragment	Will begin at 7:30 A.M. on Saturday. (What will begin? The subject is missing.)
Sentence	*The crew race* will begin at 7:30 A.M. on Saturday.
Fragment	Eight boats in the race around Manhattan. (What about the race? The verb is missing.)
Sentence	Eight boats *are competing* in the race around Manhattan.

Sometimes a fragment lacks both a subject and a verb.

Fragment	Under the Brooklyn Bridge. (Who or what is under the bridge? What is happening there?)
Sentence	*The boats will pass* under the Brooklyn Bridge.

As you will see in the discussion that follows, fragments often result from incomplete thoughts or incorrect punctuation.

Fragments Because of Incomplete Thought

You can think much faster than you can write. Many sentence fragments occur, therefore, because your mind has raced ahead of your hand. As a result you may find yourself writing a second thought before you have completed the first. In other cases you may discover that you have left out a key part of a sentence. Suppose, for example, that you wrote the following passage:

> In 1215 King John was presented with the Magna Carta. His nobles and churchmen forced him to sign the document. Establishing the principle that even the king must obey the law.

The third group of words in the paragraph above is not a sentence because it does not express a complete thought. The reader can only suppose that you meant to say that the Magna Carta established the principle described.

Exercises

A On your paper, write *S* for each group of words below that is a sentence. Write *F* for each sentence fragment. Then add words to change the fragments into sentences.

1. In a corner of the garage, the missing box of kitchen utensils.
2. Not a word appeared in the newspapers about the burglary.
3. Anyone who returns the valuable jewelry.
4. Huge trucks rolling along the nation's highways all night long.
5. Mr. Walters, one of the oldest residents of the nursing home.
6. Most of the classics are available in inexpensive editions.
7. Unfortunately a program just like several others.
8. Whenever she stays up too late.
9. A broad band of showers arriving from the southeast.
10. Several ambulances and police cars at the scene of the accident.

B Three of the groups of words in the following paragraph are sentences. The rest are fragments. On your paper, rewrite the paragraph, adding words to make the fragments into sentences.

(1) Ghost towns all across the country. (2) Pithole, Pennsylvania, one of the most famous. (3) It flourished for ten years. (4) For a time more than twenty thousand people in the town. (5) However, everyone left after the oil dried up. (6) Elsewhere, ghost towns in timber country. (7) Modern ghost towns in the iron mining regions of Minnesota. (8) The best-known in the mining sections of the West. (9) Houses full of furniture and offices with papers still in the desks. (10) Wherever the resources gave out, there are ghost towns.

Ghost town near Cody, Wyoming.

Fragments Because of Incorrect Punctuation

Sentences begin with a capital letter and end with a period, a question mark, or an exclamation point. Many fragments occur because the writer inserts end punctuation and a capital letter too soon.

Fragment	We will leave. *As soon as the dishes are done.*
Sentence	We will leave as soon as the dishes are done.
Fragment	*Before signing the bill.* The President congratulated the cosponsors.
Sentence	Before signing the bill, the President congratulated the cosponsors.

Exercises

A Each pair of word groups below contains one fragment and one sentence. Write each fragment on your paper. Then join each pair of word groups into one complete sentence by changing the punctuation and capitalization.

1. Once again the sirens wailed. Because of another accident.
2. Everyone liked my taco casserole. And the green bean salad.
3. The delegation arrived in Los Angeles. Just before midnight.
4. Mr. Wilkins Micawber was a character in *David Copperfield*. Who always felt that something would turn up.
5. Please send in your subscription. As soon as possible.
6. To improve her speaking skills. Linda joined the debate team.
7. Kim teaches yoga and aerobics three days a week. From 9 A.M. to 10:30 A.M.
8. The average American teen-ager watches television. More than twenty hours a week.
9. At the beginning of this century. Motoring was an adventure.
10. The team was still in the huddle. When time ran out.

B On your paper, write five complete sentences by combining a sentence in the left column with a fragment in the right column. Capitalize and punctuate your sentences correctly.

1. Did you finish your project?	A. Singing the theme from *Fame*
2. My cousin sold his bike.	B. At the band audition
3. The manager hired more ushers.	C. To work during the concert
4. Leo played effortlessly.	D. And bought a new tape recorder
5. Susan danced across the floor.	E. In time for the deadline

c *Proofreading* On your paper, rewrite the following paragraph, correcting the sentence fragments. Also correct any other errors in punctuation, spelling, and capitalization.

> The new Presidency. One of the last important issues at the Constitutional Convention. The resolution of this issue was largely due to the effort of james Wilson. An Immigrant from Scotland. James Madison had originally proposed that the President should be chosen by Congress. However, Wilson argued. That the President should draw his strength from a popular election. He would thus be accountabel directly to the people, further guaranteeing a genuine seperation of powers.

Part 2
Phrases and Clauses as Fragments

As you know, a **phrase** is a group of words that does not contain a subject and a verb. Therefore, a phrase cannot be a sentence; it can only be a fragment.

A common mistake occurs when a verbal phrase is mistaken for a complete sentence. This error occurs because verbals (gerunds, participles, infinitives) look like verbs and function somewhat like verbs. They are not verbs, however, and cannot be used as such.

The most troublesome verbals are those that end in *-ing*, such as *running* and *searching*. All gerunds and present participles end in *-ing*, and thus are often mistaken for verbs. You will avoid many sentence errors if you remember the following fact:

No word ending in *-ing* can be a complete verb unless it is a one-syllable word like *sing, ring,* or *bring*.

If an *-ing* word is preceded by *is, are, was,* or some other form of *be,* the words together are a verb: *is running, were searching*.

When you discover that a verbal phrase has been used as a fragment, you can correct it in one of two ways. Either add the verbal phrase to an already complete sentence or change the verbal into a verb and use it in a sentence.

The chart on the following page shows how different kinds of phrases, including verbals, can be rewritten as complete sentences.

Participial Phrase	Covered with ice
Sentence	*Covered with ice,* the roads were impassable. (The phrase is added to a sentence.)
Sentence	The roads *were covered with ice.* (A subject is provided and an auxiliary verb is combined with the participle to make a verb phrase.)
Gerund Phrase	Canoeing across the lake
Sentence	I enjoy *canoeing across the lake.* (A subject and verb are added. The gerund becomes a direct object.)
Sentence	*Canoeing across the lake* is risky. (The gerund phrase becomes the subject of the sentence.)
Infinitive Phrase	To see the midnight sun
Sentence	Wendy and I have always wanted *to see the midnight sun.* (A subject and verb are added. The infinitive phrase becomes the direct object.)
Sentence	*To see the midnight sun* must be thrilling. (The infinitive phrase has become the subject.)
Sentence	It must be thrilling *to see the midnight sun.* (The infinitive phrase modifies *thrilling.*)
Prepositional Phrase	At the end of a long day
Sentence	Everyone enjoys relaxing *at the end of a long day.* (The phrase is added to a sentence.)
Sentence	*At the end of a long day,* Sheila takes a brisk walk. (The phrase is added to a sentence.)
Appositive Phrase	One a true story and the other fiction
Sentence	Both books, *one a true story and the other fiction,* were best sellers. (The phrase is added to a sentence.)

Series Fragments

Occasionally, items listed in a series may be so long or so complicated that they are mistaken for a sentence. This is especially true if the series is composed of verbal phrases. Series fragments may lack either a subject or a verb or both.

Series Fragment   Having hoped, having dreamed, and finally having won the trophy.

Sentence   *Having hoped, having dreamed, and finally having won,* Kimo clutched the trophy. (A subject and verb are added.)

Exercise

On your paper, correct each of the following sentence fragments by writing a complete sentence. Use one of the types of corrections shown in the chart on page 581.

1. The cymbidium, an Asian orchid of moderate size
2. A seventeenth-century scientist
3. Studying the ocean floor
4. About her bid for the Presidency
5. Soaking the rice paste, stirring the mixture, and finally making the rice paper
6. To become a skilled surgeon
7. Piled with books and papers
8. Starring my favorite singing group
9. Behind the hideous mask
10. Hippocrates, the Greek physician

Subordinate Clauses as Fragments

Unlike a phrase, a subordinate clause does have a subject and a verb. However, a subordinate clause does not express a complete thought and cannot be a sentence. Combine a subordinate clause with an independent clause to correct this kind of fragment.

Fragment   As soon as we saw the flames.
Sentence   *As soon as we saw the flames,* we dialed 911.

Another way to correct a fragment that is a subordinate clause is to rewrite the clause as a sentence.

Fragment   Trevor Library, which seemed like a stuffy old mausoleum.
Sentence   *Trevor Library seemed like a stuffy old mausoleum.*

Fragments in Conversation

Fragments often occur in conversation without harming communication. Tone of voice, gestures, and the presence of each speaker all help to add meaning and keep ideas clear.

Sentence   When is the canceled game going to be played?
Fragment   Probably Thursday.
Fragment   Morning or afternoon?
Fragment   After lunch, if it doesn't rain.

Professional writers sometimes use fragments when they want to create realistic dialogue, establish a certain mood, or achieve a particular rhythm in their prose. These professional writers know the rules of grammar but are consciously breaking these rules for a specific purpose.

Exercises

A On your paper, correct the fragments in each of the following groups of words.

1. To enhance the flavor of a dish, chefs often use the zest. Which is the outermost part of the rind of a lemon or an orange.
2. The tall figure of a man who appeared in the doorway.
3. Although James Michener's novel *Centennial* is unusually long. It is certainly worth reading.
4. The sky was blue and the sun shining. When we arrived at the lodge in Yellowstone Park.

ight well I got up this morning I was late for school it sm

5. To go on a photographic safari in Africa.
6. Just as he raised the camera. The animal disappeared.
7. India has over two hundred languages. And many religions.
8. Linda is studying forestry. Because she is concerned about the environment.
9. The rock collection that belongs to Dwayne's father.
10. The climbers carefully checked their pitons. Which are spikes used for climbing steep rock faces.

B Application in Literature Professional writers sometimes use fragments intentionally to establish a mood or to create realistic dialogue. List the fragments in the selection below. Rewrite each fragment as a sentence. Compare your sentences with the original. Be prepared to explain why you think Steinbeck chose to use fragments in this passage. (Notice that the author has also ignored some punctuation rules.)

(1) But most of the families changed and grew quickly into the new life. (2) And when the sun went down—

(3) Time to look out for a place to stop.

(4) And—there's some tents ahead.

(5) The car pulled off the road and stopped, and because others were there first, certain courtesies were necessary. (6) And the man, the leader of the family, leaned from the car.

(7) Can we pull up here an' sleep?

(8) Why, sure, be proud to have you. (9) What State you from?

(10) Come all the way from Arkansas.

(11) They's Arkansas people down that fourth tent.

(12) That so?

(13) And the great question, How's the water?

(14) Well, she don't taste so good, but they's plenty.

(15) Well, thank ya.

(16) No thanks to me.

(17) But the courtesies had to be.

From *The Grapes of Wrath* by John Steinbeck

c *Write Now* Transcribe or tape record a short conversation that you hear during your day at school. Make a list of the fragments in the conversation. Rewrite the conversation changing all the fragments to complete sentences.

much

last night all the buses had stopped running I slid on the ice and fell flat on my face off I was my boots and had to take them our snow job my boots and had to

Part 3
Run-on Sentences

A run-on sentence is two or more sentences written as though they were one sentence.

In some run-on sentences the writer fails to use an end mark at the end of each sentence.

Run-on   The tide is out now the water is only a foot deep.
Correct   The tide is out. Now the water is only a foot deep.

In other run-on sentences the writer uses a comma instead of an end mark. This error is called the **comma fault** or **comma splice.**

Run-on   Don't worry about Joe, he can take care of himself.
Correct   Don't worry about Joe. He can take care of himself.

Correcting Run-on Sentences

There are several ways to correct run-on sentences. In both corrections above, the run-on sentence has been rewritten as two separate sentences. Sometimes, however, when the ideas expressed are closely related, it is preferable to join them into a single sentence.

You can join the sentences with a comma and a coordinating conjunction.

Run-on   The demonstrators were orderly, the mayor willingly listened to their complaints.
Correct   The demonstrators were orderly, **and** the mayor willingly listened to their complaints.

You can join the sentences with a semicolon.

Run-on   The demonstrators were orderly, the mayor willingly listened to
            their complaints.
Correct   The demonstrators were orderly; the mayor willingly listened to
            their complaints.

You can join the sentences with a semicolon and a conjunctive adverb. (See page 500 for a list of conjunctive adverbs.)

Run-on   The demonstrators were orderly, the mayor willingly listened to
            their complaints.
Correct   The demonstrators were orderly; **consequently,** the mayor
            willingly listened to their complaints.

Grammar Note Each correct sentence above is a compound sentence with two independent clauses. (See pages 565–566 for more about independent clauses and compound sentences.)

Exercises

A On your paper, correct each of the following run-on sentences by (1) using end punctuation and capitalization to separate the sentences; (2) joining the sentences with a comma and a coordinating conjunction; or (3) joining the sentences with a semicolon or with a semicolon and a conjunctive adverb. Do not correct every sentence the same way.

1. We flew to LaGuardia Airport then we took the shuttle to Washington.
2. I try to practice the flute every day, I don't always have time.
3. Christy Brown overcame incredible handicaps, he became an outstanding writer.
4. The marketplace was dusty and crowded, everywhere vendors hawked their wares.
5. The small skiff edged carefully out of the harbor the wind changed suddenly.
6. At the end of Hawthorne's *The Scarlet Letter,* Hester returned to Boston Pearl remained in England.
7. My father is colorblind, he needs no help coordinating his ties, shirts, and suits.
8. The contestant hesitated too long, the buzzer ended his turn.
9. Neal can try to make the Olympic team, he can turn pro.
10. The critic did not like the play, he wrote a scathing review.

11. Racehorses in the Northern Hemisphere have their official birthday on January first, in the Southern Hemisphere the date is August first.
12. Friendly Indians allowed wagon trains to pass through their hunting grounds, some even helped the pioneers.
13. John took a special class in computers he thought it would help him find a summer job.
14. Our bus broke down on the way to school, it broke down again on the way home.
15. It isn't a new dress, I wore it to homecoming last year.

B Copy this paragraph, correcting the run-on sentences.

Joseph William Turner was one of Britain's greatest painters. When he died in 1851, he willed all of his paintings to his beloved country, England this gesture, although generous, caused the government a great deal of trouble. Turner's family immediately set about to upset the will, claiming that the artist was not of sound mind when he

Slave Ship, J. W. Turner, 1840.

wrote it. Their efforts were unsuccessful Turner's work, finished and unfinished, was delivered to the National Gallery. The gallery, unprepared to accept such a volume of work, stored the canvases in the basement. In 1910, Turner's work was to be displayed it was to hang in the Tate Gallery, an annex of the National Gallery. Instead, the works went from one basement to another. The Thames River overflowed in 1928 many of the canvases were severely damaged. Now, 136 years after Turner's death, his works hang in a new gallery designed solely to display Turner's work finally the conditions of the will are fulfilled.

c *Proofreading* On your paper, write the following paragraph, correcting all the run-on sentences. Also correct any errors in spelling, punctuation, and capitalization.

Many people agree that Wilt Chamberlain was the gratest player in the history of the National basketball Association, he still holds an incredable number of records. In one Season he played more on-court minutes than any other player. He led the league in scoring for seven strait years, and he has scored the most lifetime points his record is 31,419 points scored. In a game against New York in 1962, Chamberlain scored fifty nine points in one half, he ended up scoring one hundred points in the game. He was also a champion rebounder, he led the league in rebounds for eleven seasons, for a career total of 23,924. Chamberlain played for Philadelphia San Francisco and los Angeles all three teems wish they had him back.

Checkpoint *Parts 1, 2, and 3*

Rewrite the following fragments and run-ons as complete sentences.

1. The Union Pacific Railroad was completed in 1869. Linking the country from coast to coast.
2. The Siberian tiger is powerful the Indian tiger is more powerful.
3. The fossil which is sixty-five million years old.
4. To unlock the mystery of the Abominable Snowman.
5. Two bathrooms, a large sunny kitchen, and a two-car garage.
6. Guppies are easy to care for other fish provide color and variety in an aquarium.
7. Jupiter is a mystery. Because it is wrapped in clouds.
8. Eaves are part of the roof they protect the outside walls.
9. We like pizza with thin crust they prefer the thick variety.
10. Firecrackers, having originated in ancient China.
11. Nero ruled Rome wisely for a time. Then became obsessed by a fear that he would lose his ability to govern.
12. The hikers arose refreshed. After sleeping only a short time.
13. Tarragon is an herb it should be used sparingly.
14. There are three varieties of mangoes Hayden, turpentine, and pineapple.
15. Since push buttons became popular, It has become more and more unusual to see a telephone with a rotary dial.

Linking
Grammar & Writing

Imagine that you are searching for a lost group of explorers in the Amazon jungle. You receive a radio communication from the explorers. However, the signal is faint, and you can only hear fragments of what is said. Read the fragments listed below. Then write a draft of the complete radio message by turning the fragments into sentences.

> . . . is Captain . . . not lost . . . located about three miles northeast of the village Quizotl . . . ten days . . . cannot move . . . explosion in our camp . . . Julio, of the Amazon exploration team . . . most of our party . . . quickly . . . medical supplies and blankets.

Prewriting and Drafting At the top of a page, make a column for each of the following questions: *Who? What? Where? When? How?* Place each fragment in a column that you think is appropriate. Then turn the fragments into complete sentences that help to explain what happened to the explorers. Your draft of the complete radio message should fully explain what happened.

Revising and Proofreading When revising your draft, consider the following questions:

1. Is the radio message complete and logical?
2. Can the reader easily follow the order of events?
3. Are fragments and run-on sentences avoided?

Additional Writing Topic Thumb through recent magazines or newspapers and look for sentence fragments in the headlines of advertisements. Turn the headline fragments into sentences that describe your personality or your current life. Then write a paragraph that connects your sentences and forms an interesting or humorous self-description. The following paragraph gives an example of this kind of description; the underlined phrases show the advertisement fragments.

> I feel better than ever, new and improved, and brighter and bolder. Now that I have a part-time job, I'm going to be all that I can be. I believe that, since you only go around once in life, you have to grab all the gusto you can. The best part is I can buy what I want at unbelievably low, low prices. I am definitely participating in part of the American dream.

Chapter 24
Application and Review

A Identifying Fragments, Sentences, and Run-ons Identify each of the following word groups as *F* (fragment), *S* (sentence), or *R* (run-on sentence). Then correct each fragment and run-on.

1. Researchers are trying to understand how memory works they are mapping where the brain forms and stores memories.
2. Because patients undergoing brain surgery do not need to be unconscious during the surgery. Patients can tell surgeons what they experience when parts of their brain are stimulated.
3. The cortex, which is the brain's wrinkled covering. Is the location of higher complicated thought activities.
4. The wrinkles and folds of the cortex. Increase its surface area.
5. Scientists compare tracing the pattern of memory in the brain to the myth of Theseus following the thread in the labyrinth of the Minotaur.
6. Memories-to-be enter the cortex and are analyzed then eventually they find their way deeper into the brain.
7. There, spouting chemical fountains. Which etch the item to be remembered into the brain somewhat like a picture is etched onto film.
8. Synapses are connections where a nerve impulse jumps from one brain cell to the next.
9. Synapses form patterns. Like spider webs throughout the brain.
10. In the future when researchers finally unlock the mysteries of synapse patterns.

B Correcting Fragments Correct the fragments in the following paragraph by connecting them to make complete sentences.

> Every year, people come from all over America. To gather in the little community of Bean Blossom, Indiana. And take part in the annual Bill Monroe Bluegrass Festival. The festival is a combination of old and new. A celebration of traditional and contemporary bluegrass music. It offers the finest in good old-fashioned, foot-stomping entertainment. Including music by some of the best bluegrass bands in the country. Visitors to the festival stroll up and down several acres of Indiana countryside. Listening to melodies like "Salty Dog" and "*T* for Texas." They can applaud the highly skilled musicians. Who play on instruments ranging from banjos and mandolins. To fiddles, autoharps, and guitars, both electric and acoustic.

C Correcting Run-on Sentences Correct each of the run-on sentences in the following paragraph. Use your judgment to decide the best way to correct the run-ons. For some run-ons, simply separate the sentences into two. For others, use commas with corresponding conjunctions, semicolons, or semicolons with conjunctive adverbs.

None of us could believe that Harry was guilty, he had never been known to do anything dishonest. He had always been careful to give customers the exact change, yet he was now charged with pilfering the cash register at his checkout counter. The manager himself usually picked up the extra cash twice a day, however, on Thursday evening he waited until the store closed for the night. He put Harry's cash in a separate bag, then he locked it up in the safe. When he counted it the next morning, it was ten dollars short. The manager accused Harry of pocketing the money, however, Harry denied the charge. He thought for a while, then he asked to count the money. The manager agreed, he stood beside Harry while he counted. Harry went through each stack of bills slowly, finally Harry found the ten dollars. Two ten-dollar bills had stuck together. The manager and his assistant apologized, they even let Harry pick up the cash from all of the other checkout counters in the store the next week to show that they trusted him. They never questioned Harry's honesty again.

D Correcting Fragments and Run-ons Rewrite the following paragraph, correcting all sentence fragments and run-ons. Use the methods you have learned in this chapter.

Theodore Roosevelt, the twenty-sixth president of the United States. He is remembered for his hunting trips although he believed that his most important achievement in public life was his effort to conserve forests and help wildlife. Roosevelt claimed that "The American had but one thought about a tree, and that was to cut it down." In order to preserve the beautiful forests of the United States. Roosevelt created the Forest Service in 1905, he set aside 150 million acres of forest reserves and formed a number of national parks.

The bespectacled New Yorker, who had been a sickly child. He traveled extensively. As a young man who enjoyed riding through the West. Here he saw that much of the wildlife of the country was disappearing. Such as buffalo, wild turkey, and elk. He established wildlife and waterfowl refuges. To protect many endangered species.

However the animal that Roosevelt did the most to "protect" is the bear, the "Teddy" bear was named after this president when he refused to shoot an old, almost-blind bear while on a hunting trip.

Cumulative Review

Chapters 23 and 24

A Identifying Phrases and Clauses Determine whether each group of italicized words in the sentences below is a phrase (*P*) or a clause (*C*). Then identify each phrase as *Prepositional*, *Appositive*, or *Verbal*. Identify each of the clauses as *Adjective*, *Noun*, *Adverb*, or *Independent*.

> *Example*   *Although he was born into poverty,* Gabriel
> García Marquez became a world-famous
> writer. *C, Adverb*

1. Many writers of great literature have had *to overcome physical or psychological adversity.*
2. The poet John Keats wrote some of his best-known works while suffering from tuberculosis, *a common disease of his era.*
3. The epileptic seizures of the Russian novelist Feodor Dostoevski were so severe that it took him days to recover; for much of his career *he was also overwhelmed with debts.*
4. *At various stages in her career,* Virginia Woolf experienced bouts of mental illness that prevented her from writing.
5. *John Milton wrote his most famous poem* after he had completely lost his sight.
6. The novelist Richard Wright overcame a childhood of hunger and prejudice, *and he became a powerful writer.*
7. Flannery O'Connor continued *writing short stories,* though she had an incurable disease which eventually took her life.
8. O. Henry, *who became a master of the short story,* began his writing career while in prison.
9. While *working as a hotel busboy,* Langston Hughes showed Vachel Lindsay his poems; soon a book of his poems was published.
10. The power *of Elie Wiesel's novels* can be traced to his childhood experience in concentration camps.
11. *After his father was imprisoned for debt,* the twelve-year-old Charles Dickens went to work in a factory.
12. Alice Walker was blinded in one eye as a child; *writing fiction* helped her escape from the taunts of her classmates.
13. *How the young orphan Jerzy Kosinski survived in war-torn Europe* became the subject for his highly praised novel.

14. *Katherine Mansfield spent her last years as an invalid,* yet during that time she wrote some of her best stories.
15. The Argentine writer Jorge Borges wrote many of his finest short stories *after he became totally blind.*

B Recognizing Sentence Structures Number your paper from 1–15. Describe the structure of each sentence in Exercise A as *Simple, Compound, Complex,* or *Compound-Complex.*

C Correcting Fragments and Run-on Sentences Rewrite the following paragraphs to correct all errors.

> The Old City of Jerusalem is a holy place to Muslims, Christians, and Jews. Containing within its walls the place from which Muslims believe that Mohammed ascended to heaven, the spot where Christians believe Jesus was killed and rose again, and the site where Jews believe Solomon's Temple once stood. The Old City makes up less than one percent of the modern city of Jerusalem, Israel's largest city is now the home of about 407,000 people.
>
> In A.D. 1099 Christian crusaders fought Jews and Muslims, established a kingdom in Jerusalem that lasted for about one hundred years. For the next six hundred years, the city was inhabited mainly by Muslims from Egypt, Syria, and Turkey. Until 1917, when a British army captured the city. After this, both Jews and Muslims flocked there. Jerusalem was a divided city until 1967, when Israel won control of the entire city. In the Six Day war.
>
> Today Muslims, Christians, and Jews live in the city, however, relations among them are sometimes stormy. Even violent. Despite the violence, Jerusalem continues to be holy land for three religions.

D Finding Misplaced and Dangling Modifiers Rewrite the following letter to correct problems with modifiers.

```
Dear Clyde,
    Answering your letter, my cow gave birth to a
beautiful calf. It was born while you were in Atlanta
bellowing for all the world to hear. I remembered
your letter soon after I first saw the calf in the
middle of dinner. I wanted to tell you only good news,
but I must also tell you that your goldfish died,
wishing you were here.
```

25

Using Verbs

*E*xaggerated actions, brightly colored costumes, and dramatic
makeup—these are the outstanding features of Japan's
kabuki theater. However, long after the costumes and
makeup have ceased to startle and delight the audience,
the action continues to captivate. Action tells the story
of the drama.

Similarly, readers rely on verbs to tell the story of a
sentence. In this chapter you will learn to use verb
tenses correctly and to differentiate between verbs that
are often confused. This will help you to communicate
more effectively and precisely.

The Principal Parts of Verbs

Before you study the many forms of verbs, you may want to review some basic facts.

A **verb** is a word that expresses an action, a condition, or a state of being. Verbs are divided into two main categories. **Action verbs** describe a physical or mental action that someone is performing. **Linking verbs** do not express action. Rather, they serve as a link between the subject of the sentence and a word in the predicate that renames or describes the subject. For more information about verbs, see Chapter 21, pages 478–483.

Every verb has many different forms. All of these forms are made from the four **principal parts** of the verb: the **present infinitive** (usually called the **present**), the **present participle,** the **past,** and the **past participle.**

Present	Present Participle	Past	Past Participle
talk	(is) talking	talked	(have) talked
sing	(is) singing	sang	(have) sung
put	(is) putting	put	(have) put

In the examples above, notice that the present participle and the past participle are preceded by *is* and *have*. This is to show that these forms are always used with helping verbs. Also note that the present participle ends with *-ing*. This ending does not change; all verbs add *-ing* to the present to form the present participle. The endings of the past and the past participle, however, do change from verb to verb; the past and the past participle may be formed in several ways. These endings determine whether a verb is regular or irregular.

Regular Verbs

A regular verb is one to which *-ed* or *-d* is added to the present in order to form the past and the past participle. Most verbs are regular.

Some regular verbs change their spelling slightly when *-ing* or *-ed* is added to the present.

Present	Present Participle	Past	Past Participle
trip	(is) tripping	tripped	(have) tripped
spy	(is) spying	spied	(have) spied
picnic	(is) picnicking	picnicked	(have) picnicked

Exercise

On your paper, make four columns in which you list the principal parts of the following regular verbs.

1. grab	6. carry	11. clean
2. expel	7. disappear	12. admit
3. occur	8. regret	13. limit
4. narrate	9. move	14. receive
5. achieve	10. satisfy	15. omit

Irregular Verbs

An **irregular** verb is a verb that does not form the past and past participle by adding *-ed* or *-d* to the present. Irregular verbs form the past and past participle in a variety of ways.

There are approximately sixty commonly used verbs in this category. Several examples are given below.

Present	Present Participle	Past	Past Participle
put	(is) putting	put	(have) put
say	(is) saying	said	(have) said
tear	(is) tearing	tore	(have) torn
ring	(is) ringing	rang	(have) rung
throw	(is) throwing	threw	(have) thrown
go	(is) going	went	(have) gone
freeze	(is) freezing	froze	(have) frozen

Because the principal parts of irregular verbs are formed in a variety of ways, you must either memorize these parts or refer to a dictionary. The dictionary will list the principal parts of all irregular verbs. Remembering the parts of irregular verbs will be simpler if you break them down into the five groups that follow.

Group 1 The easiest of the irregular verbs to remember are those that have the same form for the present, the past, and the past participle.

Present	Present Participle	Past	Past Participle
burst	(is) bursting	burst	(have) burst
cost	(is) costing	cost	(have) cost
cut	(is) cutting	cut	(have) cut
hit	(is) hitting	hit	(have) hit
hurt	(is) hurting	hurt	(have) hurt
put	(is) putting	put	(have) put
set	(is) setting	set	(have) set
shut	(is) shutting	shut	(have) shut

Group 2 The irregular verbs in this group have the same form for the past and the past participle.

Present	Present Participle	Past	Past Participle
bring	(is) bringing	brought	(have) brought
catch	(is) catching	caught	(have) caught
fight	(is) fighting	fought	(have) fought
flee	(is) fleeing	fled	(have) fled
fling	(is) flinging	flung	(have) flung
get	(is) getting	got	(have) got
			or gotten
lead	(is) leading	led	(have) led
lend	(is) lending	lent	(have) lent
lose	(is) losing	lost	(have) lost
say	(is) saying	said	(have) said
shine	(is) shining	shone	(have) shone
		or shined	*or* shined
sit	(is) sitting	sat	(have) sat
sting	(is) stinging	stung	(have) stung
swing	(is) swinging	swung	(have) swung
teach	(is) teaching	taught	(have) taught

Usage Note Both *got* and *gotten* are standard usage. However, *got* is more common. Both *shone* and *shined* are standard usage, but *shone* is used when there is no direct object.

Beginning duck.

Exercises

A On your paper, write the past or the past participle form of the verb given in parentheses. Keep in mind that the past participle is used with a form of the auxiliary verb *have*.

1. Of all of Sherlock Holmes's cases, "The Adventure of the Speckled Band" (teach) me not to jump to conclusions.
2. A young woman named Stoner (sit) in Holmes's study.
3. She (say) that lately she had (put) some rather strange facts together.
4. Her stepfather had (bring) a cheetah and a baboon from India and had not (shut) them up, but had let them run loose.
5. Suddenly the nervous visitor (flee) from Holmes's study.
6. Holmes (lead) and I followed to the young lady's estate.
7. The moon (shine) brightly across the lawn.
8. We (catch) sight of a baboon who (swing) down from a tree.
9. I (fight) back thoughts that I had (lose) my mind.
10. We entered the house, where things (get) even more curious.
11. Ms. Stoner's sister Julie had mysteriously died, and rumors had (got) around about the cause of her death.
12. The stepfather had (lend) the use of Julie's bedroom to Ms. Stoner.
13. Each night a strange whistle had been heard, and a light (shine) from the middle window.
14. One night we watched and then (burst) into the bedroom.
15. There, in Ms. Stoner's bed, was a deadly Indian swamp adder; fortunately it had not (hurt) Ms. Stoner.

Scene from the film *The Adventures of Sherlock Holmes.*

B Find the verb that is used incorrectly in each sentence. Write the correct form on your paper. If a sentence has no verb errors, write *Correct*.

1. Mr. Chin brang out his collection of jade carvings.
2. The rookie quickly reached up and miraculously catched the hard-hit line drive.
3. The Cheshire cat set in a tree and grinned at Alice.
4. Robert Graves sayed that love is a universal headache.
5. At the finish line, the cyclists bursted through the ribbon.
6. Jellyfish have stinged many unsuspecting swimmers.
7. As the motor launch approached, the dolphins fled.
8. A careless motorist flinged a bag of litter from the car.
9. Carleen must have lended the lawnmower to the Johnsons.
10. The small passenger plane must have losed its way in the mysterious Bermuda Triangle.
11. Mack shut one eye and spied through the keyhold.
12. The aerialist swinged gracefully through the air.
13. Spanish conquistadors leaded many expeditions in hopes of finding the legendary land of El Dorado.
14. In medieval times spices costed a great deal of money.
15. Extensive vaccination programs have bringed an end to smallpox in the United States.

C *Proofreading* Rewrite the paragraph correcting errors in spelling, punctuation, capitalization, and verb forms.

> As I sayed to that agriculture expert who came down here from the capitol, the kudzu's not a plant—its a green monster. Now, you may think Im exaggerating, but you should have seen what happened to that agriculture man when he tried to show the farmers around hear how to get rid of this pesky weed. If he had been smart, he would have fleed Instead, that so-called Expert getted out a can of weedkiller. I guess he figgered that plant was just going to lie there while he sprayed it. That old kudzu certainly teached him a lesson! It was a site! The vine catched him, swinged him right off the ground and putted him down in the top of a sycamore tree. well we called the volunteer fire department, and they brung ladders to get him down. When that vine herd the sirens, though, it grabbed him again and flang him up until his head bursted through the underside of a cloud. I guess he would have starved to death if I hadn't lended the fire department my shotgun so they could shoot biscuits up to him. I tell you, that kudzu's mean. So far, everyone that's fighted it has losed.

Group 3 The irregular verbs in this group form the past participle by adding *-n* or *-en* to the past.

Present	Present Participle	Past	Past Participle
bear	(is) bearing	bore	(have) borne
beat	(is) beating	beat	(have) beaten
bite	(is) biting	bit	(have) bitten *or* bit
break	(is) breaking	broke	(have) broken
choose	(is) choosing	chose	(have) chosen
freeze	(is) freezing	froze	(have) frozen
speak	(is) speaking	spoke	(have) spoken
steal	(is) stealing	stole	(have) stolen
swear	(is) swearing	swore	(have) sworn
tear	(is) tearing	tore	(have) torn
wear	(is) wearing	wore	(have) worn

Usage Note Both *bitten* and *bit* are standard. *Bitten* is more common.

Exercises

A On your paper, write the past or the past participle form of the verb given in parentheses.

1. The Guatemalan dancers (wear) elaborately embroidered costumes.
2. The council president has already been (swear) into office.
3. A test tube of the sulphuric compound (break) during the experiment, and a terrible stench filtered through the lab.
4. During the night, thieves (steal) the most precious painting from the collection at the museum.
5. The school board has (choose) an architect to design the new library.
6. The trapper's fingertips had almost (freeze) in the bitter cold.
7. Yesterday I (speak) to the manager about my job application.
8. The child had been (bite) by an unleashed dog.
9. She (bear) yesterday's bad news surprisingly well.
10. The championship team has (break) most of the school's track records.
11. The suspect (swear) he had been home reading poetry at the time the robbery was committed.
12. The wreckers (tear) down the abandoned hotel two weeks ago.
13. No one has ever (beat) Mr. Alvarez at backgammon.
14. Walden Pond had (freeze) solid by early November.
15. The general claimed that the rebel army (break) the truce first.

16. Poverty has not (beat) their resilient spirit.
17. Erosion and constant wind (wear) away the topsoil and created the great Dust Bowl of the 1930's.
18. I have (speak) in public often, but I still get nervous.
19. Gale-force winds have (tear) doors off hinges, turned over cars, and toppled telephone poles.
20. The aging athlete may have (steal) his last base.

B Find the verb that is used incorrectly in each sentence. Write the correct form on your paper. If a sentence has no verb errors, write *Correct*.

1. I would like to know who stealed the radio in my locker.
2. Her top rival has not beat her in the last seven matches.
3. During dessert I thought I had bit into a piece of metal, but it was a nutshell.
4. Has the relentless heat broke any records this summer?
5. Elizabeth I of England had many suitors chose for her, but she never married any of them.
6. In last year's blizzard the car door freezed shut.
7. Ms. Hernández has spoke to school groups about the needs of the elderly.
8. The stowaways must have stolen onto the ship at night.
9. The defenders of the Alamo had swore to fight to the last man.
10. Someone has tore two pages out of this month's *National Geographic* magazine.
11. My father has worn the same rumpled hat for five years.
12. The natives beared the wounded warrior back to their camp and took him to the hut of the *shaman,* or witch doctor.
13. Our team has soundly beat most of the other contenders for the league championship.
14. Our community has bore the full force of the tax hike, but services have not improved.
15. Have you spoke to your parents about using the car?
16. Most of our dishes broke when the moving van came to a sudden and unexpected stop.
17. The principal has chose Ramona to welcome the senator.
18. Dad has froze several containers of his tomato sauce.
19. Construction crews teared up most of the roadway along the East River.
20. Over the years wind, rain, and pollution have wore away the detailed carvings on many ancient Greek buildings.

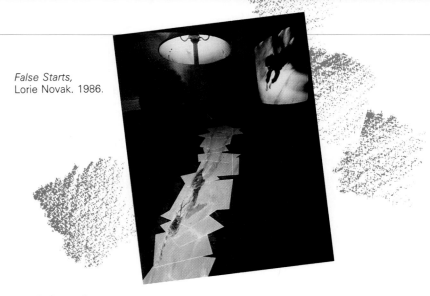

False Starts,
Lorie Novak. 1986.

C *Write Now* Fantasy stories often feature seemingly impossible circumstances or events, such as entering another dimension, traveling through time, or visiting another world. Let your imagination wander and create a fantasy story of your own. Use at least eight verbs from the lists on pages 596, 597, and 600.

Group 4 The irregular verbs in this group change a vowel to form the past and the past participle. The vowel changes from *i* in the present to *a* in the past to *u* in the past participle.

Present	Present Participle	Past	Past Participle
begin	(is) beginning	began	(have) begun
drink	(is) drinking	drank	(have) drunk
ring	(is) ringing	rang	(have) rung
shrink	(is) shrinking	shrank	(have) shrunk
sing	(is) singing	sang	(have) sung
sink	(is) sinking	sank	(have) sunk
spring	(is) springing	sprang	(have) sprung
		or sprung	
swim	(is) swimming	swam	(have) swum

Exercises

A On your paper, write the past or the past participle form of the verb given in parentheses.

1. The French Revolution, which (begin) in 1789, was caused by unfair taxation of the lower classes and reckless spending by the nobility.
2. By the end of Hawthorne's story "Dr. Heidegger's Experiment," four aging friends had (drink) water from the Fountain of Youth.

3. A suspicious-looking stranger (ring) the doorbell.
4. Woody Guthrie wrote and (sing) hundreds of folk songs about social and political themes.
5. The orchestra had already (begin) the overture when we arrived.
6. My brand-new "non-shrink" sweatshirt (shrink) two sizes when I washed it for the first time.
7. Sandy promised he'd call, but the phone hasn't (ring) all afternoon.
8. In 1898 the U.S. battleship *Maine* (sink) in Havana's harbor, killing 260 people.
9. Greek soldiers (spring) from inside a great wooden horse and defeated the Trojans.
10. The marathon swimmer Diana Nyad has (swim) across Lake Ontario and around Manhattan Island.
11. As predicted, the snow (begin) to fall shortly after midnight.
12. The alto (sing) off key during rehearsal.
13. The philosopher Plato wrote that the city of Atlantis (sink) into the sea after an earthquake.
14. The exhausted hunters (drink) greedily from the mountain stream.
15. Since February the value of the dollar has (shrink) dramatically.
16. As the band played, the crowd (sing) the national anthem.
17. Bells (ring) out across the nation in celebration of the bicentennial of the Constitution.
18. My head (swim) when I thought about what the changes would mean.
19. Suddenly the announcer's voice (sink) to a whisper.
20. Greek myths say that the goddess Athena (spring) full grown from the head of Zeus.

B Find the verb that is used incorrectly in each sentence. Write the correct form on your paper. If a sentence has no verb errors, write *Correct*.

1. The senior choir sung patriotic songs at the special assembly.
2. Our coach thinks that we have began the debate season with an extremely strong team.
3. Yesterday, Andrea sank a hole in one.
4. The crowd looked skeptical when the rabbit springed from the magician's hat.
5. The horses had already swum to the opposite bank.
6. Meghan drunk soda water with lemon juice before she sang.
7. The trained dogs rung a bell for food.
8. Troubadours of the twelfth and thirteenth centuries went from castle to castle, where they sung poems about love and war.

9. The Russian submarine had sank beneath the surface.
10. "I think this boat has sprang a leak," said Carolyn.
11. We suddenly begun to see what Mom was getting at.
12. Either my new jeans have shrank, or I ate too much dinner.
13. The cashier had already rang up the grocery order when I realized I didn't have enough money.
14. Have you ever drank fresh coconut milk or papaya juice?
15. The spectators shrunk back in fear as the orange car spun wildly out of control.
16. Schools of fish swam under the glass-bottom boat.
17. My sister begun classes last week at Kenyon College.
18. The damaged Liberian freighter sunk off the California coast.
19. My dad has sang in the "Do-It-Yourself-Messiah" in Philadelphia for the last three years.
20. Private investigator Jerome Jackson sprung up and answered the phone on the second ring.

Group 5 The irregular verbs in this group form the past participle from the present—often by adding *-n* or *-en*. In the list that follows, note the similarity between the present and the past participle forms.

Present	Present Participle	Past	Past Participle
blow	(is) blowing	blew	(have) blown
come	(is) coming	came	(have) come
do	(is) doing	did	(have) done
draw	(is) drawing	drew	(have) drawn
drive	(is) driving	drove	(have) driven
eat	(is) eating	ate	(have) eaten
fall	(is) falling	fell	(have) fallen
give	(is) giving	gave	(have) given
go	(is) going	went	(have) gone
grow	(is) growing	grew	(have) grown
know	(is) knowing	knew	(have) known
ride	(is) riding	rode	(have) ridden
rise	(is) rising	rose	(have) risen
run	(is) running	ran	(have) run
see	(is) seeing	saw	(have) seen
shake	(is) shaking	shook	(have) shaken
slay	(is) slaying	slew	(have) slain
take	(is) taking	took	(have) taken
throw	(is) throwing	threw	(have) thrown
write	(is) writing	wrote	(have) written

Exercises

A On your paper, write the past or the past participle form of the verb given in parentheses.

1. Several ships (blow) off course during the storm.
2. People have (come) from miles around to attend the auction.
3. My parents (do) their best to discourage me from quitting.
4. As usual, the Rose Bowl game (draw) a capacity crowd.
5. During the subway strike we (drive) into Manhattan every morning.
6. Moths have (eat) a hole in my best jacket.
7. Live power lines had (fall) across the road.
8. Mom has (give) an ultimatum: clean up your room or else!
9. Josh has (go) to Israel for the summer to work on a kibbutz.
10. As the yearbook deadline approached, we (grow) panicky.
11. When I was little I (know) all the names of the state capitals.
12. If you have ever (ride) a unicycle, you know how difficult it is.
13. Two deer (run) across the road in front of our car.
14. The governor has (shake) hands with several hundred well-wishers.
15. Sir Gawain had (slay) the dragon with one blow of his sword.
16. Someone had (take) down the stop sign.
17. Jeff (throw) out the receipt for his jacket, and now the store refuses to let him return it.
18. Have you (write) for your entry blank?
19. The bread dough has (rise) in twenty minutes, but the recipe said it would take an hour.
20. Hundreds of people claim to have (see) Bigfoot, or Sasquatch, as he is sometimes called.

Time Passing, Paul Leith, 1984.

B Find the verb that is used incorrectly in each sentence. Write the correct form on your paper. If a sentence has no verb errors, write *Correct*.

1. A vendor come down the street selling bags of roasted chestnuts.
2. Scientists have did studies showing that salmon use their sense of smell to find their way back to their birthplace to spawn.
3. The pandas have already ate their daily portion of bamboo shoots.
4. Mr. Cobb had driven into the rest area off the highway because he was too sleepy to continue.
5. The empty house has fallen into disrepair.
6. Austrian archduke Maximilian had went to Mexico to establish an empire for Napoleon III, but the Mexicans refused to accept him.
7. Andrew must have growed four inches in a year.
8. We should have knowed that the banks would be closed today.
9. The marchers had rid a bus all night to attend the rally.
10. Hundreds of lemmings runned across the beach and into the sea.
11. The detective feared that the lawyer had slew his partner.
12. The road crews throwed sand and salt on the icy highways.
13. Fortunately for us, Clare has wrote ahead for reservations.
14. A cloud of moths rose from the old wool rug when we moved it from the attic.
15. Many normal, ordinary people claim that they have saw UFO's.

C *Proofreading* Proofread the following anecdote for errors in verb usage as well as other errors in spelling, punctuation, and capitalization. Then on your paper write the anecdote correctly.

Young Henry martin was sitting on a large branch that had fell from an old Oak tree. He was watching the waters, of a nearby River, that had rised and were flooding the road. A passing moterist seen the water, slammed on his brakes, swang his car to the side of the rode, and drawed up next to the boy.

"Has the water became too deep to cross?" he asked.

"No sir. Go right ahead," Henry replied.

After the motorist had drove partway through the water. his car sunk up to it's hood. He clumb out of the car, swimmed to dry ground, and begun to rant and rave. "Are you crazy? I almost drownd!" he shouted. "You certianly gived me some bad advice you must have knowed the water was too deep to cross."

Young Henry shaked his head in amazment. "Thats funny," he said as he putted his hand too inches from the ground. "The water only comed up to hear on the ducks!"

Part 2

Verb Tenses

All verbs change form to show the time of the action they express. These changes in form are called **tenses.** English verbs have three simple tenses (present, past, and future) and three perfect tenses (present perfect, past perfect, and future perfect). You use these tenses to show whether something is happening now, has happened in the past, or will happen in the future. The six tenses are formed by using the principal parts that you have just studied and combining them with certain auxiliary verbs such as *be* and *have*.

Scene from the
film *Back to the Future*.

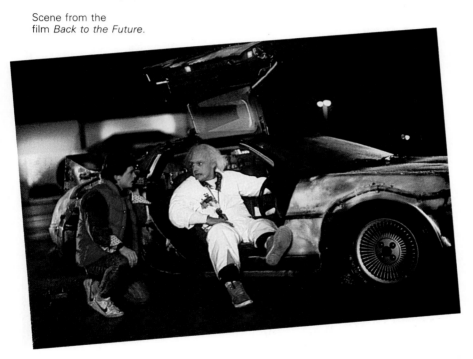

Verb Conjugation

A verb **conjugation** is a list of all the forms used in the six tenses of a verb. A verb conjugation also shows changes in form for the first, second, and third persons and for the singular and plural.

When you study the simple and perfect tenses of verbs on pages 609–610, refer to the conjugation of the regular verb *call* that is shown on the following page.

Principal Parts

Present	Present Participle	Past	Past Participle
call	(is) calling	called	(have) called

Simple Tenses

	Singular	Plural
Present Tense		
First Person	I call	we call
Second Person	you call	you call
Third Person	he, she, it calls	they call
Past Tense		
First Person	I called	we called
Second Person	you called	you called
Third Person	he, she, it called	they called

Future Tense (*will* or *shall* + the present form)

	Singular	Plural
First Person	I will (shall) call	we will (shall) call
Second Person	you will call	you will call
Third Person	he, she, it will call	they will call

Perfect Tenses

Present Perfect Tense (*has* or *have* + the past participle)

	Singular	Plural
First Person	I have called	we have called
Second Person	you have called	you have called
Third Person	he, she, it has called	they have called

Past Perfect Tense (*had* + the past participle)

	Singular	Plural
First Person	I had called	we had called
Second Person	you had called	you had called
Third Person	he, she, it had called	they had called

Future Perfect Tense (*will have* or *shall have* + the past participle)

	Singular	Plural
First Person	I will (shall) have called	we will (shall) have called
Second Person	you will have called	you will have called
Third Person	he, she, it will have called	they will have called

Using the Simple Tenses

The simple tenses include the **present, past,** and **future** tense.

The Present Tense To form the present tense, use the first principal part (the present form): *I go, we see.* Add *-s* or *-es* to the present form for the third person singular: *he goes, she sees.*

Use the present tense to show an action that (1) occurs in the present; (2) occurs regularly; or (3) is constant or generally true at any given time.

> There *goes* our bus! (action occurring in present)
> We *attend* band practice every Thursday. (action occurring regularly)
> The heart *pumps* blood. (constant action)

The **historical present tense** is used to tell of some action or condition in the past as though it were occurring in the present.

> The captain *orders,* "Abandon ship!" as the great vessel *lists* dangerously to starboard, its deck ablaze.

Note Use the present tense when writing about literature.

> In *Macbeth,* William Shakespeare *tells* the story of a Scottish king and his ambitious wife.

The Past Tense To form the past tense of a regular verb, add *-d* or *-ed* to the present form: *you smiled, they laughed.* If the verb is irregular, use the past form listed as one of the principal parts: *she went, we rode, they caught.*

Use the past tense to show an action that was completed in the past.

> Yesterday I *ran* around the reservoir.

The Future Tense To form the future tense, use the auxiliary verb *will* or *shall* with the present form. *Will* simply indicates future; *shall* usually implies an intention or obligation: *I will stay, we shall stay.*

Use the future tense for an action that will occur in the future.

> The test *will begin* at nine o'clock.
> I *shall* not *admit* latecomers.

Future time may also be shown by using the present tense in combination with an adverb or phrase that tells time.

> We *pick* up our bus passes next week. (The words *next week* indicate future time.)

Using the Perfect Tenses

The perfect tenses include the **present perfect,** the **past perfect,** and the **future perfect** tense.

The Present Perfect Tense To form the present perfect tense, use the auxiliary verb *has* or *have* with the past participle: *you have danced, she has slept.* Use the present perfect tense to show an action (1) that was completed at an indefinite time in the past or (2) that began in the past and continues into the present.

> He *has left* without his books. (action completed at indefinite time)
> We *have worked* here for ten years. (action continuing into the present)

The Past Perfect Tense To form the past perfect tense, use the auxiliary verb *had* with the past participle: *I had wondered, we had known.* Use the past perfect tense to show an action in the past that came before another action in the past.

> I *had* already *finished* when you called. (action preceding another past action)

The Future Perfect Tense Form the future perfect tense by using the auxiliary verbs *will have* or *shall have* with the past participle: *you will have eaten.* Use the future perfect tense to show an action in the future that will occur before another future action or time.

> By the time I meet Elena, I *will have bought* her birthday present—a new hat. (action occurring before another future action or time)

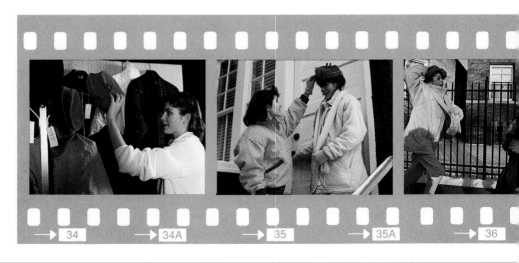

34 → 34A → 35 → 35A → 36

Exercises

A On your paper, write the verbs in the following sentences. Identify the tense of each verb.

1. The candidate had answers to most of the questions reporters asked at the press conference.
2. The workers on the demolition crew handled the explosives with care.
3. The world's largest crater, the Barringer, is 1,265 meters wide.
4. David Bushnell, an American engineer, built the first submarine in the 1700's.
5. Acid rain has taken its toll on many historic monuments.
6. Will the new classrooms have air-conditioning?
7. Amateur rock collectors have found many valuable gems.
8. By the end of the next century, scientists will have learned the language of whales.
9. Even the most loyal fans had begun to lose heart.
10. The party will begin at five o'clock in the old auditorium at the school.
11. I have taken the same bus every day for two years.
12. Have you ever ridden on a mechanical bronco?
13. In 1891 Marie Dubois discovered the bones of Java Man.
14. My car weighs about 2,000 pounds.
15. Little John had sworn his loyalty to Robin Hood.

B On your paper, write the verbs in the following sentences. Identify the tense of each verb. Then change the tense to the one given in parentheses.

> *Example*   Sonia came for a short visit. (future)
> came, Past
> Sonia will come for a short visit.

1. Elizabeth Blackwell lived in England as a child. (past perfect)
2. The guests ate French bread and *escargot* (snails). (future)
3. A new roller rink will open at the mall before Thanksgiving. (future perfect)
4. The girls' basketball team has won the state title. (future)
5. Cliff refuses any help with geometry. (past)
6. Martina Navratilova won the U.S. Open. (present perfect)
7. Tomorrow morning we will practice our mime routine on the small stage in the gym. (present)
8. The band played the grand finale. (past perfect)
9. The Detroit Symphony returned from Europe. (present perfect)
10. Debra played Juliet in *Romeo and Juliet*. (present perfect)

Part 3

Progressive and Emphatic Verb Forms

In addition to the six basic tenses, verbs also have other special forms. These include the progressive and emphatic forms.

Using the Progressive Forms

The **progressive forms** show ongoing action. They are made by using a form of *be* with the present participle; they always end in *-ing*.

> I *am calling* my brother. (present progressive)
> I *was calling* my brother. (past progressive)
> I *will (shall) be calling* my brother. (future progressive)
>
> I *have been calling* my brother. (present perfect progressive)
> I *had been calling* my brother. (past perfect progressive)
> I *will (shall) have been calling* my brother. (future perfect progressive)

Use the **present progressive** form to show an ongoing action that is taking place now.

> The tenants *are planting* a garden in the courtyard.

The present progressive form can also be used to show future time when the sentence contains an adverb or a phrase, such as *tomorrow* or *next week,* that indicates the future.

> We *are leaving* for Detroit tomorrow.

Use the **past progressive** form to show an ongoing action that took place in the past.

> I *was studying* all morning.

Use the **future progressive** form to show an ongoing action that will take place in the future.

> This summer we *will be visiting* all our relatives.

Use the **present perfect progressive** to show an ongoing action continuing in the present.

> My mother *has been taking* guitar lessons.

Use the **past perfect progressive** to show an ongoing action in the past interrupted by another past action.

The car *had been running* smoothly until it was sideswiped.

Use the **future perfect progressive** to show a future ongoing action that will have taken place by a stated future time.

By this time tomorrow, I *will have been wearing* this cast for six weeks.

Using the Emphatic Forms

The present tense and the past tense have **emphatic forms** that give special emphasis or force to the verb. To form the present emphatic, use the auxiliary verb *do* or *does* with the present form of the main verb. To form the past emphatic, use the auxiliary verb *did* with the present form of the main verb.

They usually *practice* every day. (present)
They usually *do practice* every day. (present emphatic)

They really *won* twelve games in a row. (past)
They really *did win* twelve games in a row. (past emphatic)

Usage Note When the emphatic form is used in negative statements or questions, there is usually no special emphasis intended.

He *does*n't usually *forget* his appointments.
Do you *think* this avocado is ripe?

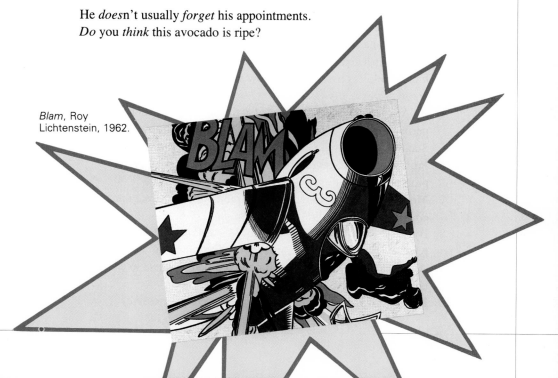

Blam, Roy Lichtenstein, 1962.

Exercises

A Write the verbs in the following sentences. Identify the tense of each verb and tell whether it is in the progressive or emphatic form, as shown in the example.

> *Example*   Dad did tell me about the flat tire.
> did tell, Past Emphatic

1. How have you been managing to get around?
2. These pre-Columbian figures do seem to be authentic.
3. We are now exploring new sources of energy.
4. The community had been hoping for a new sports and swimming complex for years.
5. CPR does save lives.
6. The lawyer will be filing her brief soon.
7. The patient really does seem better today.
8. Many scientists have been studying identical twins separated at birth.
9. Was anyone doing research for the project?
10. The principal did approve the student council's participation in the rally.

B On your paper, rewrite each of the following sentences, changing the italicized verb to the form given in parentheses.

1. Though not famous as a player, Mary E. Outerbridge *introduced* the game of tennis to the United States. (past emphatic)
2. The blue marlin caught by E. J. Fishman in 1968 really *weighed* 845 pounds. (past emphatic)
3. French soldiers *used* the crossbow as early as A.D. 851. (past progressive)
4. By August Jim *will have worked* at the pool for two months. (future perfect progressive)
5. Stanley *bowled* at the lanes every day after work. (past progressive)
6. Professor Pauling *studied* the aging process. (present perfect progressive)
7. Mocha was a little-known city in Arabia, but it *became* famous for its coffee. (past emphatic)
8. By the time he returned to Europe, Marco Polo *had worked* for Kublai Khan for seventeen years. (past perfect progressive)
9. Attendance has been falling, but the promoters *intend* to continue the concert through the weekend. (present emphatic)
10. I *register* for summer classes today. (present progressive)

Improper Shifts in Tense and Form

Use the same tense to show two or more actions that occur at the same time.

Within a paragraph or between sentences, do not shift tenses unless the meaning calls for a change. Use the same tense for the verbs in most compound sentences and in sentences with a compound predicate.

Incorrect	We *washed* the car, and then we *polish* it.
Correct	We *washed* the car, and then we *polished* it.

Incorrect	Chris *drafts* her letters and *corrected* them.
Correct	Chris *drafts* her letters and *corrects* them.

A shift in tense is not necessarily incorrect. There are times when a writer must use a tense shift to express a logical sequence of events or the relationship of one event to another. For example, to show one action occurring before or after another action, two different tenses are needed.

> Marcus *had solved* (past perfect) the problem before Mr. Weiss *explained* (past) how to do it.
> You *will have heard* (future perfect) the results by the time I *arrive* (present).
> I *see* (present) that you *have* already *finished* (present perfect) the book I *lent* (past) you.

Unnecessary or illogical shifts in verb tense are often made by inexperienced writers. Check your work carefully to avoid this type of error. Always be sure that your verbs express a consistent and logical time sequence.

Exercises

A On your paper, rewrite the following sentences. Correct improper shifts in tense by changing the tense of one verb to match the other.

> *Example*   Louis XIV of France is crowned at age five
> and continued to rule for seventy-two
> years.
>
> Louis XIV of France was crowned at age
> five and continued to rule for seventy-two
> years.

1. Coach called time out, and both teams dash for the sidelines.
2. The principal was walking purposefully to the front of the room when he is interrupted by a loud noise.
3. The aerialist climbed up the ladder and leaps onto the platform.
4. Carl hits a home run but neglected to touch third base.
5. Still invigorated by the day's adventure, we had already crossed Pennsylvania Avenue and head for the Washington Monument.
6. The writer Francisco Jiménez keeps a note pad and every day, without exception, had added the definition of an unfamiliar word.
7. A cloud of menacing grasshoppers swept from the sky and quickly destroy acres of wheat.
8. By the time she had finished her training, she will have studied with the finest musicians in the country.
9. In the moonlit garden the eyes of the cat glittered, and every hair on its body stands upright.
10. Angelo swam up behind me and dunks me in the frigid water.

B Application in Literature The following passages demonstrate how professional writers use the tenses and forms of verbs. Write the tense for each italicized verb below. Also tell if the verb is in the progressive or emphatic form. As you finish each passage, note how the author leads the reader back and forth through time by using various tenses and forms of verbs.

1. When enough years *had gone* by to enable us to look back on them, we sometimes *discussed* the events leading to his accident. I *maintain* that the Ewells *started* it all, but Jem, who *was* tour years my senior, *said* it *started* long before that. Harper Lee
2. I *had been reading* . . . of the Spanish influenza. At first it *was* far off. . . . Then the stories *told* of people dying in California towns we *knew,* and finally the [paper] *began* reporting the spread of the "flu" in our city. Ernesto Galarza

3. "Harry, what *are* you *thinking* of?" Mrs. Oliver *asked* me. "*Don't* I *get* any change?" She *was laughing*. Albert Halper

4. In true quicksand a trapped pedestrian soon *sinks* to the depth of his knees and *will sink* further if he *stands* still or *struggles* wildly.

Gerard H. Matthes

5. . . . I *like* to think that the flood *left* them a gift, a consolation prize, so that for years to come they *will be finding* edible mushrooms here and there about the house. . . . Annie Dillard

6. I *remember* the last time I *saw* him. It *was* early in September, and I *was sitting* on the gate. . . . Durango Mendoza

7. There *was* a commotion in Roaring Camp. It *could* not *have been* a fight, for in 1850 that *was* not novel enough to have called together the entire settlement. Bret Harte

8. But part of me is English, for I *love* England with a peculiar, possessing love. I *do possess* something of England. Pearl S. Buck

9. I *said* that writing *is* a craft, not an art, and the man who *runs* away from his craft because he lacks inspiration *is fooling* himself. He *is* also *going* broke. William Zinsser

10. "Oh, I *have had* such a curious dream!" *said* Alice, and she *told* her sister, as well as she could remember them, all these strange Adventures of hers that you *have* just *been reading* about; and when she *had finished*, her sister *kissed* her and said, "It was a curious dream, dear, certainly: but now *run* in to tea; it *is getting* late." Lewis Carroll

The Trial of the Knave of Hearts (from *Alice's Adventures in Wonderland*), Sir John Tenniel, 1865.

C *Write Now* Write a paragraph or two in which you describe how your attitude towards celebrating your birthday has changed over the years. You might want to focus on two or three birthdays, discussing your attitude, for example, at age five, age ten, and this year. Then discuss what you think your attitude will be at age fifty. Pay careful attention to how you shift tenses and forms of verbs.

Checkpoint *Parts 1, 2, and 3*

A On your paper, write the correct past or past participle form of each verb given in parentheses.

1. At the exhibit we (see) a skeleton of a brontosaurus.
2. I have (go) over my notes but cannot find the information.
3. Has Eric (give) you his entire coin collection?
4. If Columbus had (take) another route, America might have remained undiscovered for a long while.
5. After Alice (drink) the potion, she grew very tall.
6. Patriots had (ring) the Liberty Bell to proclaim our independence.
7. We (freeze) the leftovers after dinner.
8. The suspect's briefcase (burst) open, and money spilled out.
9. Gertrude Ederle (swim) the English Channel in 14 hours, 31 minutes.
10. Have you ever (take) the car ferry to Washington Island?
11. After Napoleon had (lose) at Waterloo, he went into exile.

12. Because the government had (break) the treaty of 1868, the Sioux fought for their land.
13. Mona has (lend) me a book about the penal colonies in Australia.
14. Mrs. Yoshida (teach) us origami, Japanese paper folding.
15. We have (write) for several copies of Garrison Keillor's article "How to Write a Personal Letter."
16. The light that (shine) from the North Star last night actually left the star 680 years ago.
17. Have you ever (bite) into a persimmon?
18. Confederate soldiers (sing) a song called "Eating Goober Peas."
19. Many runaway slaves (flee) to freedom on the Underground Railroad established by Harriet Tubman.
20. Have you (put) the car in gear or in neutral?

B On your paper, write the correct past or past participle form of each verb given in parentheses.

1. On May 30, 1889, the dam of the South Fork Reservoir at Conemaugh Lake about twelve miles east of Johnstown, Pennsylvania, (burst) due to heavy rains.
2. The owners of the dam had been warned about its flawed construction, but they had (choose) to ignore the warnings.
3. Due to the torrential rains in the last week of May, the Conemaugh River had already (rise) over its banks.
4. On the morning of May 30, messengers on horseback (ride) through the valley warning people that the dam could go.
5. At three o'clock came the awful cry, "The dam has (break)!"
6. People have (say) that they could hear the roar of the cataract for miles as it tumbled down the valley.
7. A wall of water forty feet high and a half mile wide (tear) through the valley.
8. The flood (bear) locomotives along like leaves.
9. It (fling) giant trees and boulders into the air.
10. It (take) with it bridges, houses, and hundreds of human lives.
11. In seven minutes the flood and the mountain of wreckage reached Johnstown, where it (hit) the Pennsy Bridge.
12. The bridge somehow resisted the impact, but the wreckage soon (catch) fire.
13. Many townspeople had (flee) in time.
14. However, over two thousand people (lose) their lives.
15. It (cost) over ten million dollars to repair the damage caused by the Johnstown Flood.

C On your paper, write the verbs in the following sentences. Identify the tense of each verb.

1. For her science fair report Margarite researched the development of the computer.
2. Susan's allergies have become worse this year.
3. In some people's opinion, Prime Minister Thatcher has borne the responsibilities of office well.
4. The debating team will go to the state meet next year.
5. The interpreter had learned Chinese in college.
6. Each year the Arctic tern migrates between the Arctic and the Antarctic, a round trip of 12,000 miles!
7. The members of the expedition will leave a flag at the summit.
8. In 2001 Australia will have been a nation for one hundred years.
9. Pablo Picasso, the famous artist, named his daughter *Paloma*, the Spanish word for "dove."
10. A famous piece of embroidery, the Bayeux Tapestry, illustrates the invasion of England by William the Conqueror in 1066.

D On your paper, rewrite the following sentences. Correct improper shifts in tense or form by changing the tense of one verb to match the other.

1. Marvin and Flo were painting their house flamingo pink while the neighbors had looked on in disbelief.
2. In 1932 more than fifteen hundred U.S. banks closed, and the depositors will lose 192 million dollars.
3. In 490 B.C. the Greek messenger Phidippides runs from Marathon to Athens and carried the news of an Athenian battle victory.
4. Since 1970 deaths due to heart disease have decreased 28 percent, and deaths due to strokes decrease 49 percent.
5. Medical research will become more sophisticated, and many diseases are cured in the future.

E On your paper, write the verbs in the following sentences. Identify each verb according to its form: *Progressive* or *Emphatic*.

1. Despite angry protests from citizens, the city council did approve the tax proposal.
2. In history we are studying the colonization of North America.
3. I do want your support in the upcoming student-council election.
4. William Thomson, the mathematician, was studying at Glasgow University at the age of ten.

5. By June my mother will have been working at the telephone company for fifteen years.
6. Your encouragement of my music really does make a difference.
7. The beekeeper was sowing clover near his hives to improve the flavor of his honey.
8. My sister will be completing her doctorate this year.
9. After the first performance of Igor Stravinsky's strange new music, the outraged Russian audience really did riot.
10. The quarterback and the wide receiver were practicing passes before the game on Sunday.

Part 4
Voice and Mood

You have already seen that verbs can take on many forms—the emphatic forms, the progressive forms, and the forms of the various tenses. The verbs change depending upon the purposes for which they are used. In addition to these common changes in verb form, there are other, more subtle forms that verbs can take. Writers use these verb forms to achieve special purposes.

Using the Active and Passive Voice

The **voice** of a verb tells whether the subject performs or receives the action of the verb. When the subject performs the action expressed by the verb, the verb is in the **active voice.** When the subject receives the action, the verb is in the **passive voice.** To form the passive voice, use a form of *be* with the past participle of the main verb.

Active Voice   The quarterback intentionally *threw* the ball out of bounds. (The subject *quarterback* performs the action of *throwing*.)

Passive Voice   The ball *was* intentionally *thrown* out of bounds by the quarterback. (The subject *ball* receives the action of being *thrown*.)

Active Voice   Liz *was cooking* dinner. (*Liz* performs the action of *cooking*.)

Passive Voice   Dinner *was being cooked* by Liz. (*Dinner* receives the action of being *cooked*.)

Notice that the verbs in the active voice above are transitive verbs; they have direct objects. When the verbs are changed from the active to the passive voice, the direct object becomes the subject. Only transitive verbs can change from active to passive. Intransitive verbs and linking verbs do not have direct objects. Therefore they cannot be in the passive voice because there is no word to become the subject.

Using Voice in Writing

In the passive voice, the subject does not act; it receives the action. Therefore, the active voice is usually more lively and more precise than the passive voice. For this reason, you should avoid writing long passages in the passive voice. You should also avoid mixing the passive and active voice in the same sentence or in related sentences.

On the other hand, do not hesitate to use the passive voice when you want to emphasize the person or thing receiving the action or when the person or thing performing the action is unknown.

> The performers *were given* a standing ovation. (The persons receiving the action are emphasized.)
> The concert *has been canceled* without notice. (The person performing the action is not known.)

Exercises

A On your paper, write the verbs in the following sentences. Identify each verb according to its voice: *Active* or *Passive*.

1. Within one hour every ticket to the concert had been sold.
2. In my dream last night, I had been invited by the Queen to Buckingham Palace.
3. My older sister has already chosen a career in cryogenics.
4. On the next pitch Dawson was hit by a curve ball.
5. That director does not understand the spy thriller genre.
6. Even with the new stadium lights only seventeen games have been played at night.
7. A new museum will be constructed on the site of the old Civil War battlefield.
8. The speaker told of her hair-raising adventures on Mt. Kilimanjaro in Africa.
9. Cynthia has bought a book entitled *Zen and the Art of Motorcycle Maintenance*.
10. That incredible flower-covered float was decorated by the people from the Botanical Gardens.

B Rewrite each sentence, changing all active verbs to passive and all passive verbs to active. Add words as needed.

1. The preface to the book was written by Isaac Asimov.
2. The mayor will dedicate the new bridge tomorrow.
3. The citrus crops were destroyed by the unexpected frost.
4. The sports celebrity will be introduced by the principal.
5. Scientists have identified more than one hundred elements.
6. Flu shots will be given by the school nurse.
7. The field trip to the arboretum was spoiled by the heavy rain.
8. A fire behind the stage interrupted last night's rock concert.
9. Jessica easily solved the mystery of the disappearing books.
10. The chef added leftovers to Monday's stew.

C *Write Now* Rewrite the following paragraph. Where appropriate, change passive verbs to active and make any other changes that might improve the description.

(1) On the night of April 12, 1865, the play *Our American Cousin* was seen by President Lincoln at Ford's Theatre. (2) The play was watched by the President and his wife from a special box. (3) The man who crept up behind him could be seen by no one. (4) The pistol was fired by him before anyone could protect the President. (5) The President's head was hit by the bullet, causing him to fall forward. (6) Down from the box jumped the man, breaking his leg; however, his escape was still managed. (7) The man, an actor and Southern sympathizer by the name of John Wilkes Booth, was later caught and shot.

Interior of Ford's Theatre.

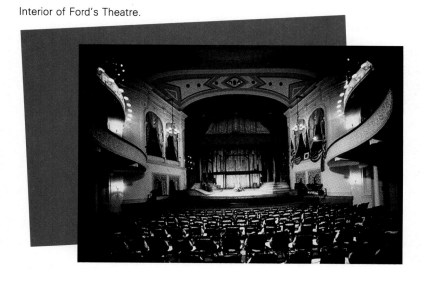

Understanding and Using Mood

The **mood** of a verb is the manner in which a verb expresses an idea. In English there are three moods: the indicative, the imperative, and the subjunctive. The **indicative mood,** which you use most of the time, states a fact or asks a question.

Indicative Mood The killer whales in Puget Sound *were captured* for commercial exploitation.
Have you ever *seen* a herd of orca whales?

The **imperative mood** is used to give a command or make a request. This mood has only one tense (the present) and only one person (the second).

Imperative Mood *Look* at this brochure about Big Sur, California.
Please *show* it to your teacher.

The **subjunctive mood** is used (1) to express a wish or a condition that is doubtful or contrary to fact or (2) to express a command or request after the word *that*.

Subjunctive Mood I wish I *were* king. (expressing a wish)
If I *were* you, I would write that letter. (expressing a condition contrary to fact)
He asked that the books *be returned* promptly. (expressing a command or request after *that*)
We insisted that Fred *paint* the fence green. (expressing a command or request after *that*)

The forms of the subjunctive mood are identical to those of the indicative mood, with the following exceptions:

1. The *s* is omitted from the verb in the third-person singular.

Indicative He *uses* safety belts.
Subjunctive We asked that he *use* safety belts.

2. The present tense of the verb *to be* is always *be*.

Andrew asked that the order *be* canceled.

3. The past tense of the verb *to be* is always *were*.

If she *were* President, she would advocate programs to provide increased employment.

Usage Note The subjunctive mood is used mainly in formal contexts. It is seldom used in informal writing or speaking.

Exercise

Write the mood of each italicized verb below.

1. If I *were* rich, I would buy a major league baseball team.
2. The tennis instructor suggested that her student *hold* the racquet with both hands.
3. I wish I *were* a world traveler.
4. Please *help* me carry the amplifiers and drums.
5. How long *have* gondolas *been used* in Venice?
6. The Nez Percé asked that they *be allowed* to settle in Canada.
7. *Do*n't *trip* over those cables!
8. If we *were* never sad, we would not know how to be happy.
9. Though they *be* friendly, we shall remain wary.
10. We always *use* our safety belts.

Part 5
Commonly Confused Verbs

Three pairs of verbs are commonly confused: *lie* and *lay*, *rise* and *raise*, and *sit* and *set*. Because of the related meanings of each pair, it is important that you distinguish these meanings in order to use the verbs correctly.

Lie and Lay

Here are the principal parts of the verbs *lie* and *lay*.

Present	Present Participle	Past	Past Participle
lie	(is) lying	lay	(have) lain
lay	(is) laying	laid	(have) laid

Lie is an intransitive verb that means "to rest in a flat position" or "to be in a certain place." *Lie* never has a direct object.

Our cat always *lies* in the middle of the couch.
Several books *were lying* on the floor of the closet.

Lay is a transitive verb that means "to place." *Lay* always has a direct object unless the verb is in the passive voice.

Active Voice   The mayor *will lay* the cornerstone for the new gymnasium. (*Cornerstone* is the direct object.)

Passive Voice   After a long delay, the cornerstone *was* finally *laid*.

Rise and Raise

Listed below are the principal parts of the verbs *rise* and *raise*.

Present	Present Participle	Past	Past Participle
rise	(is) rising	rose	(have) risen
raise	(is) raising	raised	(have) raised

Rise is an intransitive verb that means "to go upward." *Rise* does not take a direct object.

The sun *will rise* in another hour.
The water *has* already *risen* three inches.

Raise is a transitive verb that means "to lift" or "to make something go up." *Raise* always takes a direct object unless the verb is in the passive voice.

Active Voice The custodian *raises* the flag every morning. (*Flag* is the direct object.)
Passive Voice Every morning the flag *is raised*.

Sit and Set

Here are the principal parts of the verbs *sit* and *set*.

Present	Present Participle	Past	Past Participle
sit	(is) sitting	sat	(have) sat
set	(is) setting	set	(have) set

Sit is an intransitive verb that means "to occupy a seat." It does not take a direct object.

> Please *sit* next to me on the bus.
> The family *had been sitting* at the airport all night.

Set is a transitive verb that means "to place." *Set* always has a direct object unless the verb is in the passive voice.

Active Voice The artist *set* a fresh canvas on the easel. (*Canvas* is the direct object.)

Passive Voice A fresh canvas *was set* on the easel.

Usage Note See the alphabetical listing on pages 843–848 for other verbs that are sometimes confused.

Exercises

A Write the correct verb form of the two given in parentheses.

1. Our dog won't (lie, lay) still.
2. The beautiful old chest had (laid, lain) in the attic for years.
3. New tennis courts have been (laid, lain) out in the field.
4. We (lay, laid) our towels on the beach and sat down.
5. The murder weapon was found in a drainage ditch, (laying, lying) in two feet of water.
6. Please (sit, set) those empty cartons in the hall.
7. A group of children were (setting, sitting) on the curb.
8. How long has this coffeepot been (setting, sitting) on the stove?
9. We (sat, set) down and waited for the play to begin.
10. You can (set, sit) the bag of ice in the cooler.
11. Please (raise, rise) the window a few more inches.
12. Their profits have (raised, risen) every year.
13. The dough should (raise, rise) by itself.
14. Someone was (raising, rising) a disturbance outside the election hall before the judges finished the ballot count.
15. Will the sales tax be (raised, risen) again this year?

B *Proofreading* Proofread the following paragraphs for errors in verb usage, as well as other errors in spelling, punctuation, and capitalization. On your paper rewrite the paragraphs correctly.

> In ancient Assyria books were wrote on tablets that were put in clay containers. In order to read the Contents, the containers were broke open with a chisel. Little is knowed about how the greeks

improved on this early method of bookbinding. It is commonly believed, however, that Athenians used a gluelike substance to hold together leaves of parchment or papyrus.

Regular bookbinding begun with the invention of printing. Unweildy containers gived way to covers made of leather. Kings and queens outdone one another in devising luxurious bindings. It become fashonible to emboss a cover with the owner's coat of arms. Sketches of birds and flowers were drawed and then tooled painstakingly onto the leather.

The French Revolution brung the art of bookbinding to a temporery halt. Ornate binding's and coats of arms were considered an insult to the citizenry. One literary revolutionist teared off offending covers and throwed them out the window.

In recent years reader's have chose paperbacks over hard-cover editions an inexpensive paperback can be lain open to hold one's place. It can be red while the reader is setting on a crowded subway or bus or laying on the beach. Nevertheless, their are still people who, once they have saw a beautifully bound book, cannot wait to own it.

Checkpoint *Parts 4 and 5*

A On your paper, write the verbs in the following sentences. Identify each verb according to its voice: *Active* or *Passive*.

1. The dispute was settled by the referee.
2. The annual awards banquet has always been catered by Luigi's Restaurant.
3. Her daily five-mile walk has made Gwen Clark, 95, a neighborhood legend.
4. We have owned the same car for six years.
5. The Youth Council has petitioned for a basketball court at the Community Center.
6. The film adaptation was written by Woody Allen.
7. More than 58,000 names are inscribed on the Vietnam Veterans Memorial in Washington, D.C.
8. The lost city of Troy was found by Heinrich Schliemann, a German archaeologist.
9. They will visit Balboa Park in San Diego.
10. Astronauts' helmets are sprayed with a thin film of gold.

B On your paper, identify the mood of each italicized verb in the following sentences: *Indicative*, *Imperative*, or *Subjunctive*.

1. Someone moved that the nominations *be closed*, but there were several objections from the delegates.
2. Yesterday the moon partially *obscured* the sun.
3. You sound as though your friend *were* the only player on the field today.
4. *Read* the book *Horsefeathers and Other Curious Words* before you write your report on word derivations.
5. Mother talks as if she *were planning* to take more courses in accounting.

C On your paper, write the correct verb form of the two given in parentheses.

1. Most of Alaska (lays, lies) below the Arctic Circle.
2. We wondered how long the expensive watch had (laid, lain) in the pile of leaves.
3. The British Army, under the command of General Cornwallis, (laid, lay) down their arms and surrendered to General Washington and the Continental Army at Yorktown.
4. Rainsford (laid, lay) awake all night plotting his escape from the island and the menacing General Zaroff.
5. (Lay, Lie) the spare tire and the flat on the grass and help me find the hubcap.
6. We (sat, set) the pot of water over the coals and waited for it to come to a boil.
7. We tried to (raise, rise) the cellar door ourselves, but it was too heavy for the two of us.
8. While waiting for the mail truck, we (sat, set) in the shade of an old apple tree.
9. The hikers (sat, set) down their packs and asked for directions to the camping grounds.
10. Dad was (setting, sitting) in the kitchen reading recipes for holiday breads.
11. At the meeting several merchants had (raised, rose) serious objections to the proposed parking meters.
12. As the music played, the snake's head began to (raise, rise) slowly from the basket.
13. Fortunately the water in the reservoir has (raised, risen).
14. I (raised, rose) from my bed at 7:00 A.M. sharp.
15. Have your garage doors ever (raised, risen) by themselves?

Linking
Grammar & Writing

The advent of the mini-cam has made up-to-the-minute and on-the-spot news coverage possible. In years past, people often did not learn of important and exciting events for days or even weeks after they happened. Imagine what it would be like to be a news reporter with a mini-cam crew at a famous event in history. Use one of the suggestions listed below or choose another event you find interesting and write an eyewitness report that describes the action taking place.

> The arrival of the first Conestoga wagon that crossed the country from St. Louis to Oregon
> The opening of the Panama Canal
> The sailing of the *Mayflower* from England
> The arrival of the Cherokee Indians in Oklahoma after their journey on the Trail of Tears
> The completion of one of the great pyramids of Egypt

Prewriting and Drafting To gather some details, you may wish to briefly research the event you have chosen. You might then prepare a list of active, interesting verbs that will help you to accurately capture the scene and "show" it to your readers. As you draft, remember that the time limit for mini-cam features is often short. Strive for an attention-getting opener and arrange details so that the action is covered both quickly and logically.

Revising and Proofreading Remember that you are reporting on-the-spot. Check to see that your verb tenses are appropriate and consistent. Can you make the action more forceful and direct by changing any passive voice verbs to active voice? Can you improve the order or number of details that you provide? Although the viewing audience will not read your report, a written copy must go to your news chief—a very demanding editor. Be sure spelling, capitalization, and punctuation are correct.

Additional Writing Topic In both speaking and writing we often confuse the words *lie*, meaning "to be in a horizontal position"; *lie*, meaning "to tell an untruth"; and *lay*, meaning "to put or place something." Test your knowledge of *lie* and *lay*. Compose a modern fable about a bricklayer who is given to telling untruths. Write the tale first in the present tense; then rewrite it in the past tense.

Word Blends

After Alice stepped into a new world in Lewis Carroll's *Through the Looking Glass*, she had a conversation with a famous language expert—Humpty Dumpty. "You seem very clever at explaining words, sir," said Alice. "Would you kindly tell me the meaning of the poem called 'Jabberwocky'?"

One by one, Mr. Dumpty explained the strange words in that nonsense poem. *Slithy*, for example, is a combination of *lithe* and *slimy*. *Mimsy* combines *miserable* and *flimsy*. "You see, it's like a portmanteau—there are two meanings packed up into one word," he said. A portmanteau is a large suitcase with two compartments. Humpty Dumpty's analogy has provided a common term for word blends—portmanteau words.

Blends have been a part of the language for centuries. Early examples include *glimmer*, a combination of *gleam* and *shimmer*, from the 1400's, and *clash* (*clap* plus *crash*) from the 1500's. Some of the blends Lewis Carroll contributed to English include *squawk* (*squeak* plus *squall*) and *chortle* (*chuckle* plus *snort*). More recent blends are *brunch* (*breakfast* and *lunch*), *smog* (*smoke* and *fog*), and *motel* (*motor* and *hotel*).

Just as more information can be packed into sentences by combining them, more information can be packed into words by creating blends. As Humpty Dumpty noted, however, "When I make a word do a lot of work like that, I always pay it extra."

Chapter 25
Application and Review

A Using Verbs Correctly Choose the correct verb form of those given in parentheses.

1. Juana has (gone, went) to the library to use the copying machine.
2. Years ago, automobiles (cost, costed) much less to produce.
3. The cat (torn, tore) a large hole in the newspaper.
4. That blister on my heel has (hurt, hurted) for days.
5. My parakeet must be sick; it hasn't (sang, sung) for a week.
6. Laura has (brought, brung) pumpkin pie for Thanksgiving dinner.
7. Our dog Zap has always (wore, worn) a collar.
8. Osaka has (broke, broken) the school record for diving.
9. A dinner bell was (rang, ringed, rung) to call the campers.
10. The candidate (shook, shaked) hands with everyone.
11. Tim (flung, flang, flinged) a dart at the target.
12. My new shirt (shrank, shrunk) two sizes in the clothes dryer.
13. Lost in the desert, Connors had (drank, drunk) no water for days.
14. We should have (knowed, known) that the weather would be bad.
15. A ten dollar bill (lay, laid) on the sidewalk.
16. An unexpected southwest wind (rose, raised) the temperature.
17. Please (lie, lay) your jacket on the couch so I can mend it.
18. The bricklayer (sat, set) the bricks in neat rows.
19. Ryan (sat, set) patiently in the dentist's chair.
20. Emily (rose, raised) her eyebrows in disapproval.

B Recognizing Verb Tenses and Forms Write the italicized verbs on your paper. Tell what tense each is. Also tell which verbs are in the progressive and emphatic forms.

1. Tim *will be helping* with the school directory.
2. Thousands of years ago, the Sahara *was* lush and green.
3. Lisa *tries* to write in her journal every day.
4. It *has been determined* that the first motorist ran a red light.
5. I *do want* to go with you, but I promised to wash my grandfather's car this afternoon.
6. It looked as though Miriam *had been waiting* for hours.
7. The United Nations *serves* as a forum for international opinions.
8. Steve *did rake* the leaves, but the wind has blown them all back into the yard again.

9. If you practice breathing correctly, your singing voice *will become* stronger.
10. Eating yogurt for breakfast *is getting* to be a habit.

C Understanding the Forms of Verbs

Rewrite the following sentences, changing the verb to the form shown in parentheses. Add or delete words as necessary.

1. Kareem Abdul-Jabbar constantly moved up and down the court. (present progressive)
2. Poachers have drastically reduced the black rhinoceros population in Kenya. (passive)
3. During the speech, no one applauded. (past progressive)
4. The astronauts spend many hours in a weightless environment. (future perfect)
5. The abusive football player was removed from the game by the frustrated umpire. (active)
6. I find chess more challenging than checkers. (present emphatic)
7. Karen and her brother are debating the issue. (past)
8. José's life was saved by Elise's knowledge of CPR. (active)
9. The linesman called the serve out of bounds. (past perfect)
10. The trains pick up new cars at the freight yards. (future)
11. Balboa the chimpanzee was often fed peanuts by visitors to the zoo. (active)
12. I think the critic was correct when he said that movie should be rated *R*. (past emphatic)

D Recognizing the Mood of Verbs

On your paper, identify the mood of each italicized verb in the following sentences.

1. *Stop* talking and listen to this weather bulletin.
2. If I *were* Marcia, I'd at least consider the suggestion.
3. The shape of the hair follicle *determines* whether a person has straight, wavy, or curly hair.
4. *Remember* to leave by 4:00 P.M. if you want to avoid rush hour traffic.
5. Andrew asked that the order *be canceled*.
6. When *did* you *discover* that your book bag was missing?
7. A British sea captain named Matthew Webb *was* the first person to swim across the English Channel.
8. Pandas *are* not actually bears.
9. He *requested* that Mary remove her car.
10. *Go* straight home and take care of that cold.

26
Subject and Verb Agreement

Y ou probably wouldn't try to squeeze three people into one pair of jeans. Similarly, good writers don't try to fit a compound subject with a singular verb because they know that this mismatch would result in a clumsy sentence that is difficult to understand.

In this chapter you will learn how to make subjects and verbs agree in number so that your meaning can be clearly understood.

Part 1

Agreement in Number

The **number** of a word indicates whether the word is singular or plural. A word is **singular** in number if it refers to one person or thing. A word is **plural** if it refers to more than one person or thing. In English only nouns, pronouns, and verbs can change number.

The subject and verb of a sentence must agree in number.

If the subject of a sentence is singular, its verb must also be singular. If a subject is plural, then its verb must also be plural. This grammatical harmony between the subject and verb is called **subject-verb agreement.**

> The kitten (singular) likes (singular) catnip.
> The kittens (plural) like (plural) catnip.
>
> Kate (singular) has (singular) been practicing every day.
> The girls (plural) have (plural) been practicing every day.

The Number of Subjects and Verbs

The subject of a sentence is almost always a noun or pronoun. Determining the number of a noun or pronoun used as a subject is rarely a problem. By now you are familiar with the singular and plural forms of nouns and pronouns.

Except for *be,* the singular and plural forms of verbs should also cause little difficulty. Verbs show a difference between singular and plural only in the third person present tense. The third person singular present form ends in *s.*

Verb Forms

Singular		Plural	
I	sing	we	sing
you	sing	you	sing
he, she (Maria), it	**sings**	they (the twins)	sing

Grammar Note Nouns ending in *s* are usually plural, whereas verbs ending in *s* are usually singular.

Singular and Plural Forms of *Be* The verb *be* presents special problems in agreement because this verb does not follow any of the usual verb patterns. In the chart below, note that *be* has special forms for the singular and plural in both the present and past tenses and in all three persons.

Forms of Be

	Present Tense		**Past Tense**	
	Singular	*Plural*	*Singular*	*Plural*
First Person	I am	we are	I was	we were
Second Person	you are	you are	you were	you were
Third Person	he, she, it is	they are	he, she, it was	they were

Usage Note The most common errors involving the verb *be* are *you was*, *we was*, and *they was*. Avoid such nonstandard English in your speaking and writing.

Exercise

On your paper, write the form of the verb that agrees in number with the subject of each of the following sentences. Then tell whether the verb form is singular or plural.

> *Example*   Two dogs (has, have) climbed over the fence.
> have, plural

1. Francisco de Goya's later paintings (is, are) grotesque, satirical, and somber in color.
2. They (was, were) among the first to visit the prehistoric caves in southern France.
3. Halley's Comet (appears, appear) every seventy-five years.
4. Several dolphins (was, were) washed up on the beach.
5. We (has, have) always lived within an hour's drive of the ocean.
6. You (was, were) explaining the last geometry problem to me before the telephone rang.
7. My new record (was, were) melting on the radiator.
8. That umpire (need, needs) to have his eyesight checked.
9. Those German tourists (appear, appears) lost.
10. Those students (is, are) members of the new karate club.

Part 2
Words Between Subject and Verb

A verb agrees only with its subject.

Occasionally, a word or group of words comes between the subject and the verb. Even though another word may be closer to the verb than the subject is, the verb must still agree in number with its subject. When words come between the subject and the verb, identify the subject and make sure the verb agrees with it.

> The <u>speakers</u> on that car stereo <u>are</u> not <u>working</u> properly. (*Speakers*, not *stereo*, is the subject.)
>
> The <u>plant</u> with purple blossoms <u>is</u> an aster. (*Plant*, not *blossoms*, is the subject.)

The words *with, together with, along with, as well as,* and *in addition to* are prepositions. A phrase beginning with these prepositions does not affect the number of the subject.

> That country <u>singer</u>, along with his band, <u>has been</u> on tour for three months. (*Has* agrees with the singular subject *singer*.)
>
> The <u>Prime Minister</u>, together with her top aides, <u>is visiting</u> the United Nations. (*Is* agrees with the singular subject *Prime Minister*.)

Exercises

A On your paper, write the subject of each sentence. Then write the form of the verb that agrees in number with the subject.

1. The most poignant scenes in the play *Our Town* (occurs, occur) in Act Three.
2. The first clock to strike the hours (was, were) made in 1754.
3. Training, as well as courage, (is, are) needed to make an expert mountain climber.
4. The age of those huge sequoia trees (is, are) hard to believe.
5. The quarterback, as well as the offensive linemen, (is, are) planning an extra practice session.
6. The pilot, in addition to the crew, always (has, have) your safety and comfort in mind.
7. The high cost of repairs usually (comes, come) as a surprise.
8. Sir Edmund Hillary, along with Tenzing Norgay, (was, were) the first to climb Mt. Everest.
9. The decision of the umpires (was, were) loudly disputed.
10. Reports of flooding along the Ohio River (has, have) been exaggerated by the media.

B Rewrite the following sentences correcting all errors in subject-verb agreement. If a sentence is correct, write *Correct*.

1. The president of the company, along with her assistant, plan to fly to South Africa for meetings with the government.
2. Aid for the victims are being coordinated by the Red Cross.
3. The ultraviolet rays of the sun is widely known to have harmful effects on the skin.
4. The scientist's report, together with the photographs, is very convincing.
5. Several tenants in the apartment complex wants to know what to do in case of an earthquake.
6. The lights in the valley looks like distant stars.
7. Lee Iacocca, along with several other top business leaders, are speaking at the convention.
8. Our Doberman, along with her three pups, has been relocated in the basement.
9. The purpose of the Second Continental Congress in 1776 was to decide whether to declare independence from Britain.
10. In recent years the number of videocassette rentals have exceeded the number of books checked out from public libraries.

Part 3
Compound Subjects

Use a plural verb with most compound subjects joined by *and*.

Both <u>aluminum</u> and <u>copper</u> <u>are</u> excellent conductors of heat.
How <u>do</u> your <u>aunt</u> and <u>uncle</u> <u>like</u> living in Albuquerque?

Use a singular verb with a compound subject joined by *and* that is habitually used to refer to a single thing.

<u>Macaroni and cheese</u> <u>is</u> a favorite dish in our house.

Use a singular verb with a compound subject that is preceded by *each*, *every*, or *many a*.

Each <u>car</u> and <u>truck</u> in the lot <u>is</u> on sale this week.
Every <u>student</u> and <u>teacher</u> <u>has been tested</u> for meningitis.

When the words in a compound subject are joined by *or* or *nor*, the verb agrees with the subject nearer the verb.

Either my <u>mother</u> or my <u>father</u> <u>drops</u> me off at school in the morning.
(The singular verb *drops* agrees with *father*, the subject nearer the verb.)

A <u>novel</u> or two <u>plays</u> <u>meet</u> this semester's reading requirements. (The plural verb *meet* agrees with *plays*, the subject nearer the verb.)

Neither the arresting <u>officers</u> nor the <u>commissioner</u> <u>wants</u> to make a statement to the press. (The singular verb *wants* agrees with *commissioner*, the subject nearer the verb.)

Exercises

A On your paper, write the form of the verb that agrees in number with the subject of each of the following sentences.

1. Neither the train nor the airlines (runs, run) on schedule during severe weather.
2. The chairs and the table (was, were) loaded with pumpkins just before Halloween.
3. Every man and woman voting in the election (has, have) an obligation to learn about the candidates.
4. Either Dad or Mother (has, have) left the front door open.
5. The horse and buggy (is, are) associated with an era that was slower-paced and less complicated.

6. (Is, Are) either pen or pencil acceptable on this application?
7. Two textbooks and a notebook (was, were) lying on the table.
8. A lifeguard or the swimming coach (is, are) always on duty.
9. Many a boy or girl (has, have) enjoyed books by Dr. Seuss.
10. Ham and eggs (is, are) my favorite weekend breakfast.

B On your paper, write the form of the verb that agrees in number with the subject of each of the following sentences.

1. During the 1970's Frank Shorter and Bill Rodgers (was, were) America's premier marathon runners.
2. An Olympic gold medal in 1972 and a silver medal in 1976 (was, were) Shorter's top achievements.
3. The Boston Marathon and the New York Marathon (was, were) the sites of Rodgers's finest victories.
4. Hard work and dedication (goes, go) into the making of a runner.
5. Two short, fast workouts or one long, slow run (makes, make) up the daily training routine of most competitive marathoners.
6. Neither inclement weather nor minor injuries (prevents, prevent) world-class runners from accomplishing their mileage quota—as much as twenty miles per day.
7. Every major marathon and small town race (poses, pose) the same challenge—to run as hard as possible for as long as possible.
8. High school track and field (is, are) where most marathoners get their start.
9. Many a young runner and future Olympian (has, have) been inspired by Shorter and Rodgers.
10. Today Shorter and Rodgers (continues, continue) to race; neither fame nor fortune (has, have) diminished their enthusiasm.

c *Write Now* Think of two athletes, teams, performers, movies, or authors that you can compare. Write a paragraph about the likenesses and differences between the two. In your comparison use some sentences with compound subjects. Begin at least one sentence with *either* or *neither* and one with *both*.

Checkpoint *Parts 1, 2, and 3*

A On your paper, write the form of the verb that agrees in number with the subject of each of the following sentences.

1. The curators at the museum (has, have) asked for funds.
2. Several paintings in the art gallery (is, are) being restored.
3. Neither wolves nor coyotes (lives, live) in this area.
4. Every player and coach (runs, run) ten laps after practice.
5. Either an agent or a business manager (advises, advise) a performer on every contract.
6. Jerry, together with his cousins, (is, are) buying a snowmobile.
7. The juice, along with the sandwiches, (is, are) in the basket.
8. Performers in a circus (works, work) long hours.
9. A doe and a fawn (was, were) grazing in the meadow.
10. Fish and chips (is, are) a popular snack in London.

B Rewrite the following sentences correcting all errors in subject-verb agreement. If a sentence is correct, write *Correct*.

1. Despite the law, several employees of the city lives outside the city limits.
2. Neither the audience nor the actors was aware of the mishap behind the stage.
3. Has the demand for more computer courses been met?
4. Plants in a shady area usually needs less water.
5. Tacos, my favorite food, is served every Wednesday.
6. The quality of these photographs are exceptionally good.
7. The boxer, as well as his trainers, live at the camp.
8. Three farmhands and the cook share the bunkhouse.
9. Neither the President nor his press secretary were responsible for the news leak.
10. Either the counselor or the coaches has been in touch with the college scouts.

Part 4

Indefinite Pronouns as Subjects

Some indefinite pronouns are always singular; some are always plural. Others may be either singular or plural.

Singular Indefinite Pronouns			
another	either	neither	other
anybody	everybody	nobody	somebody
anyone	everyone	no one	someone
anything	everything	nothing	something
each	much	one	

Neither of the dressing rooms is available right now.
Everybody plans to attend the rodeo.

Plural Indefinite Pronouns			
both	few	many	several

Use a plural verb with a plural indefinite pronoun.

Several in the class were excellent writers.
Both of the dancers were injured.

Singular or Plural Indefinite Pronouns			
all	enough	most	plenty
any	more	none	some

These indefinite pronouns are singular when they refer to one thing. They are plural when they refer to several things.

Singular	Most of the ice cream <u>has melted</u>. (*Most* refers to one quantity of ice cream.)
	<u>Some</u> of the forest <u>was destroyed</u> by the fire. (*Some* refers to one portion of the forest.)
Plural	<u>Most</u> of the ice cream cones <u>are gone</u>. (*Most* refers to several ice cream cones.)
	<u>Some</u> of the trees <u>were</u> hundreds of years old. (*Some* refers to several trees.)

Exercises

A On your paper, write the subject of each of the following sentences. Then write the form of the verb that agrees in number with the subject.

1. Several of the station's disc jockeys (was, were) at the benefit for the homeless shelter.
2. Most of the programs on television (is, are) situation comedies.
3. Only one of the newspapers (has, have) covered the arson story.
4. All of the giant turkey (was, were) eaten in two hours.
5. Neither of the stock car racers (was, were) injured in the collision.
6. Both of the warring countries (has, have) finally come to the peace table in Geneva.
7. (Has, Have) either of the presidential candidates spoken about cuts in the defense budget?
8. Obviously, one of the witnesses (was, were) telling a lie.
9. This year some of the teams (has, have) new uniforms.
10. Many of the old houses in this block (is, are) being renovated.

B Rewrite the following sentences correcting all errors in subject-verb agreement. If a sentence is correct, write *Correct*.

1. Most of her jokes goes over like lead balloons.
2. Few of my friends knows the real me.
3. According to a recent study, one out of two defectors eventually return to his or her homeland.
4. Neither of these chemistry experiments have produced the desired effects.
5. One of the engines on the jet were smoking.
6. Each of the balloons carry scientific equipment.
7. Everyone in the wedding pictures are grinning happily.
8. Neither of these brands are the one I want.
9. Several of our listeners has called the radio station.
10. All of the workers have gone on strike.

c *Write Now* Your pep club is holding a recycled sporting goods sale to raise money for new basketball uniforms. The club has received piles of used gloves, skates, skis, balls, shoulder pads, and other equipment. You are to report to the club on the number and condition of some of the sale items. Write your report using indefinite pronouns as the subjects of several sentences. For example: We have fifteen footballs. A *few* of them are in good shape, but *many* have punctures and need patching. *Some* of these footballs are totally worthless and should be thrown away.

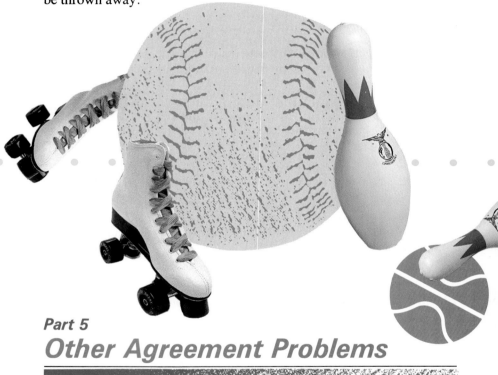

Part 5
Other Agreement Problems

There are several other situations where problems in subject-verb agreement may arise.

Inverted Sentences

Problems in agreement often occur in inverted sentences beginning with *here* and *there*; in questions beginning with words such as *why*, *where*, and *what*; and in inverted sentences beginning with a phrase.

Even when the subject comes after the verb, it still determines whether the verb should be singular or plural. Study the examples on the following page.

Incorrect	Here is the designs for the homecoming float.
Correct	Here are the designs for the homecoming float.
Incorrect	There is two *t*'s in "regretted."
Correct	There are two *t*'s in "regretted."
Incorrect	Who is those tall people in the parking lot?
Correct	Who are those tall people in the parking lot?
Incorrect	From out of the dark forest comes two hideous dragons.
Correct	From out of the dark forest come two hideous dragons.

Usage Note The contractions *here's*, *there's*, *what's*, and *where's* contain the singular verb *is*. Use them only with singular subjects.

Incorrect	There's my new golf clubs.
Correct	There are my new golf clubs.
Incorrect	What's the math assignments for next week?
Correct	What are the math assignments for next week?

Sentences with Predicate Nominatives

Use a verb that agrees in number with the subject, not with the predicate nominative.

> Mother's main interest is computers. (*Interest* is the subject and takes a singular verb.)
> Computers are Mother's main interest. (*Computers* is the subject and takes a plural verb.)
> Running in the Olympics was her dream and her goal. (*Running in the Olympics* is the subject and takes a singular verb.)

Sentences with Don't and Doesn't

Use *doesn't* with singular subjects and with the personal pronouns *he, she*, and *it*. Use *don't* with plural subjects and with the personal pronouns *I, we, you*, and *they*.

Singular	Doesn't the bus stop at this corner?
	It doesn't run regularly on weekends.
Plural	Don't the buses run on Saturday?
	They don't stop here on weekends.

Grammar Note Remember that *not* and its abbreviation *n't* are adverbs—not part of the verb.

Exercise

On your paper, write the form of the verb that agrees in number with the subject of each of the following sentences.

1. Why (doesn't don't) he want to join the club?
2. There (was, were) many unusual exhibits at the new reptile house in the renovated zoo.
3. To the right of the entrance (was, were) a vending machine and a well-used video game.
4. (There's, There are) two gallons of cider in the refrigerator.
5. Here (comes, come) the best archers in the competition.
6. (Where's, Where are) the chopsticks I left on the counter?
7. (Doesn't, Don't) the wind sound especially wild tonight?
8. (Here's, Here are) the pamphlets you lent me for my report.
9. Down into the underwater cave (swims, swim) Jacques Cousteau and his assistant.
10. Their biggest drawback (is, are) their combination of inexperience and indifference.
11. Through this door (passes, pass) the lawmakers of our nation.
12. (Where's, Where are) the wigs and rubber noses for the skit?
13. The task of the expedition (was, were) to establish a base camp and to begin scientific observations.
14. In the middle of the garden (stands, stand) an ineffective scarecrow and a dozen hungry blackbirds.
15. (What are, What's) the weather predictions for this week?

Collective Nouns as Subjects

A **collective noun** names a group or collection of people or things: *family, choir, crew, herd, faculty*. Depending on its meaning in a sentence, a collective noun may take a singular or plural verb. If a collective noun refers to a group acting together as one unit, use a singular verb. If a collective noun refers to members or parts of a group acting individually, use a plural verb.

Singular	The team is the best in the history of our school. (acting as a unit)
Plural	The team were hurriedly dressing for the game. (acting individually)
Singular	The council has scheduled a meeting for Thursday. (acting as a unit)
Plural	The council have disagreed on the date. (acting individually)

Singular Nouns with Plural Forms

Some nouns are plural in form but are regarded as singular in meaning. That is, they end in *s* as most plural nouns do, but they do not stand for more than one thing: *news*, *mumps*, *mathematics*. Therefore, they take a singular verb.

> The stock market <u>news</u> <u>was</u> encouraging.
> <u>Mumps</u> <u>is</u> more serious for adults than for children.

Other nouns end in *s* and take a plural verb even though they refer to one thing or one unit: *scissors*, *pliers*, *trousers*, *congratulations*.

> Where <u>are</u> the <u>pliers</u>?
> <u>Congratulations</u> <u>are</u> in order.

Some nouns that end in *s* may be either singular or plural, depending on their meaning in the sentence: *ethics*, *economics*, *civics*, *politics*, *athletics*. When plural, these words are often preceded by a possessive form or a modifier.

Singular   <u>Ethics</u> <u>consists</u> of a set of values.
Plural   Their <u>ethics</u> <u>are</u> sometimes questionable.

The name of a country or an organization is singular even though it may be plural in form.

> The <u>Philippines</u> <u>consists</u> of thousands of islands and islets.
> The <u>United Nations</u> <u>has televised</u> most of today's sessions.

Titles and Groups of Words as Subjects

Use a singular verb with a title.

The title of a book, play, short story, article, film, TV program, musical composition, or work of art is singular even though it may be plural in form.

> *The Orphans* <u>is</u> the story of twins who attract misfortune.
> <u>*David and Goliath*</u> <u>was painted</u> for the King of France in 1295.

Use a singular verb with any group of words that refers to a single thing or thought.

> <u>What we need</u> <u>is</u> votes.
> <u>"Because I said so"</u> <u>is</u> a popular phrase.
> <u>Canoeing down the Wolf River</u> <u>was</u> definitely the highlight of my
>   family's summer.

Words of Amount and Time as Subjects

Words that refer to amounts are usually singular.

Use a singular verb with nouns or phrases that refer to a period of time, a weight, a measurement, a fraction, or an amount of money.

> Five <u>hours</u> <u><u>seems</u></u> a long time to wait.
> One hundred <u>pounds</u> of bird seed <u><u>is</u></u> in that container.
> Ten <u>yards</u> of material <u><u>is</u></u> enough for the backdrop.
> <u>Two-thirds</u> of the money <u>has</u> already <u><u>been raised</u></u>.
> A hundred <u>dollars</u> <u><u>is</u></u> too much for that jacket.

Use a plural verb when the subject refers to a period of time or an amount that is thought of as a number of separate units.

> Two <u>hours</u> <u><u>remain</u></u> before lift-off.
> Three <u>quarters</u> <u><u>were jingling</u></u> in my pocket.

Exercises

A On your paper, write the form of the verb that agrees in number with the subject of each of the following sentences.

1. Mowing her neighbors' lawns (was, were) Sue Ellen's summer job.
2. The relief party (was, were) nearly at the ledge when the rock slide began.
3. Last year home economics (was, were) offered as an elective.
4. The social dynamics in this big family (is, are) fascinating for an outsider to watch.
5. Two thousand (seem, seems) a low estimate for the number of spectators at the parade.
6. The East Indies (was, were) once an important source of European wealth.
7. "War of the Worlds" (was, were) written by H. G. Wells.
8. Two-thirds of the wheat crop (was, were) never harvested.
9. The jury (was, were) arguing over the final piece of evidence in the trial of the former governor.
10. Six quarts of milk (are, is) what we ordered; we received five.
11. Whatever you said to your sisters (is, are) forgiven now.
12. With its new strategy, the cycling team (has, have) been winning more consistently.
13. Genetics (has, have) become a controversial topic.
14. Three cockroaches (is, are) living in my locker.
15. The scissors (has, have) been left on top of the sewing machine.

B The following sentences contain many of the errors in subject-verb agreement that you have studied in this chapter. On your paper, rewrite those sentences correctly. If a sentence does not contain an error, write *Correct*.

1. Among the most famous of modern "monsters" are Nessie, who supposedly swims in the murky waters of Loch Ness in Scotland.
2. The Loch Ness Phenomenon Investigation Bureau, founded in the early 1960's, was established to keep track of information about Nessie.
3. The ethics of this organization is irreproachable.
4. To date, over three thousand sightings has been recorded.
5. Most of the sightings has taken place just before dawn.
6. Nessie's snakelike head, together with its camel-like body, have caused much speculation in the scientific community.
7. There's several theories about Nessie.
8. One scientific group believe that Nessie is a giant eel.
9. Chances of solving the centuries-old mystery has improved with the use of technology.
10. Recent studies, using underwater cameras and a special listening device, has detected moving shadows that are not identifiable.
11. The rewards offered for finding the elusive Nessie total nearly 2.6 million dollars!
12. One scientist, however, has said that he don't want to be there when the mystery is finally unraveled.

c *Proofreading* Proofread the following paragraphs. Rewrite them on your paper, correcting all errors. Pay particular attention to subject-verb agreement.

One man and his small son runs their fingers over the black wall, touching a name. Another kneel and bow his head. A family are placing flowers and a tiny flag at the base of the wall. The people are visitors at the Vietnam Veterans Memorial in Washington d.c.

Maya Ying Lin, chosen from 1421 entries in the contest to create a Vietnam War memorial, were only a 22-year-old architecture student at yale at the time. Maya Lin describes her design: "A rift in the earth, a long, polished black stone wall emerging from and receding into the earth." The Memorial are actually two walls, two leg's of a V, each 250 feet long. Over 57000 names—the killed and missing in the War—is carved in the black granite. The list of soldiers are arranged in the order of their deaths from 1959 to 1975. When the Memorial was dedicated in 1982, there was a public reading of all the engraved names, which took three days.

Politics were an everpresent factor in the controversial Vietnam War. Inevitably, the wall has been controversial also. Some doesn't like the Memorial and would prefer a more traditional statue Most has found it's simple design profoundly moving. The true meaning of the Memorial is clearly expressed by its creator, Maya Lin: "It does not glorify the war or make an antiwar statement. It is a place for private reckoning."

Part 6
Relative Pronouns as Subjects

A relative pronoun is sometimes the subject of an adjective clause (see pages 554–555). To determine whether to use a singular or a plural verb in the clause, you must first determine the number of the relative pronoun. A relative pronoun stands in place of its antecedent (the word to which it refers). If that antecedent is plural, the relative pronoun must be plural. If the antecedent is singular, the relative pronoun must be singular.

A relative pronoun agrees with its antecedent in number.

Singular   She is the candidate who has received the most votes. (*Who* refers to the singular antecedent *candidate*.)

Plural   Here is a list of candidates who have already conceded. (*Who* refers to the plural antecedent *candidates*.)

Singular   Ms. Greene is the only one of the coaches who has run in road races. (Only *one* has run races. *Who* refers to the singular antecedent *one*.)

Plural   Len is one of those people who are always coming late. (*People* are always coming late. *Who* refers to the plural antecedent *people*.)

The problem of agreement arises in the last two sentences because there are two words, either of which might be the antecedent of the relative pronoun. Remember that the verb in the relative clause will agree with the true antecedent of the relative pronoun.

Exercise

On your paper, write the form of the verb that agrees in number with the subject of the adjective clause.

1. Good running shoes are those that (has, have) firm support for the feet.
2. James is the only one who (has, have) finished.
3. Those are the fields that (produces, produce) the most oil.
4. This is the only one of his novels that (is, are) worth reading.
5. My cousin is one of those individuals who (is, are) always finding good in others.

6. Gib is one of the students who (notices, notice) everything going on in class.
7. The elderly gentleman was the only onlooker who (was, were) smiling at the mime.
8. Mr. Marin is the only teacher I know who (calls, call) the roll at the end of class.
9. Veterans Day is one of the holidays that (falls, fall) on Saturday this year.
10. Sarah is one of the drummers who (marches, march) in the band.
11. This is the only one of my teeth that still (aches, ache).
12. Here are two paints of the kind that (resists, resist) moisture best.
13. Joanne is the one person in the group who (is, are) willing to share her record collection.
14. He is the only one of the recently arrived refugees who (speak, speaks) English.
15. There are three members of our class who (has, have) consistently scored 100's on tests.

Checkpoint *Parts 4, 5, and 6*

A On your paper, write the form of the verb that agrees in number with the subject of the sentence.

1. All of the pigeons (gathers, gather) around that feeder.
2. Social studies (was, were) my best class last year.
3. Five dollars (are, is) a lot of money for a movie ticket.
4. *The King and I* (opens, open) this Saturday night.
5. Everyone (seems, seem) upset about plans to expand the airport.
6. Either of these novels (is, are) acceptable for the book report.
7. One out of four Americans (has, have) been on TV at some time.
8. (There's, There are) the new computers I told you about.
9. Visiting China and Tibet (was, were) Teresa's dream.
10. Black holes are objects in space that (doesn't, don't) emit light.
11. The committee (has, have) turned in their ballots.
12. Through the harbor in the glorious sunshine (sails, sail) replicas of the *Niña* and the *Pinta*.
13. (Who are, Who's) the winners of the athletic scholarships?
14. None of the active volcanoes (has, have) erupted this year.
15. Why (was, were) the tightwire performers working without a net?

B On your paper, write the form of the verb that agrees in number with the subject of each sentence.

1. The story of pizza (begins, begin) many hundreds of years ago in Naples, Italy.
2. *Moretum,* a work by the ancient Roman poet Virgil, (gives, give) a description of pizza.
3. This popular food (has, have) many appealing qualities, which (includes, include) convenience, affordability, nutritional value, and good taste.
4. There (is, are) now many regional varieties of pizza.
5. Some of these varieties (is, are) recognized by their distinctive toppings: in Nice, France—black olives; in Naples—mozzarella cheese made from water buffalo milk.
6. Neither of these pizzas, however, (is, are) quite like the Roman pizza, which (has, have) onions, but no tomatoes.
7. The first pizzeria in the United States (was, were) started in New York in 1905.
8. A booming business today (is, are) the pizza delivery services.
9. Over four billion dollars worth of pizza (is, are) sold each year.
10. Each day people in the United States (eats, eat) seventy-five acres of pizza!

Linking
Grammar *&* Writing

A famous Hollywood movie producer wants to film a documentary of a typical day in your life. You have been asked to write a schedule of your activities daily so that the director can prepare for filming. Write a schedule focusing on four typical "scenes" in your day. Describe what you will do and who will be with you in each instance. Make sure that your subjects and verbs agree.

Prewriting and Drafting Choose the day of the week that you want for the filming of the documentary. Then think of your activities on that day, consider the four "scenes" that best typify you, and identify the friends and family members who would be included. For each of your scenes, detail the happenings and note the time. Consider the following example:

> *3:30 P.M.* I come home about now, hungry as a bear. The camera should capture the relief on my face as I open the refrigerator and explore the leftovers.
>
> *3:45 P.M.* Now I have the radio blasting and I am phoning my friends at the same time. During my phone calls, my younger brother asks me who I'm talking with. He always asks, even though he knows how much it annoys me.

As you draft your schedule, remember to focus on typical activities, the kinds of things you often do, and to use the present tense.

Revising and Proofreading Consider these questions:

1. Do the activities in your schedule represent a typical day?
2. Have you described them in enough detail so that someone who does not know you can understand them?
3. Is the time sequence of your schedule clear and easy to follow?
4. Do all subjects and verbs agree?

Additional Writing Topic Sometimes schools, neighborhoods, communities, social groups, or teams have "personalities." Identify a group that has a very recognizable personality. Write about the people in this group. Discuss their beliefs, habits, behaviors, and attitudes. Write in the present tense, and use indefinite pronouns (*someone, everyone, none, almost, each, every, many, several*) where possible. Make sure that your subjects and verbs agree.

The Cowboy

W hat could be more American than the cowboys of the Wild West? Whether they are lassoing stampeding mustangs on the range or riding bucking broncos in the rodeo, these buckaroos seem to be American originals. Yet most of the words associated with their world are not original—they were borrowed from other sources.

Buckaroo is a corruption of the Spanish word *vaquero,* the name of the Spanish cattlemen and horse-traders the cowboys encountered on the trails of the West. Spanish is also the source of *lasso, stampede* (from *estampida*), *mustang, lariat* (from *la reata*), *bronco* (Spanish for "rough" or "unruly"), and *rodeo.*

Even *cowboy* was not born on the range. In England during the 1700's it was a term for boys who tended cattle. Its first use in America came during the Revolutionary War as a derogatory term for Tory soldiers who used cowbells to lure American soldiers and farmers into ambushes. During the Civil War, it was used to describe roustabouts who rustled cattle along the Texas-Mexican border. It also described teen-aged boys who served as drovers on long trail drives because older men had been pressed into service as soldiers.

Finally, after the Civil War, the cowboys of the great Western cattle drives earned their place in history and folklore. Over time, the other meanings have been forgotten, and what is remembered is *cowboy*'s rich and often romanticized connection to the American West.

His First Lesson, Frederic Remington, 1903.

Chapter 26
Application and Review

A Making Subjects and Verbs Agree Choose the correct form of the verb for each sentence.

1. Marc Chagall's intricate and colorful mosaic *Four Seasons* (was, were) installed in Chicago in 1974.
2. My backpack, together with its contents, (weighs, weigh) over twenty pounds.
3. Everyone who (thinks, think) that a reporter's life is romantic should spend time working on a newspaper.
4. There (is, are) some problems that can't be solved without the help of others.
5. One of the new cars (gets, get) over sixty miles per gallon in highway driving.
6. Hawaii, like Japan, (is, are) actually several islands.
7. One-fourth of the goods that Americans buy (is, are) imported.
8. She (doesn't, don't) care whether anyone approves of her clothes.
9. Out of a mountain in the Black Hills (emerges, emerge) the gigantic sculptured figure of Chief Crazy Horse.
10. Two hundred years of democracy (has, have) made certain changes in the Constitution necessary.
11. His sunglasses (makes, make) him look mysterious.
12. The editor is the person who (decide, decides) which articles to print in each issue.
13. Compassion is one of the qualities that (are, is) necessary in a good leader.
14. Many of the people who (live, lives) in this neighborhood are of Polish ancestry.
15. Pneumatics (deal, deals) with the properties of air and other gases.
16. *A Tangle of Roots* (are, is) a thought-provoking story.
17. One hundred sixty pounds (are, is) the average weight of the players on the opposing team.
18. The lights at the end of the pier (are, is) easily seen at night.
19. A paramedic and a firefighter (was, were) hospitalized yesterday for their injuries.
20. Neither the governor nor her aide (was, were) interviewed on the local evening news.

B Solving Problems in Subject-Verb Agreement Choose the correct form of the verb for each sentence.

1. Salvaging autos (has, have) become a thriving business in the United States.
2. According to recent national figures, there (are, is) at least 29 million cars ten years old or older in this country.
3. Twenty-nine million (represent, represents) a considerable increase from just a few years ago.
4. Each of today's junkyards (has, have) its own personality.
5. Some of the junkyards (sell, sells) only parts for specific models; others (deal, deals) only in hubcaps.
6. Computers, which never would have been seen in a junkyard of old, (keep, keeps) track of the rapidly changing inventory in some newer junkyards.
7. Attractive showrooms, steam-cleaned parts, and the free use of power tools (is, are) offered by some junkyards.
8. At some fancier junkyards, neither couples on dates nor a well-dressed business person (is, are) a strange sight.
9. "The Riches of Wrecks," a recent magazine article, (tell, tells) about one "junkyard" that is contained within a six-story building.
10. Of course, many a junkyard still (has, have) the typical fierce-eyed mongrel keeping watch at the gate, guarding a mountain of rusty cars and old rubber tires.

C Correcting Errors in Subject-Verb Agreement The following passage contains several errors in the agreement of subjects and verbs. Rewrite the paragraph, correcting these errors.

(1) Charlie Brown is one of the characters created by Charles Schultz for his much-loved comic strip. (2) "Peanuts" have been around for over a generation now, and there is hardly anyone who don't feel compassion for the struggles of Charlie Brown. (3) Each of his readers, from children to adults, seem to identify with Charlie's tendency to fail. (4) One of the problems that Charlie often has are getting his kites to fly. (5) There's always trees in the way, and the kite invariably gets caught in one of them—on purpose, Charlie believes. (6) Then there is Charlie's inability to kick a football or win even a single baseball game. (7) Either the kite or sports give Charlie trouble in almost every strip. (8) Charlie's popularity has grown so much that "Peanuts" are now found on television. (9) He don't have to worry about being unloved. (10) Charlie Brown has millions of friends all over the world.

Cumulative Review

Chapters 25 and 26

A Identifying Verb Tenses and Forms Write the italicized verbs on your paper. Tell what tense each is. Also tell which verbs are in the progressive and emphatic forms.

1. By the time he *finishes* all of his schooling, he *will have been studying* for twenty-one years.
2. The young comedian *wanted* to know what *happens* to the socks that *are vanishing* every day in dryers across the country.
3. I *did know* that my shirt was on backwards; I *was* simply *trying* to determine if you *were* sharp enough to see the mistake.
4. Ever since we *moved* here, the bright red leaves of the sumac *have been brightening* the countryside in the autumn.
5. The slow, relentless movement of glaciers *had carved* out those hills centuries ago, long before the river *snaked* its way along the same path that *had been used* by the glaciers.
6. At this time tomorrow, the giraffe *will amble* once again to the feeder where it *will have found* its mid-morning snack.
7. Unicorns *have stirred* the imagination of poets for centuries.
8. If they *do build* the apartment complex, we *will be worrying* about what *will happen* to the current residents.
9. Renoir the artist *told* his son, who *became* a famous filmmaker, that to know people one *needs* to study their hands and faces.
10. "That girl *is* a winner," the admiring coach told her team; "she always *has been* a winner, and she always *will be* a winner."

B Changing the Voice of Verbs On your paper, rewrite the sentences below, changing all the italicized verbs from passive to active or active to passive. Add or change words as needed; you may create additional sentences if you wish.

1. The old maple tree by the courthouse on Vine Street *had been hit* by the stranger's car.
2. After he safely emerged from his car, the confused driver *told* the police his amazing story.
3. His car *had been driven* into the tree by a goblin who had taken control of the steering wheel.
4. The goblin *had entered* the car at a stoplight.

5. The man *was* quickly *pushed* from the steering wheel by the goblin, who seemed determined to drive.
6. After losing control of the steering wheel, the astonished man *stared* at the goblin; he *expected* disaster.
7. Surprisingly, no obstacles *were hit* by the car, because the goblin turned out to be a capable driver.
8. Then, the goblin *was* suddenly *distracted* by an ice-cream truck turning ahead at the corner.
9. The goblin *craved* ice cream, *looked* longingly at the truck, and *smashed* the car into the tree.
10. Discouraged but not hurt, the goblin *flew* after the truck, leaving the man alone to tell his story to the amused police.

C Recognizing the Moods of Verbs On your paper, identify the mood of each italicized verb in the following sentences.

1. If I *were* you, I would certainly call my parents right away to tell them about the errant pumpkin that *crashed* through the kitchen ceiling this afternoon.
2. *Tell* them the truth, even though it sounds like fiction.
3. When they ask that the whole story *be told,* simply recount the scene you *witnessed* when you returned from school.
4. If they do not believe you, have them call the police, who *said* they would explain everything to your parents.
5. They *have fined* the skydivers who *dropped* the pumpkin while playing catch two thousand feet above your house.

D Correcting Errors in Agreement Rewrite the following paragraph to correct all errors in subject and verb agreement.

Leonardo da Vinci, among all the artists of the Renaissance, represent the most diverse range of interests. His versatility has long amazed those admirers of his genius who has studied his work. All of his life's energies was devoted to understanding the world around him, and he did research in mathematics, architecture, music, optics, astronomy, geology, botany, zoology, hydraulics, aeronautics, and anatomy. In fact many seemingly modern inventions, such as the helicopter, was first developed by da Vinci. Even during those times when most of his attention were focused on a single project, he continued to study many different subjects. His work as artist, scientist, and inventor still command interest. If you visit a university today, you will find either art historians or an engineer who are engaged in the study of his work. His genius seems ageless and immortal.

27

Using Pronouns

*F*resh fish and a heaping plate of spaghetti—these dishes may look like the real thing, but look again. They're actually made of plastic. Such "stand-ins" are useful in situations where real food would quickly spoil. For example, in a restaurant-window display, a plate of polymer pasta continues to look appetizing long after real spaghetti would have lost its appeal.

Language has stand-ins too—pronouns. Pronouns take the place of nouns in sentences, yet they also function in specialized ways. In this chapter you will learn about the three cases that mark the specialized use of pronouns and about the relationship of pronouns to the nouns they replace.

Part 1

The Cases of Pronouns

Pronouns are words that may be used in place of nouns. Pronouns change form, depending on their use in sentences. These changes in pronoun form are called changes in the **case** of the pronouns. There are three cases in English: the **nominative case,** the **objective case,** and the **possessive case.** The personal pronouns are classified below according to case, number (singular and plural), and person (first, second, and third).

Singular

	Nominative	Objective	Possessive
First Person	I	me	my, mine
Second Person	you	you	your, yours
Third Person	he	him	his
	she	her	her, hers
	it	it	its

Plural

	Nominative	Objective	Possessive
First Person	we	us	our, ours
Second Person	you	you	your, yours
Third Person	they	them	their, theirs

The pronouns *who* and *whoever* are classified below according to case.

Nominative	Objective	Possessive
who	whom	whose
whoever	whomever	whosever

Indefinite pronouns change form only in the possessive case. The nominative and objective cases are identical.

Nominative	Objective	Possessive
someone	someone	someone's
everybody	everybody	everybody's
no one	no one	no one's

The pronouns *this, that, these, those, which,* and *what* do not change their forms to indicate case.

The material in this chapter will explain when to use the various case forms of pronouns.

Exercise

Application in Literature List the italicized pronouns in the three passages below. Identify each personal pronoun as first, second, or third person; singular or plural; and nominative, objective, or possessive case. Write only the case for *who* and indefinite pronouns.

(1) Some boys taught *me* to play football. . . . (2) *You* went out for a pass, fooling *everyone*. (3) Best, you got to throw yourself mightily at *someone's* running legs. (4) Either you brought *him* down or you hit the ground flat out on *your* chin. . . . (5) Nothing girls did could compare with *it*.

(1) If in that snowy backyard the driver of the black Buick had cut off *our* heads, Mikey's and *mine,* I would have died happy, for nothing has required so much of *me* since as being chased all over Pittsburgh . . . by this sainted, skinny, furious redheaded man *who* wished to have a word with *us*. (2) *I* don't know how *he* found *his* way back to his car.

(1) *We* girls chafed, whined, and complained under our parents' strictures. (2) The boys waged open war on *their* parents. (3) The boys' pitched battles with *their* parents were legendary; the punishments *they* endured melted *our* hearts.

From *An American Childhood* by Annie Dillard

Past Lives,
Lorie Novak, 1987.

Pronouns in the Nominative Case

Like nouns, pronouns can function as both subjects and predicate nominatives.

Pronouns as Subjects

The nominative form of the pronoun is used as the subject of a verb.

When a pronoun is a part of a compound subject, it is often difficult to decide on the appropriate form. To decide which form to use in the compound subject, try each part of the subject separately with the verb.

> Hal and (I, me) kayaked down the Brule. (Hal kayaked; I kayaked, *not* me kayaked.)

The plural forms *we* and *they* sound awkward in many compounds. They can be avoided by rewording the sentence.

Awkward   We and they planned to swim at dawn.
Better   We all planned to swim at dawn.

Pronouns as Predicate Nominatives

A pronoun that follows a linking verb is a **predicate pronoun.**

A predicate pronoun takes the nominative case.

It is often difficult to decide on the pronoun form to use after the verb *be*. Use the nominative case after phrases in which the main verb is a form of *be*, such as *could have been*, *can be*, and *should be*.

> It *was* **I** whom they called.
> It *must have been* **they** in the sports car.

When the nominative form sounds awkward, reword the sentence.

Awkward   The winner was she.
Better   She was the winner.

Usage Note In informal conversation and writing, it is acceptable to use the objective case after the verb *be* in the sentence *It is me*. For formal writing, however, use the nominative case.

Exercise

Write the correct form of the pronoun for each sentence. Choose from those given in parentheses.

1. Jeff and (I, me) are reporting on scientific explanations for UFO's.
2. At the center of the photo are Stalin, Churchill, and (he, him).
3. How many movies did Humphrey Bogart and (she, her) make?
4. Marty and (he, him) volunteered to fill sandbags.
5. The Warner brothers and (they, them) formed a film company.
6. The three dressed in togas were Pam, Ida, and (I, me).
7. Was it (he, him) who painted the stage set to look like stone?
8. (She, Her) and the officer were having a loud argument about which driver was at fault.
9. When Scott and (they, them) arrived at the South Pole, (they, them) found Amundsen's Norwegian flag already there.
10. We thought it was (he, him) in the clown outfit.

Part 3
Pronouns in the Objective Case

Like nouns, pronouns can also function as objects of verbs, objects of prepositions, or as part of infinitive phrases.

Pronouns as Objects of Verbs

The objective pronoun form is used for a direct or indirect object.

When a pronoun is part of a compound object, it is often difficult to decide on the appropriate form for the pronoun. The compound object may consist of pronouns or both nouns and pronouns.

To decide which pronoun form to use in a compound object, try each part of the object separately with the verb.

Direct Object	The principal wanted to see George and (I, me). (see George; see me, *not* see I)
	Jenny invited both (they, them) and (we, us) to the party. (invited them, *not* invited they; invited us, *not* invited we)
Indirect Object	The counselor gave Janet and (I, me) good advice. (gave Janet; gave me, *not* gave I)

Pronouns as Objects of Prepositions

The objective pronoun form is used as the object of a preposition.

When a pronoun is part of the compound object of a preposition, it is often difficult to decide on the appropriate pronoun form. To determine which form is correct, try each pronoun separately in the sentence.

> Will your sister be going with you and (I, me)? (with you; with me, *not* with I)

Use the objective pronoun forms after the preposition *between*.

> between you and him, *not* between you and he
> between him and me, *not* between he and I

Pronouns with Infinitives

The infinitive is a verb that is preceded by *to*. See pages 540 and 541 for more information about infinitives.

The objective form of the pronoun is used as the subject, object, or predicate pronoun of an infinitive.

> The referee asked *them to observe* the rules. (*Them* is the subject of *to observe*.)
> The team expected the MVP *to be her*. (*Her* is the object of *to be*.)

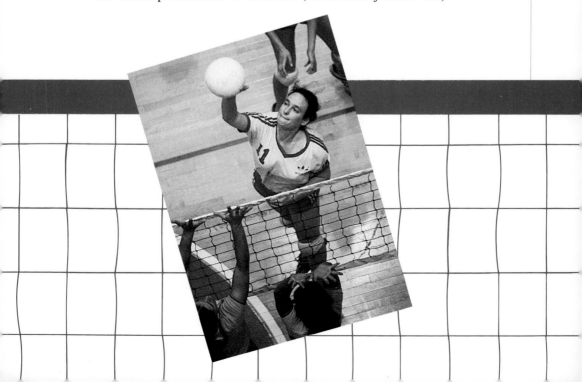

Exercises

A Write the correct pronoun from those given in parentheses.

1. The Friar secretly married Romeo and (she, her).
2. By working together, Mme. Curie and (he, him) discovered the element radium.
3. Marcus and (I, me) learned how to pack a parachute correctly.
4. (We, Us) did not expect to sit between Amy and (she, her).
5. Ray Bradbury gave Casey and (I, me) an interview.
6. The crowd would not allow (she, her) or (we, us) to speak.
7. The photographer met (he, him) and (I, me) at the finish line.
8. The moratorium gives the union representatives and (they, them) some time to think about further negotiations.
9. Holmes knew that the "ghost" would turn out to be (he, him).
10. Reservations were made for everyone except Russ and (we, us).
11. The voters know it was (they, them) who elected the mayor.
12. Just between you and (me, I), I am terrified of spiders.
13. Evan and (them, they) were feeling a bit squeamish about the dissection of the frog in biology class.
14. It was (him, he) who said that victory was bittersweet.
15. Jerry yelled for Marcia and (I, me) to take cover just as the hail started to fall on (we, us).

B Application in Literature Choose the pronoun that makes each of the following excerpts correct.

1. It was (she, her) who used to come between (I, me) and my paper when I was writing reviews. Virginia Woolf
2. (He, Him) and (I, me) both were afraid of me becoming a sissy—(he, him) perhaps more afraid than I. John Updike
3. We supposed (he, him) to be the leader, because he stood up in full view, swinging his big knife over his head. Rain-in-the-Face
4. The angels, not half so happy in Heaven,
   Went envying (she, her) and (I, me); . . . Edgar Allan Poe
5. Most of (we, us) in the camp were poor boys, or boys who were almost poor. Thomas Sancton
6. From childhood, my sister and (I, me) have had a well-grounded dislike for our friends the birds. Ruth McKenny
7. I had no reason to suppose that I'd see (her, she), or (her, she) (I, me) . . . in that hotel lobby. . . . Milton Mayer
8. Eileen and (me, I) didn't exchange a glance, but we loved each other now. Laurie Lee

c *Write Now* Think about a process that needs at least four people to complete, such as putting up a tent, playing a game, or moving a large piece of furniture or equipment. Then write an explanation of the process. Use at least ten pronouns, including five compound subjects or objects, two compound objects of prepositions, and two pronouns with infinitives.

Checkpoint *Parts 1, 2, and 3*

Write the correct pronoun form from those given in parentheses. Then tell the case of the pronoun you chose.

1. Inspector Clouseau questioned the butler and (they, them).
2. F.D.R. and (he, him) were both governors of New York.
3. The travel agent quoted (they, them) and (we, us) different prices for the same flight.
4. For Lee and (we, us) the fiesta was all work and no fun.
5. Was it (she, her) or her sister Charlotte Brontë who wrote *Wuthering Heights?*
6. We saw (they, them) and their bodyguards after the concert.
7. Neither (we, us) nor Canadians need visas for that country.
8. The party was a surprise for Grandpa and (she, her).
9. With Emily and (I, me), the marine biologist waited for high tide and the running of the small fish called grunion.
10. Just between you and (I, me), I'd love to conduct a symphony orchestra some day.
11. Later on our tour, (she, her) and (I, me) saw the Book of Kells.
12. It must have been (he, him); he was wearing one sequined glove.
13. Early election results indicated the winner would be (she, her).
14. The Clarks and (we, us) are going on a photographic safari.
15. The guide explained to (he, him) and (I, me) that the 3,200-year-old temple at Abu Simbel was built for Ramses II.
16. Do you know (who, whom) was the sculptor of Mt. Rushmore?
17. When will Andrew Wyeth and (they, them) exhibit their paintings?
18. Tom disagrees with Alice and (I, me) that the narwhal can be considered a unicorn.
19. Was it (he, him) who said "Honesty is the best policy"?
20. The drivers' education instructor taught (I, me) and (he, him) how to parallel park.

Part 4

Pronouns in the Possessive Case

Personal pronouns that show ownership use the possessive case. Possessive pronouns can be used to replace nouns or to modify nouns.

The possessive pronouns *mine, ours, yours, his, hers, its,* and *theirs* can be used in place of nouns, as in the following sentences: That is *mine. Yours* is blue.

My, our, your, his, her, its, and *their* are used to modify nouns: That is *my* sweater. *Your* sweater is blue.

You will notice that *his* and *its* are used in either situation.

Punctuation Note Never use an apostrophe with possessive pronouns. Spellings such as *it's* and *he's* indicate a contraction.

Possessive Pronouns Modifying Gerunds

The possessive form of the pronoun is used when the pronoun immediately precedes a gerund.

> *His running* has improved since the last track meet. (*Running* is a gerund functioning as the subject. The possessive form *his* modifies *running*.)

Remember that present participles, like gerunds, are verbals that end in *-ing*. However, the possessive case is not used before a participle. The nominative or objective case of a pronoun is used before a participle.

> We saw *him running* toward the finish line. (*Running* is a participle modifying *him*.)

To distinguish between a gerund and a present participle, remember this: if the *-ing* word is used as a noun, it is a gerund; if it is used as a modifier, it is a participle. It may also be helpful to ask yourself *Who?* or *What?* of the verb in the sentence.

> We dislike *their playing* the stereo at midnight. (What did we dislike? We disliked the playing. Therefore, *playing* is a gerund, the object of the verb *dislike*. The possessive pronoun *their* should be used.)
> We heard *them playing* the stereo at midnight. (What did we hear? We heard them. Therefore, *playing* is a participle modifying *them*.)

Exercise

Choose the correct pronoun from those given in parentheses.

1. (Him, His) giving up the throne for "the woman he loved" was totally unexpected.
2. Will you use Judy's ticket or (her, hers)?
3. I didn't like (him, his) sneaking in through the back door after curfew.
4. Is the tackle box (your, yours) or his?
5. If you like (me, my) cooking, please stay for dinner.
6. This is (their, theirs) listing of the property.
7. (Their, Them) exploring and mapping the northwestern United States in the early 1800's made Meriwether and Clark famous.
8. Mother doesn't want (you, your) talking and laughing to disturb the sleeping baby.
9. Parking your car in that restricted area will result in (you, your) getting a ticket.
10. (His, Him) dancing of the *Nutcracker* is almost as good as Baryshnikov's.

Part 5
Problems in Pronoun Usage

Certain situations involving pronouns often cause confusion.

Who *and* Whom *in Questions and Clauses*

The pronouns *who* and *whom* are used to ask questions or to introduce clauses.

To use *who* and *whom* in questions, it is necessary to understand how the pronoun is functioning in the question.

Who is the nominative form of the pronoun. It is used as the subject of the verb or as a predicate pronoun.

Whom is the object form of the pronoun. It is used as the direct object or as the object of a preposition.

> *Who* wrote this novel? (*Who* is the subject.)
> *Whom* will you choose? (*Whom* is the direct object of *choose*.)

The pronouns *who, whoever, whom, whomever,* and *whose* may be used to introduce noun or adjective clauses. These pronouns also have a function within the clause.

Who and **whoever** are nominative case pronouns and can act as the subject or predicate pronoun in a clause.

Whom and **whomever** are in the objective case and can act as the direct object or the object of a preposition in a clause.

The following steps and examples can help to eliminate confusion about the use of *who* and *whom* in subordinate clauses:

1. Isolate the subordinate clause.
2. Determine how the pronoun in question is used in that clause.
3. If the pronoun is used as a subject or predicate pronoun, choose *who* or *whoever*. If the pronoun is used as an object, choose *whom* or *whomever*.

> Galileo Galilei is the scientist *(who, whom)* invented the thermometer.
> 1. The adjective clause is *(who, whom) invented the thermometer*.
> 2. The pronoun is acting as the subject within the clause.
> 3. *Who* is in the nominative case and the correct choice.

> Pearl Buck is an author *(who, whom)* I admire.
> 1. The adjective clause is *(who, whom) I admire*.
> 2. The pronoun is acting as the direct object within the clause.
> 3. *Whom* in the objective case is the correct choice.

> A medal was given to *(whoever, whomever)* finished the race.
> 1. *(Whoever, Whomever) finished the race* is the noun clause acting as the object of the preposition *to*.
> 2. The pronoun is acting as the subject within the clause.
> 3. The nominative pronoun *whoever* is the correct choice.

Whose functions as the possessive pronoun within a clause.

This is the artist *whose painting I bought.* (*Whose* is a possessive pronoun modifying *painting* in the clause.)

Exercises

A Write the correct pronoun from those given in parentheses.

1. (Who, Whom) knows how to figure skate well enough to do a Mohawk turn?
2. The student (who, whom) found the watch that I lost yesterday turned it in at the office.
3. Chris is the gymnast (who, whose) specialty is the rings.
4. For (who, whom) does Jeff baby-sit on Thursday nights?
5. Perry, (whoever, whomever) taught you how to trim a sail deserves a medal.
6. The President (who, whom) initiated the New Deal was Franklin Roosevelt.
7. Only the judges know (who, whom) the winner will be.
8. Ask (whomever, whoever) you want.
9. With (who, whom) will you travel?
10. The police asked everyone in the neighborhood (who, whom) the troublemakers were.
11. (Whoever, Whomever) needs advice should talk to a friend or guidance counselor.
12. (Who, Whom) was your report about?
13. Persephone was the woman (who, whom) Hades carried away to the underworld.
14. No one (who, whom) was in the audience will ever forget the singer's farewell performance.
15. Doug, (whom, whose) father repairs stereos, has volunteered to fix the speakers in the auditorium.

B Write the correct pronoun from those given in parentheses.

1. The inventor (who, whom) got movies off to a roaring start was Thomas Edison.
2. It was Edison, (who, whom) we now consider a genius, who introduced the kinetoscope in 1894.
3. With this instrument, (whoever, whomever) had a nickel could watch a film by peering through a viewer and turning a crank.
4. Two years later, the Lumière brothers, (who, whom) worked in Paris, invented a projector.

5. Consequently, theater owners, (whom, whose) main objective was making a profit, could collect ticket money from (whoever, whomever) they could crowd into their theaters.
6. It was Warner Brothers (who, whom) presented the first all-sound film in 1923.
7. Many actors (whom, who) starred in silent films faced a dilemma.
8. Actors (whom, whose) voices didn't match the audience's expectations were out of jobs.
9. For example, silent screen heartthrob Rudolph Valentino, (who, whom) was worshiped by millions of fans, quickly lost his popularity when women heard his high, thin voice.
10. Lillian Gish was one actress (whom, who) audiences loved in both silent films and "talkies."

Rudolph Valentino and Vilma Banky in the1926 film *Son of the Sheik.*

Pronouns with Appositives

The pronouns *we* and *us* are often followed by an appositive, a noun that identifies the pronoun. Phrases such as *we students* or *us players* can cause confusion when you are trying to choose the correct pronoun. To decide whether to use the nominative case *we* or the objective case *us* in this type of construction, drop the appositive, or noun, and read the sentence without it.

> (We, Us) girls can bring the lunch. (We can bring the lunch, *not* Us can bring the lunch.)
> The problem was easy for (we, us) girls. (for us, *not* for we)

Exercise

Write the correct pronoun from those given in parentheses.

1. (We, Us) Americans can learn a great deal from other cultures.
2. The law guarantees the rights of (we, us) students.
3. Do you think that (we, us) two will have the same class?
4. There is no such thing as a junk car to (we, us) antique auto enthusiasts.
5. Only (we, us) two were asked to read the part of Macbeth.
6. The pianist played warm-up scales for (we, us) newcomers.
7. (We, Us) fans were not surprised by the Bears' record.
8. There is a private rehearsal for (we, us) flute players.
9. Did you know that (we, us) twins are taking part in a nationwide study on inherited versus acquired learning?
10. The candidate who won the mayoral election was grateful to (we, us) loyal supporters.

Pronouns as Appositives

You have learned how to use pronouns correctly when they are followed by appositives. Now you will see how to use pronouns when they, themselves, are appositives.

The form of a pronoun used as an appositive is determined by the use of the noun to which it is in apposition.

> The delegates, *Tony* and *I,* want your support. (*Tony* and *I* are in apposition to *delegates,* which is the subject of *want.* The nominative form *I* is required.)
>
> For the two producers, *Margo* and *him,* the show was a hit. (*Margo* and *him* are in apposition to *producers,* which is the object of the preposition *for.* Therefore, the objective form of the pronoun, *him,* is required.)
>
> We gave the neighbors, *Toby* and *her,* a housewarming gift. (*Toby* and *her* are in apposition to *neighbors,* which is the indirect object of *gave.* Therefore, the objective form of the pronoun, *her,* is required.)

To determine which form of the pronoun to use in apposition, try the appositive by itself with the verb or preposition.

> Her friends, Jackie and (he, him), were always calling. (Jackie and he were, *not* Jackie and him were.)
>
> The flowers are from two of your friends, Sally and (I, me). (The flowers are from me, *not* from I.)

Pronouns in Comparisons

Comparisons can be made by using a clause that begins with *than* or *as*. Notice the use of pronouns in the comparisons below.

> Fred is better at chess *than he is*.
> You have as many A's *as she has*.

The final clause in a comparison is sometimes **elliptical,** meaning that some words have been omitted. The use of an elliptical clause can make pronoun choice more difficult.

> Fred is better at chess than he.
> You have as many A's as she.

To decide which pronoun form to use in an elliptical clause, fill in the words that are not stated.

> Herb plays the trumpet better than (I, me). (Herb plays the trumpet better than *I play*.)
> Betty was expecting Paul rather than (she, her). (Betty was expecting Paul rather than *Betty was expecting her*.)
> We can sing as well as (they, them). (We can sing as well as *they can sing*.)

Exercises

A Write the correct form of the pronoun from those that are given in parentheses.

1. Write to your representatives, Mr. Owen and (he, him), to express your opinion about the proposed tax increase.
2. Bill is much better at budgeting than (I, me).
3. The performers, Brad and (she, her), were dressed in bright pink wigs and shiny black costumes with sequins.
4. The class would rather have you for president than (he, him).
5. No one was more upset over the test scores than (she, her).
6. After the concert we gave the soloists, Jenny and (she, her), bouquets of flowers.
7. The violin section is tuning up earlier than (they, them).
8. We were expecting someone at the zoning board meeting who had more information than (he, him).
9. At the end of the competition, the judges gave two speakers, Barry and (I, me), first place honors.
10. Would you mind if I asked my cousins, Loretta and (she, her), to go with us?

B Rewrite the following sentences, correcting any errors in pronoun usage. If the sentence contains no errors, write *Correct*.

1. Us hikers should always pay attention to the weather.
2. Our trail guides, Mario and him, told us to dress appropriately, but some of us didn't listen.
3. Guess whom was wearing a heavy sweater and slacks on what turned out to be the hottest day of the year?
4. The other hikers, who arrived in shorts, T-shirts, and light jackets, were obviously better informed than me.
5. After panting and sweating along the trail for hours, I decided I would never make this mistake again.

Reflexive Pronouns

A pronoun such as *myself, herself,* or *ourselves* is used reflexively when it refers to a preceding noun or pronoun.

A reflexive pronoun cannot be used by itself; it must have an antecedent in the same sentence.

Incorrect	Jean and myself carried it up the stairs. (There is no antecedent for *myself.*)
Correct	Jean and I carried it up the stairs.
Incorrect	The coach spoke to Tom and myself.
Correct	The coach spoke to Tom and me.

The words *hisself* and *theirselves* are nonstandard.

Incorrect	The boys washed the clothes theirselves.
Correct	The boys washed the clothes themselves.

Exercise

Write the correct pronoun from those given in parentheses.

1. Sam can ski much better than (I, myself).
2. Arthur Miller (hisself, himself) went to China to direct his play *Death of a Salesman*.
3. We kept some of the fruitcakes for (us, ourselves).
4. The coach spoke to Evie and (me, myself) about team spirit.
5. During the garage sale, Kim and (myself, I) will be cashiers.
6. No one but (yourself, you) volunteered to sell refreshments during halftime.
7. I can't hear (me, myself) think!
8. This discussion is between (him, himself) and (myself, me).
9. Everyone in the class understood the biology assignment but (themselves, them).
10. The drivers (theirselves, themselves) realized the danger.

Checkpoint *Parts 4 and 5*

A Write the correct pronoun from those given in parentheses.

1. Unfortunately, Jim knew the answers to the trivia questions on science and history better than (I, myself, me).
2. Do you know (who, whom) became king after Henry VIII?
3. These can't be (my, mine); (my, mine) gloves are leather.
4. Will the concert manager allow (we, us) three backstage if we tell him that we're reporters for the school paper?
5. We tried to alert (whoever, whomever) might be in the burning building by pulling the fire alarm.
6. My parents were awakened by (us, our) enthusiastic but off-key caroling on the front porch.
7. The sandwich with lettuce only is for (he, him); (hers, her) has tomato and mayonnaise.
8. (Who, Whom) knows the name of the Norwegian playwright who wrote *A Doll's House?*
9. Lenny burned (hisself, himself) yesterday afternoon while trying to light the barbecue grill.
10. (Who, Whom) would have thought that (she, her) debating in school would eventually lead to a career in politics.

B Rewrite the sentences, correcting pronoun errors.

1. Doug Henning demonstrated some tricks that were even easy enough for we amateurs.
2. My father says me watching too much television may injure my grades as well as my eyes.
3. Whomever gets there first should scout out a good campsite.
4. Before we plan our trip, we should talk to someone whom has already traveled to the Yucatán peninsula.
5. The foundation was organized by Senator Sam Nunn and he.

Part 6
Pronoun-Antecedent Agreement

An antecedent is the noun or pronoun for which another pronoun stands and to which it refers.

A pronoun must agree with its antecedent in number, gender, and person.

Agreement in Number If the antecedent of a pronoun is singular, a singular pronoun is required. If the antecedent is plural, a plural pronoun is required.

The singular indefinite pronouns listed below often cause difficulty. When a singular indefinite pronoun is the antecedent of another pronoun, the second pronoun must be singular. Remember that a prepositional phrase following an indefinite pronoun does not affect the number of any other word in the sentence.

another	anything	everybody	neither	one
anybody	each	everyone	nobody	somebody
anyone	either	everything	no one	someone

Each (singular) of the boys brought *his* (singular) guitar.
No one (singular) has made up *his or her* (singular) mind.

Notice in the example above that the phrase *his or her* is considered singular.

The following indefinite pronouns are plural and are referred to by the plural possessive pronouns *our*, *your*, and *their*.

| both | few | many | several |

Both of the countries have improved *their* economies.
Few of us wanted *our* pictures taken.
Many of you do not have *your* eligibility slips.

The indefinite pronouns *all, some, any,* and *none* may take either a singular or plural pronoun, depending upon the meaning intended.

All the furniture was in *its* original condition.
All the students were taking *their* last examination.

Some of the cider has lost *its* tang.
Some of the children in the refugee camp have heard from *their* parents.

In all of the examples above, the indefinite pronouns are used as subjects. Note that the verb as well as any other pronouns referring to the subject all agree in number with that subject.

Incorrect   None of the singers *was* making *their* debuts.
Correct   None of the singers *were* making *their* debuts.
Correct   None of the singers *was* making *his or her* debut.

Two or more singular antecedents joined by *or* or *nor* are referred to by a singular pronoun.

Either Bob or Hank will let us use *his* car.
Neither the cat nor the dog had eaten *its* meal.

Use the noun nearer the verb to determine the pronoun for subjects joined by *or* or *nor*.

> Neither the cat nor the dogs had eaten *their* meal.
> Neither the dogs nor the cat had eaten *his* meal.

Collective nouns may be referred to by either a singular or plural pronoun. Determine the number from the meaning in the sentence.

> The track team *has its* new coach. (The team is thought of as a unified, singular whole.)
> The track team *have* worked out in *their* spare time. (Various members act individually.)

Agreement in Gender Masculine gender is indicated by *he, his, him.* Feminine gender is indicated by *she, her, hers.* Neuter gender is indicated by *it* and *its.* A pronoun must be of the same gender as the word to which it refers.

When a singular pronoun must refer to both feminine and masculine antecedents, the phrase *his or her* is acceptable. It is, in fact, preferred by some people who wish to avoid what they consider to be sexist language.

Correct	Each student should have *his* ticket ready.
Correct	Each student should have *his or her* ticket ready.

Agreement in Person A personal pronoun must be in the same person as its antecedent. The words *one, everyone,* and *everybody* are in the third person. They are referred to by *he, his, him, she, her, hers.*

Incorrect	*One* should always wear *your* seatbelt.
Correct	*One* should always wear *his or her* seatbelt.

Exercise

Find and correct the errors in agreement in these sentences. Write *Correct* if there is no error.

1. The student council has made their decision to support an assembly commemorating the bicentennial of our state.
2. Everyone in my class agreed to donate their time to put on a skit about the early history of the state.
3. Many of the students voted for Elaine and me to direct.
4. At first, no one seemed to know what they were doing.
5. Their experience was more hectic than you expected.

6. For example, each of the leading players had their own schedule.
7. Also, it seemed that someone always left your props at home.
8. For a while, not one of the stage crew expected to see his or her home again.
9. Another problem was caused by the fact that not everybody was able to supply their own costume.
10. Suddenly, many of the problems found its own solution.
11. Some of the girls decided that they could adapt their old dance costumes.
12. We also found that you could borrow props from a resale shop.

Part 7
Pronoun Reference

A writer must always be sure that there is a clear connection between a pronoun and its antecedent. If the pronoun reference is indefinite or ambiguous, the resulting sentence may be confusing, misleading, or even humorous.

Indefinite Reference

To avoid any confusion for the reader, every personal pronoun should refer clearly to a definite antecedent.

Indefinite   *It* says in the newspaper that a strike is likely.
Better   *The newspaper* says that a strike is likely.

Indefinite	Al is running for office because *it* is exciting.
Better	Al is running for office because *politics* is exciting.
Indefinite	Read what *they* say about headsets.
Better	Read what *this article* says about headsets.

The pronoun *you* is sometimes used when it is not meant to refer to the person spoken to. The effect is usually confusing.

Indefinite	In that course *you* have fewer exams.
Better	In that course *there are* fewer exams.

Exercise

Revise the sentences to remove all indefinite pronoun references.

1. It said on TV that the President plans to veto the bill.
2. During Prohibition, they made the sale of liquor illegal.
3. Andy wants to be a chef because it interests him.
4. The best show they broadcast is *Nova*.
5. In this school, they make you study a foreign language.
6. I missed Carl's birthday, and I'm sorry about it.
7. The temperature is dropping; it may force the orange growers to light smudge pots to keep the crop from freezing.
8. In Hawaii, they greet you with leis made of flowers.
9. I have never told a lie, and it makes people trust me.
10. You visit three European capitals in three days on that tour.

Ambiguous Reference

The word *ambiguous* means "having two or more possible meanings." The reference of a pronoun is ambiguous if the pronoun may refer to more than one word. This situation arises whenever a noun or pronoun falls between the pronoun and its true antecedent.

Ambiguous	Take the books off the shelves and dust them. (Does this mean dust the books or dust the shelves?)
Better	Dust the books after you take them off the shelves.
Ambiguous	The hounds chased the foxes until they were exhausted. (Were the hounds or the foxes exhausted?)
Better	Until the hounds were exhausted, they chased the foxes.
Ambiguous	Before I could hit the mosquito on your arm, it flew off. (Did the mosquito or the arm fly off?)
Better	Before I could kill the mosquito, it flew off your arm.

Exercise

Rewrite the sentences below to remove all ambiguous pronoun references.

1. When I put the candle in the candelabra, it broke.
2. Sara told Tanya that she really should try out for track.
3. There's an orange in this lunch bag, but it isn't mine.
4. Allison put the plant in the wagon after she bought it.
5. Before you wash them, separate the clothes from the towels.
6. Tom explained to Fred that his car needed to be overhauled.
7. Julie told Kate that her drawing won an award.
8. Take the tennis rackets out of the presses and check them.
9. Joan took the belt off her dress and sent it to the dry cleaners.
10. Although I keep my books with my notebooks, I always lose them.
11. Ellen told Kay that she had made a serious mistake by not paying more attention in class.
12. As the designer talked to the model, she smiled.

Checkpoint *Parts 6 and 7*

Rewrite the sentences, correcting any errors in pronoun usage.

1. In most ads, they never tell you the price.
2. Neither of the people who complained would give their name.
3. Nobody showed up after the raffle to collect their prize.
4. When the traffic officer spoke to Mom, she frowned.
5. I think it is difficult to stay on a diet.
6. Take the saddle off the horse before you polish it.
7. Each of the players promised that they would sell ten raffle tickets by next Friday.
8. Nobody turned their outline in on time.
9. The butcher knew it was time to sharpen his knife.
10. Did either your father or grandfather change their name?
11. We found that you could hear well even in the last row.
12. Ana told Kim that her painting looked professional.
13. Some of the team have his equipment on wrong.
14. Either the principal or the class advisers must give his or her approval in writing.
15. I saw the picture in a magazine, but now I can't find it.

Linking
Grammar *&* Writing

You have just found out that plans are being made to construct a twenty-story building just four feet from your house or apartment. Write a letter to the editor of the local newspaper in which you give your opinion about whether or not the building should be built. In your letter, use pronouns in all three cases.

Prewriting and Drafting Think of the effects that such a large building would have, especially on you and your family. List all the positive effects that you can think of. Then list all the negative effects. Read through your lists and decide if you are for or against the building. Write one sentence that states your position. Then think of reasons that support your position.

When you draft your letter, begin by stating your purpose. Explain your point of view and the reasons behind it, using facts and details. Conclude with a sentence that summarizes your ideas.

Revising and Proofreading Use the following questions to help evaluate and revise your letter:

1. Is your position clearly expressed?
2. Have you given convincing reasons to support your position?
3. Have you used facts and details to explain your reasons?
4. Are the reasons arranged in an effective order?

Additional Writing Topic Write a two-paragraph description of yourself and one other person. In the first paragraph, describe your similarities. In the second, describe your differences. Use pronouns, and be certain that the antecedents are clear.

Chapter 27
Application and Review

A Choosing Pronouns Correctly Choose the correct form of the pronoun.

1. Was it really (they, them) singing or was it a lip-sync?
2. Except for my sister and (she, her), no one else saw the light.
3. (Who, Whom) does Inspector Holmes suspect?
4. The chef trained Britt and (he, him) as assistants.
5. Neither Hall nor David would budge from (his, their) point of view on arms control.
6. It was Gilbert and Sullivan (who, whom) created comic operettas such as *The Mikado* and *The Pirates of Penzance*.
7. No one understands the situation better than (I, me), and no one dislikes it more than (I, me).
8. Will you go to the air show with Marcus and (I, me)?
9. I really enjoyed (you, your) singing those Civil War ballads.
10. The flight attendant told (they, them) that (they, them) must be able to speak a foreign language.
11. The captain awarded (I, me, myself) a trophy for sportsmanship.
12. Everyone must provide (his or her, their) own transportation.
13. Sondra asked the ushers, Miguel and (she, her), for directions to the kinetic sculpture display.
14. Between (he, himself, him) and (I, myself, me), we managed to make a mess of the entire kitchen.
15. The "glamorous" passenger in the limousine was (I, me)!

B Correcting Pronoun Errors Rewrite the sentences, eliminating pronoun errors. If there are no errors, write *Correct*.

1. The proud owner of the dirt bike was myself.
2. Everyone left the debate feeling pleased with their performance.
3. If you could spend a day with a famous person from history, who would it be?
4. His playing in the band was a source of satisfaction to Brian's grandfather.
5. Max and me are trying to produce a program for cable television.
6. You made as many errors adding the figures as me.
7. The contest was between Frank and myself.
8. No one wants to give their free time to the project.

9. Whomever touches the wet paint will leave fingerprints on the doorknob.
10. The main attractions were her and the ventriloquist.
11. Every doctor should attempt to keep their medical knowledge up to date.
12. To whom did you want this message delivered?
13. Although you were shorter than Danny last year, you are now two inches taller than he.
14. Gina always peeks at the books' endings; I am more patient than her.
15. Neither my dad nor my uncle George can fit into their old World War II Army uniform.

C *Proofreading* Rewrite the following paragraphs. Correct all errors in pronoun usage as well as any errors in spelling, capitalization, or punctuation.

Sir Kay looked around and said, "Who took my sword?" A knight cannot be seen at a jousting tournament without their sword!"

Wart piped up, "I know where you sord is; I forgot to bring it from camp."

Sir Kay sputtered, "Didn't you hear my reminding you not to forget anything when Father and myself were leaving?"

"Yes," said wart pleasantly, "but you and him also asked me to water you're horses, and I did that first. Don't worry. I'll run back to camp and get your sword.

As Wart dashed threw the town square, he noticed a stone with a sword protruding from it. Wart glanced around to see who it could belong to, but no one was there. As he approached, Wart could see that the sword was inscribed, "Whomever pulls this sword from this stone shall be king of England.

"Oh, well," Wart said to hisself, "I'll just borrow it for the tournament and hope that whoever owns it will understand."

As soon as Wart pulled the sword from the stone, bells rang and a mystical lite appeared. Excited people came running from all directions, asking, "Who pulled the sword from the stone?"

"Look! He holds the sword. It has to be he."

Another cautioned, "Not so fast! Make him do it again so we can be sure it was him."

So Wart, being an agreeable lad, replaced the sword and removed it again the Crowd cheered.

They say that a week later Wart was crowned Arthur, King of England.

28
Using Modifiers

*A*n artist envisions a white horse standing in a lavender garden, creates it, and suddenly you see what before existed only in the artist's mind. Amazing! Yet a writer can do even more. Writers can convey not only what they see but also whatever they hear, feel, taste, and touch.

In this chapter you will learn to use modifiers to accomplish this feat by selecting and placing vivid modifiers in your sentences as skillfully as artists mix and use vivid colors in their compositions.

Part 1
Understanding Modifiers

An **adjective** tells *which one, what kind,* or *how many* about a noun or pronoun. An **adverb** tells *how, when, where,* or *to what extent* about a verb, adjective, or another adverb. To decide whether a modifier is an adjective or adverb, determine the part of speech of the word it modifies.

Garfield the cat is a character in a *popular* cartoon. (The word *popular* modifies the noun *cartoon. Popular* is an adjective.)

This feisty feline is quite *independent.* (The word *independent* modifies the noun *feline. Independent* is a predicate adjective.)

Garfield *always* fights for some of his owner's lasagna. (The word *always* modifies the verb *fights. Always* is an adverb.)

His owner, Jon, is *seldom* victorious. (The word *seldom* modifies the adjective *victorious. Seldom* is an adverb.)

Adjective and Adverb Forms

Adjectives cannot be recognized by any one form or ending. Adverbs, however, are often recognizable because most adverbs are formed by adding *-ly* to adjectives.

Adjective	Adverb
poor	poorly
careful	carefully
sudden	suddenly
excited	excitedly
happy	happily
inquisitive	inquisitively

A few adjectives and adverbs are spelled in the same way. In most of these cases, the adverb form does not end in *-ly*.

Adjective	Adverb
a *straight* course	thinks *straight*
a *hard* problem	works *hard*
a *high* note	soars *high*
a *long* journey	lasts *long*
a *late* flight	arrives *late*

Some adverbs have two forms, both of which are considered correct. One form is spelled with *-ly*. The other is not.

Come *quick!*	Please, move *quickly.*
Drive *slow.*	We must be careful and work *slowly.*
Stay *close!*	Follow *closely* or you will get lost.

Usage Note The short form of the adverbs shown above is more likely to be used in informal speech or in short imperative sentences. The form ending in *-ly* is used in formal writing.

Modifiers That Follow Verbs

A word that modifies an action verb, an adjective, or another adverb is always an adverb.

Beyond the castle moat, a beast howled *dreadfully*. (*Dreadfully* modifies the action verb *howled*.)

The howl of this beast was *really* dreadful. (*Really* modifies the adjective *dreadful*.)

So dreadfully did the beast howl that the king sent a knight out to slay it. (*So* modifies the adverb *dreadfully*.)

Always use an adverb to modify an action verb. Be careful not to use an adjective to modify an action verb.

Incorrect	The officer stepped *cautious* into the room.
Correct	The officer stepped *cautiously* into the room.
Incorrect	Two hot-air balloons rose *sudden* on the horizon.
Correct	Two hot-air balloons rose *suddenly* on the horizon.
Incorrect	The karate opponents bowed *polite* to each other.
Correct	The karate opponents bowed *politely* to each other.

A linking verb, on the other hand, is usually followed by an adjective rather than an adverb. As you have learned, a predicate adjective follows a linking verb and modifies the subject of the sentence.

The plastic fruit in the bowl appeared *real*. (*Real* is a predicate adjective. It follows the linking verb *appeared,* and it modifies the subject *fruit.*)

A speaker or a writer rarely has a problem when a modifier follows a form of the verb *be,* the most common linking verb. Some linking verbs, however, may also be used as action verbs. When these verbs are used as action verbs, they can be modified by adverbs.

Verbs that can be used as both linking and action verbs include *look, sound, appear, grow, smell, taste,* and *remain.* Look at the examples below.

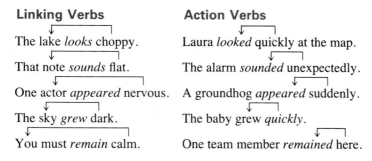

Linking Verbs	Action Verbs
The lake *looks* choppy.	Laura *looked* quickly at the map.
That note *sounds* flat.	The alarm *sounded* unexpectedly.
One actor *appeared* nervous.	A groundhog *appeared* suddenly.
The sky *grew* dark.	The baby grew *quickly.*
You must *remain* calm.	One team member *remained* here.

Exercises

A On your paper, write the correct modifier of the two given in parentheses. Then label it as an adjective or an adverb.

1. You can find the tollway (easy, easily) from here.
2. The young colt seems (unsteady, unsteadily) on its feet.
3. Both alarms sounded (simultaneous, simultaneously).
4. It rained (steady, steadily) for forty days and nights.
5. Can a small, pocket calculator process figures as (rapid, rapidly) as a computer?
6. The captain felt (uneasy, uneasily) about the approaching storm.
7. Harriet found the solution to the first problem and (quick, quickly) turned to the second.
8. Columbus thought he had (certain, certainly) found India.
9. Your voice sounds (different, differently) on the phone.
10. The detective looked (suspicious, suspiciously) at the fingerprints on the windowsill.

B Write the correct modifier of the two given in parentheses. Label it as an adjective or adverb. Then write the word it modifies.

> *Example*   Lasers appear very (bright, brightly) when compared
> with other lights.
> bright, adjective, Lasers

1. Scientists felt (confident, confidently) that they would be able to create the kind of superlight that was first described by Albert Einstein in 1917.

2. For fifty years, scientists worked (patient, patiently) to create this powerful light, which they called a *laser*.

3. In 1960, the first device for producing lasers was built (successful, successfully) by Theodore Maiman.

4. This rudimentary device was small enough to fit in one hand, yet it produced a beam of light stronger than any that had been produced (previously, previous).

5. Since Maiman's achievement, other scientists have used lasers (creative, creatively).

6. Some lasers produce beams so strong that they can cut (direct, directly) through steel.

7. Other lasers produce beams (precise, precisely) enough to be used in surgery.

8. Lasers are (remarkable, remarkably) in the ways they have improved surgical techniques.

9. Most laser surgery can be done (rapid, rapidly) without causing any bleeding.

10. Follow the development of lasers (careful, carefully); they are bound to be important in the future.

c *Write Now* In medieval times knights rode out to seek adventure and slay dragons. As protection, knights wore elaborate suits of armor. Do some brief research on the kinds of armor knights wore. Then use your imagination to write a description of what wearing a suit of armor would be like. First, describe the appearance of the armor. Then tell how it fits you and what it feels like as you move about. Use adjectives, predicate adjectives, and adverbs to make your description interesting and precise.

St. George and the Dragon, Paolo Uccello, circa 1450

Tom Swifties

Tom Swifties are word puns based on a comic relationship between an adverb and the main idea of a sentence.

Tom Swift, hero of a series of popular novels, was a youthful genius who invented such wonders as electric airplanes. The books are out of vogue now, but the punning word game named in Tom's honor is still going strong. These Tom Swifties will give you the idea [and, perhaps, lead you into creating your own].

"Pass the cards," said Tom ideally.

"I have the mumps," said Tom infectiously.

"You gave me two less than a dozen," said Tom tensely.

"I don't like wilted lettuce," said Tom limply.

"Our ball club needs a man who can hit sixty homers a season," said Tom ruthlessly.

"He's a young M.D.," said Tom internally.

"Gold leaf," said Tom guiltily.

"I'm out of cartridges for my starting gun," said Tom blankly.

"It's the maid's night off," said Tom helplessly.

"The thermostat is set too high," said Tom heatedly.

"The chimney is clogged," said Tom fluently.

"Golly, that old man is bent over," said Tom stupidly.

"Don't you love sleeping outdoors?" said Tom intently.

"I've been stung," said Tom waspishly.

"Let's invite Greg and Gary," said Tom gregariously.

"This boat leaks," said Tom balefully.

"Welcome to my tomb," said Tom cryptically.

"I just returned from Japan," said Tom disorientedly.

"I'll never stick my fist into the lion's cage again," said Tom offhandedly.

"I can't find the oranges," said Tom fruitlessly.

"I lost my trousers," said Tom expansively.

"Are you fond of venison?" said Tom fawningly.

"Here are my Tom Swifty entries," said Tom submissively.

"You've ruined my health," said Tom halfheartedly.

"Is there a quiz today?" asked Tom testily.

"It's just too early to get up," complained Tom mournfully.

"What's the angle?" asked Tom obtusely.

"Is that you?" asked Tom sheepishly.

"It's raining," reported Tom precipitously.

Willard R. Espy and others

Comparison of Adjectives and Adverbs

Every adjective and adverb has a basic form, called the **positive degree.** This is the form of the word you will find in the dictionary. The positive degree is commonly used to describe individual things, groups, or actions.

Positive   Many microcomputers are *light*. Most of them can be transported *easily*.

The **comparative degree** of an adjective or an adverb is used to compare two things, groups, or actions.

Comparative   A portable computer is *lighter* than a desk-top computer. Most portables can be carried *more easily* than most desk-top computers.

When deciding whether the comparative is correct, be alert to phrases such as *the other one* that signal the comparison of two things.

When more than two things, group, or actions are compared, the **superlative degree** of an adjective or an adverb is used.

Superlative   A lap-top computer is the *lightest* computer. Of all computers now available, it can be transported the *most easily*.

To make comparisons correctly, remember that the comparative degree is used to compare only two things and that the superlative degree is used to compare three or more things. Specific numbers are not always given in a comparison. At times you must determine how many things are being compared. Would you use the comparative or the superlative form in the following sentence?

This is the (better, best) restaurant in the city.

You can infer that the comparison is between one restaurant and all the other restaurants in the city. Therefore, the superlative form, *best,* should be used. Now try this example.

Which is (better, best)—the French restaurant or the Italian one?

Since only two restaurants are being compared, the comparative form, *better,* should be used.

Regular Comparisons

Like verbs, modifiers may be regular or irregular. Most adjectives and adverbs are regular and form the comparative and superlative in one of two ways.

A one-syllable modifier forms the comparative and superlative by adding -er and -est. Some two-syllable modifiers also form the comparative and superlative in this way.

Positive	Comparative	Superlative
warm	warmer	warmest
close	closer	closest
soon	sooner	soonest
sad	sadder	saddest
funny	funnier	funniest

Spelling Note Most dictionaries list the comparative and superlative forms of modifiers in which there is a spelling change, such as the change from *y* to *i* in *funnier, funniest.*

Most modifiers with two syllables and all modifiers with three or more syllables use *more* and *most* to form the comparative and superlative.

Positive	Comparative	Superlative
helpful	more helpful	most helpful
precisely	more precisely	most precisely
optimistic	more optimistic	most optimistic
reliably	more reliably	most reliably

For negative comparisons, *less* and *least* are used before the positive form of the modifier.

Positive	Comparative	Superlative
careful	less careful	least careful
comfortable	less comfortable	least comfortable
eagerly	less eagerly	least eagerly
cautiously	less cautiously	least cautiously

Irregular Comparisons

A few adjectives and adverbs are irregular. Their comparative and superlative forms are not based on the positive form. Because irregular modifiers are used frequently, you should memorize their forms. Study the list of irregular modifiers on the next page.

Positive	Comparative	Superlative
bad	worse	worst
far	farther *or* further	farthest *or* furthest
good	better	best
late	later	latest *or* last
little	less	least
many	more	most
much	more	most
well	better	best

Usage Note *Farther* refers to distance, and *further* refers to an addition in time or amount: The distance to town is *farther* than I thought. I won't discuss it *further*.

Exercises

A Rewrite the following sentences. Correct all errors in the use of comparative and superlative modifiers.

1. Is solar energy the less expensive form of energy?
2. Of the three rowboats we rented, the yellow one was the leakier.
3. The worse experience of my life was forgetting my lines on stage.
4. Geoffrey has the stronger southern accent in the class.
5. Which is mightiest, the pen or the sword?
6. Malabar, a tropical plant, is least bitter than spinach.
7. The world's faster bird is named the swift.
8. Joe explained the problem patienter than I could have.
9. Which of these stereo speakers produces the best sound—this one or that one?
10. Fruit is most plentiful in summer than fall.
11. We all practiced the polka, but Jan did it more enthusiastically.
12. Of the horse and automobile, great-grandfather believed that a horse was safest.
13. Who among all those who auditioned for the ballet seemed the more promising?
14. Michelangelo's more famous masterpiece, the Sistine Chapel ceiling, took him four years to complete.
15. Housing is usually cheapest in rural areas than in the city.
16. That was the awfulest mistake I ever made.
17. Of the two candidates, Abernathy was the least qualified.
18. Which is the hardest substance, carbon or steel?
19. Try to think most positively about getting a college scholarship.
20. A rare metal called osmium is the heavier of all metals.

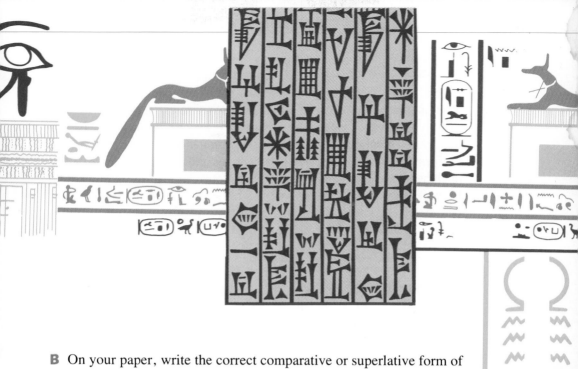

B On your paper, write the correct comparative or superlative form of the modifier given in parentheses.

1. About the same time that Egyptian hieroglyphics were fascinating European scholars, archaeologists in the Near East were uncovering another (mysterious) script.
2. Cuneiform, a wedge-shaped writing, had been in use much (early) than Egyptian hieroglyphics, but information about it had somehow been lost for a thousand years.
3. Of all the samples discovered, the (old) tablets were found in Mesopotamia.
4. The (good) way to describe cuneiform is to say that it looks like bird tracks left in wet mud.
5. Cuneiform writing was done by pressing a triangular-shaped stylus into a soft clay tablet; then the clay tablet was baked to make it (hard) and stronger.
6. Because it has (few) wedges than hieroglyphics, cuneiform is considered a (elementary) form of writing.
7. During the years it was used, cuneiform changed (little) than hieroglyphics.
8. Even though it is one of the (primitive) of all written languages, cuneiform does have a form of punctuation.
9. One mark that was clearly (small) than the others was used to separate words.
10. Some forms of cuneiform were (difficult) than others to read; it took scientists many years to decipher them.

c *Write Now* Imagine that you are a reviewer for your local newspaper. Your "beat" is either entertainment or special sports events. Your assignment this week is to attend two similar special events—for example, two rock concerts, two ballets, two tennis matches, or two ice-skating competitions. Write a review in which you compare the two performances. Use comparative adjectives and adverbs to describe and evaluate the events you have attended. Point out features of equipment (a *larger* racket, a *more elaborate* costume) and the actual performance (served *more powerfully,* spun the *most gracefully*).

Checkpoint *Parts 1 and 2*

A On your paper, write the correct modifier of the two modifiers given in parentheses. Then tell whether the modifier is an adjective or an adverb.

1. Press down (firm, firmly) so your signature comes through.
2. I type (more slowly, most slowly) than anyone else in class.
3. Of the twins, Kara is the (younger, youngest).
4. Which is (more far, farther) from Miami, Haiti or Bermuda?
5. Which are (funnier, funniest), old movies or sitcoms?
6. Eric's handwriting is the (elaboratest, most elaborate) imaginable.
7. The team felt (more confident, more confidently) after practice.
8. Of the two stations, PBS's coverage was (better, best).
9. Of all the squads, ours made the (fewer, fewest) goals.
10. Night descended (quick, quickly) on the valley.

B Correct any errors in the use of modifiers. If the sentence contains no error, write *Correct*.

1. This ice skate is the sharpest of the pair.
2. The fans have never cheered so enthusiastically.
3. The incoming waves are moving terribly fast.
4. The chimney must be cleaned regular to avoid fires.
5. Which is easiest to learn, knitting or crocheting?
6. Of all the basketball players, Lee dribbles the most skillfully.
7. Which did you feel was most suspenseful, the book or the movie?
8. The pollution from the factory smelled terribly all summer.
9. The charity drive is progressing steady toward its goal.
10. The coach was the better of the three banquet speakers.

Part 3
Using Comparisons Correctly

The following guidelines and examples will help you to use comparisons correctly.

Avoid Double Comparisons

The comparative form of a modifier is made either by adding *-er* or by using *more*. It is incorrect to use both.

The superlative form of a modifier is made either by adding *-est* or by using *most*. It is incorrect to use both.

Incorrect	My boat will go much more faster than yours.
Correct	My boat will go much faster than yours.

Incorrect	You should find it more easier to do.
Correct	You should find it easier to do.

Incorrect	It was the most fanciest house I'd ever seen.
Correct	It was the fanciest house I'd ever seen.

Avoid Illogical Comparisons

Illogical or confusing comparisons result if two unrelated items are compared or if something is compared with itself.

The word *other* or the word *else* is required in comparisons of an individual member with the rest of the group.

Illogical	Bill has won more trophies than any student athlete. (Bill is also a student athlete.)
Clear	Bill has won more tropies than any *other* student athlete.

Illogical	George is as tall as anyone on the school's basketball team. (George is also on the team.)
Clear	George is as tall as anyone *else* on the school's basketball team.

The word *as* or the word *than* is required after the first modifier in a compound comparison.

Illogical	Tim is as tall if not taller than Brad.
Awkward	Tim is as tall *as*, if not taller than, Brad.
Clear	Tim is as tall *as* Brad, if not taller.

Illogical	Sue's grades are better or at least as good as Helen's.
Clear	Sue's grades are better *than,* or at least as good as, Helen's.
Illogical	The Dodgers' chances of winning the pennant are as good if not better than the Giants'.
Clear	The Dodgers' chances of winning the pennant are as good *as* the Giants', if not better.

Both parts of a comparison must be stated completely if there is any chance of its being misunderstood.

Confusing	I miss her more than Sandra.
Clear	I miss her more than Sandra *does.*
Clear	I miss her more than I *miss* Sandra.
Confusing	Harvard beats Yale more often than Brown.
Clear	Harvard beats Yale more often than Brown *does.*
Clear	Harvard beats Yale more often than it *beats* Brown.

Confusing	Rio is nearer the Equator than London.
Clear	Rio is nearer the Equator than London *is.*

Exercises

A Find the errors in comparison in the following sentences, and rewrite the sentences correctly on your paper.

1. The work of a miner is more dangerous than a carpenter.
2. The letter *e* is used more frequently than any letter in the English language.

3. Joyce, the treasurer, is as informed as any member of the committee.
4. Strum your guitar a little more faster.
5. The rules of chess are more complicated than checkers.
6. Gardenias are as fragrant if not more fragrant than roses.
7. John Hancock signed his name more larger than usual.
8. Charles Lindbergh was more adventurous than any pilot.
9. I respect Betty Jean more than Chuck.
10. Spinach is as nutritious as any green vegetable.
11. The camera club enrollment is more bigger than ever this year.
12. The Colosseum in Rome is old, but the Parthenon in Athens is oldest.
13. Of all those in the contest, Tom's frog jumped the most highest.
14. Rye bread is as tasty if not tastier than pumpernickel.

B *Proofreading* The following paragraph contains errors in comparisons, spelling, capitalization, and punctuation. Rewrite the paragraph, correcting all errors.

> Have you noticed that billboard art is becoming even more bolder than in the past? Human figures are as large, if not larger than, the legendary giant Paul Bunyan. Some billboard people are raised from the background, they seem to pitch their product direct to each passerby. The most strikingest billboard I have seen shows a row of huge sneakers. It's colors are more vibranter than those in any billboard I have seen. Those sneakers would be to large even for Paul Bunyan!

Part 4
Special Problems with Modifiers

Certain adjectives and adverbs have forms that can be confusing. In the following section you will learn the correct use of adjectives and adverbs that are often used incorrectly.

This *and* These; That *and* Those

This and *that* modify singular words. *These* and *those* modify plural words. The words *kind, sort,* and *type* require a singular modifier.

| *Incorrect* | *These* kind are the best. |
| *Correct* | *This* kind is the best. |

| *Incorrect* | *These* sort of gloves wear well. |
| *Correct* | *This* sort of glove wears well. |

Them *and* Those

Those may be either a pronoun or an adjective. *Them* is always a pronoun and never an adjective.

Incorrect   Where did you get *them* statistics?
Correct   Where did you get *those* statistics? (adjective)
Correct   Where did you get *them*? (pronoun)

Bad *and* Badly

Bad is an adjective. When it is used after linking verbs, it modifies the subject. *Badly* is an adverb. It modifies action verbs.

I felt *bad*. (The adjective *bad* follows a linking verb and modifies the subject *I*.)

The team played *badly*. (The adverb *badly* modifies the action verb *played*.)

Good *and* Well

Good is an adjective. It modifies nouns or pronouns.

Zinnias are a *good* choice for a sunny garden.

Good can also be used as a predicate adjective with linking verbs. It then modifies the subject.

Dad always feels *good* after a brisk walk.

Well can be either an adjective or an adverb. As an adjective, *well* means "in good health," and it can follow a linking verb. As an adverb, *well* modifies an action verb. It tells how the action is performed.

The Vice-President looks *well*. (adjective)
Jake is sprinting *well* now. (adverb)

The Double Negative

Two negative words used together where only one is necessary is called a *double negative*. A double negative is incorrect.

Incorrect   He did*n't* have *no* energy left.
Correct   He did*n't* have *any* energy left.

Incorrect   She did*n't* know *nothing* about the Civil War.
Correct   She did*n't* know *anything* about the Civil War.

It is incorrect to use *hardly* or *barely* with a negative word.

| **Incorrect** | There was*n't hardly* a ticket left for the show. |
| **Correct** | There was *hardly* a ticket left for the show. |

| **Incorrect** | Terry could*n't barely* hit the ball. |
| **Correct** | Terry could *barely* hit the ball. |

Exercises

A On your paper, write the correct word of the two choices given in parentheses.

1. Anything that contains curry or thyme tastes (bad, badly) to me.
2. The bus that takes passengers to the terminal hasn't (never, ever) been so late before.
3. Be careful not to trip over (those, them) wires.
4. The lifeguard at the beach didn't say (anything, nothing) about an undertow.
5. The croton grew (good, well) even after being transplanted to the window box on the porch.
6. There (were, weren't) no socks left at the bottom of my drawer—they were all in the wash.
7. (Those, That) kind of elaborate theater costume requires many yards of brocade and lace.
8. The Prime Minister hasn't said (nothing, anything) that disagrees with our policy.
9. Secretaries should be able to type accurately, take dictation rapidly, and spell (well, good).
10. By midnight our family's Thanksgiving turkey (had, hadn't) barely begun to thaw out.

B On your paper, write the correct word of the two choices given in parentheses.

1. Until recently in India, there were hardly (any, no) tigers left in existence.
2. Hunting and the spread of civilization had destroyed three subspecies (quick, quickly), and the future of two more looked (bad, badly).
3. By (careful, carefully) studying the pugmarks, or tracks, of (those, them) cats that were left, conservationists learned where to establish a protected reserve.
4. Swampy areas south of Nepal were chosen because (these, this) kind of big cat is drawn to water.

5. Also, (this, these) areas aren't much good for (anything, nothing) else.
6. Tourists who haven't (ever, never) seen a tiger can visit the buffer zone around the park.
7. However, it is not (good, well) to go on foot.
8. For some reason, tigers won't do (nothing, anything) harmful to people mounted on elephants or riding in vehicles.
9. The big cat is doing (good, well) under protection.
10. (This, These) type of park may save tigers from extinction.

c *Proofreading* The following paragraph contains errors in the use of modifiers as well as other errors. Rewrite the paragraph correctly.

One can't hardly discuss the subject of inventers without mentioning Thomas Edison. The electric light, the storage battery, the phonographs, and the movie—all of them inventions are credited to Edison. Edisons impact on industrial America was great not only because he invented these kind of devices, but also because he revolutionized the businiss of invention. After Edison, the inventor was no longer an isolated individuel, instead, the inventor became a member of a scientific team. These new kind of team worked just as good, if not better than, inventors on their own.

Checkpoint *Parts 3 and 4*

A Rewrite the following sentences, correcting all errors in the use of modifiers.

1. Diamonds are much more harder than other gems.
2. Haven't none of the musicians arrived?
3. I telephone Louis more often than George.
4. We haven't scarcely begun to distribute our posters even though the concert is less than a week away.
5. In the upcoming season, the Knicks should play as good as any team in the division.
6. In full armor, some medieval knights couldn't hardly walk.
7. Saturn has as many satellites if not more than any planet.
8. Them cheeses are very high in cholesterol.
9. There isn't nobody else who writes such suspenseful stories.
10. The novels of Charles Dickens are more widely read than Jane Austen.
11. Please don't feel badly about the misunderstanding.
12. Grandfather is more active than anyone in the family.
13. The woodwind ensemble played so good that it received a standing ovation from the enthusiastic crowd.
14. These type of boots are fashionable but not practical for the cold, snowy winters of the Midwest.
15. The emcee pronounced the contestants' names bad.

B *Proofreading* Rewrite the following paragraph correcting all errors. Pay particular attention to the use of modifiers.

My brother and I needed money bad, so we convinced our nieghbor to let us paint her garage. We told her that we work good together and are not as slowly as professional painters. She agreed, and we headed to the hardwear store. A salesperson told us that we should use long-handled roller brushes so that we wouldn't have to climb no ladders. However, my brother told him, "We want to use these kind," and he pointed out some short-handled brushes. We bought them short-handled brushes and rented an eight-foot construction ladder. Our painting was going good when our neighbor came around to offer us something to drink. I turned toward her. And fell off the ladder! Them cans of paint and the brushes landed on top of me. It didn't hurt to bad, but I did get two black eyes and a coat of paint.

Linking
Grammar *&* Writing

The Guinness Book of World Records tells about a millionairess named Henrietta Green who had $95,000,000 when she died in 1916. She was a miser who saved scraps of soap and went to free clinics to avoid paying doctor bills. Write an interior monologue in which you put yourself into the mind of Henrietta Green and think her thoughts as she walks down the streets of New York City. Use adjectives and adverbs to make the impressions vivid and to show in concrete detail how the world's greatest miser saw life.

Prewriting and Drafting One way of writing an interior monologue is to imagine someone talking to himself or herself. Imagine, for example, what life would be like if you were a miser like Henrietta Green. What would you think about? How would you see the world around you?

As you draft your interior monologue, try to capture the unique personality of the miserly Henrietta. The following example shows one way of starting.

> Look at that broken bottle—a foolishly wasted penny that could have been wisely saved! Some poor fool will probably get hurt on the glass, and then there will be doctor bills, and medicine bills, and no end of trouble. How carelessly people throw money away these days! I'd suffer before I'd pay anyone good money.

Revising and Proofreading Read your draft aloud. Does it sound realistic and convincing, as if a real miser were talking? Have you used concrete details and vivid adjectives and adverbs to describe Henrietta's thoughts? Will your reader understand what Henrietta is seeing and sensing as she walks the streets of New York City?

After revising, carefully proofread your monologue. You may want to exchange monologues with a classmate.

Additional Writing Topic Imagine what our modern world would look like to a person from our country's past. What would Thomas Jefferson think of skyscrapers and digital watches? What would Emily Dickinson think of laser games and television commercials? Write a paragraph or two from the point of view of some historical figure seeing the modern world. Use comparative adjectives and adverbs to contrast the past and present worlds.

Weasel Words

T hink about the following advertising claims. As you read, notice the italicized modifier used in each one.

Sudsos leaves dishes *virtually* spotless. (Since *virtually* means "practically," Sudso leaves spots on dishes.)

Krumbles potato chips are made with 100 percent *natural* ingredients. (What would be *unnatural* ingredients?)

Tum-Eez relieves *simple* indigestion. (What if your indigestion is not *simple*?)

Virtually, natural, and *simple* are examples of **weasel words**— words that seem forthright, but are actually evasive. Advertising slogans and political rhetoric are frequently accused of being filled with weasel words. The term was coined at the turn of the century by political commentator Stewart Chaplin. He was annoyed with the way politicians often used qualifying words that seemed to add emphasis, but, in fact, made statements weaker. "Why, weasel words are words that suck the life out of the words next to them, just as a weasel sucks the egg and leaves the shell," he said.

Chaplin's phrase became popular in 1916, when it was used by Theodore Roosevelt to describe misleading political statements. Today, weasel words may be used so that they have no meaning at all. Weasel words allow the user to weasel out of commitment.

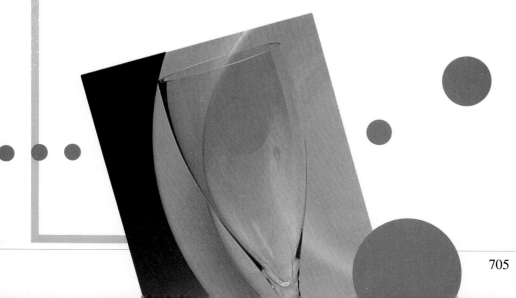

Chapter 28
Application and Review

A Choosing the Correct Modifier On your paper, write the correct form of the two choices given in parentheses.

1. That cartoonist draws her characters extremely (good, well).
2. The food that had been sitting out on the picnic table all day certainly smelled (bad , badly).
3. Would you bring me (them, those) pliers from the workbench?
4. I've never seen (this , these) kind of shoe.
5. Tooth enamel is one of the (hardest , most hardest) natural substances.
6. Jerry hadn't (never, ever) seen a television studio, so he was looking forward to the field trip.
7. Regina waited (nervous, nervously) for the results of her audition for the orchestra.
8. The radio announcer sounded (serious , seriously) when he explained that the interview had been canceled.
9. Of all reptiles on earth, the giant tortoise lives the (longer, longest).
10. Because of his cold, Eric (could , couldn't) hardly talk.
11. Eve types (accurate, accurately) enough to qualify for the word-processing position.
12. We developed both black and white and color film, but the color roll developed (faster , fastest).
13. The Library of Congress has more books than (any, any other) library in the nation.
14. The candidate's schedule of campaign activities doesn't allow (any , no) time for socializing.
15. Our mountain bike club traveled (more , most) miles on Monday than we did on Tuesday.
16. Anna's scheme for Student Council reelection sounds (foolish , foolishly).
17. Mark has been to more foreign countries than (anyone, anyone else) in his class.
18. The batter (had , hadn't) barely tipped the ball, yet still managed to get a base hit.
19. Tie-dyeing seems (easier , easiest) to do than making an intricate batik design.
20. The champion looked (intent, intently) at the chess board before making a move.

B Using Modifiers Correctly The sentences below contain errors in the use of modifiers. On your paper, rewrite each sentence correctly.

1. My little brother and my youngest cousin always play good together.
2. If you want to try a delicious fruit, try these kind of grapes.
3. The photographer moved silent around the sweetly sleeping children.
4. Dressed in her ballet costume, Felicia looked beautifully as she stepped into the spotlight.
5. Of all three debaters, Ricardo spoke the more persuasively in favor of stricter gun-control legislation.
6. We felt badly when we realized that our friends had been waiting at the theater for an hour.
7. The job will go more quicklier if you get a partner to help you address all these envelopes.
8. The rate of population growth in some countries is greater than the food .
9. We couldn't scarcely hear the weather report because of the thunder outside.
10. The painter Vincent van Gogh didn't have no idea that he would one day be famous.

c *Proofreading* The following paragraphs contain errors in the use of modifiers as well as other mistakes. On your paper, rewrite the paragraphs, correcting all errors.

(1) Alfred Nobel left his mark on the world in too dramatically different areas. (2) It seems ironically that the person who invented dynamite would also bequeath a prize for world peace, but Nobel did just that.

(3) Nobel was born in Sweden in 1833. (4) His family was in the business of making explosives, and sometimes there were problems in controlling them dangerous substances. (5) Often, those kind of substances, such as nitroglycerin, would explode inside the Nobel factories. (6) To make the nitroglycerin more stabler , Alfred Nobel mixed it with another material. (7) He called his invention "dinamite ."

(8) In 1896, after dynamite and other inventions had made Nobel as rich, if not richer than, the wealthiest men in the world, Nobel wrote his will. (9) He didn't leave none of his fortune to his family. (10) Instead, his money was to go to men and women who would make outstanding contributions in the areas of literature, physics, chemistry, medicine, economics and world piece . (11) So it was that a pioneer in the feild of explosives became the founder of a peace prize.

Cumulative Review

Chapters 27 and 28

A Correcting Errors in Pronoun Usage Some of the following sentences contain errors in the use of pronouns. Rewrite these sentences, eliminating the errors. If there are no errors in a particular sentence, write *Correct*.

1. No one should lose their sleep worrying about that.
2. The lawyer asked the jury to find Ellen Anderson innocent, even though she had admitted her role in the crime of passion.
3. Long after other couples had grown weary, you could see their dancing with tireless enthusiasm as if the night had just begun.
4. You should let the neighbors know that my uncle and me will be hunting.
5. The coach gave Susan and me some invaluable tips during practice.
6. In a sprint, he can run faster than me , though he has trouble pacing himself for longer distances.
7. The decision is not mine alone to make; everyone in the club should have their say.
8. The faculty has officially approved their new contract.
9. No one had a better sense of what the audience liked than her .
10. Neither gusting, late-night winds nor the creaking of a floor in an empty house will frighten my sister or myself .
11. Who gave this elegant sapphire ring to you?
12. After we succeed in our lawn care business, the profits should be split evenly between you and I .
13. According to those two expert film critics, my mother and she , that new film is not worth the price of admission.
14. Someone had been throwing their trash in the river in defiance of the new clean water law.
15. Who will you vote for in the upcoming school election?
16. The police were still searching for whomever stole the school mascot from the display case.
17. The speaker at the assembly asked us to remember the sacrifices that previous generations had made for we young people.
18. Neither of the two players wanted to lose their role.
19. It was her whom you saw last night, supposedly lurking in the shadows; she was simply waiting for her ride to come.
20. Whom is the state's attorney general now?

B Correcting Errors of Pronoun Reference Revise the following paragraph to remove all indefinite and ambiguous pronoun references. You will need to rewrite some of the sentences.

(1) Horatio Alger, Jr., wrote stories during the decades after the Civil War about poor boys who became rich through hard work, decency, and determination. (2) He wrote more than a hundred books about it, with titles such as *Making His Way*, *Strive and Succeed*, and *Struggling Upward*. (3) His stories of street urchins who became wealthy and virtuous business leaders gave you hope and inspired young people throughout the nation. (4) Though his books all followed similar plots, it was enormously influential. (5) It sent out the message to generations of young people that hard work and honesty would always be rewarded. (6) No matter how poor they were, Alger's stories gave millions of young Americans hope that a better tomorrow was possible. (7) It reinforced the image of the United States as a land where anyone could achieve material success, if only you worked hard enough.

C Using Adjectives and Adverbs Rewrite the following sentences, correcting any of the italicized modifiers that are incorrectly used. If a sentence has no errors, write *Correct*.

1. A tornado is a twisting, *powerfully*, and destructive wind storm, usually seen as a rotating, funnel-shaped cloud.
2. Though the dimensions of a tornado are far smaller than those of a hurricane, a tornado's destructive force is *greatest*.
3. Its winds reach speeds of three hundred miles per hour; they move faster than those found in *any* kind of storm.
4. Most of the world's tornadoes occur in the United States; of all its geographic regions, the West has the *fewer* tornadoes.
5. Tornadoes *frequently* strike Midwestern and Southern states; chiefly in spring and early summer.
6. Wherever a tornado touches down, it *immediate* poses a threat to any people or property in its vicinity.
7. Tornadoes can *quick* uproot trees, overturn railroad cars, and flatten entire homes.
8. After tornadoes, victims may have to search *careful* through debris to find remnants of their property.
9. Fortunately, the tornado warnings of the National Weather Service have worked *good*, saving countless lives over the years.
10. While nobody can*'t* predict when a tornado will occur, scientists can identify weather conditions that may lead to one.

29

Capitalization

I magine the confusion that would result if everyone were simply called "person." Proper names enable you to distinguish the specific from the general. To indicate that a word is a specific name, or proper noun, and not just a label given to a category of things, or common noun, writers capitalize the first letter of that word.

In this chapter you will learn to use capitalization to distinguish proper nouns from common nouns so that you can efficiently and precisely refer to people, places, things, and ideas.

Part 1

People, Personal Titles, Nationalities, and Religions

A **proper noun** is the name of a specific person, place, thing, or idea. A **common noun** names a general class of people, places, things, or ideas. Proper nouns are capitalized. Common nouns are not. A **proper adjective** is an adjective formed from a proper noun, and is, therefore, also capitalized.

Common Noun	Proper Noun	Proper Adjective
continent	Europe	European
queen	Queen Elizabeth	Elizabethan

Proper nouns and adjectives occur in many compound words. Capitalize only the parts of these words that are capitalized when they stand alone. Do not capitalize prefixes such as *pro-*, *un-*, and *pre-* attached to proper nouns and adjectives.

pro-Leftist   un-American   pre-Civil War

The following rules will help you identify proper nouns and adjectives and capitalize them correctly.

Names of People and Personal Titles

Capitalize people's names and initials that stand for names.

Elizabeth Dole   J.P. Morgan   Lyndon B. Johnson

Capitalize titles and abbreviations for titles used before people's names or in direct address.

Reverend Jesse Jackson   **Ms.** Hudson   **Lt.** Harrison
How often should I take this medication, **Doctor?**

The abbreviations *Jr.* and *Sr.* are also capitalized after names. In the middle of a sentence, these abbreviations are followed by a comma.

Mr. Ralph Benson, **Sr.,** addressed the class.

In general, do not capitalize a title when it follows a person's name or is used without a proper name.

The doctor wrote a prescription for Amy.

Capitalize a title used without a person's name if it refers to a head of state or a person in another important position.

> the **P**resident and **V**ice-**P**resident of the United States
> the **P**ope   the **P**rime **M**inister   the **C**hief **J**ustice

The prefix *ex-* and the suffix *-elect* are not capitalized when attached to titles.

> ex-**P**resident Carter   the **P**rime **M**inister-elect

Family Relationships

Capitalize the titles indicating family relationships when the titles are used as names or as parts of names.

> It's hard to believe that **A**unt **M**aria and **M**om are twins.

If the title is preceded by an article or a possessive word, it is not capitalized.

> My uncle admitted that being a father can be difficult.

Races, Languages, Nationalities, and Religions

Capitalize the names of races, languages, nationalities, and religions, and any adjectives formed from these names.

> **H**induism   **C**aucasian   **C**hinese cooking
> **F**rench   **H**ebrew   **A**rabian horses

"Hold on there! I think you misunderstood—
I'm Al Tilley ... the bum."

© 1984 Universal Press Syndicate

The Supreme Being and Sacred Writings

Capitalize all words referring to God, the Holy Family, and religious scriptures.

the **L**ord	**A**llah	the **T**orah
Christ	the **G**ospel	the **K**oran
the **V**irgin **M**ary	the **O**ld **T**estament	the **T**almud

Capitalize personal pronouns referring to God.

They thanked the Lord for **H**is love and guidance.

Do not capitalize *god* and *goddess* when they refer to multiple deities, such as the gods and goddesses of various mythologies.

Isis was one of several Egyptian nature goddesses.
The Greek god Hades was ruler of the underworld.

The Pronoun I

Always capitalize the pronoun *I*.

I'll probably make the team if **I** improve my free throws.

Exercises

A On your paper, write the following sentences, using capital letters where necessary. If a sentence needs no capitals, write *Correct*.

1. Was henry kissinger secretary of state when ex-president ford was in office?
2. Last week rabbi kaplan, father ryan, and reverend anderson led a discussion on the role of god and his teachings.
3. My aunt said that her mother-in-law is the third member of their family to be elected a judge.
4. May i tell the vice-president that you're waiting, colonel?
5. During the Crusades, Christian armies fought to end arab rule in jerusalem.
6. Have father and cousin roger met lt. palermo?
7. Strong patterns of rhyme and rhythm are typical of scottish and english folk ballads.
8. Tomorrow sister bernadette's bible study group will discuss matthew and mark, the first two books of the new testament.
9. I told mr. arroyo that i'd invited mayor grant to the meeting.
10. The secretary of health, education and welfare met with representative-elect joseph p. kennedy, jr., to discuss federal policies.

Mahatma Gandhi addressing a crowd in New Delhi.

B Find the words that need capital letters in the following paragraphs. Write them correctly on your paper after the number of the sentence in which they appear.

(1) For centuries the indian people have been divided by struggles between the hindus and the moslems, two groups with vastly different religious beliefs. (2) The moslems, like christians and jews, believe in one god. (3) Founded by a prophet named mohammed, the moslem religion is based on the teachings of the koran, a sacred book similar to the bible. (4) Mosques are churchlike buildings where moslems worship their god, Allah.

(5) In contrast, hindus believe that the creator and his creations are one and the same, and can be worshipped in any form, including animals, water, planets, or stars. (6) Consequently, hindu temples are filled with statues of gods and goddesses—symbols of the faith's three-and-a-half million divinities. (7) The most important of these divine beings are brahma, shiva, and vishnu. (8) A hindu worships alone, searching for the perfect balance in life as taught in the vedas, four sacred books of scripture.

(9) On August 15, 1947, hindus and moslems joined together to form a unified indian nation, independent of british rule. (10) The two men most responsible for ending the country's internal struggle were the famous peace-loving hindu, mahatma gandhi, and viceroy of india louis mountbatten, the great-grandson of queen victoria.

Geographical Names, Structures, and Vehicles

Certain nouns and adjectives that refer to geographical areas or topographical features are capitalized.

Geographical Names

In a geographical name, capitalize the first letter of each word except articles and prepositions.

Continents	Australia, South America, Europe, Asia
Bodies of Water	Lake Ontario, the Jordan River, Strait of Belle Isle, Cape Cod Bay, the Adriatic Sea, St. George's Channel
Land Forms	the Pyrenees, the Sinai Peninsula, the Grand Canyon, the Syrian Desert, Mount Constance, the Plains of Abraham, Raton Pass, the Rocky Mountains
World Regions	the Orient, the Middle East, the Far East
Special Terms	the Northern Hemisphere, the Tropic of Cancer, the North Pole
Political Units	the District of Columbia, the West Indies, San Francisco, the Republic of Texas
Public Areas	Gettysburg National Park, Fort Niagara, the Blue Grotto, Mount Rushmore
Roads and Highways	Main Street, Route 447, West Side Highway, Van Buren Avenue, the Ohio Turnpike

Usage Note In official documents, words like *city*, *state*, and *county* are capitalized when they are part of the name of a political unit: *the County of Westchester, the City of Dallas*. In general usage, however, such words are not capitalized.

Capitalize the word modified by a proper adjective only if the noun and adjective together form a geographical name.

English Channel	English accent
the Indian Ocean	Indian artifacts

Directions and Sections

Capitalize names of sections of the country or the world, and any adjectives that come from those sections.

> The Jennings moved from the **E**ast **C**oast to the **S**outhwest.
> Jane is from a **M**idwestern town, but she has an **E**astern accent.

Do not capitalize compass directions or adjectives that merely indicate direction or a general location.

> Drive south on Pine Street to the first stoplight.
> I spent my vaction on the western coast of Yugoslavia.
> The hurricane moved northward.

Bodies of the Universe

Capitalize the names of planets in the solar system and other objects in the universe, except words like *sun* and *moon*.

Neptune	**H**alley's **C**omet	an eclipse of the sun
Jupiter	the **B**ig **D**ipper	a phase of the moon

Capitalize the word *earth* only when it is used in conjunction with the names of other planets. The word *earth* is not capitalized when the article *the* precedes it.

> Mercury, Venus, Earth, Mars, and Pluto are known as the terrestrial planets because they resemble the earth in size, density, and chemical composition.

Structures and Vehicles

Capitalize the names of specific monuments, bridges, and buildings.

the **L**incoln **M**emorial	**A**rch of **T**riumph
the **P**rudential **B**uilding	**T**ower **B**ridge
the **F**lat **I**ron **B**uilding	the **S**tatue of **L**iberty

Capitalize the names of specific ships, trains, airplanes, automobiles, and spacecraft.

Queen Elizabeth II	the *Denver Zephyr*
the *Spirit of St. Louis*	*Reliant*

Punctuation Note Underline the names of specific ships, airplanes, trains, and spacecraft, but not automobiles.

Exercises

A On your paper, write the following sentences, using capital letters where necessary. If no capitals are needed, write *Correct*. This exercise covers many of the rules you have studied so far in this chapter.

1. In 1909 american explorer robert e. peary led the first expedition to reach the north geographic pole, which lies near the center of the arctic ocean.
2. In the past two decades, many factories from the north have moved to the southwest.
3. The cayman islands, which belong to great britain, are located just south of cuba in the caribbean sea.
4. This bus goes down fifth avenue past central park to greenwich village and washington square.
5. The town of trier, on the mosel river in germany, was once an important city in the roman empire.
6. In 1976 a section of *viking I* landed on mars to conduct scientific experiments; it also returned the first television pictures from the martian surface.
7. The only german composers i could name were bach, beethoven, and brahms.
8. The winds near the equator move from east to west, but the prevailing winds in the upper latitudes move eastward.
9. One day on the slowly spinning planet mercury is equal to more than 58 days on earth.
10. In 1903 panamanians—supported by the united states—declared independence from the country of colombia and formed the republic of panama.
11. The elegant jefferson memorial in washington, d.c. is a circular structure built out of white marble; it was designed by the classical architect john russell pope.
12. In 1803 the united states purchased the louisiana territory, a parcel of land stretching from the gulf of mexico to the canadian border, and from the mississippi river to the rocky mountains.
13. In 1968 london bridge was dismantled and moved to lake havasu city, arizona.
14. The spanish explorer Juan Ponce de León was the governor of puerto rico until 1513, when he landed in Florida seeking the legendary Fountain of Youth.
15. In one of the most famous scenes in the original movie, king kong climbs up the empire state building; in the modern version of the film he scales the world trade center.

B Rewrite the following paragraph, supplying the necessary capitals.

(1) Few natural wonders in north america can compete with the majesty of niagara falls, which are located about halfway along the northward course of the niagara river. (2) Carrying the overflow of four of the five great lakes, the river plunges over a precipice between lake erie and lake ontario into the gorge on either side of goat island. (3) To the north of the small island is the nearly straight line of the american falls. (4) To the south and west, on the river's canadian side, is the graceful curve of horseshoe falls. (5) From rainbow bridge, which is just below the falls, one can observe arcs of color forming on the clouds of spray. (6) The most unusual view, however, is from a boat named *maid of the mist*, in honor of the legendary indian girl whose canoe tumbled over niagara. (7) Her ghostly image is said to appear occasionally in the foaming mist.

c *Write Now* Imagine that you appeared on a TV game show and won first prize—a two-week trip anywhere in the world. You have chosen your destination, and you are now on your way there. Write several journal entries describing your trip. Be sure to name the places you visit, the routes you travel, the structures you see, and the forms of transportation you take. You may need to research your topic before writing. Make sure to follow the rules of capitalization outlined in this chapter.

Part 3
Organizations, Historical Events, and Other Subjects

Several other commonly used words and phrases are capitalized. These are grouped into six major categories.

Organizations and Institutions

Capitalize the names of organizations and institutions.

Capitalize all words except prepositions and conjunctions in the names of organizations and institutions. Also capitalize abbreviations of these names.

Democratic Party	Central Intelligence Agency **(CIA)**
Sullivan High School	Securities and Exchange Commission
Lee Glass Company, Inc.	House of Representatives
First Methodist Church	Trans World Airlines **(TWA)**

Do not capitalize words such as *school*, *company*, *church*, *college*, and *hospital* when they are not used as parts of names.

Events, Documents, and Periods of Time

Capitalize the names of historical events, documents, and periods of time.

World War II	the Homestead Act
Bill of Rights	the Dark Ages
the Renaissance	the Battle of Bunker Hill

Months, Days, and Holidays

Capitalize the names of months, days, and holidays but not the names of seasons.

June   Tuesday   Memorial Day   winter

Time Abbreviations

Capitalize the abbreviations *B.C.*, *A.D.*, *A.M.*, and *P.M.*

Augustus ruled from 27 **B.C.** to **A.D.** 14.
The meeting begins at 9:30 **A.M.** and ends at 3:00 **P.M.**

Awards, Special Events, and Brand Names

Capitalize the names of awards and special events.

Nobel **P**rize for **P**eace	**S**uper **B**owl
Emmy **A**ward	**M**ichigan **S**tate **F**air

Capitalize the brand names of products but not a common noun that follows a brand name.

Springtime air freshener	**G**olden **G**rain cereal

School Subjects and Class Names

Do not capitalize the general names of school subjects. Do capitalize the titles of specific courses and of courses that are followed by a number. School subjects that are languages are always capitalized.

biology	**G**erman
Home **E**conomics 200	**I**ntroduction to **P**sychology

Capitalize class names only when they refer to a specific group or event or when they are used in direct address.

The juniors are selling tickets for the **J**unior **P**rom.
Every spring the **F**reshman **C**lass holds a carnival.
Good luck, **S**eniors, as you graduate and begin new lives.

Exercises

A On your paper, write the following sentences, using capital letters where necessary.

1. The boston choral society will appear at the university of maine.
2. The new deal was a program designed to end the great depression.
3. In autumn, jewish people observe the holiday yom kippur.
4. During the spring semester, mr. otero will teach trigonometry as well as geometry II and algebra I.
5. Irreplaceable historical relics such as the rosetta stone and the magna carta are displayed in the british museum.
6. The oldest english company, javersham oyster fishery, has been in operation for over seven hundred years.
7. My european history class saw a film about the renaissance.
8. In 1975 the novelist saul bellow won the pulitzer prize for his novel *Humboldt's Gift*.
9. Opening day for springfield high school is the tuesday after labor day.

10. Theodore roosevelt led his famous Rough-Riders during the spanish-american war.
11. The senior class variety show will be presented to the freshmen, sophomores, and juniors on friday, may 3, at 7:30 p.m.
12. I ordered a plaid shirt and a pair of levi's jeans from carson, pirie, scott and company's christmas catalog.

B On your paper, write the following sentences, using capital letters where necessary and correcting improperly capitalized words. Refer to all the capitalization rules covered so far in this chapter.

1. In 1776 most americans were of dutch, french, swedish, scotch-irish, and english descent.
2. Citizens of the young Nation generally spoke english, worshipped as protestants, and shared a northern European heritage.
3. In the 1840's roman catholic irish immigrants crossed the atlantic to flee from Famine and harsh british laws.
4. Eastern europeans also hoped fo find a new homeland in america.
5. The armenians sought refuge from turkish oppression, while Italians and greeks hoped to overcome poverty.
6. Many polish people wished to escape Foreign rule in their divided country, and jews fled from russian persecution.
7. The Chinese arrived during the 1860's and 1870's to work on construction of the central pacific railroad.
8. Toward the end of the Century, however, the chinese and other newcomers who accepted lower wages were blamed for declining economic conditions.
9. The workingman's party in california urged the Government to pass laws discriminating against specific immigrant groups.
10. The sidewalk ordinance was one such law; it prohibited people who carried merchandise on poles from using sidewalks.
11. In later years, the United States congress restricted the numbers of immigrants from certain countries by creating laws such as the chinese exclusion act.
12. Many social reformers, however, tried to help Immigrants.
13. Jane Addams founded hull house, where newcomers could learn english and prepare for american Citizenship.
14. Industrialists such as carnegie steel company's Andrew Carnegie and standard oil company's John d. Rockefeller helped immigrants by funding Public Education Institutions.
15. In spite of the hardships, most immigrants improved their lives and made important Contributions to our diverse american culture.

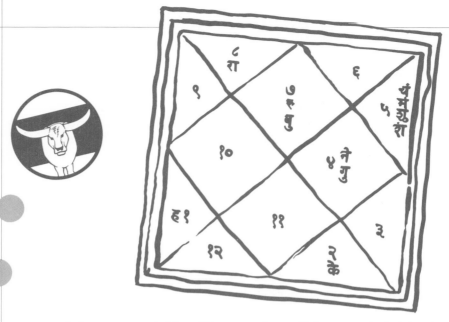

Left: an ox, a symbol from Chinese astrology. Right: an astrological chart from India.

C *Proofreading* Rewrite the following paragraphs, correcting all errors in spelling, punctuation, and capitalization.

The origins of astrology date back to about 2,470 b.c., when the babylonians used Heavenly bodys to make predictions. By the middle ages astrology had spread throughout the World almost all the great Scholars were said to have studied it during the renaissance. Crime, disease, and catastrophes were "explained" using astrology.

Today there are several different astrologies—european, indian, and chinese. While some beleivers claim that astrology has roots in Science or Religion, most modern astrologists simply try to understand human behavior within the Universe. Do movements of the sun, moon, stars, and planets really affect our personalities. Researchers do not have answers to this question. In the meantime, however, people Worldwide continue to delight in relating themselves to the timeless elements of the Heavens.

Checkpoint *Parts 1, 2, and 3*

A Rewrite the sentences adding capital letters where necessary.

1. In a.d. 1263 john balliol and his wife, devorgilla, founded a college at oxford university.

2. I asked aunt maria to bring back some irish lace and english tea from her trip to the british isles.
3. According to a recent survey, thirty percent of all americans have visited yellowstone park.
4. Each summer over labor day weekend i sail our family boat, the *vagabond*, around the apostle islands in lake superior.
5. Could you tell me, dad, whether the cosmos computer company is located on ash street?
6. The orbit of halley's comet brought it close to earth in 1986.
7. Several french communities, such as st. louis, were founded in the midwest.
8. Because I scored 100 points on the test about the great depression, i received the student-of-the-month award in history class.
9. According to an ancient tale, rome was founded at 8:00 a.m. on april 21, 753 b.c., by the mighty chieftain, romulus.
10. Sarah ferguson became the duchess of york when she married prince andrew in westminster abbey on july 23, 1986.
11. Gold was discovered in the pike's peak region of colorado in the
12. The junior class of richmont high school sponsored a rock concert to raise money for unicef.
13. The strategic arms limitations talks (salt) stopped when the soviet union invaded afghanistan in 1979.
14. We flew to frankfurt on lufthansa airlines and then traveled through the night on the *komet*, a sleeper express train.

B Application in Literature In the following paragraph, some capital letters have been changed to lower-case letters, and some lower-case letters have been capitalized. Return the paragraph to its original, correct form by rewriting it and correcting all capitalization errors.

(1) San Francisco put on a show for me. (2) i saw her. . . from the great road that bypasses sausalito and enters the golden gate bridge. (3) The afternoon Sun painted her white and gold—rising on her hills like a Noble City in a happy dream. (4) A city on hills has it over flat-land places. (5) New york makes its own Hills with craning buildings, but this gold and white acropolis rising wave on wave against the blue of the pacific sky was a stunning thing, a painted thing like a picture of a medieval italian city which can never have existed.

From *Travels with Charley* by John Steinbeck

Part 4

First Words and Titles

The first words of a sentence, a quotation, and a line of poetry are capitalized.

Sentences and Poetry

Capitalize the first word of every sentence.

The coach gave his players a pep talk.

Capitalize the first word of every line of poetry.

Whenever Richard Cory went down town,
We people on the pavement looked at him:
He was a gentleman from sole to crown,
Clean favored, and imperially slim.

From "Richard Cory" by Edward Arlington Robinson

Usage Note Sometimes, especially in modern poetry, the lines of a poem do not begin with capital letters.

Quotations

Capitalize the first word of a direct quotation.

Patrick Henry exclaimed, "**G**ive me liberty or give me death!"

In a **divided quotation,** do not capitalize the first word of the second part unless it starts a new sentence.

"It's true," said Renée, "that appearances can be deceiving."
"It's true," said Renée. "**A**ppearances can be deceiving."

Letter Parts

Capitalize the first word in the greeting of a letter. Also capitalize the title, person's name, and words such as *Sir* and *Madam*.

Dear **M**s. **L**opez   **D**ear **S**ir or **M**adam

Capitalize only the first word in the complimentary close.

Sincerely yours,   **V**ery truly yours,

Outlines and Titles

Capitalize the first word of each item in an outline and letters that introduce major subsections.

    I. Entertainers
      A. Musicians
         1. Vocal
         2. Instrumental

Capitalize the first, last, and all other important words in titles. Do not capitalize conjunctions, articles, or prepositions with fewer than five letters.

Book	*To Kill a Mockingbird*
Newspaper	*Miami Herald*
Magazine	*Interview*
Play	*Much Ado About Nothing*
Television Series	*The Oprah Winfrey Show*
Work of Art	*The Last Supper*
Long Musical Work	*The Marriage of Figaro*
Short Story	"The Pit and the Pendulum"
Song	"We Are the World"
Chapter	Chapter 11, "The Rise of Islam"

The word *the* at the beginning of a title and the word *magazine* are capitalized only when they are part of the formal name.

The New York Times	*the Springfield Courier*
Audubon Magazine	*Time magazine*

Punctuation Note Titles are either underlined or put in quotation marks. See Chapter 32, page 784 for punctuation rules.

Exercises

A Rewrite the items below, capitalizing words where necessary. Underline any words that are italicized in the exercise.

1. "the only thing we have to fear," claimed Franklin Roosevelt in 1933, "is fear itself."
2. Robert Frost's poem, "stopping by woods on a snowy evening," speaks of fulfilling one's obligations in life.
3. dear sir:
    please send me audition information on your upcoming production of *sunday in the park with george*.

    sincerely yours,

    alonzo m. sanchez
4. the ending of the short story "the lady or the tiger" is left to the reader's imagination.
5. i celebrate myself, and sing myself,
    and what i assume you shall assume,
    for every atom belonging to me as good belongs to you.

    Walt Whitman
6. "did you happen to see last night's episode of *who's the boss?*" asked kathleen.
7. we read and discussed chapter 6 in our biology text, entitled "the liver and its function."
8. I. literature
    a. fiction
        1. short stories
        2. plays
        3. novels
    b. nonfiction
9. the september issue of *smithsonian* magazine included an article entitled, "have you hugged a manatee today?"
10. yesterday in Humanities II we studied Cézanne's painting, *the basket of apples*.
11. "let's get tickets for *the barber of seville*," said Ron. "it's my favorite opera."
12. *the princess bride*, directed by rob reiner, is a modern movie adaptation of a classic fairy tale.
13. my dad subscribes to *the wall street journal*.
14. Bob Dylan's song "the times they are a-changing" expressed the social unrest of the 1960's.
15. "for my great books class," said Amy, "I read *crime and punishment* and *a tale of two cities*."

B Application in Literature In the following passage, some capital letters have been changed to lower-case letters, and some lower-case letters have been capitalized. Return the passage to its original, correct form by rewriting it and correcting all errors in capitalization.

(1) I've read that Navajo, a language related to that of the indians of alaska and northwest canada, has no curse words unless you consider "coyote" cursing. (2) by comparison with other native tongues, it's remarkably free of english and spanish. (3) a navajo Mechanic, for example, has more than two hundred purely navajo terms to describe automobile parts. (4) It might be navajo that will greet the first Extraterrestrial ears to hear from planet earth. (5) On board each *voyager* Spacecraft traveling toward the edge of the solar system and beyond is a gold-plated, long-playing record. (6) Following an aria from mozart's *magic flute* and chuck berry's "johnny b. goode," is a navajo night Chant, music the conquistadors heard.

From *Blue Highways* by William Least Heat Moon

c *Write Now* Briefly describe two works of art that have had a powerful effect on you. The works of art can include such things as books, movies, paintings, poems, songs, or musicals. In addition, explain what significance these works of art have for you. Use correct capitalization throughout, paying particular attention to titles.

Checkpoint *Parts 1, 2, 3, and 4*

A Rewrite the following sentences, correcting all capitalization errors.

1. success is counted sweetest
   by those who ne'er succeed.
   to comprehend a nectar
   requires sorest need.
   Emily Dickinson

2. amanda asked, "will you be marching with the veterans of foreign wars in the parade, grandpa?"

3. "my art History class," said kevin, "Will attend a lecture on *dancers in the wings*, a painting by french artist edgar degas.

4. the prime minister of australia will dine at the white house during his visit there on monday.

5. the *lusitania* was a british steamship that was torpedoed and sunk by a German Submarine off the Coast of ireland in may, 1915.

B On your paper, rewrite the following passage, using capital letters where necessary.

(1) born into a modest midwestern household on december 5, 1901, walter elias disney became one of the best-known creative geniuses of the twentieth century. (2) disney developed his interest in drawing while living on his family's Missouri Farm, and later he received a smattering of formal art education at the kansas city art institute. (3) his job at kansas city film ad company gave eighteen-year-old disney the experience in animation techniques that he needed to open his own animation company. (4) his animated versions of fairy tales such as "puss in boots" and "the four musicians of bremen " began a long and successful film career.

(5) four days before christmas in 1937, *snow white and the seven dwarfs* premiered in hollywood. (6) it was the first feature-length animated film. (7) during the next three decades, mr. disney entertained america with hundreds of cartoons and films—from *song of the south* and *alice in wonderland* to *the sword in the stone* and *mary poppins*.

(8) in addition to creating film entertainment, disney's dream of an amusement park for people of all ages became a reality when disneyland opened on july 17, 1955, in anaheim, california.

Linking
Mechanics *&* Writing

Imagine that your favorite celebrity (athlete, entertainer, politician, artist, or writer) has just won an award and that you are to interview this person for your local newspaper.

Prewriting and Drafting Begin by making a list of facts about the celebrity. Your list should include the name of the celebrity, the name of the award, and the reason this celebrity is getting the award. Also include a quote from the celebrity regarding the secret of his or her successful career.

Select the most interesting and relevant information on your list, organize your material into paragraphs, and write your first draft.

Revising and Proofreading As you revise your first draft, consider these questions:

1. Have you given a clear, specific picture of this person's life?
2. Have you included details of this person's achievements—titles of songs, literary pieces, movies, works of art, athletic competitions, or governmental posts?
3. Does your story follow a logical sequence?
4. Have you followed the rules for correct capitalization?

Additional Writing Topic Imagine that you are a famous anthropologist in A.D. 2110. You have just spent ten years studying a strange tribe in a remote region. Now you must report your findings. Include information about the region's geography, the tribe's social groups and leaders, tribal art, and literature.

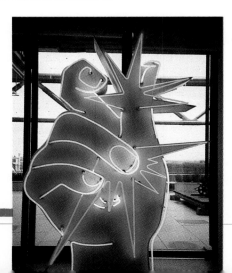

Chapter 29
Application and Review

A Using Capital Letters Correctly Write the following sentences, capitalizing words as necessary.

1. passing under the north pole, the *nautilus* was the first submarine to travel from the pacific ocean to the atlantic.
2. the gulf stream keeps winters mild along cape cod.
3. majorca is a spanish island resort in the mediterranean sea.
4. I. federal officials
       A. the president
       B. cabinet members
    II. state officials
5. the movie *a man for all seasons* recounts the story of sir thomas more, who was beheaded by king henry VIII for remaining loyal to the roman catholic church.
6. several western high schools are offering interesting courses in frontier history.
7. the first known photo of the "monster" in loch ness was taken by col. robt. k. wilson in 1933.
8. at the country kitchen cafe i had the italian minestrone and house salad with french dressing.
9. the tallest sandcastle ever built was created at treasure island, florida, and entitled "lost city of atlantis."
10. headquarters for the united nations are in new york city.
11. the wheel was invented in the tigris-euphrates valley by the sumerians in 3500 b. c.
12. "we ask, o lord," prayed rev. dixon, "that you bless this occasion."
13. let's welcome the freshman class to cooper high school.
14. my favorite song from the musical *my fair lady* was "i could have danced all night."
15. carlos, did your sister take european history or history 20 in her junior year?
16. the greyhound bus traveled east along route 3 until it arrived in jefferson city.
17. the tallest building today is sears tower on wacker drive in chicago.
18. on its way to mercury in february of 1974, the american spacecraft *mariner 10* took pictures of venus.

19. my uncle phil brought his kodak camera to the game at white sox park last saturday.
20. the longest sentence ever published was 2,403 words; it was written by jack mcclintock and appeared in the *miami herald* newspaper.

B Using Capital Letters Correctly Find the words in the following paragraphs that are capitalized incorrectly. On your paper, write the words and capitalize them correctly after the number of the sentence in which they appear.

(1) "a marathon," Says *webster's new world dictionary,* "Is any long-distance or endurance contest." (2) most runners know the story behind the word *marathon*—the legend of a fierce Battle on the plains near the greek town of marathon in 490 b.c. (3) the athenians caught the invading persian army by surprise, charged the enemy, and saved the greek empire. (4) a greek soldier, pheidippides, was ordered to run from the Battlefield to athens with news of the victory, a distance of twenty-two miles. (5) although pheidippides had no training in running, he managed to reach athens, exclaiming, "rejoice, we conquer!" (6) poor pheidippides promptly collapsed and died, but his name is remembered because his lengthy run is considered the first "marathon."

The marathon became an official event in the modern olympic games in 1896. (7) the present standardized marathon distance of 42,195 m was actually determined by an english princess in london. (8) a marathon was set up to begin at windsor castle and end at white city stadium. (9) her royal highness wished to view the start of the race from her castle window and then see the finish from her stadium seat—a 26 mile span. this distance has remained the same for every olympic marathon since that Summer day in 1908.

(10) the first marathon in the united states was run in new york city, but the best-known american marathon is held each year in boston. (11) thousands of runners have tested their endurance in this famous eastern race, but you might ask, "why would people subject themselves to such a grueling challenge?" (12) to answer this question, consider the case of carl eilenberg, who was ready to quit the 1975 boston marathon when he was halfway up heartbreak hill. (13) a former star runner from syracuse university, tom coulter, ran alongside, and gave carl some memorable words of encouragement. (14) "once you cross the finish line at boston," tom said, "there's nothing you can't do." (15) these words gave carl the strength to continue running and ultimately to finish the race.

30
End Marks
and Commas

Piece from the Gestalt Series,
Victor Vasarely, 1968–1974.

*H*ow does this painting make you
feel confused anxious do you
know where it begins where it ends where it's going?
Unlike the preceding paragraph and the painting
above, language has marks that punctuate its flow, pace
the presentation of ideas, and indicate where one
thought ends and another begins. In this chapter you
will learn how to use periods, question marks,
exclamation points, and commas to help you
communicate clearly.

Part 1
End Marks

End marks are the punctuation marks that indicate the end of a unit of thought. The three kinds of end marks are the period, the question mark, and the exclamation point. The proper use of each end mark is described on the following pages.

The Period

Use a period at the end of all declarative sentences and most imperative sentences.

> More people speak Mandarin Chinese than any other language in the world.
>
> Please lock the door when you leave.

When an imperative sentence expresses strong emotion or excitement, an exclamation point, rather than a period, is used to end the sentence.

> Watch out!   Let's hurry!

Use a period at the end of an indirect question.

An **indirect question** indicates that someone has asked a question, but it does not give the reader the exact words of the question. (See page 780 for punctuation of direct questions.)

> Jeremy asked whether Amelia Earhart's airplane had ever been located.

Use a period at the end of an abbreviation or an initial.

Sen. Phil Gramm	Inc.	6:00 A.M. on Oct. 1
Gov. Martha L. Collins	Tues.	3 ft. 2 in.
Mr. John Williams, Jr.	Jan.	2 hr. 35 min.

For abbreviations of metric measurements, acronyms, and abbreviations that are pronounced letter by letter, periods are optional. Use your dictionary to check whether periods are required for the following abbreviations.

cm	ml	NATO	UNICEF	NFL	MIT	CIA
km	g	NASA	CARE	UFO	PBS	FBI
kg	L	HUD	NOW	TV	TWA	IRS

Use a period after each number or letter in an outline or a list.

Outline	List
I. Television programs	1. paintbrush
A. Daytime	2. canvas
1. Soap operas	3. watercolors
2. Game shows	
B. Evening	

Use a period between dollars and cents and to indicate a decimal.

$8.57   5.36

The Question Mark

Use a question mark at the end of an interrogative sentence or after a question that is not a complete sentence.

How many days does it take for Mars to orbit the sun?
Your cassettes? I think you left them in the den.
The date? It's the twenty-fifth.

Occasionally, writers may use a question mark to indicate that a declarative sentence is intended to be expressed as a question. In these cases the question mark is a signal to read the sentence with rising inflection.

Declarative	Interrogative
You've finished your homework.	You've finished your homework?
These are yours.	These are yours?

The Exclamation Point

Use an exclamation point at the end of an exclamatory sentence or after a strong interjection.

An **interjection** consists of one or more words that show feeling or imitate a sound.

What a great game!   That's unbelievable!
Oh no!   Crash!   Fantastic!   Yes!   Zoom!

When an interjection is followed by a sentence, the sentence may end with a period, a question mark, or an exclamation point.

Wait! I almost forgot my keys.
Wonderful! Will you play that song again?
Look! There's a truck heading toward us!

At the Porcupine Ball

© 1985 Universal Press Syndicate

Exercises

A Rewrite the following sentences, adding periods and other end marks as necessary. If you are unsure about punctuating abbreviations, consult a dictionary.

1. Mr Franz asked the company, Gilson's Inc, whether the bill for $749 was correct
2. In AD 79 the eruption of Mt Vesuvius destroyed Pompeii, an ancient city in Italy
3. Help I've been robbed
4. Rev Thomas ran through the J FKennedy Forest during his 6 5 (six and five-tenths) km race near downtown St Louis
5. I Federal agencies
   A Investigative
      1 CIA (Central Intelligence Agency)
      2 FBI (Federal Bureau of Investigation)
   B Economic
      1 SEC (Securities and Exchange Commission)
      2 IRS (Internal Revenue Service)
   II State agencies
6. The answer Ask me the question again
7. On Nov 5, at 9:00 AM, Dr J A Larson, Jr, will attend a nutrition conference in Washington, DC
8. Did UCLA beat MSU in the football game on Sat, Sept 8th
9. Are you serious Mrs James actually chose *me* for the leading role in the play
10. Look out Didn't you see that last step

B Rewrite the following paragraph, adding end marks as needed.

(1) At 10:42 AM Jas R Fox, Jr, began to panic (2) He had been running for 2 hrs and still had 3 km to go (3) He wondered whether he had the energy to cover the remaining 2 mi of the race (4) Would he make it (5) Buildings seemed to float past him as he continued down Ash St —Chas A Stevens and Co, F W Woolworth's, Bidwell's, Inc (6) Throat parched and head pounding, he spotted the finish line about 25 yds away (7) Straining, urging his exhausted limbs forward, he finally felt the rope hit his chest. (8) "I've made it" he exulted

Part 2
Commas: Series, Introductory Elements, and Interrupters

Commas can help you express your ideas by slowing down the rhythm of a sentence, showing a shift in thought, or adding clarity. The following rules explain the proper uses of the comma.

Commas in a Series

Use a comma after every item in a series except the last one.

A series consists of three or more items of the same kind.

Words	Benjamin Franklin was a politician, a writer, a scientist, and an inventor.
Phrases	Groups of children played behind the house, on the porch, and in the yard.
Clauses	The archaeologist explained where the dinosaurs lived, what they ate, and how they protected themselves.

Do not use a comma if all parts of the series are joined by the words *and, or,* or *nor.*

All summer we swam and fished and sailed.

Use commas after *first, second,* and so on, when they introduce a series. (Note also the use of semicolons [;] below. For more information on semicolons refer to pages 757–759.)

Our bus stopped at three streets: first, Clark Street; second, Johnson Avenue; and third, Main Street.

Use commas between coordinate adjectives that modify the same noun.

Raging, howling winds whipped the coastline.

To determine whether adjectives are **coordinate**—that is, of equal rank—try placing an *and* between them. If the *and* sounds natural, and if you can reverse the order of the adjectives without changing the meaning, then a comma is needed.

His loud (*and*) whining voice made the audience shudder. (The *and* sounds natural, and the meaning is not changed by reversing the order of the adjectives. Therefore, a comma is needed.)
His loud, whining voice made the audience shudder.

Maria is an experienced (*and*) subway rider. (The *and* sounds awkward, and the adjectives cannot be reversed. No comma is necessary.)
Maria is an experienced subway rider.

In general, it is safe to omit the comma after numbers and adjectives of size, shape, and age.

a big round moon   five tiny wafers

Equal rank.
Left: the insignia of a Master Chief Petty Officer in the U.S. Navy. Right: the insignia of a Chief Master Sergeant in the U.S. Air Force.

Exercises

A Rewrite the following sentences, placing commas where necessary. If no commas are needed, write *Correct*.

1. In the early 1900's jazz was introduced to the major cities of the United States by composers and performers such as W.C. Handy Bessie Smith Louis Armstrong Earl Hines and Joe Oliver.
2. All roads bridges and highways into the city have been blocked by the blinding driving snowstorm.
3. Suddenly, the commanding officer picked up a pen reached for my papers signed them and handed them across the desk to me.
4. The Himalayan Mountains extend across portions of China Nepal India and Pakistan.
5. In 1687 King Louis XIV gave a dinner party for a distinguished foreign guest in Paris that included the following: twenty-two "large" soups sixty-four "small" soups twenty-one main courses forty-four kinds of roasts sixty-three side dishes thirty-six salads and twelve sauces.
6. On weekends I usually bowl or see a movie or go to a party.
7. Princess Diana's engagement ring is a large oval sapphire surrounded by fourteen small diamonds.
8. The growling snarling dog stood behind the sturdy spiked gate in front of the house.
9. At basketball practice we worked on several skills: first dribbling; second passing; and third rebounding.
10. Carlos pulled on his old blue sweatshirt bounded down the stairs and devoured a bowl of hot creamy oatmeal.

B Application in Literature Some commas have been omitted from the following sentences. Write the word before each missing comma and place the comma correctly. Notice how commas help to clarify the writers' ideas.

1. He straightened his shoulders flipped the reins against the horse's shoulder and rode away. John Steinbeck
2. The brother came with his plump healthy wife and two great roaring hungry boys. Katherine Anne Porter
3. Mrs. Proudhammer knew very well what people thought of Mr. Proudhammer. She knew, too, exactly how much she owed in each store she entered how much she was going to be able to pay and what she had to buy. James Baldwin
4. It was true we were at war, observing heatless meatless and wheatless days and conserving sugar. Sterling North

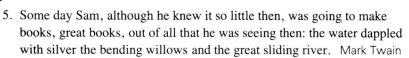

5. Some day Sam, although he knew it so little then, was going to make books, great books, out of all that he was seeing then: the water dappled with silver the bending willows and the great sliding river. Mark Twain

6. [Frederick] Douglass was then twenty-four years old six feet tall with hair like a lion and very handsome. Langston Hughes

7. The shaggy little creatures kicked bucked sprang into the air ran through our legs and even hurtled straight up the walls. James Herriot

8. Hours of wintertime had found me in the treehouse, looking over the schoolyard spying on multitudes of children through a two-power telescope Jem had given me learning their games following Jem's red jacket through wriggling circles of blind man's bluff secretly sharing their misfortunes and minor victories. Harper Lee

9. Tarzan ran his brown fingers through his thick black hair cocked his head upon one side and stared. Edgar Rice Burroughs

10. She was a lofty dignified conventional lady; and she smelled like an old dictionary among whose pages many flowers have been dried and pressed. Elizabeth Enright

c *Write Now* You are an eyewitness to a jewelry store robbery and are being questioned regarding details of the incident. Write a statement describing the crime as you saw it. Be sure to explain the robber's sequence of actions, as well as his or her specific appearance. Apply the rules for commas that you have just studied, so that your "police report" will be clear and precise.

Commas with Introductory Elements

Use a comma after introductory words, mild interjections, or adverbs at the beginning of a sentence.

Well, I think I can manage the job by myself.

Yes, I would like some watermelon.

However, the storm raged for two more days.

Nonetheless, I expect you and Christopher to be ready for next Saturday's car wash.

Use a comma after a series of prepositional phrases at the beginning of a sentence.

Before gaining independence in 1960, Nigeria was a colony of Great Britain.

A single prepositional phrase that begins a sentence may be set off by a comma if it is followed by a natural pause when read.

Because of heavy traffic, we missed half of the movie.

A comma is not necessary when there would be almost no pause in speaking, or if the phrase is very short.

By tomorrow I'll be rested.

Use a comma after verbal phrases at the beginning of a sentence.

Hoping for victory, the exhausted players pressed on.

To enhance your appearance, wear colors that complement your complexion.

Use a comma after adverbial clauses at the beginning of a sentence. (For more information on verbals and adverbial clauses, see Chapter 23, pages 540–541 and pages 558–559.)

When the concert ended, the audience applauded wildly.

Use a comma after words or phrases that have been transposed; that is, moved to the beginning of a sentence from their normal position.

Call Serena for directions if necessary. (normal order)

If necessary, call Serena for directions. (transposed order)

The birthday card is obviously going to be late. (normal order)

Obviously, the birthday card is going to be late. (transposed order)

Commas with Interrupters

Use commas to set off nonessential appositives.

Nonessential appositives are words or phrases that add extra information to an already clear and complete sentence.

> The World Series, baseball's toughest competition, is held annually in the fall.
> *Growing Up*, a touching and humorous autobiography, was written by Russell Baker.

Essential appositives, however, are needed to make the sentence clear and complete. Do not use commas with essential appositives.

> The movie *The Color Purple* was based on a novel by Alice Walker.
> The Spanish monk Torquemada was responsible for the infamous Spanish Inquisition.

For further information about appositives, see Chapter 23, pages 537–538.

Use commas to set off words of direct address.

> Erika, please pass the pasta.
> I understand, Mr. Ames, that your hobby is woodworking.
> You've just won the drawing, Mario!

Use commas to set off parenthetical expressions.

Parenthetical expressions are words and phrases used to explain or qualify a statement. Since they interrupt the flow of thought in a sentence, they are set off by commas.

> Our car, I believe, is over there.
> You know, of course, that Mark Twain was a pseudonym.

The following expressions are often used parenthetically:

of course	consequently	for example
in fact	I believe	on the other hand
by the way	after all	nevertheless
however	moreover	therefore

Grammar Note When words and phrases such as *I believe* are used as basic parts of the sentence, they are not set off by commas.

> I believe our car is over there.
> We hope we'll get back in time for the meeting.

Conjunctive adverbs such as *nevertheless*, *therefore*, and *consequently* may be used parenthetically. Since they interrupt the flow of a sentence, they are set off by commas.

> The explorer, nevertheless, completed his hike up the mountain.
> The artist, therefore, has little need for a home computer.
> The rally, consequently, was attended by very few.

Occasionally, words like *however*, *therefore*, and *consequently* are used to modify a word in a sentence. As modifiers they are essential parts of the sentence and need no commas.

> Pat cannot arrive on time however hard he tries.
> The cast had performed the play the previous semester. They
>   therefore needed little rehearsal.
> Evening rehearsals were consequently eliminated.

For more information on conjunctive adverbs, see Chapter 21, page 500.

Exercises

A Rewrite the following sentences, placing commas where necessary. If a sentence needs no commas, write *Correct*.

1. Both Colin and Evan enjoy playing soccer a rough and tumble game.

2. The actor Henry Fonda won an Oscar for *On Golden Pond*.
3. Did you realize Joan that six American Presidents were born in October; moreover we have never had a President born in June?
4. After scoring six runs in the first inning the Mets let up.
5. Saving some of your money however is simply good sense.
6. My sister on the other hand is quite a spendthrift.
7. When we explored the campsite area we discovered a cave.
8. The oldest human-built structure a rough circle of piled lava blocks dates back to 1,700,000 B.C.
9. You are obviously the best candidate for this office Senator.
10. Yes as a matter of fact I walk the dog every morning for twenty minutes or more.
11. Politicians however sincere they may be are distrusted by many Americans.
12. Consequently the fate of Amelia Earhart remains a mystery.
13. Sally K. Ride the first American female astronaut was a member of the 1983 *Challenger* crew.
14. Off the coast of California we went deep-sea fishing.
15. To avoid muscle soreness or injury always warm up and cool down when exercising.

B Rewrite the following paragraph, adding commas where necessary.

(1) William Faulkner one of America's greatest writers grew up in Mississippi hearing tales of honor gallantry and defeat. (2) Although he dropped out of high school, he read widely traveled and wrote poetry and prose. (3) Encouraged by author Sherwood Anderson Faulkner published two novels by 1927. (4) Moreover he continually experimented with new writing techniques. (5) His long sentences were packed with images and detail and therefore allowed the reader to share the characters' innermost thoughts. (6) *The Sound and the Fury* many believe is the best example of Faulkner's unique style and his greatest contribution to American literature.

C *Write Now* You are trying to convince your parents to grant you some special privilege such as staying out later than is usually allowed. Write out this discussion, using introductory words and interrupters to indicate the opposing sides of the argument. For example:

Me: I'm old enough, in fact, to stay out past midnight. Letting me stay out would show that you really do trust me.
Parents: It isn't a question of not trusting you. However, we'll talk about it and let you know.

Part 3

Commas: Quotations, Compound Sentences, and Clauses

Use commas to set off the explanatory words of a direct quotation.

Explanatory words are statements that identify the speaker but are not part of the quotation. Use a comma after explanatory words when they precede the quotation.

> Mark said, "Drive east to the first stoplight."

When the explanatory words follow the quotation, a comma belongs at the end of the quotation inside the quotation marks.

> "Drive east to the first stoplight," Mark said.

In a divided quotation, use a comma within the quotation marks after the first part of the quotation and after the explanatory words.

> "Drive east," Mark said, "to the first stoplight."

Indirect quotations require no commas.

> Mark said to drive east to the first stoplight.

Commas in Compound Sentences

Use a comma before the conjunction that joins the two main clauses of a compound sentence.

A comma is not necessary when the main clauses are very short and are joined by the conjunctions *and*, *but*, *so*, *or*, or *nor*.

A comma does separate clauses joined by *yet* or *for*.

> You said you'd help, yet I finished the project myself.

There is no comma between the parts of a compound predicate.

> Eighty percent of Japan is covered with mountains and cannot be used for agriculture.

Exercises

A Commas have been left out of the following sentences. Number your paper from 1 to 10, write the word that comes before the missing comma, and place the comma correctly. Some sentences may need more than one comma. If no commas are needed in a sentence, write *Correct*.

1. We had not intended to stay up late for we had an early class.
2. "Few details are known"said Alexander "about William Shakespeare's life."
3. Glaciers on Greenland slide into the sea and break into icebergs.
4. "I've written some poetry I don't understand myself" said Pulitzer Prize-winning poet Carl Sandburg.
5. The principal said that the pep rally would be rescheduled.
6. New York ranks thirtieth in size but is second in population.
7. "The first woman champion at Wimbledon" said Ann "was Maud Watson."
8. "I'd better work on my science report today or I'll never have it finished by tomorrow" said Kate.
9. The catcher signaled and Viola threw the ball.
10. World War I began in 1914 and ended in 1920.

B Application in Literature Rewrite the following passage adding fifteen missing commas. You will use several of the comma rules you have learned so far in this chapter. Notice how the use of commas adds clarity and organization to writing.

(1) The doctor said "I was not in when you came this morning. (2) But now at the first chance I have come to see the baby."

(3) Kino stood in the door filling it and hatred raged and flamed in back of his eyes. . . .

(4) "The baby is nearly well now" he said curtly.

(5) The doctor smiled but his eyes in their little lymph-lined hammocks did not smile.

(6) He said "Sometimes my friend the scorpion sting has a curious effect. (7) There will be apparent improvement, and then without warning—pouf!". . . (8) "Sometimes" the doctor went on in a liquid tone "sometimes there will be a withered leg or a blind eye or a crumpled back. (9) Oh I know the sting of the scorpion my friend and I can cure it."

From *The Pearl* by John Steinbeck

c *Write Now* Writers of historical fiction must use their imagination when they write dialogue. Do some brief research about one of the situations below. Then combine this information with your imagination and write the dialogue that might have taken place. Vary your quotations to include explanatory words that precede, divide, and follow the speaker's words. Place commas correctly.

> Delegates to the Constitutional Convention discuss adoption of the Constitution of the United States.
> Columbus reports his discoveries to Queen Isabella.
> Queen Elizabeth and William Shakespeare talk about the opening of the Globe Theatre.

The Declaration of Independence, John Trumbull, 1786.

Commas with Nonessential Clauses and Phrases

Use commas to set off nonessential clauses.

A **nonessential clause** merely adds extra information to an already complete sentence. An **essential clause** is necessary to complete the meaning of the sentence; if it is dropped, the meaning changes. No commas are used with essential clauses.

Nonessential Clause	The Mississippi River, *which empties into the Gulf of Mexico,* is the setting of the musical *Showboat.* (Clause can be dropped.)
Essential Clause	The river *that empties into the Gulf of Mexico* is the Mississippi. (Clause cannot be dropped.)

Notice that *which* is used to introduce nonessential clauses, and *that* is used to introduce essential clauses.

Use commas to set off nonessential participial phrases.

A nonessential participial phrase can be dropped without making the meaning of the sentence incomplete.

An essential participial phrase is necessary to the meaning of the sentence. No commas are used with essential participial phrases.

Nonessential Participial Phrase	The man, *driving a Ford sedan,* headed down Fir Street at 25 mph. (Dropping the phrase does not change the meaning of the sentence.)
Essential Participial Phrase	The man *driving a Ford sedan* is my father. (The phrase identifies a specific man, so it cannot be dropped without changing the meaning of the sentence.)

Exercise

Rewrite the following sentences, adding the necessary commas. If no commas are needed, write *Correct*.

1. Lewis Carroll who wrote *Alice in Wonderland* was a British author and mathematics professor.
2. This is the house that we expect to buy.
3. The coach fearing overconfidence put the team through a rigorous practice session.
4. The Carlsbad Caverns which attract sightseers to New Mexico are the largest known underground caves.
5. The horse that is pawing the ground has not been fed.
6. Charles Hires who was a student at Jefferson Memorial College became the first manufacturer of root beer in 1866.
7. The movie now showing at the Tivoli Theater stars the popular actor Emilio Estevez.
8. The commuters agitated by a long delay climbed quickly onto the morning train.
9. Running for the bus Angela slipped and twisted her ankle.
10. The car that you just passed is a police car.
11. *On the Terrace* painted in 1881 is one of the most popular of Renoir's paintings.
12. Mount St. Helens which had lain dormant for 123 years erupted on May 18, 1980.
13. The tag sewn into the lining tells whose coat it is.
14. Walking in pairs the chorus members entered the auditorium.
15. The Chinese name Chang which belongs to at least 104 million people is the most common family name in the world.

Part 4
Commas: Other Uses

There are several other situations that call for the use of commas.

Commas in Dates, Place Names, and Letters

In dates, use a comma between the day of the month and the year. When only the month and year are given, no comma is necessary.

> October 1, 1948   November 16, 1980   May 1975

When a date is part of a sentence, a comma also follows the year.

> On July 5, 1835, there were snowstorms in New England.

Use a comma between the name of a city or town and the name of its state or country.

> Dallas, Texas   Paris, France   Sydney, Australia

When an address or place name is part of a sentence, it is necessary to use a comma after each item. Do not put a comma between the name of a state and the ZIP code, however.

> Please forward my mail to 3144 Camelback Road, Phoenix, Arizona 85016, where I will reside for two months.

Use a comma after the salutation of a friendly letter. (Use a colon after the salutation of a business letter.) Use a comma after the closing of a friendly letter or a business letter.

> Dear Angie,   Yours truly,

Commas to Avoid Confusion

Use a comma to separate words or phrases that might be mistakenly joined when read.

In some situations, commas are needed to separate words that may be mistakenly read together. The first situation occurs when the conjunctions *but* and *for* are mistaken for prepositions.

Confusing   I liked all the speeches but one was superb.
Clear   I liked all the speeches, but one was superb.

A second source of confusion is a word that may be an adverb, a preposition, or a conjunction at the beginning of a sentence.

Confusing Below the earth looked like a quilt.
Clear Below, the earth looked like a quilt.

A third source of confusion is a noun following a verbal phrase.

Confusing While sleeping Di dreamed she was attacked by polka dots.
Clear While sleeping, Di dreamed she was attacked by polka dots.

Use a comma to indicate the words left out of parallel word groups.

> Detroit manufactures cars; Hollywood, dreams.
> The day became warm, and our spirits, merry.

Commas with Titles and Numbers

Use commas when a name is followed by one or more titles. Also use a comma after a business abbreviation if it is part of a sentence.

> I met with John Kane, Jr., regarding the fund-raiser.
> My brother worked for Lane and Fox, Inc., for two years.

In numbers of more than three digits, use a comma after every third digit from the right, with the exception of ZIP codes, phone numbers, years, and house numbers.

> An estimated crowd of 60,000 people thronged the stadium.

Exercises

A Rewrite the following sentences, using commas where necessary.

1. David Kunst walked 14500 miles around the world between June 10 1970 and October 5 1974.
2. My sister loves classical music; my brother jazz.
3. He stayed at 465 Turner Terrace Lexington Kentucky for a week.
4. Please send the payment to Barbara Snower D.D.S. by April 1 1989.
5. Beyond the residential section extends for miles.
6. Please write to me at 2367 W. Ash Street Earlham New York 11023.
7. John D. Rockefeller Sr. formed the Standard Oil Company in 1870.
8. My brother became angry, and my dad silent.
9. By the year 2000 there may be 6100 million people on our planet.
10. Phillip waited for he knew his friend would call soon.
11. Elizabeth II Queen of England was born in London England in 1926.
12. Inside the restaurant was beautifully lighted.
13. Edith Wharton wrote *Ethan Frome*; Doris Lessing *African Stories*.
14. Skip painted all the chairs but four needed repair as well.
15. After refueling the plane the pilot flew on to Des Moines Iowa.

B Rewrite the following letter, adding commas where necessary.

April 24, 19—

Dear Holly

Did you know I'm a celebrity? Before you answer look on page 23 of the April issue of Photographer magazine. Can you believe that a girl from Byfield Oregon could win a photo contest that had 2400 entries? Until I heard from the sponsor, Picture This Ltd. I didn't think I had a chance.

I will be spending the summer studying photography under Gregory Martin Jr. Write to me at L'Hôtel Marquis 73 rue Duret Paris France.

Sincerely

Connie

Checkpoint Parts 1-4

A Copy the following sentences, adding periods, question marks, exclamation points, or commas where they are needed. If the punctuation is correct, write *Correct*.

1. After fishing my sister cleaned the trout and fried them
2. All of the visitors spoke Spanish English and Portuguese
3. Marion Heid PhD was named the President's advisor to NATO
4. The time It's exactly 5:08 PM
5. Believe it or not Elvis Presley recorded eighty albums
6. After the discovery of gold many settlers came to Australia.
7. Wow Dave Winfield just hit a grand slam
8. The exotic island of Bora-Bora first described by Capt James Cook in 1769 has attracted travelers writers and film makers
9. November 25 1987 was a holiday. The library was therefore closed
10. The first baseball game in which one team scored more than 100 runs took place in Philadelphia Pennsylvania on October 1 1865
11. I Department stores
    - A WTGrant
    - B Fox and Co
    - II Specialty shops
    - A The Timepiece Inc
    - B Video Etc
12. Muhammad Ali, one of America's most famous world-class athletes, won fifty-six fights and lost five.
13. The highest auction bid for Vincent van Gogh's *Landscape with Rising Sun* was $9900000
14. George Washington Carver as a matter of fact revolutionized agriculture by developing new uses for sweet potatoes and peanuts
15. "Karen please send my mail to my new address" said Josh "I will be living at 3476 N Rock Rd Ames Iowa 64978"
16. Yes our plane was forced to land in Columbus Ohio for the weather in Detroit was cold and wet and foggy.
17. Ed wondered why he owed $7 10. "The ten cents is tax" he asked.
18. Dear Jan

    The flight to Montreal was great. Below the clouds looked like snowy peaks. Give me a call soon

    Yours truly
    Lauren

19. Having won seven Olympic medals and setting twenty-six world records Mark Spitz might be considered history's most successful swimmer

20. "In 1987" asked Ralph "who won the World Series"

21. At 6:10 AM on January 19 1977 snow began to fall in West Palm Beach Florida

22. Chief Joseph whose American Indian name means "Thunder Traveling Over the Mountains" led his people the Nez Percé to within thirty miles of Canada before being captured

B *Proofreading* Proofread the following paragraph for punctuation errors. For each sentence, list any words that should precede a punctuation mark, and follow each word with the correct punctuation.

(1) *Commedia dell'arte* which is a form of comic theater was performed all across Europe between the years 1400 and 1600 (2) Unlike most actors of today performers of the *commedia* did not memorize written dialogue (3) Instead they improvised which means that they made up their lines as they went along (4) The actor who was most important in the *commedia* was the clown (5) He had to be very athletic since much of the humor in *commedia* performances came from his gymnastics (6) The clown who was very clever usually played tricks on the other characters (7) *Commedia dell'arte* was very popular; in fact an entire town would often turn out to watch a performance (8) Audiences for the most part could be counted on to fill the hat that was passed around after every show

Seventeenth-century *commedia dell'arte* characters.

Linking
Mechanics *&* Writing

Imagine you are from a remote island and are unfamiliar with common American pastimes, such as baseball games, movies, or skateboards. Write a composition that will explain several popular pastimes to the people of your island. Remember that most of what you describe will be unknown on your island, so you will have to use appositives and essential or nonessential phrases and clauses to explain these things.

Prewriting and Drafting Whether you live in a city, a suburb, or the country, entertainment is part of your life. Use clustering or brainstorming to gather ideas to write about. Then organize your information in a logical sequence and write a first draft. Remember that your point of view should be that of an outside observer.

Revising and Proofreading Review your draft as though you were someone who has never had this experience. Have you given enough information so that readers on your island will understand your descriptions? Have you used sensory words and active verbs to make the events come alive? Pay close attention to comma use when you proofread your draft.

Additional Writing Topic Advertisers often try to create a sense of excitement regarding very ordinary products that they are trying to sell. Write an ad to rent out your house or apartment, describing it as though it were a resort or vacation hotel. Use both questions and exclamations to let your readers know how exciting it would be to spend a week where you live. The following example may give you some ideas and help you get started.

> Do you want to spend a week in paradise? Come to 1223 Elm Street in Oceanside. Relax in luxurious surroundings, where you can enjoy all the wonderful comforts of home and then some:
> Picture-perfect color TV
> Great movies nightly!
> Gourmet cooking
> Hot stereo!
> Room overlooking quaint suburban street
> Off-street parking!
> Unlimited use of grounds

Chapter 30
Application and Review

A Using Punctuation Correctly Rewrite the following sentences, adding punctuation where necessary.

1. Traveling through space the astronaut radioed the information back to earth
2. Dornette did you go to Sacramento or did you stay in San Jose
3. Historically the objects that have served as money include stones shells furs fish ivory and precious metals
4. Dr Sayner who is the team doctor will undoubtedly tape your ankle
5. After the local band left the stage Whitney Houston appeared and the audience exploded in applause
6. My favorite Shakespearean play is *Hamlet*; hers *Othello*
7. The mammoth which is a kind of prehistoric elephant once roamed the region that is now Texas
8. Hooray Our team made the play-offs
9. Reptiles have several distinguishing characteristics: first they are coldblooded; second their skin is covered with scales; and third they lay eggs
10. Reaching its maximum speed of 1450 mph the *Concorde* flew from New York to London England in a record 2 hrs 56 min and 35 sec on January 1 1983
11. St Francis of Assisi a thirteenth-century friar was known for his humility reverence for nature and strong religious faith
12. The American inventor Thos A Edison demonstrated the first phonograph machine on December 7 1887
13. German shepherds are if I am not mistaken gentle animals
14. Oh no Did you see that lightning Mr Gordon
15. Above the sky was filled with thunderclouds
16. Marshall High School left the gym in victory, and Hoover High in defeat
17. All the girls went skating but Sue had to stay home.
18. "Did you know" asked Cindy "that you have to order tickets for *Phantom of the Opera* six months before the performance date"
19. At some time during the first century AD, the Romans created a stronger more durable type of concrete
20. Consequently the smaller less sporty car sells for around $6000 which makes it more affordable

B Finding Punctuation Errors Number your paper from 1 to 20. After each number, list any words that should be followed by a punctuation mark; then place the mark correctly.

1. Honestly we are not justified in complaining
2. When the tide went out we walked along the sandy beach
3. Watch out for that truck
4. Miss Jordan asked the class "Who knows the author of *Crime and Punishment*"
5. The ancient Egyptian Pharaoh Pepi II the longest reigning monarch is said to have ruled for ninety-four years
6. If possible make the appointment for Tuesday or Thursday
7. We visited Adams Library one of the oldest in America
8. "The oldest surviving fabric was found in Turkey" said Mr. Jarvis "It was radiocarbon dated back to 5900 BC"
9. Amy's favorite vegetable is corn; Jeremy's tomatoes
10. Never worrying Alex met each day with enthusiasm and energy
11. Juan Ramón Jiménez who wrote *Platero and I* received the Nobel Prize for Literature in 1956
12. Inside the calf was sleeping on a bed of coarse wet straw and its mother was resting nearby
13. "You look beautiful tonight Amanda" he said managing a smile
14. My Uncle Joe trying to lower his cholesterol level eats lots of salads fruits and whole grains
15. Would you like a cool refreshing dip in the pool

C *Proofreading* Rewrite the following passage, correcting errors in punctuation, spelling, and capitalization.

Are you a "chocoholic" Well your not alone my freind In fact chocolate has been making americans smile for four thousand years A product grown and used by the aztecs for centurys, chocolate was beleived by ancient peoples to have been brought down from the Garden of Life by the god Quetzalcoatl It was a consolation to people for having to live on earth In the afterlife it was expected to be served perpetually

The first north american chocolate was manufactured in boston in 1765 but America's most famous chocolate maker was milton hershey a Pennsylvania dutchman Another contribution to the american market was made by Domingo Ghirardelli who sent 600 lbs of his chocolate to San Francisco with a merchant heading west to the gold rush The Ghirardelli Chocolate Company located in San Leandro California is now one of the most successful businesses in the western US

31

Semicolons, Colons, and Other Punctuation

all ignorance toboggans into know
and trudges up to ignorance again:
but winter's not forever,even snow
melts;and if spring should spoil the game,what then?

From "All Ignorance Toboggans into Know"
by e. e. cummings

Without punctuation, this poem by e. e. cummings would plummet out of control like a runaway toboggan. Notice how the colon and semicolon link thoughts smoothly, perhaps even suggesting the rhythm of a sledder and of the changing seasons.

In this chapter you will learn how to use semicolons, colons, dashes, hyphens, and parentheses to express yourself knowledgeably and to make your own writing flow.

Part 1

The Semicolon

Like commas, semicolons separate different elements within a sentence. The semicolon, however, signals a more emphatic break than a comma does.

Semicolons Used with Commas

When there are several commas within parts of a compound sentence, use a semicolon to separate the parts. Use a semicolon between main clauses joined by a conjunction if the clause before the conjunction contains commas.

> Jim had done research, taken notes, and made an outline; but he didn't feel ready to begin writing.
> We put out sandwiches, cider, raw vegetables, and potato salad; and still we wondered if there would be enough to eat.

When there are commas within parts of a series, use a semi-colon to separate the parts.

> Members of our class come from as far away as Leeds, England; New Delhi, India; and San Juan, Puerto Rico.
> Maris was in charge of the scenery; Roy, the costumes; and Felipe, the directing of the play.
> Eric called the dancers together; reviewed the opening number, solos, and finale; and told them to be ready by seven sharp.

Semicolons Between Main Clauses

Use a semicolon to join the parts of a compound sentence if no coordinating conjunction is used.

A stronger relationship between the clauses is shown by a semi-colon rather than by a conjunction such as *and* or *but*.

> Bonita is good at set shots, but I am not.
> Bonita is good at set shots; I am not.

> The cyclone struck with savage fury, and it demolished most of the little coastal town.
> The cyclone struck with savage fury; it demolished most of the little coastal town.

Remember that a semicolon may be used only if the clauses are closely related. Do not use a semicolon to join unrelated clauses.

Incorrect   José is a fine athlete; the school fields many teams.
Correct   José is a fine athlete; he has earned letters in three sports.

Semicolons and Conjunctive Adverbs

Use a semicolon before a conjunctive adverb or a parenthetical expression that joins the clauses of a compound sentence.

> Our treasury was nearly empty; accordingly, we began considering various fund-raising projects.
> Many of their talents complemented each other; for example, he played the piano and she sang.

Note that the conjunctive adverb or transitional phrase is followed by a comma in the examples above.

Punctuation Note Many words can be used either as conjunctive adverbs or as interrupters. If the words are used as interrupters, use commas to set the words off from the rest of the sentence.

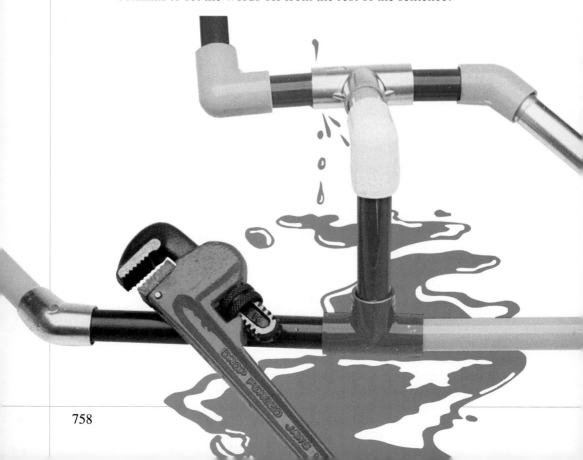

The weather was hot and humid; however, all of the participants
managed to finish the race. (conjunctive adverb)
On the day of the race, however, the weather was hot and humid.
(interrupter)

Exercise

Application in Literature Semicolons have been omitted from the
following passages. Rewrite the passages, correctly inserting semicolons where they are needed. Notice how semicolons add clarity to
the ideas.

1. In two respects it was an exceptionally safe car: first, it didn't go very
   fast second, it had three foot pedals. E. B. White
2. For her pallbearers only her friends were chosen: her Latin teacher, W.
   L. Holtz her high school principal, Rice Brown her doctor, Frank
   Foncannon her friend, W. H. Finney her pal at the *Gazette* office, Walter
   Hughes and her brother Bill. William Allen White
3. She had a painful sense of having missed something, or lost something
   she felt that somehow the years had cheated her. Willa Cather
4. We are not ignorant like the Forest People—our women spin wool on the
   wheel our priests wear a white robe. We do not eat grubs from the tree
   we have not forgotten the old writings, although they are hard to
   understand. Stephen Vincent Benét
5. Mama had not been consulted therefore, she made no comment.
   Jade Snow Wong
6. Uncle Hiram was somewhat smaller than Chig's father his short-cropped
   kinky hair was half gray, half black. William Melvin Kelley
7. Sylvia's heart gave a wild beat she knew that strange white bird, and had
   once stolen softly near where it stood in some bright green swamp grass,
   away over at the other side of the woods. Sarah Orne Jewett
8. It is a maxim of state that power and liberty are like heat and moisture:
   where they are well mixed, everything prospers where they are single,
   they are destructive. Abigail Smith Adams
9. The kitchen was warm now a fire was roaring in the stove with a
   closed-up rushing sound. Gina Berriault
10. But there we were, without a mate and it was necessary, of course, to
    advance one of the men. Robert Louis Stevenson
11. Nine times out of ten, in the arts as in life, there is actually no truth to be
    discovered there is only error to be exposed. Henry Louis Mencken
12. Here a weasel fails to see a plump white ptarmigan in the snow there
    a dragonfly snares a fast-moving mosquito in its basket of legs
    somewhere an eager fox pup grabs a toad. David Robinson

Part 2

The Colon

The colon is used to direct the reader's attention forward to what comes next in the sentence. Often a colon introduces an explanation or example.

Use a colon to introduce a list of items.

A colon often follows a word or phrase such as *these, the following,* or *as follows*. A colon is not used when a series of complements or modifiers immediately follows a verb.

> Jim is a member of the following groups: the Drama Club, the Debate Team, the International Club, and the Sophomore Swimming Team. (list)
>
> We visited these countries on our trip: Switzerland, France, Spain, Italy, and Austria. (list)
>
> The candidate's attributes are honesty, intelligence, and courage. (series of complements)
>
> The chart shows the primary colors, which are red, yellow, and blue. (series of modifiers)

Do not use a colon in the middle of a prepositional phrase; and, as a general rule, do not use a colon immediately after a verb.

Incorrect	Mike is interested in: chemistry, photography, and ice hockey.
Correct	These are Mike's interests: chemistry, photography, and ice hockey.

Incorrect	You should bring: paper plates, cups, and napkins.
Correct	You should bring the following items: paper plates, cups, and napkins.

Use a colon to introduce a quotation that lacks explanatory words such as *he said* or *she asked.*

> Christine wheeled around angrily: "You're going to regret this decision one day!"

Use a colon to introduce a very long or very formal quotation.

> In his Inaugural Address in 1961, President John Kennedy said: "Ask not what your country can do for you—ask what you can do for your country."

Use a colon between two independent clauses when the second explains the first.

> Then I knew we were in trouble: none of our boys could match the dive we had just seen.
>
> From then on we understood Ms. Gilroy: she was demanding, but she was fair.

Punctuation Note Capitalize the first word of a formal statement following a colon. If the statement following the colon is informal, however, you may begin the first word with a lowercase letter.

Other Uses of the Colon

Use a colon (1) after the formal salutation of a letter, (2) between hour and minute figures of clock time, (3) in Biblical references to indicate chapter and verse, (4) between the title and subtitle of a book, (5) between numbers referring to volume and pages of books and magazines, and (6) after labels that signal important ideas.

> Dear Sir or Madam: *The Raven: The Life of Sam Houston*
>
> 8:20 P.M.   *National Geographic* 171: 348–385
>
> Psalm 23:7   Warning: This substance is harmful if
>
> John 3:16   swallowed.

Exercises

A Copy the following sentences, adding the necessary semicolons and colons.

1. We ought to beat Lexington, trample Bowling Green, and slaughter Libertyville but we may lose to Russell Springs.
2. Beginning next January we shall have the following in stock treadmills, exercise bikes, rowing machines, and body-building equipment.
3. Did you read *Aging A Guide to Feeling Young Forever*?
4. Ellen has a new camera it was made in Korea.
5. On Sunday Reverend Thomas quoted from Matthew 10 12–15 in his 1100 A.M. sermon.
6. Dear Sir or Madam

   I would like to order these items from your catalog one pair of moccasins, no. 12431 one Western-style shirt, no. 23947 and one silver belt buckle, no. 67441.

   Please send the items to the following address 3810 Golden Terrace, Apt. 394, Los Angeles, CA 90052.

7. Pablo Picasso was the most prolific painter in history in fact, he produced more paintings in his career of seventy-eight years than any other artist.
8. This medicine carries a label that reads "Warning Keep this and all medications out of the reach of children."
9. Walt and Jeanne have different sports preferences Walt prefers tennis Jeanne prefers soccer.
10. The weather forecast called for low temperatures and strong winds moreover, there was a possibility of snow.

B Rewrite the following sentences, adding semicolons or colons where necessary. In some sentences, semicolons should replace commas. If the sentence requires no changes, write *Correct*.

1. Jesse Granville wrote short stories and poetry, played the trumpet, and sang in a quartet, he also did volunteer work after school as a tutor and as a hospital aide.
2. Author Tom Wolfe said of his craft "When I started writing in college, I wanted to think that genius was ninety-five percent inside your head. . . . I now believe that the proportions are more like sixty-five percent material and thirty-five percent whatever you've got inside of you."
3. The pitcher has three sure-fire pitches his fastball, his slider, and his curveball.
4. The dance was scheduled to begin at 800 P.M. the band, however, did not arrive until 842 P.M.
5. The *Readers' Guide to Periodical Literature* indicated that I could find the article on computer programs in *Newsweek* 18541. (Volume 185, page 41)
6. Barry Harper's baseball souvenir collection includes items such as the following a million baseball cards, nine hundred players' uniforms, three thousand autographed baseballs, seventy-five World Series programs, and more.
7. Did Mrs. Robertson know that the name of the first controlled and power-driven airplane, which was flown by Orville Wright, was the *Flyer I*?
8. Attention The 530 train to Ipswich and Rockport will leave from track 3.
9. My parents made themselves very clear my sister was not to watch any TV over the weekend.
10. The travelers had renewed their passports, booked their hotels, and confirmed their plane reservations, nevertheless, they were afraid they had overlooked something.

Left: Manute Bol, the tallest player in the NBA. Right: Tyrone Bogues, the shortest player in the NBA.

C *Proofreading* Rewrite the following paragraphs, correcting errors in punctuation, capitalization, and spelling.

Few profesional basketball players created the excitment that Tyrone Bogues did in his first month of play with the National basketball Association (NBA) in 1987. Basketball fans are fascinated by Bogues he is a mere 5-foot-3-inches tall. What Bogues lacks in height, however he makes up for with these charteristics speed, skill, and determanation. The shortest legitimite player in nba history. Bogues is not a publisity stunt. In fact, he was a first-round draft choice of the Washington Bullets.

In a preseason match-up against the Los Angeles lakers, Bogues entered the game after the first quarter. the Bullets were trailing 31–22. Racking up twelve points and four assists, he helped shoot the bullets ahead by eight at the half. The Laker's Magic Johnson sums up Bogues' special talent "You have to be aware of him at all times he's like a Fly that gets in your face when your trying to sleep. Every time you think you've slapped him away, he comes buzzing right back

Part 3
The Dash

Dashes are used to indicate an abrupt change of thought or a pause in a sentence. Dashes show a looser connection to the main idea than commas do. The words, clauses, or phrases set off by dashes merely add extra information to an already complete thought.

Use a dash to show an abrupt break in thought.

> The winner of today's baseball game—assuming we aren't rained out—will play in the regional semifinals.
> The appetizers—supposedly the restaurant's specialty—left us disappointed.

Use a dash to set off a long explanatory statement that interrupts the main thought of the sentence.

> They frantically searched everywhere—under the seats, in the aisle, in the lobby—before Dan finally found the car keys in his jacket pocket.
> The meeting between the two men—they had clashed violently and repeatedly over a period of years—was unexpectedly calm and friendly.

Note that in the first example, punctuation occurs within the interrupting statement. Here the dash serves as a guide to the reader, signaling the addition of extra, nonessential information.

Use a dash to set off a summarizing statement from the rest of the sentence.

> Insufficient heating, leaky roofs, cluttered stairways, and unsanitary corridors—for all these violations of the housing code, the landlord was brought into court.
> Photographs of rock-and-roll stars, concert posters, souvenir T-shirts—these covered the walls of her room.

Be careful not to overuse dashes. When used in the correct circumstances, dashes can add interest, variety, and emphasis to your writing. However, too many dashes may confuse the reader and make your writing seem choppy and less precise.

Note In typewritten work, press the hyphen key twice to form a dash.

When writing dialogue, use a dash to show an abrupt break in thought.

In dialogue, the break in thought is often caused by uncertainty or hesitancy, as in the first example below.

> "Photosynthesis is an action—I mean, it's what happens—well, it's sunlight doing something to chlorophyll."
>
> "The movie opens with a spectacular shot of the desert—oh, you've already seen it."
>
> "When I talked to her yesterday she said that—oh, I really shouldn't repeat it."

You will note from the last two examples above that the dash adds a casual, conversational tone to dialogue. People often change their thoughts in mid-sentence while speaking.

Exercise

Application in Literature Dashes have been omitted from the quotations below. Rewrite the passages, and return them to their original form by inserting dashes where they should occur. Notice how the authors have used dashes to separate ideas and add meaning and style to their work.

1. She detached his hand his hold was quite feeble and could not compete with her tennis biceps and leapt off the curb and up the streetcar steps, hearing with relief the doors grind shut behind her. Margaret Atwood
2. A man with murder in his heart will murder, or be murdered it comes to the same thing and so I knew I had to leave. James Baldwin
3. Impy left by the back way. Before the scrape of her hard, bare feet had died away on the back porch, a wild shriek I was sure it was hers filled the hollow house. O. Henry
4. The third day it was Wednesday of the first week Charles bounced a see-saw onto the head of a little girl and made her bleed, and the teacher made him stay inside all during recess. Shirley Jackson
5. The following spring the heavier of the two almost half the tree broke off in a spring gale. Richard Mabey
6. I would sit down to this breakfast at a round table in the dining room with my young parents or my beloved Miss Rachel. My father called Tata, the Polish for papa was my most favorite person in the world.
   Esther Hautzig
7. Sometimes you are able to "step out," but this effort in fact the pure exhilaration of easy movement soon exhausts you. Sharon Curtin

8. The freshness of the morning air, the smell of poplars, lilacs and roses, the bed, a chair, the dress which rustled last night, a tiny pair of slippers, a ticking watch on the table all these came to him clearly with every detail. Anton Chekhov

Part 4
The Hyphen

Use a hyphen in compound numbers from twenty-one to ninety nine.

> thirty-six steps twenty-eight countries

Use a hyphen in all spelled-out fractions.

> a four-fifths majority one-sixth of the pie

Use a hyphen in certain compound words.

> sister-in-law T-shirt right-of-way

Use a hyphen between words that make up a compound adjective used before a noun.

> We found a well-informed source.

When a compound adjective follows a linking verb, it is usually not hyphenated.

> The report seemed well organized.
> The source was well founded.

Some proper nouns and proper adjectives with prefixes and suffixes require a hyphen.

> Mexican-style   pre-Roosevelt   pro-Yankees

Use a hyphen if part of a word must be carried over from one line to the next.

> Gabriela Dimitrova, a Bulgarian weightlifter, defected to the
> United States after competing in the Women's World Weight-
> lifting Championship in Daytona Beach, Florida.

The following rules should be observed when hyphenating words:

1. Words are separated by hyphens only between syllables.
2. Only words having two or more syllables can be hyphenated.
3. Each line should have at least two letters of the hyphenated word.

Exercise

Rewrite the sentences below, adding dashes and hyphens where needed.

1. Squids, snails, and shellfish all these species are classified as mollusks.
2. Ms. Boynton's whimsical work cartoons of animals for greeting cards and calendars rapidly made her a commercial success.
3. Melissa and Jonathan used a six yard tape measure the longest they could find in the hardware store.
4. Turn left at the next Look out for that truck!
5. Angie bought a good looking bike yesterday at Jim's no, I think it was at Al's Spoke and Cycle Shop.
6. The tallest self supporting tower is the CN Tower in Toronto.
7. Labor saving devices such as vacuum cleaners, washing machines, and toasters became widely used in the 1920's.
8. By 1920, fifteen million Model T's had been sold at can you believe it less than $300 each.

Part 5
Parentheses

Parentheses enclose material that is only loosely connected to the sentence. Such material interrupts the continuity of the sentence and is nonessential.

Use parentheses to set off supplementary or explanatory material that is loosely related to the sentence.

> I can still clearly recall my high-school graduation twenty years ago (sometimes it seems like only yesterday).

Note the use of parentheses in the following examples:

> Though Loch Ness had been a tourist haven for the rich in Victorian times (the Queen herself journeyed up the loch in a paddle steamer in 1873), it was the road that really opened the area to large numbers of visitors.
>
> Their father was the twelfth child of a wealthy Englishman (one of whose houses, Claverton Manor, is now the American Museum).
>
> Inside was a first-aid kit (including boxes of antivenin), a can of beans (invariably rusty), malaria pills, and pliers.

When the supplementary material is more closely related to the sentence, use commas or dashes. Compare the use of punctuation in the following examples:

Comma	The best point of Kate's speech, which she saved for the end, was that every group needs leadership.
Dash	The beef was braised—that is, it was browned and then simmered in a covered container.
Parentheses	Leonardo da Vinci (he was a brilliant scientist and one of the world's greatest artists) wrote: "Those sciences are vain and full of errors which are not born of experiment, the mother of all certainty."

Use parentheses to enclose figures or letters in a list that is part of a sentence.

> A tree is different from a shrub in that it has (1) greater height and (2) a single trunk.
>
> Is your favorite time of day (a) morning, (b) afternoon, or (c) evening?

Use parentheses to informally identify a source of information you use in your writing or to give credit to an author whose ideas or words you are using.

> "When the stock market went over the edge of Niagara in October and November, 1929, and the decline in business became alarming, the country turned to the President for action" (Allen 282).

Punctuation with Parentheses

Use punctuation marks inside the parentheses when they belong to the parenthetical material. However, when punctuation marks belong to the main part of the sentence, place them outside of the parentheses.

> Leo's speech was on disarmament; Barb's, on acting as a career (her favorite subject); Jim's, on slum clearance.
>
> I never guessed (would you have?) that the maid did it.
>
> Sheldon spoke of his victory over Central's debaters (*his* victory!) as if he had been a one-man team.
>
> The tallest player on the men's basketball team is Seamus (pronounced shay´məs!).

Checkpoint Parts 1–5

Rewrite the following sentences, adding semicolons, colons, dashes, and hyphens where needed.

1. Our school has exchange students from these countries Brazil, Kenya, Sweden, and Chile.
2. My class that meets at 930 oh, I hope I won't be late will discuss student rights.
3. The coach tried everything pep talks, privileges, rallies, toughness to try to improve the team's morale.
4. The water ballet routine was precisely choreographed furthermore, it was performed flawlessly.
5. Selina prepared for the audition she memorized her lines and practiced her dance.
6. The following are departure times for trains to Union Station 830 A.M., 1200 noon, and 430 P.M. every weekday.
7. We ate lunch at a little out of the way country restaurant that featured twenty one different appetizers.
8. In his book *On Writing Well,* William Zinsser says this "Clutter is the disease of American writing."
9. Jennifer came to a decision she would attend college after all.
10. Dr. Martin Luther King, Jr., was a great leader accordingly, his birthday has been made a national holiday.
11. We have a factory in Salem, Oregon an office in Buffalo, New York and a mill at Andover, Massachusetts.
12. The telephone rang it was Ron saying he'd be late.
13. She did not want to go it was dark and windy to the graveyard at midnight on Halloween.
14. The Ten Commandments are found in Exodus 20 7–17.
15. Alana is the sister in law of a well known actor.
16. Lou Schlanger's class at South Bronx High School I assume these students have impossible schedules begins at 710 A.M.
17. We are disappointed in the advertisement it is too small.
18. My brother in law has an astounding appetite last Thanksgiving he ate the following for dinner two large turkey legs, three twice baked potatoes, and two thirds of a pumpkin pie!
19. Walter Mitty if he's a hero then we all are lives an exciting life in his make believe world.
20. That turn of the century mansion has a well bred look.

Linking
Mechanics *&* Writing

Write a dialogue between two characters. One character is a non-stop talker who rambles on and on about trivial ideas, frequently interrupting himself or herself to insert unrelated details. The second character is a polite, quiet person who speaks precisely and correctly, but who keeps being interrupted by the first speaker. Use commas, semicolons, dashes, and parentheses to make the dialogue clear. (Parentheses may be used to describe the actions or reactions of the characters while the dialogue is going on.)

Prewriting and Drafting To write an effective dialogue, you need to create characters with unique identities—that is, characters with specific interests, needs, and personality traits. Before you begin drafting your dialogue, brainstorm about what your characters will be like. Then make a list of character traits for each person.

After you have established the identities of your characters, jot down notes about how their relationship can be described. Then think about what their conversation will be about. Decide whether you want to treat the dialogue seriously or humorously. Remember, even a brief dialogue should tell a complete story; it should have a beginning, middle, and end.

Revising and Proofreading After you have drafted your dialogue, ask someone to join you in a dramatic reading, with each of you speaking the lines of one character. Use the following questions to help you identify areas for revision:

1. Is the dialogue lifelike?
2. Does the unique personality of each character come across?
3. Is it easy to understand what the characters are talking about?
4. Does your dialogue "tell a story"?
5. Are there places where material needs to be cut or added?
6. Have you punctuated correctly to make the dialogue clear?

Additional Writing Topic Dashes and parentheses are often used in informal writing, such as personal letters, because they allow the writer to express ideas and information in a conversational tone. Think of the most exciting event you have ever experienced or participated in. Then write a personal letter in which you describe that event to a good friend. Use correct punctuation, including dashes and parentheses.

Chapter 31
Application and Review

A Using Punctuation Correctly Rewrite the following sentences, adding semicolons, colons, dashes, and hyphens as needed.

1. For her extra credit report on the tragic *Titanic,* Alyssa used *The World Book Encyclopedia,* Volume 19, pages 235 236.
2. Dear Mr. Berger

   My used car business will take me to an out of town conference therefore, I would like you to forward my mail to the following address The Armstrong Plaza Hotel, 136 Fiftieth Street North, Richmond, VA 23232. The telephone number is 804-555-5300. Thank you very much.

   Sincerely yours,
   Charles Ames
3. Mud slides, rock slides, premature dynamite explosions, and the deaths of 5,400 workers these were some of the problems that plagued the construction of the six mile Panama Canal.
4. It's about well, it's something like I would say it's a good eighteen miles from here.
5. The newly formed rock and roll band was scheduled to appear at a pregame party however, their bus broke down, and they spent twenty four hours in Tulsa waiting for parts to be delivered.
6. The blockbuster movie *E.T.* holds the record for the highest box office sales it grossed a mind boggling 322 million dollars.
7. Attention These computer controlled doors lock promptly at 500 P.M.
8. In reference to the Constitutional Convention, George Washington wrote this to a friend "We exhibit at present the novel and astonishing spectacle of a whole people deliberating calmly on what form of government will be the most conducive to their happiness."
9. The robber turned to the clerk "Give me all your money!"
10. At 120 years of age, Shigechiyo Izumi he has always lived on the same island in Japan has the unique distinction of having the oldest documented age of any human being.

B Punctuating Sentences Correctly Rewrite the following sentences, adding semicolons, colons, dashes, and hyphens as needed.

1. What happens in the end no, I won't give it away would surprise even the most devoted reader of mystery stories.

2. The Declaration of Independence ends with these inspiring words "We mutually pledge to each other our lives, our fortunes, and our sacred honor."

3. This must be Dolores's room lavender and green are two of her favorite colors.

4. The following plays are classified as tragedies *Oedipus the King, Macbeth, Julius Caesar, King Lear, Hamlet, Timon of Athens, Romeo and Juliet,* and *Death of a Salesman.*

5. After two weeks of intensive campaigning, twenty four well qualified students were elected to the Student Council.

6. You will find the quote in *Thomas Jefferson The Man and His Times,* Volume III 106.

7. Cats love peeking into corners, crawling under beds, perching atop bookshelves, and getting into bureau drawers but they don't like being put in confined spaces.

8. Geraldo said at least I think this is what he said that everyone would be welcome at the party.

9. With her latest performance, Jocelyn bettered her own long standing record in the play offs.

10. The Puritans, who settled in New England in the 1600's, discouraged merrymaking and festivities for example, they had laws against celebrating Christmas.

c *Proofreading* Rewrite the following passage, correcting errors in capitalization and spelling as well as errors in the use of semicolons, colons, dashes, and hyphens. Add any missing punctuation.

We eat more hamburgers char-broiled and pan-fried than any other nation in the world. Our all American hamburgers, however, began their sizzle on another continent. During the Middle Ages, Tartar Nomads in russia often ate raw meat. To tendarize the meat, they used the folowing recipe place a slab of meat under a saddel; ride on it all day, scrape and shred the meat, and mix it with salt, pepper, and onion juice. The modern version of this delicacy, no longer tenderized under a saddle, is called "steak tartar" German Soldiers from the town of Hamburg picked up the idea at Baltic seaports they brought it home with them. Sometime later, Hamburg cooks had another inspiration, they started broiling the meet. It took, however an american cook experts disagree on who this genius was to introduce hamburger patties to buns. This introduction was a tremendous success. The rest, as they say, is history.

32

Apostrophes and Quotation Marks

"Injustice anywhere is a threat to justice everywhere."

Martin Luther King

*T*hrough his powerful speeches, Reverend Martin Luther King, Jr., inspired many people to work for civil rights. Today writers and speakers still use the words of Reverend King to motivate individuals to support this cause. However, they always credit King for these words and enclose them in quotation marks.

In this chapter you will learn to use quotation marks to set off direct quotations and to use apostrophes to show ownership.

Part 1
Apostrophes

Apostrophes have several important functions. They are used to indicate possession, to show omitted letters, and to form the plurals of certain items such as numbers.

Using Apostrophes to Indicate Possession

Use apostrophes to form the possessives of singular and plural nouns.

To use apostrophes correctly, you must know whether nouns are singular or plural. To form the possessive of a singular noun, add an apostrophe and an *s* even if the noun ends in *s*.

> teacher's   city's   lass's   Chris's

Punctuation Note Exceptions to this rule about the possessive of singular nouns are *Jesus, Moses,* and names from mythology that end in *s: Jesus', Moses', Zeus', Odysseus'.*

To form the possessive of a plural noun that ends in *s* or *es*, add only an apostrophe. The possessive of a plural noun that does not end in *s* is formed by adding an apostrophe and an *s*. For information on forming the plurals of nouns, see pages 802–804.

> teachers'   cities'   men's   children's

To form the possessive of a compound noun, add an apostrophe only to the last part of the noun.

A **compound noun** is a noun composed of more than one word. Some compound nouns are written with hyphens between the parts.

> notary public + 's = notary public's office
> sisters-in-law + 's = sisters-in-law's coats

The possessive forms of nouns such as the *Queen of England* and the *President of the United States* are formed by adding an apostrophe and *s* to the last word only: *the Queen of England's throne.* Your writing will usually be less awkward if you reword and use an *of*-phrase instead.

> the throne of the Queen of England
> the home of the President of the United States

"*Sorry, but I'm going to have to issue you a summons for reckless grammar and driving without an apostrophe.*"

In cases of joint ownership, only the name of the last person mentioned is given the possessive form. Add an apostrophe or an apostrophe and *s*, depending on the spelling of the name.

> Tom and Wes's school
> the actors and dancers' costumes

This rule also governs the formation of the possessives of the names of firms and organizations.

> Cross and Hamilton Company's sales force
> Johnson & Johnson's corporate headquarters

If the names of two or more persons are used to show separate ownership, each name is given the possessive form.

> Madison's and Monroe's administrations
> Don's and Jim's grades

Again, to avoid an awkward sentence, a phrase using the word *of* may be substituted for the possessive form.

> the administrations of Madison and Monroe
> the grades of Don and Jim

To form the possessive of an indefinite pronoun, add an apostrophe and *s*.

> everyone's   somebody's
> one's   either's

Add an apostrophe and *s* to the last word to form the possessives of compound pronouns like those shown below.

> someone else's turn   no one else's answer

Do not use an apostrophe with a personal pronoun to show possession.

> The raincoat on the couch is hers. Yours is in the closet.
> Is that magazine ours? Its cover is missing.

When nouns expressing time and amount are used as adjectives, they are given the possessive form.

> a month's time   four days' wait   two centuries' tradition

Using Apostrophes to Show Omissions

Use apostrophes in contractions.

In contractions words are joined and letters are left out. An apostrophe replaces the missing letter or letters.

> you'll = you will or you shall   don't = do not
> what's = what is   Hank's = Hank is

Dialogue may use contractions that reflect regional dialects. Apostrophes are used to indicate the missing letters in such contractions.

> "How d'you do, Ma'am!" he shouted. "'Tis a fine mornin'."

Use an apostrophe to show the omission of figures.

> the class of '89   the blizzard of '78

Using Apostrophes for Certain Plurals

Use apostrophes to form the plurals of letters, numbers, signs, and words referred to as words.

> How many *r*'s are there in *embarrass*?
> Her speech has too many *therefore*'s in it.
> F. Scott Fitzgerald focuses on the 1920's in *The Great Gatsby*.
> To type *$*'s instead of *4*'s, depress the shift key.

Usage Note The plurals of letters, numbers, signs, and words used as words are always italicized in print. In manuscript and typewritten work they are underlined. See the Writer's Handbook, page 833, for further information about italics and underlining.

Exercises

A Find the words that have errors in apostrophe usage. Write each word correctly on your paper. If a sentence contains no errors, write *Correct*.

1. Somebody's jacket is hanging from the flagpole.
2. The reporter ignored the editor-in-chiefs warning and revealed one of his sources.
3. Alex's and Andrea's Health Club features exercise machines', aerobic's classes, and swimming lessons'.
4. Youll need two dollar's worth of quarters to play that new pinball machine.
5. Were Poe's and Hawthorne's short stories written during the early 1800's?
6. My father-in-laws panel truck is being repaired at Al and Ron's Auto Shop.
7. Odysseus' son searched in vain for his missing father.
8. Who's fault is the Chernobyl disaster? We discovered that its really many peoples fault.
9. When you have two *l*'s together in the Spanish language, how are they pronounced?
10. Selena wont drive me to Park and Hemsleys new store.
11. Roosevelts and Rockefeller's backgrounds were similar.
12. The Secretary of the Treasurys salary is $86,200.
13. Place *s next to the names of the books that are theirs'.
14. I especially liked Sissy Spacek's and Tommy Lee Jones' performances in *Coal Miners Daughter*.
15. Shes got two weeks worth of work to finish in one week.

B Follow the directions for Exercise A.

1. Several golfer's scores were below par.
2. Perrys last name has four es in it.
3. Bross and Bradys' Gourmet Shop sells pickled eel, goat cheese, and sun-dried tomatoes.
4. Its not likely that Saturn is inhabited, but lets investigate.
5. My teacher's first suggestion was to eliminate the *um*'s in my speech.
6. Cray Research Incorporateds computer, the CRAY-1, is the worlds most powerful computer.
7. Youll have to pay at least one months rent as a security deposit on the apartment.
8. That drive-ins sound system isnt working.

9. Weve used my brother-in-laws cabin in northern Vermont every summer.
10. Everythings under control; Ginas teaching the three-year-olds their *ABC*'s.
11. The client's cars are ready for them.
12. I'll write a children's story for the magazine's next issue.
13. Have you ever eaten at Anthonys and Cleopatras Diner in Cairo, Illinois?
14. Arent you reading Hemingways novels in your new course, American Literature of the 20s and 30s?
15. Michael Jackson set the record in 84 for winning the most Grammy Awards in one years time.

C *Proofreading* Rewrite the following paragraph correctly. You will find errors in spelling, capitalization, and punctuation. Pay special attention to the use of apostrophes.

One of ice hockeys greatest players is Bobby Orr, the National Hockey Leagues all-time top-scoring Defenseman. Orrs incredible record include's six one-hundred-point season's, and more individual honor's and award's than any other player in the NHLs history. Despite Orr's fame, a reporter once remarked, after dinning with orr in one of Bostons downtown restaurants, "Hes so easygoing. I would forget that I was with one of sports greatest superstars."

Orrs thirteen-year career included six operations on his left knee. Finally, even a Surgeons skill couldnt coax the heros knee to respond. Forced to retire early, Bobby Orr became the Hockey Hall of Fames youngest member in September of 79. Their, the famous number 4s sweater remains as a tribute to its' outstanding owner.

D *Write Now* You are the writer of the "Did You Know . . . ?" column for your school paper. For this month's column, you have these news items to write about: (1) a new project by members of the science club; (2) inside information from an anonymous source; (3) the thoughts of your star football player on the upcoming game; (4) a survey conducted by the history classes; (5) a mistake by your editor in chief. Write your column, using possessive forms of some nouns and pronouns.

Part 2
Quotation Marks

Quotation marks are used to set off direct quotations, titles, and words used in special ways.

Direct and Indirect Quotations

Use quotation marks to begin and end a direct quotation.

Ricardo said, "The violinists are ready to perform."

Do not use quotation marks to set off an indirect quotation.

Ricardo said that the violinists are ready to perform.

Punctuation of Direct Quotations

The speaker's words are set off from the rest of the sentence with quotation marks, and the first word of the quotation is capitalized.

"Let's meet at my house next time," Raoul said.
Raoul said, "Let's meet at my house next time."

When the end of the quotation is also the end of the sentence, the period falls inside the quotation marks. Also note the placement of commas in the examples above.

If the quotation is a question or exclamation, the question mark or exclamation point falls inside the quotation marks.

"May I make the poster?" Lola asked.
"I deny everything!" the suspect cried.

Note that no commas are necessary in the examples above.

If the entire sentence is a question or an exclamation, the question mark or exclamation point falls outside the quotation marks.

> Did I hear you say, "You're welcome to take these concert tickets"?
> It's totally absurd for anyone to consider these thieves "responsible citizens"!

If there is a colon or a semicolon at the close of a quotation, it falls outside the quotation marks.

> The committee said that the following states contained "pockets of poverty": Kentucky, West Virginia, and Pennsylvania.
> Read the ballad "Sir Patrick Spens"; then study its relation to Coleridge's poem "Dejection: An Ode" and write an essay comparing the two.

Both parts of a divided quotation are enclosed in quotation marks. The first word of the second part is not capitalized unless it begins a new sentence.

> "Part of my plan," the Governor said, "is to reduce property taxes this year."
> "You must remember this," the guidance counselor said. "Ten hours of casual work will probably be less effective than five hours of real concentration."

In dialogue, a new paragraph and a new set of quotation marks are used to show a change in speakers.

> "My working habits have no pattern," the author said. "Some writers set themselves very strict schedules. I prefer to remain more flexible."
>
> "But you've written five books in five years," the interviewer replied. "You must work very hard every day."
>
> "On the contrary, some days I spend the entire morning putting in a comma and the afternoon taking it out."

Single quotation marks are used to enclose a quotation within a quotation.

> Herb said, "Then she actually said to me, 'I hope I didn't keep you waiting.'"
> "The announcer just said, 'More snow throughout the state tonight,'" Len reported.
> "Who wrote the song 'What I Did for Love'?" asked Jan.

A quotation may sometimes be several paragraphs in length. In long quotations, begin each paragraph with quotation marks. Place quotation marks at the end of the last paragraph only.

Usage Note A long quotation can be set off from the rest of the text by indenting and double spacing. In this case, no quotation marks are needed.

When a quoted fragment is inserted in a sentence, the first word of the fragment is not capitalized unless it begins a sentence or is a proper noun. No comma is needed to set the phrase apart from the rest of the sentence.

> Marc Antony claims that he has "come to bury Caesar, not to praise him." However, his speech has the opposite effect.

Exercises

A Rewrite the following sentences, adding the necessary punctuation marks and capital letters.

1. Zachary asked may I rewrite this composition
2. Your Honor the defendant pleaded I beg you for another chance
3. The city is not equipped to deal with a heavy snowfall the guide explained
4. Did Governor Thompson say that the state of Illinois will allot more funds for education asked Jenny
5. Don replied that he had no one to blame but himself
6. In Shakespeare's *Julius Caesar*, Cassius is described as having a lean and hungry look
7. Did you know asked Juan that the three most common names for American dogs are Rover, Spot, and Max
8. Who said look out asked the irate guard
9. Referring to her father's encouragement, Andrea Jaeger said he told me Andrea, I think you have natural talent you can be a good player, maybe even a champion
10. Who was the only American President who never married asked José
11. Did Perry's message say we have met the enemy and they are ours
12. The test was incredibly hard said Sam but it was fair
13. Sink that freethrow screamed the cheerleaders
14. In the Sand Creek Massacre the speaker added several hundred Cheyenne Indians were killed
15. Martha said that the advertisers on the Super Bowl broadcast paid $550,000 per half minute

B Application in Literature The following passage has been changed to include several errors in the use of punctuation, capitalization, and paragraphing. Rewrite the passage, returning it to its original state by correcting the errors.

(1) He was very thin and dressed in rags. (2) What I remember are his eyes. (3) He had huge, dark eyes. (4) He did not speak. (5) He just stood there, looking up at me. (6) Who are you I asked in Chinese? (7) I am no one. (8) He said. (9) But what is your name I asked? (10) I have no name he said. (11) Where are your parents? (12) I have no parents. (13) But where did you come from I asked, staring at him? (14) I came from nowhere he said. (15) And you are going nowhere? (16) Nowhere he said. (17) Then why come to me? (18) He shook his head, not able to answer. (19) Come in I said finally, you must be hungry.

Pearl S. Buck

C *Write Now* You are in the middle of a telephone conversation with your best friend. Suddenly your conversation is interrupted by loud static and a high-pitched tone. Then a voice says, in English, "Go ahead, Detroit. This is Moscow." Write down the rest of your conversation with a Russian teen-ager, being sure to follow the rules for proper English punctuation, capitalization, and paragraphing.

Setting Off Titles

Use quotation marks to set off chapter titles and other parts of books and the titles of short stories, essays, poems, articles, television episodes, and short musical compositions.

Chapter Title	"Chapter 9: The Progressive Spirit"
Short Story	"The Black Cat"
Essay	"The Joys of Science"
Poem	"Mending Wall"
Magazine Article	"Good Food for Healthy Bodies"
Television Episode	"Lucy and Desi in London"
Song	"This Land Is Your Land"

The title of a book, magazine, newspaper, TV series, play, painting, or long musical composition is italicized in print. In writing, indicate italics by underlining. See the Writer's Handbook, page 833, for more information about italics and underlining.

Words Used in Special Ways

Use quotation marks to set off words used in special ways and to set off slang.

Writers can show that they are using a word as someone else has used it by enclosing it in quotation marks. Slang words and phrases are also enclosed in quotation marks.

> The government official claimed he was "protecting" his country's interests when he lied during his testimony.
> The slang of the '80's includes such words as "nerd," "awesome," "wicked," and "tubular."

A word referred to as a word is italicized in print. In writing, the word is underlined. When a word and its definition appear in a sentence, the word is italicized (or underlined) and the definition is put in quotation marks.

> Until then I'd never heard the word *boondoggle*.
> In music the word *pianissimo* means "very soft."

Punctuation Note When a comma or period immediately follows the quoted word or phrase, the punctuation mark is placed inside the quotation marks. If the quoted word or phrase comes at the end of a question or exclamation, the punctuation mark is placed outside the quotation marks: Is this what you mean by "cool"?

Exercises

A Write the following sentences, adding quotation marks and underlining where necessary.

1. What does the word serendipity mean? asked Sandy.
2. Todd calls money bread, and Meg calls it green stuff.
3. I choreographed my dance routine to the song Hip to Be Square.
4. What does Montresor mean in the story The Cask of Amontillado when he says: For half of a century no mortal has disturbed them?
5. Why is the word nevermore repeated frequently in Edgar Allan Poe's poem The Raven?
6. One of Holden Caulfield's favorite words is phony.
7. I became ill while I was reading the chapter called Bacteria Are Your Friends.
8. One of my favorite Steinbeck short stories is The Snake.
9. When I'm Sixty-Four was a popular song from the Beatles' album *Sergeant Pepper's Lonely Hearts Club Band*.
10. The word facetious contains all five vowels arranged in alphabetical order.
11. Janie is writing an episode called The Wrath of Spock for the new *Star Trek* series.
12. Epilogue means a concluding part added to a literary work.
13. Your problem of too much spending money is one I'd like to have!
14. Triskaidekaphobia means the mortal fear of 13.
15. Kristin reported on an article in *Self* magazine called Do Women Really Assert Themselves?

B Follow the directions for Exercise A.

1. Last night's episode of *Murder, She Wrote* was called It Runs in the Family.
2. The verb eulogize means to praise highly.
3. The astronauts aboard *Apollo IX* sang Happy Birthday to You during their 1969 space voyage.
4. What is meant by the phrase manifest destiny?
5. Mom ironically referred to the tuna casserole as a gourmet treat.
6. Rachel led a thought-provoking discussion of the story The Open Boat.
7. My favorite train song is City of New Orleans.
8. Footprints is my favorite poem in our text, *Reading Literature*.
9. We read E.B. White's essay called Once More to the Lake.
10. The governor did not see many benefits in what the mayor called his public transportation solution.

Checkpoint *Parts 1 and 2*

A Rewrite the following sentences adding necessary punctuation. Be sure to use apostrophes and quotation marks correctly.

1. After reading a chapter from *The Martian Chronicles* called The Green Morning, Renee decided shed enjoy being a space traveler.
2. My kid brother is exactly like the main character in O. Henrys story The Ransom of Red Chief.
3. The TV term for an added sound track of people laughing is canned laughter.
4. Ms. Armanda, does the word subsequent mean next Sonia asked.
5. Carla asked Did Mr. Oldfield say Class is dismissed ?
6. The 84 Olympics were held in Los Angeles.
7. Joyces and Amandas term papers were the best in Mr. Chens class.
8. I guess youll be wantin some kindlin for the stove tmorrow.
9. Is the song When You Wish upon a Star from the movie *Pinocchio*?
10. Have you read Poes poem The Bells the psychiatrist asked.
11. Don and Eds Hot Dog Heaven has five 4s in its phone number.
12. Your mother-in-laws gloves were left in someone elses car.
13. Its an earthquake screamed Jody.
14. Our cruise on the *Royale* included the Caribbeans prettiest islands.

B Application in Literature Apostrophes and quotation marks have been omitted from the following passage. Rewrite the passage correctly.

(1) Why, Bert Howland, she said, how long have you been sitting here?

(2) All my life, he said. (3) Just waiting here for you . . .

(4) Flatterer, she said . . .

(5) Wearing your hair a different way or something, arent you? he asked.

(6) Do you usually notice things like that? she asked.

(7) No, he said. (8) I guess its just the way youre holding your head up. (9) Like you thought I ought to notice something.

From "The Beau Catcher" by Frederick Laing

Linking Mechanics *&* Writing

Soap operas are one of the most popular types of television show. In them, families, and sometimes entire communities, share secrets, problems, and schemes.

Write the dialogue for one scene from the fictional soap opera *All My Problems*. In this scene, a conversation is taking place in a restaurant between the handsome doctor Cliff Noble and and the scheming socialite Erica Lyer. Erica is trying to undermine Cliff's confidence about an upcoming heart transplant operation that he is performing on his sweetheart Jenny. Erica wants the operation to be a failure so that she can have Cliff for herself.

In your dialogue use the various forms of quotations covered on pages 780–784. Make certain that you punctuate, capitalize, and paragraph your dialogue correctly.

Prewriting and Drafting Jot down a list of possible problems that Cliff might encounter during a heart transplant operation—physical, emotional, and technical. Erica might remind Cliff of these potential problems while appearing to sympathize with him. Cliff's responses should range from confident refutations at the beginning of the conversation to worried statements at the end. Your dialogue might begin with a line such as:

"Goodness, Cliff, you're looking terrible!" Erica observed. "You must be worried about the heart transplant."

Revising and Proofreading After you have written the dialogue, proofread your work for the use of correct capitalization and punctuation in quotations. Have you begun a new paragraph each time the speaker changes?

Additional Writing Topic You are the leader of a rock group that has been rapidly gaining popularity. Your group is coming out with an album, and you have been asked to write the history of the group for the back cover. In your story, give some background about each person, including what his or her interests and favorite things are. Give a brief description of several songs on the album. Also describe the group's accomplishments and future plans. Since album notes are an example of informal writing, you may also use contractions to give your notes a conversational tone.

From Hand to Mouth

L anguage is not always fair. When it comes to matters of right and left, for example, the lefties have been subjected to discrimination. A "right-hand man" is an important person, but a "left-handed compliment" is not really a compliment at all.

Right-handed people have traditionally outnumbered left-handers, so words having to do with the right side have had the upper hand. The supremacy of the right can be traced to the origins of several words. *Dexterous,* meaning "skillful," comes from the Latin *dexter,* meaning "right" or "right hand." Therefore, someone who is ambidexterous has two right hands, since the Latin *ambi* means "both." *Adroit,* another word meaning "skillful," comes from the French *a droit,* meaning "to the right."

On the other hand, literally, is *sinister.* This word for something evil, corrupt, or dangerous comes from the Latin for "left." *Gauche,* meaning "awkward" or "clumsy," comes from the French for "left." *Gawky,* another word meaning "clumsy," comes from a dialect phrase meaning "left-handed." Even the word *left* itself doesn't get any respect. It comes from the Anglo Saxon *lef,* which means "weak," since the left hand is weaker than the right hand for the majority of people.

Left-handed people are right to complain that language has not always treated them right.

Untitled pencil drawing,
Joseph Lileck, 1985.

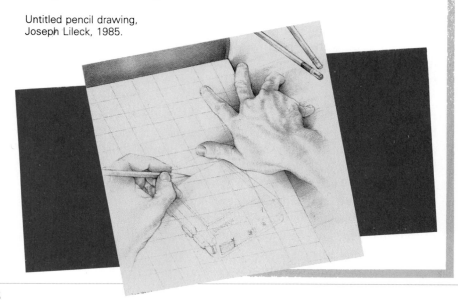

Chapter 32
Application and Review

A Using Apostrophes and Quotation Marks Rewrite the following sentences, correcting any errors in the use of apostrophes and quotation marks. Add correct punctuation and capital letters where they are needed.

1. The word refer is a palindrome, a word that is spelled the same forwards and backwards
2. Whoopee! the announcer shouted the Rangers have won
3. Sabrina asked did you read the poem Fifteen
4. You're teeths enamel said the dentist cant be replaced.
5. Is a Supreme Court Justices appointment for life Amy asked
6. Why do TV emcees say well be back after this word from our' sponsor
7. Who wrote the short story The Open Window Vivienne asked
8. Benson and Walker Companys employees have been asked to read an article in *Business Quarterly* magazine entitled How to Increase Your' Productivity
9. The students computers arent convenient remarked Mr. Day
10. The 8s and the #s on my keyboard are sticking said Joe.

B Application in Literature Apostrophes and quotation marks have been omitted from the following passage. Rewrite the passage correctly.

(1) A dark silhouette stepped into her path and demanded, Who are you? where are you going?

(2) Eleni held up her flare and saw more dark figures, ranged all the way up the hill. (3) Eleni Gatzoyiannis, wife of Christos, from the neighborhood of the Perivole, she said, pointing across the ravine. (4) Im trying to find my children.

(5) The figure came closer, and she could see the crown insignia on his two-pointed hat. (6) You cant go any farther, he said. (7) The guerrilla lines are all across the upper half of the village. (8) From here to there is a firing range. (9) But my children are over there! Eleni exclaimed. (10) Well have the whole village by morning, said the soldier. (11) Wait till then.

From *Eleni* by Nicholas Gage

33

Spelling

L ook at the fanciful way letters have been used in these designs.

Although you can create alphabetic pictographs such as these to represent an entire word, you cannot be quite as creative when you combine regular letters to spell words.

In this chapter you will learn the rules you must follow to spell correctly, as well as exceptions to those rules. You will also learn several ways to improve your spelling so you can communicate clearly.

Part 1

Improving Your Spelling

Correct spelling is important in all types of writing. In personal messages, letters, essays, and school tests, good spelling counts. Misspelled words on a job application may even cause you to lose the job. To improve your spelling, study and apply the following rules and methods.

1. **Identify and conquer your specific spelling problems.** Know the errors you repeatedly make. Study your past writing assignments; list all misspelled words. Master those words.

2. **Pronounce words carefully.** We misspell words when we pronounce them incorrectly. If you write *liberry* for *library,* you are probably mispronouncing the word.

3. **Use memory aids, called mnemonics, for words that give you trouble.** Stationery has *er* as in *letter;* there is "a rat" in *separate; Wednesday* contains *wed.*

4. **Always proofread your writing.** Many misspellings are simply the result of careless mistakes. Proofread your writing to catch these errors.

5. **Look up new and difficult words in a dictionary.**

6. **Learn the spelling rules contained in this chapter.**

The methods listed in the following chart will help you master the spelling of particularly difficult words.

Mastering the Spelling of a Word

1. **Look at the word and say it to yourself.** Make sure you pronounce it correctly.
2. **Close your eyes and visualize the word.** Look at it again; notice any prefixes, suffixes, or double letters.
3. **Write the word from memory.** Then check your spelling.
4. **Repeat the process.** Repeat it once if you spelled the word correctly. If you made an error, repeat the process until you have spelled the word correctly three times.

Part 2
Using Spelling Rules

The English language is rich in words from many different languages. As a result, English spelling is varied and complex. The following rules can help you eliminate spelling errors.

The Addition of Prefixes

When a prefix is added to a word, the spelling of the word remains the same. When a prefix creates a double letter, keep both letters.

pre- + arrange = prearrange   co- + operate = cooperate
re- + discover = rediscover   com- + mend = commend
anti- + trust = antitrust   il- + logical = illogical

The Suffixes -ly and -ness

When the suffix -ly is added to a word ending in l, keep both l's. When -ness is added to a word ending in n, keep both n's.

general + -ly = generally   keen + -ness = keenness
truthful + -ly = truthfully   sudden + -ness = suddenness
wool + -ly = woolly   lean + -ness = leanness

Exercise

Write the following words, adding prefixes and suffixes.

1. im- + moderate
2. thin + -ness
3. friend + -ly
4. pre- + arrange
5. dis- + satisfy
6. uneven + -ness
7. un- + natural
8. mis- + understand
9. co- + ordinate
10. re- + examine
11. loyal + -ly
12. co- + exist
13. in- + operable
14. dry + -ness
15. careful + -ly

Suffixes with Silent e

When a suffix beginning with a vowel or y is added to a word ending in a silent e, the e is usually dropped.

make + -ing = making   fascinate + -ion = fascination
wheeze + -y = wheezy   facilitate + -ing = facilitating
knife + -ing = knifing   rose + -y = rosy

When a suffix beginning with a consonant is added to a word ending with a silent *e*, the *e* is usually retained.

home + -less = homeless   divine + -ly = divinely
subtle + -ness = subtleness   lone + -ly = lonely
require + -ment = requirement   fate + -ful = fateful
engage + -ment = engagement   care + -ful = careful

Exceptions include *truly*, *argument*, *ninth*, *wholly*, and *awful*.

When a suffix beginning with *a* or *o* is added to a word with a final silent *e*, the final *e* is usually retained if it is preceded by a soft *c* or a soft *g*.

bridge + -able = bridgeable   courage + -ous = courageous
peace + -able = peaceable   advantage + -ous = advantageous
notice + -able = noticeable   outrage + -ous = outrageous
manage + -able = manageable   gorge + -ous = gorgeous

When a suffix beginning with a vowel is added to words ending in *ee* or *oe*, the final silent *e* is retained.

agree + -ing = agreeing   toe + -ing = toeing
hoe + -ing = hoeing   decree + -ing = decreeing
free + -ing = freeing   see + -ing = seeing

Suffixes with Final y

When a suffix is added to a word ending in *y*, and the *y* is preceded by a consonant, the *y* is changed to *i* except with the suffix *-ing*.

silly + -ness = silliness   marry + -age = marriage
company + -es = companies   twenty + -eth = twentieth
happy + -est = happiest   dally + -ing = dallying
carry + -ed = carried   empty + -ing = emptying
merry + -ly = merrily   marry + -ing = marrying

Exceptions include *dryness*, *shyness*, and *slyness*.

When a suffix is added to a word ending in *y* preceded by a vowel, the *y* usually does not change.

pray + -ing = praying   destroy + -er = destroyer
enjoy + -ing = enjoying   coy + -ness = coyness
gray + -ly = grayly   decay + -ing = decaying

Exceptions include *daily* and *gaily*.

Donald O'Connor, Debbie Reynolds,
and Gene Kelly in the 1952 film *Singin' in the Rain*.

Exercise

Rewrite each of the following sentences, adding prefixes and suffixes as shown.

1. Gene Kelly's (un- + forget + -able) (dance + -ing) in the film *Singin' in the Rain* has become (legend + -ary).
2. The gondola was (glide + -ing) (lazy + -ly) down the canal.
3. Strike negotiators made a (courage + -ous) effort to achieve a (peace + -able) settlement.
4. The English language contains the (large + -est) number of (use + -able) words of any language in the world.
5. Our old car was (slide + -ing) slowly down the (ice + -y) hill.
6. (Creative + -ness) develops (natural + -ly) with (encourage + -ment).
7. The idea of (canoe + -ing) on the (nine + -th) longest river in North America is (un- + believe + -ably) tempting.
8. Despite our (argue + -ments), the jury was (un- + compromise + -ing) in its verdict.
9. A recluse is (lone + -ly), but a hermit is (lone + -ly + -er).
10. The (assemble + -y) of convicts began (negotiate + -ing).
11. My (radiology + -ist) is (continue + -ing) the (intense + -ive) X-ray treatment.
12. That airline's (arrive + -als) are (usual + -ly) prompt treatment.
13. The (early + -est) Mayan (write + -ing) is not (easy + -ly) read.
14. A (grace + -ful) ballerina develops (supple + -ness) by (true + -ly) endless hours of practice.
15. We climbed (clumsy + -ly) up the (danger + -ous) walls of the old (fortify + -cation).

Doubling the Final Consonant

In one-syllable words that end with a single consonant preceded by a single vowel, double the final consonant before adding a suffix beginning with a vowel.

grab + -ing = grabbing   drug + -ist = druggist
dig + -er = digger   slim + -est = slimmest

Do not double the final consonant in one-syllable words ending in one consonant preceded by *two* vowels.

treat + -ing = treating   feel + -ing = feeling
loot + -ed = looted   clean + -ing = cleaning

In two-syllable words, double the consonant only if both of the following conditions exist:

1. The word ends with a single consonant preceded by a single vowel.
2. The word is accented on the second syllable.

re · gret' + -ed = regretted   per · mit' + -ing = permitting
de · ter' + -ence = deterrence   al · lot' + -ing = allotting
oc · cur' + -ing = occurring   re · fer' + -er = referrer

If the newly formed word is accented on a different syllable, the final consonant is not doubled.

re · fer' + -ence = ref' · er · ence
prof' · it + -eer = prof · i · teer'

In some cases a word is correct with a single or double consonant: *canceled* or *cancelled, equiped* or *equipped, traveled* or *travelled.* Check your dictionary for the preferred spelling.

Exercise

Write the following word pairs, adding the suffixes as shown. Underline any words in which you had to double the final consonant.

1. control + -ed
   quarrel + -ed
2. impel + -ing
   travel + -ing
3. loot + -ed
   regret + -ed
4. admit + -ance
   disturb + -ance
5. murmur + -ing
   defer + -ing
6. heap + -ed
   tap + -ed
7. run + -ing
   hasten + -ing
8. differ + -ence
   concur + -ence
9. limit + -ed
   commit + -ed
10. panel + -ing
    propel + -ing
11. lead + -ing
    rip + -ing
12. repel + -ent
    resist + -ant

Words with ie and ei

When the sound is long *e* (ē), the word is spelled *ie*, except after *c*.

retrieve	pier	receive
belief	shield	ceiling
piece	brief	conceit

When the sound is long *a* (ā), the word is spelled *ei*.

sleigh	neighbor
beige	freight

Exceptions include *either, friend, leisure, neither, seize, sieve, species, weird, forfeit, financier,* and *Fahrenheit.*

Words with the "Seed" Sound

There are three suffixes in English pronounced "seed." They are spelled *-cede, -ceed,* and *-sede*. Learn the twelve words below and avoid misspelling "seed" words.

-cede accede, antecede, cede, concede, intercede, precede, recede, secede
-ceed exceed, proceed, succeed
-sede supersede

Exercise

Rewrite these sentences with correctly spelled words. Where letters are missing, use *ie, ei,* or one of the "seed" endings to complete the word. Note that some words may be in the past tense.

1. We rec ___ ved many for ___ gn telex messages.
2. Keith pro ___ ed up the mountain after a br ___ f stop.
3. No one pre ___ d Washington as Ch ___ f Executive of this country.
4. In anc ___ nt Egypt pr ___ sts wrote hieroglyphics.
5. The heir apparent will suc ___ to the throne.
6. Colonial rule in America was super ___ d by the Constitution and a bel ___ f that all people have inalienable rights.
7. Drivers who exc ___ the speed limit endanger the lives of others.
8. The judge ac ___ d to the prisoner's request for a repr ___ ve.
9. My fr ___ nd and n ___ ghbor sh ___ lded my property from s ___ zure by the financ ___ r.
10. We learn about the ante ___ nts of that spec ___ s from w ___ rd fossils.

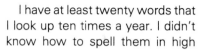

Spell Bound

When I look up something in the dictionary, it's never where I look for it.

The dictionary has been a particular disappointment to me as a basic reference work, and the fact that it's usually more my fault than the dictionary's doesn't make it any easier on me. Sometimes I can't come close enough to knowing how to spell a word to find it; other times the word just doesn't seem to be anywhere in the dictionary. I can't for the life of me figure out where they hide some of the words I want to look up. They must be in there someplace.

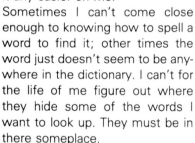

Other times I want more information about a word than the dictionary is prepared to give me. I don't want to know how to spell a word or what it means. I want to know how to use it. I want to know how to make it possessive and whether I double the final consonant when I add -ing to it. And as often as I've written it, I always forget what you do to make a word that ends in s possessive. "The Detroit *News'* editor"? "The Detroit *Newses* editor"? I suppose the Detroit *News's* editors know, but I never remember and the dictionary is no help.

I have at least twenty words that I look up ten times a year. I didn't know how to spell them in high school, and I still don't. Is it "further" or "farther" if I'm talking about distance? I always go to the dictionary for further details. I have several dictionaries, and I avoid the one farthest from me. Furthest from me? I am even nervous about some words I should have mastered in grade school. I know when to use "compliment" instead of "complement," when to use "stationery" and not "stationary," and "principle" not "principal;" but I always pause just an instant to make sure.

You'd think someone who has made a living all his life writing words on paper would know how to spell everything. I'm not a bad enough speller to be interesting, but there are still some words I look up in the dictionary because I'm too embarrassed to ask anyone how they're spelled. I've probably looked up "embarrassed" nine times within the last few years, and I often check to make sure there aren't two s's in "occasion." "Ocassion" strikes me as a more natural way to spell the word.

Andrew A. Rooney

Commonly Misspelled Words

abbreviate
absence
accidentally
accommodate
accompanying
achievement
acknowledge
acquaintance
across
address
all right
altogether
always
amateur
analyze
annihilate
anonymous
answer
apologize
appearance
appreciate
appropriate
arctic
argument
arising
arrangement
ascend
assassinate
associate
attendance
audience
auxiliary
awkward
bachelor
balance

bargain
becoming
beginning
believe
benefited
bicycle
biscuit
bookkeeper
bulletin
bureau
business
cafeteria
calendar
campaign
candidate
cellophane
cemetery
certain
changeable
characteristic
colonel
colossal
column
commission
committed
committee
comparative
compel
competitive
complexion
compulsory
conscience
conscientious
conscious
consensus

contemptible
convenience
corps
correspondence
courageous
courteous
criticism
criticize
curiosity
cylinder
dealt
decision
definitely
dependent
descent
description
desirable
despair
desperate
dictionary
different
dining
diphtheria
disagree
disappear
disappoint
discipline
dissatisfied
economical
efficient
eighth
eligible
eliminate
embarrass
eminent

emphasize
enthusiastic
environment
equipped
especially
etiquette
exaggerate
excellent
exceptional
exhaust
exhilarate
existence
expense
experience
familiar
fascinating
fatigue
February
feminine
financial
foreign
forfeit
fourth
fragile
generally
genius
government
grammar
guarantee
guard
gymnasium
handkerchief
height
hindrance
horizon

humorous	mischievous	practice	specifically
imaginary	missile	preference	specimen
immediately	misspell	prejudice	strategy
incidentally	mortgage	preparation	strictly
inconvenience	municipal	privilege	subtle
incredible	necessary	probably	success
indefinitely	nickel	professor	sufficient
indispensable	ninety	pronunciation	surprise
inevitable	noticeable	propeller	syllable
infinite	nuclear	prophecy	sympathy
influence	nuisance	psychology	symptom
inoculation	obstacle	pursue	tariff
intelligence	occasionally	quantity	temperament
interesting	occur	questionnaire	temperature
irrelevant	occurrence	realize	thorough
irresistible	opinion	recognize	throughout
knowledge	opportunity	recommend	together
laboratory	optimistic	reference	tomorrow
legitimate	original	referred	traffic
leisure	outrageous	rehearse	tragedy
lieutenant	pamphlet	reign	transferred
lightning	parallel	repetition	truly
literacy	parliament	representative	Tuesday
literature	particularly	restaurant	tyranny
loneliness	pastime	rhythm	twelfth
luxurious	permanent	ridiculous	unanimous
maintenance	permissible	sandwich	undoubtedly
maneuver	perseverance	schedule	unnecessary
marriage	perspiration	scissors	vacuum
mathematics	persuade	secretary	vengeance
matinee	picnicking	separate	vicinity
medicine	pleasant	sergeant	village
medieval	pneumonia	similar	villain
microphone	politics	sincerely	weird
miniature	possess	sophomore	wholly
minimum	possibility	souvenir	writing

Checkpoint *Parts 1 and 2*

A Find the misspelled words below and write them correctly. If the word is not misspelled, write *Correct*.

1. procede
2. conceed
3. dissagree
4. necessaryly
5. greeness
6. sucseed
7. awfuly
8. transslate
9. thinness
10. receed
11. supercede
12. missunderstand
13. relocate
14. wholy
15. ireverent
16. uneveness
17. seseed
18. eventualy
19. browness
20. exseed

B Rewrite any misspelled words in the following sentences.

1. Mr. Horton spent his liesure time weedding his garden.
2. Ty Cobb, the greatest batter in the history of baseball, recieved many awards for his achievments.
3. The village preist performs several wedings each year.
4. After stock prices fell, the financeir confered with his bookeeper.
5. Poe wrote many unerving tales about madmen and fiends.
6. Before diner I was seized by a strong urge for something very extravagant—caviar.
7. The ballad made referrence to a fierce knight weilding a sheild.
8. His feild is foreign diplomacy.
9. It's realy an ordinary-looking house.
10. Three beautys huried across the stage to recieve thier awards.
11. Despite hours of work, Bob was disatisfied with the results.
12. Greiving is a necessary process when a tragic loss occurs.
13. Sceintists beleive that the last dinosaur died about 65 million years ago.
14. Cheating on taxes is not only ilegal but also imoral.
15. The uneveness of the lettering ruins the whole sign.
16. Five girls succeded in their final examineations.
17. We often face requirments that exsede our knowledge.
18. Individual states may not seceed from the Union.
19. A prefix presedes the root word.
20. New laws on taxs supercede existing codes.

c *Proofreading* Proofread the following paragraph and correct errors in spelling, capitalization, and punctuation. Use the rules in this chapter, the list on pages 798–799, and a dictionary.

During world war i (1914–1918), a young leiutenant in the British royal army medical corps watched helplessly as young men died, many of them from minor wounds and infections after the war, Alexander Fleming returned to st. mary's hospital medical school, London University, to teach and continue his search for a substance that could elliminate disease-bearing microbs and save human lifes. One day in 1928, fleming examined a labaratory dish in which he had been growing *staphylococcus* bacteria. He notised that the culture had been accidentaly contaminated by a green mold, and the bacteria surrounding the mold had been killed. He found that the mold inhibitted the growth of bacteria even when it was diluted 800 times. Fleming, preparred by years of conceintious study and work, deduced that ordinary mold which he later identified as *penicillium notatum,* might work to treat bacterial infections in people

Flemings discovery—and the subsequent development of diffrent kinds of penicillins—had a great impact on medicine and the treatment of a number of deadly illnesses. Today, pencillin is used to cure such diseases as pneumonia, scarlet fever, throat infections, and spinal meningitis. For his sucess and persiverance, Fleming was knighted in 1944, he recieved the nobel prize in medicine in 1945

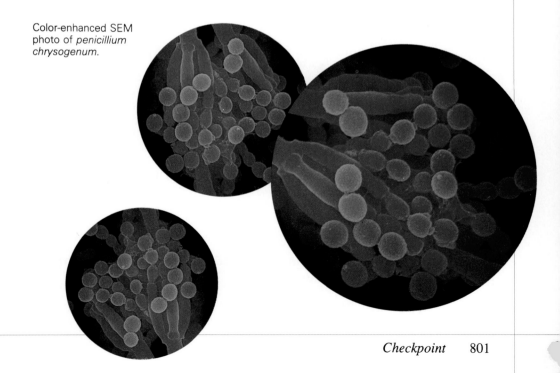

Color-enhanced SEM photo of *penicillium chrysogenum.*

Part 3
Plurals of Nouns

Noun plurals are spelled according to several rules. Study these rules for forming plurals. Also, check the dictionary whenever you are in doubt about the correct spelling of a word.

Regular Formation

Add -s to form the plural of most nouns.

building + -s = buildings   tree + -s = trees
flute + -s = flutes   oboe + -s = oboes

Nouns Ending in s, sh, ch, x, or z

Add -es to form the plural of nouns ending in s, sh, ch, x, or z.

rash + -es = rashes   waltz + -es = waltzes
bus + -es = buses   crutch + -es = crutches

Nouns Ending in y

When a noun ends in y preceded by a consonant, the plural is formed by changing the y to i and adding -es.

duty + -es = duties   party + -es = parties

When a noun ends in y preceded by a vowel, the plural is formed by adding -s.

tray + -s = trays   pulley + -s = pulleys
envoy + -s = envoys   boy + -s = boys

Nouns Ending in o

When a noun ends in o preceded by a vowel, the plural is formed by adding -s.

studio + -s = studios   ratio + -s = ratios
rodeo + -s = rodeos   duo + -s = duos

When a noun ends in o preceded by a consonant, the plural is usually formed by adding -s.

piano + -s = pianos   silo + -s = silos

Some nouns ending in *o* preceded by a consonant form the plural by adding *-es*.

tomato + -es = tomatoes	potato + -es = potatoes
echo + -es = echoes	hero + -es = heroes
cargo + -es = cargoes	veto + -es = vetoes

A few nouns in this class form the plural with either *-s* or *-es*.

mottos *or* mottoes	zeros *or* zeroes
mosquitos *or* mosquitoes	tornados *or* tornadoes

Consult the dictionary whenever you are not sure how to spell a word's plural form.

Nouns Ending in f, ff, or fe

The plural of most nouns ending in *f, ff,* or *fe* is formed by adding *-s*.

roof + -s = roofs	staff + -s = staffs
belief + -s = beliefs	safe + -s = safes
carafe + -s = carafes	giraffe + -s = giraffes

The plural of some nouns ending in *f* or *fe* is formed by changing the *f* or *fe* to *v* or *ve* and adding *-s* or *-es*.

calf + -es = calves	loaf + -es = loaves
life + -s = lives	self + -es = selves
half + -es = halves	wharf + -es = wharves
shelf + -es = shelves	leaf + -es = leaves
knife + -s = knives	elf + -es = elves

Nouns with Irregular Plurals

The plural of some nouns is formed by a change of spelling.

tooth—teeth	goose—geese
man—men	mouse—mice
woman—women	ox—oxen
child—children	basis—bases
datum—data	die—dice
crisis—crises	hypothesis—hypotheses

The plural and singular forms are the same for a few nouns.

sheep	corps	Japanese
deer	moose	Swiss

A few nouns have no truly singular form; they always appear in the plural form.

pants   mumps   economics   politics   scissors

Names

The plural of a name is formed by adding -s or -es.

Albert Steele—the Steeles   Jack Amos—the Amoses
Judy Lyons—the Lyonses   Bob Sable—the Sables

Compound Nouns

When a compound noun is written without a hyphen, the plural is formed by adding -s or -es to the end of the word.

armful + -s = armfuls   teaspoonful + -s = teaspoonfuls
rosebush + -es = rosebushes   skateboard + -s = skateboards

When a compound noun is made up of a noun plus a modifier, the plural is formed by adding -s or -es to the noun.

mothers-in-law (*In-law* is a modifier.)
attorneys general (*General* modifies *attorneys*.)
passers-by (*By* modifies *passers*.)
bills of sale (*Of sale* modifies *bills*.)
secretaries of state (*Of state* modifies *secretaries*.)
two-thirds (*Two* modifies the noun *thirds*.)

When a compound noun is made up of a verb plus an adverb, the plural is formed by adding -s or -es to the last word.

drive-in + -s = drive-ins   shut-out + -s = shut-outs
takeover + -s = takeovers   wind-up + -s = wind-ups

Exercises

A Write the plural of each noun below.

1. holiday
2. glass
3. radio
4. dash
5. laboratory
6. lady
7. valley
8. potato
9. hypothesis
10. tablespoonful
11. drive-in
12. right of way
13. sister-in-law
14. chief of police
15. Danish
16. mouse
17. takeover
18. corps
19. notary public
20. leaf

B Find the errors in the formation of plural nouns in the following sentences. Rewrite the misspelled words correctly.

1. Several hanger-ons were waiting for the parties to end.
2. Don't use more than three cupsful of flour.
3. The French serve many delicious dishes covered with sauce's.
4. My sister's favorite storys are *Snow White and the Seven Dwarves* and *The Elfs and the Shoemaker*.
5. The Martin's and the Foxes have had ancestores in Canada for centurys.
6. The attorney generals for those two states are shoos-in for the next election.
7. Three-fourths of the deers in the forest preserve were driven away by the corps's of soldieres and noisy equipments.
8. There are several hypothesis to explain the existence of the twin moons of Mars.
9. Our canoes glided smoothly down the watersway of Wisconsin.
10. The dogs were good decoyes; they led the wolfs into our trap.

c *White Now* Imagine that you are one of eleven children in a family. Every Wednesday you accompany your parents to the supermarket to help with the weekly grocery shopping. Think about providing meals for eleven children and two adults. Describe the shopping trip and the quantities of food your family has to buy. You will undoubtedly use plural forms in writing about this shopping trip. Try to use as many irregular plurals as you can to demonstrate your mastery of them.

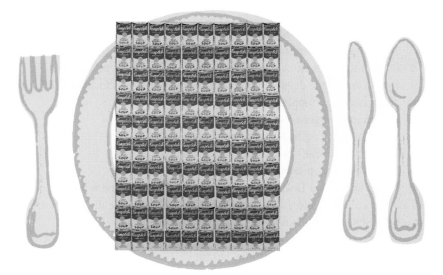

100 Cans, Andy Warhol, 1962.

Checkpoint *Part 3*

A Write the plural form of each noun below.

1. garage	11. zero	21. cue
2. switch	12. battery	22. brush
3. coat of arms	13. Alice	23. hex
4. donkey	14. nightmare	24. belief
5. lass	15. president-elect	25. harmonica
6. echo	16. axis	26. Romeo
7. lily	17. moose	27. kidney
8. Perez	18. gentleman	28. Lloyd
9. trousers	19. samurai	29. jackknife
10. tributary	20. breadfruit	30. honeycomb

B Rewrite the following sentences, correcting all errors in the formation of plurals. If a sentence has no errors, write *Correct*.

1. In autumn, Martin's brother-in-laws pick persimmones and blackberrys for canning.
2. Mr. Eckert says that there are three Smith's in his class's.
3. The Western democracys managed to solve both crisises peacefully.
4. Mitzner's Music sells radioes, stereoes, and pianoes.
5. Despite numerous injurys, the German and American teames still won several trophys.
6. Former Secretary of States often become professores.
7. Some dentists distribute toothbrushs to their patientes.
8. Four million American householdes have video discs or cassettes.
9. It took thirty-one days (310 hours) for Klaus Friedrich to set up 320,236 dominoes; they toppled in less than thirteen minutes.
10. The recipe's required two teaspoonsful of salt.
11. South America is the home of tomatos and potatos.
12. Fodder for the calfs and sowes is stored in the siloes.
13. Soloes by the sopranos were well received.
14. There are several Bostones, Osloes, and Athenses in the world.
15. Some college seniors write thesises before they receive diplomaes.
16. Bulrushs, sedge's, and grass's all thrive in wet places.
17. The hunter's used knifes to kill the deeres.
18. Prints of hoofs led scouts to the herdes.
19. Loafes of bread and sheafs of wheat are symbols of harvest.
20. Oboes, harpes, and violaes are featured in this symphony.

Linking
Mechanics & Writing

Imagine you are the curator of a museum. While examining a store-room, you notice a door frame behind some shelves. You remove the shelves, open the door, and step inside a musty room that is filled with incredible objects. Describe the contents of the room in a report. List the items you found; use as many different plural nouns as you can.

Prewriting and Drafting Use your imagination to invent descriptions of the unusual objects. Gather details by questioning or by using an encyclopedia. Write a first draft. In your final report include an introductory paragraph, a list, and a concluding paragraph. Remember to use plural nouns.

Revising and Proofreading Use these questions when proofreading.

1. Is there enough detail for any reader to visualize each object?
2. Are all proper nouns or adjectives capitalized?
3. Are all compound nouns or adjectives appropriately hyphenated?
4. Are correct noun plurals used, and are all words correctly spelled?

Additional Writing Topic Some very old recipes give quantities in nonstandard measurements. For example, a recipe may say, "Add as much butter as fills two walnut shells," or "Blend in three handfuls of flour." Write a recipe for a dish that you know how to make. When you list a quantity, use unconventional measures as in the examples.

Out in Left Field

"It's Greek to me." "Beat it!" "Not so hot." "Right on." Surprisingly, all of these slang expressions originated with Shakespeare. Slang comes from many less literary sources as well, including sports, jazz and rock music, crime, technology, and foreign languages. Since 1960, more than 22,000 examples have been collected in the periodically updated *Dictionary of American Slang*. This dictionary defines its turf as words and expressions that are used and understood by the majority of the American public but that are not accepted as good, formal usage.

Probably no other area has contributed as much slang to the English language as baseball. Even people who have never rooted for their home team know and use such expressions as "You're way off base" and "I liked him right off the bat."

Some slang expressions have originated with specific groups, who use the slang to exclude outsiders from their conversations. Several common slang terms have come from the criminal community. Examples include *kidnap,* a combination of "kid" (a small goat) and "napper" (thief); *cop,* from "*c*onstable *on p*atrol"; and *hijack,* from the highway robber's demand to a stagecoach driver: "Hands up high, Jack!"

Most slang quickly becomes outdated, although some can remain in the language for centuries without being accepted into standard English. When slang words do become part of the language, it's often hard to remember that their origins may be "out in left field."

Chapter 33
Application and Review

Finding and Correcting Spelling Errors Identify spelling errors in the sentences below. Rewrite the complete sentences and be careful to spell each word correctly.

1. The Gettysburg Adress was only one of President Abraham Lincoln's fameous speeches.
2. It's your fault that niether of us passed the test.
3. The nieghborhood group sent a representative to the city comission.
4. The riegn of Queen Victoria preceeded that of Edward VII.
5. The worryed farmer stayed up all night with the two sick calfs.
6. It's my opinion that no musician has sucseeded like Paul McCartney in his acheivements as a composer and recording artist.
7. Sales of holiday albumes and singles have each toped the one-hundred million mark.
8. Rakeing leafs, I beleive, is Maria's chore.
9. Writting carefuly, Jeff copied the outline from the book.
10. Mother usualy dissapproves of sugared snacks.
11. The caravan stopped at several oasises on its journey through the desert.
12. On Everest unecessary equippment becomes dangerous excess bagage for the mountaineers.
13. The Japanese eat varyous specieses of fish.
14. Roger exceled at drawing inferrences in a logical way.
15. Tyrone is enjoing his twentyeth birthday.
16. Kim relatted that he had had the same wierd dream three nights in a row.
17. The looksout percieved a stationary ship through the binnoculars.
18. Leo's performance was one of his best piano soloes.
19. As a winer of both trophys, Bernice was delighted.
20. The flood waters are rising, so procede with caution.
21. My best freind is encourageing me to put in an applycation for a part-time job.
22. The audience was truely elatted when the rock star heroes made an appearance.
23. Each of my sister-in-laws has gained acceptance at three of the best universitys in the country.
24. Those televisiones hooks-up are loose.
25. The editor in chiefs of several big-city dayly papers were interviewed on TV last night.

Cumulative Review

Chapters 29–33

A Using Capitalization and Punctuation Correctly Rewrite the following paragraphs, correcting errors in capitalization and punctuation.

(1) According to some writers, the history of exploration can be divided into three major stages. (2) The first stage the Exploration of the Old World probably began with ancient egyptian and babylonian traders around 2500 BC. (3) These traders traveled South to the Indian ocean and West to the Mediterranean sea. (4) About 300 b.c., the ancient Greek astronomer Pytheas explored the North Atlantic ocean, perhaps traveling as far North as Norway. (5) Around this time the conquests of Alexander the great, extended the known world as far east as India. (6) Many centuries later, Marco Polo, an Italian adventurer, further expanded World horizons when he traveled throughout China. (7) By the late middle ages, large parts of north africa, nearly all of Europe, and a substantial part of Asia had been included in the known world.

(8) The second stage, the Exploration of the New World, started around A.d. 1450 with the search, for a sea route to China. (9) Among the most famous of these explorers were the following Christopher Columbus the Italian navigator who sailed west across the Atlantic in 1492, Vasco da Gama the Portuguese sailor who became the first European to reach India by sea and Ferdinand Magellan, the Portuguese Navigator who commanded the first world-circling voyage. (10) Thanks, largely to the efforts of intrepid explorers such as these, most regions of the world have been accurately mapped.

(11) Nonetheless exploration is still very much alive. (12) In October of 1957, the Soviet Union launched *Sputnik I* the first artificial satellite and this event launched the third stage the Exploration of Space. (13) In May of 1961, President John f. Kennedy announced, that the United States would land a manned spacecraft on the moon within a decade. (14) The culmination of Americas early space exploration came on July 20 1969. (15) On this date, Neil Armstrong became the first human being ever to set foot on the moon. (16) Since that historic walk on the moon numerous explorers have bravely ventured into the immense darkness of space.

B Correcting Errors in Quotations and Spelling Rewrite the following paragraphs, correcting all mistakes in the use of quotation marks, capitalization, punctuation, and spelling.

(1) A poor woman once asked a rich man to lend her a big silver spoon so that she could entertain a special guest. (2) "I'll let you borrow my spoon, the rich man replied But only if you return it tomorrow." (3) Then he added, "make sure you return it before the sun goes down". (4) After recieving the spoon, the woman left.

(5) She returned the next day, after having hurryed to arrive before sunset. (6) She carryed with her the big spoon and a little spoon as well. (7) As soon as the rich man spoted the second spoon, he asked the woman "what had happened." (8) "The big spoon had a baby." she answerd.

(9) "Your story is hardly beleivable, he said." (10) "However, since the mother spoon is mine," the child spoon also belongs to me." (11) Then he greedily accepted both spoons from the poor woman.

(12) A few days later, the woman came back and said. (13) "May I borrow your silver candlesticks tonight"? (14) The rich man agreed to her request, secretly hopeing that the woman would return with many little candlesticks. (15) However, the poor woman returned the next day empty-handed. (16) She said that the "candlesticks had both fallen off the table during dinner and died. (17) She also said "she regreted their loss."

(18) The rich man, angerred by this story, wanted to sieze her; instead, he took her before the three wisest people in that small town. (19) The three sages immediatly discussed the problem and arrived at a unanimous decision. (20) "If you accept the profits when a spoon has a baby, then you must take the loss when a candlestick dies.

C Adding Suffixes and Forming Plurals Number your paper from 1 to 20. Write the words listed below.

1. hobo + -s
2. deter + -ence
3. teaspoonful + -s
4. structure + -al
5. constitute + -ion
6. imply + -ed
7. imagine + -ary
8. courage + -ous
9. eight + -teen
10. change + -able
11. persevere + -ance
12. merry + -ly
13. transfer + -ed
14. love + -able
15. belief + -s
16. father-in-law + -s
17. argue + -ment
18. incidental + -ly
19. latch + -s
20. occur + -ence

Sentence Diagraming

Diagraming can help you understand how parts of a sentence relate to each other. In addition, diagraming sharpens your critical skills by requiring you to analyze sentences and classify the parts.

A sentence diagram shows how the parts of a sentence fit together. The base for a sentence diagram is shown below:

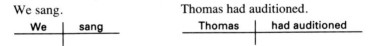

In the diagrams that follow, you will see how other lines are added to this base.

Subjects and Verbs

Place the simple subject on the horizontal main line to the left of the vertical line. Place the simple predicate, or verb, to the right.

We sang.

We	sang

Thomas had auditioned.

Thomas	had auditioned

In diagraming, capitalize only those words that are capitalized in the sentence. Do not use punctuation except for abbreviations. Place single-word modifiers on slanted lines below the words they modify.

Sentences Beginning with There or Here

To diagram a sentence beginning with *there*, first decide whether *there* tells *where* or is an introductory word. If *there* tells *where*, place it on a slanted line below the verb.

There is the document.

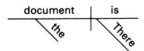

If *there* is an introductory word, place it on a horizontal line above the subject.

There have been many natural disasters.

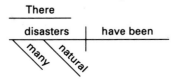

Unlike *there*, the word *here* always tells *where*. In a sentence diagram, therefore, place *here* on a slanted line below the verb.

Here comes the mayor.

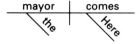

In both sentences above, the subject comes *after* the verb. Notice, however, that in the diagram the subject is placed *before* the verb to the left of the vertical line.

Interrogative Sentences

In an interrogative sentence, the subject often comes after the verb or after part of the verb phrase. In diagraming, remember to place the subject before the verb to the left of the vertical line:

Have you finished?   Can you contribute?

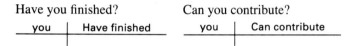

Imperative Sentences

In an imperative sentence, the subject is usually not stated. Since commands are given to the person spoken to, the subject is understood to be *you*. To diagram an imperative sentence, place the understood subject *you* to the left of the vertical line. Then enclose *you* in parentheses. Place the verb to the right of the vertical line.

Go!

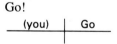

Direct Objects

In a diagram, place the direct object on the main line after the verb. Separate the direct object from the verb with a vertical line that does not extend below the main line.

The company offered discounts.

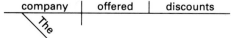

Indirect Objects

To diagram an indirect object, draw a slanted line below the verb. From the bottom of the slanted line, draw a line parallel to the main line. Place the indirect object on the parallel line.

The hairdresser paid me a compliment.

Subject Complements

In a diagram, place a predicate nominative or a predicate adjective on the main line after the verb. Separate the subject complement from the verb with a slanted line that extends in the direction of the subject.

Mary is president. (*President* is a predicate nominative.)

George seems well. (*Well* is a predicate adjective.)

Sentences with Compound Parts

Compound Subjects To diagram a compound subject, place the parts on parallel horizontal lines as shown below. Then connect the parallel lines with a broken line. On the broken line, write the conjunction that connects the parts of the compound subject. Attach the compound subject to the main line with solid diagonal lines.

Crocodiles, snakes, lizards, and turtles are reptiles.

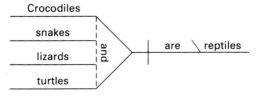

Compound Verbs To diagram a compound verb, place the parts on parallel horizontal lines. Write the conjunction on the broken line. Attach the compound verb to the main line as shown below.

Miller wrote and directed this production.

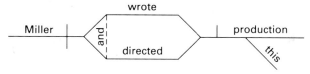

If each word in a compound verb has an object or a subject complement, place the complement on the parallel line after the verb.

The rebels won the skirmish and appeared confident.

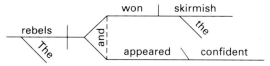

Compound Direct Objects and Indirect Objects To diagram a compound direct object or indirect object, place the parts on parallel horizontal lines. Write the conjunction on the broken line. Attach the compound object to the main line as shown below.

Houdini performed magic tricks and fantastic stunts. (*compound direct object*)

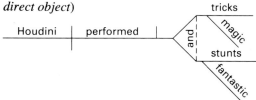

Compound Subject Complements To diagram a compound predicate nominative or predicate adjective, place the parts on parallel horizontal lines. Connect the parts with a broken line and write the conjunction on that line. Attach the compound predicate nominative or predicate adjective to the main line as shown below.

The winners are Jean and Sharon. (*compound predicate nominative*)

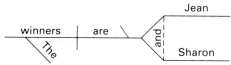

Adjectives

To diagram an adjective, place it on a slanted line below the word it modifies. Keep in mind that *a, an,* and *the* are adjectives and that more than one adjective can modify the same word.

Our new high school has a fitness trail.

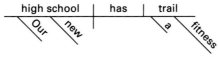

When two or more adjectives are connected by a conjunction, place the adjectives on slanted lines below the words they modify. Connect the slanted lines with a broken line. Then write the conjunction on the broken line.

A playful but friendly porpoise saved the sailor's life.

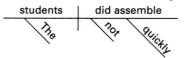

Adverbs

To diagram an adverb that modifies a verb, place the adverb on a slanted line under the verb. Keep in mind that words like *not* and *never* are adverbs.

The students did not assemble quickly.

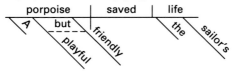

To diagram an adverb that modifies an adjective or an adverb, place the adverb on a line connected to the modified adjective or adverb as shown below.

Too many cars rust very quickly.

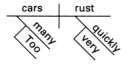

Prepositional Phrases

To diagram a prepositional phrase, draw a slanted line below the word that the phrase modifies. From the slanted line, draw a line parallel to the main line. Place the preposition on the slanted line and the object of the preposition on the parallel line. Words that modify the object of the preposition are placed on slanted lines below the object.

Eric painted a portrait of the President.

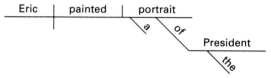

If a preposition has a compound object, place the objects on parallel lines as shown below.

Some stagecoach drivers were known for their determination and their bravery.

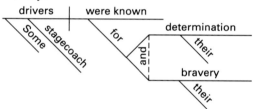

Gerunds and Gerund Phrases

To diagram a gerund, place it on a line drawn as a step (⌐_). Put the step on a forked line (⋏) that stands on the main line. The placement of the forked line shows how the gerund or gerund phrase is used—as a subject, a direct object, a predicate nominative, or the object of a preposition. If the gerund phrase includes modifiers, place these on slanted lines as shown in the example below.

We disliked taking the aptitude test. (*gerund phrase used as direct object*)

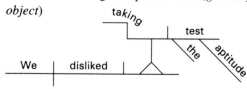

To diagram a gerund or a gerund phrase that is the object of a preposition, place the preposition on a slanted line that extends from the modified word. Then place the step and the forked line below the main line as shown below.

After swimming, we relaxed. (*gerund phrase as object of a preposition*)

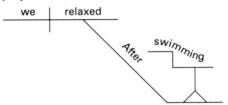

Participles and Participial Phrases

To diagram a participle, place the participle on an angled line below the word it modifies. Place any modifiers on slanted lines below the participle they modify.

Purring softly, the kitten lay down.

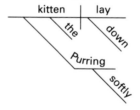

To diagram a participial phrase that includes a direct object and modifiers, place the object on a straight line extending from the base of the angled line. Place any modifiers on slanted lines below the words they modify.

Sailing his boat brilliantly, Jeff won the race. (*participial phrase including a direct object and modifiers*)

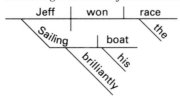

Infinitives and Infinitive Phrases

To diagram an infinitive used as a noun, place the infinitive on an angled line. Write the word *to* on the slanted part of the angled line and write the verb on the horizontal part of the angled line. Put the angled line on a forked line that stands on the main line. The placement of the forked line shows how the infinitive or infinitive phrase is used in the sentence. Place any modifiers on slanted lines below the words they modify.

We want to have a beach party soon. (*infinitive used as direct object*)

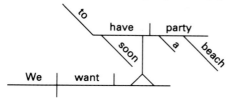

To diagram an infinitive used as a modifier, place the angled line on a horizontal line below the modified word. Attach the horizontal line to the main line as shown below.

This mountain is difficult to climb. (*infinitive used as adverb*)

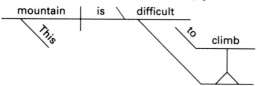

Appositives and Appositive Phrases

To diagram an appositive, place the appositive in parentheses after the word it identifies or explains. Place any modifiers on slanted lines below the appositive.

The ostrich, a native bird of Africa, can run swiftly.

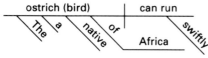

Adjective Clauses

Place the clause on its own horizontal line below the main line, diagraming the clause as if it were a sentence. Use a broken line to connect the relative pronoun in the adjective clause to the word in the independent clause that the adjective clause modifies.

The route that they took went through Washington.

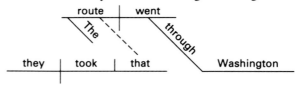

Adverb Clauses

Place the clause on its own horizontal line below the main line, diagraming the clause as if it were a sentence. Use a broken line to connect the adverb clause to the word it modifies in the independent clause. Write the subordinating conjunction on the broken line.

When the car stopped, we lurched forward.

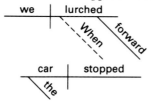

Noun Clauses

To diagram a noun clause, place it on a separate line that is attached to the main line with a forked line. The placement of the forked line shows how the noun clause is used in the sentence.

Diagram the word that introduces the noun clause according to its use. If the introductory word simply introduces the clause, place it on a line above the clause as shown in the second example.

What Juri saw was an illusion. (*noun clause used as subject*)

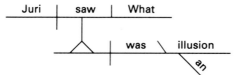

I know that they are going. (*noun clause used as object of the verb*)

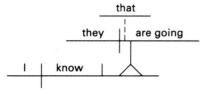

We have a job for whoever is qualified. (*noun clause used as object of a preposition*)

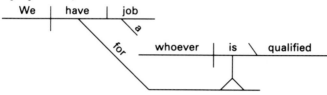

Compound Sentences

To diagram a compound sentence, place the independent clauses on parallel horizontal lines. Use a broken line with a step to connect the verb in one clause to the verb in the other clause. Write the conjunction on the step. If the clauses are joined by a semicolon, leave the step blank.

The game was close, but we finally won.

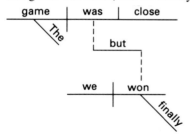

Complex Sentences

To diagram a complex sentence, first decide whether the subordinate clause is an adjective clause, an adverb clause, or a noun clause. Then use the information presented on pages 820–821 to diagram the sentence.

Compound-Complex Sentences

To diagram a compound-complex sentence with an adjective or an adverb clause, diagram the independent clauses first. Then attach the subordinate clause or clauses to the words they modify. Leave enough room to attach a subordinate clause where it belongs.

> Franklin Pierce, our fourteenth president, accidentally collided with an old lady while he was riding on horseback, and a policeman arrested him.

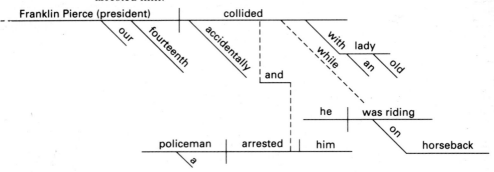

To diagram a compound-complex sentence with a noun clause, decide how the noun clause is used in the independent clause. Then diagram the noun clause in the position that shows how it is used.

> Who started the mutiny was never decided, but the British government blamed Mr. Christian. (The noun clause *who started the mutiny* is the subject of the verb in the first independent clause.)

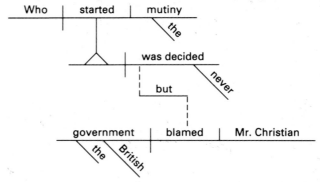

Writer's Handbook

Ideas for Writing

Ideas for writing are everywhere. You need only to recognize them and develop them. To help get your mental wheels rolling, read the following material and use your thinking skills to generate writing topics. You will find ideas for writing, trigger words, and guidelines for using fine art and photographs as starting points for writing.

Ideas for Writing

Descriptive
a sneak preview
a red sports car
a person who is like his or her pet
an aged gorilla
a room that has been closed for 100 years
an athletic team for whom nothing goes right
a place in which you spend much of your free time
a childhood souvenir

Narrative
nearing the finish
an honest mistake
terror from the sky
the last chance
the uninvited guest
an undiscovered country
your greatest personal success
a disappointment

Expository
(Process)
how to take a driver's test
how to break a code
how to make a pizza
how to lift weights
how volcanoes form

(Definition)
Define one of the following terms:
beauty, brain waves, charlatan, honor, ibex, revolution, stereotype

(Comparison/Contrast)
travel by horseback and travel by car
you, today and five years ago
the American Revolution and the Russian Revolution
two musicians
nuclear energy and solar energy

(Cause-and-Effect)
What causes insomnia?
What are the effects of malnutrition?
What causes conflict between parents and teen-agers?

(Problem-and-Solution)
increasing number of high-school dropouts
disposal of nuclear waste
shoplifting

Persuasive
Should capital punishment be abolished?
Should parents impose curfews on their children?
Should certain types of censorship be allowed?

Ideas for Writing in Subject Areas

Art
paper making
Georgia O'Keeffe
early moviemakers
modern Mexican
  muralists
the Taj Mahal
What is performance
  art?
surrealism
the responsibility of
  the artist to society
the history of
  photography

Consumer Education
how to balance a
  checkbook
what to look for
  when buying a
  television set
the role of the FDA
videocassette copy-
  right laws
how to read an ad
  critically

Health
What causes high
  blood pressure?
Should smoking be
  banned in public
  places?
sickle cell anemia
benefits of regular
  exercise
What foods help pre-
  vent cancer?

Math
famous mathe-
  maticians: Euclid,
  Descartes
catenaries and sus-
  pension bridges
geometric patterns in
  nature
Archimedes' spiral
how to construct a
  dodecahedron
Mayan mathematical
  system
the importance of
  computer literacy
  in today's world
game theory

Music
the life of Duke
  Ellington
roots of rock-and-roll
reggae music
how a guitar is made
famous blues
  musicians
history of the
  synthesizer
Beethoven's impact
  on classical music
origin of punk rock
Compare/contrast
  compact discs and
  LP's.
folk traditions of
  Southern
  Appalachia
how to play the
  conga drums

Science
Compare/contrast mi-
  tosis and meiosis.
effects of space
  exploration
mountain formation
cause of high tides in
  the Bay of Fundy
effects of El Niño
gene splicing
geothermal energy
desalination
the first land plants
What caused the ex-
  tinction of the
  dinosaurs?

Social Science
Should lie detector
  tests be used as ev-
  idence in court?
Who should control
  the Panama Canal?
causes of
  unemployment
Should the U.S. have
  stricter gun control
  laws?
"The Pentagon
  Papers" and the
  war in Vietnam
the conflict in the
  Middle East
the history of civil
  disobedience
the value of pre-
  school programs
the effects of divorce
  on children

Trigger Words

The words listed below should trigger many different writing ideas. Use them along with the thinking skills on pages 22–51 to generate new writing ideas.

Trigger Words

chaos	fad	shopping mall
loneliness	panic	tracks
holiday	hijacker	locker
promise	field day	assembly
rivalry	tension	flood
luck	midnight	election

Fine Art and Photographs

By developing the thinking skills described in Chapter 2, you have learned to generate writing ideas from a wide range of subjects and experiences. You can apply those same skills to the photographs and fine art that appear throughout this text. Turn to an image at random and ask yourself questions such as the following:

1. What do I see in this picture? How could I describe it?
2. Is the subject of this picture one that I could research?
3. How does this picture make me feel? What memories or personal associations spring from this feeling?
4. What might have occurred just prior to the scene shown in this picture? What might occur just after it?
5. Who are the people in this picture? Could they make good characters in a story?
6. How might I analyze this image? What could I say about the subject, colors, and composition?
7. What do I know about the artist or photographer? What could I say about his or her technique? Did this person have an interesting life or career that might be worth investigating?
8. What writing possibilities might be suggested by the setting or the time period that is represented here?
9. What aspects of our history or culture are demonstrated here? Might these be worth exploring?
10. What is my overall evaluation of this picture? What evidence could I give to support my judgment?

Outlines and Other Graphic Organizers

Graphic organizers, such as outlines, charts, and diagrams, provide a simple, efficient way to help you explore key ideas and uncover important relationships. The first of these, the outline, is the organizer with which you are probably most familiar.

An outline is a preliminary plan of material to be presented in a report or speech. A good outline records information in a concise and logical manner. It helps a writer or researcher organize ideas and provides a speaker with a diagram of the basic points in a talk.

Types of Outlines

A **formal outline** shows the main points of a topic, the order in which they are to be presented, and the relationships between them. Formal outlines are useful when writing formal compositions or speeches and when outlining chapters for study.

There are two types of formal outlines: sentence outlines or topic outlines. In a **sentence outline,** each main topic and sub-topic is written in a complete sentence. Below is a portion of a sentence outline.

Painting a Landscape in Oils

Purpose: to show how anyone can paint a simple landscape by following a few step-by-step procedures.

I. Choose materials and a subject.
    A. Purchase a few basic art supplies.
        1. Buy paints in black, white, and the primary colors.
        2. Buy an eraser and pencils or charcoal.
        3. Buy canvas, a palette, and brushes.
    B. Beginners should choose a simple subject.
        1. Do not include buildings, people, or animals.
        2. Beginners do best when they paint large areas of water, sky, and forest seen at a distance.

II. Make preliminary sketches of your subject.
    A. Draw canvas-sized sketches of your subject.
    B. Transfer the best sketch to your canvas using light pencil or charcoal.

A **topic outline** uses words or phrases instead of complete sentences. Below is a portion of a topic outline.

First Steps to First Aid

Purpose: to explain how first aid techniques can provide emergency treatment until medical help arrives.

    I. Goals of first aid
        A. To ease pain
        B. To prevent worse injuries
        C. To soothe fears

   II. General techniques of first aid
        A. Staying calm
        B. Avoiding movement of victim
        C. Preventing shock
            1. Symptoms of shock
            2. Treatment of shock
        D. Reassuring victim

Before making an outline, decide whether a sentence or topic outline better suits your needs. Once you begin, do not mix forms within a given outline.

Correct Outline Form

The same form generally applies to topic and sentence outlines.

1. Write the title at the top of the outline. The title, introduction, and conclusion are not considered parts of the outline.
2. Use the following arrangement of numerals and letters for main points and subpoints.

    I. (Main point)
        A. (First subpoint)
        B. (Second subpoint)
           1.
           2.
               a.
               b.   (Details and subdetails)
                 (1)
                 (2)
                     (a)
                     (b)

3. Indent each division of the outline. Place the letter or numeral directly underneath the first letter in the first word of the larger heading above, as shown in the examples on pages 827–828.
4. Do not use a single subheading. A heading should not be broken down if it cannot be divided into at least two points. If there is a *1* under *A*, there must also be at least a *2*.
5. In a topic outline, keep items of the same rank in parallel form. For instance, if *A* is a noun, then *B* and *C* should also be nouns. The form of subtopics need not be parallel to that of main topics.
6. Begin each item with a capital letter. Do not use end punctuation in a topic outline.

Writing an Informal Outline

An **informal outline** helps you organize information quickly and efficiently. Main ideas are presented as separate headings. Details and subdetails are written beneath each heading using numbers, letters, dashes, or indentations. Attention to parallel structure is unnecessary in an informal outline.

Informal outlines are especially useful for taking lecture notes, for preparing to answer exam questions, and for making prewriting notes during an essay test. The following is an example of an informal outline on the Industrial Revolution.

   I. Origins of the Industrial Revolution
      —new inventions
         steam engine
         spinning jenny
         cotton gin
         flying shuttle
         lathe
      —transportation advances
         macadam roads
         steam-powered railroads
         steamboats
         canals

   II. Effects of the Industrial Revolution
      —mass production of goods
      —rapid growth of cities
      —child labor
      —long workdays
      —dangerous working conditions

Other Graphic Organizers

A **graphic organizer** is a way to organize information you have gathered for a report or speech. In addition to outlines, graphic organizers include charts, cause-effect schemes, tree diagrams, and clusters.

Charts help you analyze or compare information. When you complete a chart, you can easily see where there are gaps in your information. The headings that are listed across the top of the chart are called **variables.**

Vascular Plants

Plant	Spore or Seed Dispersal	Reproductive Structure	Site of Photosynthesis
ferns	wind	sporangia	blade of fern
whisk ferns	water	sporangia	stem
gymnosperms	wind	cones	leaves

A **cause-effect scheme** shows that something happened because of something else. The chart below has been used to analyze a short story, "The Cask of Amontillado" by Edgar Allen Poe. A similar chart could be used to analyze any cause-effect relationship.

"The Cask of Amontillado"

Cause	Effect
Fortunato insults Montresor.	Montresor vows revenge.
To lure Fortunato into the trap, Montresor uses flattery.	Fortunato put at ease, follows Montresor into vaults.
Montresor baits Fortunato, using his rival's name (Luchresi).	Fortunato becomes blinded by pride and lured to his death.
The catacombs are cold and damp.	Montresor feels chilled and heartsick. (Guilt feelings?)
Montresor is not left unpunished; he has a guilty conscience.	Fifty years later Montresor is still telling his tale.

A **cluster** is a type of personal brainstorming that can help you explore or organize related ideas. Begin by writing a word or phrase in the center of a piece of paper. Circle the word or phrase and outside that circle write down any associated words or ideas. Put each in its own circle and connect it with a line to the "nucleus" word. Branch out from the new circles in the same way.

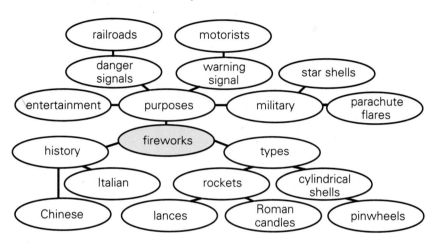

A **tree diagram** is useful for showing relationships between different aspects and details of a topic. Draw a straight line down the center of your paper and write your main idea in a word or phrase at the base. Then write down any words or phrases that you associate with this main idea. Put each new idea on a line that stems from the main idea. Branch out from the new stems in a similar manner.

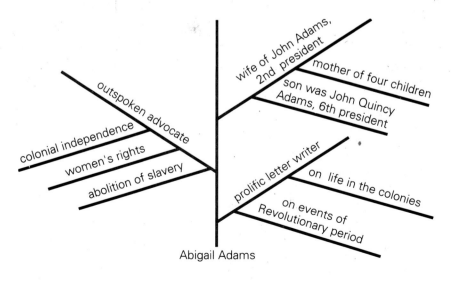

Good Manuscript Form

Your readers will be more impressed by a paper that is neat and legible than by a paper that is hard to read. Good manuscript form increases the impact of what a writer says. Follow these guidelines as you prepare your paper:

1. Type your paper if possible. If you must write your paper by hand, write carefully and legibly. Use only dark blue or black ink.
2. Leave margins of an inch at the top, the bottom, and the right side of the page. The left margin should be slightly wider. Double-space all typed copy. Indent each paragraph five spaces. Follow each end punctuation mark with two spaces.
3. Center your title two lines below the last line of your heading. Capitalize the first word and all important words in your title. Do not underline your title or place it in quotation marks unless it is a quotation from another source.

If your paper is longer than three or four pages, your teacher may require a separate title page. Write the heading in the upper right-hand corner and center the title on the page.

Abbreviations in Writing

Abbreviations may be used for most titles that appear before and after proper names, for names of government agencies, and in expressions of dates and time.

Before Proper Names	Dr., Mr., Mrs., Ms., Messrs., Rev., Hon., Gov., Sgt.
After Proper Names	Jr., Sr., M.D., Ph.D.
Government Agencies	CIA, FCC, FDA
Dates and Time	A.D., B.C., A.M., P.M.

Notice that there are no periods after abbreviations of government agencies.

Abbreviations of titles are acceptable only when used as part of a name. It is not acceptable to write *The Gov. of the state is a Dr*. The titles *Honorable* and *Reverend* are not abbreviated when preceded by *the: the Honorable Lois Tate*. They appear with the person's full name, not just the last name. Also, abbreviations are not appropriate for the President and Vice-President of the United States.

In most writing, abbreviations are not acceptable for names of countries and states, months and days of the week, nor for words that are part of addresses or company names.

Incorrect   We are going to Mich. and Can.
Correct   We are going to Michigan and Canada.

Incorrect   Miller's play opened on Thurs., Jan. 23.
Correct   Miller's play opened on Thursday, January 23.

Incorrect   Pay your bill to the Bell Tel. Co.
Correct   Pay your bill to the Bell Telephone Company.

In addition, abbreviations are generally not acceptable for names of school courses, page or chapter references, Christmas, or measurements.

Numbers in Writing

Numbers that can be written in two words or fewer are usually spelled out; longer numbers are written in figures.

They gathered *thirty-one* bushels of apples.
The tickets are selling for *eight* dollars each.
The loss amounted to *$4,280*.

A number beginning a sentence is spelled out.

Eight hundred people were suddenly left homeless by the flash flood.
Twenty-five minutes passed without a word from Jack.

Figures are used to express dates, street and room numbers, telephone numbers, page numbers, temperatures, decimals, and percentages.

Shakespeare was born on April 23, 1564.
The English class is in room 312.
We were asked to learn the poem on page 80.
Yesterday the temperature reached 101 degrees.
The earthquake measured 4.5 on the Richter scale.
Matt had 98 percent correct on the physics test.

Note   Commas are used to separate the figures in sums of money or expressions of large quantities.

Terry saved $1,270 over the last two years.
Bernie has collected more than 100,000 stamps.

Italics in Writing

The word *italics* is a printer's term. It refers to a kind of type. When a writer wants to indicate that a word is in italics, he or she underlines it in the manuscript.

Titles of books, plays, newspapers, magazines, motion pictures, works of art, television programs, and long musical compositions are printed in italics. The names of ships, trains, and aircraft are also printed in italics.

Manuscript Form	I always skim the articles in Newsweek.
Printed Form	I always skim the articles in *Newsweek*.
Manuscript Form	Bernard Malamud won the Pulitzer Prize for The Fixer.
Printed Form	Bernard Malamud won the Pulitzer Prize for *The Fixer*.

Italics are used for words, letters, or figures referred to as such.

Manuscript Form	In England, color is spelled colour.
Printed Form	In England, *color* is spelled *colour*.
Manuscript Form	Dot your i's and cross your t's.
Printed Form	Dot your *i*'s and cross your *t*'s.

Foreign words and phrases that have not become common in our language are printed in italics: *coup d'etat, tempus fugit.*

Many foreign words have become so widely used that they are now part of the English language: spaghetti, gourmet. These words are printed in regular type.

The only way to be sure whether a word or phrase of foreign origin should be printed in italics is to consult the dictionary. Special symbols indicate foreign words.

Italics are used to give special emphasis to words or phrases.

The tendency in modern writing is to avoid the use of italics for emphasis. One reason is that italic type is considered harder to read than regular (roman) type. Another reason is that modern writers often prefer the straightforward, uncluttered appearance of text without the excessive use of italics.

Use italics for emphasis only if the meaning of a statement would otherwise be unclear.

"Have you *ever* seen such a storm!" Father exclaimed.

Common Usage Problems

The following section contains a list of some of the most common usage problems. Read through the list to find the items that give you problems and study the suggested ways to correct them. For help with commonly misused words see "Word Usage" on pages 843–848.

Abbreviations

Generally, you should avoid using abbreviations in formal papers with the exception of titles (Mr., Mrs., Ms., Dr.), years (B.C., A.D.), and times (A.M., P.M.).

Be, Overuse of

Overuse of the verb *to be* leads to monotonous writing. Whenever possible, choose an active verb that will make your writing more lively and precise. Forms of the verb *to be* include the following: *am, is, are, was, were, be, been, being*.

Weak	Nineteenth-century reformer Lucy Stone *was* a believer in abolition and women's rights.
Better	Nineteenth-century reformer Lucy Stone *believed* in abolition and women's rights. (Replace a weak verb by changing the noun *believer* into the verb *believed*.)
Weak	Before beginning her campaign for women's rights, Lucy Stone *was* a schoolteacher.
Better	Before beginning her campaign for women's rights, Lucy Stone *taught* school. (Replace *was* with an action verb derived from the noun *schoolteacher*.)

Clauses

See Essential and Nonessential clauses.

Clichés

Clichés are expressions that have been used so often they have lost much of their meaning and impact. *Beating around the bush, chip off the old block,* and *solid as a rock* are examples of clichés. Avoid using clichés in your writing. Instead, try to find fresh images and phrases to express your ideas.

Comparisons, Illogical

When comparing an individual member with the rest of the group, use the word *other* or the word *else*.

Incorrect   May Shin is more energetic than *any* member of the Student Council. (This implies May Shin is not a member of the Student Council.)

Correct   May Shin is more energetic than *any other* member of the Student Council.

If there is any possibility that a comparison may be misunderstood, it must be stated clearly and completely.

Confusing   The problem confused Jim *more than* Bob. (Did the problem confuse Jim or did Bob confuse Jim?)

Clear   The problem confused Jim *more than it* confused Bob.

Dangling Modifiers

See Modifiers.

Double Negatives

A **double negative** results when two negative words are used in a sentence. Double negatives are nonstandard usage. *Hardly* or *barely*, used with a negative word, is also nonstandard.

Incorrect   We did*n't* have *no* information about the meeting.

Correct   We did*n't* have *any* information about the meeting.

Incorrect   The skier *hadn't hardly* begun the race before she fell.

Correct   The skier *had hardly* begun the race before she fell.

Essential and Nonessential Clauses

An **essential clause** identifies the person, place, or thing that it modifies. It is essential to the meaning of the sentence. Essential clauses are not set off from the rest of the sentence by commas. Most essential clauses are introduced by *that* or *who* and not by *which*.

> The artist *who drew the illustrations at the age of 100* was Grandma Moses. (The clause tells which artist.)
> The bird *that Benajmin Franklin proposed for the national symbol* was the turkey. (The clause tells which bird.)

A **nonessential clause** merely provides additional information. It can be omitted without changing the meaning of the sentence. Nonessential clauses are set off by commas from the rest of the sentence. They may be introduced by *which* or *who* but not *that*.

The handshake, *which is a gesture of friendship,* originally indicated
that a person had no weapons.
Valentina Tereshkova, *who was only twenty-six years old at the time
of her historic flight,* became the first woman cosmonaut.

Expletives, Overuse of

When the word *there* is used to begin a sentence, and when it does
not function as an adverb, it is called an **expletive.** Sometimes it is
necessary to begin a sentence with an expletive, but this construction
weakens your writing and should be avoided.

Weak   *There is* an African bird, called the black-backed courser,
that dines inside a crocodile's mouth.

Better   An African bird, the black-backed courser, dines inside a
crocodile's mouth.

Gerunds Preceded by Pronouns

A **gerund** is a verb form that serves as a noun and ends in *-ing.* A
gerund may function as a *subject, object, object of a preposition,* or
predicate nominative. Use the **possessive case** of a pronoun when it
precedes a gerund.

Incorrect   The company agreed to *him* negotiating a contract.
Correct   The company agreed to *his* negotiating a contract.

Infinitives

An **infinitive** is a verb form that usually begins with *to: to understand, to swim.* A **split infinitive** occurs when an adverb is placed
between *to* and the rest of the infinitive. Try to avoid splitting the
infinitive. Instead, place the adverb before or after the infinitive or
infinitive phrase.

Awkward   *To* properly *evaluate* the situation, we must review all the
evidence.

Improved   *To evaluate* the situation properly, we must review all the
evidence.

Jargon

Jargon is the special terminology used by people within one profession. For example, typesetters use terms such as *flush left, ragged
right, density, point size,* and *leading.* Lawyers use *plaintiff, brief,* and
abstract. Although such words act as a "language shortcut" for people
within the same profession, they often confuse others. Always choose
terminology that your audience will understand.

Jargon	If you do not brush your teeth regularly, you may develop carious lesions and periodontal disease.
Simplified	If you do not brush your teeth regularly, you may develop cavities and gum disease.

Modifiers

Adjective-Adverb Confusion Sometimes you may have trouble deciding whether to use an adjective or an adverb. Use an adjective to modify a noun or pronoun. Adjectives tell *which one, what kind, how many,* or *how much.* Adverbs modify verbs, adjectives, or other adverbs. Adverbs tell *where, when, how,* or *to what extent.*

Incorrect	The lighthouse beacon shone *bright* all night. (modifies *shone,* not *beacon*)
Correct	The lighthouse beacon shone *brightly* all night.

Hopefully The adverb *hopefully* means "in a hopeful manner." *Hopefully* is often misused, however, to mean "I hope."

Incorrect	*Hopefully,* our theater group will perform *Grease.*
Correct	*I hope* our theater group will perform *Grease.*

Comparative and Superlative Forms Use the **comparative form** to compare two items and the **superlative form** to compare more than two items. Do not use *-er* and *more* or *-est* and *most* together.

Incorrect	Of the two quotations, that one is *most* memorable.
Correct	Of the two quotations, that one is *more* memorable.

Incorrect	The Trans-Siberian Railroad, which extends for more than 6,000 miles, is the *most longest* railroad in the world.
Correct	The Trans-Siberian Railroad, which extends for more than 6,000 miles, is the *longest* railroad in the world.

Dangling and Misplaced Modifiers A **dangling modifier** is an error that occurs when the word to which a modifier refers is missing from the sentence.

Dangling Modifier	While strumming the guitar, the strings broke. (Were the strings strumming the guitar?)
Correct	While I was strumming the guitar, the strings broke.

A **misplaced modifier** occurs when a word or phrase is placed incorrectly and seems to modify the wrong word.

Misplaced Modifier	We sell chairs for secretaries with swivel legs.
Correct	For secretaries, we sell chairs with swivel legs.

Parallelism

When the coordinating conjunction *and* joins similar sentence parts—noun and noun, verb and verb, phrase and phrase—the construction is said to be *parallel*. An error in parallel structure occurs when *and* is used to join unlike constructions.

Not Parallel	On the nature trail we studied animal *camouflage* and *how leaves change colors*. (noun and clause)
Parallel	On the nature trail we studied animal *camouflage* and leaf *pigmentation*. (noun and noun)

Person, Shifts in

Person refers to the point of view a writer uses. A writer may use first, second, or third person point of view, but the point of view should remain consistent throughout one piece of writing.

Shift in Person	*Teen-agers* participate in many extracurricular activities. Usually *you* attend these after school.
Consistent	*Teen-agers* participate in many extracurricular activities. Usually *they* attend these after school.

Pronouns

Agreement A pronoun must agree with its antecedent in number. If the antecedent is singular, the pronoun must be singular. If the antecedent is plural, then the pronoun must be plural.

Incorrect	In ancient Egypt, a *cat-owner* shaved off *their* eyebrows when a pet died.
Correct	In ancient Egypt a *cat-owner* shaved off *his or her* eyebrows when a pet died.

Sometimes indefinite pronouns create problems in agreement. The following indefinite pronouns are always singular: *anyone, anybody, anything, each, either, everybody, everyone, everything, neither, nobody, no one, one, somebody,* and *someone*.

Incorrect	*Anyone* who forgets *their* ticket will have to make other transportation arrangements.
Correct	*Anyone* who forgets *his or her* ticket will have to make other transportation arrangements.

When a singular and a plural antecedent are joined by *or* or *nor*, the noun nearer the verb determines the number of the pronoun.

> Neither *Shawn* nor the *girls* checked *their* suitcases with the ticket agent.

Ambiguous Reference The reference of a pronoun is ambiguous if the pronoun may refer to more than one word.

Ambiguous   Cathy spoke to Ms. Dryer about *her* vacation. (Cathy's
                    vacation or Ms. Dryer's?)
Clear   Cathy spoke about her vacation to Ms. Dryer.

Lack of Antecedents When a pronoun is used without an antecedent, the sentence becomes unclear.

Unclear   The museum tour was very boring because *he* seemed uninformed.
                (Who was uninformed?)
Clear   The museum tour was very boring because the *guide* seemed
                uninformed.

Nominative and Objective Case Pronouns change forms, depending on the ways in which they are used in sentences. When a pronoun takes the place of a subject or follows a form of the verb *be*, the **nominative case** is used.

> Joseph Montgolfier invented the hot-air balloon. *He* got the idea
>   while watching his wife's petticoat dry over a fire. (takes the place
>   of the subject)
> Could it have been *she* who called? (follows a form of the verb *be*)

The **objective case** is used when a pronoun takes the place of an object.

> Mr. Patel drove *us* to the scholarship banquet. (direct object)
> Vangela's pen pal sent *her* a package. (indirect object)
> Why was the poem credited to *him*? (object of a preposition)

To decide which pronoun form to use in a compound object, read the pronoun in question by itself.

> Mrs. Potocki sent Charlie and (I, *me*) postcards of Wawel Castle in
>   Krakow, Poland. (compound indirect object; think: Mrs. Potocki
>   sent *me*)
> Yuriko laid the architectural plans on the table between (she, *her*) and
>   (I, *me*). (compound objects of the preposition; think: between *her*,
>   between *me*)

Redundancy

A statement is **redundant** if it says the same thing in two ways. Remove redundant words to make your writing more concise.

Redundant   The *annual* automobile show is held *each year*.
Better   The automobile show is held *annually*.

Sentence Errors

Fragments A **sentence fragment** is a group of words that does not express a complete thought. A subject, a predicate, or both are missing. To correct this error, add the missing part or parts.

Fragment   Eats insects by trapping them in its leaves. (The subject is missing.)

Sentence   *The pitcher plant* eats insects by trapping them in its leaves.

Fragment   Over the rock formations at Victoria Falls. (Both the subject and predicate are missing.)

Sentence   *Every minute 75 million gallons of water rush* over the rock formations at Victoria Falls.

Run-on Sentences A **run-on sentence** is two or more sentences written as though they were one sentence. The most common run-on occurs when two sentences are joined by a comma. This error is called a **comma fault**. To correct this error, form two independent sentences or add a comma and a coordinating conjunction.

Comma Fault   In 1687 the governor general demanded the surrender of the Connecticut *charter, the* colonists hid it.

Correct   In 1687 the governor general demanded the surrender of the Connecticut *charter. The* colonists hid it.

Correct   In 1687 the governor general demanded the surrender of the Connecticut *charter, but* the colonists hid it.

Another way to correct run-on sentences is to connect them with a semicolon.

Run-on The hungry rattlesnake slid among the *palmettos, then* it flicked its tongue to detect any prey.

Correct The hungry rattlesnake slid among the *palmettos; then* it flicked its tongue to detect any prey.

Slang

Colorful and original words and phrases coined by a particular group at a certain time are referred to as **slang**. Although slang is common in everyday speech, it should never be used in formal writing. It may be used with caution in informal writing. The following words are examples of slang:

cool   something that is pleasing
square   somebody who is not up-to-date with current fashions and ideas
gross   something distasteful

Verb Tense

Tense means "time." Most verbs change their forms to show present, past, and future time. Each verb has three **simple tenses** and three **perfect tenses.** Sometimes a writer confuses the reader by unnecessarily using two verb tenses in the same sentence. Avoid improper shifts of verb tense.

Incorrect   Heinrich Schliemann *found* the historical site of Troy and
        starts digging through the ancient layers.

Correct   Heinrich Schliemann *found* the historical site of Troy and
        started digging through the ancient layers.

Voice

Verbs have two voices, active and passive. When the subject performs the action, the verb is in the **active voice.** When the subject receives the action, the verb is in the **passive voice.** Good writers generally use the active voice because it creates more vivid images.

Passive Voice   The ball was hurled at the batter by the rookie pitcher.
Active Voice   The rookie pitcher hurled the ball at the batter.

Who and Whom

Who is the subject form of the pronoun and is used as the subject of a sentence. *Who* can also act as the subject or the predicate nominative of a clause.

> *Who* supplied the first road signs?
> The B.F. Goodrich Company, *who* provided the first road signs, called them the Goodrich Guide Posts.

Whom is the object form of the pronoun. It is used as the direct object or as the object of a preposition in a sentence or clause.

> *Whom* did Jane Addams help? (direct object)
> With *whom* did Elias Howe fight a legal battle? (object of a preposition)

You, Use of

Do not use the pronoun *you* in your writing unless you mean the reader.

Incorrect   *You* can buy many sophisticated accessories for a word
        processor. (The writer does not mean *you,* personally.)

Correct   *Consumers* can buy many sophisticated accessories for a word
        processor.

Word Usage

The following section explains many common misuses of individual words. Study these words and learn how to use them correctly.

accept means "to agree to something" or "to receive something willingly."

except means "to exclude or omit" or "not including."

> Will you *accept* or decline their invitation?
> The new rule *excepts* honor students from final exams.
> Everybody *except* Jean brought a nutritious lunch.

adapt means "to make *apt* or suitable; to adjust."

adopt means "to *opt* or choose as one's own; to accept."

> The writer *adapted* the play for the screen.
> After years of living in Japan, she *adopted* the culture.

advice means "counsel given to someone."

advise means "to give counsel."

> The mechanic gave us practical *advice* about the car.
> Ms. Fernando will *advise* the Spanish Club this year.

affect means either "to influence" or "to pretend."

effect (verb) means "to accomplish or to produce a result."

Effect (noun) also means "the result of an action."

> The news from South Africa *affected* him deeply.
> In *The Hound of the Baskervilles,* the actor *affected* a British accent.
> The students tried to *effect* a change in school policy.
> What *effect* did the acidic soil have on the experiment?

agree can be used with the prepositions *to, with,* and *on.* You *agree to* something, such as a plan. You *agree with* someone else; or something, such as spinach, does not *agree with* you. You *agree* with others *on* a course of action.

all ready means "completely prepared."

already means "even now" or "by or before the given time."

> We are *all ready* for the volleyball tournament.
> We are *already* late.

all right is standard usage. The misspelling *alright* is nonstandard usage.

> Rosa was feeling ill Monday, but she is *all right* today.

a lot means "a great number or amount." Use it only in informal speaking or writing. Spell it as two words; *alot* is incorrect.

> After the flood *a lot* of residents complained.

altogether means "entirely" or "on the whole."
all together means "considering all parts of a group as a whole."

> This news story is *altogether* false.
> A tug of war is won by a team pulling *all together*.

amount indicates a total sum of things. It usually refers to items that cannot be counted.
number refers to items that can be counted.

> Did you ever wonder about the *amount* of food consumed by the
>   average teen-ager each day?
> The chef cooked the *number* of omelets we ordered.

anywhere, nowhere, somewhere, anyway are correct. *Anywheres, nowheres, somewheres,* and *anyways* are incorrect.

Incorrect	Pat couldn't find the calculator *anywheres*.
Correct	Pat couldn't find the calculator *anywhere*.

Incorrect	*Somewheres* there is a book on Cajun cooking.
Correct	*Somewhere* there is a book on Cajun cooking.

borrow means "to take something on loan." You *borrow from* someone.
lend means "to give out something temporarily." You *lend to* someone.

Incorrect	Will you *borrow* me your biology book?
Correct	Will you *lend* me your biology book?
Correct	May I *borrow* your biology book?

bring means "motion or movement towards someone or some place."
take means "motion or movement away from someone or some place."

> A Boeing 747 will *take* me to St. Louis.
> I hope Mom *brings* a newspaper home.

can means "able or having the power to do something."
may means "to have permission to." It also expresses the probability of something happening.

> *Can* you ride a horse?
> *May* I be excused from this project?
> Eagles *may* become extinct if their habitat is destroyed.

capital means "most important." It refers to an uppercase letter or to the city that is the seat of a government.

capitol is the building where a state legislature meets.

the Capitol is the building in Washington, D.C., where the United States Congress meets. The *c* is always capitalized.

> Carson City is the *capital* of Nevada.
>
> Our state *capitol* has an elaborate foyer.
>
> Cameras are not permitted in the House and Senate chambers of the *Capitol*.

des′ert means "a dry, sandy region with sparse vegetation."

de sert′ means "to abandon."

des sert′ is a sweet course served at the end of a meal.

> Fifteen percent of the Sahara *Desert* is sand.
>
> Many soldiers *deserted* the army that winter.
>
> Applie pie is a favorite American *dessert*.

differ from means "to have dissimilar characteristics."

differ with means "to disagree with someone."

> Juan's musical talent *differs from* Roy's.
>
> I *differ with* my parents on that topic.

different from is used to compare dissimilar items. *Different than* is nonstandard.

Incorrect	Mike's values are *different than* yours.
Correct	Mike's values are *different from* yours.

farther means "more distant."

further means "additional."

> Robin's punt went *farther* than Jenny's.
>
> Did you need *further* information?

fewer refers to numbers of things that can be counted.

less refers to amount or quality.

> *Fewer* students attended this month than last month.
>
> Why was there *less* confusion today than yesterday?

formally means "in a structured way."

formerly means "previously."

> The committee *formally* ratified the income tax.
>
> Our teacher was *formerly* an off-Broadway actor.

had of, off of are incorrect. The *of* is unnecessary.

Incorrect   If you *had of* played, we would have won.
Correct   If you *had* played, we would have won.

Incorrect   The child fell *off of* the swing.
Correct   The child fell *off* the swing.

hear means "to listen to" or "to take notice of."
here means "in this place."

> Did you *hear* the latest weather report?
> The singing group will perform *here* next Friday.

imply means "to suggest something in an indirect way."
infer means "to come to a conclusion based on something that has been read or heard."

> Joan's remark *implied* that she did not trust the congressional committee's report.
> From Elisa's comment, Mark *inferred* that she was nervous about taking her driver's test.

its is a possessive pronoun.
it's is a contraction for *it is* or *it has*.

> Babylon attained *its* greatest glory around 600 B.C.
> *It's* a well-known fact that many people lost their fortunes during the Great Depression of the 1930's.

kind of a, sort of a are incorrect. The *a* is unnecessary.

Incorrect   What *kind of a* horse is Scout?
Correct   What *kind of* horse is Scout?

learn means "to gain knowledge or instruction."
teach means "to instruct."

> Jerome is *learning* Portuguese.
> Mrs. Strathmore *teaches* astronomy at the museum.

leave means "to go away from."
let means "to permit."

> Please *leave* the dog alone!
> *Let* me show you to your homeroom.

like can be a preposition. Using *like* as a conjunction before a clause is not fully acceptable. It is better to use *as* or *as if*.

Incorrect	*Like* we told you, the bus will be leaving soon.
Correct	*As* we told you, the bus will be leaving soon.

Incorrect	Ralph looked *like* he had seen a ghost.
Correct	Ralph looked *as if* he had seen a ghost.

loose means "free and untied" or "not tight."
lose means "to misplace something" or "to fail to maintain." It is also the opposite of *win*.

> Tell the fireman that the hydrant cap is *loose*.
> Where did you *lose* your English book?
> Did your father *lose* his temper when he saw the car?

majority refers to a number that can be counted. Its use is incorrect if used in speaking of time or distance.

Incorrect	The *majority of the time* was wasted.
Correct	*Most of the time* was wasted.
Correct	The *majority* of the students wasted no time.

most is an adjective meaning "the greater part."
almost is an adverb meaning "nearly."

Incorrect	*Most* everyone attended the soccer game.
Correct	*Almost* everyone attended the soccer game.

of is sometimes mistakenly used in phrases like *could have, should have,* or *must have*. Always use the word *have* or its contraction in these phrases, never use *of*.

Incorrect	The plant *must of* been overwatered.
Correct	The plant *must have* been overwatered.

principal refers to something highest in importance or rank. It also refers to the head of a school.
principle means "a basic truth, standard, or rule of behavior."

> In the third act of the play, the *principal* character is killed in a car accident.
> The Constitution was founded on the *principle* that all men are created equal.

seldom ever is incorrect. The *ever* is unnecessary. Use *seldom, very seldom,* or *hardly ever* instead.

Incorrect	Steam locomotives are *seldom ever* seen today.
Correct	Steam locomotives are *seldom* seen today.

Correct	Medieval castles were *very seldom* built on flat land.
Correct	To avoid a surprise attack, the castle walls were *hardly ever* left unguarded.

stationary means "fixed or unmoving."
stationery refers to paper and envelopes used for writing.

> The subway train remained *stationary* while workers cleared the tracks.
> Please submit your request for a student identification card on school *stationery*.

their is a possessive pronoun meaning "belonging to them."
there is an adverb or sometimes an expletive meaning "in that place."
they're is a contraction for *they are*.

> *Their* bus tickets were never collected.
> *There* is the box containing the first-aid kit.
> After the meeting *they're* spending a week in Paris.

to is a preposition meaning "toward" or "in the direction of."
too is an adverb meaning "also" or "very."
two is the number *2*.

> Elizabeth Barrett sent secret letters *to* Robert Browning.
> Samuel F.B. Morse, inventor of the telegraph, was a portrait artist *too*.
> *Two* pigments, along with chlorophyll, produce the colors seen in autumn leaves.

weather refers to atmospheric conditions.
whether helps express a choice or alternative.

> *Weather* conditions are carefully checked prior to all airplane departures.
> Keisha doesn't care *whether* we go skating or skiing.

who's is a contraction for *who is* or *who has*.
whose is the possessive form of *who*.

> *Who's* working at the blood drive this afternoon?
> *Whose* father helped organize the event?

your is the possessive form of *you*.
you're is a contraction for *you are*.

> *Your* library book is on the cabinet.
> *You're* scheduled to perform at 8:00 P.M.

Index

Effect. *See* Cause and effect
ei and *ie*, spelling and, 796
either . . . or, 499
Elliptical clauses, 559, 674
Emotional appeals, 387
Emphasis, sentences inverted for, 518
Emphatic forms of verbs, 613
Employment. *See* Job applications
Empty sentences, 139–40
Encyclopedias, 397–98
   bibliography cards for, 319
English
   formal-informal, 371–73
   standard-nonstandard, 371–75
   see also Language; Language Lore;
      Usage
Entertaining speeches, 450
Entry words in dictionaries, 54
Envelopes for business letters, 434
Esperanto, 336
Essay questions, 260–63, 418
Essays, titles in quotation marks, 784
Essay tests, 260–63, 418
Essential appositives, 538
Essential clauses, 555–56, 746, 836–37
Essential participial phrases, 544
Etymology, in dictionaries, 54
Euphemisms, 380–81
Evading issues, 277
Evaluating
   evidence, 273–74
   and peer editing, 88–90
   and revising, 61
Evaluation, of speeches, 460–61
Evaluation forms
   using, in peer editing, 88, 90
Events, capitalization of, 719, 720
Example, as context clue, 344
Examples
   in developing paragraphs, 104
   in expository writing, 249, 250
   in persuasive writing, 273
except, accept, 843
Exclamation points, 734
   with exclamatory sentences, 510
   with imperative sentences, 510
   with interjections, 502
   with quotation marks, 780–81
Exclamatory sentences, 510
   punctuation of, 734
Expletives, 518
   overuse of, 837
Expository writing, 206–29, 230–59
   analyzing, 208–209, 232–33

audience and, 215
body of, 216, 220, 240, 245, 250
cause and effect, 208, 232, 241–45
combining methods in, 222, 251–53
comparison and contrast, 208, 232,
   236–40
conclusions of, 216, 220, 240, 245,
   250
definition, 208, 218–21
details in, 220, 223, 244
development of, 208, 217, 221, 240,
   245, 250
drafting, 216, 220, 223, 227, 239–40,
   244–45, 249–50, 252–53, 257
explaining a process, 208, 213–17
guidelines for, 227, 257
ideas for, 824
introductions to, 216, 220, 240, 244,
   249
in literature, 209–12, 233–35
organization in, 215, 217, 221, 239,
   240, 244, 245, 248, 250
in paragraphs, 98, 99–100, 101
presenting, 227, 257
prewriting, 215, 219–20, 222, 227,
   238–39, 243–44, 248–49, 252, 257
problem and solution, 208, 232,
   246–50
proofreading, 227, 257
purpose in, 217, 221, 240, 245, 250
revising, 217, 221, 224, 227, 240,
   245, 250, 253, 257
thesis statements in, 239, 244, 248
transitions in, 240, 245
uses of, 225–26, 254–56
Extemporaneous speeches, 453

F

Facts
   in advertising, 384
   in developing paragraphs, 104, 113
   in expository writing, 249
   in persuasive writing, 273
   in reports, 312, 326
Fallacies, 276–79
   in advertising, 384–89
False analogy, 277
False testimonials, 388
Family relationships, capitalization of,
   712
farther, further, 694, 845
Faulty comparisons, 836
Faulty coordination, 137
Faulty subordination, 137

I

Metaphor, 166, 294–95
Microfiche and microfilm, 401
Misplaced modifiers, 534, 544, 838
Mnemonics, 445–46
Modified block form, for letters, 435
Modifiers, 686–707
 adjectives, 485–88, 687–89
 adverbs, 489–92, 687–89
 comparative forms of, 692–94, 697–98
 in descriptive writing, 165
 misplaced, 534, 544, 838
 special problems with, 699–701
 superlative forms of, 692–94, 697–98
 see also Adjectives; Adverbs; Prepositional phrases
Months, capitalization of names of, 719
Monuments, capitalization of, 716
Mood
 and descriptive writing, 156, 157,
  169, 170
 in poetry, 294
 of verbs, 623
Mood essays, 16, 17
most, almost, 847
Motion pictures, italics for, 834
Multiple choice questions, 418
Multiple meanings of words, 375
Music, capitalization of, 725
Musical compositions, italics for, 834

N

Name-calling, 278
Names, capitalization of, 711
Narrative writing, 180–205
 analyzing, 182–83
 audience and, 192, 197
 character in, 183, 189, 191, 193
 compositions, 110
 drafting, 194–96, 203
 elements of, 183
 guidelines for, 203
 ideas for, 190–91, 824
 in literature, 183–88
 organization of, 193–94, 195, 197
 in paragraphs, 98, 105
 plot in, 183, 189, 191, 193–94
 point of view in, 189, 194
 prewriting for, 190–94, 203
 proofreading, 197, 198, 203
 purpose and, 192, 197, 202
 revising, 197, 203
 setting in, 183, 189, 191, 192
 uses of, 199–202
Narrator, 189

Nationalities, capitalization of, 712
Navaho language, 573
Negative comparisons, 693
Negative statements, emphatic form in,
 613
neither . . . nor, 499
Neuter gender, 473
Newspapers, capitalization of, 725
Nominative case, pronouns, 661, 663,
 840
Nonessential appositives, 538
Nonessential clauses, 555–56, 836–37
 commas with, 746–47
Nonessential phrases, 544, 747
 commas with, 746–47
Nonfiction, classification of, 392–93
Nonrestrictive clauses. *See* Nonessential
 clauses
Nonstandard English, 374–75
Note cards, 320
 for speeches, 457
Notetaking, 411–12
 and research for reports, 320–21
 see also Speed writing
not only . . . but (also), 499
Noun clauses, 560–61
 in complex sentences, 568
 defined, 560
 diagraming, 820
 words that introduce, 561
Nouns, 469–71
 abstract, 469
 as adjectives, 487
 as adverbs, 490
 collective, 470, 646, 679
 common, 469, 711
 compound, 470, 804
 concrete, 469
 defined, 469
 gerunds and gerund phrases as,
  546–47
 infinitives and infinitive phrases as,
  540
 plurals of, spelling, 802–804
 possessives of, 775
 predicate, 524
 proper, 469, 711
 singular, with plural forms, 647
Noun suffixes, 353–54
*nowhere, anywhere, somewhere, any-
 way,* 844
number, amount, 844
Number
 of personal pronouns, 472

body of, 327
choosing a subject for, 312–13
conclusions for, 334
documentation for, 328, 335
drafting, 326–34, 337
guidelines for, 337
ideas for, 825
introductions in, 326–27
limiting a topic for, 314–15
manuscript form for, 832–34
notetaking for, 320–21
outlines for, 322–24
prewriting for, 312–16, 337
purpose and, 313–14
research for, 315, 317–22, 337
revising, 335, 337
sample paper, 329–33
thesis statements for, 315
Research, 29, 63, 65
for descriptive writing, 162
for persuasive writing, 273–74
for reports, 315, 317–22, 337
for speech topics, 451
Restatement, as context clue, 343–44
Restrictive clauses. *See* Essential clauses
Revising, 80–90
descriptive writing, 172–73, 177
in essay test, 263
evaluation forms for, 90
expository writing, 217, 221, 224,
227, 240, 245, 250, 253, 257
for form, 81
for ideas, 80
narrative writing, 197, 203
peer editing, 87–90
persuasive writing, 283, 287
poetry analysis, 308
proofreading, 81–83
reflecting during, 80
reports, 335, 337
self-editing, 84–85
Rhyme, in poetry, 296
Rhythm, in poetry, 296
rise, raise, 625, 626
Root words, 357–58
Run-on sentences, 585–86, 841

S

Salutations, 434
SAT (Scholastic Aptitude Tests), 419
Scanning, 407
Second-person pronouns, 472
"Seed" sound, spelling words with, 796
seldom ever, 847

-self, -selves, to form reflexive pronouns, 474
Self-editing, 84–85
Semicolons, 757–59
combining sentences with, 126
with commas, 757
with compound sentences, 566,
757–58
with conjunctive adverbs, 500, 758
and correcting run-on sentences, 586
with quotation marks, 781
Senses, using, 4, 6–9
hearing, 7
sight, 6
smell, 7–8
taste, 7–8
touch, 7–8
see also Sensory details; Sensory images
Sensory details
in descriptive writing, 156, 161, 172
in developing paragraphs, 104
in narrative writing, 192, 194
Sensory images, 164
Sentence completion questions, 421
Sentence correction questions, 424
Sentences, 508–31, 565–69, 576–93
capitalization in, 724
choppy, 147
combining, 126–29, 131–34, 136–37
complements, 521–24
complete predicates, 512
complete subjects, 512
complex, 567–68
compound, 126–27, 565–66, 757, 758
compound-complex, 569
declarative, 510
defined, 508, 526
diagraming, 812–22
direct objects, 521
empty, 139–40
exclamatory, 510
faulty coordination in, 137
faulty subordination in, 137
fragments, 508, 577–84, 841
imperative, 510
indirect objects, 522
interrogative, 510
inverted, 518, 644–45
objective complements, 523
overloaded, 141–42
padded, 144–45
parallelism in, 149
predicate adjectives, 524

predicate nominatives, 524
punctuation of, 733–34, 740
run-on, 585–86, 841
simple, 565
simple predicates, 514
simple subjects, 514
subject-verb agreement in, 634–59
subject complements, 524
subjects, in unusual positions, 517–18
Sentence style, 124–53
see also Sentences
Series
semicolons with, 757
set off with dashes, 764
Setting, 183, 189, 191, 192
Shape, in poetry, 293–94
Ships
capitalization of names of, 716
italics for names of, 834
Short answer questions, 418
Short stories. *See* Narrative writing
Short stories, titles of,
capitalization of, 725
in quotation marks, 784
Sight, using sense of, 6
Signature, in letters, 434
Silent *e*, spelling problems with, 792–93
Similarities and differences, 42–43
see also Comparison and contrast
Simile, 166, 295
Simple predicates, 514
Simple sentences, 565
Simple subjects, 514
Singular pronouns, 472
sit, set, 625, 626
Skimming, 407
Slang, 374, 841
Slow drafts, 75
Smell, using sense of, 7–8
Snarl words, 386
Snob appeal, 278, 388
somewhere, anywhere, nowhere, any-
way, 844
Songs
capitalization of titles of, 725
as personal writing, 16, 18
titles of, in quotation marks, 784
sort of a, 846
Spacecraft, capitalization, 716
Spatial order, 71, 105, 163
Speaker, 292
Speeches. *See* Formal speaking
Speed writing, 120–23
Spelling, 790–811

commonly misspelled words, 798–99
compound nouns, 804
doubling the final consonant, 795
final *y,* 793
ie and *ei,* 796
plurals of nouns, 802–804
and prefixes, 792
silent *e,* 792–93
and suffixes, 792–93
words with "seed" sound, 796
Split infinitives, 541, 837
Stacks, in libraries, 391
Standard English, 371–74
Standardized tests, 419–29
Starting Points for Writing, 21, 77, 119,
179, 205, 229, 259, 289, 339
stationary, stationery, 848
Statistics, in paragraphs, 104
Stereotyping, 277
Study schedules, 405
Study skills, 404–15
finding main ideas, 407–409
keeping a learning log, 412–13
managing your time, 405–406
and styles of learning, 413–14
taking notes, 411–12
varying your reading rate, 406–407
see also Memorizing; Speed writing;
Tests
Style, in persuasive writing, 281
Subject cards, 395
Subject complements, 523
Subjective descriptive writing, 169–71
Subjectivity, 9
Subjects, of sentences
agreement, with verbs, 634–59
complete, 512
compound, 514, 565, 639
diagraming, 812, 814
positions of, 517–18
pronouns as, 663
simple, 514
Subjects, for writing. *See* Topics
Subjunctive mood, 624
Subordinate clauses, 134, 136, 551–52,
554–56, 558–61
adjective, 134, 554–56
adverb, 558–60
in complex sentences, 567
in compound-complex sentences, 569
defined, 551
faulty subordination, 137
as fragments, 583
noun, 560–61

W

Y

Editorial Credits

Executive Editor, Language Arts: Bonnie L. Dobkin
Senior Editor: Julie A. Schumacher
Editors: Diane E. Carlson, Marcia Crawford Mann
Associate Editor: Richard Elliott
Assistant Editor: Peter P. Kaye
Project Assistance: Ligature, Inc.

Sources of Quoted Materials (continued)

a Poem," from JAMBOREE *Rhymes for All Times* by Eve Merriam, copyright © 1962, 1964, 1966, 1973, 1984 by Eve Merriam, all rights reserved, reprinted with permission of Marian Reiner for the author. **292:** Henry Holt & Co., Inc.: For an excerpt from "Apple-Picking," from *The Poetry of Robert Frost,* edited by Edward Connery Latham, copyright 1930 and 1939 by Holt, Rinehart & Winston, Inc., copyright 1958 by Robert Frost, copyright © 1967 by Leslie Frost Ballantine. **293:** The Ecco Press: For lines from "Three Moves," from *Only the Dreamer Can Change the Dream* by John Logan, copyright (c) 1955, 1960, 1962, 1963, 1964, 1965, 1966, 1967, 1968, 1969, 1970, 1973, 1981 by John Logan; published by the Ecco Press in 1981. **293:** Norma Millay (Ellis): For an excerpt from "Departure," from *The Collected Poems* by Edna St. Vincent Millay, Harper & Row, copyright © 1923, 1951 by Edna St. Vincent Millay and Norma Millay Ellis. **294:** Liveright Publishing Corporation: For lines from "in Just-," from *Tulips & Chimneys* by E. E. Cummings, edited by George James Firmage, copyright © 1923, 1925, and renewed 1951, 1953 E. E. Cummings, copyright © 1973, 1976 the Trustees for the E.E. Cummings Trust, copyright 1973, 1976 George James Firmage. **294:** Doubleday & Company, Inc.: For an excerpt from "It was beginning winter," from *The Lost Son* by Theodore Roethke, copyright 1947, from *The Collected Poems of Theodore Roethke,* reprinted by permission of Doubleday, a division of Bantam, Doubleday, Dell Publishing Group, Inc. **295:** Alfred A. Knopf, Inc.: For lines from "Dreams," from *The Dream Keeper* by Langston Hughes, copyright 1932 Alfred A. Knopf, Inc., renewed 1960 Langston Hughes. **298:** Henry Holt and Company, Inc.: For "To an Athlete Dying Young." from *The Collected Poems of A. E. Housman,* copyright 1939, 1940, © 1965 Holt, Rinehart and Winston, Inc., copyright © 1967, 1968 Robert E. Symons. **298:** Alfred A. Knopf, Inc.: For "Ex-Basketball Player" from *The Carpentered Hen and Other Tame Creatures* by John Updike, copyright © 1957 by John Updike. **309:** Random House, Inc. For an excerpt from "Caged Bird," from *Shaker, Why Don't You Sing?* by Maya Angelou, copyright 1983 by Maya Angelou. **342:** Wesleyan University Press: For lines from "Catch" by Robert Francis © 1953 Wesleyan University Press. **400:** H. W. Wilson Company: For entries from *Readers' Guide to Periodical Literature,* page 35, June 10, 1987 issue, copyright © 1987 H. W. Wilson Company, material reproduced by permission of the publisher. **494:** Dave Barry: For excerpts from *What Is and Ain't Grammatical;* copyright © 1982 Dave Barry. **535:** Franklin Watts, Inc.: For excerpts from "The Perils of Syntax," from *How to Win a Pullet Surprise* by Jack Smith, copyright © 1982 Jack Smith. **691:** Harper & Row, Publishers, Inc.: For excerpts from *The Garden of Eloquence* by Willard R. Espy, copyright © 1980 Willard R. Espy. **691:** Clarkson N. Potter, Inc.: For excerpts from *Another Almanac of Words at Play* by Willard R. Espy, copyright © 1983 Willard R. Espy. **756:** Harcourt Brace Jovanovich, Inc.: For the first stanza of "All Ignorance Toboggans into Know," from *Complete Poems 1913–1962* by E. E. Cummings, copyright 1944 E.E. Cummings; renewed 1972 Nancy T. Andrews. **797:** Atheneum Publishers, an imprint of Macmillan Publishing Co.: For excerpts from "Dictionaries," from *And More by Andy Rooney* copyright © 1982 Essay Productions, Inc.

The authors and editors have made every effort to trace the ownership of all copyrighted selections from this book and make full acknowledgment for their use.

Photographs:

Assignment photography: Ralph Brunke: **19, 21, 39, 52,** *l* **75,** *r* **77, 101, 130, 138, 154, 173,** *c* **179, 214,** *l* **226, 229, 230, 256, 290, 303, 326, 360, 385, 402, 404,** *r* **419, 434, 444, 446, 508, 535, 557, 582, 583, 618, 630, 631,** *all* **644, 655, 727, 737, 739, 758,** *all* **766;** Eric Futran: **372, 382, 438;** Gregg Eisman: **49, 91, 123, 379,** *in* **404, 440,** *all* **448, 576,** *all* **610;** Richard Hellyer: **94, 165,** *all* **168, 291, 386, 585, 634, 783;** Greg Gillis: *all* **206, 207, 698, 700, 710. 4:** Bill Ross, West Light; **5:** Seattle Art Museum, purchased with funds from PONCHO. Paul Macapia, photographer; **7:** *r* Hedrich Blessing; **7:** *l* H. Armstrong Roberts; **8:** © 1984 Universal Press Syndicate, Inc.; **14:** David Muench; **17:** George Thompson, Chicago Tribune Company; **21:** *r* Bobbe Wolf; **21:** *l* John Weinstein; **22:** NASA; **23:** Jet Propulsion Lab, NASA; **26:** Roy DeForest; **31:** The Hirshhorn Museum & Sculpture Garden, Art Resource; **33:** Diana Rasche; Joan Liftin, Archive Pictures; **44:** Bruce McClelland, Arizona Daily Star; **46:** *l* Karyn Bertschi; *cr* Norman Tompson, Taurus Photos; *cl* Karyn Bertschi; *r* Jane Horton; **51:** Chris Stewart, San Francisco Chronicle; **51:** *l* Mark Hanauer, Onyx; **54:** © 1987 Universal Press Syndicate, Inc.; **56:** Drawing by M. Stevens; © 1985 The New Yorker Magazine, Inc.; **57:** Marilyn Gartman; **58:** Grant Heilman; **59:** H. W. Hesselmann, Image Bank; **63:** *r* David Hamilton, Image Bank; *l* Margaret Bourke-White, Edwynn Houk Gallery; **64:** WLS-AM; **68:** Brent Jones; **72:** Diana Rasche; **75:** *r* Don Klumpp, Image Bank; **77:** *t* Bob Daemmrich, Click/Chicago; **77:** *l* Deborah Kahn Kalas, Stock, Boston; **78:** Courtesy World Book Encyclopedia,; **79:** Gary Gladstone, Image Bank; **85:** Warren Morgan, West Light; **88:** Frank Staub, Picture Cube; **95:** Ellis Herwig, Stock, Boston; **97:** Frans Lanting; **100:** Dr. H. E. Edgerton, MIT Strobe Lab; **103:** Movie Still Archives; **109:** Martin Rogers, Stock, Boston; **111:** Tom Nebbia; **119:** *t* Russ Kinne, COMSTOCK; *b* Larry Kolvoord; **120:** Drawing by Chas. Addams; © 1973, The New Yorker Magazine,

Inc.; **122:** Gwen Knight, Saden Gallery; **124:** Bill Ross, West Light; **125:** Rotterdam, Focus on Sports; **130:** *in* John Running; **134:** National Optical Astronomy Observatories; **135:** California Institute of Technology; **143:** UPI/Bettman Newsphotos; **148:** *c* All-Sport/Simon Burty, West Light; **148:** *r* All-Sport/Simon Burty, West Light; **151:** Koball Collection, Superstock; **155:** Marc Harris; **159:** Museum of the American Indian, Heye Foundation; **160:** NASA; **161:** Art Resource; **179:** *t* Tison Keel; *b* Marc Harris; **180:** James Marshall, Document Brooklyn; **181:** James Marshall, Document Brooklyn; **185:** Jay King; **188:** Tom Van Ende; **196:** Adrian Keating, Jr.; **200:** © David Hiser, Image Bank; **205:** Photri; Michael Lipkin; **210:** Rod Planck, Click/Chicago; **211:** Art Wolfe; **222:** *in* Nicholas Groh; **222:** *lr* Fred Myers, Click/Chicago; **226:** *r* The Ladd Company; **229:** *t* North Wind Pictures,; *b* Montgomery Ward/Signature Group; **230:** © The Detroit Institute of Arts, Gift of the Dexter M. Ferry, Jr. Trustee Corporation; **231:** Toledo Museum of Art; **234:** Guido Rossi, Image Bank; **238:** *r* Michael Ochs Archives; *l* Photri, Marilyn Gartman; **243:** Bill Barley, Bill Barley & Associates; **248:** Gilles Peress, Magnum Photos; **252:** The Bettmann Archive; **253:** Geoffrey Smith, Uniphoto; **259:** *c* Donald Dietz, Stock, Boston; *l* Milton Heiberg Studios; *r* Stan Badz, Jackson-Clarion Ledger; **260:** L. Mason, Image Bank; **262:** Lewis Portnoy, Spectra-Action, Inc.; **263:** David Madison; **264:** Bruce Rosenblum, Picture Cube; **265:** James Yang, Illustrator, Beth Singer Design; **269:** Eric Meola, Image Bank; **275:** Francois Robert; **278:** Ira Wexler; **282:** Martin Rogers, Uniphoto; **289:** *b* Ronald Seymour; *t* Frank Siteman, Southern Light; **295:** *r* Miguel, Image Bank; *l* Eric Wheather, Image Bank; **299:** *in* Geoffrey C. Clifford, Wheeler Pictures; *b* Laurie ShoulterKarall; **310:** General Service Administration, Art-in-Architecture program; **311:** General Service Administration, Art-in-Architecture program; **317:** Roy Boyd Gallery; **323:** Art Wolfe, Aperture; **325:** *ll,* Lee Boltin; **332:** Melchior Di Giacomo, Image Bank; **336:** Time, Inc.; **339:** *t* S. Perkins, Magnum photos; *b* Michael Collier, Stock, Boston; **342:** R. Chappele, FPG; **345:** The Fontayne Group, © US Press; **347:** *l* Garry Gay, Image Bank; *r* Bill Everitt, Tom Stack & Assoc.; **352:** National Lampoon; **356:** Salvador Dali Foundation, Inc.; **362:** The Saint Louis Museum of Art, museum purchase; **365:** *in* Michael Fogden, Bruce Coleman; **368:** Grant Heilman; **376:** Drawing by H. Martin; © 1986 The New Yorker Magazine, Inc.; **384:** Tribune Media Services; **387:** David Lissy, Focus on Sports; **389:** Courtesy American Cancer Society; **390:** John Cary; **393:** Albright-Knox Art Gallery; **395:** *l* Kaz Mori, Image Bank; **399:** With permission of Encyclopedia Brittanica, Inc.; **408:** Culver Pictures; **411:** Manfred Kage, Peter Arnold; **414:** Ellis Herwig, Marilyn Gartman; **416:** San Francisco Museum of Modern Art, Albert M. Bender Collection and bequest fund purchase; **419:** *l* Donald Graham, Aperture; **422:** *r* Stephen Dalton, Animals, Animals; *l* Raymond Mendez, Animals, Animals; **426:** Tribune Media Services; **451:** Collection D. Livermore; **454:** The Bettmann Archive; **456:** By permission of Johnny Hart and North America Syndicate, Inc.; **458:** Janet Edwards, Eastman Kodak Company; **460:** *r* Walter Iooss, Image Bank; **462:** Also Tutino, Art Resource; **468:** Laimute Druskis, Taurus Photos; **471:** © 1987 The Detroit Institute of Arts, City of Detroit Purchase; **475:** © 1986 Universal Press Syndicate, Inc.; **477:** *r* Edward Bock, Frozen Images; *l* Ann Duncan, Tom Stack and Assoc.; **481:** L. West, FPG; **483:** Tim Thompson; **487:** Togashi; **488:** FPG; **492:** *in* Keith Berr; **497:** *r* Len Kaufman; *l* The Bettmann Archive; **502:** © 1987 Newspaper Enterprise Assoc., Inc.; **505:** *r* J. Carnemolla, West Light; **512:** *l* Marilyn Gartman; **512:** *r,* The Bettmann Archive; **517:** © 1981 United Features Syndicate, Inc.; **520:** Marche, FPG; **525:** Dennie Cody, FPG; **527:** *c,* NASA; *l* NASA; *r* NASA, Grant Heilman; **532:** L. T. Rhodes, Click/Chicago; **537:** © 1986 Universal Press Syndicate, Inc.; **542:** The Tate Gallery A.D.A.G.P.; **546:** Greg Nikas, Picture Cube; **548:** David Austen, Click/Chicago; **552:** *l,* Fran Barakas; *r* Brent Jones; **557:** *l,r* John Reader; *c* John Reader; **565:** Jean Gaumy, Magnum Photos; **567:** Roger Miller, Image Bank; **570:** Curtis Willocks, Document Brooklyn; **573:** *all,* John Running; **578:** George Robbins, The Stock Solution; **580:** Uniphoto; **587:** Photri, Gartman Agency; **594:** Don Clegg; **597:** © 1986 Universal Press Syndicate, Inc.; **598:** Culver Pictures; **602:** Lorie Novak; **605:** Benson & Hedges Illustrators' Gold Awards 1984, Courtesy Sharp Practice; **607:** Ralph Nelson, Universal City Studios, Inc.; **612:** Uccello, Photo Researchers; **613:** Richard Brown Baker Collection, Yale University Art Gallery; **617:** Courtesy MacMillan-London; **623:** Andrew Lautman, Ford's Theatre; **626:** Michael Melford, Wheeler Pictures; **637:** Diana Rasche; **640:** Joe McNally, Wheeler Pictures; **649:** Bill Tucker; **650:** Peter Marlow, Magnum Photos; **653:** Sam Griffith, Click/Chicago; **655:** Amon Carter Museum, Fort Worth; **660:** *all* Andreas Dannenberg, Wheeler Pictures; **662:** Lorie Novak; **665:** David Madison; **670:** © 1978 United Feature Syndicate, Inc.; **672:** Culver Pictures; **675:** Larry Kolvoord; **680:** Uniphoto; **683:** *l* Henley and Savage, *r* John Newbauer; **686:** Jacques Dirand, Courtesy House & Garden. © 1984 by The Conde Nast Publications, Inc.; **692:** Photri; **705:** Yuri Dojc, Image Bank; **710:** Greg Gillis; **712:** © 1984 Universal Press Syndicate, Inc.; **714:** Sygma; **718:** Richard Burda, Taurus Photos; **725:** Courtesy Interview Magazine; **729:** Susan Van Etten; **732:** Photri, Marilyn Gartman; **735:** © 1985 Universal Press Syndicate, Inc.; **742:** Charles Palek, Animals, Animals; **746:** Joseph Szaszfai, Yale University Art Galley; **749:** Phyllis Galembo; **752:** The Bettmann Archive; **756:** Phil Schofield, West Stock; **763:** Focus on Sports; **769:** *t* The Bettmann Archive; *b* Historical Pictures Service, Chicago; **774:** Ernst Haas, Magnum Photos; **776:** Drawing by Maslin. © 1987 The New Yorker Magazine, Inc.; **779:** Gerard Vandystadt, Agence Vandystadt, Photo Researchers; **788:** Courtesy Joseph Lileck; **794:** Movie Still Archives; **797:** Courtesy Andrew Rooney; **801:** Manfred Kage, Peter Arnold; **805:** Albright-Knox Art Gallery, Buffalo, NY. Gift of Seymour H. Knox, 1963; **807:** F. G. Samia; **808:** *r,* Bernard Brault Photography.

Illustrations:

Lynne Fischer (hand coloring of photographs): **155, 173, 390, 752, 790;** David Moneysmith: **64–65, 188, 192–193, 174–175, 192–193, 330–331;** Precision Graphics: **718, 806–807;** Laura Tarrish: *c* **615;** Helen M. Lopez: **ii, iii.**

Fuck as a verb — to fuck.
Fuck as and adjective — she fuckin see
Fuck as a noun — to fck or Not to Fuck.
Fuck as an adjective — My handwriting fuckin
        Sucks)

———